Lecture Notes in Computer Science 8688

Commenced Publication in 1973
Founding and Former Series Editors:
Gerhard Goos, Juris Hartmanis, and Jan van Leeuwen

Editorial Board

David Hutchison
Lancaster University, UK

Takeo Kanade
Carnegie Mellon University, Pittsburgh, PA, USA

Josef Kittler
University of Surrey, Guildford, UK

Jon M. Kleinberg
Cornell University, Ithaca, NY, USA

Alfred Kobsa
University of California, Irvine, CA, USA

Friedemann Mattern
ETH Zurich, Switzerland

John C. Mitchell
Stanford University, CA, USA

Moni Naor
Weizmann Institute of Science, Rehovot, Israel

Oscar Nierstrasz
University of Bern, Switzerland

C. Pandu Rangan
Indian Institute of Technology, Madras, India

Bernhard Steffen
TU Dortmund University, Germany

Demetri Terzopoulos
University of California, Los Angeles, CA, USA

Doug Tygar
University of California, Berkeley, CA, USA

Gerhard Weikum
Max Planck Institute for Informatics, Saarbruecken, Germany

T0212681

Angelos Stavrou   Herbert Bos
Georgios Portokalidis (Eds.)

Research in Attacks, Intrusions, and Defenses

17th International Symposium, RAID 2014
Gothenburg, Sweden, September 17-19, 2014
Proceedings

Springer

Volume Editors

Angelos Stavrou
George Mason University
Department of Computer Science
Fairfax, VA 22030, USA
E-mail: astavrou@gmu.edu

Herbert Bos
Free University Amsterdam
Department of Computer Science
1081 HV Amsterdam, The Netherlands
E-mail: herbertb@cs.vu.nl

Georgios Portokalidis
Stevens Institute of Technology
Department of Computer Science
Hoboken, NJ 07030, USA
E-mail: gportoka@stevens.edu

ISSN 0302-9743   e-ISSN 1611-3349
ISBN 978-3-319-11378-4   e-ISBN 978-3-319-11379-1
DOI 10.1007/978-3-319-11379-1
Springer Cham Heidelberg New York Dordrecht London

Library of Congress Control Number: 2014947893

LNCS Sublibrary: SL 4 – Security and Cryptology

© Springer International Publishing Switzerland 2014
This work is subject to copyright. All rights are reserved by the Publisher, whether the whole or part of
the material is concerned, specifically the rights of translation, reprinting, reuse of illustrations, recitation,
broadcasting, reproduction on microfilms or in any other physical way, and transmission or information
storage and retrieval, electronic adaptation, computer software, or by similar or dissimilar methodology
now known or hereafter developed. Exempted from this legal reservation are brief excerpts in connection
with reviews or scholarly analysis or material supplied specifically for the purpose of being entered and
executed on a computer system, for exclusive use by the purchaser of the work. Duplication of this publication
or parts thereof is permitted only under the provisions of the Copyright Law of the Publisher's location,
in ist current version, and permission for use must always be obtained from Springer. Permissions for use
may be obtained through RightsLink at the Copyright Clearance Center. Violations are liable to prosecution
under the respective Copyright Law.
The use of general descriptive names, registered names, trademarks, service marks, etc. in this publication
does not imply, even in the absence of a specific statement, that such names are exempt from the relevant
protective laws and regulations and therefore free for general use.
While the advice and information in this book are believed to be true and accurate at the date of publication,
neither the authors nor the editors nor the publisher can accept any legal responsibility for any errors or
omissions that may be made. The publisher makes no warranty, express or implied, with respect to the
material contained herein.

Typesetting: Camera-ready by author, data conversion by Scientific Publishing Services, Chennai, India

Printed on acid-free paper

Springer is part of Springer Science+Business Media (www.springer.com)

Preface

Welcome to the proceedings of the 17th International Symposium on Research in Attacks, Intrusions, and Defenses (RAID 2014). This year, RAID received an unusually large number of 113 submissions out of which the Program Committee selected 22 high-quality papers for inclusion in the proceedings and presentation at the conference in Gothenburg. In our opinion, an acceptance rate of 19% is healthy. In addition, we accepted 10 posters from 24 submissions. The acceptance rate and quality of submissions clearly shows that RAID is a competitive, high-quality conference, but avoids the insanely low probabilities of acceptance that sometimes reduce security conferences to glorified lotteries.

Running a well-established conference with many strong submissions makes the job of the program chairs relatively easy. Moreover, the chair / co-chair setup (where the co-chair of the previous year becomes the chair of the next), and the conference's active Steering Committee both ensure continuity. In our opinion, it has helped RAID to become and to remain a quality venue.

One thing we did consciously try to change in this year's edition is the composition of the Program Committee. Specifically, we believe that it is important to infuse new blood into our conferences' Program Committees – both to prepare the next generation of Program Committee members, and to avoid the incestuous community where the same small circle of senior researchers rotates from Program Committee to Program Committee. From the outset, we therefore aimed for a Program Committee that consisted of researchers who had not served on the RAID PC more than once in the past few years, but with a proven track record in terms of top publications. In addition, we wanted to introduce a healthy number of younger researchers and/or researchers from slightly different fields.

It may sound like all this would be hard to find, but it was surprisingly easy. There is a lot of talent in our community! With a good mix of seniority, background, and expertise, we were very happy with the great and very conscientious Program Committee we had this year (as well as with the external reviewers). Specifically, we made sure that all valid submissions received at least three reviews, and in case of diverging reviews, we added one or two more. As a result, the load of the Program Committee this year may have been higher than in previous years, but we are happy with the result and thank all reviewers for their hard work.

We are also grateful to the organizers, headed by the general chair Magnus Almgren and supported by Erland Jonsson (local arrangements), Georgios Portokalidis (publications), Vincenzo Gulisano and Christian Rossow (publicity), Bosse Norrhem (sponsoring), and all local volunteers at Chalmers. We know from experience how much work it is to organize a conference like RAID and that a general chair especially gets most of the complaints and too little of the credit. Not this year: hats off to Magnus for a great job!

Finally, none of this would be possible without the generous support by our sponsors: Symantec, Ericsson, Swedish Research Council, and the City of Gothenburg. We greatly appreciate their help and their continued commitment to a healthy research community in security.

We hope you enjoy the program and the conference.

July 2014   Angelos Stavrou
                                                                         Herbert Bos

Organization

Organizing Committee

General Chair

Magnus Almgren   Chalmers University of Technology, Sweden

Local Arrangement Chair

Erland Jonsson   Chalmers University of Technology, Sweden

PC Chair

Angelos Stavrou   George Mason University, USA

PC Co-chair

Herbert Bos   Vrije Universiteit, The Netherlands

Publication Chair

Georgios Portokalidis   Stevens Institute of Technology, USA

Publicity Chair

Vincenzo Gulisano   Chalmers University of Technology, Sweden
Christian Rossow   Vrije Universiteit, The Netherlands / RU
                Bochum, Germany

Sponsorship Chair

Bosse Norrhem

Program Committee Members

Leyla Bilge	Symantec Labs, Europe
Baris Coskun	AT&T Security Research Center, USA
Manuel Costa	Microsoft Research, UK
Aurelien Francillon	Eurecom, France
Flavio D. Garcia	University of Birmingham, UK
Dina Hadziosmanovic	Delft University of Technology, The Netherlands
Gernot Heiser	NICTA and UNSW, Australia
Sotiris Ioannidis	FORTH-ICS, Greece
Xuxian Jiang	North Carolina State University, USA

Emmanouil Konstantinos Antonakakis	Georgia Tech, USA
Peng Liu	Penn State University, USA
Paolo Milani Comparetti	Lastline Inc., USA
Damon Mccoy	George Mason University, USA
Fabian Monrose	University of North Carolina at Chapel Hill, USA
Hamed Okhravi	MIT Lincoln Labs, USA
Alina Oprea	RSA Laboratories, USA
Michalis Polychronakis	Columbia University, USA
Georgios Portokalidis	Stevens Institute of Technology, USA
Konrad Rieck	University of Göttingen, Germany
William Robertson	Northeastern University, USA
Christian Rossow	RU Bochum, Germany
Simha Sethumadhavan	Columbia University, USA
Kapil Singh	IBM Research, USA
Asia Slowinska	Vrije Universiteit, The Netherlands
Anil Somayaji	Carleton University, Canada

External Reviewers

Sumayah Alrwais	Indiana University, USA
Fabian van den Broek	Radboud University Nijmegen, The Netherlands
Lorenzo Cavallaro	Royal Holloway University of London, UK
Tom Chothia	University of Birmingham, UK
Joseph Gardiner	University of Birmingham, UK
Gurchetan S. Grewal	University of Birmingham, UK
Georgios Kontaxis	Columbia University, USA
Mihai Ordean	University of Birmingham, UK
Roel Verdult	Radboud University Nijmegen, The Netherlands

Steering Committee

Chair

Marc Dacier	Symantec Research, France

Members

Davide Balzarotti	Eurécom, France
Herve Debar	Telecom SudParis, France
Deborah Frincke	DoD Research, USA
Ming-Yuh Huang	Northwest Security Institute, USA
Somesh Jha	University of Wisconsin, USA

Erland Jonsson	Chalmers, Sweden
Engin Kirda	Northeastern University, USA
Christopher Kruegel	UC Santa Barbara, USA
Wenke Lee	Georgia Tech, USA
Richard Lippmann	MIT Lincoln Laboratory, USA
Ludovic Me	Supelec, France
Robin Sommer	ICSI/LBNL, USA
Alfonso Valdes	SRI International, USA
Giovanni Vigna	UC Santa Barbara, USA
Andreas Wespi	IBM Research, Switzerland
S. Felix Wu	UC Davis, USA
Diego Zamboni	CFEngine AS, Mexico

Sponsors

Symantec (Gold level)
Ericsson AB (Silver level)
Swedish Research Council
City of Gothenburg

Table of Contents

Web II

Authentication and Privacy

Network Security

Intrusion Detection and Vulnerability Analysis

Poster Abstracts

Paint It Black: Evaluating the Effectiveness of Malware Blacklists

Marc Kührer, Christian Rossow, and Thorsten Holz

Horst Görtz Institute for IT-Security, Ruhr-University Bochum, Germany
{firstname.lastname}@ruhr-uni-bochum.de

Abstract. *Blacklists* are commonly used to protect computer systems against the tremendous number of malware threats. These lists include abusive hosts such as malware sites or botnet Command & Control and dropzone servers to raise alerts if suspicious hosts are contacted. Up to now, though, little is known about the *effectiveness* of malware blacklists.

In this paper, we empirically analyze 15 public malware blacklists and 4 blacklists operated by antivirus (AV) vendors. We aim to categorize the blacklist content to understand the nature of the listed domains and IP addresses. First, we propose a mechanism to identify parked domains in blacklists, which we find to constitute a substantial number of blacklist entries. Second, we develop a graph-based approach to identify sinkholes in the blacklists, i.e., servers that host malicious domains which are controlled by security organizations. In a thorough evaluation of blacklist effectiveness, we show to what extent real-world malware domains are actually covered by blacklists. We find that the union of all 15 public blacklists includes less than 20% of the malicious domains for a majority of prevalent malware families and most AV vendor blacklists fail to protect against malware that utilizes *Domain Generation Algorithms*.

Keywords: Blacklist Evaluation, Sinkholing Servers, Parking Domains.

1   Introduction

The security community needs to deal with an increasing number of malware samples that infect computer systems world-wide. Many countermeasures have been proposed to combat the ubiquitous presence of malware [1–4]. Most notably, researchers progressively explored network-based detection methods to complement existing host-based malware protection systems. One prominent example are endpoint reputation systems. The typical approach is to assemble a blacklist of endpoints that have been observed to be involved in malicious operations. For example, blacklists can contain domains of Command & Control (C&C) servers of botnets, dropzone servers, and malware download sites [5]. Such blacklists can then be queried by an intrusion detection system (IDS) to determine if a previously unknown endpoint (such as a domain) is known for suspicious behavior.

Up to now, though, little is known about the *effectiveness* of malware blacklists. To the best of our knowledge, the completeness and accuracy of malware

A. Stavrou et al. (Eds.): RAID 2014, LNCS 8688, pp. 1–21, 2014.
© Springer International Publishing Switzerland 2014

blacklists was never examined in detail. Completeness is important as users otherwise risk to miss notifications about malicious but unlisted hosts. Similarly, blacklists may become outdated if entries are not frequently revisited by the providers. While an endpoint may have had a bad reputation in the past, this might change in the future (e.g., due to shared hosting).

In this paper, we analyze the effectiveness of 15 public and 4 anti-virus (AV) vendor malware blacklists. That is, we aim to categorize the blacklist content to understand the nature of the listed entries. Our analysis consists of multiple steps. First, we propose a mechanism to identify parked domains, which we find to constitute a substantial number of blacklist entries. Second, we develop a graph-based approach to identify sinkholed entries, i.e., malicious domains that are mitigated and now controlled by security organizations. Last, we show to what extent real-world malware domains are actually covered by the blacklists.

In the analyzed blacklist data we identified 106 previously unknown sinkhole servers, revealing 27 sinkholing organizations. In addition, we found between 40 - 85% of the blacklisted domains to be unregistered for more than half of the analyzed blacklists and up to 10.9% of the blacklist entries to be parked. The results of analyzing the remaining blacklist entries show that the coverage and completeness of most blacklists is insufficient. For example, we find public blacklists to be impractical when it comes to protecting against prevalent malware families as they fail to include domains for the variety of families or list malicious endpoints with reaction times of 30 days or higher.

Fortunately, the performance of three AV vendor blacklists is significantly better. However, we also identify shortcomings of these lists: only a single blacklist sufficiently protects against malware using *Domain Generation Algorithms* (DGAs) [3], while the other AV vendor blacklists include a negligible number of DGA-based domains only. Our thorough evaluation can help to improve the effectiveness of malware blacklists in the future.

To summarize, our contributions are as follows:
- We propose a method to identify parked domains by training an SVM classifier on seven inherent features we identified for *parked* web sites.
- We introduce a mechanism based on blacklist content and graph analysis to effectively identify malware sinkholes without *a priori* knowledge.
- We evaluate the effectiveness of 19 malware blacklists and show that most public blacklists have an insufficient coverage of malicious domains for a majority of popular malware families, leaving the end hosts fairly unprotected. While we find blacklists operated by AV vendors to have a significantly higher coverage, up to 26.5% of the domains were still missed for the majority of the malware families, revealing severe deficiencies of current reputation systems.

2   Overview of Malware Blacklists

Various malware blacklists operated by security organizations can be used to identify malicious activities. These blacklists include domains and IP addresses, which have been observed in a suspicious context, i.e., hosts of a particular

Table 1. Observed content of the analyzed malware blacklists (‡ denotes C&C blacklists)

Blacklist	Domains (in #)		Observ. (days)	Blacklist	Domains (in #)		Observ. (days)
	Current	Historical			Current	Historical	
AMaDa [8]‡	0	1,494	267				
Citadel [7]‡	4,634	0	66	Palevo Tracker [8]‡	35	147	542
Cybercrime [9]‡	1,070	0	121	Shadowserver [13]‡	0	0	832
Exposure [4]	0	107,183	559	Shallalist [14]	20,677	48	320
Malc0de [10]	2,121	20,135	832	SpyEye Tracker [8]‡	123	956	832
MDL Hosts [11]	1,653	11,996	832	UrlBlacklist [15]	127,745	281	824
MDL ZeuS [11]‡	12	1,675	829	Virustracker [16]	12,066	56,269	196
MW-Domains [12]	23,396	37,490	832	ZeuS Tracker [8]‡	759	8,042	832

type such as C&C servers or—less restrictive—endpoints associated to malware in general. Table 1 introduces the 15 public malware blacklists that we have monitored for the past two years [6]. For the majority of blacklists, we repeatedly obtained a copy every 3 hours (if permitted). The columns *Current* state the number of entries that were listed at the end of our monitoring period. The columns *Historical* summarize the entries that were once listed in a blacklist, but became delisted during our monitoring period. For reasons of brevity, we have omitted the number of listed *IP addresses* per blacklist, as we mainly focus on the blacklisted *domains* in our analyses. For all listed domains, we resolved the IP addresses and stored the name server (NS) DNS records. If blacklists contained URLs, we used the domain part of the URLs for our analysis.

Four blacklists are provided by `Abuse.ch`, of which three specifically list hosts related to the *Palevo* worm and the banking trojans *SpyEye* and *ZeuS*. The *Virustracker* project lists domains generated by DGAs, and the *Citadel* list includes domains utilized by the *Citadel* malware (that was seized by Microsoft in 2013 [7]). *UrlBlacklist* combines user submissions and other blacklists, covering domains and IPs of various categories, whereas we focus on the malware-related content. The *Exposure* [4] blacklist included domains that were flagged as malicious by employing passive DNS (pDNS) analysis. The *Abuse.ch AMaDa* and the *Exposure* lists were discontinued, yet we leverage the collected historical data.

Besides these public blacklists, we have requested information from four antivirus (AV) vendors, namely *Bitdefender TrafficLight* [17], *Browserdefender* [18], *McAfee Siteadvisor* [19], and *Norton SafeWeb* [20]. These blacklists cannot be downloaded, but we can query if a domain is listed. We thus do not know the overall size of these blacklists and omit the numbers in Table 1.

Datasets. We divide the 15 public blacklists into three overlapping datasets. The first dataset, referred to as $S_{C\&C}$, consists of domains taken from the sources primarily listing endpoints associated to C&C servers, denoted by ‡ in Table 1. We extend $S_{C\&C}$ with the IP addresses to which any of these domains at some point resolved to. The second, coarse-grained dataset S_{Mal} includes the domains that were at any time listed in any of the 15 blacklists (including $S_{C\&C}$) and the resolved IPs. Last, we generate a third dataset S_{IPs}, covering all currently listed IP addresses by any of the 15 public blacklists (i.e., 196,173 IPs in total). This dataset will help us to verify if blacklists contain IPs of sinkholing servers.

Paper Outline. Motivated by the fact that blacklists contain thousands of domains, we aim to understand the nature of these listings. We group the entries in four main categories: domains are either i) unregistered, ii) controlled by parking providers, iii) assigned to sinkholes, or iv) serve actual content. Unregistered domains can easily be identified using DNS. However, it is non-trivial to detect parked or sinkholed domains. We thus propose detection mechanisms for these two types in Section 3 (parking domains) and Section 4 (sinkholed domains). In Section 5, we classify the blacklist content and analyze to what extent blacklists help to protect against real malware. Note that a longer version of this paper with more technical details is available as a technical report [21].

3   Parking Domains

Parking domains make up the first prominent class of blacklist entries. They are mainly registered for the purpose of displaying web advertisements, so called ads. Typically no other, real content is placed on these domains. As domains associated with malicious activities tend to be parked to monetize the malicious traffic [22], we expect parked domains to constitute a substantial number of blacklist entries. Unfortunately, parking services have diverging page templates to present the sponsored ads. As such, it is not straightforward to identify these sites, e.g., with pattern-matching algorithms. In order to identify parking domains in the blacklists, we thus introduce a generic method to detect parked domains that can cope with the diversity of parking providers.

3.1   Datasets

We first assemble a labeled dataset by manually creating patterns and applying pattern-matching algorithms [23, 24]. Note that these patterns are far from complete due to the high diversity of page templates. We leverage the resulting dataset as ground truth to evaluate our generic detection model for parked domain names later on. We generate the labels based on Li *et al.*'s [22] observation that parking providers either modify the authoritative NS sections of a domain to point to dedicated parking NS or employ web-based (i.e., HTTP-, HTML-, or JavaScript-based) redirections to forward users to the final parking content.

Based on our recorded DNS information, we first label domains following the DNS-based type of redirection. That is, we analyze the 233,772 distinct name servers aggregated while processing the blacklist data. We split the NS hostnames into tokens and searched for terms indicating parking such as `park`, `sell`, and `expired` and labeled NS whose hostnames match one of these terms as potential parking name servers. We monitored a fraction of parked domains that switched their authoritative NS to a different parking provider. As a result, we extracted the domains that used the parking NS identified in the previous step from the aggregated DNS data, requested latest NS records for each domain, and inspected the most frequently used NS. In addition, we consulted the *DNS DB* [25], a *passive DNS* (pDNS) database. That is, for each identified parking NS, we requested

50,000 randomly selected domains the NS was authoritative for, obtained current NS records for each domain, and again checked the NS hostnames against terms indicating parking behavior. Overall, using these techniques and manual inspection, we identified 204 NS operated by 53 parking providers.

A minority of parking services employ web-based techniques to redirect users to the actual parking content. The DNS-based methods discussed so far did not detect these providers. However, we identified parked domains that are often transferred between providers, thus we assume that some domains found in pDNS data of the previously identified parking NS at some point have relocated to providers utilizing web-based redirection techniques. To identify these services, we extracted 10,000 randomly chosen domains from the pDNS data of each parking NS, analyzed the domain redirection chains, and identified 14 patterns of *landing pages* [21] to which users are redirected to when visiting parked domains. These landing pages belong to parking, domain, and hosting providers.

Finally, we use the parking NS and landing pages to manually extract 47 descriptive strings, in the following referred to as *identifiers* (IDs) [21]. These IDs can be found in the HTTP responses of many parked domains (e.g., `<frame src="http://ww[0-9]{1,2}` and `landingparent`). We use these IDs to create the *parked domains* dataset $\mathcal{P}$ that consists of 5,000 randomly chosen domains from the pDNS database we find to utilize a verified parking NS or include at least one identifier. We further create a dataset $\mathcal{B}$ of benign (i.e., non-parked) domains. We utilize the Top 5,000 domains taken from the Alexa Top Ranking [26] and verify that none of these domains trigger a landing page or ID match.

3.2   Feature Selection and Classification

Pattern matching allowed us to identify a subset of all parking services. However, we seek to identify intrinsic characteristics of parking websites that are more generic than the manually assembled classification described above. We thus studied subsets of our benign and parked domain sets and identified two, respectively, five generic features based on HTTP and HTML behavior.

The first HTTP-based feature is determined by the redirection behavior when domains are directly accessed without specifying any subdomains. For benign domains, automated redirection to the common `www` subdomain is often enforced. Parked domains, in contrast, typically do not exhibit similar behavior.

Our second feature is based on the observation that parked domains deliver similar content on random subdomains and the domains itself while benign domains tend to serve differing content for arbitrary subdomains (if at all). We measure the normalized Levenshtein ratio [27] between the HTML content gathered by accessing the domain and a randomly generated subdomain. If the HTTP request for the subdomain failed (e.g., due to DNS resolution), the feature is set to -1, otherwise the value is in the range from 0 (no similarity) to 1 (equal).

The first HTML-based feature is derived from the observation that many parked domains display sponsored ads while the textual content is negligible. Contrary, most benign domains deliver a substantial amount of human-readable content in the form of coherent text fragments. Our third feature thus defines the ratio of human-readable text in relative to the overall length in returned web content after removing HTML tags, JavaScript codes, and whitespaces.

Next, we outline three features to express the techniques that landing pages utilize to embed parking content. That is, we account for the observation that most parked domains use JavaScript or frames to display sponsored ads. In the fourth feature, we measure the ratio of JavaScript code. In the fifth feature, we count the number of `<frame>` tags on landing pages. As many page templates utilizing frames contain only the basic HTML structure and the frameset, the frame count is particularly powerful in combination with the ratio of human-readable text (feature 3). A fraction of parked domains, however, do not rely on JavaScript or frames and directly embed the referral links into the HTML code. We observed many of these parking providers to specify rather long attributes in the referral `<anchor>` tags (e.g., multiple mutual IDs in the `href` attribute). As parked domains tend to serve numerous referral links, the average length of `<anchor>` tags is expected to be considerably higher than in content served by the majority of benign domains, as expressed in the sixth feature.

The seventh feature is defined by the `robots` value specified in the `<meta>` tag. Parked domains in our dataset either did not specify a `robots` value (thus using the default `index + follow`) or defined one of the values `index + nofollow`, `index + follow`, or `index + follow + all`. Parking providers monetize the domains and are interested in promoting their domains, thus permitting indexing by search engines. In contrast, benign sites often customize the indexing policies—we identified 31 different `robots` values. As the `robots` value is a concatenation of tokens, we mapped all possible single tokens to non-overlapping bitmasks and use the numerical value of the bit-wise OR of all tokens as feature.

Most parking services rely on JavaScript to display referral links and advertisements. The HTML-based features (3 - 7) thus require JavaScript execution when aggregating the feature values. As the initially served content before executing JavaScript and the final content after executing JavaScript both are characteristic for parked domains (and might be entirely different, e.g., when JavaScript is used for redirection), we obtain two feature values for each of the HTML-based features accordingly, resulting in 12 feature values per domain.

We use these 12 feature values to classify domains as either parked or benign (i.e., non-parking). We evaluated our approach for different types of machine-learning algorithms using RapidMiner [21, 28] and achieved the best results for *support vector machines* (SVMs) using the *Anova* kernel [29].

3.3   Evaluation

Cross-Fold Validation. We evaluate the feature set with a 10-fold cross validation using all domains in our *benign* $\mathcal{B}$ and *parking* $\mathcal{P}$ sets and achieve an average detection rate of 99.85% correctly classified domains while the false positive (FP) rate is at 0.11% and the false negative (FN) rate at 0.04%.

Individual Dataset. To evaluate our approach on an individual dataset and discuss false positives and negatives as suggested by Rossow *et al.* [30], we split the 10,000 labeled *benign* and *parked* domains into a training set S_{Train} consisting of 1,000 benign and 1,000 parked domains and a test set S_{Test} that includes the remaining 8,000 domains. The resulting detection model correctly classifies 7,969 domains in S_{Test} (99.6%) as benign or parked, resulting in 5 FPs (0.1%) and 26 FNs (0.3%). When investigating the FPs, we find each domain to have a ratio of less than 20% for human-readable text (feature 3) in combination with a high average length of <anchor> tags (feature 6). Further, all domains respond to random subdomain requests and serve similar web content (i.e., the normalized Levenshtein ratio ≥ 0.9). When analyzing the 26 FNs, we find domains that either switched between redirecting to parking and benign content or delivered parking content on the second visit. As we visited each domain only once during feature attribution, we did not observe parking behavior for these domains.

Real-World Data. Finally, we verify our approach on real-world data containing significantly more unlabeled domains. We obtained the Top 1M domains from the Alexa Ranking 12 weeks after the Top 5k domains were gathered for the *benign set B*. We expect only a few parked domains in this dataset, thus we mainly are interested if our approach can handle the diverse page structures of benign web pages without high FP rates. We could aggregate feature values for 891,185 domains while the remaining domains either did not resolve to IP addresses or provide web content within a time frame of 15 seconds, respectively, replied with blank content or HTTP error codes. We further remove 957 domains already covered by S_{Train}, thus the resulting set S_{Alexa} is defined by 890,228 domains. We then match the content of each domain against the IDs and landing pages introduced in Section 3.1 to estimate a lower bound of FPs and FNs. We cannot ensure the correctness of the IDs, hence might erroneously flag benign domains as parked. We thus manually verify potential false classifications.

As shown in Table 2, we achieve a correct detection rate (CD; the sum of true positive and true negative rate) of 99.5%, a FP rate of 0.4%, and a FN rate of 0.1%. The IDs flag 5,208 domains as parked, yet we find 71 of the domains to be incorrectly flagged. The classifier marks 8,709 domains as parked of which 4,596 domains are verified by the IDs. Of the remaining domains we find 626 to be parked that are not detected by the IDs, resulting in 5,222 parked domains detected by the classifier. These results indicate that 0.6% of the Alexa 1M domains, i.e., more than 1/200 of the most popular domains, are parked. More specifically, we identify 36 parked domains in the Alexa Top 10k while 432, respectively, 1,170 domains are parked in the Top 100k and Top 250k, showing that the majority of parked domains are not ranked in the Top 250k Alexa. During the manual verification process,

Table 2. Results of S_{Alexa} and $S_{Current}$ (Parked = Domains flagged as parked by IDs or classifier (CL), INT = Intersection of domains flagged as parked by IDs and CL, FI = Domains falsely flagged as parked by IDs, New = Domains detected by CL but not found by IDs)

Subset	Size	Parked (#)			#FI	#New	Rates (%)		
		ID	CL	INT			CD	FP	FN
S_{Alexa}	890,228	5,208	8,709	4,596	71	626	99.5	0.4	0.1
$S_{Current}$	33,121	3,747	5,623	3,027	28	2,336	(98.7)	0.8	(0.5)

we find the vast majority of parked domains to be associated to domain resellers such as *Above*, *GoDaddy*, and *Sedo* [21].

We now turn back to our original goal, i.e., classifying the content of blacklists. We thus extracted currently blacklisted domains from our blacklist set S_{Mal} twelve weeks after generating the *benign* B and *parking* P sets used for S_{Train}. We name this dataset $S_{Current}$ and again remove domains already included in S_{Train}. Of the 158,648 currently listed domains, we obtained feature values for 33,121 domains. The remaining domains either were unregistered or replied with HTTP error codes. The classifier defines 5,623 domains as parked, of which 3,027 domains are verified by the IDs. When manually investigating the remaining 2,596 domains flagged by the classifier, we identify 2,336 parked domains not detected by the IDs and 260 FPs (0.8%). The FPs are mostly caused by adult content and web directory sites with similar characteristics as parked domains. When taking a closer look at the initial high number of 692 FNs, we find 538 domains not serving parking content at all (i.e., referral links). More precisely, one domain reseller causes most of the FNs, as we identify 506 domains (73.1% of all FNs) redirecting to `hugedomains.com`, providing web content not exhibiting common parking behavior. To evaluate if our approach fails to detect domains associated with this reseller due to missing training data, we adjusted S_{Train} to cover a partition of these domains and find the detection model to correctly classify these domains as parked, reducing the FN rate to 0.5%.

4   Sinkholes

Next to parking domains, also so called sinkholing servers (*sinkholes*) are prominent types of blacklist entries. Sinkholes are operated by security organizations to redirect malicious traffic to trusted hosts to monitor and mitigate malware infections. In order to track sinkholes in our blacklist data, we first identify intrinsic characteristics of these servers. We thus obtained an incomplete list of sinkhole IPs and domains by manual research and through collaboration with partners. In pDNS, we then observed that domains associated with sinkholes tend to resolve to the corresponding IPs for a longer period of time, thus the monitored DNS A records are persistent. Contrary, malicious domains tend to switch to various IPs and Autonomous Systems (AS) within a short time frame to distribute their activities to different providers [5]. We also found sinkholed domains switching to other sinkholes provided by the same organization or located in the same AS, and discovered domains that were relocated to other sinkhole providers.

Sinkhole operators often use their resources to monitor as many domains of a malware family as possible. We thus find sinkhole IP addresses to be typically assigned to numerous (up to thousands of) domains. In the majority of cases, the domains resolving to a specific sinkhole IP shared the same NS such as `torpig-sinkhole.org` or `shadowserver.org`. We thus argue that if multiple domains resolve to the same IP address but do not utilize the same NS, the probability that this IP is associated with a sinkhole is considered to be low.

Another observation is the content sinkholes serve upon HTTP requests. When requesting content from randomly chosen sinkholed domains using `GET / HTTP/1.1`, we find sinkholes to either not transfer any HTML data (i.e., closed HTTP port or web servers responding with 4xx HTTP codes) or serve the same content for all domains as monitored for `zinkhole.org`. We thus assume that domains resolving to the same set of IP addresses but serving differing content do not belong to sinkholes and are rather linked to services such as shared hosting.

4.1   Sinkhole Identification

Based on these insights we introduce our approach to identify sinkholes in the blacklist datasets $S_{C\&C}$ and S_{Mal}. The datasets consist of currently listed and historical domains and the IPs to which any of the domains resolved to. For each domain, we aggregate current DNS records and web content while we obtain reverse DNS records, AS and online status details, and web content for all IPs.

Filtering Phase. In a first step, we aim to filter IP addresses sharing similar behavior as sinkholes to eliminate potential FPs. We thus remove the IPs associated with parking providers using the detection mechanism introduced in Section 3. To identify IPs of potential shared hosting providers serving benign or malicious content, we analyze the aggregated HTTP data. We define IPs to be associated with shared hosting when we obtain varying web content (i.e., normalized Levenshtein ratio ≤ 0.9) for the domains resolving to the same set of IPs. Furthermore, we expect sinkholes to be configured properly, thus we do not consider web servers as sinkholes that delivered content such as `it works`.

As our datasets might include erroneously blacklisted benign domains, we filter likely benign IPs such as hosting companies and *Content Delivery Networks* with the following heuristic: we do not expect the Alexa Top 25k domains to be associated to sinkholing servers. We thus obtained the HTTP content of each domain, extracted further domains specified in the content, and requested DNS A records for all domains. The resulting dataset S_{Benign} includes 105,549 presumably benign IPs. We acknowledge that this list does not remove all false listings in the blacklist datasets, however, this heuristic improves our data basis.

To further reduce the size of the datasets, we eliminate IPs associated to *Fast Flux* with the following heuristic: we define an IP to be associated with Fast Flux when at least 50% of the blacklisted domains currently resolving to this IP are found to be Fast Flux domains, whereas we define a Fast Flux domain as follows: i) the domain resolved to more than 5 distinct IPs during our observation time and ii) at least half of these IPs were seen within two weeks. As we expect the ratio of fast flux domains associated to individual sinkhole IP addresses to be rather low, we assume to not remove any sinkholing servers.

Graph Exploration. The actual sinkhole identification follows the intuition that IPs of sinkholes mostly succeed malicious IPs in the chain of resolved IPs for a high number of domains and are persistent for a longer period of time. For each dataset $S_{C\&C}$ and S_{Mal}, we map this assumption onto a separate directed graph $G = (V, E)$, whereas the domains and IPs in the datasets are represented as vertices $v \in V$. The edges $e \in E$ are determined by the relationship between the domains and IPs. We define $u \in V$ to be a parent node of v when there exists a directed edge $e = (u, v)$ and define $w \in V$ to be a child node of v when there exists a directed edge $e = (v, w)$. The edges $e \in E$ are defined as follows:

(i) For each domain $v \in V$, we add a directed edge $e = (v, w)$ if domain v at some point resolved to IP $w \in V$.

(ii) For each domain $v \in V$, we add an edge $e = (w_o, w_n)$ if v resolved to IP $w_o \in V$, switched to a new IP $w_n \in V$, and never switched back to IP w_o.

In step (i), we assign the resolved IPs to each domain in our datasets. In step (ii), we add a domain's history of A records (i.e., resolved IPs) to the graph.

We name $deg^-(v)$ the in-degree of node v, resembling the number of parent nodes. In our graph model, the in-degree represents the number of domains that currently are or were once resolving to node v and the number of IPs preceding v in the resolver chain. For sinkholes, the in-degree is considerably higher than the average in-degree as sinkholes usually succeed malicious IPs in the chain of resolved IPs and a single sinkhole IP is often used to sinkhole multiple domains.

We further refer to $deg^+(v)$ as the out-degree of node v, resembling the number of child nodes, e.g., IP addresses that followed node v in the resolver chain. We find the out-degree of sinkhole IPs to be significantly lower than the average out-degree because sinkhole IPs are persistent for a longer period of time. As a result, the ratio $R = \frac{deg^-(v)}{deg^+(v)}$ is expected to be high for sinkholes.

We use the resulting graph to create a list of potential sinkholes S_{pot} by adding all IP addresses $v \in V$ which meet these requirements:

(i) The IP address must respond to ICMP Echo or HTTP requests.

(ii) At least D domains are currently resolving to this IP, whereas the value D is defined by the average number of active domains per IP in our set.

(iii) The ratio R exceeds a threshold T, whereas T is defined as the average ratio of all IP addresses $v \in V$.

(iv) All domains associated with a single IP address utilize the same NS.

We then manually verify each IP in S_{pot} whether it is a FP or associated with a sinkhole by analyzing the utilized NS, served web content, reverse DNS record, and AS details, and also employ a service provided by one of our collaboration partners listing known sinkhole IPs. Verified sinkholes are added to the set S_{ver}.

We chose these rather hard requirements as most sinkhole operators have little incentive to disguise the existence of their sinkholes. We thus hypothesize that this list of requirements will even hold once our sinkhole detection technique is known. However, as we might have missed sinkhole IPs due to the strict requirements for S_{pot}, we explore the neighboring IP addresses of S_{ver} in the second phase of the sinkhole identification. Before doing so, we extract the NS of the domains resolving to the IPs in S_{ver}, manually check whether the NS are specifically used in conjunction with sinkholed domains and if so, we add the NS to a trusted set S_{NS}. Further on, to also detect inactive sinkholes at a later stage, we create a mapping of trusted NS and the AS the corresponding sinkhole $s \in S_{ver}$ is located in, defined by $S_{NS\_AS} = \{(ns_s, AS_s) \mid ns_s \in S_{NS}\}$.

Sinkhole operators might relocate domains to different sinkholes in the same organization and AS, thus we explore the parent and child nodes of each sinkhole to identify yet unknown sinkholes. For each $ip \in V$, we check whether ip is a parent or child node of a known sinkhole $s \in S_{ver}$, whereas we only consider IPs abiding $AS_{ip} = AS_s$. If ip is found to be a neighboring node of at least two sinkholes, we define ip to be a potential sinkhole and add it to S_{pot}. Further, ip is added to S_{pot} when it is a parent or child node of at least one sinkhole in the same AS and the domains resolving to both IP addresses share the same NS.

To identify sinkholes which cannot be found by exploring parent and child nodes, we leverage the trusted name servers $ns \in S_{NS}$. As we defined these NS to be exclusively used for sinkholed domains, we check if the authoritative NS of the domains currently resolving to each IP $ip \in V$ can be found in S_{NS}.

The previous exploration mechanisms traced active sinkholes only as we require domains to resolve to the IPs of potential sinkholes. Our blacklist dataset also includes historical data, thus we are interested in obtaining a list of sinkholes which were active in the past. Inactive sinkholes presumably do not have domains currently resolving to them, hence we cannot leverage the NS data as conducted in the previous step. Instead, we examine the domains which once resolved to each $ip \in V$ in our dataset, obtain the currently most utilized name server ns, and check if ns is covered by S_{NS}. If $ns \in S_{NS}$ is true, the ip is either of malicious character and the domains once resolving to ip are now sinkholed or we identified an inactive sinkhole and the domains were relocated to other sinkholes. To distinguish between malicious and sinkhole IP we check if (ns_{ip}, AS_{ip}) is listed in S_{NS_AS}. If this is true, we add ip to S_{pot} as we assume that malicious IPs are not located in the same AS in which we found verified sinkholes.

4.2   Evaluation

We now evaluate our method on the datasets $S_{C\&C}$ and S_{Mal}. On $S_{C\&C}$, the filtering step removed 1,144 IPs listed in S_{Benign} or associated with parking providers or Fast Flux. The resulting graph consists of 41,269 nodes and 371,187 edges. In the first phase of the graph exploration our approach adds 20 IPs to S_{pot}, which we manually verified to be associated with sinkholes. In the second phase, we identify 6 sinkholes by exploring the parent and child nodes of the already verified sinkholes, 11 sinkholes by analyzing the actively used NS, and 8 sinkholes by exploring the NS of historically seen domains. Table 3 outlines the operators of the verified sinkholes and the number of distinct AS. The sinkholes listed as *Others* are associated with organizations such as *Abuse.ch* and *Echo-Source*. In total, we discovered 45 sinkholes in $S_{C\&C}$ without any false positives.

On the larger and more distributed dataset S_{Mal}, we filter 7,349 IPs, resulting in a graph of 277,315 nodes and 4,690,369 edges. The first phase of the graph exploration identifies 80 IPs to be potential sinkholes. We are able to verify 59 of these IPs to be associated with sinkholes and find 10 IPs to serve 403 (Forbidden) and 404 (Not Found) HTTP error codes or empty HTTP responses for all associated domains. Another 7 IPs do not accept HTTP requests due to the HTTP port being closed. We assume that these 17 IPs are either associated with sinkholes or hosting companies, which deactivated misbehaving accounts or servers. The remaining 4 IPs in S_{pot} are considered to be FPs as two IPs serve benign content (i.e., related to adult content and the DNS provider noip.com), one IP replies with a single string for all known domains, and the last IP is still distributing malicious content. Based on the 59 verified sinkholes, we perform the second phase and detect 14 sinkholes by exploring the parent and child nodes, 19 sinkholes by monitoring the actively utilized NS, and 14 sinkholes by exploring the NS of previously seen domains. In *Others*, we summarize operators such as *Fitsec*, *Dr.Web*, and the *U.S. Office of Criminal Investigations*.

Our detection technique identified 106 IP addresses, which we verified to be associated with sinkholes, 17 IP addresses of potential sinkholes, and 4 IP addresses, which are falsely added to S_{pot} in the first exploration phase. The second phase does not cause any FPs but doubles the number of sinkholes.

Table 3. Sinkhole IPs identified in $S_{C\&C}$ and S_{Mal}

		$S_{C\&C}$		S_{Mal}	
Organization	# AS	Active	Inactive	Active	Inactive
Anubis Networks	1	1	0	4	0
Cert.pl	1	4	0	4	0
GeorgiaTech/SinkDNS	5	0	0	8	1
Microsoft	3	7	2	11	2
Others	17	4	1	18	4
PublicDomainRegistry	7	10	7	20	11
Shadowserver	1	0	0	5	0
Torpig-Sinkhole	2	4	1	8	2
Zinkhole	1	4	0	7	1

5 Blacklist Evaluation

Based on the findings in the previous sections, we now proceed to analyze the content of the monitored malware blacklists in regards to multiple characteristics.

5.1 Classification of Blacklist Entries

We introduced detection mechanisms for parked domains and sinkholing servers, which are covered by blacklists. Table 4 outlines how many of the currently listed domains ($S_{Current}$) and IPs (S_{IPs}) can be assigned to one of these categories.

Table 4. Classification of $S_{Current}$ and S_{IPs}

	(in %)		Sinkholed		
Blacklist	Unreg.	Parked	Domains	(% / #)	# IPs
Citadel	23.6	0.2	70.4	3,263	n/a
Cybercrime	40.1	1.6	4.2	45	0
Malc0de	12.0	1.5	0.0	0	0
MDL Hosts	18.0	3.0	0.4	6	n/a
MDL ZeuS	41.6	0.0	8.3	1	0
MW-Domains	52.1	2.4	2.8	659	n/a
Palevo Tracker	0.0	0.0	2.9	1	1
Shallalist	45.7	10.9	0.9	190	1
Shadowserver	n/a	n/a	n/a	n/a	4
SpyEye Tracker	47.2	0.0	19.5	24	2
UrlBlacklist	72.3	3.1	1.7	2,211	3
Virustracker	85.1	8.7	3.5	426	n/a
ZeuS Tracker	52.0	0.3	0.1	1	0

The Abuse.ch blacklists as well as *MDL ZeuS* include a low number of parked domains. In contrast, we observe a high number of parked domains for blacklists that have only a few historical entries (cf. Table 1 in Section 2). Particularly for *Shallalist* and *UrlBlacklist*, we assume that the listed domains are not reviewed periodically as more than 57%, respectively, 77% of all domains are either non-existent, parked, or associated to sinkholes while the number of historical entries is almost negligible. When taking a look at *Virustracker*, we find 8.7% of the currently listed domains to be parked. *Virustracker* consists of DGA-based domains next to a partition of hard-coded malware domains that are valid and blacklisted for a longer period of time. The classification results indicate that the hard-coded domains are parked significantly more often than the DGA-based domains, i.e., when inspecting a random subset of 25 DGA-based and 25 hard-coded domains, only a single DGA-based domain was parked while more than 40% of the hard-coded domains were associated to parking. We thus assume that many of the persistent domains are parked to monetize the malicious traffic.

5.2   Blacklist Completeness

Next, we aim to answer how complete the blacklists are, i.e., we measure if they cover all domains for popular malware families. We thus turn from analyzing *what is* listed to evaluating *what is not* blacklisted. To the best of our knowledge, we are the first to analyze the completeness of malware blacklists. Estimating the completeness is challenging as it requires to obtain a ground truth first, i.e., a set of domains used by each malware family. To aggregate a dataset of malicious domains we leverage analysis reports of our dynamic malware analysis platform SANDNET [31]. We inspect the network traffic of more than 300,000 malware samples that we analyzed since Mar. 2012 and identify characteristic patterns for the C&C communication and egg download channels of 13 popular malware families. Our dataset includes banking trojans, droppers (e.g., *Gamarue*), ransomware (e.g., *FakeRean*), and DDoS bots (e.g., *Dirtjumper*), thus represents a diverse set of malware families. Per malware family, we manually identify typical communication patterns and extract the domains for all TCP/UDP connections that match these patterns. Next to regular expressions, we use traffic analysis [32] and identify encrypted C&C streams using probabilistic models [33] to classify the malware communication. We ensured that these fingerprints capture generic characteristics per malware family, guaranteeing that the number of false negatives is negligible (see [32] and [33] for details). We manually verified a subset of the suspicious communication streams and did not identify any false classifications. Admittedly, our dataset is limited to a small subset of the overall malware population only. Given the subset of malware samples, the set of extracted domains is thus by no means complete. However, our dataset serves as an independent statistical sample. In addition, polymorphism creates tens of thousands new malware *samples* daily, whereas the number of new malware *variants* (e.g., using different C&C domains) is much lower [30]—indicating that our dataset achieves reasonable coverage, as also indicated in the experiments.

We evaluate the completeness of the blacklists by computing the ratio of the malware domains observed in SANDNET that are also blacklisted. Table 5 outlines our evaluation results per family. The second column shows the number of domains we obtained from SANDNET per family. The remaining columns represent the results for particular blacklist datasets as introduced in Section 2, while S_{AV} is defined by the union of all four AV vendor blacklists. Our analysis shows that the public blacklists detect less than 10% of the malicious domains for eight ($S_{C\&C}$) and five (S_{Mal}) malware families, respectively. As a result, the detection capabilities of an IDS or AV software using these blacklists is insufficient, even when combining multiple blacklists that employ different listing strategies. The public blacklists do achieve detection rates higher than 50% for particular families because of highly specialized listing policies such as in the `Abuse.ch` trackers and Microsoft's list of *Citadel* domains, yet they fail to detect the other families—even though families such as *Sality* are known since 2003.

Table 5. Coverage of malware domains

Family	#Dom.	Public (%)		AV Vendors (%)		
		$S_{C\&C}$	S_{Mal}	S_{AV}	S_{BD}	S_{MA}
Citadel	225	87.6	89.3	96.0	57.3	79.1
Dirtjumper	47	2.1	2.1	80.9	63.8	40.4
FakeRean	34	0.0	17.7	73.5	50.0	58.8
Gamarue	127	6.3	18.9	86.6	62.2	47.2
Gbot	321	0.0	0.0	100.0	77.3	100.0
Palevo	58	51.7	58.6	93.1	63.8	89.7
Ponyloader	210	4.3	21.0	95.7	71.4	65.7
Pushdo	42	0.0	9.5	92.9	64.3	78.6
Rodecap	9	11.1	11.1	100.0	66.7	44.4
Sality	417	0.0	1.2	82.3	73.4	27.3
SpyEye	145	56.6	57.9	83.4	26.9	61.4
Tedroo	7	0.0	0.0	85.7	57.1	28.6
ZeuS	47	51.1	53.2	95.7	51.1	61.7

Three of the blacklists operated by AV vendors perform significantly better. Looking at the union of the blacklists, at least 70% of the domains per family are detected. More than 90% of the domains were listed for seven of the 13 families. We also look at the breakdown of S_{AV}, i.e., how well the individual blacklists perform. Table 5 includes the two blacklists that perform best: S_{BD} is operated by *Bitdefender* and S_{MA} by *McAfee*. Surprisingly, these blacklists have a non-negligible separation—combining them significantly increases the overall coverage for many families. We do not list the remaining two blacklists due to space constraints, however, note that *Norton* performs similar to *Bitdefender* and *McAfee* while *Browserdefender* fails to detect any domain for the majority of families and covers only 2 - 7% of the domains for the other malware families.

5.3   Reaction Time

For the domains seen in SANDNET which are also covered by S_{Mal}, we additionally estimate the *reaction time* of the blacklists. That is, we measure how long it takes to blacklist the domains once they were seen in SANDNET. As the domains could have been performing malicious activities before we observed them in SANDNET, the presented reaction times are lower bounds. We therefore obtained pDNS records and VirusTotal [34] analysis results to investigate the history of each domain. In total, we could aggregate pDNS records for 81.3% of all domains and obtained information from VirusTotal for 98% of the domains.

We determined the reaction times for each combination of public blacklist and malware family. Yet, for reasons of brevity we focus on a few interesting combinations only. Figure 1 illustrates a CDF of the reaction times of four blacklists, respectively, blacklist combinations. The y-axis shows the reaction time per blacklist entry in days and the x-axis depicts the ratio of domains with this reaction time. Negative y-values indicate that the domain was first seen in the blacklists and then observed in SANDNET, pDNS, or VirusTotal. Positive y-values denote that a blacklist lagged behind. The y-values of blacklisted domains that are not found in pDNS or VirusTotal are set to the negative infinity.

The black solid line represents the reaction time of the blacklists provided by **Abuse.ch** (*Palevo, SpyEye,* and *ZeuS*) and the corresponding domains as seen in SANDNET. About 23.3% of the domains were listed by the blacklists before they appeared in SANDNET, respectively, 76.7% of the domains were seen in SAND-NET first. As depicted by the black dotted line, we find 37.9% of the domains to be blacklisted before appearing in VirusTotal. Approximately 64.7% of the domains were seen in SANDNET and added to the blacklists on the same day. The reaction time of **Abuse.ch** was less than a week for 80.2% of the SANDNET domains and the blacklists included already 96.6% of the domains within 30 days. The results show an adequate reaction time for the **Abuse.ch** blacklists, although the completeness is not ideal (cf. Section 5.2). The black dashed line illustrates the results obtained for the **Abuse.ch** blacklists and pDNS. We could not obtain pDNS records for 27.6% of the domains, i.e., these domains, although monitored in multiple sandbox environments, were never seen in the *DNS DB* database. Another 3.4% of the domains were blacklisted before the domains appeared in pDNS, while 10.4% of the domains were blacklisted and seen in pDNS on the same day. The remaining 58.6% of the domains were seen in pDNS on average 334 days before appearing in the blacklists. These domains either performed malicious activities before becoming blacklisted or—more likely—performed benign actions before turning malicious.

We observe different results for the reaction times of the other three blacklists shown in the graph. The reaction time of *UrlBlacklist* was higher than a month for 53.5% of the domains. Similarly, the blacklist *MW-Domains* has a reaction time of at least 30 days for 39.7% of the domains. After four months, the cover-

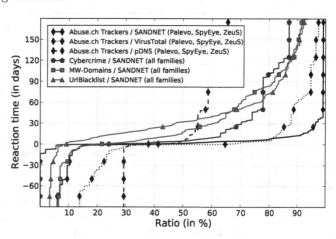

Fig. 1. Reaction times of selected blacklists

age of all three blacklists was still below 90%. In general, the low number of domains that appeared in SANDNET *after* they were blacklisted (negative y-values) indicates that our ground truth dataset is up-to-date.

5.4   DGA-Based Domains

Malware that employs DGAs to dynamically create domains—typically derived from the current date—imposes additional difficulties to blacklist operators. First, DGA-based domains are valid for a limited time span, thus often change. Ideally, blacklists would include these domains *before* they become valid. Second, most of the domains are never registered or seen active, e.g., when dynamically analyzing malware samples. Yet, DGA-based malware is on the rise [3], hence networks protected by blacklists would benefit from DGA-based listings.

We evaluate the coverage of DGA-based domains in the blacklists for five prevalent malware families. We implemented the DGAs for these families after obtaining the algorithms from partners or using reverse engineering. Four families generate domains every day, whereas the *ZeuS P2P* domains are valid for 7 days. We again measure the completeness and determine the reaction time for each family, i.e., how many days it takes to blacklist a domain once it becomes valid. We further estimate the rate of registered domains in S_{Mal} by leveraging the recorded DNS data (i.e., we check if the domains resolved to IP addresses at the time the domains were valid). As the dataset S_{Mal} contains all the domains that were listed by *any* of the 15 public blacklists at some point in time since 2012, it should also include DGA-based domains that were valid in the past.

Table 6 illustrates the listing behavior we monitored in the period Jan. 2012 to Mar. 2014 for the public blacklists (first major column) and on a typical weekday in Mar. 2014 for the AV vendor blacklists (second major column).

Table 6. Coverage of DGA-based domains

| Family | S_{Mal} | | | | S_{AV} | | |
| | # Domains | Listed | Reg. | t_{React} | # Domains | Listed | Reg. |
		Ratio (%)				Ratio (%)	
Bamital	84,136	21.9	11.7	-1	104	75.0	50.0
Conficker	7,354,415	1.6	0.2	1	50,500	94.3	4.8
Flashback	4,045	18.0	15.3	71	5	0.0	100.0
Virut	8,089,752	0.2	0.004	13	10,000	97.9	1.7
ZeuS P2P	131,000	28.9	0.2	1	1,000	99.5	4.5

In total, less than 1.2% of all domains were listed by the public blacklists. On the positive side, blacklists have a low reaction time for three families (if they blacklist a domain). On the downside, 82.1% of the matches are found in the blacklist *Virustracker* only. When removing *Virustracker* from S_{Mal}, the reaction times increase significantly for most families (i.e., *Bamital*: 12 days, *Conficker*: 12 days, *Flashback*: 381 days, *Virut*: -271 days, and *ZeuS P2P*: 16 days). Before removing *Virustracker* from S_{Mal}, we find 0.2% of the *Virut* domains to be blacklisted. After removing *Virustracker*, we find merely 167 domains (0.002%) to be listed. Due to the generic structure of *Virut* domains, we assume that these domains are not listed to protect against *Virut* in particular but rather because they were related to other malicious activities. The reaction time confirms our assumption as it is not reasonable to blacklist domains 271 days before they become active for a single day.

We also determine the coverage of the AV vendor blacklists regarding DGA-based domains. To avoid requesting millions of domain names, we divide our analysis into two steps. To measure if the blacklists protect against threats of DGA-based domains that are currently active, we request listing information and DNS A records for all the domains that are valid on the day we perform this experiment (i.e., 03/24/2014). Second, we analyze if blacklists include domain names which become active in the future. We thus also request a sample of DGA-based domain names (i.e., a random selection of at most 10 domains per day and malware family, respectively, type for *Conficker*) that will be valid between 03/25/2014 and 04/24/2014, i.e., up to 31 days ahead of the day of requesting.

For the domains valid on the day of performing our experiment, we find 76.1%, respectively, 28.9% of the *ZeuS P2P* domains to be blacklisted by *McAfee* and *Bitdefender* and observe the best coverage for *Norton* as most of the results in Table 6 are caused by this blacklist—with a single exception. *Norton* lists 95.5% of the *ZeuS P2P* domains while the union of all AV vendor blacklists increases the coverage up to 99.5%. For the remaining blacklists and malware families, we find a negligible number of listed domains (if domains are listed at all). When taking a closer look at the registered domains that day, we find half of the *Bamital* domains and most of the domains for *Conficker B/C* and *Flashback* to be sinkholed. Further on, four domains of *ZeuS P2P* are sinkholed while the 168 registered *Virut* domains are associated to parking providers and benign web pages. In conclusion, a partition of valid domains is sinkholed by security researchers, yet the remaining domains could be used for malicious activities. We thus recommend to blacklist each DGA-based domain for security reasons (i.e., to trigger alerts). For the domains getting active in the near future, we again find the blacklist provider *Norton* to perform best. Except for *Flashback* (no listed domain) and *Bamital* (coverage of 46.5%), we find *Norton* to include at least 94.5% of the domains for each of the remaining families. For the other families and blacklists, we again observe a negligible number of listed domains.

Our analysis shows that as of today, only one blacklist can reasonably protect against any of the five DGAs used in our experiments. This is surprising to us, given the fact that—once the DGA is known—the DGA-based domains can be accurately predicted unless there are external dependencies (e.g., DGAs utilizing lists of popular feeds from social network web pages). One of the reasons could be that DGAs are often used as a C&C backup mechanism only. For example, *Zeus P2P* uses a DGA only if its peer-to-peer communication fails [35]. Another reason could be that DGA-based domains may, by coincidence, collide with benign domains. Still, as these issues can be overcome, the potential of including DGA-based domains is unused in most of the nowadays blacklists.

6   Discussion and Future Work

We showed that our parking detection approach can effectively distinguish parked and benign domains. As our features depend on the content delivered by parking services such as sponsored ads, domain resellers serving benign content and parked domains exhibiting parking behavior different from the expected however cannot be effectively identified by our detection model. This is particularly problematic when parking providers block us, e.g., for sending too many requests.

Parking services employ different types of blocking (e.g., provide error messages, benign content, or the parking page template without any referral links). To avoid getting blocked, we could distribute the requests to several proxy servers or rate-limit our requests. Further, domains might perform cloaking [36], i.e., provide malicious content for real users while serving parking content for automated systems. We leave a detection of cloaking domains for future work and acknowledge that a large number of parked domains alone does not necessarily imply that a blacklist is not well-managed. We also have to keep in mind that the parking IDs might be biased in respect to the language of the blacklist content, as we obtained the IDs by leveraging the NS used by the blacklisted domains. However, our dataset does not include any national blacklists, which primarily list domains of a specific country or language. While performing the manual verification for the real-world datasets in Section 3.3, we monitored many domains providing content in foreign languages that were flagged as parked by the classifier. This shows that our approach is largely language-independent.

The proposed sinkhole detection method relies on the blacklists to observe behavior that can be attributed to sinkholes. As such, our detection capabilities are limited to sinkholes that are blacklisted. We could use the identified sinkhole dataset as ground truth and leverage techniques such as passive DNS analysis to identify further potential sinkholes [37]. Additionally, the quality of our approach depends on the accuracy of the blacklists. If blacklists contain too many benign domains that cannot be filtered, e.g., by removing Alexa Top 25k, parking, and shared hosting IPs, we might flag benign IP addresses as potential sinkholes.

Our evaluation on the completeness of blacklists is limited to estimating lower bounds as SANDNET only covers a random subset of all samples of the active malware families. Consequently, we may have missed malicious domains in SANDNET. We aim to scale up malware execution to achieve a higher coverage.

We classified the blacklist content as parked, sinkholed, or unregistered and analyzed the completeness of the blacklists in regards to domains of various malware families. Yet, the blacklists also include domains we could not classify accordingly, leaving 23.7% of the currently blacklisted domains to be unspecified. These domains might also include potential false listings, e.g., caused by erroneous setups of analysis back-ends or insufficient verification of domains that are flagged to be potentially malicious. False listings, however, are hard to identify as each blacklist applies its own listing strategy and might include domains of malware families that are not present in SANDNET and the DGA-based domain dataset. Analysis techniques to identify potential false listings thus require a thorough evaluation of correctness. We leave the categorization of the so far unclassified domains for future work.

7   Related Work

The effectiveness of malware blacklists is still largely unstudied. In prior work, we proposed a system to track blacklists and presented first details regarding blacklist sizes [6]. With this paper, we extend our work and evaluate malware blacklist effectiveness—motivated by promising results others reported with blacklists in a different context. For example, Thomas *et al.* [38] looked at blacklists in Twitter. Similarly, Sinha *et al.* [39], Rossow *et al.* [40], and Dietrich *et al.* [41] evaluated the strength of blacklists in the context of email spam, while Sheng *et al.* [42] analyzed phishing blacklists.

Concurrent to our sinkhole identification work, Rahbarinia *et al.* developed a system called SinkMiner [37] to identify sinkhole IPs. They leverage pDNS data and *a priori* information about sinkholes to extrapolate to other sinkholes. Our approach does not rely on an initially-known set of sinkholes and, in its simple form, works without pDNS. In addition, we found sinkholes which were not linked to other sinkholes—many of which SinkMiner would miss. Nevertheless, a combination of SinkMiner and our graph-based approach could identify yet unknown sinkholes, as SinkMiner analyzes the global history of domains using pDNS while we are limited to the history of blacklisted domains. We further proposed a more advanced mechanism to identify parking providers. Rahbarinia *et al.* filter for NS that include the term *park* in their hostnames. Yet, of the 204 parking NS identified in Section 3.1 we find 59 NS to not specify this term in their hostnames. Halvorson *et al.* [23, 24] identify parked domains by applying regular expressions to the aggregated web content. Instead, we introduced characteristic features for parking behavior and—to the best of our knowledge—are the first to propose a generic mechanism to identify parked domains.

Orthogonal to our work, a number of proposals aim to increase the quality of existing blacklists. Neugschwandtner *et al.* [43] proposed SQUEEZE, a multi-path exploration technique in dynamic malware analysis to increase the coverage of C&C blacklists. Stone-Gross *et al.* [44] proposed FIRE, a system to identify organizations that demonstrate malicious behavior by monitoring botnet communication. Our findings show that usage of such systems should be fostered.

8 Conclusion

We have shown that blacklists have to be employed with care as the nature of the listings is diverse. First, one needs to keep in mind that also sinkholes may be blacklisted. Second, many parking providers re-use popular malware domains. This is crucial to know, e.g., when blacklists raise false positives or one aims to attribute a reputation to certain providers based on blacklist data. In addition, our evaluation of blacklist coverage indicates how blacklists can be improved in the future as none of the public blacklists is sufficiently complete to protect against the variety of malware threats we face nowadays. We further have shown that most blacklists operated by AV vendors do not cover DGA-based malware to effectively protect users, although integration would be straight-forward. We are confident that our analyses will help to improve blacklists in the future.

Acknowledgment. We would like to thank our shepherd Manos Antonakakis for his support in finalizing this paper. We also would like to thank the anonymous reviewers for their insightful comments. This work was supported by the German Federal Ministry of Education and Research (Grant 01BY1110, MoBE).

References

1. Kolbitsch, C., Livshits, B., Zorn, B., Seifert, C.: Rozzle: De-Cloaking Internet Malware. In: Proceedings of the 2012 IEEE Symposium on Security and Privacy, SP 2012, pp. 443–457. IEEE Computer Society, Washington, DC (2012)
2. Antonakakis, M., Perdisci, R., Lee, W., Vasiloglou, I.N., Dagon, D.: Detecting Malware Domains at the Upper DNS Hierarchy. In: Proceedings of the 20th USENIX Conference on Security, SEC 2011, p. 27. USENIX Association, Berkeley (2011)
3. Antonakakis, M., Perdisci, R., Nadji, Y., Vasiloglou, N., Abu-Nimeh, S., Lee, W., Dagon, D.: From Throw-Away Traffic to Bots: Detecting the Rise of DGA-Based Malware. In: Proceedings of the 21st USENIX Conference on Security Symposium, Security 2012, p. 24. USENIX Association, Berkeley (2012)
4. Bilge, L., Kirda, E., Kruegel, C., Balduzzi, M.: EXPOSURE: Finding Malicious Domains Using Passive DNS Analysis. In: 18th Annual Network and Distributed System Security Symposium. The Internet Society, San Diego (2011)
5. Rossow, C., Dietrich, C., Bos, H.: Large-Scale Analysis of Malware Downloaders. In: Flegel, U., Markatos, E., Robertson, W. (eds.) DIMVA 2012. LNCS, vol. 7591, pp. 42–61. Springer, Heidelberg (2013)
6. Kührer, M., Holz, T.: An Empirical Analysis of Malware Blacklists. Praxis der Informationsverarbeitung und Kommunikation 35(1), 11–16 (2012)
7. Microsoft Corp.: Citadel Botnet (2014), http://botnetlegalnotice.com/citadel
8. Abuse.ch Malware Trackers (2014), http://www.abuse.ch/
9. CyberCrime Tracker (2014), http://cybercrime-tracker.net
10. Malc0de.com (2014), http://malc0de.com/
11. Malware Domain List (2014), http://www.malwaredomainlist.com/
12. Malware-Domains (2014), http://www.malware-domains.com/
13. Shadowserver: Botnet C&C Servers (2014), http://rules.emergingthreats.net
14. Shalla Secure Services (2014), http://www.shallalist.de/
15. URLBlacklist (2014), http://urlblacklist.com/
16. Kleissner & Associates (2014), http://virustracker.info/
17. Bitdefender TrafficLight (2014), http://trafficlight.bitdefender.com/
18. BrowserDefender (2014), http://www.browserdefender.com
19. McAfee SiteAdvisor (2014), http://www.siteadvisor.com/
20. Norton Safe Web (2014), http://safeweb.norton.com/
21. Kührer, M., Rossow, C., Holz, T.: Paint it Black: Evaluating the Effectiveness of Malware Blacklists. Technical Report HGI-2014-002, University of Bochum - Horst Görtz Institute for IT Security (June 2014)
22. Li, Z., Alrwais, S., Xie, Y., Yu, F., Wang, X.: Finding the Linchpins of the Dark Web: A Study on Topologically Dedicated Hosts on Malicious Web Infrastructures. In: Proceedings of the 2013 IEEE Symposium on Security and Privacy, SP 2013, pp. 112–126. IEEE Computer Society, Washington, DC (2013)
23. Halvorson, T., Szurdi, J., Maier, G., Felegyhazi, M., Kreibich, C., Weaver, N., Levchenko, K., Paxson, V.: The BIZ Top-Level Domain: Ten Years Later. In: Taft, N., Ricciato, F. (eds.) PAM 2012. LNCS, vol. 7192, pp. 221–230. Springer, Heidelberg (2012)
24. Halvorson, T., Levchenko, K., Savage, S., Voelker, G.M.: XXXtortion?: Inferring Registration Intent in the .XXX TLD. In: Proceedings of the 23rd International Conference on World Wide Web, WWW 2014, pp. 901–912. International World Wide Web Conferences Steering Committee, Geneva (2014)
25. Farsight Security, Inc.: DNS Database (2014), https://www.dnsdb.info/
26. Alexa Internet, Inc.: Top 1M Websites (2013), http://www.alexa.com/topsites/

27. Damerau, F.J.: A Technique for Computer Detection and Correction of Spelling Errors. Commun. ACM 7(3), 171–176 (1964)
28. RapidMiner, Inc. (2014), http://rapidminer.com/
29. Hofmann, T., Schölkopf, B., Smola, A.J.: Kernel Methods in Machine Learning. Annals of Statistics 36, 1171–1220 (2008)
30. Rossow, C., Dietrich, C.J., Kreibich, C., Grier, C., Paxson, V., Pohlmann, N., Bos, H., van Steen, M.: Prudent Practices for Designing Malware Experiments: Status Quo and Outlook. In: Proceedings of the 2012 IEEE Symposium on Security and Privacy, SP 2012. IEEE Computer Society, San Francisco (2012)
31. Rossow, C., Dietrich, C.J., Bos, H., Cavallaro, L., van Steen, M., Freiling, F.C., Pohlmann, N.: Sandnet: Network Traffic Analysis of Malicious Software. In: Proceedings of the First Workshop on Building Analysis Datasets and Gathering Experience Returns for Security, BADGERS 2011, pp. 78–88. ACM, NY (2011)
32. Dietrich, C.J., Rossow, C., Pohlmann, N.: CoCoSpot: Clustering and Recognizing Botnet Command and Control Channels using Traffic Analysis. Comput. Netw. 57(2), 475–486 (2013)
33. Rossow, C., Dietrich, C.J.: ProVeX: Detecting Botnets with Encrypted Command and Control Channels. In: Rieck, K., Stewin, P., Seifert, J.-P. (eds.) DIMVA 2013. LNCS, vol. 7967, pp. 21–40. Springer, Heidelberg (2013)
34. VirusTotal (2014), http://www.virustotal.com/
35. Rossow, C., Andriesse, D., Werner, T., Stone-Gross, B., Plohmann, D., Dietrich, C.J., Bos, H.: P2PWNED: Modeling and Evaluating the Resilience of Peer-to-Peer Botnets. In: Proceedings of the 2013 IEEE Symposium on Security and Privacy, SP 2013, pp. 97–111. IEEE Computer Society, Washington, DC (2013)
36. Kolbitsch, C., Livshits, B., Zorn, B., Seifert, C.: Rozzle: De-cloaking Internet Malware. In: Proceedings of the 2012 IEEE Symposium on Security and Privacy, SP 2012, pp. 443–457. IEEE Computer Society, Washington, DC (2012)
37. Rahbarinia, B., Perdisci, R., Antonakakis, M., Dagon, D.: SinkMiner: Mining Botnet Sinkholes for Fun and Profit. In: 6th USENIX Workshop on Large-Scale Exploits and Emergent Threats. USENIX, Berkeley (2013)
38. Thomas, K., Grier, C., Ma, J., Paxson, V., Song, D.: Design and Evaluation of a Real-Time URL Spam Filtering Service. In: Proceedings of the 2011 IEEE Symposium on Security and Privacy, SP 2011, pp. 447–462. IEEE Computer Society, Washington, DC (2011)
39. Sinha, S., Bailey, M., Jahanian, F.: Shades of Grey: On the effectiveness of reputation-based "blacklists". In: 3rd International Conference on Malicious and Unwanted Software, MALWARE 2008, pp. 57–64 (2008)
40. Rossow, C., Czerwinski, T., Dietrich, C.J., Pohlmann, N.: Detecting Gray in Black and White. In: MIT Spam Conference (2010)
41. Dietrich, C.J., Rossow, C.: Empirical Research on IP Blacklisting. In: Proceedings of the 5th Conference on Email and Anti-Spam, CEAS (2008)
42. Sheng, S., Wardman, B., Warner, G., Cranor, L.F., Hong, J., Zhang, C.: An Empirical Analysis of Phishing Blacklists. In: Proceedings of the Sixth Conference on Email and Anti-Spam (2009)
43. Neugschwandtner, M., Comparetti, P.M., Platzer, C.: Detecting Malware's Failover C&C Strategies with Squeeze. In: Proceedings of the 27th Annual Computer Security Applications Conference, ACSAC 2011, pp. 21–30. ACM, NY (2011)
44. Stone-Gross, B., Kruegel, C., Almeroth, K., Moser, A., Kirda, E.: FIRE: FInding Rogue nEtworks. In: Proceedings of the 2009 Annual Computer Security Applications Conference, ACSAC 2009, pp. 231–240. IEEE Computer Society, Washington, DC (2009)

GOLDENEYE: Efficiently and Effectively Unveiling Malware's Targeted Environment

Zhaoyan Xu[1], Jialong Zhang[1], Guofei Gu[1], and Zhiqiang Lin[2]

[1] Texas A&M University, College Station, TX
{z0x0427,jialong,guofei}@cse.tamu.edu
[2] The University of Texas at Dallas, Richardson, TX
zhiqiang.lin@utdallas.edu

Abstract. A critical challenge when combating malware threat is *how to efficiently and effectively identify the targeted victim's environment*, given an unknown malware sample. Unfortunately, existing malware analysis techniques either use a limited, fixed set of analysis environments (not effective) or employ expensive, time-consuming multi-path exploration (not efficient), making them not well-suited to solve this challenge. As such, this paper proposes a new dynamic analysis scheme to deal with this problem by applying the concept of speculative execution in this new context. Specifically, by providing multiple dynamically created, parallel, and virtual environment spaces, we speculatively execute a malware sample and adaptively switch to the right environment during the analysis. Interestingly, while our approach appears to trade space for speed, we show that it can actually use less memory space and achieve much higher speed than existing schemes. We have implemented a prototype system, GOLDENEYE, and evaluated it with a large real-world malware dataset. The experimental results show that GOLDENEYE outperforms existing solutions and can effectively and efficiently expose malware's targeted environment, thereby speeding up the analysis in the critical battle against the emerging targeted malware threat.

Keywords: Dynamic Malware Analysis, Speculative Execution.

1 Introduction

In the past few years, we have witnessed a new evolution of malware attacks from blindly or randomly attacking all of the Internet machines to targeting only specific systems, with a great deal of diversity among the victims, including government, military, business, education, and civil society networks [17,24]. Through querying the victim environment, such as the version of the operating system, the keyboard layout, or the existence of vulnerable software, malware can precisely determine whether it infects the targeted machine or not. Such *query-then-infect* pattern has been widely employed by emerging malware attacks. As one representative example, advanced persistent threats (APT), a unique category of targeted attacks that sets its goal at a particular individual or organization, are consistently increasing and they have caused massive damage [15]. According to an annual report from Symantec Inc, in 2011 targeted malware has a steady uptrend of over 70% increasing since 2010 [15], such overgrowth

A. Stavrou et al. (Eds.): RAID 2014, LNCS 8688, pp. 22–45, 2014.
© Springer International Publishing Switzerland 2014

has never been slow down, especially for the growth of malware binaries involved in targeted attacks in 2012 [14].

To defeat such massive intrusions, one critical challenge for malware analysis is how to effectively and efficiently expose these environment-sensitive behaviors and in further derive the specification of environments, especially when we have to handle a large volume of malware corpus everyday. Moreover, in the context of defeating targeted attacks, deriving the malware targeted environment is an indispensable analysis step. If we can derive the environment conditions that trigger malware's malicious behavior, we can promptly send out alerts or patches to the systems that satisfy these conditions.

In this paper, we focus on *environment-targeted malware*, i.e., malware that contains *query-then-infect* features. To analyze such malware and extract the specification of their targeted environment, we have to refactor our existing malware analysis infrastructure, especially for dynamic malware analysis. Because of the limitation of static analysis [38], dynamic malware analysis is recognized as one of the most effective solutions for exposing malicious behaviors [38,37]. However, existing dynamic analysis techniques are not effective and efficient enough, and, as mentioned, we are facing two new challenges: First, we need *highly efficient techniques* to handle a great number of environment-targeted malware samples collected every day. Second, we require the analysis environment to be more *adaptive* to each individual sample since malware may only exhibit its malicious intent in its targeted environment. (More details are explained in Section 2.)

As such, in this paper we attempt to fill the aforementioned gaps. Specifically, we present a novel dynamic analysis scheme, GOLDENEYE, for agile and effective malware targeted environment analysis. To serve as an efficient tool for malware analysts, GOLDENEYE is able to *proactively* capture malware's environment-sensitive behaviors in progressive running, *dynamically* determine the malware's possible targeted environments, and *online* switch its system environment *adaptively* for further analysis.

The key idea is that by providing several dynamic, parallel, virtual environment spaces during a single malware execution, GOLDENEYE proactively determines what the malware's targeted environment is through a specially designed speculative execution engine to observe malware behaviors under alternative environments. Moreover, GOLDENEYE dynamically, adaptively switches the analysis environment and lets malware itself expose its target-environment-dependent behaviors. Although GOLDENEYE trades space for speed, interestingly our experimental results show that GOLDENEYE could actually use less memory space while achieving much higher speed than existing multi-path exploration techniques.

In summary, this paper makes the following contributions:

- We present a new scheme for environment-targeted malware analysis that provides a better trade-off between effectiveness and efficiency, an important and highly demanded step beyond existing solutions. As a preliminary effort towards systematic analysis of targeted malware, we hope it will inspire more future research in targeted and advanced persistent threat defense.
- We design and implement GOLDENEYE, a new lightweight dynamic analysis tool for discovering malware's targeted environment by applying novel speculative execution in dynamic, parallel, virtual environment spaces. The proposed approach

can facilitate the analysis on new emerging targeted threats to reveal malware's possible high-value targets. Meanwhile, it also facilitates conducting large volumes of malware analysis in a realtime fashion.

– We provide an in-depth evaluation of GOLDENEYE on real-world malware datasets and show that GOLDENEYE can successfully expose malware's environment-sensitive behaviors with much less time or fewer resources, clearly outperforming existing approaches. We also show that GOLDENEYE can automatically identify and provide correct running environment for tested well-known targeted malware families. To further improve the accuracy and efficiency, we also propose a distributed deployment scheme to achieve better parallelization of our analysis.

2   Background and Related Work

2.1   Objectives

The focal point of this paper is on a set of malware families, namely *environment-targeted malware*. In our context, we adopt the same definition of *environment* in related work [36], i.e., we define an *environment* as a system configuration, such as the version of operating system, system language, and the existence of certain system objects, such as file, registry and devices.

Environment-targeted malware families commonly contain some customized environment check logic to identify their targeted victims. Such logic can thus naturally lead us to find out the malware's targeted running environment. For instance, Stuxnet [13], an infamous targeted malware family, embeds a PLC device detection logic to infect machines that connect to PLC control devices. Banking Trojans, such as Zeus [21], only steal information from users who have designated bank accounts. Other well-known examples include Flame [6], Conficker [43] and Duqu [4].

As a result, different from the traditional malware analysis, which mainly focuses on malware's behaviors, environment-targeted malware analysis has to answer the following two questions: (1) Given a random malware binary, can we tell whether this sample is used for environment-targeted attacks? (2) If so, what is its targeted victim or targeted running environment?

Consequently, the goal of our work is to design techniques that can (1) identify possible targeted malware; (2) unveil targeted malware's environment sensitive behaviors; and (3) provide environment information to describe malware's targeted victims.

2.2   Related Work

Research on Enforced/Multi-path Exploration. Exposing malicious behaviors is a research topic that has been extensively discussed in existing research [33,30,27,23,36,47,46].

One brute-forced path exploration scheme, forced execution, was proposed in [46]. Instead of providing semantics information for a path's trigger condition, the technique was designed for brute-force exhausting path space only. Most recently, X-Force [42] has made this approach further by designing a crash-free engine. To provide the semantics of the trigger, Brumley *et al.* [25] proposed an approach that applies taint analysis and symbolic execution to derive the condition of malware's hidden behavior. In [34], Hasten was proposed as an automatic tool to identify malware's stalling code and deviate the execution from it. In [35], Kolbitsch *et al.* proposed a multipath execution scheme for Java-script-based malware. Other research [29,46] proposed techniques to enforce execution of different malware functionalities.

One important work in this domain [37] introduced a snapshot based approach which could be applied to expose malware's environment-sensitive behaviors. However, this approach is not efficient for *large-scale* analysis of environment-targeted malware: it is typically very expensive and it may provide too much unwanted information, thus leaving truly valuable information buried. This approach essentially requires to run the malware multiple times to explore different paths. After each path exploration, we need to rewind to a previous point (e.g., a saved snapshot), deduce the trigger condition of branches and explore unobserved paths by providing a different set of input, or sometimes enforce the executing of branches in a brute-force way. Obviously this kind of frequent forward execution and then rolling back is very resource-consuming, thus making it not very scalable to be applied for analyzing a large volume of malware samples collected each day. Moreover, this scheme is a typical sequential model which makes the analysis hard for parallel or distributed deployment, e.g., in a cloud computing setting. Last but not least, the possible path explosion problem [37] is another important concern for this approach.

Research on Malware's Environment-Sensitive Behaviors. Another line of research [27,23,28,36,44,40] discusses malware environment-sensitive behaviors. These studies fall into three categories: (1) Analyzing malware's anti-debugging and anti-virtualization logic [23,28]; (2) Discovering malware's different behaviors in different system configurations [36]; (3) Discovering behaviors in network-contained environment [32]. The main idea in these studies is to provide *possible target environments* before applying the traditional dynamic analysis. The possible target environment could be a running environment without debuggers [28], introspection tools [23], or patched vulnerabilities involved.

In a recent representative study [36], the authors provided several statically-configured environments to detect malware's environment sensitive behaviors. While efficient (not carrying the overhead of multi-path exploration), this approach is not effective, i.e., the limitation is: *we cannot predict and enumerate all possible target environments in advance.* In particular, in the case of targeted malware, we often are not able to predict malware's targeted environments before the attack/analysis.

Summary. We summarize the pros and cons of previous research in Table 1. We analyze these techniques from several aspects: *Completeness, Flexibility, Prerequisites, Resource Consumption, Analysis Speed, Assisting Techniques, and Deployment Model.*

Table 1. Summary of Existing Techniques

Approach Category	I	II
Representative Work	[25,37,46]	[36,23]
Completeness	High	Low
Flexibility	High	Low
Prerequisites	Low	High
Resource Consumption	High	Low
Analysis Speed	Slow	Fast
Assisting Techniques	Symbolic Execution, Tainted Analysis, Execution Snapshot	Trace Comparison
Deployment Model	Sequential	Sequential/Parallel

As illustrated, the first category of solution, such as [37,25], has theoretically full-completeness but with high resource consumption. It requires the execution to periodically store execution context and roll back analysis after one-round exploration, thus very slow. Meanwhile, it requires some assisting techniques, such as symbolic execution which is slow and has some inherent limitations [22]. Last but not least, it is not designed for parallel deployment, making it not able to leverage modern computing resources such as clouds.

For the second category, such as [23,36], these approaches support both sequential and parallel deployment. Meanwhile it has less resource consumption and fast analysis speed. However, all the environments require manual expertise knowledge and need to be configured *statically beforehand*. Hence, it is not flexible nor adaptive. More importantly, it is incomplete, limited to these limited number of preconfigured environments, and has a low analysis coverage.

3   Overview of GOLDENEYE

An overview of our approach is presented in Figure 1. As illustrated, our scheme consists of three phases. In phase I, we screen malware corpus and identify the possible targeted malware samples. In phase II, we employ dynamic environment analysis to iteratively unveil the malware candidates' targeted running environments. In phase III, we summarize the analysis result with detailed reports. The reports contain the information about malware's sensitive environments and their corresponding behavior differences.

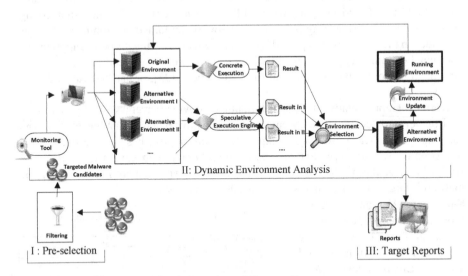

Fig. 1. Overview of GOLDENEYE

In this section we briefly overview the basic idea of our key novel design in GOLDENEYE, i.e., *progressive speculative execution in parallel spaces*, and leave the rest system details to Section 4.

The first key design of GOLDENEYE is to *dynamically* construct parallel spaces to expose malicious behaviors. To overcome the limitation of previous work [36], which statically specifies multiple analysis environments beforehand, our design is to dynamically construct multiple environments based on malware's behaviors, *the call of environment query APIs*. In particular, through labeling these APIs beforehand, we can understand all possible return values of each environment query. For each possible return value, we construct one environment for that. For example, if we find the malware queries system call GetKeyboardLayout, we can prepare multiple return values such as 0x0004 for Chinese and 0x0409 for United States, and simulate two parallel running environment with Chinese and English keyboards for analyzing malware behaviors. As shown in Figure 2, the parallel environments is constructed alongside with malware's execution, therefore, it prevents running the same sample by multiple times. As long as our API labeling (introduced in Section 4) can cover the environment query, we believe GOLDENEYE can automatically detect/expose all environment-sensitive behaviors of samples.

Our second novel design is to apply speculative execution in these parallel environments. Observing the limitation of existing work [37], which consumes a huge amount of time and memory on rolling back the analysis on alternative paths, we apply the concept of speculative execution [31], which refers to the situation when a computer system performs some task that may not be actually needed but to trade off some other optimize needs. The merit of applying speculative execution in our context is to keep the execution forward as far as possible. Thus, we consider to construct multiple possible environments online and speculatively execute malware in each environment instance. Through determining the most possible malicious execution path, we can also determine what the running environment is in order to reach certain path.

To embrace speculative execution in our new problem domain, we need to solve new technical challenges. First, since the executed instructions in each environment vary, it is practically infeasible to predict the execution in an online dynamic fashion. We solve this challenge by *progressively* performing the speculative execution at the *basic block level*. In particular, we execute each basic block in all alternative environment settings. Since there is no branch instruction inside each basic block, the instructions are the same for all environments. When we reach the branch instruction at the end of a block, we apply several heuristics to determine which is the possible malicious path. Consequently, we reduce the space by only keeping the settings that most likely lead to the desired path.

Second, speculative execution is essentially a trade-off scheme between speed and space (i.e., trading more memory consumption for speedup) [31]. In our design, we also try to reduce the memory consumption by two novel designs: (1) We only speculatively execute the instructions that generate different results for different environments. We choose to employ taint analysis to narrow down the scope to the instructions which operate on environment-related data. (2) We monitor the memory usage to prevent the explosion of alternative environments.

In general, we introduce the following speculative execution engine: We conduct speculative execution at the granularity of code block to emulate the malware's execution in multiple parallel environment spaces. We first *prefetch* a block of instructions.

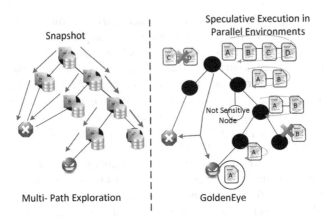

Fig. 2. Illustration of Differences between GOLDENEYE (right) and Multi-path Exploration [37] (left)

Next, we apply taint analysis on the pre-fetched instructions and taint each byte of the API/instruction output (*environment element*) as the tainted source. The reason to use taint analysis is to filter those instructions that are not related to the environment, which can reduce the overhead of full speculative execution. We propagate tainted labels and when we hit one instruction with the tainted operands, we accordingly update the execution context in all alternative environments. We continue such propagation until we reach the end of the block, which is a branch instruction. For the branch instruction, we determine whether it could be affected by the tainted bytes or not. If it is an environment-sensitive branch, we continue to the next step, i.e., branch selection and update. If not, speculative execution will start a new pre-fetch operation.

For environment-sensitive branches, we attempt to prevent the overhead caused by roll-back operation in [37]. We design our scheme to proactively select the branches based on the information provided in the speculative execution. The intuition is: if we can tell which branch is more likely the malware author's intended branch, we can dynamically adjust the environment to enforce the malware to only execute some designated branch. In principle, whenever we find a branch that belongs to a possible malicious path, we will re-examine the alternative environments and only select the environment that could be used to enforce the desired branch. Our solution to find the possible malicious branch is to apply similar techniques as *branch evaluation* [47] to predict the possible malicious branches. The detail will be presented in Section 4.2.

To differentiate GOLDENEYE with other approaches, we illustrate the high-level idea of GOLDENEYE in Figure 2 by comparing with an existing multi-path exploration approach [37]. For the multi-path exploration approach (the left part in Figure 2), the redundant overhead comes from exploring all the possible paths by depth-first execution and storing roll-back snapshots for all deviation branches. GOLDENEYE works in a different way. It applies branch prediction that follows a breath-first execution scheme to quickly locate possible malicious paths, which saves the effort of exploring all possible paths. Second, it enumerates all the possible alternative environments, e.g., ABCD in Figure 2, dynamically. It ensures the analysis continuously keep forward and saves the roll-back operations. Thus, it is not necessary to store snapshots for every branch. Lastly, we use taint analysis to skip many non-environment-sensitive branches to further save the exploration overhead.

Meanwhile, from the figure we can also notice how the speculative execution technique is performed in parallel environments. Essentially, our speculative execution is periodically progressing for each code block. We need to iterate all the environments and synchronize their running results for each instruction in the code block. At the end of a basic block, the parallel space will be curtailed and GOLDENEYE clears all the environments settings that unlikely lead to targeted paths.

4 Detailed Design

4.1 Phase I: Pre-selection of Malware Corpus

The first phase of GOLDENEYE is to quickly obtain the malware samples which are candidates of environment-targeted malware. As defined in Section 2.1, our criteria for the pre-processing is to find any malware that is sensitive to its running environment.

Our scheme of pre-selection is achieved by tainting the return values of certain environment query API/instructions and tracking whether the tainted bytes affect the decision on some branch instructions, such as changing CFlag register. If the tested sample is sensitive to its environment querying, we keep the sample for further steps.

API Labeling. The most common way for malware to query its running environment is through certain system APIs/instructions. To capture malware's environment queries, we need to hook these APIs/instructions. Furthermore, it is important to derive all possible return values of these APIs/instructions because these return values are used to define parallel denvironments. In GOLDENEYE, we label three categories of environment queries:

- *Hook system-level environment query APIs.* The operating system provides a large set of system APIs to allow programmers query the running environment. They have also been commonly used by malware to achieve the similar goal.
- *Hook environment-related instructions.* Some X86 instructions such as CPUID can also be thought as a way to query environment information.
- *Hook APIs with environment-related parameter(s).* Some system files/registries can be used to store environment configuration. Thus, we also hook file/registry operation APIs and examine their parameters. If the parameters contain some keywords, such as version, we also treat as a query attempt.

For each labeled API/instruction, we examine its return value as the reference to initialize parallel environments. In general, we construct one speculative execution context for each possible return value. To narrow down the alternative choices of the environment, we define the following four basic sets of return values.

- *BSET(n)* defines a two-choice (binary) set. One example for NtOpenFile is *BSET(0)* for the return value NTSTATUS, which accepts 0 (success) or other value (failure).
- *SET([...])* defines a normal enumeration of values, such as enumeration for LANGID in the default system language.
- *RANGE(A, B)* set contains a range of possible return values.

Based on these three sets, we construct the parallel contexts. For example, we simply construct two parallel contexts for *BSET(n)* element. Note that a large amount of system objects, whose querying API returns -1 as *non-existence* and *random value* as the *object handle*, belong to this type. We consider all these objects as *BSET(n)* element.

For *SET([...])* with n different values, we accordingly initialize n parallel settings based on the context.

For *RANGE(A, B)* set, we examine whether the range set can be divided into some semantically independent sub-ranges. For example, the different range of native call NtQuerySystemInformation's return specifies different type of the system information. For these cases, we construct one context for each semantically-independent sub-range. Otherwise, we initially construct one context for each possible value.

One current limitation of our labeling is that we cannot provide parallel environments for API functions whose return values are not enumerable. For example, some malware logic may depend on the content of certain file. However, it is not possible for us to construct all possible (correct) file contents in advance. One possible solution is to combine symbolic execution [22] in the analysis step at the cost of extra analysis overhead. However, to achieve better balance between efficiency and effectiveness, we do not adopt such solution at the moment.

4.2   Phase II: Dynamic Environment Analysis

Dynamic environment analysis is the main component of GOLDENEYE. In this section, we present its detailed design. We use Conficker [43] worm's logic as a working example. As illustrated in Figure 3, in this example, Conficker worm queries the existence of specific mutex and the version of the running operating system. The malicious logic is triggered only after the check succeeds.

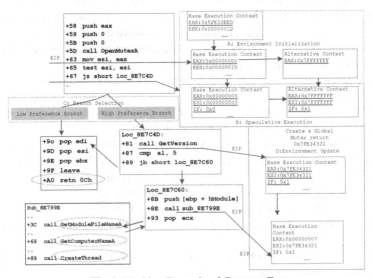

Fig. 3. Working Example of GOLDENEYE

Initialization of Malware Environment Analysis. After the preprocessing, we first initialize the analysis by constructing parallel environments when we find malware's environment query. We define a running environment with a set of environment elements as

$$env = \{e_1, ..., e_i, ...e_n\}$$

For each e_i, it is defined as a tuple:

$$< identifier, API, type, value >$$

where $identifier$ uniquely denotes the name of each environment element, such as the mutex name or the title of GUI windows; API is the invoked API to query the element; $type$ specifies the type of element, such as system setting (system language, os version, etc.) or system objects (the existence of files, registries, etc.); and $value$ states *what are possible values of each element*, such as true/false or a set of hex values.

Context Maintenance of Speculative Execution. After GOLDENEYE captures malware's environment query, a set of initialized environment contexts are maintained by our speculative execution engine. The main overhead of our speculative execution comes from continuously maintaining those parallel contexts.

To save space, the key design for context maintenance is based on our progressive execution scheme. Since the execution in parallel can be naturally synchronized by each instruction (it follows the same code block(s)), we choose to only record the modification of parallel contexts. As illustrated in Figure 3 Step A and B, we have no need to maintain the full execution context, such as all general registers value and execution stack, in each parallel space. We only track the different data, which is EAX and ESI in the example. We maintain such alternative contexts using a linked list. When an environment update operation starts, we only update the *dirty* bytes that have been modified since the previous block(s). In further, we organize each progressive context using linked-list to track the modified bytes.

Taint-assisted Speculative Execution. Another key design to prevent redundant overhead is to applying taint tracking on environment-sensitive data. In particular, we taint each byte of the environment query's return and propagate the tainted labels by each instruction. When we encounter an instruction without tainted operation, we continue with concrete execution. Otherwise, when we encounter an instruction with the tainted operands, we accordingly update the execution context in all alternative environments. We continue such propagation until we reach the end of a basic block. For the branch instruction, we also determine whether it could be affected by the tainted bytes or not (whether CFlag has been tainted or not). If it is an environment-sensitive branch, we continue the branch selection and environment update. If not, speculative execution starts a new pre-fetch operation to continue analyzing a new code block.

The advantage of using taint analysis is to efficiently assist the analysis in three ways: (1) Our speculative execution is only conducted on the instructions whose operands have been tainted. It allows us to skip (majority) untainted instruction for speculative execution to save analysis effort. (2) Tainted propagation can help us to determine the environment-sensitive branches. Our environment prediction/selection is based on the correct identification of these sensitive branches. (3) Tracking the status of the tainted label helps us to maintain parallel environment spaces and delete/merge untracked environments.

Heuristics for Branch Selection. Next, we present how we evaluate the branches and determine which branch is more possible in the targeted environment. In GOLDEN-EYE, we apply three heuristics to determine what is a possible branch in the targeted environment:

- If a branch contains a function call that calls some exit or sleep functions, such as ExitProcess, ExitThread, and sleep, it means this branch may terminate the program's execution. We treat another branch as the possible targeted branch.
- If a branch contains function calls that create a new process or thread, such as CreateProcess and CreateThread, or start network communication, such as socket and connect, we treat this branch as the possible targeted branch. Similar function calls could be some representative malicious calls, such as functions for process injection, auto-booting, and kernel hijacking [45].
- If a branch directly interacts with the environment, we treat this branch as the possible targeted branch. For example, if malware creates a file before the branch, we treat the branch that directly operates on the created file as the targeted branch. Essentially, if one branch contains instructions intensively operating on tainted data, we consider it as the targeted branch.

After examining these three heuristics, if we still cannot decide the possible targeted branch in a given time window or we find some conflicts among different heuristics, inspired by the multi-path exploration work [37], we will save the snapshot at the branch point and conduct the concrete execution for both branches. While this may lead to more overhead (as in [37]), our experimental result shows that such cases are very rare (less than 5% cases require rolling back).

Determining Targeted Branch. Our scheme of branch evaluation is to *foresee* k (e.g., $k = 50$) instructions and find whether any of them contains code of our interest. The foreseeing operation is conducted by statically disassemble the code in the blocks after the addresses of two branches. It is gradually processed until we have collected enough evidence for predicting the branch.

In particular, we start with disassembling one code block at a time. We also need to disassemble all the possible branches after each code block. Then we scan each instruction to check whether it (1) has a CALL instruction or (2) operates on some tainted data.

For the first case, we need to examine the destination address of CALL. Beforehand, we need to maintain two API address lists: the first records the address of possible malicious functions such as CreateProcess and socket, and the second records the dormant/termination functions such as sleep and ExitProcess. Thus, if CALL's destination address belongs to either of the lists, we set the corresponding preference to the explored branch.

For the second case, we examine each instruction along two alternative paths to see whether any instruction operates on the tainted data or not. We achieve that by examining the source operands of each instruction. If the source operand is tainted before, we consider the instruction operates on tainted data. Then we deduce the path that contains more instructions using tainted data.

If we cannot make a decision after we examine k instructions, we apply enforced execution [46] to explore both branches. In this case, we need an extra round of analysis for each branch (which is very rare in practice, as shown in our evaluation).

In Figure 3 Step C, we illustrate our strategy by evaluating two branches after the JZ instruction. As shown in the left branch, the execution may direct to leave and retn while the right branch exhibits possible malicious logic, such as CreateThread. Then, we choose the right branch and identify the alternative context as our preferred execution context.

Environment Update. The result of target branch prediction is to decide whether to remain in the current running environment or to switch to another alternative environment. If the environment switching is needed, there are three basic environment switching operations: (1) Creation, (2) Removal, (3) Substitution.

The key requirement of our design is to update the environment online. Hence, our environment update step is performed directly after the speculative execution engine has committed its execution context.

Creating an element is a common case for an environment update. Especially when malware tries to query the existence of certain system object, we would thus create such an object to ensure that the following malware operation on this object will succeed. To this end, we create a dummy object in the system, such as creating a blank file with certain file name or creating a new registry entry. Accordingly, deleting the element is the opposite operation and we can simply achieve that by deleting the corresponding existing system object. While the dummy objects may not always work because fundamentally we may not have the exact same knowledge as malware and its targeted environment to fill the actual content, this scheme works quite well in our evaluation. And we leave a full discussion of GOLDENEYE limitations in Section 7.

The substitution operation usually occurs when malware requires different system configuration from the current running environment. A main approach to find out the correct environment setting is through the result of the speculative execution. Since the speculative execution tells us the condition to ensure the selected branch, we can concretely set up the value to satisfy this requirement. For example, we can modify some registry entries to modify certain software version. As a more generic solution, we design an API manipulation scheme. When a substitution occurs, we hook the previously captured APIs or instructions, and return a manipulated value to malware for every query.

The environment update for our working example is illustrated in Figure 3 Step D. The first step is to update the base execution context as the selected context. In the example, we first update the ESI and ZF register. Secondly, since EAX is the object handle of the mutex object, we need to create the mutex for current context and bind EAX to the mutex handle. In our implementation, we do not concretely create the mutex. Instead, we record the handle value and when any system call operates on the handle, we enforce the SUCCESS to emulate the existence of the object.

Handling Space Explosion. As one notable problem for parallel space maintenance in the speculative execution engine, explosion of parallel spaces could dramatically increase the overhead of GOLDENEYE, especially when the combination of multiple environment elements happens (Cartesian Effect). We solve the problem by periodically pruning the parallel spaces. More specially, we enforce the space adjustment when current memory occupation exceeds some predefined threshold, ρ_h. During the analysis, we associate a timestamp T with each environment element. The time stamp denotes the last instruction that accesses the corresponding taint label of the element. When the current memory usage overflows ρ_h, the speculative execution engine fetches the environment element with the oldest time stamp. Then, the update operation merges all the parallel spaces which have different values for the pruned elements. This process is recursively performed till the current memory capacity is below a predefined lower bound, ρ_l. In practice, among all of our test cases, the average number of concurrent parallel spaces is below 200. It means that, with minor memory overhead (below 500B) for each space, the space pruning rarely occurs in the practical analysis task.

5   Distributed Deployment of GOLDENEYE

While the above scheme works very well in practice (as shown in our experiment), there are still some concerns: (1) To prevent rolling-back, we adopt branch evaluation to select the most likely malicious branch, which might not always be accurate. (2) Our environment update step is conducted online. Thus, some analysis is possibly conducted on a set of inconsistent environments. (3) The possible environment explosion may overburden one analysis instance.

To further improve the accuracy and efficiency, we propose a distributed deployment scheme of GOLDENEYE. The scheme is essentially taking advantage of parallel environments created by the speculative engine and distributing them to a set of worker machines for further analysis.

In detail, when the speculative engine detects an environment-sensitive branch, it can choose to push a request R into a shared task queue and allow an idle worker (virtual) machine to handle the further exploration. The worker machine monitoring (WMM) tool pulls each request and updates the environment settings before analyzing a malware sample. After the booting of a malware sample, the WMM tool will monitor the execution status and enable the speculative execution if some unobserved malicious logic has occurred.

There are two tasks for each WMM: (1) *Updating analysis environment*, which is a set of operations to update its environment before analysis, such as *create/delete environment element* or *modify current environment value*. After that, we create one customized environment for each analysis task. (2) *Starting speculative execution*, which is to conduct a series of EIP and basic context registers comparison before restarting the speculative execution. By skipping the instructions which have been analyzed before, we can focus on exploring new malicious behaviors.

The merits of our design are twofold. First, the analysis environment is dynamically changed and the setting is dynamically generated based on the malware execution and analysis progress. It is essentially different from the parallel/distributed deployment of existing analysis techniques [36,23] because their settings are statically preconfigured. Second, it saves a huge amount of system resources including memory and storage. Snapshot-based schemes such as [33,37] are mainly used as sequential execution. If one attempts to parallelize its deployment, a great deal of resources need to be used to store/transmit/restore the snapshots. In our design, each worker machine just maintains *one* initial snapshot locally and consumes little memory to transmit the environment request. In this sense, our scheme achieves a better balance between effectiveness and efficiency.

6   Evaluation

We have implemented GOLDENEYE, which consists of over 4,000 lines mixed C and python code. Our monitoring tool, taint tracking tool, and speculative execution engine are implemented based on the open-source binary instrumentation framework, DynamoRIO [5] by first translating the X86 instructions into an intermediate language BIL [26], then performing data and control flow analysis afterwards. We write our semantic rule module as an independent C library, which receives the output of the monitoring tool and parses each instruction. Our environment selector is based on an open source disassembly library, *distorm*[3]. We also implement a lightweight emulated execution engine inside the module to perform branch evaluation. In addition, our environment update module is implemented as an API hook tool based on DynamoRIO and a set of dummy object creation/deletion scripts, which can be directly invoked by our environment update module. In this section, we present our evaluation results.

6.1   Experiment Dataset

Our test dataset consists of 1,439 malware samples, collected from multiple online malware repositories such as Anubis [1] and other sources [10]. This dataset is randomly collected without any pre-selection involved. We analyze these 1,439 malware using a free virus classification tool [20] and classify them into 417 distinct malware families. Analyzing the classification result, we further categorize these 417 malware families into four classes: *Trojan, Worm, Spyware/Adware*, and *Downloader*. The statistics about our dataset is listed in Table 2. Meanwhile, we also collect a small dataset that includes some well-known malware samples which are environment-targeted, such as Conficker [43], Duqu [4], Sality [12], and Zeus [21]. For each malware family, we collected several variant samples.

Table 2. Malware's Classification from VirusTotal

Category	# Malware Samples	Percent	Distinct Families
Trojan	627	43.57%	263
Adware/Spyware	284	19.73%	59
Worm/Virus	185	12.85%	27
Downloader	343	23.83%	68
Total	1,439	100%	417

6.2   Experiment Setup

In our experiment setting, we manually labeled 112 system/library APIs with 122 output parameters, and hooked them in our analysis. All our experiments are conducted in a machine with Intel Core Duo 2.53GHz processor and 4GB memory.

6.3   Experiments on General Malware Corpus

We conduct the following experiments to evaluate GOLDENEYE on the larger malware dataset with $1,439$ samples.

Measurement of Effectiveness. First, we study the effectiveness of our approach in terms of the code coverage in analysis. To measure that, we first collect a baseline trace by naturally running each malware sample in our virtual environment for 5 minutes. Then we apply GOLDENEYE to collect a new trace in the adaptively-changing environment(s). In our evaluation, we measure the relative increase in the number of native system calls between the base run and analysis run. The distribution of increased APIs among all malware samples is shown in Figure 4. As seen in Figure 4, over 500 malware samples exhibit over 50% more APIs in the new run. It shows that our system can expose more malware's environment-sensitive behaviors. From the result, we also find that over 10% Adware/Spyware exhibits 100% more behaviors. It may imply that Spyware is more sensitive to the running environment compared with other malware categories. This is reasonable because Spyware normally exhibits its malicious behavior after it collects enough information about the infected user. This further proves the usefulness of our system. Examining the quantitative results of other categories, it is evident that our system can efficiently discover malware's environment-sensitive functionalities.

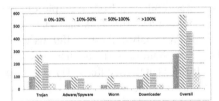

Fig. 4. Relative Increase of Native APIs

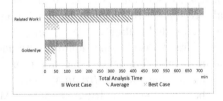

Fig. 5. Analysis Time Comparison

Comparison with Related Work. The last set of our experiment is to compare the effectiveness and efficiency of GOLDENEYE with other approaches. To this end, we first implemented the approach presented in the related work [37] (labeled as Related Work I), which needs to explore multiple possible paths of environment-sensitive branches. Secondly, we configure four virtual environments according to the descriptions in related work [36] (labeled as Related Work II). We test malware samples in all four environments and choose the best one as the result. Then we randomly select 100 malware samples from each category of malware and collect the traces generated by GOLDEN-EYE, Related Work I, and II, respectively. When collecting each execution path trace, we terminate the analysis if no further system calls are observed for 30 seconds (e.g., sample terminates or sleeps), or if it reaches maximum analysis time which we set as 300 seconds (5 minutes) for GOLDENEYE and Related Work II. For Related Work I, since it needs to explore all possible paths, we have to let it run for a much longer time. However, it could possibly take forever. Hence, in this experiment we limit its maximum analysis time to 12 hours.

Table 3. Performance comparison with two representative existing approaches

Approach	Malware	Percent of Increased APIs				# of Rolling Back			Memory/Disk Usage		
		<10%	10%-50%	50%-100%	>100%	<50	50-500	>500	<1MB	1MB-5MB	>5MB
GOLDENEYE	Trojan	31%	36%	27%	6%	74%	26%	0%	67%	33%	0%
	Adware/Spyware	29%	34%	28%	9%	86%	14%	0%	56%	44%	0%
	Worm	39%	47%	11%	3%	84%	16%	0%	24%	76%	0%
	Downloader	43%	29%	24%	4%	69%	31%	0%	32%	68%	0%
Related Work I[37]	Trojan	21%	34%	29%	16%	0%	2%	98%	0%	0%	100%
	Adware/Spyware	16%	32%	33%	19%	0%	1%	99%	0%	0%	100%
	Worm	27%	28%	37%	8%	0%	0%	100%	0%	0%	100%
	Downloader	19%	41%	23%	17%	0%	2%	98%	0%	0%	100%
Related Work II[36]	Trojan	94%	5%	1%	0%	-	-	-	-	-	-
	Adware/Spyware	99%	0%	1%	0%	-	-	-	-	-	-
	Worm	96%	4%	0%	0%	-	-	-	-	-	-
	Downloader	98%	2%	0%	0%	-	-	-	-	-	-

The result is presented in Table 3. We use the following metrics for the comparison:

– Increased APIs. For each of three approaches, we pick the longest trace during any single run to compare with the normal run. For each approach, we record the percentage of malware samples whose increased APIs belonging to $0 - 10\%$, $10 - 50\%$, $50 - 100\%$, or 100% and above. From the result, we can see that Related Work I performs the best among all approaches, which is obvious because this approach blindly explores all possible paths and we select the path with most APIs in the comparison. Meanwhile, in our test, pre-configured environment (Related Work II) can seldom expose malware's hidden behaviors; on average it only increase 5% more APIs. Thus, even though pre-configured environment has no extra overhead for the analysis, it cannot effectively analyze targeted malware. It further confirms that it is impractical to predict malware's targeted environment beforehand. Our approach clearly performs significantly better than Related Work II, and very close to Related Work I.

– Number of Rolling Backs, which is a key factor to slow down analysis. For exploring both branches, Related Work I has to roll back the execution. In theory, for each environment-sensitive branch, it requires one roll back operation. From the result, we can see that most of the samples have to roll back over 500 times to finish the analysis. However, our GOLDENEYE can efficiently control the number of rolling back because it only occurs when branch prediction cannot determine the right path to select. The largest number of rolling back in our test is 126 and median number is 39. It means that we can save more than 90% overhead when compared with multi-path exploration.

– Memory Usage. According to the description in [37], average snapshot for rolling back consumes around 3.5MB memory. Considering their approach needs to recursively maintain the context for branches and sub-branches, the memory/disk overhead should be over 5MB. However, the highest memory/disk usage of GOLDENEYE is only around 1-2MB, which is much less than half of the memory overhead in Related Work I. Hence, for memory usage, our system also outperforms the compared solution.

Finally, we also compare the total time to complete analysis for GOLDENEYE and Related Work I. For each malware, both GOLDENEYE and Related Work I may generate multiple traces and we sum up all the time as the total time to complete the analysis of the malware. The result is summarized in Figure 5. As we can see, for GOLDENEYE, the average analysis time per malware is around 44 minutes, while the average time for Related Work I is 394 minutes, which is around 9 times slower. Furthermore, the worst case for GOLDENEYE never exceeds 175 minutes while there are 12% of tested malware takes longer than 12 hours for Related Work I (note that if we do not set the 12 hour limit, the average for Related Work I will be much longer). This clearly indicates that GOLDENEYE is much more efficient.

In summary, it is evident that our approach has better performance regarding the trade-off of effectiveness and efficiency. We believe the main reason that other solutions have a higher overhead or lower effectiveness is because they are *not* designed to analyze malware's targeted environment. In other words, our approach is more *proactive* and *dynamic* to achieve the goal of targeted malware analysis.

6.4   Experiment on Known Environment-Targeted Malware Dataset

In this experiment, we aim to verify that our system can extract known targeted environments for malware samples. We began our experiment from collecting the ground truth of some malware set. We look up multiple online resources, such as [43], for the documentation about our collected malware samples. In particular, we first verified that all of them are environment-targeted malware, which means they all need to check some environments and then expose their real malicious intention. Secondly, we manually examine their analysis report and summarize their interested environment elements. We group them into five categories: *System Information*, *Network Status*, *Hardware*, *Customized Objects*, and *Library/Process*. For instance, if one sample's malicious logic depends on some system-wide mutex, we consider it as sensitive to *Customized Objects*. We record our manual findings about our test dataset in Table 4(a).

Table 4. Test on Targeted Malware

	System	Network	Hardware	Customized Object	Library Process
Conficker[43]	√	√		√	√
Zeus[21]	√	√	√	√	√
Sality[12]	√	√			
Bifrost[2]	√	√	√	√	
iBank[7]	√	√	√	√	√
nuclearRAT[9]	√	√	√	√	√
Duqu[4]	√	√	√	√	√
Nitro[16]	√	√	√		
Qakbot[11]	√			√	√

(a) Ground Truth

	System	Network	Hardware	Customized Object	Library Process
Conficker	√	√		o	√
Zeus	√	√	√	√	o
Sality	√	√			
Bifrost	√	√	√	o	
iBank	√	√	×	×	√
nuclearRAT	√	×	√	o	o
Duqu	o	√	√	√	√
Nitro	o	√	o		
Qakbot	o			√	√

(b) GOLDENEYE Environment Extraction Result
√: Correctly Extracted, o: Similar Element
×: Not Extracted

There are several caveats in the test. First, if the documentation does not clearly mention the sample's MD5 or the sample with the specific MD5 cannot be found online, it may bring some inaccurate measurement for the result. One example is the Trojan iBank [7] case. We analyze some of its variants and they may not exhibit the same behaviors as the documented states. Second, we conclude the extraction result in three types: (a) *Correctly Extracted* means GOLDENEYE can extract the exact same environment element. (b) *Similar Element* means GOLDENEYE finds some element that acts the similar functionality as mentioned in the document, but such element may have different name as the document described. We suspect it is probably because the element name is dynamically generated based on different information. For this type, we consider GOLDENEYE successfully extracts the environment information, because the correct element name could be derived through further manual examination or automatic symbolic execution [22]. (c) *Not Extracted* means GOLDENEYE fails to extract the environment element.

From the result, we can see that our GOLDENEYE can correctly detect most of the targeted environment elements (41 out of 44) within the 5-min analysis time limit. However, our system fails to extract 3 elements out of 44 cases. After we manually unpack the code and check the reason of the failures, we find there are two main reasons: (1) Some hardware query functions are not in our labeled API list (e.g., in the case of iBank). This could be solved if we improve our labeled API list. (2) Some element check only occurs after the malware successfully interacts with a remote (C&C) server (e.g., in the case of nuclearRAT). However, these servers may not be alive during our test thus we fail to observe such checks.

6.5 Case Studies

Next, we study some cases in our analysis. We list several environment targets which may trigger malware's activities.

Targeted Location. For Conficker A, GOLDENEYE successful captures the system call `GetKeyboardLayout` and automatically extracts malware's intention of not infecting the system with Ukrainian keyboard [43]. For some variants of Bifrost[2], GOLDENEYE finds they query the system language to check whether the running OS is Chinese system or not, which is their targeted victim environment. For these cases, GOLDENEYE can intelligently change the query result of APIs, such as `GetKeyboardLayout`, to make malware believe they are running in their targeted machine/location.

User Credentials. We found several malware samples target at user credentials to conduct their malicious activities. For example, we found that Neloweg[19] will access registry at `Microsoft/Internet Account Manager/Accounts key`, which stores users' outlook credentials. Similar examples also include Koobface[8], which targets at user's facebook credentials. GOLDENEYE successfully captures these malicious intentions by providing fake credentials/file/registry to malware and allowing the malware to continue execution. While the malware's further execution may fail because GOLDENEYE may not provide the exact correct content of the credential, GOLDENEYE can still provide enough targeted environment information to malware analysts.

System Invariants. In our test, GOLDENEYE extracted one mutex from Sality [12] whose name is `uxJLpe1m`. In the report, we found that the existence of such mutex may disable Sality's execution. This turns out to be some common logic for a set of malware to prevent multiple infections. Similar logic has also been found in Zeus [21] and Conficker [43]. For these cases, even though the clean environment, which does not contain the mutex, is the ideal environment for analysis, we can still see that GOLDEN-

EYE's extracted information is useful, potentially for malware prevention, as discussed in [48].

Displayed Windows and Installed Library. iBank [7] Trojan is one example that is sensitive to certain displayed windows and installed library. In particular, GOLDENEYE detects that IBank tries to find the window "`_AVP.Root`", which belongs to Kasperky software. Meanwhile, it also detects that IBank accesses `avipc.dll` in the home path of Avira Anti-virus software. Our GOLDENEYE further detects if such library or window exists, the malware exhibits more behaviors by calling the function `AvIpcCall` in the library to kill the AV-tools. IBank samples tell us that if our analysis is performed in an environment without AV tools installed, we will miss these anti-AV behaviors. Hence, as a side effect, GOLDENEYE could be a good automatic tools for analysts to detect malware's anti-AV behaviors.

Others. Last but not least, we always assume exposing more malicious behaviors is better. However, detecting some path with less malicious behaviors may be also interesting. One example we find in our dataset is Qakbot [11]. The malware exhibits some behaviors related to some registry entry. This malware tries to write `_qbothome_qbotinj.exe` into a common start up registry key `CurrentVersion\Run`. The further logic for Qakbot needs to check the existence of such registry entry and if it fails, malware goes to sleep routine without directly exhibiting some malicious behaviors. This case is interesting for us because we find that by changing environment setting, we could even observe some *hidden dormant* functionality. Discovering such hidden dormant functionality may help defenders to make some schemes for slowing down the fast-spreading of certain malware.

6.6 Experiment on Distributed Deployment of GOLDENEYE

Finally, we evaluate the performance overhead of our distributed deployment of GOLDENEYE. In this experiment, we measure three cases:

- Case I: Generate a parallel task for all environment-sensitive branches.
- Case II: Generate a parallel task only when the branch evaluation cannot decide a branch after measuring the branch selection heuristics.
- Case III: Do not generate a parallel task and do not conduct rolling back, i.e., using a single machine instead of distributed deployment (for undetermined paths, we select the default environment as desired).

We use additional four worker (virtual) machines for this measurement (Case I and II). Each virtual machine installs original unpatched Windows XP SP1 operating system. We randomly select 100 malware samples and run each sample for at most 300 seconds in each configuration. We compare performance with the baseline case, which is running each malware in the default environment.

The result is summarized in Figure 6. As seen in the figure, we study the effectiveness by measuring the increased ratio of native APIs. As expected, Case I and II expose over 30% more behaviors than Case III. However, the standard deviation of Case I is higher than Case II. It shows that, with the same analysis time, the first approach may not outperform the second case because exploring all environment-sensitive paths is

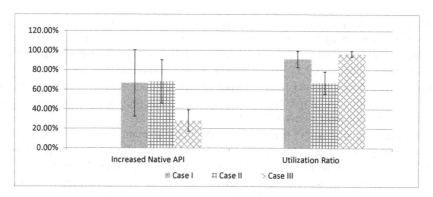

Fig. 6. Measurement of Distributed GOLDENEYE

not efficient enough. We also measure the utilization ratio of the analysis machine(s), which is defined as the percentage of time for an analysis machine to run the analysis task within the given 300 seconds. The average utilization ratio from VMs in Case I is over 90%, which is much higher than Case II. In short, we conclude that Case II configuration of GOLDENEYE, i.e., combining the branch selection scheme with the distributed deployment, seems to achieve the best balance between effectiveness and resource consumption among the three cases.

7   Discussion

Exposing malicious behaviors of environment-targeted malware is a challenging research task for the whole malware defense community. As a new step towards systematic environment-targeted malware analysis, our solution is not perfect and not targeting to completely solve the problem. We now discuss limitations/evasions below.

Correctness of Path Selection/Prediction. One limitation of our approach is that the correctness of our branch evaluation depends on whether malware's behavior fits our heuristics. One solution for this problem is to explore all possible branches by multi-round snapshot-and-recover analysis, as in [37]. However, this scheme may cause much higher overhead because of the *path explosion* problem. Hence, to trade off the performance, we choose to apply snapshot-and-recover only when we cannot apply the heuristics. Other dynamic analysis approaches such as previous work [39,41] can also be applied to make the analysis more efficient.

Possible Problems of Taint Analysis. In our scheme, we apply taint analysis at the stages of preprocessing and speculative execution. For preprocessing, taint analysis can help us filter out the malware which are not sensitive to the environment. For speculative execution, taint analysis helps to save execution overhead from multiple aspects. However, as discussed in related work [22], taint analysis could have limitations of *over-tainting* and *under-tainting*. Even though it may cause the problem of imprecise results, for our cases, the limitation can seldom affect our analysis. This is because: (1) Even though over-tainting costs more overhead for speculative execution, our scheme is still more lightweight than existing approaches. (2) The under-tainting problem may mislead our branch prediction. However, by using stricter branch selection criteria, we could avoid such wrong branch. Meanwhile, conducting more roll-backing operations on some critical branches can also improve the overall accuracy. (3) Our analysis can be independently conducted even without taint analysis. In this case, our speculative execution engine has to be executed at all branches to truncate undesired environments. Even though it may cause more overhead, we believe it still outperforms other approaches because it prevents unnecessary rolling-back.

Evasion through Misleading the Analysis. The implementation GOLDENEYE is built upon on binary instrumentation, and because of the similar limitation as VMM-based approaches[28], it is possible for malware to detect the existence of GOLDENEYE.

By knowing our heuristics for branch selection, the attacker could mislead our analysis through injecting some certain APIs in the branches. However, some heuristics (e.g., environment interaction, process termination) are relatively hard to be evaded because otherwise they will be against the malware's execution intention. We note that even in the worst case (we have to rewind to explore another branch, similar to existing multi-path solutions), our solution is still better than a blind multi-path exploration scheme.

Another way to evade the analysis is to query environment information and process it at a very later time. To handle this issue, we could increase the capacity of parallel spaces and track the tainted environment elements throughout the whole analysis by paying a little more analysis overhead.

Malware can insert some dormant functions such as `sleep` because GOLDENEYE may not prefer to choose branches in which malware could enter a dormant status. To handle such cases, GOLDENEYE can examine more code blocks in the foreseeing operation in order to make a more accurate branch selection or could simply generate a parallel task for another worker machine.

Last but not least, current implementation of GOLDENEYE does not handle implicit control flow, a common issue to many dynamic analysis systems. Hence, malware authors may evade the analysis by including implicit control flow. However, this issue could be partially solved by conducting symbolic execution on indirect branches. We leave it as our future work.

Environment-Uniqueness Malware. A recent study [27] discussed a novel anti-analysis technique, which applies environment primitives as the decryption key for the malware binary. In the real world, flashback [18] malware has exhibited similar interesting attributes. To the best of our knowledge, there is no research or tool can automatically analyze such kind of malware. Even though our approach cannot provide correct analysis environment for the captured sample, we believe our analysis can still discover more information than traditional automatic analysis techniques. For example, our approach can detect malware's query for system environment and deduce what are likely environment elements that compose the decryption key. We leave the analysis of such malware to our future work.

8   Conclusion

In this paper, we have presented a new dynamic analysis system, GOLDENEYE, to facilitate targeted malware analysis by efficiently and effectively exposing its targeted environments. To achieve our goal, we design several new dynamic analysis techniques based on speculative execution, such as parallel environment spaces construction and branch evaluation, to solve the technical challenges faced by targeted malware analysis. To further improve the accuracy and efficiency, we deploy GOLDENEYE onto a distributed computing model. In the evaluation, we show that our scheme can work on a large real-world malware corpus and achieve a better performance trade-off compared with existing approaches. While not perfect, we believe this is a right step towards an interesting new topic, i.e., targeted threat analysis and defense, which needs further research from the community.

Acknowledgments. This material is based upon work supported in part by the National Science Foundation under Grant CNS-0954096 and the Air Force Office of Scientific Research under Grants FA9550-13-1-0077 and FA-9550-12-1-0077. Any opinions, findings, and conclusions or recommendations expressed in this material are those of the authors and do not necessarily reflect the views of NSF and AFOSR.

References

1. Anubis: Analyzing unknown binaries, http://anubis.iseclab.org/
2. Bifrost, http://www.symantec.com/security_response/writeup.jsp?docid=2004-101214-5358-99
3. Disassembler library for x86/amd64, http://code.google.com/p/distorm/
4. Duqu,
   http://www.kaspersky.com/about/press/major_malware_outbreaks/duqu
5. DynamoRIO,
   http://dynamorio.org/
6. Flame,
   http://en.wikipedia.org/wiki/Flame_malware
7. IBank,
   http://www.sophos.com/en-us/threat-center/threat-analyses/viruses-and-spyware/Troj~IBank-B/detailed-analysis.aspx
8. Koobface,
   http://www.symantec.com/security_response/writeup.jsp?docid=2008-080315-0217-99&tabid=2
9. NuclearRAT,
   http://en.wikipedia.org/wiki/Nuclear_RAT
10. Offensive Computing, http://www.offensivecomputing.net/
11. Qakbot,
    http://www.symantec.com/connect/blogs/w32qakbot-under-surface
12. Sality,
    http://www.symantec.com/security_response/writeup.jsp?docid=2006-011714-3948-99
13. Stuxnet, http://en.wikipedia.org/wiki/Stuxnet
14. Symantec intelligence quarterly,
    http://www.symantec.com/threatreport/quarterly.jsp
15. Symantec: Triage analysis of targeted attacks, http://www.symantec.com/threatreport/topic.jsp?id=malicious_code_trend

16. The Nitro Attacks: Stealing Secrets from the Chemical Industry, `http://www.symantec.com/security_response/whitepapers.jsp`
17. Trends in targeted attacks, `http://www.trendmicro.com/cloud-content/us`
18. Trojan BackDoor.Flashback, `http://en.wikipedia.org/wiki/Trojan_BackDoor.Flashback`
19. Trojan.Neloweg, `http://www.symantec.com/security_response/writeup.jsp?docid=2012-020609-4221-99`
20. Virustotal, `https://www.virustotal.com/`
21. Zeus Trojan horse, `http://www.symantec.com/security_response/writeup.jsp?docid=2010-011016-3514-99`
22. Avgerinos, T., Schwartz, E., Brumley, D.: All you ever wanted to know about dynamic taint analysis and forward symbolic execution (but might have been afraid to ask). In: Proc. of IEEE S&P 2010 (2010)
23. Balzarotti, D., Cova, M., Karlberger, C., Kruegel, C., Kirda, E., Vigna, G.: Efficient detection of split personalities in malware. In: Proc of NDSS 2010 (2010)
24. Bilge, L., Dumitras, T.: Before we knew it: An empirical study of zero-day attacks in the real world. In: Proc. of CCS 2012 (2012)
25. Brumley, D., Hartwig, C., Liang, Z., Newsome, J., Poosankam, P., Song, D., Yin, H.: Automatically identifying trigger-based behavior in malware. In: Lee, W., Wang, C., Dagon, D. (eds.) Botnet Analysis and Defense. AIS, vol. 36, pp. 65–88. Springer, Heidelberg (2008)
26. Brumley, D., Jager, I., Avgerinos, T., Schwartz, E.J.: BAP: A binary analysis platform. In: Gopalakrishnan, G., Qadeer, S. (eds.) CAV 2011. LNCS, vol. 6806, pp. 463–469. Springer, Heidelberg (2011)
27. Royal, P., Song, C., Lee, W.: Impeding automated malware analysis with environment-sensitive malware. In: Proc. of HotSec 20 12 (2012)
28. Chen, X., Andersen, J., Mao, M., Bailey, M., Nazario, J.: Towards an Understanding of Anti-Virtualization and Anti-Debugging Behavior in Modern Malware. In: Proc. of DSN 2008 (2008)
29. Comparetti, P.M., Salvaneschi, G., Kirda, E., Kolbitsch, C., Krugel, C., Zanero, S.: Identifying dormant functionality in malware programs. In: Proc. of S&P 2010 (2010)
30. Dinaburg, A., Royal, P., Sharif, M., Lee, W.: Ether: Malware analysis via hardware virtualization extensions. In: Proc of CCS 2008 (2008)
31. Gonzlez, J., Gonzlez, A.: Speculative execution via address prediction and data prefetching. In: Proc. of ICS 1197 (1997)
32. Graziano, M., Leita, C., Balzarotti, D.: Towards network containment in malware analysis systems. In: Proc. of ACSAC 2012 (December 2012)
33. Kolbitsch, C., Milani Comparetti, P., Kruegel, C., Kirda, E., Zhou, X., Wang, X.: Effective and efficient malware detection at the end host. In: Proc. of USENIX Security 2009 (2009)
34. Kolbitsch, C., Kirda, E., Kruegel, C.: The power of procrastination: Detection and mitigation of execution-stalling malicious code. In: Proc. of CCS 2011 (2011)
35. Kolbitsch, C., Livshits, B., Zorn, B., Seifert, C.: Rozzle: De-cloaking internet malware. In: Proc. of S&P 2012 (2012)
36. Lindorfer, M., Kolbitsch, C., Milani Comparetti, P.: Detecting Environment-Sensitive Malware. In: Sommer, R., Balzarotti, D., Maier, G. (eds.) RAID 2011. LNCS, vol. 6961, pp. 338–357. Springer, Heidelberg (2011)
37. Moser, A., Kruegel, C., Kirda, E.: Exploring Multiple Execution Paths for Malware Analysis. In: Proc. of S&P 2007 (2007)

38. Moser, A., Kruegel, C., Kirda, E.: Limits of static analysis for malware detection. In: Proc. of ACSAC 2007 (2007)
39. Nadji, Y., Antonakakis, M., Perdisci, R., Lee, W.: Understanding the Prevalence and Use of Alternative Plans in Malware with Network Games. In: Proc. of ACSAC 2011 (2011)
40. Nappa, A., Xu, Z., Rafique, M.Z., Caballero, J., Gu, G.: Cyberprobe: Towards internet-scale active detection of alicious servers. In: Proc. of NDSS 2014 (2014)
41. Neugschwandtner, M., Comparetti, P.M., Platzer, C.: Detecting Malware's Failover C&C Strategies with SQUEEZE. In: Proc. of ACSAC 2011 (2011)
42. Peng, F., Deng, Z., Zhang, X., Xu, D., Lin, Z., Su, Z.: X-force: Force-executing binary programs for security applications. In: Proceedings of the 2014 USENIX Security Symposium, San Diego, CA (August 2014)
43. Porras, P., Saidi, H., Yegneswaran, V.: An Analysis of Conficker's Logic and Rendezvous Points (2009), http://mtc.sri.com/Conficker/
44. Shin, S., Xu, Z., Gu, G.: Effort: Efficient and effective bot malware detection. In: Proc. of INFOCOM 2012 Mini-Conference (2012)
45. Sikorski, M.: Practical Malware Analysis: The Hands-On Guide to Dissecting Malicious Software (2012) (No Starch Press)
46. Wilhelm, J., Chiueh, T.-c.: A forced sampled execution approach to kernel rootkit identification. In: Kruegel, C., Lippmann, R., Clark, A. (eds.) RAID 2007. LNCS, vol. 4637, pp. 219–235. Springer, Heidelberg (2007)
47. Xu, Z., Chen, L., Gu, G., Kruegel, C.: PeerPress: Utilizing enemies' p2p strength against them. In: Proc.of CCS 2012 (2012)
48. Xu, Z., Zhang, J., Gu, G., Lin, Z.: AUTOVAC: Towards automatically extracting system resource constraints and generating vaccines for malware immunization. In: Proc. of ICDCS 2013 (2013)

PillarBox: Combating Next-Generation Malware with Fast Forward-Secure Logging

Kevin D. Bowers[1], Catherine Hart[2,*], Ari Juels[3,*], and Nikos Triandopoulos[1]

[1] RSA Laboratories, Cambridge, USA
[2] Bell Canada, Vancouver, Canada
[3] Cornell Tech (Jacobs Institute), New York, USA

Abstract. *Security analytics* is a catchall term for vulnerability assessment and intrusion detection leveraging security logs from a wide array of *Security Analytics Sources (SASs)*, which include firewalls, VPNs, and endpoint instrumentation. Today, nearly all security analytics systems suffer from a lack of even basic data protections. An adversary can *eavesdrop* on SAS outputs and advanced malware can *undetectably suppress* or *tamper* with SAS messages to conceal attacks.

We introduce *PillarBox*, a tool that enforces *integrity* for SAS data even when such data is buffered on a compromised host within an adversarially controlled network. Additionally, PillarBox (optionally) offers *stealth*, concealing SAS data and potentially even alerting rules on a compromised host. Using data from a large enterprise and on-host performance measurements, we show experimentally that PillarBox has minimal overhead and is practical for real-world systems.

Keywords: Security analytics, forward-secure logging, log integrity and secrecy, self-protecting alerting, secure chain of custody.

1 Introduction

Big data security analytics is a popular term for the growing practice of organizations to gather and analyze massive amounts of security data to detect systemic vulnerabilities and intrusions, both in real-time and retrospectively. 44% of enterprise organizations today identify their security operations as including big data security analytics [17]. To obtain data for such systems, organizations instrument a variety of hosts with a range of *Security Analytics Sources* (SASs) (pronounced "sass"). By SAS here, we mean generically a system that generates messages or alerts and transmits them to a *trusted server* for analysis and action.

On a host, for instance, a SAS can be a Host-based Intrusion Detection System (HIDS), an anti-virus engine, any software facility that writes to syslog, or generally any eventing interface that reports events to a remote service, e.g., a Security and Information Event Monitoring (SIEM) system. Further afield, a SAS could be a dedicated Network Intrusion Detection System, or, in an embedded device, a feature that reports physical tampering. A SAS could also be the reporting facility in a firewall or proxy.

---

* Work performed while at RSA Laboratories.

A. Stavrou et al. (Eds.): RAID 2014, LNCS 8688, pp. 46–67, 2014.
© Springer International Publishing Switzerland 2014

SASs play a central role in broad IT defense strategies based on security analytics, furnishing the data to detect systemic vulnerabilities and intrusions. But a big data security analytics system is only as good as the SAS data it relies on. Worryingly, current-generation SASs lack two key protections against a local attacker.

First, an attacker can *undetectably suppress or tamper with* SAS messages. Today's approach to securing SAS messages is to transmit them immediately to a trusted server. By disrupting such transmissions, an attacker can create false alarms or prevent real alarms from being received. Even a SAS with a secure host-to-server channel (such as SSL/TLS) is vulnerable: An attacker can undetectably blackhole/suppress transmissions until it fully compromises the host, and then break off SAS communications. (We demonstrate the feasibility of such an attack in Section 5.) And logged or buffered SAS messages are generally vulnerable to deletion or modification after host compromise.

Consider, for instance, a rootkit Trojan that exploits a host vulnerability to achieve privilege escalation on an enterprise host. A HIDS or anti-virus engine might immediately detect the suspicious privilege escalation and log an alert, "Privilege Escalation." An attacker can block transmission of this message and, once installed, the rootkit can modify or remove critical logs stored locally (as many rootkits do today, e.g., ZeroAccess, Infostealer.Shiz, Android.Bmaster).[1] Because any buffered alert can be deleted, and any transmission easily blocked, an enterprise server receiving the host's logs will fail to observe the alert and detect the rootkit.

A second problem with today's SASs is that an attacker can *discover* intelligence about their configuration and outputs. By observing host emissions on a network prior to compromise, an attacker can determine if and when a SAS is transmitting alerts and potentially infer alert-generation rules. After host compromise, an attacker can observe host instrumentation, e.g., HIDS rule sets, logs, buffered alerts, etc., to determine the likelihood that its activities have been observed and learn how to evade future detection.

For enterprises facing sophisticated adversaries, e.g., *Advanced Persistent Threats* (APTs) (e.g., Aurora, Stuxnet and Duqu) such shortcomings are critical. Threat-vector intelligence is widely known to play a key role in defense of such attacks, and its leakage to cause serious setbacks [15].

Thus an attacker's ability to suppress alerts undetectably and obtain leaked alert intelligence in today's SAS systems is a fundamental vulnerability in the host-to-server chain of custody and a considerable flaw in big data security analytics architectures.

PillarBox. As a solution to these challenges, we introduce a tool called *PillarBox*.[2] PillarBox securely relays alerts from any SAS to a trusted analytics server. It creates a secure host-to-server chain of custody with two key properties:

1. **Integrity:** PillarBox protects a host's SAS messages against attacker tampering or suppression. It guarantees that the server receives all messages generated *prior* to host compromise (or detects a malicious system failure). PillarBox also aims to secure real-time alert messages *during* host compromise faster than the attacker can

---

[1] Many rootkits remove or obfuscate logs by modifying the binary of the logging facility itself.

[2] A *pillar box* is a Royal Mail (U.K.) mailbox in the form of a red metal pillar. It provides a secure and stealthy chain of custody, with integrity (only postal workers can open it), message hiding (it's opaque), and delivery assurance (if you trust the Royal Mail).

intercept them. *After* host compromise, PillarBox protects already generated SAS messages, even if an attacker can suppress new ones.

2. **Stealth:** Optionally, PillarBox conceals when and whether a SAS has generated alerts, helping prevent leakage of intelligence about SAS instrumentation. It does so against an attacker that sniffs network traffic before compromise and learns all host state after compromise. Stealth can also involve making SAS alert-generation rules *vanish* (be erased) during compromise.

Counterintuitively, PillarBox *buffers SAS messages on the (vulnerable) host.* As we show, this strategy is better than pushing alerts instantly to the server for safekeeping: It is equally fast, more robust to message suppression, and important for stealth.

Challenges. While PillarBox is useful for any type of SAS, the most stringent case is that of *self-protection*, which means that *the SAS messages to be protected regard the very host producing the messages*, potentially while the host is being compromised (as with, e.g., a HIDS). Thus, integrity has two facets. First, a host's buffered alerts must receive ongoing integrity protection even *after host compromise*. Second, alerts must be secured *quickly*—before an attacker can suppress or tamper with them as it compromises the host. We show experimentally that even in the most challenging case of self-protection, PillarBox secures SAS alerts before a fast attacker can suppress them— *and even if the attacker has full knowledge of and explicitly targets PillarBox.*

Stealth (optional in PillarBox) requires that the host's internal data structures be invariant to SAS message generation, so that they reveal no information to an attacker after host compromise. Message buffers must therefore be of fixed size, making the threat of overwriting by an attacker an important technical challenge. Additionally, to protect against an adversary that controls the network, stealth requires that PillarBox transmissions resist traffic analysis, e.g., do not reveal message logging times. A final challenge in achieving stealth is the fact that an attacker that compromises a host learns the host's current PillarBox encryption keys.

Contributions. In this paper we highlight and demonstrate the transmission vulnerability in security analytics systems and propose a solution, which we call PillarBox. In designing PillarBox, we also specify the properties of integrity and stealth, which are general and fundamental to the architecture of any security analytics system. We show how to combine standard forward-secure logging and activity-concealment techniques to simultaneously achieve both properties in the self-protection SAS mode of operation.

We present an architecture for PillarBox and a prototype end-to-end integration of the tool with syslog, a common SAS. We show experimentally that PillarBox can secure alerts in the challenging self-protection case before an attacker can suppress them by killing PillarBox processes. Since the majority of host compromises involve privilege escalation, we also show that for a common attack (the "Full-Nelson" privilege escalation attack), an alerter can be configured to detect the attack and the resulting SAS message can be secured before the attacker can shut down PillarBox. Additionally, we use alert-generation data from a large enterprise to confirm that PillarBox can be parameterized practically, with low performance overhead on hosts.

We emphasize that we do not address the design of SASs in this paper. How SAS messages are generated and the content of messages are outside the scope of this paper.

PillarBox is a practical, general tool to harden the host-to-server chain of custody for any SAS, providing a secure foundation for security analytics systems.

Organization. Section 2 introduces PillarBox's threat model and design principles, while Section 3 describes its architecture and integration with a SAS. Section 4 gives technical details on buffer construction and supporting protocols. Section 5 demonstrates a simple attack on existing SAS systems and presents an experimental evaluation of PillarBox. We review related work in Section 6 and conclude in Section 7. More technical details, which have been omitted from this version due to space constraints, can be found in the full version of this paper [4].

2 Modeling and Design Principles

We first describe the threat model within which PillarBox operates. We then explain how host-side buffering serves to secure SAS alerts within this model and follow with details on the technical approaches in PillarBox to achieving integrity and stealth.

2.1 Threat Model

Our threat model considers three entities, the *SAS* or the *host*, the *attacker*, and the *server*, which itself is a trusted entity, not vulnerable to attack. We model the attacker to be the strongest possible adversary, one attacking a host in the self-protecting setting. (Achieving security against this strong adversary ensures security against weaker ones, e.g., those attacking only the network or a firewall whose SAS only reports on network events.) Recall that in the self-protecting case, a SAS reports alerts about the host itself: While the compromise is taking place, the SAS generates one or more alert messages relevant to the ongoing attack and attempts to relay them to the server.

The adversary controls the network in the standard Dolev-Yao sense [6], i.e., the attacker can intercept, modify, and delay messages at will. When its intrusion is complete, the attacker achieves what we call a *complete compromise* of the host: It learns the host's complete state, including all memory contents—cryptographic keys, alert messages, etc.—and fully controls the host's future behavior, including its SAS activity.

To violate integrity, the attacker's goal is to compromise the host *without*: (1) any unmodified alerts reaching the server and (2) the server learning of any modification or suppression of alerts by the attacker. The SAS can only start generating meaningful alerts, of course, once the intrusion is in progress. After the attacker has achieved complete compromise, it can shut down the SAS or tamper with its outputs. So a SAS produces valid and trustworthy alerts only *after* intrusion initiation but *prior* to complete compromise. We call the intervening time interval the *critical window* of an attack, as illustrated in Figure 1. This is the interval of time when intrusions are detectable and alerts can be secured (e.g., buffered in PillarBox) before the attacker intercepts them.

Conceptually, and in our experiments, we assume that the attacker has full knowledge of the workings of the SAS, including any mechanisms protecting alerts en route to the server, e.g., PillarBox. It fully exploits this knowledge to suppress or modify alerts. The attacker doesn't, however, know host state, e.g., cryptographic keys, prior to complete

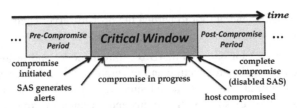

Fig. 1. Event timeline of host compromise

compromise nor does it know the detection rules (behavioral signatures) used by the SAS, i.e., the precise conditions leading to alert generation.

To violate stealth, the attacker tries to learn information about SAS rules and actions, e.g., if the SAS has issued alerts during an attack, by making adaptive use of the network and of post-compromise host state, e.g., PillarBox's buffer. SAS detection rules can also be used to infer behavior, but are outside the scope of PillarBox. Vanishing rules (rules that are deleted if they ever trigger an alert) can be used to protect against adversarial rule discovery in the SAS. By analogy with cryptographic privacy definitions, a concise definition of stealth is possible: An attacker violates stealth if, for any SAS detection rule, it can distinguish between PillarBox instantiations with and without the rule.

2.2 Secure Alert Relaying via Buffering

A key element in our design is the use of a host-side *PillarBox buffer*, for brevity called the *PBB*, where alerts are secured. The objective is to secure alerts in the PBB during the critical window, as shown in Figure 2. Once in the PBB, alert messages are protected in two senses: They are both integrity-protected and "invisible" to the attacker, i.e., they support systemic stealth. (Informally, the PBB serves as a "lockbox.") Also, as we explain, either alerts reliably reach the server, or the server learns of a delivery failure.

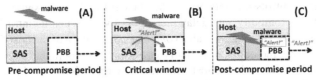

Fig. 2. PillarBox across compromise phases: (A) The host has not yet been attacked. (B) The SAS detects in-progress compromise and places an alert in PBB. (C) The host is under the attacker's full control, but PBB securely stores and transmits the alert.

We first explain why buffering is important to secure the SAS chain of custody in PillarBox and then how we address the technical challenges it introduces.

Why Buffering Is Necessary. The approach of most SAS systems today, e.g., syslog and HIDSs, is to push alerts to a remote server in real time, and thus secure them at the server during the critical window. But there are many important cases, both adversarial and benign, in which SAS messages *cannot be pushed reliably*, for two main reasons:

- *Imperfect connectivity:* Many host SAS systems lack continuous connectivity to the server (e.g., laptops shuttling between an office and home have limited connection with corporate security servers but are open to infection in the home). Lightweight embedded devices often cannot ensure or even verify delivery of transmitted messages (e.g., wireless sensor networks often experience transmission failures).

– *Network attacks*: An attacker can actively suppress on-the-fly SAS transmissions by causing malicious network failures. It can selectively disrupt network traffic, via, e.g., ARP stack smashing (e.g., see CVE-2007-1531 and CVE-2010-2979), or flood target hosts to achieve denial-of-service (DoS) during a compromise, causing message delay or suppression. The result is complete occlusion of server visibility into the critical window—potentially appearing to be a benign network failure. (We describe our own implementation of such an alert-suppression attack below.)

But even if reliable, immediate SAS message-pushing were generally feasible, it would *still* have an undesirable effect:

– *SAS intelligence leakage:* If a host pushes alerts instantaneously, then its outbound traffic reveals SAS activity to an attacker monitoring its output. An attacker can then probe a host to learn SAS detection rules and/or determine after the fact whether its intrusion into a host was detected. Note that encryption does not solve this problem: Traffic analysis alone can reveal SAS rule-triggering. (As noted above, PillarBox overcomes this problem via regular alert-buffer transmission.)

Thus, *message buffering*, as opposed to on-the-fly event-triggered transmission, is of key importance in a SAS chain of custody and the cornerstone of PillarBox. Such buffering, though, poses new security challenges. If an attacker completely compromises a host, there is no way of course to prevent it from disabling a SAS or tampering with its future outputs. But there is a separate problem after host compromise: Inadequately protected buffered SAS messages are vulnerable to modification/suppression and intelligence leakage. We next elaborate on how PillarBox solves these problems.

Achieving Integrity. A main challenge in creating a secure chain of custody in PillarBox is the need to secure alert messages *after* compromise, while they are still buffered and exposed to an attacker. Log-scrubbing malware can attempt to modify buffered alerts (e.g., replace the strong alert "Privilege Escalation" with the more benign "Port Scan Observed") or just purge alerts. *Post-compromise integrity protection* for buffered SAS messages is thus crucial in PillarBox—but at first glance, this might seem unachievable.

Indeed, a digital signature or message authentication code (MAC) alone, as proposed, e.g., for syslog [12], does not protect against tampering: After host compromise an attacker learns the signing key and can forge messages. Message encryption similarly does not protect messages against deletion, nor does tagging them with sequence numbers, as an attacker with control of a host can forge its own sequence numbers.

Fortunately, post-compromise alert integrity is achievable using the well-known cryptographic technique of *forward-secure* integrity protection. The main idea is to generate new (signing) keys on the host after every alert generation and delete keys immediately after use. This technique is commonly used for forward-secure logging (e.g., [14, 19, 25, 26]),[3] an application closely related to SAS protection. Similarly,

---

[3] Such systems are designed mainly for forensic purposes rather than detection (e.g., to protect against administrator tampering after the fact), thus they often "close" logs only periodically.

PillarBox uses forward-secure pseudorandom number generation (FS-PRNG) to create MAC keys. Each key is used to secure a single message and then deleted. An FS-PRNG has the property that past keys cannot be inferred from a current key, preventing tampering of messages that have already been secured. The server runs this FS-PRNG to compute the (same) shared keys with the host, allowing it to detect tampering or erasure.

What is new in the use of forward security in PillarBox is primarily its application for self-protecting alerting: Indeed, the main aspect of integrity here is securing alerts in the PBB as fast as possible during a compromise, i.e., in the critical window. Effectively, PillarBox engages in a race to secure alerts before the attacker intercepts them, and winning this race is not a matter of cryptography, but of system design, including the design choice of host-side buffering! An important contribution of our work is an experimental validation (in Section 5) that winning this race, and thus the whole PillarBox approach to securing alerts, is feasible. This is shown to hold even against a fast, local, PillarBox-aware attacker that kills PillarBox processes as quickly as possible.

Achieving Stealth. Stealth, as we define it, requires concealment of the entire alerting behavior of a SAS, including detection rules, alert message contents, alert generation times, and alert message existence in compromised hosts. Stealth is a key defense against sophisticated attackers. (One example: Host contact with "hot" IP addresses can help flag an APT, but an attacker that learns these addresses can just avoid them [15].)

Straightforward encryption alone does not achieve stealth: If buffer alerts are encrypted on a host, an attacker can infer alert generation simply by counting buffer ciphertexts upon host compromise. Similarly, encrypted host-to-server traffic leaks information: An attacker can determine via traffic analysis when a host has triggered an alert or even perform black-box probing against a host to test attacks and infer which are or are not detectable. Instead, stealth in PillarBox requires a combination of several ideas.

In particular, PillarBox employs a buffer size T, and buffer transmission-time interval μ, that are *fixed*, i.e., invariant. Each message is also of fixed size (or padded to that size). When PillarBox transmits, it re-encrypts and sends the entire fixed-size buffer, not just fresh (encrypted) alerts. Such fixed-length transmissions prevent an attacker from determining when new alerts have accumulated in the host buffer, while its fixed communication patterns defeat traffic analysis. As the host buffer is of fixed size T, PillarBox writes messages to it in a round-robin fashion. Thus, *messages persist in the buffer until overwritten.*[4] This feature creates a need for careful parameterization: T must be large enough to hold all alert messages generated under benign conditions within a time interval μ; this condition ensures that if round-robin overwriting occurs, PillarBox implicitly signals to the server a "buffer-stuffing" attempt by an attacker.[5]

PillarBox generates encryption keys in a forward-secure way to protect against decryption attacks after an attacker compromises a host's keys. To protect against an attacker that controls the network and eventually the host as well, encryption is applied in *two layers*: (1) To *buffered messages*, to ensure confidentiality after host compromise, and (2) to *host-to-server buffer transmissions* to ensure against discovery of alert data

---

[4] Thus messages may be transmitted multiple times. Such persistent transmission consumes bandwidth but it may allow temporarily suppressed messages to eventually reach the server.

[5] Below we develop a framework for parameterization of T and μ and then explore practical settings by analyzing real-world alert transmission patterns in a large enterprise.

from buffer ciphertext changes.[6] Finally, as these two encryption layers ensure confidentiality in the buffer and over the network, but not in the SAS alerting engine itself, a key complement to stealth in PillarBox is concealment of detection rules in hosts: Our experiments show the viability of instrumenting the SAS with *vanishing rules*.

Complete stealth in PillarBox carries an unavoidable cost: Periodic rather than immediate transmissions can delay server detection of intrusions. But we note that stealth is an optional feature in PillarBox: It can be removed or weakened for limited attackers.

3 Architecture

We next describe PillarBox's general architecture, main software components and operating configuration, used to secure the host-to-server chain of custody in a SAS system.

3.1 Interface with SAS

Being agnostic to message content, PillarBox works with any SAS. It can serve as the main channel for SAS alerts or can deliver SAS alerts selectively and work in parallel with an existing transport layer. Exactly how SAS messages are produced at the host or consumed at the receiving server depends on SAS instrumentation and alert-consuming processes. (As such, it's outside the scope of our work.) Similarly, our architecture abstracts away the communication path between the host and server, which can be complicated in practice. In modern enterprises, networks carry many SAS-based security controls that alert upon malfeasance. Typically, alerts are sent via unprotected TCP/IP transmission mechanisms, such as the syslog protocol (which actually uses UDP by default), the Simple Network Messaging Protocol (SNMP), or the Internet Control and Messaging Protocol (ICMP). These alerts are typically generated by endpoint software on host systems (such as anti-virus, anti-malware, or HIDS) or by networked security control devices. These devices are commonly managed by a SIEM system, which may be monitored by human operators. For the purposes of our architecture, though, we simply consider a generic SAS-instrumented host communicating with a server.

Alerter. We refer generically to the SAS component that generates alert messages as an *alerter* module.[7] This module monitors the host environment to identify events that match one of a set of specified alert *rules*. When an event triggers a rule, the alerter outputs a distinct alert message. An alert template may either be static (predefined at some setup time for the host) or dynamic (updated regularly or on-demand through communication with the server). Rules may take any form. They may test individual state variables (specified as what is generally called a *signature*) or they may correlate more than one event via a complicated predicate or classifier. As mentioned before, the SAS may tag select rules as "vanishing." When such a rule is triggered, it is erased from the current rule set to further enhance the stealth properties provided by PillarBox.

---

[6] Buffer encryption alone is insufficient: If identical buffer ciphertexts leave a host twice, the attacker learns that no new alert has been generated in between. Semantically secure public-key encryption would enable use of just one layer, but with impractically high cost overheads.

[7] Of course, a SAS includes other components, e.g., a transport layer, update functionality, etc.

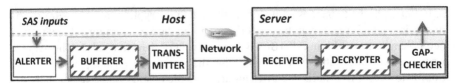

Fig. 3. PillarBox architecture and data flow. Shaded areas show the PillarBox components; striped ones comprise PillarBox's crypto-assisted core reliable channel.

In our basic architecture, the alerter's interface with PillarBox is unidirectional. The alerter outputs alert messages, and PillarBox consumes them. Although many architectures are possible, given PillarBox's emphasis on critical alerts, in our canonical operational setting, the SAS may send only *high severity* messages (e.g., those that seem to indicate impending compromise) to PillarBox, and relay regular logs through its ordinary low-priority transport layer.

3.2   PillarBox Components

The general message flow in PillarBox is fairly simple. Most of the complexity is hidden by the PBB "lockbox." PillarBox consists of five modules, shown in Figure 3.

Bufferer. This module controls the core message buffer, the PBB (which is detailed in Section 4). It accepts two calls: A Write call from the alerter to insert a message into the PBB (in encrypted form) and a Wrap call from the transmitter—described below— requesting export of the current buffer contents (also in a securely encapsulated form). This module is also responsible for maintaining the secret state of the PBB and updating the cryptographic (MAC and encryption) keys, which are effectively used to securely label messages and buffers with sequence numbers. The bufferer does not discard messages from the buffer when they are transmitted: A message is encapsulated and transmitted until overwritten, offering the extra feature of persistence.[8]

Transmitter. This module schedules and executes buffer transmissions from the host to the server. Transmissions may be scheduled every μ seconds, for parameter μ, like a "heartbeat." The module sends Wrap requests to the bufferer and transmits encapsulated buffers to the server over the network using any suitable protocol.

Receiver. This module receives encapsulated-buffer transmissions on the server from the host-based transmitter over the network. When it receives a transmission pushed from the host, it relays it with a Read instruction to the decrypter.

Decrypter. In response to a Read request from the receiver, the decrypter decrypts and processes an encapsulated buffer. It verifies the buffer's integrity and outputs either its constituent messages, or else a $\perp$ symbol indicating a buffer corruption. It also labels the buffer and its messages with their corresponding (verified) sequence numbers.

Gap-checker. The gap-checker's main task is to look for lost messages in the SAS message stream, which cause it to output an alert that we call a *gap alert*. These may be caused by one of two things: (1) A flood of alerts on the host (typically signalling an intrusion) or (2) Overwriting of alerts in the buffer by malicious buffer-stuffing on the

---

[8] This byproduct of stealth can be leveraged to accommodate lossy networks, as explained later.

compromised host (see also Section 4). As messages are labeled with verified sequence numbers, gap checking requires verification that no sequence numbers go missing in the message stream. Because messages continue to be transmitted until overwritten, note that in normal operation sequence numbers will generally *overlap* between buffers. The gap-checker can optionally filter out redundant messages. To detect an attacker that suppresses buffer transmission completely, the gap-checker also issues an alert if buffers have stopped arriving for an extended period of time, as we discuss below.

3.3   Parameterizing PillarBox

The gap-checker always detects when a true gap occurs, i.e., there are no false-negatives in its gap-alert output. To ensure a low false-positive rate, i.e., to prevent spurious detection of maliciously created gaps, it is important to calibrate PillarBox appropriately.

The size T of the PBB dictates a tradeoff between the speed at which alerts can be written to the buffer and the rate at which they must be sent to the server. Let τ denote an estimate of the maximum number of alerts written by the host per second under normal (non-adversarial) conditions. Then provided that the encapsulation interval μ (the time between "snapshots" of buffers sent by the host) is at most T/τ seconds, a normal host will not trigger a false gap alert. We characterize τ, the maximum SAS message-generation rate of normal hosts, in Section 5. Using a moderate buffer size T we are able to achieve extremely low false-positive gap-alert rate in most cases. In networks vulnerable to message loss, the persistence feature of PillarBox can be useful: The larger T, the more repeated transmissions of every message.

Also, if an attacker suppresses buffer transmission completely, the gap-checker will cease to receive buffers. The gap-checker issues a *transmission-failure alert* if more than β seconds have elapsed without the receipt of a buffer, for parameter setting $\beta > T/\tau$.

PillarBox cannot itself distinguish benign from adversarial transmission failures (although network liveness checks can help). While there are many possible policies for transmission-failure alerts, in reliable networks, PillarBox is best coupled with an access policy in which a host that triggers a transmission-failure alert after β seconds is *disconnected from network services other than PillarBox.* Any disconnected services are restored only when PillarBox's decrypter again receives a buffer from the host and can detect alerts. In a benign network outage, this policy will not adversely affect hosts: They will lack network service anyway. An adversary that suppresses PillarBox buffer transmission, though, will cut itself off from the network until PillarBox can analyze any relevant alerts. Such interfacing of PillarBox with network-access policies *limits the attackers ability to perform online actions while remaining undetected.*

4   PillarBox Buffer and Protocols

We now present the main component of PillarBox, the PBB, and its protocols (run by the bufferer and decrypter), which realize a reliable messaging channel, as well as the functionality exported to the alerter and gap-checker to secure the SAS chain of custody.

Ideal "Lockbox" Security Model. Conceptually, the PBB serves as a "lockbox" for message transport: It's a buffer of T fixed-size slots that supports two basic operations:

1. `write`: The *sender* S (the client in PillarBox) inserts individual messages into the buffer via `write` in a *round-robin* fashion. Given currently *available* position $I \in \{0, \ldots, T-1\}$ (initially set at random), a new message is written in slot I (replacing the oldest message), and I is incremented by 1 $(\bmod\ T)$.
2. `read`: The *receiver* R (the server in PillarBox) invokes `read`, which outputs the (monotonically increasing) sequence numbers j of the buffer and s_j of the last inserted message, along with the T messages in the buffer starting at position I, with wraparound.

Messages buffered in this ideal "lockbox" can only be read via the `read` interface and can only be modified (authentically) via the `write` interface. When read by R, a message m_i stored at slot i is guaranteed to be either the most recent message written to slot i (the empty symbol $\emptyset$ if no message was ever written), or a special corruption symbol $\bot$ that indelibly replaces all the buffer's contents if the buffer was tampered with or modified otherwise than by `write`.

The goal of an attacker on compromising a host is to learn SAS actions and suppress alerts buffered during the critical window. The ideal `read` interface of the "lockbox" buffer protects against violations of stealth (the attacker cannot observe when R reads the buffer). Given the `write` interface, the attacker can only violate buffer integrity in the post-compromise period in one of four ways:

1. *Buffer modification/destruction:* The attacker can tamper with the contents of the buffer to suppress critical-window alerts. As noted above, this will cause decryption errors indicated by the special symbol $\bot$.
2. *Buffer overwriting:* The attacker can exploit buffer wraparound by writing T relatively benign messages into it to *overwrite* and thereby destroy messages generated during the critical window.
3. *Buffer dropping:* The attacker can simply drop buffers or delay their transmission.[9]
4. *Transmission stoppage:* The attacker can break the PBB completely, causing no buffer transmission for an extended period of time, or indefinitely.

During the critical window, the attacker can alternatively try to attack so quickly that the critical window is nearly zero. In this case, there is not sufficient time for PillarBox to take in a SAS alert message and put it in the PBB. Our experiments in Section 5 show in some settings of interest that this attack is unlikely.

Adversarial buffer modification or destruction, as explained above, is an easily detectable attack. It causes the server to receive a symbol $\bot$, indicating a cryptographic integrity-check failure. The gap-checker in PillarBox detects both buffer overwriting attacks and buffer dropping attacks by the same means: It looks for lost messages, as indicated by a gap in message sequence numbers.[10] Figure 4 depicts a normal buffer transmission and one, ostensibly during an attack, in which messages have been lost to an alert flood or to buffer overwriting. A transmission stoppage is detectable simply

---

[9] The attacker can also potentially cause buffers to drop by means of a network attack during the critical window, but the effect is much the same as a post-compromise attack.

[10] I.e., a gap alert is issued when the sequence numbers s_j and $s_{j'}$ of (of the last inserted messages in) two successively received buffers j and j' are such that $s_{j'} - s_j \geq T$.

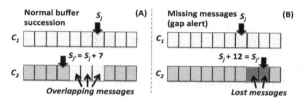

Fig. 4. Gap rule example on successively received buffers C_1, C_2, indexed by sequence numbers j, j' and $T = 10$: (A) Normal message overlap between buffers; (B) A detectable gap: Messages with sequence numbers $s_j + 1$ and $s_j + 2$ have been lost

when the server has received no buffers for an extended period of time, producing a transmission-failure alert, as noted above.

Security Definitions. Our implementation of this ideal "lockbox" consists of the PBB and three operations: (i) The sender S runs Write to insert a message into the PBB and (ii) Wrap to encapsulate the PBB for transmission, and (iii) The receiver R runs Read to extract all messages from a received, encapsulated PBB. We denote by C the contents of the PBB after a series of Write operations by S, and by $\hat{C}$ a cryptographic encapsulation transmitted to R. We require two security properties, *immutability*, and *stealth* and two non-cryptographic ones, *persistence* and *correctness*.

Informally, *correctness* dictates that under normal operation any sequence of messages of size at most T added to C by S can be correctly read by R in an order-preserving way; in particular, the T *most recent* messages of C and their *exact order* can be determined by R. *Persistence* means that by encapsulating the buffer C repeatedly, it is possible to produce a given message in C *more than once*.

For our two cryptographic properties, we consider a powerful adaptive adversary A that operates in two phases: (1) Prior to compromise, A fully controls the network, and may arbitrarily modify, delete, inject, and re-order transmissions between S and R; A may also determine when S encapsulates and sends the PBB, and may also choose its time of compromise; (2) On compromising S, A corrupts S, learns its secret state, and fully controls it from then on.

Immutability means, informally, that pre-compromise messages in C are either received unaltered by R in the order they were written, or are marked as invalid; i.e., even after compromising S, A cannot undetectably drop, alter or re-order messages in C. *Stealth* means, informally, that A cannot learn any information about messages buffered prior to compromise. It is stronger than confidentiality. Not only cannot A learn the contents of messages, it also cannot learn the number of buffered messages— or if any were buffered at all. This holds even after A has compromised S.

Detailed Construction. Our construction employs (and we assume basic familiarity with) a *forward-secure pseudorandom number generator* FS-PRNG (e.g., [10]) that exports two operations GenKey and Next to compute the next pseudorandom numbers, as well as an *authenticated encryption scheme* (e.g., [2]) that exports operations AEKeyGen, AuthEnc and AuthDec to encrypt messages m of size k to ciphertexts of size $g(k) \geq k$.

Operation Write

Input: secret key (r_i, r'_j, i, j), message $m \in \{0, 1\}^\ell$, buffer C

Output: new secret key $(r_{i+1}, r'_j, i+1, j)$, updated buffer C

1. $C[C[T]] = (\text{AuthEnc}_{r_i}(m), i)$
2. $C[T] = C[T] + 1 \bmod T$
3. $(r_{i+1}, r'_j, i+1, j) \leftarrow \text{KEvolve}(r_i, r'_j, i, j, 1, \text{low})$
4. delete r_i
5. return $[(r_{i+1}, r'_j, i+1, j), C]$

Operation Wrap

Input: secret key (r_i, r'_j, i, j), buffer C

Output: new secret key $(r_i, r'_{j+1}, i, j+1)$, encaps. buffer $\hat{C}$

1. $\hat{C} = (\text{AuthEnc}_{r'_j}(C), j)$
2. $(r_i, r'_{j+1}, i, j+1) \leftarrow \text{KEvolve}(r_i, r'_j, i, j, 1, \text{high})$
3. delete r'_j
4. return $[(r_i, r'_{j+1}, i, j+1), \hat{C}]$

Operation Read

Input: secret key (r_i, r'_j, i, j), encapsulated buffer $\hat{C}$

Output: new secret key $(r_l, r'_{j'}, l, j')$, $(m_0, \ldots, m_{T-1})$

1. if $j' \leq j$ then return $[(r_i, r'_j, i, j), \perp]$
2. $(r_i, r'_{j'}, i, j') \leftarrow \text{KEvolve}(r_i, r'_j, i, j, j' - j, \text{high})$
3. $(C[0], \ldots, C[T]) = C \leftarrow \text{AuthDec}_{r'_{j'}}(c'); I = C[T]$
4. if $C = \perp$ then return $[(r_i, r'_j, i, j), \perp]$
5. for $0 \leq k < T$ do
   (a) $(c, l) = C[k + I \bmod T]$
   (b) if $k = 0 \wedge l \leq i$ then return $[(r_i, r'_j, i, j), \perp]$
   (c) if $k \neq 0 \wedge l \neq LAST + 1$ then return $[(r_i, r'_j, i, j), \perp]$
   (d) $(r_l, r'_{j'}, l, j') \leftarrow \text{KEvolve}(r_i, r'_{j'}, i, j', l - i, \text{low})$
   (e) $m_k \leftarrow \text{AuthDec}_{r_l}(c); LAST = l$
6. return $[(r_{l-T+1}, r'_{j'}, l - T + 1, j'), (m_0, \ldots, m_{T-1})]$

Fig. 5. Operations Write, Wrap and Read

In particular, the sender $\mathcal{S}$ maintains the following data structure:

1. a *secret key* σ (also kept by the receiver $\mathcal{R}$);
2. a *buffer* C, $C = (C[0], C[1], \ldots, C[T-1])$, initially filled with *random data*, that takes the form of an array of size $T + 1$, where $C[i]$, $0 \leq i \leq T$, denotes the ith position in C; we set the size of each slot $C[i]$ to be $s = g(\ell)$, where ℓ is an appropriate given message length (defining message space $\{0, 1\}^\ell$).[11]
3. a *current index* I, initialized at a *random* position in C, and itself stored at $C[T]$.

Key management operates as follows. Given a security parameter κ, algorithm KGen first initiates an authenticated encryption scheme as well as two FS-PRNGs, one *low-layer* to generate sequence $r_0, r_1, \ldots$ (for message encryption) and one *high-layer* to generate sequence $r'_0, r'_1, \ldots$ (for buffer encryption). It then initializes the secret states of $\mathcal{S}$ and $\mathcal{R}$, which take the (simplified) form (r_i, r'_j, i, j), denoting the *most recent*

---

[11] In our EAX encryption implementation: $\ell = 1004$ and $g(\ell) = 1024$.

forward-secure pseudorandom numbers for the low and high layers, along with their sequence numbers. Also, given the current secret state (r_i, r'_j, i, j), an integer t and a control string $b \in \{\texttt{low}, \texttt{high}\}$, algorithm KEvolve creates the corresponding low- or high-layer t-th next forward-secure pseudorandom number.

Then our main protocols operate as shown in Figure 5. First, given secret writing key (r_i, r'_j, i, j), message m and buffer C, Write securely encodes m, adds it in C and updates the secret key. Then, given secret writing key (r_i, r'_j, i, j) and a buffer C, Wrap securely encapsulates C to $\hat{C}$ and updates the secret key. Finally, given secret reading key (r_i, r'_j, i, j) and an encapsulated buffer $\hat{C}$, Read decrypts the buffer and all of its contents returning a set of T messages and updates the secret key.

For simplicity, we here consider a fixed-size PBB that holds fixed-size messages (parameters T and $g(\ell)$ respectively). Note that PillarBox can be easily extended to handle variable-length messages and to dynamically enlarge the PBB buffer, as needed, in order to prevent loss of alert messages (due to overwriting) during prolonged PBB-transmission failures; we omit these extensions due to space limitations.

5   Experimental Evaluation

We developed a prototype of PillarBox in C++. To implement authenticated encryption we utilize an open-source version of EAX-mode encryption. We also implemented a custom FS-PRNG as a hash chain for generating the necessary cryptographic keys (for both low- and high-layer secure processing of messages and buffers).

We next experimentally validate the effectiveness of PillarBox in securing alerts during the critical window. We first demonstrate the merits of our alert-buffering approach via a generic attack against alert-pushing methods. We then show that PillarBox is fast enough to win the race condition against an attacker trying to disrupt the securing of alert messages. Surprisingly, even when an attacker already has the privilege necessary to kill PillarBox, the execution of the kill command itself can be secured in the PillarBox buffer before the application dies. Finally, we validate the feasibility of PillarBox as a practical alert-relaying tool.

5.1   Demonstrating Direct-Send Vulnerability

We motivate the need for securing the chain of custody in SASs and justify our design choice of host-side buffering, rather than immediately putting alerts on the wire, by showing the feasibility of an attacker intercepting on-the-wire host alert transmissions silently (without sender/receiver detection) in a rather simple setting.

Using the Ettercap tool [1] we inserted an attack machine (attacker) as a man-in-the-middle between our client and server communicating over a switch. The attacker performed ARP spoofing against the switch, to which most non-military-grade hubs and switches are vulnerable. Because it attacked the switch, neither endpoint observed the attack. Once inserted between the two machines, our attacker was able to drop or rewrite undesired packets on the fly. Even if the client and server had been communicating over a secured channel (a rarity in current practice), alert messages could still easily have been dropped, preventing any indication of the attack from reaching the server.

If executed within a subnet, the attack described here would rarely be detected, even by a forensic tool performing network packet capture, as these tools are typically deployed to monitor only inbound/outbound traffic, or at best across subnets.

Given the ease with which we were able to not only prevent communication between a client and server, but moreover modify what the server received, without detection, it should be clear just how important chain-of-custody is in SASs. If the messages being transmitted are of any value, then they need to be protected. Otherwise an attacker can simply block or modify all SAS communication while attacking a host, after which he can turn off or otherwise modify what the SAS sends from the client side. Attacking in such a way makes it impossible for the server to detect anything has gone wrong and motivates our desire to provide a better way to secure log messages.

5.2   Race-Condition Experiments

We now show that it is feasible for a SAS combined with PillarBox to detect an attack in progress and secure an alert before an attacker can disrupt PillarBox operation (i.e., that the critical window is non-zero in size). PillarBox depends on both an alerter (in our case, syslog), and a named pipe used to communicate from the alerter to the bufferer. Both of these components, as well as PillarBox itself, can be attacked, creating a race condition with the attacker. If any of the components can be shut down fast enough during an attack, alerts may not be secured in the PBB. Surprisingly, we show that even an attacker with the necessary (root) privilege rarely wins this race ($\approx 1\%$ of the time).

To bias our experiments in favor of an attacker, we assume the attacker has gained access to a privileged account that already has the necessary permissions to kill any of the components. We record time required for the attacker to issue a *single command* to kill the process and show that the command itself gets secured by PillarBox before the targeted component is terminated. Our tests were performed on an 2.5GHz Intel Core 2 Duo T9300 processor with 4 GB of memory and Ubuntu 12.04 as the operating system.

Killing PillarBox. PillarBox is a simple application that is easily terminated by an attacker, although it can be run as root to provide some protection. To be secured, alerts must be generated, routed by syslog to the named pipe, and then picked up by PillarBox, encrypted and added to the buffer. An attacker's best bet at disrupting the securing of alerts is to try and shutdown PillarBox itself. If run as root, PillarBox can be terminated by invoking root privilege and issuing a kill command.[12] Calling kill with the −9 signal immediately terminates any program, unless it is in the process of making a system call; it then terminates when the system call returns. Using sudo runs the command as root, but also generates an alert message which syslog picks up. The full one-line command sudo kill − 9 < PillarBox_pid > immediately terminates PillarBox, but usually not before a log event is created, routed by syslog through the named pipe, and secured.

As Table 1 shows, in the majority of runs the alert message is locked away in $\approx$ 4ms.[13] Alert messages are, on average, secured in PillarBox before it is killed with

---

[12] kill or pkill could be used to terminate the process: pkill takes in the process name, while kill takes a process id; otherwise they operate the same.

[13] PillarBox accounts for only a minuscule fraction of this total time.

Table 1. Average time from the start of a command until log is secured in PillarBox and total time for command completion

	Secured	Std. Dev.	Disrupted	Std. Dev.	Command
Syslog (typical)	4.09ms	0.30ms	8.86ms	2.43ms	sudo kill − 9 < syslog_pid >
Syslog (worst)[14]	32.33ms	5.38ms	9.32ms	2.81ms	sudo kill − 9 < syslog_pid >
Named pipe	6.36ms	3.02ms	8.99ms	3.30ms	sudo rm named_pipe
PillarBox	4.01ms	0.19ms	6.95ms	0.37ms	sudo kill − 9 < PillarBox_pid >

almost 3ms to spare.[14] However, in about 1% of our experiments, PillarBox was killed before receiving the alert message and encrypting it. All of the commands in Table 1 were run 100 times with averages and standard deviations shown.

Impacts of System Load. To further test the ability of the attacker to beat PillarBox, we also ran tests under varying amounts of disk, memory, and CPU load. Disk load appeared to have little to no effect on either the success of PillarBox, or the timing measurements. As expected, load on the system memory slowed everything down—lengthening both the time to secure, but also the time until the kill completes—but did not appear to impact the success of PillarBox winning the race condition. For unexplained reasons, CPU load did seem to impact PillarBox on our test machine. Oddly, PillarBox did well (0% failure) at near 100% load, but relatively poorly (< 4% failure) at 20% load. These tests were run 1000 times to further reduce noise. Additionally, we re-ran our tests on a 2.13 GHz Intel Xeon E5506 Quad Core processor with 3GB of RAM running Red Hat Enterprise Linux WS v5.3 x86_64. On that machine we again noticed ≈ 1% of tests failing, but did not find a correlation between load and failure rate. We expect CPU scheduling to be at fault but leave a more thorough investigation of the effects of load as well as the impact of virtualization or greater numbers of cores as future work. If CPU scheduling is indeed the cause, running PillarBox with higher priority should further lower the probability of an attacker winning the race condition.

Killing the Named Pipe. We also considered attacks against the other components (syslog and the named pipe). We use a named pipe to pass alerts from syslog to PillarBox. A named pipe is a permanent pipe created in the filesystem which can be read from and written to by any process. To destroy a named pipe created by root an attacker would need to run sudo rm named_pipe. Again, the invocation of sudo (or otherwise transitioning to root privilege) generates a log event. As Table 1 shows, the log messages created pass through the pipe before it is closed. There were no failures in these tests.

Killing Syslog. The alerter (syslog) is the first to handle the log message, and can be shutdown or killed by running sudo kill − 9 < syslog_pid >.[15] Table 1 shows that the log message is sent by syslog before it is killed. However, presumably due to process scheduling, in several runs the kill command returns before the alert message is secured

---

[14] Due to presumed OS scheduling interruptions, in about 1/3 of the runs the kill command returns before the message is *successfully* secured in PillarBox. These results show the timings observed in those cases.

[15] The alerter could be more integrated into the kernel itself, making it even harder to intercept and/or kill. In our case, syslog channels log messages generated by the kernel and doesn't actually generate them itself.

Table 2. Timeline of events related to the execution of the attacker's command
sudo cp /etc/rsyslog.d/vanish.conf /home/vanish.copy

Event	Start	Message Secured	Rule Deleted	Copy Fails
Avg. Time (ms)	0.00	4.00ms	4.04ms	7.21ms
Std. Dev.	N/A	0.44ms	0.44ms	0.81ms

in the PBB. Because the message *always* arrives in the PBB (again, there were no failures), we assume these represent runs where the alert is passed to the named pipe before syslog terminates and then read from the pipe when the PillarBox process is later scheduled by the OS. This issue is diminished in the tests against the named pipe and PillarBox, explaining their perceived lower average timings (and standard deviations).

Vanishing Rules. When PillarBox provides stealth, it is best combined with vanishing SAS rules to prevent critical information leakage. Recall that if an attacker cannot prevent PillarBox from securing events in the critical window, the attacker benefits from at least learning how the system is instrumented and what alerts were likely to have been generated. In our test setup, the vanishing alerts generate an alert whenever a root user logs in. To test the race condition, we instrumented PillarBox to delete the vanishing alerts configuration file after securing the alert message. The attacker attempts to create a copy of the sensitive alerter configuration file. As it is shown by the relative timing of events over 100 test runs in Table 2, after securing the alert message, PillarBox always successfully deletes the configuration file at least 2.72 ms. before the attempted copy.

Privilege Escalation. Having shown that PillarBox can win the race conditions related to securing alerts and causing them to vanish, even in the pessimistic case where the attacker *starts with the necessary permissions*, we now consider the issue of privilege escalation. The concern is that if the attacker exploits vulnerabilities the transition to root privilege may not get logged. We assume that most privilege escalations could be detected given the proper instrumentation and that disrupting any of the necessary components in our system (e.g. corrupting its memory address space) without root privilege is infeasible given current architectures (e.g., Address Space Randomization [21], etc.).

As an example of a common privilege escalation, we consider the "Full Nelson" attack, which exploits CVE-2010-4258, CVE-2010-3849, and CVE-2010-3850 to gain root access. We find that this attack generates kernel messages that syslog can pick up and pass through the named pipe and into the PBB before the exploit completes and the attacker terminates essential SAS or PillarBox components or reads the configuration file. In fact, the attack includes a necessary sleep command that further benefits timely securing of alerts in PillarBox. Even in the most pessimistic case, in which the exploit code uses the kill system call before ever launching a shell, and the sleep command is removed (causing the exploit to fail), the log messages are *still* locked away in PBB before the exploit program tries to disrupt PillarBox. Since the system must be restored after the privilege escalation, we were not able to run 100 instances, but we repeatedly demonstrated that the kernel log messages can be secured in PBB before being killed.

While the "Full Nelson" attack is representative of other local privilege escalation attacks, this by no means guarantees that faster or quieter privilege escalations don't exist. What it does demonstrate is that the event signaling the end of the critical window

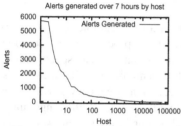

Fig. 6. Host-generated alerts over 7h

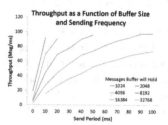

Fig. 7. Throughput vs. |PBB|, μ

(the elevation of privilege giving the attacker full control) can itself often be detected and secured in PillarBox before such privilege enables disruption of the PillarBox tool.

Asynchronous logging. We have also tested PillarBox in a more asynchronous setting using Snort as our alert generator to detect a remote SSH exploit. Once the attacker has shell access it escalates privilege and then shuts down PillarBox. Table 3 shows that in the average case all of the defenders actions (detecting the attack, securing the log in PillarBox and deleting the stealthy rule) complete a whole second before the attacker even gains shell access. The high standard deviation (measured over 100 runs) indicates that the attacker may be able to learn detection rules on rare occasion (this was never observed in our experiments), but cannot prevent the securing of the log messages.

Table 3. Race condition timings (measured from the launch of the attack)

Defender Event	Attack detected	Log secured	Rule deleted	
Average	1,645.441ms	1,645.609ms	1,645.772ms	
Std. Dev.	1,069.843ms	1,069.842ms	1,069.840ms	
Attacker Event	Remote shell	Privilege escalation	Rules copied	Log file deleted
Average	2,692.536ms	2,693.474ms	2,696.524ms	2,696.590ms
Std. Dev.	1,324.419ms	1,324.432ms	1,324.919ms	1,324.990ms

5.3 Observed Alerting Frequencies

We performed an analysis of a large enterprise (>50,000 users) dataset across a period of 7 hours. This dataset contains all collectable logs from this network, including servers, laptops, network devices, security appliances, and many more. The goal was to derive information about the typical alert frequency across a representative work day.

It is critical to note that only certain messages pertaining to, e.g., indicators of compromise, will be selected for inclusion in the PillarBox protected queue. As such, the data found here represents an overloaded maximum: It is unlikely that most networks will generate such volumes of alerts, and most alerts will not be applicable to PillarBox.

Figure 6 shows the distribution of alerts coming from hosts within the enterprise. The x-axis is in log scale, showing that the majority of machines send very few alert messages, while a small subset send the majority. Over a 7-hour window, the busiest machine generated 8603 alerts, but the average across all machines (59,034 in total) was only 18.3 alerts. Clearly, therefore, if we design the system to handle a throughput of one alert per second (3600 alerts an hour) our system will be able to handle even the busiest of alerters. The maximum observed rate in our dataset was 1707 alerts / hour.

5.4 Throughput Experiments

We now show that PillarBox can process events at a practical rate. Given a constant stream of events, the host-based application was able to process nearly 100,000 messages per second, higher than any rate recorded in our dataset. The speed with which PillarBox can encode messages naturally depends on a number of factors, e.g., message size, the cost of computing FS-PRNGs, PBB's size, and the frequency μ with which the buffer is re-encrypted and sent. Obviously the larger the messages, the longer they take to encrypt. The standard log messages generated on our Linux system were typically a few hundred characters long. We note that our hash-chain FS-PRNG required one computation per produced number, thus minimizing key-generation overhead.

Figure 7 explores tradeoffs between buffer size and send frequency in terms of their impact on maximum throughput. Some combinations of buffer size and send rate led to buffer overflows, and were removed. Performance seems to increase as buffer size increases and send frequency decreases, as expected. A large buffer that is rarely re-encrypted for sending can process events more quickly that a small, frequently sent buffer. As Figure 7 shows, throughput seems to top out just shy of 100 messages / ms, further evidence of the minimal overhead of PillarBox.

6 Related Work

PillarBox uses host-side buffering to secure alerts for transmission to a remote server. An alternative is a trusted receiver within a protected environment on the host itself. A *hypervisor*, or virtual machine monitor (VMM), for instance, has higher privilege than a guest OS, isolating it from OS-level exploits. Thus, as an alternative to PillarBox, messages could be sent from a SAS to a same-host hypervisor. Hypervisor-based messaging can be blended with even stronger security functionality in which the hypervisor protects a SAS (or other monitoring software) itself against corruption as in, e.g., [22], and/or is itself protected by trusted hardware, as in Terra [7]. Where available, a hypervisor-based approach is an excellent alternative or complement to PillarBox.

Hypervisor-based approaches, however, have several notable limitations. Many hosts and devices today are not virtualized and some, e.g., embedded devices, probably will not be for a long time. Operating constraints often limit security administrators' access to hypervisors. For instance, IT administrators may be able to require that personal devices in the workplace (e.g., laptops, tablets, and smartphones) contain an enterprise-specific VMM or application, but they are unlikely to obtain full privileges on such devices. Finally, hypervisors themselves are vulnerable to compromise: Some works have noted that the code sizes, privilege levels, and OS-independence of modern VMMs belie common assertions of superior security over traditional OSes [24, 11].

PillarBox builds in part on funkspiel schemes, introduced by Håstad et al. [9]. A funkspiel scheme creates a special host-to-server channel whose existence may be known to an adversary; but an adversary cannot tell if or when the channel has been used, a property similar to stealth in PillarBox. (By implication, an adversary cannot recover message information from the channel either.) As in our work, a funkspiel scheme resists adversaries that see all traffic on the channel and ultimately corrupt the sender.

Funkspiel schemes, though, are designed for a specific use case: Authentication tokens. The transmitter either uses its initialized authentication key or swaps in a new, random one to indicate an alert condition. A funkspiel scheme thus transmits only a single, one-bit message ("swap" or "no swap"), and is not practical for the arbitrarily long messages on high-bandwidth channels in PillarBox.

Another closely related technique is forward-secure logging (also called tamper-evident logging), which protects the integrity of log messages on a host after compromise by an adversary (see, e.g., [5, 3, 14, 23, 19, 25, 26, 13, 20, 16]). As already discussed, while these systems use forward-secure integrity protection like PillarBox, they are not designed for self-protecting settings like PillarBox. They aim instead for forensic protection, e.g., to protect against retroactive log modification by an administrator. Some schemes, e.g., [3, 19, 13, 20], are designed to "close" a log, i.e., create forward security for new events, only periodically, not continuously. Additionally, existing forward-secure logging systems do not aim, like PillarBox, to achieve stealth.

Finally, in a different context than ours, the Adeona system [18] uses forward-secure host-side buffering in order to achieve privacy-preserving location tracking of lost or stolen devices. Adeona uses cryptographic techniques much like those in PillarBox to cache and periodically upload location information to a peer-to-peer network. Adeona does not offer integrity protection like PillarBox, nor does it address the complications of high throughput, buffer wraparound, and transmission failures in our setting.

7 Conclusion

Today's big data security analytics systems rely on untrustworthy data: They collect and analyze messages from Security Analytics Sources (SASs) with inadequate integrity protection and are vulnerable to adversarial corruption. By compromising a host and its SAS, a strong attacker can suppress key SAS messages and alerts. An attacker can also gather intelligence about sensitive SAS instrumentation and actions (potentially even just via traffic analysis).

We have introduced PillarBox, a new tool that provides key, missing protections for security analytics systems by securing the messages generated by SASs. Using the approach of host-side buffering, PillarBox provides the two properties of *integrity* and *stealth*. PillarBox achieves integrity protection on alert messages even in the worst case: hostile, self-protecting environments where a host records alerts about an attack in progress while an attacker tries to suppress them. Stealth, an optional property in PillarBox, ensures that at rest or in transit, a SAS message is invisible to even a strong adversary with network and eventually host control.

Our experiments with PillarBox validate its practicality and protective value. We show, e.g., that PillarBox can "win the race" against an adversary mounting a local privilege escalation attack and disabling PillarBox as fast as possible: PillarBox secures alert messages about the attack before the attacker can intervene. Our study of alerting rates in a large (50,000+ host) environment and of local host performance confirms the low overhead and real-world deployability of PillarBox. We posit that PillarBox can offer practical, strong protection for many big data security analytics systems in a world of ever bigger data and more sophisticated adversaries.

Acknowledgments. We thank the anonymous reviewers for their helpful comments, and also Alina Oprea, Ting-Fang Yen and Todd S. Leetham for many useful discussions.

References

[1] Ettercap, http://ettercap.sourceforge.net/

[2] Bellare, M., Namprempre, C.: Authenticated encryption: Relations among notions and analysis of the generic composition paradigm. J. Cryptol. 21, 469–491 (2008)

[3] Bellare, M., Yee, B.: Forward-security in private-key cryptography. In: Joye, M. (ed.) CT-RSA 2003. LNCS, vol. 2612, pp. 1–18. Springer, Heidelberg (2003)

[4] Bowers, K.D., Hart, C., Juels, A., Triandopoulos, N.: PillarBox: Combating next-generation malware with fast forward-secure logging. Cryptology ePrint Archive, Report 2013/625 (2013)

[5] Crosby, S.A., Wallach, D.S.: Efficient data structures for tamper-evident logging. In: USENIX Sec., pp. 317–334 (2009)

[6] Dolev, D., Yao, A.C.: On the security of public key protocols. IEEE Trans. on Inf. Theory 29(2), 198–207 (1983)

[7] Garfinkel, T., Pfaff, B., Chow, J., Rosenblum, M., Boneh, D.: Terra: A virtual machine-based platform for trusted computing. In: SOSP, pp. 193–206 (2003)

[8] Goldwasser, S., Micali, S., Rivest, R.L.: A digital signature scheme secure against adaptive chosen-message attacks. SIAM J. Comput. 17(2), 281–308 (1988)

[9] Håstad, J., Jonsson, J., Juels, A., Yung, M.: Funkspiel schemes: An alternative to conventional tamper resistance. In: CCS, pp. 125–133 (2000)

[10] Itkis, G.: Handbook of Inf. Security, Forward Security: Adaptive Cryptography—Time Evolution. John Wiley & Sons (2006)

[11] Karger, P.A.: Securing virtual machine monitors: what is needed? In: ASIACCS, pp. 1–2 (2009)

[12] Kelsey, J., Callas, J., Clemm, A.: RFC 5848: Signed syslog messages (2010)

[13] Kelsey, J., Schneier, B.: Minimizing bandwidth for remote access to cryptographically protected audit logs. In: RAID, p. 9 (1999)

[14] Ma, D., Tsudik, G.: A new approach to secure logging. Trans. Storage 5(1), 2:1–2:21 (2009)

[15] Mandiant. M-trends: The advanced persistent threat (2010),
http://www.mandiant.com

[16] Marson, G.A., Poettering, B.: Practical secure logging: Seekable sequential key generators. In: Crampton, J., Jajodia, S., Mayes, K. (eds.) ESORICS 2013. LNCS, vol. 8134, pp. 111–128. Springer, Heidelberg (2013)

[17] Oltsik, J.: Defining big data security analytics. Networkworld, 1 (April 2013)

[18] Ristenpart, T., Maganis, G., Krishnamurthy, A., Kohno, T.: Privacy-preserving location tracking of lost or stolen devices: Cryptographic techniques and replacing trusted third parties with DHTs. In: USENIX Sec., pp. 275–290 (2008)

[19] Schneier, B., Kelsey, J.: Cryptographic support for secure logs on untrusted machines. In: USENIX Sec., p. 4 (1998)

[20] Schneier, B., Kelsey, J.: Tamperproof audit logs as a forensics tool for intrusion detection systems. Comp. Networks and ISDN Systems (1999)

[21] Shacham, H., Page, M., Pfaff, B., Goh, E.J., Modadugu, N., Boneh, D.: On the Effectiveness of Address-Space Randomization. In: CCS, pp. 298–307 (2004)

[22] Sharif, M.I., Lee, W., Cui, W., Lanzi, A.: Secure in-VM monitoring using hardware virtualization. In: CCS, pp. 477–487 (2009)

[23] Waters, B.R., Balfanz, D., Durfee, G., Smetters, D.K.: Building an encrypted and search-able audit log. In: NDSS (2004)

[24] Chen, Y., Chen, Y., Paxson, V., Katz, R.: What's new about cloud computing security? Technical Report UCB/EECS-2010-5, UC Berkeley (2010)

[25] Yavuz, A.A., Ning, P.: BAF: An efficient publicly verifiable secure audit logging scheme for distributed systems. In: ACSAC, pp. 219–228 (2009)

[26] Yavuz, A.A., Ning, P., Reiter, M.K.: Efficient, compromise resilient and append-only cryptographic schemes for secure audit logging. In: Keromytis, A.D. (ed.) FC 2012. LNCS, vol. 7397, pp. 148–163. Springer, Heidelberg (2012)

Dynamic Reconstruction of Relocation Information for Stripped Binaries

Vasilis Pappas, Michalis Polychronakis, and Angelos D. Keromytis

Columbia University
{vpappas,mikepo,angelos}@cs.columbia.edu

Abstract. Address Space Layout Randomization (ASLR) is a widely used technique for the prevention of code reuse attacks. The basic concept of ASLR is to randomize the base address of executable modules at load time. Changing the load address of modules is also often needed for resolving conflicts among shared libraries with the same preferred base address. In Windows, loading a module at an arbitrary address depends on compiler-generated *relocation* information, which specifies the absolute code or data addresses in the module that must be adjusted due to the module's relocation at a non-preferred base address. Relocation information, however, is often stripped from production builds of legacy software, making it more susceptible to code-reuse attacks, as ASLR is not an option.

In this paper, we introduce a technique to enable ASLR for executables with stripped relocation information by incrementally adjusting stale absolute addresses at runtime. The technique relies on runtime monitoring of memory accesses and control flow transfers to the original location of a relocated module using page table manipulation techniques. Depending on the instruction and memory access type, the system identifies stale offsets, reconstructs their relocation information, and adjusts them so that subsequent accesses to the same locations proceed directly, without any intervention. To improve performance further, the reconstructed relocation information is preserved across subsequent runs of the same program. We have implemented a prototype of the proposed technique for Windows XP, which is transparently applicable to third-party stripped binaries, and have experimentally evaluated its performance and effectiveness. Our results demonstrate that incremental runtime relocation patching is practical, incurs modest runtime overhead for initial runs of protected programs, and has negligible overhead on subsequent runs.

1 Introduction

Keeping systems up-to-date with the latest patches, updates, and operating system versions, is a good practice for eliminating the threat of exploits that rely on previously disclosed vulnerabilities. Major updates or newer versions of operating systems and applications also typically come with additional or improved security protection and exploit mitigation technologies, such as the stack buffer overrun detection (/GS), data execution prevention (DEP), address space layout

A. Stavrou et al. (Eds.): RAID 2014, LNCS 8688, pp. 68–87, 2014.
© Springer International Publishing Switzerland 2014

randomization (ASLR), and many other protections of Windows [27], which help in defending against future exploits.

At the same time, however, updates and patches often result in compatibility issues, reliability problems, and rising deployment costs. Administrators are usually reluctant to roll out new patches and updates before conducting extensive testing and cost-benefit analysis [34], while old, legacy applications may simply not be compatible with newer OS versions. It is indicative that although Windows XP SP3 went out of support on April 8th, 2014 [7], many home users, organizations, and systems still rely on it, including the majority of ATMs [1]. In fact, the UK and Dutch governments we forced to negotiate support for Windows XP past the cutoff date, to allow public-sector organizations to continue receiving critical security updates for one more year [6].

As a step towards enhancing the security of legacy programs and operating systems that do not support the most recent exploit mitigation technologies, application hardening tools such as Microsoft's EMET (Enhanced Mitigation Experience Toolkit) [25] can be used to retrofit these and even newer (sometimes more experimental) protections on third-party legacy applications. An important such protection is address space layout randomization, which aims to defend against exploitation techniques based on code reuse, such as return-to-libc [15] and return-oriented programming (ROP) [36].

ASLR randomizes the load address of executables and DLLs to prevent attackers from using data or code residing at predictable locations. In Windows, though, this is only possible for binaries that have been compiled with *relocation* information. In contrast to Linux shared libraries and PIC executables, which contain position-independent code and can be easily loaded at arbitrary locations, Windows portable executable (PE) files contain absolute addresses, e.g., immediate instruction operands or initialized data pointers, that are valid only if an executable has been loaded at its preferred base address. If the actual load address is different, e.g., because another DLL is already loaded at the preferred address or due to ASLR, the loader adjusts all fixed addresses appropriately based on the relocation information included in the binary.

Unfortunately, PE files that do not carry relocation information cannot be loaded at any address other than their preferred base address, which is specified at link time. Relocation information is often stripped from release builds, especially in legacy applications, to save space or hinder reverse engineering. Furthermore, in 32-bit Windows, it is not mandatory for EXE files to carry relocation information, as they are loaded first, and thus their preferred base address is always available in the virtual address space of the newly created process. For these reasons, tools like EMET unavoidably fail to enforce ASLR for executables with stripped relocation information. Consequently, applications with stripped relocation information may remain vulnerable to code reuse attacks, as DEP alone can protect only against code injection attacks. Furthermore, recently proposed protection mechanisms for Windows applications rely on accurate code disassembly, which depends on the availability of relocation information, to apply control flow integrity [45] or code randomization [28].

In this work, we present a technique for reconstructing the missing relocation information from stripped binaries, and enabling safe address space layout randomization for executables which are currently incompatible with forced ASLR. The technique is based on discovering at runtime any stale absolute addresses that need to be modified according to the newly chosen load address, and applying the necessary fixups, replicating in essence the work that the loader would perform if relocation information were present. As transparency is a key requirement for the practical applicability of protections tailored to third-party applications, the proposed approach relies only on existing operating system facilities (mainly page table manipulation) to monitor and intercept memory accesses to locations that need fixup.

We have evaluated the performance and effectiveness of our prototype implementation using the SPEC benchmark suite, as well as several Windows applications. Based on our results, incremental runtime relocation patching is practical, incurs modest runtime overhead for initial runs of protected programs, and has negligible overhead on subsequent runs, as the reconstructed relocation information is preserved. Besides forced ASLR, the proposed technique can also be used to resolve conflicts between stripped binaries with overlapping load addresses, a problem that occasionally occurs when running legacy applications, and to significantly improve code disassembly.

The main contributions of this work are:

– We present a technique for dynamically reconstructing missing relocation information from stripped binaries. Our technique can be used to enable forced ASLR or or resolve base address conflicts for third-party non-relocatable binaries.
– We have implemented the proposed approach as a self-contained software hardening tool for Windows applications, and describe in detail its design and implementation.
– We have experimentally evaluated the performance and correctness of our approach using standard benchmarks and popular applications, and demonstrate its effectiveness.

2   Background

The wide support for non-executable memory page protections [27,30] in recent operating systems and processors has given rise to code reuse attacks, such as return-to-libc [15] and return-oriented programming (ROP) [36], which allow the exploitation of memory corruption vulnerabilities by transferring control to code that already exists in the address space of the vulnerable process. Return-oriented programming, in particular, has become the primary exploitation technique for achieving arbitrary code execution against Windows applications. In contrast to return-to-libc, the reused code in ROP exploits consists of small instruction sequences, called *gadgets*, scattered throughout the executable segments of the targeted process.

To reuse code that already exists in the address space of a vulnerable process, an attacker needs to rely on a priori knowledge of its exact location (although in some cases the location of code can be inferred dynamically during exploitation [8, 10, 20, 23, 35, 42, 43]). Address space layout randomization (ASLR) [11, 27, 29] protects against code reuse attacks by randomizing the location of loaded executable modules, breaking the assumptions of the attacker about the location of any code of interest. Besides address space randomization, process diversity [13, 16] can also be increased by randomizing the code of executable segments, e.g., by permuting the order of functions [2, 11, 12, 22] and basic blocks [3, 5], or by randomizing the code itself [19, 28, 44].

In Windows, which is the main focus of this work, ASLR support was introduced in Windows Vista. By default, it is enabled only for core operating system binaries and programs that have been configured to use it through the /DYNAMICBASE linker switch. For legacy applications, not compiled with ASLR support and other protection features, Microsoft has released the Enhanced Mitigation Experience Toolkit (EMET) [25], which can be used to retrofit ASLR and other exploit mitigation technologies on third-party applications. A core feature of EMET is Mandatory ASLR, which randomizes the load address of modules even if they have not been compiled with the /DYNAMICBASE switch, but do include relocation information. This is particularly important for applications that even though have opted for ASLR, may include some DLLs that remain in static locations, which are often enough for mounting code reuse attacks [17, 21, 47]. EMET's ASLR implementation also provides higher randomization entropy through additional small memory allocations at the beginning of a module's base address. Many of the advanced ASLR features of EMET have been incorporated as native functionality in Windows 8, including forced ASLR.

The above recent developments, however, are not always applicable on legacy executables. Typically, when creating a PE file, the linker assumes that it will be loaded to a specific memory location, known as its *preferred base address*. To support loading of modules at addresses other than their preferred base address, PE files may contain a special .reloc section, which contains a list of offsets (relative to each PE section) known as "fixups" [38]. The .reloc section contains a fixup for each absolute addresses at which a delta value needs to be added to maintain the correctness of the code in case the actual load address is different [32]. Although DLLs typically contain relocation information, release builds of legacy applications often strip .reloc sections to save space or hinder reverse engineering. This can be achieved by providing the /FIXED switch at link time. Furthermore, in older versions of Visual Studio, the linker by default omits relocation information for EXEs when performing release builds, as the main executable is the first module to be loaded into the virtual address space, and thus its preferred base address is always expected to be available.

As modules (either EXEs or DLLs) with stripped relocation information cannot be loaded at arbitrary addresses, the OS or tools like EMET cannot protect them using ASLR. Legacy applications may also occasionally encounter address conflicts due to different modules that attempt to use the same preferred base address. Our system aims to enable the randomization of the load address of modules with stripped relocation information by incrementally adjusting stale absolute addresses at runtime.

3   Approach

Our approach to the problem of relocating stripped binaries relies on reconstructing the missing relocation info by discovering such relocatable offsets at runtime. We note here that a static approach, i.e., using disassembly to find all the relocatable offsets, would be much more difficult, if not infeasible in many cases—the reason being that stripped binaries also lack debugging symbols, so complete disassembly coverage would be impossible in most cases.

3.1   Overview

The basic idea of our approach is to load the stripped binary at a random location and monitor any data accesses or control transfers to its original location. Any such access to the original location is either a result of using a relocatable offset or an attack attempt (the attacker might try to reuse parts of the original code, not knowing that the binary was relocated). The next step is to identify the source of the access by checking whether it was indeed caused by a relocatable offset. In this case, the offset it located, its value is fixed to the new random base, and the relocation info is reconstructed so as next time the same program is executed a fixup for that address can be automatically applied.

Although there are a few different ways to monitor memory access and control transfers at runtime, we followed an approach that minimizes its effects and dependencies on third-party components. For instance, instruction-level dynamic binary instrumentation was not considered for this reason, as it requires the installation of third-party dynamic binary instrumentation frameworks (and typically incurs a prohibitively high runtime overhead). Our monitoring facility is built around basic operating system functionality, mostly memory protection mechanisms. More precisely, after a binary is loaded to a random location, we change the permissions of its original location to inaccessible, so as each time a memory access or control transfer happens to one of the original locations, a memory violation exception is raised. This type of exception usually contains the location of the instruction that caused it, the faulting address (can be the same as the instruction location), and the type of access (read or write).

The main challenge of our approach now becomes to identify whether an access to the original binary location is caused by a relocatable offset and how to trace it back to that offset. To better explain this issue, consider the following example. Assume that an instruction updates the contents of a global variable using its absolute address (e.g., 0x1000). When the instruction is executed from the new, randomly chosen location of the binary, an exception will be raised. At this point, we know the location of the instruction and the faulting address (0x1000). After analyzing the faulting instruction, we see that one of its operands is actually the faulting address. In this case, we have to fix the operand by adjusting it to the new random base, and also reconstruct the relocation info of this offset.

The example above is the most straightforward case of identifying a relocatable offset. In practice, in most cases the relocatable offset is not part of the faulting instruction. For example, consider the case of dereferencing a global pointer. There is an instruction to load the value of the pointer, probably in a register, and another instruction to read the contents of the memory location stored in the register. In this case, the faulting address is not directly related with the faulting instruction. Even worse, there are cases in which the relocatable offset has been changed before it is used. For example, accessing a field from a structure in a global array would only require a single relocatable address (the location of the array) and would result in many runtime accesses within the range of the array. It is very difficult to trace such an access reliably back to its source relocatable offset.

However, code-reuse attacks rely solely on the knowledge of the code's location, regardless of the location of data. Based on this observation, and due to the problematic nature of data pointer tracing, we focus on randomizing the load address of code segments only. Code pointers are usually guaranteed not to support any arithmetic—it would be difficult to imagine code that depends on expressions such as adding a few bytes to the location of a function start, at least for compiler-generated code. An exception to this is jump tables that contain relative offsets, but this is a case that can be easily covered, as we will see later on. This simplifies the overall approach, without sacrificing any of the security guarantees.

Figure 1 shows a high-level overview of our approach. When a stripped binary is loaded for execution (left side), its code segment is moved to a random location, while the original location becomes inaccessible (right side). Then, whenever there is a memory access or control transfer to the original location (solid arrow), the faulting address along with the instruction that caused it are analyzed. Based on this analysis, the source relocatable offset is pinpointed, gets fixed, and its relocation information is reconstructed. In the following, we describe in more detail how this analysis is being performed.

3.2   Access Analysis

The series of steps performed after a memory access violation exception is raised due to a memory access in the original code location is depicted in Figure 2. Broadly speaking, access violations are grouped into two categories based on their root cause: (i) reading the contents of the original code segment, and (ii) control transfers to the original code segment. To distinguish between the two, the system checks whether the value of the instruction pointer is within the original code segment.

In practice, the first case corresponds mostly to indirect jump instructions that read their target from the code segment. These are typically part of jump tables, which are used for the implementation of switch statements in C. In the second case, control is transfered to the original code segment because a code

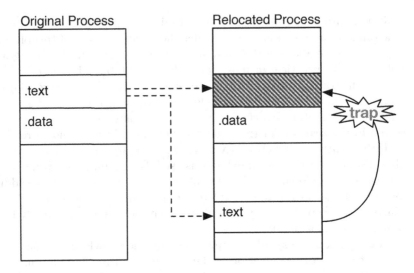

Fig. 1. High-level overview of runtime relocation fixup. The code segment of a stripped binary is loaded to a randomly chosen location, and its original memory area is marked as inaccessible. Memory accesses and control transfers to any of the original locations are trapped. Relocation information is then reconstructed by analyzing the faulting instruction.

pointer that has not been relocated is used. This could be a simple function pointer, part of a C++ virtual table (vtable), or a static one, represented as an immediate value in an instruction. In the following subsections we describe in detail how each of these cases is handled.

When control is transferred to locations in the original code segments for which there is no code pointer, or when we can not verify it as a legitimate code pointer, these transfers are flagged as code-reuse attempts (see Fig. 2). This effectively allows attackers to reuse code paths for which there are legitimate code pointers (e.g., function entries or jump table targets), given that they have not been reconstructed yet. Arguably, this leaves a very limited set of gadgets for the attacker, which quickly shrinks further as relocatable code pointers are identified.

3.3 Jump Tables

A jump table is an array of code targets that is usually accessed through an indirect jump. The following is an example of such a jump table in x86 assembly (taken from gcc's binary):

```
.text:004D5CCE     jmp   ds:off_4D6864[eax*4] ; switch jump
...
; DATA XREF: _main+2CE ; jump table for switch statement
.text:004D6864 off_4D6864     dd offset loc_4D5D53
```

```
.text:004D6868              dd offset loc_4D5D63
.text:004D686C              dd offset loc_4D5D93
.text:004D6870              dd offset loc_4D5D8B
```

When the jmp instruction is executed from the new random location, an exception is going to be raised, with the faulting address being (0x4D6864 + eax * 4). This is handled as follows: i) starting from the location pointed to by the faulting address, we scan the bytes before and after that location for more addresses and fix them, and ii) we also fix the relocatable offset in the address operand of the indirect jump instruction. In case of jump tables with relative offsets, we just skip the first step.

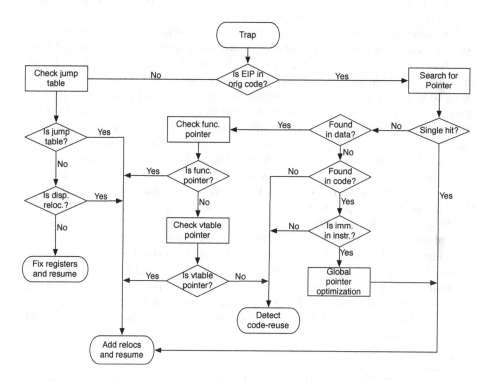

Fig. 2. Flow graph of the procedure followed after a memory access exception (trap) is generated. If the instruction pointer (EIP register) at the time of the exception is within the original code segment, the system performs pointer verification, otherwise the faulting instruction is fixed.

3.4   Pointer Verification

After jump tables are covered, we only expect to see control flow transfers to the locations of the original code. In these cases, the location of the faulting instruction is also the faulting address—there is no information about the source instruction. Given a faulting address, the whole code segment and initialized data are scanned for all its occurrences. If there is a single occurrence, we assume that it is a relocatable offset, which is handled appropriately. Otherwise, for each occurrence in the code segment, we verify that it is indeed part of a valid instruction—more precisely, an immediate operand.

Occurrences found in the initialized data segments are a bit more complicate to cover. Usually, for such a hit to be indeed a relocatable offset, it has to be a variable holding a function pointer, so there should be a way of accessing that variable. To verify this, we just need to find a data reference to that variable. In addition, function pointers can be parts of structures, arrays, or a combination of both. In general, we verify that an occurrence of the faulting address in the data segment is a relocatable offset that needs to be fixed if we can find a reference to or near its location (given as a parameter).

The following example illustrates the function pointer verification process. Assume there is a global variable that is statically initialized with the address of a function. Also, there is an indirect call instruction that reads the value of the global variable and transfers control to its value. At runtime, the value is going to be read (because the data segment is not relocated) and an exception is going to be raised when control is transfered to the function. Both the faulting address and the faulting instruction will correspond the beginning of the target function. At this point, we find an occurrence in the code segment and verify that it belongs to an instruction—which is the indirect call in this case.

Another use of function pointers is in C++ virtual tables, which is how dynamic class methods are represented. These pointers are handled a bit differently than simple function pointers, and, for this reason, we have introduced special checking rules. We first verify that there is a move instruction that copies the head of the table to a newly created class instance, by finding a move instruction that references a memory location close to the place where the code pointer was found. We then also verify that the control was transferred by an indirect call through a register, by reading the current value at the top of the runtime stack (return address) and disassembling the instruction right before the location it points to. Bellow is a real example taken from the eon binary of the SPEC benchmarks suite:

```
;; function call
.text:004017F9     mov     eax, [ecx]      ; ecx is this ptr
.text:004017FB     mov     eax, [eax+24h]
.text:004017FE     push    edx
.text:004017FF     mov     edx, [ebp+arg_4]
.text:00401802     push    edx
.text:00401803     mov     edx, [ebp+arg_0]
.text:00401806     push    edx
.text:00401807     call    eax

.....
```

```
;; vtable (the static part)
; DATA XREF: sub_409B40+8o    ; sub_40B0E0+2Fo
.rdata:00461D24 off_461D24      dd offset sub_40AAD0
.rdata:00461D28                 dd offset sub_409BB0
.rdata:00461D2C                 dd offset sub_409BC0
.....
;; copying the head of the table
.text:0040B10C      lea    ecx, [esi+4]     ; this
.text:0040B10F      mov    dword ptr [esi], offset off_461D24
```

The top part of the example shows the code that loads the function pointer from the vtable to the eax register and then transfers control there by calling it. The call instruction at the end will actually going to raise an exception. While handling the exception, we check (i) the table that contains the faulting address at 0x461D24 (middle part) is referenced by a move instruction at 0x40B10F (bottom part), and (ii) the instruction before the return address is a call instruction with a register operand (at 0x401807).

3.5 Dynamic Data

Although in order to reconstruct the missing relocation information we need to locate relocatable offsets within the image of the executable module, copies of such values also appear in dynamic data (e.g., in the stack or heap). This is the result, for example, of a global pointer being copied in a structure field that was dynamically allocated. In this case, an exception is going to be raised when the copy of the pointer (in the structure) is used. As described before, our technique is going to trace the original relocatable offset. This is sufficient for reconstructing the relocation information for this pointer, and avoid dealing with the same problem next time the same program is executed. However, we do not take any further actions to deal with copies in dynamic data. Thus, we might have to handle more than one exceptions for the same relocatable value during the same run in which it was first discovered. This, of course, does not affect the correctness and robustness of the technique in any way, but can affect overall performance.

To avoid the performance penalty under some cases, while not weakening our original approach, we added a simple optimization for global pointers. Each time a relocatable offset is fixed, and it is found to be the source operand of an instruction that copies it over to a global data location, we check whether the destination memory location contains the same value and relocate that copy, too. Below is an example of a few such instructions (taken from gcc's binary):

```
.text:004D5A69      mov    dword_550968, offset loc_4D1F10
.text:004D5A73      mov    dword_550AAC, offset loc_4D1C20
.text:004D5A7D      mov    dword_5509C4, offset nullsub_1
```

The first mov instruction in the above example copies the (relocatable) offset loc_4D1F10 to the global data memory location 0x550968. At the time an exception is raised because control was transfered to address 0x4D1F10, the source operand of the first mov instruction will be fixed, and, if the same value is found at address 0x550968, that will be fixed as well. In this way, future copies of the relocatable offset will point to the new code location, and no more exceptions will be raised for this instance.

In general, when this optimization is not applicable and there are many copies of relocatable offsets being repeatedly used, we have the option to set an access threshold, beyond which the system can inform the user that restarting the program would greatly increase its performance. Still, we believe that this is a minor issue, as it might occur only in the first few times a program is executed. After that, the relocation information of the majority of the relocatable offsets will have been reconstructed.

4   Implementation

We built a prototype of the described technique for the Windows platform. Most of the development of the tool was done on Windows XP. However, as the APIs we use have not changed in more recent versions of the operating system, our prototype supports even the latest version, which is Windows 8.1 at the time of writing.

The most significant part of the implementation is built on top of the Windows Debugging API [26], with the addition of some other standard functions (e.g., CreateProcess). This API is designed to work between two processes: the parent process is responsible for spawning a child process, and then capture and analyze any debug events the child generates. Debug events include memory access violation exceptions, process/thread startup/termination, and so on. Our implementation is bundled as a single application (about 1.5 KLOC) which can be executed from the command prompt, and receives the path of the target program to be protected as a command-line argument.

At a higher level, there are two phases of operation: initialization and runtime. We discuss both in sufficient detail in the rest of this section.

4.1   Initialization

The first step during the initialization phase is to spawn the process, while passing the appropriate arguments in order to enable debugging. The very first debug event generated by the child process is a process creation event, which is handled by the parent by performing the following tasks before resuming the execution of the child process. Initially, the Portable Executable (PE) headers are parsed. These headers include information such as the boundaries of each section (data, code, etc.) and the entry point of the code. Given that information, we proceed by copying the code section to a new, randomly chosen location using the ReadProcessMemory and WriteProcessMemory API functions, while changing the memory protections of the original code segment to inaccessible using VirtualProtectEx.

In order to improve the performance of certain runtime operations, a hash table of all possible code pointer values is built. This is done by scanning all sections and inserting any four-byte values (assuming 32-bit processes) that fall into the address range of the original code segment. Finally, we check whether there is a file that contains relocation information that was discovered as part of previous runs, and apply them.

4.2   Runtime

After initialization is completed and control is given back to the child process, the parent blocks while waiting for the next debugging event. Usually, we expect memory access violation exceptions to be generated after this stage. New DLL loaded events might happen as well, but rarely. Whenever a new DLL is loaded in the address space of the child process, the system checks whether it contains relocations. In case it does not, the same initialization steps that were previously described are performed.

As described in Section 3, the core of our technique is implemented as part of the handling mechanism of memory access violation exceptions. Each exception record contains information about the location of the instruction that caused it, along with the faulting address. Based on this information, we distinguish between two main cases: i) the instruction pointer falls within the address range of the original (inaccessible) code segment (instruction address and faulting address are the same), and ii) an illegal memory access was made by an instruction located in the relocated code segment (instruction address and faulting address are different).

If the instruction pointer after a memory exception is received falls within the original code segment, this means that the control flow was transfered there and the program failed when it tried to execute the next instruction. In this case, the faulting address corresponds to the location of the instruction in the exception record. The exception is handled by first looking up the faulting address in the hash table—which is constructed during the initialization phase. A single hit is the simplest case, because it means that this is the source of the exception. If there are more than one hits, each one is verified using the rules described in Section 3 for immediate values or function pointers.

Alternatively, if the faulting instruction belongs to the relocated code segment, this means that one of its operands caused the fault. This happens under two circumstances: the instruction is an indirect jump, reading a jump table target from the original code location, or an instruction that uses a copy of a relocatable value from dynamic data.

5   Evaluation

In this section we present the results of the experimental evaluation of our prototype in terms of correctness and performance overhead. For the largest part of our evaluation, we used benchmarks from SPEC CPU2006 [4], as well as some real-world applications, such as Internet Explorer and Adobe Reader. All the experiments were performed on a computer with the following specifications: Intel Core i7 2.00GHz CPU, 8GB RAM, 256GB SSD with 64-bit Windows 8.1 Pro.

5.1 Statistics

We started our evaluation with the goal of getting a better feeling on the differences of applying our technique to programs with distinct characteristics. First, we selected all the test programs in the integer suite that come with the SPEC benchmark and stripped the relocation information from the compiled binaries. Out of the twelve programs in that set, only libquantum had to be left out because it uses some C99 features that are not supported by Visual C++ (as noted in the SPEC configuration file Example-windows-ia32-visualstudio.cfg). Then, we executed each one using our prototype and gathered some valuable statistics that provide insights about the runtime behaviour of our technique. At the same time, we checked that the output of the benchmark test runs was correct, which in turn verified the correctness of our implementation under these cases.

Table 1 shows the results of this run. The first column contains the name of each SPEC test program, followed by the number of possible pointers that we identified for each during the initialization phase. The next three columns show the number of identified jump tables and the number of verified pointers along with the percentage of them that had a single hit in the possible pointers set. Next, we have the number of times that an already fixed relocatable offset reappeared at runtime because of copies of it in dynamic data, followed by the number of global pointer copies that we were able to apply the optimization described in the last part of Section 3. Finally, the number of actual relocatable offsets that we were able to reconstruct their relocation information in shown in the last column.

Table 1. Statistics from running the SPEC benchmarks using the reference input data (largest dataset)

Program	Possible Pointers	Jump Tables	Verified Pointers	Single Hit	Dynamic Data	Global Opt.	Reconst. Reloc.
perlbench	31,260	118	633	83.0%	43M	41	2,614
bzip2	2,147	4	11	84.6%	25	4	76
gcc	98,955	510	1,008	65.2%	73M	269	7,849
mcf	1,875	1	13	100.0%	19	–	22
gobmk	69,852	21	968	63.5%	4M	54	1,270
hmmer	4,798	15	17	94.4%	42	2	152
sjeng	8,460	12	17	100.0%	18	–	135
h264ref	17,526	17	27	71.0%	320K	61	209
omnetpp	24,861	13	1,509	90.6%	269K	8	1,669
astar	2,690	2	20	100.0%	31	–	42
xalancbmk	141,246	54	4,402	84.2%	9M	24	5,392

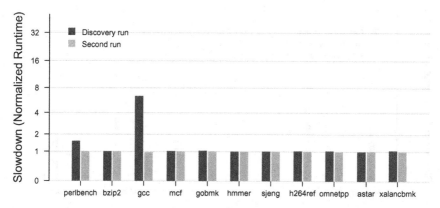

Fig. 3. Normalized slowdown compared to normal execution (no relocation). Dark-colored bars show the slowdown during the first run, where most of the relocations are discovered and there are still copies of them in dynamic data. Light-colored bars show the slowdown during the second run (and any subsequent runs) where most of the relocations have already been discovered.

An interesting observation is that most of the times we have a single hit during the verification of a code pointer, which simplifies the overall procedure. Another interesting thing to note is that there is a very high variation in the number of times that a copy of an already fixed relocatable offset in dynamic data is used. This ranges from a few tens to tens of millions using these test cases. At the same time, we note that there does not seem to be any significant correlation of this number and the actual number of the reconstructed relocatable offsets.

5.2 Performance Overhead

Next, we focus on evaluating the performance overhead. As already mentioned, the only case where we expect our technique to affect the performance of a target application is during the first (or, few first) times we execute it, where most of the relocations are being discovered. Any consecutive execution should have a minimal runtime overhead impact.

Figure 3 shows the normalized slowdown for the first execution of the SPEC programs under our prototype (Discovery run) and another execution after the relocations have been discovered (Second run). In both cases, the slowdown is compared to a normal execution without relocating the program (baseline). Also, the input data used for this experiment was the reference dataset (i.e., the largest dataset), where the average completion time for each test program is a couple of minutes. As expected, we see that the overhead of the second run is minimal (less than 5% on average) and mostly attributed to the unoptimized way of applying the discovered relocation information. Currently, in our prototype implementation we relocate every offset separately. For each of them, we read its value, change the memory permissions, update its value and restore the memory permissions. The unusually high performance overhead that we observed when

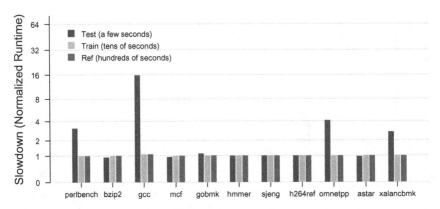

Fig. 4. Avoiding the performance hit during the dynamic relocation discovery phase (first run) by gradually increasing the input size on each execution. The overall time in this case is much less compared to running a program using large input the first time.

executing gcc is due to the fact that it contains a high number of relocatable offset copies in dynamic data (see Table 1). Although, that overhead does disappear in any consecutive execution, there is not much we can do at this point, except asking the user to restart the execution of the program in order to take advantage of the already discovered relocatable offsets. An alternative strategy is to ask the user to start with a very small input and progressively increase the workload of the program during the first few executions, until the majority of the relocations are discovered.

To demonstrate the effectiveness of that strategy, we applied it on the SPEC CPU2006 benchmarks. These test programs come with three different inputs: a very small test dataset used for verifying the functionality of the programs, a medium-sized train set used for feedback-directed optimizations and the reference dataset, which is much larger that the other two. For all the results up to this point, we have used the reference dataset. Figure 4 shows the normalized slowdown of applying our technique to the same SPEC programs, but while increasing the workload (from test, to train and reference) this time. Also, during each execution, we allow our prototype to use any reconstructed relocation information that has been discovered from previous executions. The slowdown of the reference dataset is much less compared to the one reported in Figure 3. Moreover, the overall discovery phase (which is now broken down to three executions) is much quicker compared to Figure 3, in absolute numbers. Even though gcc seems to have a larger slowdown with the test dataset than before, this accounts for 22 seconds, plus a few minutes for the next two executions, compared to 48 minutes when using the large reference dataset during the first execution.

5.3   Use Cases

The final part of our evaluation focuses on the feasibility of applying our technique on popular, real-world applications. For this purpose, we installed older versions of both Internet Explorer and Adobe Reader, where the relocation info of their EXE files was stripped. The exact versions we used were 6.0.2900.5512 and 8.1.2, respectively. In both cases, the code size of the non-relocatable EXE was relative small, approximately 10KB. Using our prototype implementation of our technique we were able to successfully relocate the code segments to a new and random location, while not breaking the functionality of the applications. The number of relocatable offsets for which we reconstructed their relocation information was 18 for Internet Explorer and 3 for Adobe Reader. Although it is just a small number of relocations, reconstructing this information is crucial in protecting these applications.

6 Related Work

We divide the related work into two parts. First, we review work that is related to address space layout randomization. Reconstructing relocation information enables or improves the accuracy of these proposals. Second, we review work from the field of dynamic data structure excavation, where similar techniques to ours are used.

6.1 Code Randomization and Disassembly

As code-reuse attacks require precise knowledge of the structure and location of the code to be reused, diversifying the execution environment or even the program code itself is a core concept in preventing code-reuse exploits [13, 16]. Address space layout randomization [27, 29] is probably one of the most widely deployed countermeasures against code-reuse attacks. The problem of randomizing non-relocatable executable files was identified early on, with the first ASLR implementations for Linux by the PaX project, and an approach based on the interception of page faults to the original locations was proposed [31]. Our work is based on the same core idea, but our implementation focuses on Windows executables, we extend it with patching support to reduce runtime overhead, and experimentally evaluate it.

In practice, however, the effectiveness of ASLR is hindered by code segments left in static locations [17,21,47], while, depending on the randomization entropy, it might be possible to circumvent it using brute-force guessing [37]. Even if all the code segments of a process are fully randomized, vulnerabilities that allow the leakage of memory contents can enable the calculation of the base address of a DLL at runtime [8, 10, 20, 23, 35, 42, 43].

To overcome the limitations of the original design, more fine-grained forms of randomization [19,28,44] have been proposed. These can be statically applied on stripped binaries and randomize code at the instruction level (instead of randomizing the base address only). Their accuracy and correctness, however, heavily depends on the accuracy of disassembly and control flow graph extraction, which is improved when relocation information is available.

Control flow integrity [9] is another protection scheme that confines program execution within the bounds of a precomputed profile of allowed control flow paths. Although its original implementation depends on debug symbols for the complete extraction of the control flow graph, recent proposals have demonstrated how more relaxed forms of the same technique can be applied on stripped binaries [45, 46]. Again, for legacy applications, these techniques would benefit from the improved control flow extraction based on the availability of relocations.

Finally, although binary rewriting is still possible in the absence of relocation information, it relies on dynamic instrumentation for indirect calls/jumps [41]. This makes the overall runtime overhead of the technique to depend on the number of executed indirect calls/jumps, which are very frequent in C++ applications.

6.2   Dynamic Data Structure Excavation

Another body of work that uses related techniques to ours is dynamic data structure excavation [14, 18, 24, 39, 40]. By looking at memory access patters dynamically at runtime, these techniques are able to infer the type of binary data, such as data structures and arrays.

Laika [14] employs Bayesian unsupervised learning to detect data structures. Possible object positions and sizes are identified by using potential pointers in the process' memory image. Although sufficient for cases like evaluating the similarity between malware samples, Laika's output is not precise enough for debugging or reverse engineering. Similar to Laika, Rewards [24] reconstructs type information dynamically, based on abstract structure identification [33]. A fundamental limitation of this approach is that it is not capable of identifying data structures that are internal to a module. Howard [40] improves on the precision of data structure excavation by applying a set of specific rules to identify data structures dynamically. Arrays, structure fields, etc. are recognized based on runtime memory access patterns.

7   Conclusion

Address Space Layout Randomization (ASLR) has proven to be a very effective mitigation against code reuse attacks, making successful exploitation much harder. Unfortunately, ASLR depends on some information that is often stripped from executable files.

As a step towards addressing this limitation, we designed and implemented a technique to dynamically reconstruct this missing information, which effectively enables ASLR even on programs that are otherwise incompatible. The results of our experimental evaluation focusing on performance measurements and use cases with real-world applications clearly show the practicality of the proposed approach.

Acknowledgements. This work was supported by the US Air Force, the Office of Naval Research, and DARPA through Contracts AFRL-FA8650-10-C-7024, N00014-12-1-0166 and FA8750-10-2-0253, respectively, with additional support by Intel Corp. This material is based upon work supported by (while author

Keromytis was serving at) the National Science Foundation. Any opinions, findings, conclusions, or recommendations expressed herein are those of the authors, and do not necessarily reflect those of the US Government, the Air Force, ONR, DARPA, NSF, or Intel.

References

1. ATMs Face Deadline to Upgrade From Windows XP, http://www.businessweek.com/articles/2014-01-16/atms-face-deadline-to-upgrade-from-windows-xp
2. /ORDER (put functions in order), http://msdn.microsoft.com/en-us/library/00kh39zz.aspx
3. Profile-guided optimizations, http://msdn.microsoft.com/en-us/library/e7k32f4k.aspx
4. SPEC CPU2006 Benchmark, http://www.spec.org/cpu2006.
5. Syzygy - profile guided, post-link executable reordering, http://code.google.com/p/sawbuck/wiki/SyzygyDesign
6. UK government pays Microsoft 5.5m to extend Windows XP support, http://www.theguardian.com/technology/2014/apr/07/uk-government-microsoft-windows-xp-public-sector
7. Windows, X.P.: SP3 and Office, Support Ends (April 8, 2003), http://www.microsoft.com/en-us/windows/enterprise/endofsupport.aspx
8. MWR Labs Pwn2Own 2013 Write-up - Webkit Exploit (2013), http://labs.mwrinfosecurity.com/blog/2013/04/19/mwr-labs-pwn2own-2013-write-up---webkit-exploit/
9. Abadi, M., Budiu, M., Erlingsson, Ú., Ligatti, J.: Control-flow integrity. In: Proceedings of the 12th ACM Conference on Computer and Communications Security, CCS (2005)
10. Bennett, J., Lin, Y., Haq, T.: The Number of the Beast (2013), http://blog.fireeye.com/research/2013/02/the-number-of-the-beast.html
11. Bhatkar, E., Duvarney, D.C., Sekar, R.: Address obfuscation: An efficient approach to combat a broad range of memory error exploits. In: Proceedings of the 12th USENIX Security Symposium (2003)
12. Bhatkar, S., Sekar, R., DuVarney, D.C.: Efficient techniques for comprehensive protection from memory error exploits. In: Proceedings of the 14th USENIX Security Symposium (August 2005)
13. Cohen, F.B.: Operating system protection through program evolution. Computers and Security 12, 565–584 (1993)
14. Cozzie, A., Stratton, F., Xue, H., King, S.T.: Digging for data structures. In: Proceedings of the 8th USENIX Conference on Operating Systems Design and Implementation, OSDI 2008, pp. 255–266. USENIX Association, Berkeley (2008)
15. Designer, S.: Getting around non-executable stack (and fix), http://seclists.org/bugtraq/1997/Aug/63
16. Forrest, S., Somayaji, A., Ackley, D.: Building diverse computer systems. In: Proceedings of the 6th Workshop on Hot Topics in Operating Systems, HotOS-VI (1997)
17. Roglia, G.F., Martignoni, L., Paleari, R., Bruschi, D.: Surgically returning to randomized lib(c). In: Proceedings of the 25th Annual Computer Security Applications Conference, ACSAC (2009)

18. Guo, P.J., Perkins, J.H., McCamant, S., Ernst, M.D.: Dynamic inference of abstract types. In: Proceedings of the 2006 International Symposium on Software Testing and Analysis (ISSTA), Portland, ME, USA, July18-20, pp. 255–265 (2006)
19. Hiser, J., Nguyen-Tuong, A., Co, M., Hall, M., Davidson, J.W.: ILR: Where'd my gadgets go? In: Proceedings of the 33rd IEEE Symposium on Security & Privacy, S&P (2012)
20. Hund, R., Willems, C., Holz, T.: Practical timing side channel attacks against kernel space ASLR. In: Proceedings of the 34th IEEE Symposium on Security & Privacy, S&P (2013)
21. Johnson, R.: A castle made of sand: Adobe Reader X sandbox. CanSecWest (2011)
22. Kil, C., Jun, J., Bookholt, C., Xu, J., Ning, P.: Address space layout permutation (ASLP): Towards fine-grained randomization of commodity software. In: Proceedings of the 22nd Annual Computer Security Applications Conference, ACSAC (2006)
23. Li, H.: Understanding and exploiting Flash ActionScript vulnerabilities. CanSecWest (2011)
24. Lin, Z., Zhang, X., Xu, D.: Automatic reverse engineering of data structures from binary execution. In: Proceedings of the 17th Annual Network and Distributed System Security Symposium (NDSS 2010), San Diego, CA (February 2010)
25. Microsoft. Enhanced Mitigation Experience Toolkit, http://www.microsoft.com/emet
26. Microsoft. Windows Debugging API, http://msdn.microsoft.com/en-us/library/windows/desktop/ms679303v=vs.85.aspx
27. Miller, M., Burrell, T., Howard, M.: Mitigating software vulnerabilities (July 2011), http://www.microsoft.com/download/en/details.aspx?displaylang=en&id=26788
28. Pappas, V., Polychronakis, M., Keromytis, A.D.: Smashing the gadgets: Hindering return-oriented programming using in-place code randomization. In: Proceedings of the 33rd IEEE Symposium on Security & Privacy, S&P (2012)
29. PaX Team. Address space layout randomization (2003), http://pax.grsecurity.net/docs/aslr.txt
30. PaX Team. Non-executable pages design & implementation (2003), http://pax.grsecurity.net/docs/noexec.txt
31. PaX Team. Non-relocatable executable file randomization (2003), http://pax.grsecurity.net/docs/randexec.txt
32. Pietrek, M.: An in-depth look into the Win32 portable executable file format, part 2, http://msdn.microsoft.com/en-us/magazine/cc301808.aspx
33. Ramalingam, G., Field, J., Tip, F.: Aggregate structure identification and its application to program analysis. In: Symposium on Principles of Programming Languages (POPL), pp. 119–132 (1999)
34. Rescorla, E.: Security holes.. Who cares? In: Proceedings of the 12th USENIX Security Symposium, pp. 75–90 (August 2003)
35. Serna, F.J.: CVE-2012-0769, the case of the perfect info leak (February 2012), http://zhodiac.hispahack.com/my-stuff/security/Flash_ASLR_bypass.pdf
36. Shacham, H.: The geometry of innocent flesh on the bone: return-into-libc without function calls (on the x86). In: Proceedings of the 14th ACM Conference on Computer and Communications Security, CCS (2007)
37. Shacham, H., Page, M., Pfaff, B., Goh, E.-J., Modadugu, N., Boneh, D.: On the effectiveness of address-space randomization. In: Proceedings of the 11th ACM Conference on Computer and Communications Security, CCS (2004)

38. Skape.: Locreate: An anagram for relocate. Uninformed, 6 (2007)
39. Slowinska, A., Stancescu, T., Bos, H.: Dde: Dynamic data structure excavation. In: Proceedings of the 1st ACM SIGCOMM Asia-Pacific Workshop on Systems (ApSys), pp. 13–18 (2010)
40. Slowinska, A., Stancescu, T., Bos, H.: Howard: A dynamic excavator for reverse engineering data structures. In: Proceedings of the Network and Distributed System Security Symposium, NDSS (2011)
41. Smithson, M., Anand, K., Kotha, A., Elwazeer, K., Giles, N., Barua, R.: Binary rewriting without relocation information. University of Maryland, Tech. Rep. (2010)
42. Snow, K.Z., Davi, L., Dmitrienko, A., Liebchen, C., Monrose, F., Sadeghi, A.-R.: Just-in-time code reuse: On the effectiveness of fine-grained address space layout randomization. In: Proceedings of the 34th IEEE Symposium on Security & Privacy, S&P (2013)
43. Vreugdenhil, P.: Pwn2Own (2010), Windows 7 Internet Explorer 8 exploit, http://vreugdenhilresearch.nl/Pwn2Own-2010-Windows7-InternetExplorer8.pdf
44. Wartell, R., Mohan, V., Hamlen, K.W., Lin, Z.: Binary stirring: Self-randomizing instruction addresses of legacy x86 binary code. In: Proceedings of the 19th ACM Conference on Computer and Communications Security (CCS), pp. 157–168 (October 2012)
45. Zhang, C., Wei, T., Chen, Z., Duan, L., Szekeres, L., McCamant, S., Song, D., Zou, W.: Practical control flow integrity & randomization for binary executables. In: Proceedings of the 34th IEEE Symposium on Security & Privacy, S&P (2013)
46. Zhang, M., Sekar, R.: Control flow integrity for cots binaries. Presented as part of the 22nd USENIX Security Symposium, pp. 337–352. USENIX, Berkeley (2013)
47. Zovi, D.A.D.: Practical return-oriented programming. SOURCE Boston (2010)

Evaluating the Effectiveness of Current Anti-ROP Defenses

Felix Schuster, Thomas Tendyck, Jannik Pewny, Andreas Maaß,
Martin Steegmanns, Moritz Contag, and Thorsten Holz

Horst Görtz Institute for IT-Security (HGI), Ruhr-Universität Bochum,
Bochum, Germany

Abstract. Recently, many defenses against the offensive technique of *return-oriented programming* (ROP) have been developed. Prominently among them are *kBouncer*, *ROPecker*, and *ROPGuard* which all target legacy binary software while requiring no or only minimal binary code rewriting.

In this paper, we evaluate the effectiveness of these Anti-ROP defenses. Our basic insight is that all three only analyze a limited number of recent (and upcoming) branches in an application's control flow on certain events. As a consequence, an adversary can perform dummy operations to bypass all employed heuristics. We show that it is possible to generically bypass kBouncer, ROPecker, and ROPGuard with little extra effort in practice. In the cases of kBouncer and ROPGuard on Windows, we show that all required code sequences can already be found in the executable module of a minimal 32-bit C/C++ application with an empty main() function. To demonstrate the viability of our attack approaches, we implemented several proof-of-concept exploits for recent vulnerabilities in popular applications; e. g., Internet Explorer 10 on Windows 8.

Keywords: ROP, Exploit Mitigation, Memory Corruptions

1 Introduction

Defensive measures against memory corruption and control flow hijacking attacks have been considerably improved recently, especially on the software side. Widely deployed techniques such as *address space layout randomization* (ASLR) and *data execution prevention* (DEP) often greatly hamper successful exploitation of a given vulnerability or even succeed in preventing the attack at all. In many cases, however, an advanced and dedicated attacker is still able to ultimately bypass these defenses and achieve reliable exploitation [1, 7, 16, 27].

An offensive technique that is used in many of today's successful attacks is called *return-oriented programming* (ROP) [17, 28]. With this technique, an attacker does not inject her own shellcode as part of the attack payload, but she reuses existing code and chains small code fragments (so called *gadgets*) together that perform malicious computations. Due to the effectiveness of this approach, it comes as no surprise that in the last few years many defensive mechanisms specifically targeting ROP have been proposed. Three recent representatives of such methods are *kBouncer* [25], *ROPecker* [8], and *ROPGuard* [10].

A. Stavrou et al. (Eds.): RAID 2014, LNCS 8688, pp. 88–108, 2014.
© Springer International Publishing Switzerland 2014

In this paper, we evaluate the effectiveness of these proposed methods and demonstrate their limitations. We first analyze kBouncer, a defensive mechanism that aims at detecting and preventing ROP-based attacks against user mode applications on the Windows operating system. kBouncer leverages the *last branch recording* (LBR) feature incorporated in current AMD and Intel x86-64 CPUs [3, 15] to check for suspicious control flows. kBouncer received broad attention not only from the research community when its first version [24] was announced as the $200,000 winner of the *Microsoft BlueHat Prize* [2]. We show that kBouncer's latest version [25] can be circumvented in virtually all realistic 32-bit and 64-bit attack scenarios with little extra effort. More specifically, we demonstrate how three recent ROP-based exploits—e.g., for Microsoft *Internet Explorer* on Windows 8—can be modified to bypass kBouncer. Furthermore, we show that even the `.text` section of a minimal 32-bit C/C++ application compiled with Microsoft's Visual Studio contains all necessary gadgets required to bypass kBouncer. We demonstrate how successful attacks against kBouncer in practice often also circumvent ROPGuard. This method placed second at the BlueHat Prize and has since been incorporated into Microsoft's *Enhanced Mitigation Experience Toolkit* (EMET).

The third defensive measure we examine is ROPecker [8]. This approach was presented in 2014 and it also leverages the LBR feature to protect applications on Linux from ROP-based attacks. We show that ROPecker suffers from conceptual weaknesses similar to kBouncer. In its published form, ROPecker can be circumvented in a generic way by an adversary. We empirically verify our attack and demonstrate a successful low-overhead bypass for a recent vulnerability of the popular web server software *Nginx*.

In summary, the contributions of this paper are as follows:

- We discuss several kinds of commonly available 32-bit and 64-bit gadgets that an attacker can utilize to perform malicious computations in a way resembling benign control flow.
- We demonstrate that ROP defenses based on analyzing a limited number of branches can be bypassed by an attacker in a generic way and that such a bypass requires little extra effort.
- We empirically verify our proposed approaches and present successful attacks against the three recent ROP defenses *kBouncer*, *ROPecker*, and *ROPGuard*.
- We assess the practical susceptibility of kBouncer and ROPecker to false positive detections of attacks using independently implemented emulators. We discover for both schemes that false positives are not unlikely to occur for at least certain popular applications.

2   Technical Background

We briefly review the basic concepts behind *return-oriented programming* and *last branch recording* that are fundamental to understand the rest of the paper.

2.1 Return-Oriented Programming

Generally speaking, an attacker's goal is the execution of certain code (referred to as *shellcode*) of her choice in the context of a vulnerable application. Typically, an attacker initially exploits some kind of software bug (e.g., a memory corruption vulnerability or a dangling pointer) to hijack an application's control flow.

As DEP has become prevalent, adversaries often resort to reusing (native) code already present in an application instead of directly injecting new shellcode, for example via exploitation techniques such as *return-to-libc* [23] or *return-oriented programming* (ROP) [17,28]. With ROP, small code fragments—called *gadgets*—ending in a *return* instruction are consecutively executed: an attacker can "program" the desired semantics by writing a chain of addresses of gadgets to the stack of one of the target application's threads in such a way that each gadget "returns" to its successor. This chain of gadgets is often referred to as *ROP chain*. On x86-64 platforms, gadgets can be *aligned* as well as *unaligned* with the original instruction stream produced by the compiler, as instructions may start at any offset into a code page. Typically, suitable gadgets for ROP attacks exist in sufficient quantities in most non-trivial applications [9,13]. There are also ROP-compilers [14,31,32] that can for example automatically convert a given shellcode into an application-specific ROP chain. Advanced techniques closely related to ROP have been presented that leverage gadgets not ending in return instructions but typically some kind of indirect jumps [4,6]. Accordingly, these techniques are also known as *jump-oriented programming* (JOP). In the following, we use the term *ROP* inclusively for *JOP*.

One widely deployed generic countermeasure against ROP is ASLR: modules are loaded at pseudo-random base addresses resulting in the whereabouts of gadgets being hard to predict. If not stated otherwise, we assume in the following discussions that the attacker has ways to gain knowledge on the base address of at least one executable module of sufficient size. We stress that this is no ambitious assumption as it is generally fulfilled for real-world ROP-based exploits [1,7,16].

2.2 Last Branch Recording

kBouncer and ROPecker rely on the *Last Branch Recording* (LBR) feature of contemporary AMD and Intel processors [3,15] to examine an application's past control flow on certain events.

The LBR can only be enabled and accessed from kernel mode. It can be configured to only track certain types of branches. Both kBouncer and ROPecker utilize this feature and they limit the LBR to indirect branches in user mode. For each recorded branch, an entry containing the *start* and *destination* address is written to the corresponding CPU core's *LBR stack*. In Intel's latest Haswell architecture, an LBR stack is limited to only 16 entries. For each newly recorded branch, the oldest entry in an LBR stack is overwritten. At any given time, an LBR stack may not only contain entries from a single process/thread, but from multiple ones running on the same core [8]. In the following, we do not consider this effect, though, it might in practice facilitate attacks. Instead, for simplicity, we assume that the LBR stack is always saved/restored on context switches.

3   Security Assessment of kBouncer

The latest version of the kBouncer runtime ROP exploit mitigation approach was presented by Pappas et al. in 2013 [25]. kBouncer checks for suspicious branch sequences hinting at a ROP exploit whenever a Windows API (WinAPI) [29] function considered as possibly harmful is invoked in a monitored process. kBouncer's authors list 52 WinAPI functions which they consider as possibly harmful. Among these functions are for example `VirtualAlloc()` and `VirtualProtect()` that are notoriously abused by attackers. Pappas et al. acknowledge that the list is possibly not complete and could be extended in the future.

kBouncer is composed of a user mode component and a kernel driver. The user mode component hooks all to-be-protected WinAPI functions in a monitored process. Whenever the control flow reaches one of these hooks, the kernel driver is informed via the WinAPI function `DeviceIoControl()`. Subsequently, the driver examines the LBR stack for traces of a ROP chain. Since kBouncer's user mode component uses two indirect branches to inform the driver, only 14 of the LBR stack's 16 entries are of value to the driver's ROP detection logic [25]. In case no attack is detected, the driver saves a corresponding "checkpoint" in kernel memory for the respective thread. Whenever a system call corresponding to a hooked WinAPI function is invoked, the driver consumes the matching checkpoint; if none is found, an attack is reported. According to Pappas et al., the purpose of the checkpoint system is to prevent exploit code from simply skipping over the top-level WinAPI functions and calling similar lower level functions (e. g., `NtCreateFile()` instead of `CreateFileW()`). The reason for kBouncer not monitoring system calls directly is the observation that between WinAPI functions' and their corresponding system call often many legitimate indirect branches are executed that would often overwrite traces of ROP chains in the LBR stack [25].

In order to evaluate kBouncer's practical applicability and defensive strength, we created a standalone emulator for kBouncer based on certain pieces of source code generously provided to us by Pappas et al. The emulator uses the *Pin* [18] dynamic analysis framework to instrument monitored applications at runtime. To the best of our judgment, the emulator accurately captures all of kBouncer's core concepts as described by Pappas et al. [25].

3.1   Examination of Indirect Branch Sequences

When examining the LBR stack corresponding to the invocation of a WinAPI function, kBouncer's kernel driver assumes an attack if at least one of the following is encountered: *(i)* a *return* to an instruction not preceded by a `call` instruction or *(ii)* a chain of a certain number of *gadgets* ending in the latest LBR stack entry. For kBouncer, gadgets are up to 20 instructions long and may contain conditional or unconditional relative jumps [25]. In the following, we refer to gadgets under this definition as k-gadgets. Gadgets outside this definition are conversely denoted as non-k-gadgets.

Listing 1.1. Simple recursive C function calculating the factorial of an integer

```
int factorial (int n)
{
  if (n <= 1) return 1;
  return factorial(n-1)*n;
}
```

Listing 1.2. Disassembly of epilogue of function `factorial()`

```
[ ... ]
lea ecx, [edi-1]
call      factorial
mul edi
pop edi
retn
```

Gadget Chain Detection Threshold. The maximum gadget chain length kBouncer can identify is 13. This is due to only 14 LBR stack entries being of value to kBouncer's detection logic and the latest effective entry always corresponding to a branch to a WinAPI function [25].

In order to determine a suitable detection threshold for the length of gadget chains, Pappas et al. examined a set of popular Windows applications (e. g., Microsoft Word and Internet Explorer) at runtime while executing certain tasks [25]. They report on having found the LBR stack to contain chains of at most *five* k-gadgets on entry to any of the 52 possibly harmful WinAPI functions across their experiments. As a result, Pappas et al. defined kBouncer to consider chains of *eight* or more k-gadgets as harmful, leaving a security margin of three against false positives.

However, longer chains of k-gadgets can easily occur in practice in benign and unsuspicious control flows. Consider for example a simple recursive function calculating the factorial of an integer as shown in Listing 1.1 and Listing 1.2. After the termination of `factorial(n)`, the LBR stack contains a legitimate chain of $n-1$ k-gadgets of the form `mul edi; pop edi; retn;`, making the control flow appear to contain a ROP chain under the kBouncer definition. Many other possible scenarios exists where legitimate control flow resembles a ROP chain under the kBouncer definition as well.

In fact, our kBouncer emulator detected k-gadget chains longer than the given detection threshold for all non-trivial applications we executed on Windows 7 SP1 64-bit while monitoring the discussed 52 WinApi functions. For example, saving a text file using the popular editor Notepad++ 5.9.8 (32-bit) reliably resulted in one detected chain of the maximum length 13. The chain is depicted in Figure 1: the chain starts towards the end of the destructor of the class `CAsyncParser` in comdlg32.dll and spans over ole32.dll and shell32.dll before ending in the protected WinAPI function `CloseHandle()`. The characteristic of the chain is that several short functions are invoked in a nested manner using indirect calls only.

Note that the discrepancy in quality and quantity of false positives detected by our emulator and the original kBouncer could have many reasons. Possibly, the dynamic disassembly provided by Pin to our emulator is more comprehensive than the static disassembly available to kBouncer's *offline gadget extraction toolkit*. It is also very well possible that kBouncer employs certain additional filtering techniques in practice. Of course we can also not entirely rule out inaccurate assumptions on our side.

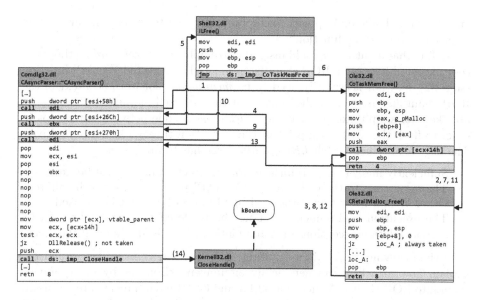

Fig. 1. Exemplary false positive chain of 13 k-gadgets as detected by our kBouncer emulator for the "Save File As" dialogue in Notepad++ 5.9.8 (32-bit) on Windows 7 64-bit. Taken indirect branches are highlighted in light gray. Branches are labeled according to the order they are executed.

3.2   Circumventing kBouncer

We now explore ways an *aware attacker* can follow to circumvent kBouncer. We consider kBouncer as bypassed when it is possible (with respect to the actual limits imposed by a vulnerability) to reliably and repeatedly conduct the following two consecutive steps without kBouncer noticing:

S1 execution of arbitrary ROP chain
S2 successful invocation of a WinAPI function protected by kBouncer

Obviously kBouncer can be safely bypassed if the last 14 indirect branches leading to a protected WinAPI function cannot be distinguished from benign control flow; regardless of the actually deployed gadget chain detection policy. This is due to kBouncer's driver being effectively only able to look at most 14 LBR stack entries into the past.

In view of this fact, Pappas et al. discuss the possibility of an attack based on a seemingly legitimate gadget chain (returns leading to call-preceded locations only and at least every eighth gadget being a non-k-gadget). They allude that such an attack would be difficult and state that "if evasion becomes an issue, longer gadgets could be considered during the gadget chaining analysis of an LBR snapshot" [25]. Furthermore, they also discuss the possibility of an attacker looking "[...] for a long-enough execution path that leads to the desired API call as part of the applications logic". They expect this kind of attack to be "[...] quite challenging, as in many cases the desired function might not be imported at all, and the path should end up with the appropriate register values and arguments to properly invoke the function".

We find that an attacker could instead also employ a simpler *third* method: the code executed between a ROP chain (step S1) and a protected WinAPI function (step S2) does not necessarily need to be *meaningful*; not in the context of the ROP chain and neither in the context of the attacked application. Hence, an attacker can simply execute arbitrary *meaningless* code between both steps in order to flush the LBR stack prior to the inspection through kBouncer's driver. The only requirements such *LBR-flushing code* has to fulfill are:

- Sufficiently many (e. g., 14) unsuspicious indirect branches must be executed.
- The arguments to the to-be-invoked WinAPI function must not be altered.
- Other WinAPI functions protected by kBouncer must not be invoked.
- The execution environment must not be rendered uncontrollable; e. g., by access violation exceptions or manipulation of the ROP chain on the stack.

In the following we *(i)* discuss suitable LBR-flushing code sequences and *(ii)* explain how attackers can generically circumvent kBouncer by incorporating them into ROP chains. Attacks for 32-bit and 64-bit environments are discussed separately as they require slightly different approaches due to divergent default calling conventions: in 32-bit applications, arguments to WinAPI functions are passed over the stack (stdcall calling convention), whereas the first four arguments are passed in registers in 64-bit applications (fastcall calling convention) [20].

We limit ourselves to gadgets/code sequences that are likely to be present in almost every process on Windows. In fact, all required gadgets/code sequences can be found in standard Windows libraries and, at least for 32-bit, in every C/C++ program created with default/common compiler and linker settings (at least *Release* or *Debug* configuration; /Od, /O1, or /O2 optimization) using Microsoft Visual Studio versions 2010, 2012, or 2013. This is even valid for the minimal C/C++ program with an empty main() whose .text section typically has an effective size of under 1 KB. We refer to this executable (*Release*, /O2) as minpe-32 and minpe-64, respectively. All code that is present in minpe-32/minpe-64 should also be present in virtually every other program compiled and linked with default settings using Visual Studio.

3.3 Circumvention for 32-Bit Applications

LBR-Flushing Code Sequences. For 32-bit programs, finding suitable LBR-flushing code sequences is easy: basically most functions that make a certain amount of sub-calls (each sub-call terminates in an indirect branch) and do not much depend on or interfere with the global state of a program comply with the listed requirements. In the following, we refer to a function with these properties as *LBR-flushing* function (lbr-ff). We found for example lstrcmpiW()[1] in kernel32.dll to be such a function. When supplied with two identical pointers to (almost) arbitrary data as arguments, we found that it reliably executed more than

---

[1] lstrcmpiW() compares two Unicode strings in a case-insensitive manner.

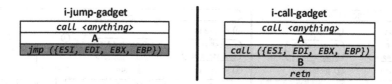

Fig. 2. Formats of the 32-bit invocation gadget types i-jump-gadget (left) and i-call-gadget (right); blocks labeled **A** and **B** may be empty or contain any sequence of instructions not rendering the execution context uncontrollable

20 unsuspicious indirect branches. The fact that the function expects two arguments is of course disadvantageous for an attacker, as this wastes precious space on the (fake) stack. In practice, an attacker could ideally choose an lbr-ff without arguments. E. g., we identified the two standard runtime library functions `pre_c_init()` (statically contained in minpe-32) and `EtwInitializeProcess()` (contained in ntdll.dll) as lbr-ffs with zero arguments. It should be clear that suitable lbr-ffs are available in abundance in most real-world applications.

Invocation Gadgets. Given an lbr-ff, the attacker's goal is to execute it between the ROP chain (step S1) and the invocation of a protected WinAPI function (step S2) in order to flush the LBR stack just before kBouncer's detection logic is triggered. Executing the lbr-ff itself is trivial: it can be part of the ROP chain just like any other gadget. Obviously though, the lbr-ff cannot simply "return" in ROP-manner to the entry point of a protected WinAPI function; kBouncer would certainly detect an attack, as entry points of WinAPI functions are never preceded by a `call` in the static instruction stream.

Instead, the control flow needs to transition from the lbr-ff to the protected WinAPI function in such a way that kBouncer cannot distinguish it from legitimate control flow. We found that for an attacker to achieve this, the availability of a call-preceded and controllable jump-based or call-based *invocation gadget* as depicted in Figure 2 is sufficient. In the following, we refer to gadgets of these formats as i-jump-gadgets and i-call-gadgets, respectively.

Given an i-jump-gadget or an i-call-gadget, a protected WinAPI function can be invoked right after an lbr-ff in such a way that the control flow appears legitimate to kBouncer. Figure 3 schematically depicts the control flows for both types of gadgets: ⓪ From the ROP chain, the control flow is transferred to the lbr-ff of choice via a traditional `retn` terminated gadget. We need to make sure that at this point the address of the instruction sequence **A** (see Figure 2) lies on top of the stack. ① This makes the lbr-ff return to **A** right behind the leading dummy `call` instruction of the i-jump-gadget/i-call-gadget. ② The protected WinAPI function is then invoked via the indirect `jmp`/`call` instruction following **A**. Typically, this instruction should branch relative to the registers `esi`, `edi`, `ebx`, or `ebp` (e. g., `jmp [ebx*4+edi]` or `call esi`). These registers are premiere choices here, because they are defined to be callee-saved in all common C/C++ calling conventions for x86 [20]. Hence, these registers can be assumed to be

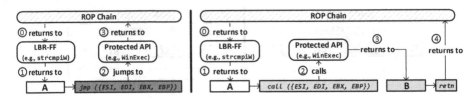

Fig. 3. Schematic control flow of the invocation of a protected WinAPI (32-bit); **left:** i-jump-gadget **right:** i-call-gadget

unaltered by the invocation of virtually any lbr-ff. This allows the attacker to set the registers using regular gadgets (*before* step ⓪). ③, ④ Depending on the invocation gadget type, the WinAPI function either returns directly to the ROP chain (i-jump-gadget) or a detour is taken over the instruction sequence **B** (i-call-gadget).

kBouncer's detection logic is triggered between steps ② and ③. At this point kBouncer cannot detect an attack anymore, as the LBR stack exclusively contains entries corresponding to branches executed *after* step ⓪. Note that the instruction sequence **A** is call-preceded. Hence, the return from the (legitimate) lbr-ff to **A** is unsuspicious to kBouncer.

Passing of Arguments. Typically, the attacker would align arguments to the WinAPI function on the stack prior to executing the lbr-ff (before step ⓪). Depending on the nature of an invocation gadget though, arguments might also be written to the stack by the instruction sequence **A**. Of course it is a requirement that the instruction sequence **A** does not alter the stack or register values in such a way that the WinAPI function cannot be invoked as intended or the control flow cannot properly resume afterward. For example, the i-jump-gadget `call <anything>; push 0; jmp edi;` would allow to invoke a WinAPI function but would inevitably lead to the function returning to the invalid address 0. Also, instructions triggering exceptions/interrupts must of course not be present in **A**. Naturally, similar requirements apply to the trailing instruction sequence **B** of the i-call-gadget.

Gadget Examples. An example for a suitable i-jump-gadget is given in Listing 1.3. The gadget's **A** sequence (lines 2–6) is composed of `xor` operations on general purpose registers. This should be unproblematic for the attacker in almost all cases.

We implemented a Python script to statically identify this and multiple other suitable i-jump-gadgets and i-call-gadgets in common Windows DLLs in an automated manner. We found this particular i-jump-gadget to be present in the 32-bit versions of kernel32.dll, kernelbase.dll, ntdll.dll, user32.dll, msvcr100.dll, msvcr110.dll, msvcr120.dll, and msvcrt.dll of both Windows 7 and Windows 8. All these DLLs are without doubt among the most frequently used ones on Windows. In fact, ntdll.dll can be found in every Windows user mode process [29]. An example for an i-call-gadget is given in Listing 1.4. We discovered this gadget in the static runtime library function `_onexit()` [21] contained in minpe-32

Listing 1.3. Aligned i-jump-gadget in `TransferToHandler()` found in multiple Windows DLLs

```
1  call       sub.7DD9D8F5
2  xor        eax , eax
3  xor        ebx , ebx
4  xor        ecx , ecx
5  xor        edx , edx
6  xor        edi , edi
7  jmp        esi
```

Listing 1.4. Aligned i-call-gadget in `_onexit()` of the standard Visual C/C++ library

```
1   call       esi
2   mov   __onexitbegin , eax
3   push       dword ptr [ebp−20h]
4   call       esi
5   mov   __onexitend , eax
6   mov dword ptr [ebp−4], 0FFFFFFFEh
7   call       $+10h
8   mov eax , edi
9   call       _SEH_epilog4
10  retn
```

(and other executables). While also allowing to generically bypass kBouncer, we found the gadget to be slightly more complicated to handle than the i-jump-gadget in Listing 1.3. Reasons are the presence of the **push** instruction in the gadget's **A** sequence (lines 2–3) and the presence of the two static calls in the **B** sequence (lines 5–9).

Obviously, one of these two gadgets should be available to the attacker in most scenarios. If not, it should in the uttermost cases be simple to find comparable gadgets given that the i-call-gadget was found in less than 1 KB of code. Knowledge of these two gadgets proved to be sufficient when we adapted high-profile real world exploits to be undetectable by kBouncer (see § 3.5).

3.4 Circumvention for 64-Bit Applications

The described 32-bit approach for bypassing kBouncer is only to some extent applicable to 64-bit. In the default 64-bit calling convention on Windows, the first four arguments to a function are not passed over the stack but in the registers `rcx`, `rdx`, `r8`, and `r9` [20]. Accordingly, an attacker would in most cases need to preload these registers *before* the invocation of the lbr-ff if the 32-bit approach was followed here. As these four registers are explicitly not callee-saved, they are likely to be altered by almost all lbr-ff. Hence, a different approach is needed for 64-bit systems.

Loop Invocation Gadget. We found a certain type of 64-bit gadget to be especially suited for both the flushing of the LBR stack and the invocation of protected WinAPI functions. A specimen contained in minpe-64 is given in Listing 1.5. The gadget is comparable to the *dispatcher gadget* that was discussed as foundation for *jump-oriented programming* by Bletsch et al. [4]. The gadget interprets `rbx` as an index into a table of code pointers. `rbx` is gradually increased and all pointers are called until `rbx` equals `rdi`. The gadget allows an attacker to execute an arbitrary number of gadgets/functions in a manner that replicates benign control flow. Of course invoked gadgets must generally not alter `rbx` or `rdi`. A very similar loop invocation gadget is for example also contained in `LdrpCallTlsInitializers()` in the 64-bit ntdll.dll. We refer to

Listing 1.5. Aligned i-loop-gadget in
`RTC_Initialize()` of the standard Visual C/C++ library

```
@loop:
mov   rax, [rbx]
test  rax, rax
jz    @skip
call  rax
@skip:
add   rbx, 8
cmp   rbx, rdi
jb    @loop
mov   rbx, [rsp+28h+arg_0]
add   rsp, 20h
pop   rdi
retn
```

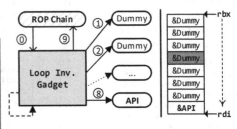

Fig. 4. Schematic control of the invocation of a WinApi function (i-loop-gadget)

this type of gadget as i-loop-gadget. An i-loop-gadget can be used to flush the LBR stack and to invoke a protected API subsequently as depicted in Figure 4: if a return-succeeded *dummy* gadget is executed at least seven times before the invocation of a protected API, the LBR stack does not contain any traces of the actual ROP chain when kBouncer's detection logic is triggered (for each dummy gadget an indirect call/return pair is executed). However, finding a suitable dummy gadget is not as easy as it might seem. Obviously, the dummy gadget must be a non-k-gadget as the i-loop-gadget in Listing 1.5 already is a k-gadget. If both are k-gadgets, then an attack is detected by kBouncer. Furthermore, the dummy gadget must neither alter the registers rbx and rdi nor the registers rcx, rdx, r8, and r9 carrying the arguments for the WinAPI function. Also, the dummy gadget of course must not render the program state uncontrollable to the attacker. We implemented a Python script to identify appropriate dummy gadgets in standard 64-bit Windows DLLs. We found a variety of long and aligned math related gadgets/functions in ntdll.dll and msvcr*.dll accessing (almost) exclusively the specialized SSE [15] floating-point registers xmm0 to xmm7. For example, `_remainder_piby2_cw_forAsm()` in msvcr120.dll contains a gadget that does not write to memory and only touches SSE registers and rax while executing at least 26 instructions. We also found several long sequences (20+) of nop instructions terminated by a return in ntdll.dll. Unfortunately, we did not find a suitable dummy gadget in the .text section of minpe-64.

In practice, the attacker might very well interleave dummy gadgets with meaningful k-gadgets, which do not alter rbx or rdi, in the invocation loop. In fact, as kBouncer per default only considers chains of more than seven k-gadgets harmful, it would be sufficient to execute a single dummy gadget at the fourth position (marked dark gray in Figure 4). This would enable the attacker to use the last three gadgets before the invocation of the WinAPI function to conveniently write arguments to the registers rcx, rdx, r8, or r9. This would result in less constraints regarding register usage for the employed dummy gadget. Generically bypassing kBouncer using an i-loop-gadget is also possible for 32-bit applications. We found for example the 32-bit equivalent of the i-loop-gadget in Listing 1.5 to be also present in minpe-32. Using the i-jump-gadgets or i-call-gadgets discussed in § 3.3 should though in most cases incur less overhead in 32-bit environments. Also, we found suitable dummy gadgets to be relatively sparse compared to lbr-ffs.

3.5 Example Exploits

To demonstrate the practicality of the described kBouncer bypasses and to assess the resulting overhead, we developed a set of example exploits which we briefly discuss now. As it is tradition, our exploits launch the Windows calculator via an invocation of WinExec(). We stress that in all cases much more complicated exploits with multiple WinAPI calls would have been easily possible. No standard Windows defensive mechanisms like ASLR and DEP were disabled or manipulated. We confirmed that our exploits would indeed circumvent kBouncer using our emulator where possible. Due to technical constraints we resorted to manual confirmation using a debugger for Internet Explorer and Firefox.

Minimal Vulnerable Programs. We extended the discussed minimal executables minpe-32 and minpe-64 to contain a simple buffer overflow vulnerability. We assumed that the attacker knew the base addresses of the main module and msvcr120.dll. In both cases we used common gadgets from msvcr120.dll like pop eax; ret; to construct a conventional ROP chain. We then used the discussed i-call-gadget and the lbr-ff in minpe-32 to invoke WinExec(); respectively for the 64-bit variant we leveraged the i-loop-gadget in minpe-64 and the discussed dummy gadget in msvcr120.dll. For 32-bit ten extra dwords (32-bit words) were needed in the ROP payload to bypass kBouncer (25 dwords vs. 35 dwords); for 64-bit 20 additional qwords (64-bit words) were required (29 qwords vs. 49 qwords). The relatively large overhead for 64-bit stems from the inclusion of the eight qword long code pointer table.

Details on the basic and augmented ROP chains for 32-bit and 64-bit can be found in our technical report corresponding to this paper [30].

MPlayer Lite. Pappas et al. used a stack buffer overflow vulnerability in *MPlayer Lite* version r33064 for Windows [1] to evaluate the effectiveness of kBouncer. MPlayer Lite is compiled with MinGW's GCC version 4.5.1. We used gadgets from the bundled avcodec-52.dll to build a conventional ROP-based exploit for the same vulnerability. To circumvent kBouncer, we augmented the ROP chain by an i-loop-gadget located in the static runtime library function TlsCallback_0() in mplayer.exe. As corresponding *dummy gadget* we chose another one of MinGW's static runtime library function. Altogether, 37 additional dwords were needed for the augmented ROP chain (21 dwords vs. 58 dwords). We found similar gadgets also in binaries compiled with different MinGW GCC versions.

Internet Explorer 10. We modified a publicly available exploit for an integer signedness error in Internet Explorer 10 32-bit for Windows 8 by *VUPEN Security* [16]. The original exploit was a winning entry at the popular 2013 Pwn2Own contest. It uses JavaScript code to dynamically construct a ROP chain consisting of 10 dwords to invoke `WinExec()`. In our modified version, four extra dwords are used to incorporate the i-jump-gadget in Listing 1.3 (kernel32.dll) and `lstrcmpiW()` as lbr-ff.

TorBrowser Bundle / Firefox 17. We modified the exploit allegedly used by the FBI to target users of the *TorBrowser Bundle* [7]. The TorBrowser Bundle is based on Firefox version 17.0.6 for Windows 7 32-bit. We use a ROP payload of 54 dwords to invoke `WinExec()`. The version bypassing kBouncer includes five additional dwords and uses the i-jump-gadget in Listing 1.3 (ntdll.dll) and `EtwInitializeProcess()` (ntdll.dll) as lbr-ff.

3.6   Possible Improvements

We now briefly review three potential improvements to address our bypasses and discuss their effectiveness.

Broadening of Gadget Definition. Pappas et al. propose that kBouncer could be improved by considering gadgets longer than 20 instructions if evasion became an issue [25]. We note that such an extension could not substantially tackle the described 32-bit attacks using i-jump-gadgets or i-call-gadgets in conjunction with lbr-ffs (see § 3.3): when kBouncer's detection logic is triggered, the effective LBR stack contains one entry corresponding to the invocation gadget and 13 to the lbr-ff. The lbr-ff's LBR entries cannot reasonably be distinguished from benign control flow, as the lbr-ff is a legit function of the attacked application (e.g., `lstrcmpiW()`). A broader definition of k-gadgets could make it harder to find dummy gadgets suitable for the (64-bit) attack approach based on i-loop-gadgets (see § 3.4). In practice though, increasing the maximum gadget length such that most suitable dummy gadgets are eliminated, would probably result in unacceptable high numbers of overall false positives. Even for a maximum length of 20, entire non-trivial functions fall already under the k-gadget definition.

Larger LBR Stack. Pappas et al. suggest that future CPU generations with larger LBR stacks "would allow kBouncer to achieve even higher accuracy by inspecting longer execution paths [...]" [25]. In such a case, our described approaches could easily be adapted to create longer sequences of indirect branches resembling benign ones. For example, the described i-loop-gadget can be used to create such sequences of almost arbitrary length. Also, finding lbr-ffs which do so is easy. The discussed `lstrcmpiW()` can for example be used to create dozens of legit indirect branches.

Heuristic Detection of Invocation Gadgets. One could attempt to extend k-Bouncer to heuristically check for LBR entries corresponding to the discussed types of invocation gadgets. This could, depending on the actual implementation, very well fend off the described attacks. However, we expect high numbers of false positives from such a measure, as the same invocation patterns can very well occur for benign control flows.

4   Security Assessment of ROPGuard

ROPGuard is a runtime ROP detection approach for user mode applications on Windows [10]. It placed 2nd to kBouncer at the BlueHat Prize and is incorporated into the *Enhanced Mitigation Experience Toolkit* (EMET) [22] that is provided as optional security enhancement for Windows. Hence, ROPGuard can be considered as the most widely spread advanced ROP countermeasure for Windows applications.

Similar to kBouncer, ROPGuard hooks a set of critical WinAPI functions in user mode processes. Whenever such a hook is triggered, ROPGuard as implemented in EMET 4.1—the most recent version at the time of this writing—tries to detect ROP-based exploits via a variety of checks. We describe the two most relevant ones now briefly [10, 19]:

- *Past and Future Control Flow Analysis*: ROPGuard verifies that the return address of a protected WinAPI function is call-preceded. Furthermore, it simulates the control flow in a simple manner from the return address onwards and checks for future non call-preceded returns. Simulation is performed until a certain threshold number of future instructions was examined or any call or jump instruction is encountered.
- *Stack Checks*: ROPGuard checks if the stack pointer points within the expected memory range for the given thread. It is common practice for attackers to divert the stack pointer to a memory region (e. g., the heap) under their control. ROPGuard also blocks attempts to make the stack executable.

Reports on how to bypass ROPGuard's implementation in EMET have already been published on the Internet (e. g., [26]). In fact, ROPGuard's original author Ivan Fratric suggests that an attacker who is aware of it "would be able to construct special ROP chains that would [...] push ROPGuard off guard" [11]. We found that our kBouncer example exploits that rely either on i-call-gadgets or on i-loop-gadgets (both *minimal vulnerable programs* and *MPlayer*) already bypassed ROPGuard's implementation in EMET. In turn, ROPGuard successfully stopped all of the three corresponding unmodified exploits. For ROPGuard, the discussed i-call-gadgets and i-loop-gadgets invoke the protected `WinExec()` via seemingly legitimate calls. These gadgets also make ROPGuard's future control flow simulation stop early due to subsequent jumps/calls. The stack-related checks do not apply to our example exploits.

5   Security Assessment of ROPecker

ROPecker, a runtime ROP exploit mitigation system, was presented by Cheng et al. in 2014 [8]. ROPecker aperiodically checks for abnormal branch sequences in an application's control flow. For that, ROPecker combines kBouncer-like examination of the LBR stack with ROPGuard-like future control flow simulation. Cheng et al. specifically report on a prototype implementation of ROPecker as a kernel module for 32-bit x86 Linux systems. Hence, we also only consider this platform. For evaluation purposes, we implemented an experimental standalone Pin-based emulator for ROPecker. We are confident that this emulator accurately captures most of ROPecker's aspects. All experiments we report on in the following were conducted on either Ubuntu 12.0.4 or Debian 7.4.0 systems.

5.1 Triggering of Detection Logic

Other than comparable approaches, ROPecker does not apply any form of binary rewriting such as API function hooking to inspect an application's control flow. Instead, ROPecker ensures that only a small fixed-size dynamic set of code pages is executable at any given time within a process. ROPecker's ROP detection logic is invoked every time an access violation is triggered due to the target application's control flow reaching a new page *outside* the set of executable pages. If no attack is detected, ROPecker replaces the oldest page in the set of executable pages with the newly reached page and resumes the execution of the corresponding thread/process. Cheng et al. refer to this technique as a "sliding window mechanism". They suggest using a window/set size of two to four executable pages, corresponding to 8 to 16 KB of executable code, because it is supposedly hard to find enough gadgets for a meaningful attack in less than 20 KB of code [8]. The pages inside the sliding window do not necessarily need to be adjacent.

For our emulator, we use a fixed sliding window size of exactly one page to achieve fine-granular capturing. Note that a smaller sliding window size results in ROPecker's detection logic being triggered more often. Hence, chances for false negatives decrease while in turn chances for false positives increase.

5.2 Examination of Indirect Branch Sequences

Each time it is triggered, ROPecker's detection logic tries to identify attacks by analyzing the past and the (simulated) future control flow of a thread/process for chains of ROP gadgets. Per default, ROPecker considers a sequence of instructions to be a gadget in case it meets the following criteria [8]: *(i)* the last instruction is an indirect branch; *(ii)* no other branch (e. g., `call` or `jnz`) is contained; *(iii)* it consists of at most six instructions. This limit was arbitrarily chosen by Cheng et al. ROPecker can be configured to consider longer gadgets. We refer to gadgets that comply with ROPecker's definition as r-gadgets.

Analysis of Past and Future Indirect Branches. Like kBouncer, ROPecker configures the CPU's LBR facility to only track indirect branches in user mode. Whenever execution reaches a page outside the sliding window, ROPecker first examines the thread's/process' *past* indirect branches for a chain of r-gadgets via the LBR stack: going backward from the most recent one, it is checked for each LBR entry (which necessarily ends in an indirect branch) if its branch destination is an r-gadget. The *past* detection stops with the first entry not matching this characteristic. After that, ROPecker simulates the thread's/process' *future*

Table 1. Exemplary max_{nor} as determined by our ROPecker emulator

Application	max_{nor}	Activity
Nginx 1.4.0	5	delivery of small web page
Adobe Reader 9.5.5	9	opening of document
Pidgin 2.10.9	9	IRC chat
Gimp 2.8.2	9	simple drawing
VLC 2.0.8	11	playback of short OGG video
LibreOffice Calc 3.5.7.2	17	creation of simple spreadsheet

indirect branches using rather complex emulation techniques going forward from the most recent LBR entry's branch destination. As soon as a code sequence is encountered that does not qualify as r-gadget, the *future* detection stops. If the accumulated length of the *past* and the *future* gadget chains is above a certain threshold, an attack is assumed.

Gadget Chain Detection Threshold. Cheng et al. suggest using a chain detection threshold between 11 and 16 r-gadgets where "an ideal threshold should be smaller than the minimum length min_{rop} of all ROP gadget chains, and at the same time, be larger than the maximum length max_{nor} of the gadget chains identified from normal execution flows" [8]. They report that various real world and artificial ROP chains analyzed by them consisted of 17 to 30 gadgets. Hence, they universally assume $min_{rop} = 17$. To assess max_{nor}, Cheng et al. examined a variety of applications (certain Linux coreutils, SPEC INT2006, ffmpeg, graphics-magick, and Apache web server) during runtime. For the code paths triggered in their experiments, they found max_{nor} overall to be 10 and for Apache even only 4; values well below their empirically determined $min_{rop} = 17$.

In practice, higher values for max_{nor} are not totally unlikely though. Consider for example again the simple recursive function `factorial()` from Listing 1.1 in § 3 whose epilogue qualifies as r-gadget. We used our experimental emulator to explore the range of max_{nor} for popular applications not covered by experiments conducted by Cheng et al. The results are listed in Table 1. The encountered chain of 17 r-gadgets for LibreOffice Calc resulted from a long chain of returns from nested function calls (similar to the `factorial()` example). We emphasize that our emulator with a sliding window size of only one page naturally catches more false positives and produces higher max_{nor} than configurations with larger sliding windows. However, these numbers suggest that ROPecker might not be equally well applicable to all kinds of applications, as in certain cases max_{nor} could be too high to allow for a reasonably low detection threshold min_{rop}.

5.3   Circumvention

We now discuss methods for the generic circumvention of ROPecker. In general, we find that the narrow definition of r-gadgets makes ROPecker only a small hurdle for aware attackers.

Cheng et al. state that ROPecker's "[...] payload detection algorithm is designed based on the assumption that a gadget does not contain direct branch

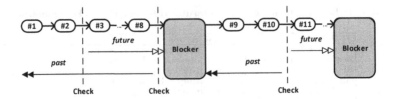

Fig. 5. Generic layout of a gadget chain bypassing ROPecker. Conventional gadgets (white) are interleaved with gadgets stopping the *past* and *future* detection logic (gray).

instructions, which is also used in the many previous work [...]. Therefore, the gadget chain detection stops when a direct branch instruction is encountered" [8]. They also acknowledge that an "[...] adversary may carefully insert long gadgets into consecutive short gadgets to make the length of each segmented gadget chain not exceed the gadget chain threshold [...]" to achieve the same. Note that these statements already describe all that is necessary in order to successfully bypass ROPecker in a generic manner. As depicted in Figure 5, attackers simply need to take care to periodically mix in a non-r-gadget (containing a branch or more than six instructions) into their gadget chains in order to stop ROPecker's *past* and *future* detection logic before the given detection threshold is reached. In the following, we refer to such a gadget as blocker-gadget.

Cheng et al. argue that to the best of their knowledge an attack using jump-containing gadgets "[...] has not been found in real-life.". We note that this observation does not necessarily imply that jump-containing (or long) gadgets are hard to use. Instead, it is in the uttermost cases trivial for an attacker to find and use such gadgets, as they do not need to be meaningful in any context. The only requirement is that they do not render the program state uncontrollable as already discussed in § 3 for kBouncer. Even entire regular functions as the ones discussed in § 3.3 can be misused by attackers here. In our example exploit against ROPecker (see § 5.4) we use for example the standard POSIX function usleep() as blocker-gadget.

5.4   Example Exploit

To demonstrate the applicability of the discussed ROPecker bypassing strategy, we created a ROP-based exploit for a stack buffer overflow vulnerability (CVE-2013-2028) [27] in the popular web server Nginx version 1.4.0. We inserted the function usleep() as blocker-gadget into the ROP chain after at least every seventh regular gadget. The entire resulting ROP payload is 107 dwords long—92 dwords are needed without ROPecker evasion—and creates a file on the target system using the system() function. Our ROPecker emulator detects a maximum chain length of nine for the exploit due to the epilogue of usleep() containing two chained r-gadgets. As this is below the default detection threshold of 11, the attack goes unnoticed.

5.5   Possible Improvements

We again briefly review potential improvements to address our bypasses and discuss their effectiveness.

Detection of Unaligned Gadgets. Cheng et al. propose that ROPecker could be improved by considering the execution of unaligned instructions as attack [8]. They note though, that it may not always be possible to decide if a given x86 instruction sequence is aligned or not. Attackers restricted to aligned gadgets would probably need longer gadget chains on average to achieve compromise. Also, finding suitable gadgets in general would be more complicated. The generic circumvention approach described in § 5.3 could though not be prevented.

Accumulation of Chain Lengths. To tackle attacks relying on blocker-gadgets, Cheng et al. suggest an extension to ROPecker that accumulates the detected chain lengths for multiple (e. g., three) consecutive sliding window updates. However, we find that an attacker could still generically avoid detection by using a (meaningless) function as blocker-gadget which updates the sliding window several times. When such a function returns to the next r-gadget, the accumulated chain length should in the uttermost cases be well below the detection threshold. We found for example the already mentioned usleep() to be a suitable function for this purpose. In our experiments, the function reliably switched pages several times before finally executing a system call.

Broadening of Gadget Definition. Lastly, Cheng et al. propose extending ROPecker in such a way that instruction sequences connected by direct jumps are also considered as gadgets, but also state that this might increase the number of false positives. In order to evaluate the practicality of such an extension, we experimentally modified our ROPecker emulator to consider kBouncer's k-gadgets (up to 20 instructions including direct jumps) instead of r-gadgets. With this hypothetical extension in place, we generally encountered high numbers of false positives often corresponding to astonishingly long benign chains of k-gadgets. For example, our emulator detected a chain of length 14 in libc for a small *hello world* application. While monitoring VLC during the playback of a short OGG video, the emulator even detected chains of lengths 77 and 82 in librsvg2 and libexpat respectively; the first being induced by a long static sequence of indirect calls to a very short function and the latter by a compact looped switch-case statement implemented using a central indirect jump. This hints at ROPecker possibly not being reasonably extendable to consider significantly more complex gadgets.

Checking for Illegal Returns. We believe that ROPecker's defensive strength could indeed be increased if it would consider returns to non call-preceded locations as indicator for an attack like kBouncer and ROPGuard do. Such an extension would effectively require attackers to largely resort to call-preceded gadgets or JOP-like concepts such as i-loop-gadgets (see § 3.4). While this would not prevent bypasses, it could significantly raise the bar. We would expect negligible overhead and close to zero additional false positives from such an extension as to the best of our knowledge returns to not call-preceded locations virtually never occur in benign control flows.

6   Related Work

To the best of our knowledge, the discussed ROP mitigation techniques have not been reviewed in other academic publications so far. Recently and concurrently to our work, Göktaş et al. demonstrate ways to bypass certain *control-flow-integrity* (CFI) systems for binary applications [12]. They show how certain types of gadgets still allow for ROP-like attacks in the presence of these systems. They mention that two of these gadget types could potentially be used to "call a function simply for tricking kBouncer" and refer to future work. We note that our described exploits would be prevented by these CFI systems. Our approaches could though be combined with the one presented by Göktaş et al.

Stephen Checkoway discusses in an article on the Internet, among others, kBouncer's first version [24] that "does not protect against return-oriented programming that doesn't use returns" [5]. This variant of kBouncer was meant to be invoked on the invocation of system calls instead of top-level WinAPI functions. Checkoway states that long enough regular code paths leading to system calls in an application could be used to erase traces of a ROP chain before kBouncer's detection logic becomes active.

The insights of both Göktaş et al. and Checkoway are similar to the foundation of our described attack techniques.

7   Conclusions

We examined the practical effectiveness of three recent approaches that attempt to prevent return-oriented programming. These are *kBouncer* [25], *ROPecker* [8], and *ROPGuard* [10]. All of them can reliably detect and prevent legacy exploits. We showed in turn that they can be bypassed in generic ways with little effort by *aware* adversaries. The basic problem is that the three approaches only analyze a limited number of recent (and upcoming) branches and an adversary can fool the employed heuristics. Both kBouncer and ROPecker rely on a custom kernel driver and employ complicated detection techniques build upon the LBR feature of modern processors. They though fall short to supply significantly higher protection levels than the much simpler ROPGuard. Our experimental results also hint at kBouncer and ROPecker being more prone to false positive attack detections than ROPGuard. We conclude that LBR, a feature that was originally designed for profiling and debugging purposes, is probably not particularly well suited for the implementation of strong defensive measures with reasonable runtime overhead.

Acknowledgments. This work has been supported by the German Federal Ministry of Education and Research (BMBF) under support code 16BP12302; EUREKA-Project SASER.

References

1. Mplayer (r33064 lite) buffer overflow + ROP exploit (2011),
   http://www.exploit-db.com/exploits/17124/
2. Microsoft BlueHat Prize (2012),
   http://www.microsoft.com/security/bluehatprize/
3. Advanced Micro Devices. AMD64 Architecture Programmers Manual Volume 2:
   System Programming, Publication no. 24593 Rev. 3.24 (December 2013)
4. Bletsch, T., Jiang, X., Freeh, V.W., Liang, Z.: Jump-oriented programming: A new
   class of code-reuse attack. In: Proceedings of ACM Symposium on Information,
   Computer and Communications Security (ASIACCS), pp. 30–40. ACM, New York
   (2011)
5. Checkoway, S.: Return-oriented programming's status is unchanged. Blog (October
   2013), https://www.cs.jhu.edu/~s/musings/rop.html
6. Checkoway, S., Davi, L., Dmitrienko, A., Sadeghi, A.-R., Shacham, H., Winandy,
   M.: Return-oriented programming without returns. In: Proceedings of ACM Conference on Computer and Communications Security (CCS), pp. 559–572. ACM,
   New York (2010)
7. Chen, W.: Here's that FBI Firefox exploit for you (CVE-2013-1690) (August 2013), https://community.rapid7.com/community/metasploit/blog/2013/
   08/07/heres-that-fbi-firefox-exploit-for-you-cve-2013-1690
8. Cheng, Y., Zhou, Z., Yu, M., Ding, X., Deng, R.H.: ROPecker: A generic and
   practical approach for defending against ROP attacks. In: Symposium on Network
   and Distributed System Security, NDSS (2014)
9. Dullien, T., Kornau, T., Weinmann, R.-P.: A framework for automated
   architecture-independent gadget search. In: USENIX Workshop on Offensive Technologies, WOOT (2010)
10. Fratric, I.: Runtime Prevention of Return-Oriented Programming Attacks, http://
    ropguard.googlecode.com/svn-history/r2/trunk/doc/ropguard.pdf
11. Fratric, I.: My BlueHat prize entry: ROPGuard – runtime prevention of return-
    oriented programming attacks. Blog (August 2012), http://ifsec.blogspot.de/
    2012/08/my-bluehat-prize-entry-ropguard-runtime.html
12. Göktaş, E., Athanasopoulos, E., Bos, H., Portokalidis, G.: Out of control: Over-
    coming control-flow integrity. In: IEEE Symposium on Security and Privacy (2014)
13. Homescu, A., Stewart, M., Larsen, P., Brunthaler, S., Franz, M.: Microgadgets:
    Size Does Matter in Turing-Complete Return-Oriented Programming. In: USENIX
    Workshop on Offensive Technologies, WOOT (2012)
14. Hund, R., Holz, T., Freiling, F.C.: Return-oriented rootkits: Bypassing kernel code
    integrity protection mechanisms. In: USENIX Security Symposium (2009)
15. Intel. Intel 64 and IA-32 architectures software developers manual, volume 1, 2A,
    2B, 2C, 3A, 3B and 3C, 325462-048US (September 2013)
16. Joly, N.: Advanced exploitation of Internet Explorer 10 / Windows 8 over-
    flow, Pwn2Own 2013 (2013), http://www.vupen.com/blog/20130522.Advanced_
    Exploitation_of_IE10_Windows8_Pwn2Own_2013.php
17. Krahmer, S.: x86-64 buffer overflow exploits and the borrowed code chunks ex-
    ploitation technique (2005), http://users.suse.com/~krahmer/no-nx.pdf
18. Luk, C.-K., Cohn, R., Muth, R., Patil, H., Klauser, A., Lowney, G., Wallace,
    S., Reddi, V.J., Hazelwood, K.: Pin: Building customized program analysis tools
    with dynamic instrumentation. In: SIGPLAN Not., vol. 40(6), pp. 190–200. ACM,
    New York (2005)

19. Microsoft Corporation. Enhanced mitigation experience toolkit 4.1—user guide (2013)
20. Microsoft Developer Network. Argument passing and naming conventions, http://msdn.microsoft.com/en-us/library/984x0h58.aspx
21. Microsoft Developer Network. C run-time library reference: _onexit (2012), http://msdn.microsoft.com/en-us/library/zk17ww08.aspx
22. Microsoft Security Research & Defense. Introducing enhanced mitigation experience toolkit (EMET) 4.1 (November 2013), http://www.microsoft.com/security/bluehatprize/
23. Nergal. The advanced return-into-lib(c) exploits: PaX case study (2001), http://phrack.org/issues/58/4.html
24. Pappas, V.: kBouncer: Efficient and transparent ROP mitigation, http://www.cs.columbia.edu/~vpappas/papers/kbouncer.pdf
25. Pappas, V., Polychronakis, M., Keromytis, A.D.: Transparent ROP exploit mitigation using indirect branch tracing. In: USENIX Security Symposium (2013)
26. Portnoy, A.: Bypassing all of the things (2013), https://www.exodusintel.com/files/Aaron_Portnoy-Bypassing_All_Of_The_Things.pdf
27. Rapid7 Vulnerability & Exploit Database. Nginx HTTP server 1.3.9–1.4.0 chunked encoding stack buffer overflow (2013), http://www.rapid7.com/db/modules/exploit/linux/http/nginx_chunked_size
28. Roemer, R., Buchanan, E., Shacham, H., Savage, S.: Return-oriented programming: Systems, languages, and applications. ACM Transactions on Information and System Security 15(1), 2:1–2:34 (2012)
29. Russinovich, M., Solomon, D.A., Ionescu, A.: Windows Internals, Part 1, 6th edn. Microsoft Press (2012)
30. Schuster, F., Tendyck, T., Pewny, J., Maaß, A., Steegmanns, M., Contag, M., Holz, T.: Evaluating the effectiveness of current anti-ROP defenses. Technical Report TR-HGI-2014-001, Ruhr-Universität Bochum (May 2014), http://syssec.rub.de/research/publications/Evaluating-Anti-ROP-Defenses/
31. Schwartz, E.J., Avgerinos, T., Brumley, D.: Q: Exploit hardening made easy. In: USENIX Security Symposium (2011)
32. Snow, K.Z., Monrose, F., Davi, L., Dmitrienko, A., Liebchen, C., Sadeghi, A.-R.: Just-in-time code reuse: On the effectiveness of fine-grained address space layout randomization. In: IEEE Symposium on Security and Privacy (2013)

Unsupervised Anomaly-Based Malware Detection Using Hardware Features

Adrian Tang, Simha Sethumadhavan, and Salvatore J. Stolfo

Columbia University, New York, USA
{atang,simha,sal}@cs.columbia.edu

Abstract. Recent works have shown promise in detecting malware programs based on their dynamic microarchitectural execution patterns. Compared to higher-level features like OS and application observables, these microarchitectural features are efficient to audit and harder for adversaries to control directly in evasion attacks. These data can be collected at low overheads using widely available hardware performance counters (HPC) in modern processors. In this work, we advance the use of hardware supported lower-level features to detecting malware exploitation in an anomaly-based detector. This allows us to detect a wider range of malware, even zero days. As we show empirically, the microarchitectural characteristics of benign programs are noisy, and the deviations exhibited by malware exploits are minute. We demonstrate that with careful selection and extraction of the features combined with unsupervised machine learning, we can build baseline models of benign program execution and use these profiles to detect deviations that occur as a result of malware exploitation. We show that detection of real-world exploitation of popular programs such as IE and Adobe PDF Reader on a Windows/x86 platform works well in practice. We also examine the limits and challenges in implementing this approach in face of a sophisticated adversary attempting to evade anomaly-based detection. The proposed detector is complementary to previously proposed signature-based detectors and can be used together to improve security.

Keywords: Hardware Performance Counter, Malware Detection.

1 Introduction

Malware infections have plagued organizations and users for years, and are growing stealthier and increasing in number by the day. In response to this trend, defenders have created commercial antivirus (AV) protections, and are actively researching better ways to detect malware. An emerging and promising approach to detect malware is to build detectors in hardware [3]. The idea is to use information easily available in hardware (typically via HPC) to detect malware. It has been argued that hardware malware schemes are desirable for two reasons: first, unlike software malware solutions that aim to protect vulnerable software with equally vulnerable software[1], hardware systems protect vulnerable software with

---

[1] Software AV systems roughly have the same bug defect density as regular software.

A. Stavrou et al. (Eds.): RAID 2014, LNCS 8688, pp. 109–129, 2014.
© Springer International Publishing Switzerland 2014

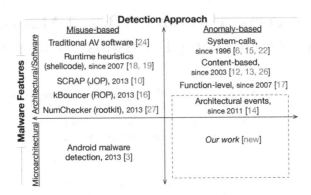

Fig. 1. Taxonomy of malware detection approaches and some example works

robust hardware implementations that have lower bug defect density because of their simplicity. Second, while a motivated adversary can evade either defense, evasion is harder in a system that utilizes hardware features. The intuition is that the attacker does not have the same degree of control over lower-level hardware features as she has with software ones. For instance, it is easier to change system calls or file names than induce cache misses or branch misprediction in a precise way across a range of time scales while exploiting the system.

In this paper we introduce techniques to advance the use of lower-level microarchitectural features in the anomaly-based detection of malware exploits. Existing malware detection techniques can be classified along two dimensions: *detection approach* and the *malware features* they target, as presented in Figure 1. Detection approaches are traditionally categorized into misuse-based and anomaly-based detection. Misuse-based detection flags malware using pre-identified attack signatures or heuristics. It can be highly accurate against known attacks but can be easily evaded with slight modifications that deviate from the signatures. On the other hand, anomaly-based detection characterizes baseline models of normalcy state and identifies attacks based on deviations from these models. Besides known attacks, it can potentially identify novel ones. There are a range of features that can be used for detection: until 2013, they were OS and application-level observables such as system calls and network traffic. Since then, lower-level features closer to hardware such as microarchitectural events have been used for malware detection. Shown in Figure 1, we examine for the first time, the feasibility and limits of anomaly-based malware detection using both architectural and low-level microarchitectural features available from HPCs.

Prior misuse-based research that uses microarchitectural features such as [3] focuses on flagging Android malicious apps by detecting payloads. A key distinction between our work and prior work is *when* the malware is detected. Malware infection typically comprises two stages, exploitation and take-over. In the exploitation stage, an adversary exercises a bug in the victim program to hijack control of the program execution. Exploitation is then followed by more elaborate take-over procedures to run a malicious payload such as a keylogger.

Our work focuses on detecting malware during exploitation, as it not only gives more lead time for mitigations but can also act as an early-threat detector to improve the accuracy of subsequent signature-based detection of payloads.

The key intuition for the anomaly-based detection of malware exploits stems from the observation that the malware, during exploitation, alters the original program flow to execute peculiar non-native code in the context of the victim program. Such unusual code execution tend to cause perturbations to the dynamic execution characteristics of the program. If these perturbations are observable, they can form the basis of detecting malware exploits.

In this work, we model the baseline characteristics of common vulnerable programs – Internet Explorer 8 and Adobe PDF Reader 9 (two of the most attacked programs) and examine if such perturbations do exist. Intuitively one might expect the deviations caused by exploits to be fairly small and unreliable, especially in vulnerable programs with extremely varied use such as in the ones we study. This intuition is validated in our measurements. On a Windows system using Intel x86 chips, our experiments indicate that distributions of measurements from the hardware performance counters are positively skewed, with many values being clustered near zero. This implies minute deviations caused by the exploit code cannot be effectively discerned directly. However, we show that this problem of identifying deviations from the heavily skewed distributions can be alleviated. We show that by using power transform to amplify small differences, together with temporal aggregation of multiple samples, we can identify the execution of the exploit within the context of the larger program execution. Further, in a series of experiments, we systematically evaluate the detection efficacy of the models over a range of operational factors, events selected for modeling and sampling granularity. For IE exploits, we can identify 100% of the exploitation epochs with 1.1% false positives. Since exploitation typically occurs across nearly 20 epochs, even with a slightly lower true positive rate, we can detect exploits with high probability. These are achieved at a sampling overhead of 1.5% slowdown using sampling rate of 512K instructions epochs.

Further we examine the resilience of our detection technique to evasion strategies of a more sophisticated adversary. We model *mimicry* attacks that craft malware to exhibit event characteristics that resemble normal code execution to evade our anomaly detection models. With generously optimistic assumptions about attacker and system capabilities, we demonstrate that the models are susceptible to the mimicry attack. In a worst case scenario, the detection performance deteriorates by up to 6.5%. Due to this limitation we observe that anomaly detectors cannot be the only defensive solution but can be valuable as part of an ensemble of detectors that can include signature-based ones.

The rest of the paper is organized as follows. We provide a background on modern malware exploits in Section 2. We detail our experimental setup in Section 3. We present our approach in building models for the study in Section 4, and describe the experimental results in Section 5. Section 6 examines evasion strategies of an adaptive adversary and their impact on detection performance. Section 7 discusses related work, and we conclude in Section 8.

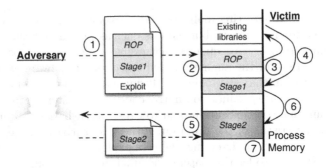

Fig. 2. Multi-stage exploit process

2   Background

Figure 2 shows a typical multi-stage malware infection process that results in a system compromise. The necessity for its multi-stage nature will become clear as we explain the exploit process in this section.

Triggering the Vulnerability. First the adversary crafts and delivers the exploit to the victim to target a specific vulnerability known to the adversary (Step ①). The vulnerability is in general a memory corruption bug; the exploit is typically sent to a victim from a webpage or a document attachment from an email. When the victim accesses the exploit, two exploit sub-programs, commonly known as the *ROP* and *Stage1* "shellcodes", load into the memory of the vulnerable program (Step ②). The exploit then uses the vulnerability to transfer control to the *ROP* shellcode (Step ③).

Code Reuse Shellcode (*ROP*). To prevent untrusted data being executed as code, modern processors provide Data Execution Prevention (DEP) to restrict code from being run from data pages. To support JIT compilation however, DEP can be toggled by the program itself. So the *ROP*-stage shellcode typically circumvents DEP by reusing instructions in the original program binary – hence the name Code Reuse Shellcode – to craft a call to the function that disables DEP for the data page containing the next *Stage1* shellcode. The ROP shellCode then redirects execution to the next stage. (Step ④) [16].

***Stage1* Shellcode.** This shellcode is typically a relatively small – from a few bytes to about 300 bytes[2] – code stub with exactly one purpose: to download a larger (evil) payload which can be run more freely. To maintain stealth, it downloads the payload in memory (Step ⑤).

***Stage2* Payload.** The payload is the final piece of code that the adversary wants to execute on the target to perform a specific malicious task. The range of functionality of this payload, commonly a backdoor, keylogger, or reconnaissance program, is unlimited. After the payload is downloaded, the *Stage1* shellcode runs this payload as an executable using reflective DLL injection (Step ⑥), a

---

[2] As observed at http://exploit-db.com

stealthy library injection technique that does not require any physical files [5]. By this time, the victim system is fully compromised (Step ⑦).

The *Stage1* shellcode and *Stage2* payload are different in size, design and function, primarily due to the operational constraints on the *Stage1* shellcode. When delivering the initial shellcode in the exploit, exploit writers typically try to use as little memory as possible to ensure that the program does not unintentionally overwrite their exploit code in memory. To have a good probability for success, this code needs to be small, fast and portable, and thus is written in assembly language and uses very restrictive position-independent memory addressing style. These constraints limit the adversary's ability to write very large shellcodes. In contrast, the *Stage2* payload does not have all these constraints and can be developed like any regular program. This is similar to how OSes use small assembly routines to bootstrap and then switch to compiled code.

The strategy and structure described above is representative of a large number of malware especially those created with recent web exploit kits [25]. These malware exploits execute completely from memory and in the process context of the host victim program. Further, they maintain disk and process stealth by ensuring no files are written to disk and no new processes are created, and thus easily evade most file based malware detection techniques.

3   Experimental Setup

Do the execution of different shellcode stages exhibit observable deviations from the baseline performance characteristics of the user programs? Can we use these deviations, if any, to detect a malware exploit as early as possible in the infection process? To address these questions, we conduct several feasibility experiments, by building baseline per-program models using machine learning classifiers and examining their detection efficacy over a range of operational factors. Here, we describe our experimental setup and detail how we collect and label the measurements attributed to different malware exploit stages.

3.1   Exploits

Unlike SPEC, there are no standard exploit benchmarks. We rely on a widely-used penetration testing tool *Metasploit* (from www.metasploit.com) to generate exploits for common vulnerable programs from publicly available information. We use exploits that target the security vulnerabilities *CVE-2012-4792*, *CVE-2012-1535* and *CVE-2010-2883* on IE 8 and the web plug-ins, *i.e.,* Adobe Flash 11.3.300.257 and Adobe Reader 9.3.4 respectively. We choose to utilize *Metasploit* because the exploitation techniques it employs in the exploits are representative of multi-stage nature of real-world exploits.

Besides targeting different vulnerabilities using different ROP shellcode from relevant library files (msvcrt.dll, icucnv36.dll, flash32.ocx), we also vary both the *Stage1* (reverse_tcp, reverse_http, bind_tcp) shellcode and the *Stage2* final payload (meterpreter, vncinject, command_shell) used in the exploits.

Additionally, we instrument the start and end of the respective malware stages with debug trap *int3* instructions (0xCC) of one byte long, to label the exploit measurements with the respective stages solely for evaluation purposes.

3.2 Measurement Infrastructure

Since most real-world exploits run on Windows and PDF readers, and none of the architectural simulators can run programs of this scale, we use measurements from production machines. We develop a Windows driver to configure the performance monitoring unit on Intel i7 2.7GHz IvyBridge Processor to interrupt once every N instructions and collect the event counts from the HPCs. We also record the Process ID (PID) of the currently executing program so that we can filter the measurements based on processes.

We collect the measurements from a VMware Virtual Machine (VM) environment, installed with Windows XP SP3 and running a single-core with 512MB of memory. With the virtualized HPCs in the VM, this processor enables the counting of two fixed events (clock cycles, instruction retired) and up to a limit of four events simultaneously. We configure the HPCs to update the event counts only in the user mode. To ensure experiment fidelity for the initial study, measurements from the memory buffer are read and transferred via TCP network sockets to a recording program deployed in another VM. This recording program saves the stream of measurements in a local file that is used for our analysis.

We experiment with various sampling interval of N instructions. We choose to begin the investigation with a sampling rate of every 512,000 instructions since it provides a reasonable amount of measurements without incurring too much overhead (See Section 5.4 for an evaluation of the sampling overhead). Each sample consists of the event counts from one sampling time epoch, the identifying PID and the exploit stage label.

3.3 Collection of Clean and Infected Measurements

To obtain clean exploit-free measurements for IE 8, we randomly browse websites that use different popular web plugins available on IE *viz.*, Flash, Java, PDF, Silverlight, and Windows Media Player extensions. We visit the top 20 websites from Alexa and include several other websites to widen the coverage of the use of the various plug-ins. Within the browser, we introduce variability by randomizing the order in which the websites are loaded across runs and by navigating the websites by clicking links randomly and manually on the webpages. The dynamic content on the websites also perturbs the browser caches. We use a maximum of two concurrent tabs. In addition, we simulate plug-in download and installation functions.

For Adobe PDF measurements, we download 800 random PDFs from the web, reserving half of them randomly for training and the other half for testing. To gather infected measurements, we browse pages with our PDF exploits with the same IE browser that uses the PDF plug-in. We use Metasploit to generate these

PDF exploits and ensure that both the clean and unclean PDFs have the same distribution of file types, for instance, same amount of Javascript.

We stop gathering infected measurements when we see creation of a new process. Usually the target process becomes unstable due to the corrupted memory state, and the malicious code typically "migrates" itself to another new or existing process to ensure persistence after the execution of the *Stage2* payload. This is an indication that the infection is complete.

While there are factors that may affect the results of our measurements, we take additional care to mitigate the following possible biases in our data during the measurement collection:

(1) **Between-run Contamination:** After executing each exploit and collecting the measurements, we restore the VM to the state before the exploit is exercised. This ensures the measurements collected are independent across training and testing sets, and across different clean and exploit runs.

(2) **Exploitation Bias:** Loading the exploits in the program in only one way may bias the sampled measurements. To reduce this bias, we collect the measurements while loading the exploit in different ways: (a) We launch the program and load the URL link of the generated exploit page. (b) With an already running program instance, we load the exploit page. (c) We save the exploit URL in a shortcut file and launch the link shortcut with the program.

(3) **Network Condition Bias:** The VM environment is connected to the Internet. To ensure that the different network latencies do not confound the measurements, we configure the VM environment to connect to an internally-configured *Squid* (from www.squid-cache.org) proxy and throttle the network bandwidth from 0.5 to 5Mbps using *Squid* delay pools. We vary the bandwidth limits while collecting measurements for both the exploit code execution and clean runs.

4   Building Models

To use HPC measurements for anomaly-based detection of malware exploits, we need to build classification models to describe the baseline characteristics for each program we protect. These program characteristics are relatively rich in information and, given numerous programs, manually building the models is nearly impossible. Instead we rely on unsupervised machine learning techniques to dynamically learn possible hidden structure in these data. We then use this hidden structure – aka model – to detect deviations during exploitation.

We rely on a class of *unsupervised* one-class machine learning techniques for model building. The one-class approach is very useful because the classifier can be trained *solely* with measurements taken from a clean environment. This removes the need to gather measurements affected by exploit code, which is hard to implement and gather in practice. Specifically, we model the characteristics with the one-class Support Vector Machine (oc-SVM) classifier that uses the non-linear Radial Basis Function (RBF) kernel. In this study, the collection of the labeled measurements is purely for evaluating the effectiveness of the models in distinguishing the measurements taken in the presence of malware code execution.

Table 1. Shortlisted candidate events to be monitored

Architectural Events		Microarchitectural Events	
Name	**Event Description**	**Name**	**Event Description**
LOAD	Load instructions (ins.)	LLC	Last level cache references
STORE	Store ins.	MIS_LLC	Last level cache misses
ARITH	Arithmetic ins.	MISP_BR	Mispredicted br. ins.
BR	Branch (br.) ins.	MISP_RET	Mispred. near return ins.
CALL	All near call ins.	MISP_CALL	Mispred. near call ins.
CALL_D	Direct near call ins.	MISP_BR_C	Mispred. conditional br.
CALL_ID	Indirect near call ins.	MIS_ICACHE	iCache misses
RET	Near return ins.	MIS_ITLB	iTLB misses
		MIS_DTLBL	D-TLB load misses
		MIS_DTLBS	D-TLB store misses
		STLB_HIT	sTLB hits after iTLB misses
		%MIS_LLC[a]	% of last level cache misses
		%MISP_BR[a]	% of mispred. br.
		%MISP_RET[a]	% of mispred. near RET ins.

[a] These *derived* events are not directly measured, but computed with two events measured by the HPCs. For example, %MISP_BR is computed as MISP_BR/BR.

4.1 Feature Selection

While the Intel processor we use for our measurements permits hundreds of events to be monitored using HPCs, not all of them are equally useful in characterizing the execution of programs. We examine most events investigated in previous program characterization works [21,9], and various other events informed by our understanding of malware behavior. Out of the hundreds of possible events that can be monitored, we shortlist 19 events for this study in Table 1. We further differentiate between the *Architectural* events that give an indication of the execution mix of instructions in any running program, and the *Microarchitectural* ones that are dependent on the specific system hardware makeup.

Events with Higher Discriminative Power. The processor is limited to monitoring up to 4 events at any given time. Even with the smaller list of shortlisted events, we have to select only a subset of events, aka features, that can most effectively differentiate clean execution from infected execution. With the collected labeled measurements, we compute the Fisher Score (*F-Score*) to provide a quantitative measure of how effective a feature can discriminate measurements in clean executions from those in infected executions. The F-Score is a widely-used feature selection metric that measures the discriminative power of features [4]. A feature with better discriminative power would have a larger separation between the means and standard deviations for samples from different classes. The F-Score measures this degree of separation. The larger the F-Score, the more discriminative power the feature is likely to have. However, a limitation to using the F-Score is that it does not account for mutual information/dependence between features, but it can guide our selection of a subset of "more useful" features. Since we are trying to differentiate samples with malicious code execution from those without, we compute the corresponding F-Scores for each event.

Table 2. Top 7 most discriminative events for different stages of exploit execution (Each event set consists of 4 event names in Bold. E.g, monitoring event set *A-0* consists of simultaneously monitoring RET, CALL_D, STORE and ARITH event counts.)

Exploit Stage	Set Label	Events ranked by F-scores						
		1	2	3	4	5	6	7
Architectural Events								
ROP	A-0	Ret	Call_D	Store	Arith	CALL	LOAD	CALL_ID
Stage1	A-1	Store	Load	Call_ID	Ret	CALL_D	CALL	ARITH
Stage2	A-2	Store	Call_ID	Ret	Call_D	CALL	ARITH	BR
Microarchitectural Events								
ROP	M-0	Misp_Br_C	%MISP_BR	Misp_Br	%MISP_RET	Mis_Itlb	Mis_Llc	MIS_DTLBS
Stage1	M-1	Misp_Ret	Misp_Br_C	%MISP_RET	%MISP_BR	Mis_Dtlbs	Stlb_Hit	MISP_BR
Stage2	M-2	Misp_Ret	Stlb_Hit	Mis_Icache	Mis_Itlb	%MISP_RET	MISP_CALL	MIS_LLC
Both Architectural and Microarchitectural Events								
ROP	AM-0	Misp_Br_C	%MISP_BR	Misp_Br	%MISP_RET	Mis_Itlb	Ret	MIS_LLC
Stage1	AM-1	Store	Load	Misp_Ret	Call_ID	RET	CALL_D	CALL
Stage2	AM-2	Store	Call_ID	Misp_Ret	Ret	CALL_D	CALL	STLB_HIT

We compute the F-Scores for the different stages of malware code execution for each event and reduce the shortlisted events to the 7 top-ranked events for each of the two categories, as well as for the two categories combined, as shown in Table 2. Each row consists of the top-ranked events for an event category and the exploit stage.

We further select top 4 events from each row to form 9 candidate event sets that we will use to build the baseline characteristic models of the IE browser. Each model constructed with one set of events can then be evaluated for its effectiveness in the detection of various stages of malware code execution. For brevity, we assign a label (such as *A-0* and *AM-2*) to each set of 4 events in Table 2 and refer to each model based on this *set label*. We note that the derived events such as %MISP_BR are listed in the table solely for comparison. Computing them requires monitoring two events and reduces the number of features used in the models. Via experimentation, we find that using them in the models does not increase the efficacy of the models. Thus, we exclude them from the event sets.

Feature Extraction. Each sample consists of simultaneous measurements of all the four event counts in one time epoch. We convert the measurements in each sample to the vector subspace, so that each classification vector is represented as a four-feature vector. Each vector, using this feature extraction method, represents the measurements taken at the smallest time-slice for that sampling granularity. These features will be used to build *non-temporal* models.

Since we observe that malware shellcode typically runs over several time epochs, there may exist temporal relationships in the measurements that can be exploited. To model any potential temporal information, we extend the dimensionality of each sample vector by grouping the N consecutive samples and combining the measurements of each event to form a vector with $4N$ features. We use $N = 4$ to create sample vectors consisting of 16 features each, so each sample vector effectively represents measurements across 4 time epochs. By grouping samples across several time epochs, we use the synthesis of these event measurements to build *temporal* models.

With the granularity at which we sample the measurements, the execution of the ROP shellcode occurs within the span of just one sample. Since we are creating vectors with a number of samples as a group, the ROP payload will only contribute to one small portion of a vector sample. So we leave out the ROP shellcode for testing using this form of feature extraction.

5 Results

5.1 Anomalies Not Directly Detectable

We first investigate if we can gain insights into the distribution of the event counts for a clean environment and one attacked by an exploit. Without assuming any prior knowledge of the distributions, we use box-and-whisker[3] plots of normalized measurements for different events. These plots offer a visual gauge of the range and variance in the measurements and an initial indication on how distinguishable the measurements taken with the execution of different malware code stages are from the *clean* measurements from an exploit-free environment.

These distribution comparisons suggest that any event anomalies manifested by malware code execution are not trivially detectable, due to two key observations. (1) Most of the measurement distributions are very positively skewed, with many values clustered near zero. (2) Deviations, if any, from the baseline event characteristics due to the exploit code are not easily discerned.

5.2 Power Transform

To address this challenge, we rely on rank-preserving power transform on the measurements to positively scale the values. In the field of statistics, the power transform is a common data analysis tool to transform non-normally distributed data to one that can be approximated by a normal distribution. Used in our context, it has the value of magnifying any slight deviations that the malware code execution may have on the baseline characteristics.

For each event type, we find the appropriate power parameter λ such that the normalized median is roughly 0.5. For each event i, we maintain and use its associated parameter λ_i to scale all its corresponding measurements throughout the experiment. Each normalized and scaled event measurement for event i, $\mathrm{normalized}_i$, is transformed from the raw value (raw_i), minimum value (min_i), maximum value (max_i) as follows:

$$\mathrm{normalized}_i = (\frac{\mathrm{raw}_i - \mathrm{min}_i}{\mathrm{max}_i})^{\lambda_i} \tag{1}$$

---

[3] The box-and-whisker plot is constructed with the bottom and top of the box representing the first and third quartiles respectively. The red line in the box is the median. The whiskers extend to 1.5 times the length of the box. Any outliers beyond the whiskers are plotted as blue + ticks.

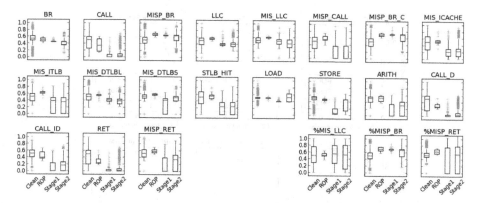

Fig. 3. Distribution of events (*after* power transform) with more discernible deviations

Using this power transform, we plot the distributions of all the events, in Figure 3. Now we observe varying deviations from baseline characteristics due to different stages of malware code execution for various event types. Some events (such as MISP_RET and STORE) show relatively larger deviations, especially for the *Stage1* exploit shellcode. These events likely possess greater discriminative power in indicating the presence of malware code execution. Clearly, there are also certain events that are visually correlated. The RET and CALL exhibit similar distributions. We can also observe strong correlation between those computed events (such as %MISP_BR) and their constituent events (such as MISP_BR).

5.3   Evaluation Metrics for Models

To visualize the classification performance of the models, we construct the *Receiver Operating Characteristic* (ROC) curves which plot the percentage of truely identified malicious samples (True positive rate) against the percentage of *clean* samples falsely classified as malicious (False positive rate). Each sample in the non-temporal model corresponds to the set of performance counter measurements in one epoch; each temporal sample spans over 4 epochs. Furthermore, to contrast the relative performance between the models in the detection of malicious samples, the area under the *ROC* curve for each model can be computed and compared. This area, commonly termed as the *Area Under Curve* (AUC) score, provides a quantitative measure of how well a model can distinguish between the clean and malicious samples for varying thresholds. The higher the AUC score, the better the detection performance of the model.

5.4   Detection Performance of Models

We first build the oc-SVM models with the training data, and evaluate them with the testing data using the non-temporal and temporal modeling on the nine event sets. To characterize and visualize the detection rates in terms of true

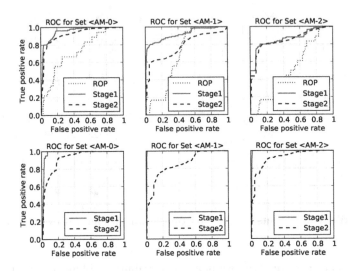

Fig. 4. Top: ROC plots for *Non-Temporal* 4-feature models for IE. **Bottom:** ROC plots for *Temporal* 16-feature models for IE.

and false positives over varying thresholds, we present the ROC curves of both approaches in Figure 4. For brevity, we only present the ROC curves for models that use both architectural and microarchitectural events. We also present the overall detection results in terms of AUC scores in Figure 5 and highlight the key observations that affect the detection accuracy of the models below.

Different Stages of Malware Exploits. We observe that the models, in general, perform best in the detection of the *Stage1* shellcode. These results suggest the *Stage1* shellcode exhibits the largest deviations from the baseline architectural and microarchitectural characteristics of benign code. We achieve a best-case detection accuracy of 99.5% for *Stage1* shellcode with *AM-1* models.

On the other hand, the models show mediocre detection capabilities for the ROP shellcode. The models does not perform well in the detection of the ROP shellcode, likely because the sampling granularity at 512k instructions is too coarse-grained to capture the deviations from the ROP shellcode in the baseline models. While the *Stage1* and *Stage2* shellcode executes within several time epochs, we measured that the ROP shellcode takes 2182 instructions on average to complete execution. It ranges from as few as 134 instructions (for the Flash ROP exploit) to 6016 instructions (for the PDF ROP exploit). Since we are keeping the sampling granularity constant, the sample that contains measurements during the ROP shellcode execution will largely consist of samples from the normal code execution.

Non-Temporal vs Temporal Modeling. We observe that the detection accuracy of the models for all event sets improves with the use of temporal information. By including more temporal information in each sample vector, we reap the benefit of magnifying any deviations that are already observable in the

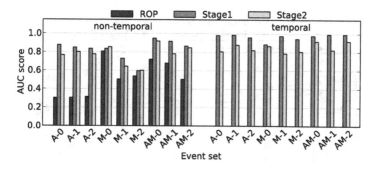

Fig. 5. Detection AUC scores for different event sets using non-temporal and temporal models for IE

non-temporal approach. For event set *M-2*, this temporal approach of building the models improves the AUC score from the non-temporal one by up to 58.8%.

Architectural vs Microarchitectural Events. We quantify the detection capabilities of our models by considering the architectural and microarchitectural features separately and in combination. Models built using only architectural events achieve AUC scores on average 4.1% better than those built solely with microarchitectural events. Combining the use of microarchitectural events with architectural ones improves the average AUC scores by 5.8% and 1.4% for microarchitectural-only and architectural-only models respectively. It is more advantageous to incorporate the use of both types of events in the detection models. For instance, by selecting and modeling both the most discriminative architectural and microarchitectural events together, we can achieve higher detection rates of up to an AUC score of 99.5% for event set *AM-1*.

Different Sampling Granularities. While we use the sampling rate of 512K instructions for the above experiments, we also examine the impact on detection efficacy for various sampling granularities. Although the hardware-based HPCs incur a near-zero overhead in the monitoring of the event counts, a pure software-only implementation of the detector still requires running programs to be interrupted periodically to sample the event counts. This inadvertently leads to a slowdown of the overall running time of programs due to this sampling overhead. To inform the deployment of a software-only implementation of such a detection paradigm, we evaluate the sampling performance overhead for different sampling rates.

To measure this overhead, we vary the sampling granularity and measure the slowdown in the programs from the SPEC 2006 benchmark suite. We also repeat the experiments using the event set *AM-1* to study the effect of sampling granularity has on the detection accuracy of the model. We plot the execution time slowdown over different sampling rates with the corresponding detection AUC scores for various malware exploit stages in Figure 6.

We observe that the detection performance generally deteriorates with coarser-grained sampling. This illustrates a key limitation of the imprecise sampling

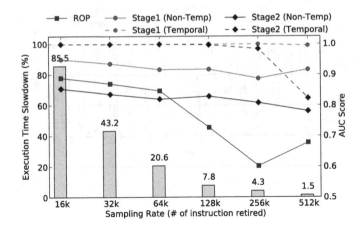

Fig. 6. Trade-off between sampling overhead for different sampling rates versus detection accuracy using set *AM-1*

technique used on Windows systems. For example, during the span of instructions retired in one sample, while we may label these measurements as belonging to a specific process PID, these measurements may also contain measurements belonging to other processes context-switched in and out during the span of this sample. The interleaved execution of different processes creates this "noise" effect that becomes more pronounced with a coarser-grained sampling rate and deteriorates the detection performance. Nonetheless, we note that the reduction in sampling overhead at coarser-grained rates far proportionately outstrips the decrease in detection performance.

Constrained Environments. To further investigate the impact of the aforementioned "noise" effect, we also assess the impact on detection accuracy in the scenario where we deploy both the online classification and the measurement gathering in the same VM. As described in Section 3.2, we collect the measurements in our study from one VM and transfer the measurements to the recorder in another VM to be saved and processed. We term this cross-remote-VM scenario where the sampling and the online classification are performed on different VMs as *R-1core*.

For this experiment, we use the event model set *AM-1* using two additional local-VM scenarios utilizing both one and two cores separately. We term these two scenarios as *L-1core* and *L-2core* respectively. We present the detection AUC scores for the three different scenarios in Table 3 (*Left*).

We observe the detection performance suffers when the online classifier is deployed locally together with the sampling driver. This may be due to possible noise introduced to the event counts while the online detector is executing and processing the stream of samples. This highlights a key limitation of the current method of periodic collection of HPC measurements on Windows systems, where we are unable to cleanly segregate the measurements on a per-process basis.

Table 3. AUC scores for: **(Left)** Constrained scenarios for IE using set *AM-1* and **(Right)** Stand-alone Adobe PDF Reader

Scenario Label	Non-Temporal			Temporal		Set Label	Non-Temporal			Temporal	
	ROP	Stage1	Stage2	Stage1	Stage2		ROP	Stage1	Stage2	Stage1	Stage2
L-1core	0.505	0.895	0.814	0.918	0.900	AM-0	0.931	0.861	0.504	0.967	0.766
L-2core	0.496	0.890	0.807	0.907	0.813	AM-1	0.857	0.932	0.786	0.999	0.863
R-1core	0.678	0.916	0.781	0.995	0.823	AM-2	0.907	0.939	0.756	0.998	0.912

To alleviate this problem, we envision a software-only implementation on a distributed or multi-core system in which the online detector is running separately from the system or core being protected. Furthermore, since this detection approach requires little more than a stream of HPC measurements, this makes it suitable as an out-of-VM deployment in a Virtual Machine Introspection (VMI)-based setting [30] for intrusion detection. This approach requires minimum guest data structures, relieving the need to bridge the semantic gap, a common problem faced by VMI works. Another potential avenue to alleviate the "noise" problem is a pure hardware implementation using a separate and secure dedicated core or co-processor for the execution of an online detector as proposed in [3].

5.5   Results for Adobe PDF Reader

Due to space constraints, we do not present the full results from our experiments on the stand-alone Adobe PDF Reader. We present the AUC detection performance of the models built with the event sets *AM-0,1,2* in Table 3 (*Right*). Compared to the models for IE, the detection of ROP and *Stage1* shellcode generally improves for the Adobe PDF Reader. We even achieve an AUC score of 0.999 with the *AM-1* temporal model. The improved performance of this detection technique for the PDF Reader suggests that its baseline characteristics are more stable given the less varied range of inputs it handles compared to IE.

6   Analysis of Evasion Strategies

In general, anomaly-based intrusion detection approaches, such as ours, are susceptible to *mimicry* attacks. To evade detection, a sophisticated adversary with sufficient information about the anomaly detection models can modify her malware into an equivalent form that exhibits similar baseline architectural and microarchitectural characteristics as the normal programs. In this section, we examine the degree of freedom an adversary has in crafting a mimicry attack and how it impacts the detection efficacy of our models.

Adversary Assumptions. We assume the adversary (a) knows all about the target program such as the version and OS to be run on, and (b) is able to gather similar HPC measurements for the targeted program to approximate its baseline characteristics. (c) She also knows the way the events are modeled, but *not* the exact events used. We highlight three ways the adversary can change her attack while retaining the original attack semantics.

Assumption (c) is realistic, given the hundreds of possible events that can be monitored on a modern processor. While she may uncover the manner the events are modeled, it is difficult to pinpoint the exact subset of four events used given the numerous possible combinations of subsets. Furthermore, even if the entire event list that can be monitored is available, there may still exist some events (such as events monitored by the power management units) that are not publicly available. Nonetheless, to describe attacks 1 and 2, we optimistically assume the adversary has full knowledge of all the events that are used in the models.

Attack 1: Padding. The first approach is to pad the original shellcode code sequences with "no-op" (no effect) instructions with a sufficient number so that the events manifested by the shellcode match that of the baseline execution of the program. These no-op instructions should modify the measurements for all the events monitored, in tandem, to a range acceptable to the models.

The adversary needs to know the events used by the model *a priori*, in order to exert an influence over the relevant events. We first explore feasibility of such a mimicry approach by analyzing the *Stage1* shellcode under the detection model of event set *AM-1*. After studying the true positive samples, we observe that the event characteristics exhibited by the shellcode are due to the unusually low counts of the four events modeled. As we re-craft the shellcode at the assembly code level to achieve the mimicry effect, we note three difficulties.

(1) **Multi-instruction No-ops:** Some microarchitectural events require more than one instruction to effect a change. For example, to raise the MISP_RET counts, sequences of RET code need to be crafted in a specific order. Insertion of no-ops must be added in multi-instruction segments.

(2) **Event Co-dependence:** To maintain the original shellcode semantics, certain registers need to be saved and subsequently restored. These operations constitute STORE /LOAD μ-operations and can inadvertently affect both STORE and LOAD events. Thus we are rarely able to craft no-op code segments to modify each event independently. For instance, among the events in *AM-1*, only the no-op instruction segment for STORE can be crafted to affect it independently. Event co-dependence makes adversarial control of values of individual events challenging.

(3) **No-op Insertion Position:** Insertion position of the no-op instruction segments can be critical to achieve the desired mimicry effect. We notice the use of several loops within the shellcode. If even one no-op segment is inserted into the loops, that results in a huge artificial increase in certain event types, consequently making that code execution look more malicious than usual.

Next, we examine the impact of such mimicry efforts on the detection performance. We pad the *Stage1* shellcode at random positions (avoiding the loops) with increasing number of each crafted no-op instruction segment and repeated the detection experiments. In Figure 7 (*Left*), we plot the box-and-whisker plots of the anomaly scores observed from the samples with varying numbers of injected no-op code. In general, the anomaly scores become less anomalous with the padding, until after a tipping point where inserting too many no-ops reverses mimicry effect. In the same vein, we observe in Figure 7 (*Right*) that the detection AUC scores

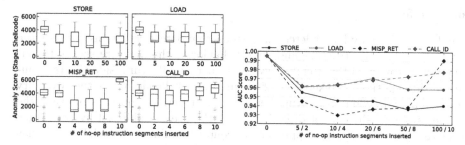

Fig. 7. Impact of inserting no-op segments on: **(Left)** The anomaly scores of *Stage1* shellcode and **(Right)** The detection efficacy of *Stage1* shellcode

decrease as the samples appear more normal. For the worst case, the detection performance suffers by up to 6.5% just by inserting *only* the CALL_ID no-ops. We do not study combining the no-ops for different events, but we believe it should deteriorate the detection performance further.

Attack 2: Substitution. Instead of padding no-ops into original attack code sequences, the adversary can replace her code sequences with equivalent variants using code obfuscation techniques, common in metamorphic malware [1]. Like the former attack, this also requires that she knows the events used by the models *a priori*. To conduct this attack, she must first craft or generate equivalent code variants of code sequences in her exploits, and profile the event characteristics of each variant. She can adopt a greedy strategy by iteratively substituting parts of her attack code with the equivalent variants, measuring the HPC events of the shellcode and ditching those variants that exhibit characteristics not acceptable to the models. However, while this greedy approach will terminate, it warrants further examination as to whether the resulting shellcode modifications suffice to evade the models. We argue that this kind of shellcode re-design is hard and will substantially raise the bar for exploit writers.

Attack 3: Grafting. This attack requires either inserting benign code from the target program directly into the exploit code, or co-scheduling the exploit shellcode by calling benign functions (with no-op effects) within the exploit code. This attack somewhat *grafts* its malicious code execution with the benign ones within the target program, thus relieving the need for the knowledge of the events that are modeled. If done correctly, it can exhibit very similar characteristics as the benign code it grafts itself to. As such this represents the most powerful attack against our detection approach.

While we acknowledge that we have not crafted this form of attack in our study, we believe that it is extremely challenging to craft such a grafting attack due to the operational constraints on the exploit and shellcode, described in Section 2. (1) Inserting sufficient benign code into the shellcode may exceed the vulnerability-specific size limits and cause the exploit to fail. (2) To use benign functions for the grafting attacks, these functions have to be carefully identified and inserted so that they execute sufficiently to mimic the normal program behavior and yet not interfere with the execution of the original shellcode. (3) The grafted code must not unduly increase the execution time of the entire exploit.

6.1   Defenses

Unlike past anomaly-based detection systems that detect deviations based on the syntactic/semantic structure and code behavior of the malware shellcode, our approach focuses on the architectural and microarchitectural side-effects manifested through the code execution of the malware shellcode. While the adversary has complete freedom in crafting her attack instruction sequences to evade the former systems, she cannot directly modify the events exhibited by her attack code to evade our detection approach. To conduct a mimicry attack here, she has to carefully "massage" her attack code to manifest a combination of event behaviors that are accepted as benign/normal under our models. This second-order degree of control over the event characteristics of the shellcode adds difficulty to the adversary's evasion efforts. On top of this, we discuss further potential defense strategies to mitigate the impact of the mimicry attacks.

Randomization. Introducing secret randomizations into the models has been used to strengthen robustness against mimicry attacks in anomaly-based detection systems [26]. In our context, we can randomize the events used in the models by training multiple models using different subsets of the shortlisted events. We can also randomize the choice of model to utilize over time. Another degree of randomization is to change the number of consecutive time-epoch samples to use for each sample for the temporal models. In this manner, the adversary does not know which model is used during the execution of her attack shellcode. For her exploit to be portable and functional on a wide range of targets, she has to modify her shellcode using the no-op padding and instruction substitution mimicry attacks for a wider range of events (and not just the current four events).

Multiplexing. At the cost of higher sampling overhead, we can choose to sample at a finer sampling granularity and measure more events (instead of the current four) by multiplexing the monitoring – we can approximate the simultaneous monitoring of 8 events across two time epochs by monitoring 4 events in one and another 4 in the other. This increases to the input dimensionality used in the models, making it harder for the adversary to make all the increased number of monitored event measurements appear non-anomalous.

Defense-in-depth. Consider a defense-in-depth approach, where this malware anomaly detector using HPC manifestations is deployed with existing anomaly-based detectors monitoring for other features of the malware, such as its syntactic and semantic structure [26,12,13] and its execution behavior at system-call level [22,6,15,20] and function level [17]. In such a setting, in order for a successful attack, an adversary is then forced to shape her attack code to conform to normalcy for each anomaly detection model. An open area of research remains in quantifying this multiplicative level of security afforded by the combined use of these HPC models with existing defenses, *i.e.* examining the difficulty in shaping the malware shellcode to evade detectors using statistical and behavioral software features, while simultaneously not exhibiting any anomalous HPC event characteristics during execution.

7   Related Work

The use of low-level hardware features for malware detection (instead of software ones) is a recent development. Demme *et al.* demonstrate the feasibility of misuse-based detection of Android malware programs using microarchitectural features [3]. While they model microarchitectural signatures of malware programs, we build baseline microarchitectural models of benign programs we are protecting and detect deviations caused by a potentially wider range of malware (even ones that are previously unobserved). Another key distinction is that we are detecting malware shellcode execution of an exploit within the context of the victim program during the act of exploitation; they target Android malware as whole programs. After infiltrating the system via an exploit, the malware can be made stealthier by installing into peripherals, or by infecting other benign programs. Stewin *et al.* propose detecting the former by flagging additional memory bus accesses made by the malware [23]. Malone *et al.* examine detecting the latter form of malicious static and dynamic program modification by modeling the architectural characteristics of benign programs (and excluding the use of microarchitectural events) using linear regression models [14]. Another line of research shows that malware can be detected using side-channel power perturbations they induce in medical embedded devices [2], software-defined radios [7] and mobile phones [11]. However, Hoffman *et al.* show that the use of such power consumption models can be very susceptible to noise, especially in a device with such widely varied use as the modern smartphone [8].

Besides HPCs, several works have leveraged other hardware facilities on modern processors to monitor branch addresses efficiently to thwart classes of exploitation techniques. kBouncer uses the Last Branch Recording (LBR) facility to monitor for runtime behavior of indirect branch instructions during the invocation of Windows API for the prevention of ROP exploits [16]. To enforce control flow integrity, CFIMon [28] and Eunomia [29] leverage the Branch Trace Store (BTS) to obtain branch source and target addresses to check for unseen pairs from a pre-identified database of legitimate branch pairs. Unlike our approach to detecting malware, these works are designed to prevent exploitation in the first place, and are orthogonal to our anomaly detection approach.

8   Conclusions

This work introduces the novel use of hardware-supported lower-level microarchitectural features to the anomaly-based detection of malware exploits. This represents the first work to examine the feasibility and limits of using unsupervised learning on microarchitectural features from HPCs to detect malware. We demonstrate that the dynamic execution of commonly attacked programs can be efficiently characterized with minimal features – the stream of event measurements easily accessible from the HPC, and used to detect lower-level perturbations caused by malware exploits to the baseline characteristics of benign programs. Unlike its misuse-based counterparts previously proposed, this anomaly-based detection approach can detect a wider range of malware, even novel ones. This work can thus be used in concert with its misuse-based counterparts to better security. Further, in modeling a class of potential mimicry attacks against our detector, we show that it can be challenging for an adversary to precisely control these hardware features to conduct an evasion attack.

Acknowledgements. We thank anonymous reviewers for feedback on this work. This work is supported by grants FA 865011C7190, FA 87501020253, CCF/SaTC 1054844 and a fellowship from the Alfred P. Sloan Foundation. Opinions, findings, conclusions and recommendations expressed in this material are those of the authors and do not necessarily reflect the views of the US Government or commercial entities.

References

1. Borello, J.M., Mé, L.: Code obfuscation techniques for metamorphic viruses. Journal in Computer Virology 4(3), 211–220 (2008)
2. Clark, S.S., Ransford, B., Rahmati, A., Guineau, S., Sorber, J., Fu, K., Xu, W.: WattsUpDoc: Power Side Channels to Nonintrusively Discover Untargeted Malware on Embedded Medical Devices. In: USENIX Workshop on Health Information Technologies (August 2013)
3. Demme, J., Maycock, M., Schmitz, J., Tang, A., Waksman, A., Sethumadhavan, S., Stolfo, S.: On the feasibility of online malware detection with performance counters. In: Proceedings of the 40th Annual International Symposium on Computer Architecture, ISCA 2013, pp. 559–570. ACM, New York (2013)
4. Duda, R.O., Hart, P.E., Stork, D.G.: Pattern Classification. John Wiley & Sons, New York (2001), J. Classif. 24(2), 305–307, pp. xx + 654 (2007)
5. Fewer, S.: Reflective DLL injection (October 2008), http://www.harmonysecurity.com/files/HS-P005_ReflectiveDllInjection.pdf
6. Forrest, S., Hofmeyr, S.A., Somayaji, A., Longstaff, T.A.: A sense of self for unix processes. In: 1996 IEEE Symposium on Security and Privacy, pp. 120–128 (1996)
7. Gonzalez, C.R.A., Reed, J.H.: Detecting unauthorized software execution in sdr using power fingerprinting. In: Military Communications Conference, MILCOM 2010, pp. 2211–2216. IEEE (2010)
8. Hoffmann, J., Neumann, S., Holz, T.: Mobile Malware Detection Based on Energy Fingerprints A Dead End? In: Stolfo, S.J., Stavrou, A., Wright, C.V. (eds.) RAID 2013. LNCS, vol. 8145, pp. 348–368. Springer, Heidelberg (2013)
9. Hoste, K., Eeckhout, L.: Comparing Benchmarks Using Key Microarchitecture-Independent Characteristics. In: 2006 IEEE International Symposium on Workload Characterization, pp. 83–92. IEEE (October 2006)
10. Kayaalp, M., Schmitt, T., Nomani, J., Ponomarev, D., Abu-Ghazaleh, N.B.: SCRAP: Architecture for signature-based protection from Code Reuse Attacks. In: HPCA, pp. 258–269 (2013)
11. Kim, H., Smith, J., Shin, K.G.: Detecting energy-greedy anomalies and mobile malware variants. In: Proceedings of the 6th International Conference on Mobile Systems, Applications, and services. pp. 239–252. ACM (2008)
12. Kong, D., Tian, D., Liu, P., Wu, D.: SA3: Automatic semantic aware attribution analysis of remote exploits. In: Security and Privacy in Communication Networks, pp. 190–208. Springer (2012)

13. Mahoney, M.V.: Network traffic anomaly detection based on packet bytes. In: Proceedings of the 2003 ACM Symposium on Applied Computing, pp. 346–350 (2003)
14. Malone, C., Zahran, M., Karri, R.: Are hardware performance counters a cost effective way for integrity checking of programs. In: Proceedings of the Sixth ACM Workshop on Scalable Trusted Computing, STC 2011, pp. 71–76. ACM (2011)
15. Marceau, C.: Characterizing the behavior of a program using multiple-length n-grams. In: Proceedings of the 2000 Workshop on New Security Paradigms, pp. 101–110. ACM (2001)
16. Pappas, V., Polychronakis, M., Keromytis, A.D.: Transparent ROP exploit mitigation using indirect branch tracing. In: Proceedings of the 22nd USENIX Conference on Security, SEC 2013, pp. 447–462. USENIX Association, Berkeley (2013)
17. Peisert, S., Bishop, M., Karin, S., Marzullo, K.: Analysis of computer intrusions using sequences of function calls. IEEE Transactions on Dependable and Secure Computing 4(2), 137–150 (2007)
18. Polychronakis, M., Anagnostakis, K.G., Markatos, E.P.: Emulation-based detection of non-self-contained polymorphic shellcode. In: Kruegel, C., Lippmann, R., Clark, A. (eds.) RAID 2007. LNCS, vol. 4637, pp. 87–106. Springer, Heidelberg (2007)
19. Polychronakis, M., Anagnostakis, K.G., Markatos, E.P.: Comprehensive shellcode detection using runtime heuristics. In: Proceedings of the 26th Annual Computer Security Applications Conference, pp. 287–296. ACM (2010)
20. Sekar, R., Bendre, M., Dhurjati, D., Bollineni, P.: A fast automaton-based method for detecting anomalous program behaviors. In: Proceedings of the 2001 IEEE Symposium on Security and Privacy, S&P 2001, pp. 144–155. IEEE (2001)
21. Shen, K., Zhong, M., Dwarkadas, S., Li, C., Stewart, C., Zhang, X.: Hardware counter driven on-the-fly request signatures. In: Proceedings of the 13th International Conference on Architectural Support for Programming Languages and Operating Systems, ASPLOS XIII, pp. 189–200. ACM, New York (2008)
22. Somayaji, A., Forrest, S.: Automated response using system-call delays. In: Proceedings of the 9th USENIX Security Symposium, vol. 70 (2000)
23. Stewin, P.: A primitive for revealing stealthy peripheral-based attacks on the computing platforms main memory. In: Stolfo, S.J., Stavrou, A., Wright, C.V. (eds.) RAID 2013. LNCS, vol. 8145, pp. 1–20. Springer, Heidelberg (2013)
24. Szor, P.: The art of computer virus research and defense. Pearson Education (2005)
25. TrendMicro: The crimeware evolution (research whitepaper) (2012)
26. Wang, K., Parekh, J.J., Stolfo, S.J.: Anagram: A content anomaly detector resistant to mimicry attack. In: Zamboni, D., Kruegel, C. (eds.) RAID 2006. LNCS, vol. 4219, pp. 226–248. Springer, Heidelberg (2006)
27. Wang, X., Karri, R.: NumChecker: Detecting kernel control-flow modifying rootkits by using hardware performance counters. In: Proceedings of the 50th Annual Design Automation Conference, DAC 2013, pp. 79:1–79:7. ACM, NY (2013)
28. Xia, Y., Liu, Y., Chen, H., Zang, B.: CFIMon: Detecting violation of control flow integrity using performance counters. In: Proceedings of the 2012 42nd Annual IEEE/IFIP International Conference on Dependable Systems and Networks, DSN 2012, pp. 1–12. IEEE Computer Society, Washington, DC (2012)
29. Yuan, L., Xing, W., Chen, H., Zang, B.: Security breaches as PMU deviation: detecting and identifying security attacks using performance counters. In: APSys, p. 6 (2011)
30. Garfinkel, T., Rosenblum, M.: A Virtual Machine Introspection Based Architecture for Intrusion Detection. In: NDSS, vol. 3 (2003)

Eyes of a Human, Eyes of a Program: Leveraging Different Views of the Web for Analysis and Detection

Jacopo Corbetta, Luca Invernizzi, Christopher Kruegel, and Giovanni Vigna

University of California, Santa Barbara
{jacopo,invernizzi,chris,vigna}@cs.ucsb.edu

Abstract. With JavaScript and images at their disposal, web authors can create content that is immediately understandable to a person, but is beyond the direct analysis capability of computer programs, including security tools. Conversely, information can be deceiving for humans even if unable to fool a program.

In this paper, we explore the discrepancies between user perception and program perception, using content obfuscation and counterfeit "seal" images as two simple but representative case studies. In a dataset of 149,700 pages we found that benign pages rarely engage in these practices, while uncovering hundreds of malicious pages that would be missed by traditional malware detectors.

We envision that this type of heuristics could be a valuable addition to existing detection systems. To show this, we have implemented a proof-of-concept detector that, based solely on a similarity score computed on our metrics, can already achieve a high precision (95%) and a good recall (73%).

Keywords: Website analysis, content obfuscation, fraud detection.

1 Introduction

Web pages available on the Internet are visited by two very different kinds of consumers: humans, surfing through their web browsers, and computer programs, such as search engines.

These consumers have dissimilar goals and constraints, which lead to significant differences in how they interpret and interact with web pages. For example, a large-scale web crawler, optimized for speed, may not run JavaScript, and thus will not capture dynamically-rendered content: To overcome this issue, search engines have established practices [13,14,28,47] that web authors should follow to make content accessible to their non-JavaScript-aware crawlers. In short, (at least) two different views exist for each page, and search engines rely on web authors to "bridge" the two worlds and make sure a human and a crawler "see" an equivalent message.

Search engines, however, have a privileged role online: Successful web sites need their pages to be indexed, so that people can find them easily; therefore,

A. Stavrou et al. (Eds.): RAID 2014, LNCS 8688, pp. 130–149, 2014.
© Springer International Publishing Switzerland 2014

web authors are highly encouraged to tailor content so that it is easily consumable by these programs. On the contrary, tools that look for cybercrime activity do not benefit from their role, as they have to face web authors that are always looking for new ways to evade detection. However, even benign web authors can present visual information to humans that is, intentionally or not, hard to digest for crawling tools, for instance by showing text through a combination of images and JavaScript code, a Turing-complete language. In the strictest sense, therefore, only programs with human-like comprehension abilities would be able to correctly "understand" even benign web pages. Whether or not this happens in practice, however, is a different question.

In this paper, we focus on how cybercriminals exploit the differences between humans and detection tools in executing, parsing, and interpreting a web page. We use two signals in our investigation. The first technique we detect is textual *content obfuscation*, with which web authors prevent non-JavaScript-aware analyzers from retrieving portions of the textual content of the page, and present a different message to humans. The second technique we detect is the presence of *fake security seal* images: cybercriminals place these seals on their websites in an attempt to deceive humans (i.e., by purporting their online rouge pharmacy is "certified" by a reputable authority), even if a program would never be fooled by this practice.

We study how these techniques are used in a dataset of 149,700 web pages, containing both benign and malicious pages. Interestingly, we found that benign pages also make use of content obfuscation for specific purposes, such as making the harvesting of e-mail addresses more difficult. However, with a few heuristics (and a clustering step to eliminate outliers) we can find malicious pages with 94% precision and 95% recall among the samples that triggered this signal. The fake seal heuristic, having almost no false positives, found 400 rogue pharmacy websites.

As a proof-of-concept of how these anti-deception heuristics could be a valuable addition to many security products, we built a "maliciousness detector" leveraging signatures extracted exclusively from pages detected by our two heuristics, using the hidden text as an additional hint. While obviously not a complete anti-fraud or anti-malware solution, our tool automatically pinpointed several scam campaigns that deceive humans without exploiting any technical vulnerability, and would therefore be out of the reach of many traditional malware detectors, unless they had specific signatures for them.

Given the importance of scam campaigns and how large exploitation campaigns were found to use content obfuscation, we estimate that our heuristics could be a valuable addition to many security products, as our proof-of-concept tool has a high precision (95%) and a good recall (around 73%) when used to find any malicious page in our dataset.

To summarize, our main contributions are:

- We introduce a novel approach to detect content obfuscation, and we study its legitimate and malicious uses in a large dataset.
- We introduce a novel approach in detecting counterfeited, or just plainly fake (with no certification authority issuing them), certification seals.

– We show that this type of heuristics can be helpful to general security tools, by introducing a similarity measure and a matching system that expand their reach.

2   Related Work

To be effective, fraud pages need to deceive twice: like any malicious site, they need to convince automated analyzers that they are legitimate sites; moreover, they need to convince humans into falling for the "phish," a trait that is unique to this cybercrime branch. To identify these sites, researchers have devised detection systems that go after both of these deceptions.

Honeyclient Evasion. Researchers have identified malware/phishing sites that perform server-side cloaking to prevent honeyclients from reaching the phishing content: only real users get to the phish, whereas honeyclients get delivered legitimate content. The cloaking may happen on the redirection chain leading to them [21], or the server hosting them [42]. Other researchers have pinpointed suspicious URLs by detecting attempts to evade honeyclients analysis, typically through fingerprinting and obfuscation [18].

Blacklist Evasion. Cybercriminals have also mitigated the efficacy of successful detections by churning through a large set of domains and URLs, with domain flux and URL fluxing [11,26,38,25]. Researchers, in turn, noting that this behavior is generally associated with malicious sites, have used it as a detection feature [20,31]. These fluxing infrastructures are also being detected mining their topology [17], the redirection chains leading to them [24,40,21], and the traffic distributors' system feeding them a stream of users to exploit [22].

Studies on Human Scamming. Another direction of research concentrates on why humans get scammed. Sheng et al. have proposed a game [37] that teaches people about how not to get scammed. Later, demographic studies have shown that education is effective in reducing the efficacy of scams [36], but it does not solve the problem alone. Wu et al. show that security toolbars do not help the users in their assessments [45]. In 2014, Neupane et al. [29] have taken these studies a step further, using fMRIs to analyze how the brain responds to phishing sites and browser countermeasures.

Browser Phishing Warnings. Traditional browser solutions to help users be aware of the phish, such as domain highlighting and phishing warnings, have shown to be not very effective [23,29]. To better inform users, researchers have proposed in-browser protection systems. Spoofguard [5] verifies that user sensitive data is not passed to sites with similar sounding domain names and that contain similar images. AntiPhish [19] tracks sensitive information and informs the user whenever those are given to any untrusted website. DOMAntiPhish [33] alerts the user whenever she visits a phishing site with a layout similar to a trusted website. All these solutions help in preventing that the user is deceived in trusting a site similar to a known site she used in the past, but they do not prevent against other categories of scams, such as fake pharmacies and rogue antiviruses [7,39]. In contrast, our system is able to track advanced, previously unseen phishing attacks.

Content Analysis. The idea of extracting text from images through OCR has been investigated in the context of e-mail spam [10]. These scams use "salting" tricks to confuse analyzers while still getting the right message to humans [4]. To counter this, researchers have proposed ways to track concept drift [8], which spammers use to thwart frequency-based content analysis. Comprehensive studies on content analysis have been proposed both for spam [30] and phishing sites [46,50]. Google is also performing phishing detection through content analysis [44], and researchers have used the search engine's index to identify scams campaigns with similar content [16]. In contrast, our system aims to identify the advanced phishing attacks that evade these content-based solutions, obfuscating their content to be resilient to static analyzers.

Visual Analysis. Phishing pages have been identified through image shingling [1], which involves fragmenting screenshots of the phishing sites into small images, and clustering the sites according to the fraction of identical images. This solution is attractive because it is resilient to small changes in the phishing site, as long as the overall template is not altered. Previous solutions involve clustering according to colors, fonts, and layout [27] to identify phishing sites visually similar to trusted sites. Hara et al. [15] show that, given a large enough dataset of phishing sites, it is possible to automatically infer the site they are mimicking. These solutions are effective as long as the phishing attack is trying to mimic the aspect of a trusted website, but they do not cover other scam categories, such as fake pharmacies, dubious online retailers, or rogue antiviruses. In contrast, our approach uses visual analysis to identify a dead giveaway of a scam: a fake security seal. Scammers use these seals to claim to be a legitimate business, even though the company generating these security seals has not assessed the scammers' business (and often does not even exist). Focusing on these seals, we can identify scamming sites that do not try to mimic a legitimate site, but are still effective in deceiving the user.

3   Dataset

Throughout the paper, we will refer to a dataset comprising the home pages of the 81,000 most popular websites according to the Alexa popularity ranking, as a baseline of benign pages. We obtained the remaining 68,000 pages from the Wepawet online analyzer [43,6].

Wepawet receives submissions from a variety of sources, including a large volume of URLs from automated feeds, both benign and malicious. As such, it represents a reasonable sample of pages that a security tool would be called to examine in practice. Notice that we used Wepawet merely as a feed of active URLs, without considering the results of its analysis.

In particular, we obtained two feeds: The first was an archive of 18,700 pages pre-filtered (via a simple keyword search in the URL) to contain a large number of fake antivirus (fake AV, [39,32]) pages, so that we could test our heuristics against this type of scam, regardless of Wepawet's ability to detect it. The second feed consisted of 50,000 submitted URLs, received in real-time so we could immediately perform our analysis on them.

Table 1. Reference truth data for the 50,000 received submissions

Page type	Samples	Percent
Pharmacy scam campaigns	2431 ± 215	$4.87 \pm 0.43\%$
"Blackhole" exploit kit	140 ± 52	$0.28 \pm 0.10\%$
Updated version of the "Blackhole" exploit kit	47 ± 29	$0.09 \pm 0.06\%$
Fake video codec scam campaign	327 ± 80	$0.65 \pm 0.16\%$
Other pages with questionable content	196 ± 62	$0.39 \pm 0.12\%$
Total number of malicious or questionable samples	3075 ± 239	$6.16 \pm 0.48\%$
Total number of benign samples	46834 ± 241	$93.79 \pm 0.48\%$

This last subset will be the basis of our final evaluation, and, as expected for a random selection, it contains a number of common scams, exploit kits, and a majority (around 94%) of benign samples. We obtained truth data for this feed through a manual review: Table 1 details our findings. For obvious time reasons, we could not examine all 50,000 pages: we opted instead for a random sample of 3,000 from which we extrapolate the totals on the entire set within a reasonable margin (Wilson confidence intervals, 85% confidence). Whenever we present these numbers, we will express them as $x \pm m$, indicating the interval $(x - m, x + m)$.

We encountered several samples with suspicious characteristics, but for which a clear benign-malicious verdict would have required a full investigation of the service provided (i.e., a "proxy service," found at several URLs under different names, and without any stated policy or identification). We marked these samples as "questionable" and have excluded them from benign and malicious sample counts.

4   Content Obfuscation

As mentioned in the introduction, many automated systems parse web pages: Examples include organizations performing large-scale crawling of the Internet or online analyzers that must evaluate the benign or malicious nature of a page within a certain time limit. These systems should view and "interpret" pages exactly like a human would, but in practice they may have to compromise accuracy in order to save bandwidth (e.g., by not downloading images) or processing time (e.g., by ignoring JavaScript, not building the actual layout of the page, not applying style sheets, etc.).

In general, content can be considered obfuscated if it would be easily seen and interpreted by the average computer user, but would be hard to interpret without simulating a full browser and the interaction of a human with it.

To refine this definition, we need to consider how automated crawlers parse pages. Details can vary a lot, but we can pick a meaningful upper bound on automated extraction capabilities and use it to differentiate the two views of a page. In particular, we conjecture that JavaScript will be a problematic feature for programs to consider, and one that many will sacrifice.

Our intuition is motivated by the consideration that analyzing a static page can be assumed to take a time that is roughly a function of its size, while executing arbitrary code introduces an unpredictable delay in the analysis. Moreover, since JavaScript code can interact with other elements on the page, the entire content must be kept in memory during the analysis (as opposed to discarding content that has already been consumed).

It is impossible to directly gauge how many web analyzers and crawlers avoid JavaScript, although, as mentioned, many search engines do provide guidelines for webmasters that are consistent with the necessity to expose content to spiders that ignore JavaScript [14,28,47] and images [12,28,48], and many published detection systems use static signature matching (e.g., [30,35,42]). The choice of this boundary between the "human-browser" world and the "automated-parser" world has also been indirectly confirmed by our findings presented in Section 4.3: Many pages (both benign and malicious) use JavaScript code to hide information they do not want exposed to automated parsers.

4.1 Heuristic

Several encapsulation and encoding schemes are used to transfer text on the web. A banking web site might, for example, provide content encoded in UTF-8, compressed by the server with *gzip* and transferred over a TLS connection. From the point of view of the client, however, these schemes are completely transparent: once the encoding layers are removed, a well-defined payload is reached for every data transfer.

A key observation is that text will almost always appear as-is in the payload.

In the simplest case an HTML page will be retrieved from the network, its content will be parsed in a tree, a layout will be constructed, and the resulting page will be presented to the user. The browser will simply copy the content of text nodes from the original payload, HTML entities being the only exception to this rule.

Web pages can also use scripts to dynamically add content to the page tree. This content may have already been present in the original payload (as a JavaScript string literal, for example), or it may come from additional network requests. This text does not have to be sent as-is: the script that loads the text is free to mangle and re-code it as it sees fit. There is, however, little reason to do so, and it seems safe to assume that legitimate websites will never engage in such practices: In fact, by comparing the dynamically constructed page with the observed payloads, we have been able to confirm that textual data is transferred as-is in the vast majority of cases.

There are a few fundamental reasons for this. For purely textual content (at the sizes typically seen in web payloads), the built-in gzip compression is better, needs no extra code transfers, and is far easier to use than custom code; in fact, none of the JavaScript code compression tools in popular use significantly alter string literals. Popular data transfer formats such as JSON and XML are also text-based. There is also a historical preference for human-readable data on the web (the HTTP protocol itself is an example), both to help debugging and to ease interoperability.

While we have observed some overly-cautious escaping of content, most cases where text was not transferred as-is were due to deliberate obfuscation attempts.

One can certainly devise obfuscation systems that necessarily require human interaction and would hide text from this and any other automated detection attempt: For example, the sensitive content can be encrypted and the password presented in an image that cannot be easily parsed automatically (using, for example, the same obfuscation techniques used for CAPTCHA test images). However, this involves asking victims to perform a task that is difficult to automate. Therefore, these techniques necessarily create significant inconvenience for the intended targets, who may not have a particularly strong motivation to interact with an almost-empty page (content shown before the verification is also available to automated analyzers) if it requires effort on their part. These kinds of expedients would also strongly differentiate the page from regular benign sites, even in the eye of an untrained user, so they are unlikely to be used in fraudulent pages and were not observed in our dataset.

4.2 Implementation

Based on the discussion above, we detect content obfuscation by first building an extractor that page authors expect to face (e.g., a static text parser) and a more powerful one (e.g., a full browser), and then observing the differences in the extracted contents.

Our detector is based on the popular Firefox web browser, modified in order to observe and record all network requests and the context in which they were made. We also store the DOM tree of the page (including frames) and take a screenshot of the website as it would be seen by a human user. Finally, the browser has been modified to automatically confirm all file save request and dismiss all JavaScript popups. While using a real web browser may be slower and less safe than using an ad-hoc solution, it also makes the simulation much more realistic and helps us avoid being fingerprinted by an attacker. The browser visits the page in a temporary VM, and is fully automated.

The system uses two viewpoints to check for text on the web page. First, the text present in the DOM tree is normalized by replacing HTML entities and URL-encoded characters, removing non-alphabetic characters, and transforming all text to lowercase. Then, the text that is present in network payloads is parsed and decoded using information recorded from the browser (for example, unzipped), and then normalized in the same way.

For every word in the body of the page (text of the DOM tree), an origin is sought in the network payloads. In particular, the presence of a word is considered "justified" if it satisfies one of the following conditions:

1. It appears as-is in the body of one of the responses from the server, including AJAX requests, requests made from iframes, etc. This rule matches most regular text.
2. It appears in one of the URLs (e.g., as part of the domain name, in the query string, etc). This rule takes care of pages that display information that is passed to them via the URL and access it via the `location` object.
3. It appears in one of the HTTP headers, which are readable by JavaScript for AJAX requests.
4. It can be obtained from the previously-mentioned sources:
   (a) as the concatenation of two words,
   (b) as the truncation of another word.
5. It is found in a whitelist of words that can be obtained directly from the JavaScript language interpreter, including type names like *none* or *HTML-ParagraphElement*, date components (e.g., month names), strings from the navigator object, etc.

These rules attempt to construct a set of benign clear-text sources that would be easily exposed to a static signature matcher, anticipate most real-world string operations (that any signature matching algorithm can and probably should take into account), and consider all page components that would possibly be exposed. Words for which an origin could not be pinpointed are considered obfuscated. For simplicity, our heuristic operates on single words only, and leaves the extension to sequences to the signature generator (Section 6.1). Purely image-based obfuscation approaches would also escape our textual detector and would require image-processing techniques for detection: similarly, we left this extension to our proof-of-concept signature matcher (Section 6.2).

The previously-described extraction rules are also applied to the domain names of URLs present in HTML attributes. This allows us to catch cases of pages that try to hide from programs the URL to which they will redirect a human viewer. Notice that text from a DOM tree is analyzed considering only network payloads that have been seen before it was retrieved, so the presence of links in a page cannot be justified with future HTTP headers.

In principle, our algorithm would also work for scripts and style sheets, but such analysis is out of scope for this paper: ordinary human users do not "parse" them, nor are they aware of their existence.[1]

4.3 Evaluation of the Detection of Obfuscated Content

Table 2 presents the samples for which we found obfuscated content (the benign, malicious, or questionable nature was established by manual review).

While obviously not perfect, our heuristic presented very few false positives in the detection of obfuscated content (that is, content incorrectly marked as

---

[1] Of course, a possible extension of our work would be to consider the two "views" of a malware analyst and of a web browser. As an example, in this model JavaScript obfuscation would be a case of content easily interpreted by a browser but cumbersome for a human to understand.

obfuscated, regardless of the benign or malicious nature of the page) in our dataset. These were often caused by incorrect parsing of the network payload, as in some cases it is difficult to replicate the exact parsing the browser will perform: unclear specifications, buggy servers, and sloppy page coding practices require browsers to rely on several heuristics, and previous research has shown that different clients can even give different interpretations to the same data [2]; it should be noted, however, that the desire to increase the number of victims can be a mitigation factor for this issue, especially for frauds: their authors have an interest in having them functional on all major browsers.

Table 2. Samples found by the content obfuscation heuristic, grouped by source

Source	Page type	Samples	In-Feed Pct.	Global Pct.
Alexa ranking (81,000 samples)	Benign	52	90%	0.06%
	Questionable	3	5.2%	0.004%
	Malicious	3	5.2%	0.004%
	total	*58*	*100%*	*0.07%*
Fake AV feed (18,700 samples)	Benign	1	0.93%	0.005%
	Questionable	4	3.7%	0.02%
	Malicious	102	95%	0.54%
	total	*107*	*100%*	*0.57%*
Received submissions (50,000 samples)	Benign	3	3.1%	0.006%
	Questionable	0	0%	0%
	Malicious	94	97%	0.19%
	total	*97*	*100%*	*0.2%*
All feeds (149,700 samples)	Benign	56	21%	0.037%
	Questionable	7	2.7%	0.005%
	Malicious	199	76%	0.13%
	total	*262*	*100%*	*0.18%*

Manual review of the 3,000 randomly selected samples from the 50,000 submissions received in real-time (Section 3), utilizing the screenshots and assisted by Optical Character Recognition software, did not uncover any false negative (obfuscated content not marked as such).

4.4   Observed Uses of Obfuscation

Even a simple `unescape` is enough to hide content from a straightforward HTML parser, and many examples in our dataset did not go much further than that. Code from exploit kits and fake antivirus scams, on the other hand, went to great lengths to obfuscate both the content and the generating script.

Beside fraudulent content, the following categories of text were commonly observed in obfuscated form:

- **E-mail addresses:** A precaution against address-harvesting spam bots. To avoid these false positives, our heuristic ignores all `mailto:` links and strings that look like e-mail addresses.

- **Domain names:** A pharmacy scam campaign and several exploit kits presented landing pages with redirection code. The target URL was obfuscated, presumably to slow down blacklist-building crawlers and human analysts.
- **Links:** Some benign websites obfuscated hyperlinks to other pages or websites, including seemingly innocuous links such as those to contact information and the terms of service. This is probably done to make sure that search engines do not focus on pages that are perceived as not significant by the webmaster; this particular technique may be an answer to Google's de-emphasizing of the `nofollow` attribute [9].

Our detector does not mark pages as questionably obfuscated if e-mail and links are the sole hidden content types, as these kinds of obfuscation are also used in benign sites.

Obfuscated target URLs, on the other hand, are definitely a strong signal of malicious content. However, the specific URLs are highly variable, easily changed, and not necessarily exposed to the user (who will likely only view and act on the first URL in the redirect chain), so they have also been ignored for the purposes of our proof-of-concept detector.

4.5   From Obfuscation Detection to Maliciousness Detection

As mentioned, our simple heuristic is, in itself, an indication that a page may contain suspicious content, but is not entirely reliable as a maliciousness detector in itself.

It does, however, find content that the page author wanted to hide: a good starting point for a more punctual detection of maliciousness. In our study, we chose to exploit the fact that cybercriminals typically run campaigns (they typically prepare many variations that implement a certain scheme) or implement general fraud schemes (such as fake pharmacies or fake antiviruses), whereas benign usages are much more likely to appear as outliers.

To this end, we leveraged obfuscated words as features for each page. Several methods exist to eliminate outliers: we opted for density-based clustering (DB-SCAN), as it performs well and can be fully automated for this purpose as long as known-benign obfuscated samples are available.[2]

This step is not strictly necessary, as far as finding interesting and suspicious pages: Without further refinement, the heuristic already pointed to 199 truly malicious pages (and 56 benign ones), many of which were not originally found by

---

[2] Specifically, we rely on the presence of a few samples originated from the Alexa set for our purposes: Intuitively we want the clustering to consider them as "noise," so (for the purpose of this step) we classify them as "benign" and everything else as "malicious". With this assignment, we have a rough estimate of how good each possible clustering is (using, for instance, the F_1 score) at discriminating between benign and malicious samples. At this point, a simple grid search can find the values for the two DBSCAN parameters (the point neighborhood size ε and the minimum cluster size) that maximize this estimated score. On Table 2's data, 0.82 and 3 were found by the grid search; the corresponding clustering is shown in Table 3.

Table 3. Samples found by the content obfuscation heuristic, automatically grouped by cluster and de-noised leveraging the obfuscated words that were detected

	Page type	Samples
Cluster 1	"Blackhole" exploit kit	41
Cluster 2	First fake-AV campaign	23
Cluster 3	"Blackhole" exploit kit	20
Cluster 4	First fake-AV campaign (minor variation)	16
Cluster 5	Second fake-AV campaign	5
Cluster 6	Third fake-AV campaign	9
Cluster 7	Updated version of the "Blackhole" exploit kit	12
Cluster 8	False positives	4
Cluster 9	Fake flash player campaign	4
Cluster 10	"Blackhole" exploit kit	12
Cluster 11	False positives	3
Cluster 12	Third fake-AV campaign (minor variation)	15
Cluster 13	Third fake-AV campaign (minor variation)	20
Cluster 14	Third fake-AV campaign (minor variation)	4
Cluster 15	Updated version of the "Blackhole" exploit kit	8
Cluster 16	False positives	3
Cluster 17	False positives	3
Samples discarded as noise	7 questionable, 3 fake-AV campaigns (all minor variations of the campaigns above), 3 pharmacy scams, 1 "Blackhole" exploit kit (bugged sample), 3 "get rich quick" scams, and 43 benign	60

Wepawet's analysis, especially among the scam campaigns that did not leverage any browser vulnerability.[3]

However, we found this step very useful both for our manual analysis and for a more punctual malicious content detection. Its results are presented in Table 3, which also serves as a recap of the nature of the pages found by the heuristic of this section. Confirming the validity of our intuition that most benign pages would appear as outliers, this clustering step was able to achieve a precision of 93.56% and a recall 94.97% in finding malicious pages among the samples that presented obfuscation.

The false positives are multiple benign sites that were obfuscating a few similar words, usually for search engine optimization purposes. All fake antivirus campaigns present in the dataset were identified correctly. As mentioned, pages from two well-known exploit kits were also identified.

---

[3] Interestingly, while reviewing the pages that were found, we even encountered several that appeared to be generated by an exploit kit, although Wepawet had not detected them as such. Further review revealed that these pages, generated by the "Blackhole" exploit kit, were fingerprinting Wepawet's JavaScript engine and disabling their malicious payload to escape detection.

As expected, campaigns tend to emerge as distinct clusters. Incidentally, we have observed a certain number of minor variations, updates, or bugs within the same campaign or usage of exploit kits: this tends to surface as a splitting of a campaign in a few distinct clusters.

5   Counterfeit Certification Seals

Our second heuristic explores an attempt to confuse human consumers without attempting to deceive automated analyzers.

In particular, we observed that in many cases scammers try to make their pages appear more legitimate by including certification seals: small images meant to convey that the site has passed a review by a trusted third party. These seals are also often displayed by legitimate online sellers to reassure users about the safety of their data. Reputable companies releasing these certifications include Symantec, GeoTrust, McAfee and other well-known certification authorities and vendors of security software.

No standard mandates the exact meaning of the certification. Some issuers just claim to periodically check the website for malware, others are meant to fully verify that the site is owned by a reputable business entity. In all cases, seals are included to make visitors more comfortable (and presumably more likely to spend time or money on the site). As such, their counterfeiting is attractive for fraudsters, even if no computer program would "understand" them or consider them in any way.

5.1   Use by Fraudsters

Unfortunately, there are also no standards on how certification seals should be included in a page and how an end user can verify their legitimacy. Unlike HTTPS certificates, browsers cannot check them on the user's behalf, as the seal is usually just another image on the page.

Issuers can mandate certain technical measures in their usage policies, such as the requirement to include a script served from an authority's server [41]. Typically, correctly included seals should react to clicks by opening a verification page hosted by the issuer.

Nothing, however, prevents a malicious seller from simply copying the seal image from a legitimate site and displaying it on a fraudulent page. Should someone click on the seal to verify it, the scammer can simply present a locally-hosted fake certification. Unless the end user specifically checks the certification page origin (and knows the correct domain name of the authority that issues the seal in question), the page will look legitimate.

Given the ease of including a copied image and the low risk of detection by untrained users, fraud perpetrators often display copious amounts of certification seals on their pages, especially on online shops such as rogue pharmacies. Figure 1 shows a few examples.

Fig. 1. Examples of counterfeit certification seals found on rogue pharmacy sites

Seal images can be completely made-up and refer to no established third-party, present alterations of logos of real certification authorities [3] or, as we most commonly observed, present copies of actual logos and faked certification pages.

5.2   Heuristic

For our study, we augmented the system described in Section 4.2 with a component that calculates a perceptual hash [49] (for resilience against small alterations) of all images with a size comparable to the ones typically used for certification seals, compares them with the known ones, and checks if they are legitimate or not.

There are few legitimate seal providers: a manual review of their terms of services and inclusion practices would allow constructing a fully reliable detector, if desired. As expected for a deception technique exclusively directed toward humans, we did not observe any attempt to hide its use from even a simple analyzer. Therefore, we opted again for a fully-automated approach in our survey: we performed optical character recognition on the 100 most common images (as aggregated by the perceptual hashing function) and looked for keywords expressing trust and protection such as "secured," "approved," "trust," and "license" to find seals, and check legitimacy simply by verifying if they link off-site or not: an imperfect approach that however highlights how easy it can be for a program to detect purely human-directed deception attempts.

While not uncovering all frauds in our dataset (not all of them use these fake seals, nor does our heuristic cover all of these images), this simple heuristic correctly flagged about 400 samples, with no false positives. All these samples originated from rogue pharmacy campaigns and, as we will show in the next section, proved to be a valuable starting point for a detector of this entire category of scams.

6   Proof-of-concept General Detector

As we have seen, the difference between a human view and an algorithmic view can indeed be useful in pointing out malicious pages, even with two simple heuristics such as ours. Of particular note is its tendency to find "pure" scam campaigns that do not involve software exploits, yet succeed due to deception.

In this section we will show if these heuristics could be useful to a complete maliciousness detection suite, in particular by seeing if the pages they uncover could enable finding more. To this end, we implemented a proof-of-concept detector that uses them as its only starting point, and we will show how it can already reach significant detection rates. It is fairly standard in its construction (signature generation and matching), but we will also use it to exemplify a similarity measure that gives a different "weight" to certain words (the ones that were obfuscated, in our case) and is resilient to the inclusion of extraneous text, as we have observed this happens with a certain frequency in scam pages when they are part of a larger page (posts in hijacked forums are an example). Incidentally, this approach would also defend against fraudsters including large amounts of irrelevant text specifically to thwart automated analysis, even if it was presented in such a way that humans would not pay attention to it (i.e., in a semi-invisible color, at the end of a long page, out of view, ...).

6.1   Signature Generation

The clusters in Table 3, with the addition of the pages detected due to seal counterfeiting, serve as the basis to generate signatures. In particular, our system tries to identify contiguous regions of text that are "typical" of a cluster, to maximize the impact of common textual elements (presumably core to the nature of those pages), while de-emphasizing regions that are variable among the different samples: A score is assigned to each word present in pages belonging to the cluster. The score is initially the number of occurrences of the word in the samples, doubled if the word was obfuscated; scores are then normalized to have zero-average (to further reduce noise, we also exclude the 100 most common English words). All the maximal-scoring contiguous regions of text are then found (this operation has linear-time complexity [34]) and identical regions are aggregated to form the "signature" regions for that cluster.

As an example, for the cluster of a simple fake-AV campaign that included a few variations, the following regions were chosen: `center initializing virus protection system`, `initializing virus protection system`, `initializing treat protection system.`, whereas for a pharmacy scam regions included both the entire common content of the typical sales page, and smaller text snippets that were present in many, but not all pages (mainly, the type of drugs sold in specific subpages).

6.2   Signature Matching

When presented with a sample, our proof-of-concept detector will perform a fuzzy matching with the signature regions, to find other similar but unknown campaigns.

Simple textual similarity measures (i.e., the Jaccard coefficient) weight the amount of common elements versus the amount of uncommon ones. As mentioned, we will propose here a slightly different approach that is more resilient to the inclusion of unrelated random words in the page, as we consider this a good property when faced with content that exclusively tries to deceive humans: in those cases, a small amount of information could very well be sufficient.

In particular, when evaluating a page:

1. A candidate match m_i is found for each of the n signature regions s_i (longest matching subsequence in the page text).[4]
2. The Jaccard distance d_i is computed for each (m_i, s_i) pair.
3. The distance of the page to the clusters is computed: $d = \min \{d_1 \ldots d_n\}$.

Notice that with this method only one zone of the page influences the final result: the one that is most similar to one of the clusters. Therefore, as opposed to inserting disturbances anywhere, an author that wished to avoid detection would have to modify several words right in the middle of their most relevant content, likely changing the message perceived by a potential victim.

At this point we can mark a page as benign or malicious based, using a threshold on d. To make sure the threshold is neither too low nor too high, we used a separate training phase to select a good value.[5]

To exemplify extra robustness precautions that would be included in a complete detector, we added two image-based matching systems based on a page screenshot. One recovered text through Optical Character Recognition (which can then be used as normal HTML text), the other directly compared the page screenshot with those of the pages found by the two heuristics.

6.3 Evaluation

We evaluate the overall performance of our proof-of-concept system on the (otherwise unlabeled) 50,000 samples obtained from real-time submissions. As mentioned in Section 3, this set includes a variety of scam sites, traditional drive-by download exploit pages, and benign pages.

Table 4 provides a numerical overview of its performance. Overall, the system flagged 1,833 pages as malicious. Based on manual analysis of these instances, we confirmed 1,746 cases as true positives (first line): a significant increase from the 95 detected by the content obfuscation heuristic (Table 2) and the 400 detected by the seal-counterfeiting one; the remaining 87 flagged pages were incorrect

---

[4] If desired, each match m_i could also be enlarged by a percentage to achieve extra resiliency against the insertion of random "stopping" words in the middle of an otherwise matching page section.

[5] We used a procedure similar, in its principle, to the one employed in Section 4.5: Pages from the Alexa feed were all marked as benign, then a well-scoring threshold value was computed for each cluster. Again, those known-benign pages are used to get a rough estimate of the amount of false positives that each given value would cause. A linear search is then used, starting from a low threshold value and increasing it until the false positive rate surpasses a certain percentage: 2%, in our case. We protect from possible outliers in the Alexa feed by requiring the presence of at least three of its samples before the search is terminated. While this procedure requires a sizable number of benign samples, it is applicable in many cases: such samples are easily gathered from widely-available rankings or website directories.

detections of benign pages (second line). As anticipated in Section 3, negatives are expressed as confidence intervals (lines three and four, and dependent scoring values in the remaining lines).

Table 4. Performance of the proof-of-concept detector

True positives (flagged, malicious)	1,746
False positives (flagged, benign)	87
True negatives (not flagged, benign)	$47,524 \pm 192$
False negatives (not flagged, malicious)	643 ± 192
Precision	95.25%
Recall	$73.08 \pm 5.86\%$
F_1 *score*	$82.69 \pm 3.75\%$
True positive rate	$73.08 \pm 5.86\%$
False positives rate	$0.18 \pm 0.00\%$

True positives included pharmacy scams from several different campaigns or sellers and many fake-AV variants, underlining how the findings from these heuristics generalize well and improve detection (most scam campaigns, for instance, were not originally marked as suspicious or malicious by Wepawet). Examples of false negatives are posts on hijacked forums that contained relatively little malicious content, or scams that significantly differed from the samples found by our two simple heuristics. For cases where the samples were related (although quite different and possibly originating from different criminal operations), our system showed excellent detection.

While not enough to create a complete security system, these results confirm our intuition that detection of this "view difference" (even in the two simple heuristic forms we presented) can be a useful addition to many analyzers. As an example, referring to Table 1, a honeyclient or exploit-based detector is unlikely to catch the (otherwise very common) scam campaigns without a method such as ours.

Finally, we note that even just removing content obfuscation and counterfeit certifications from the fraudsters' tool arsenal could be a desirable result in itself. In fact, a general property of heuristic like ours is that they present attackers with a problematic choice: from their point of view, if they choose to exploit the difference between the two "worlds" of programs and humans they risk giving away the nature of their operation (and possibly uncover other similar scams). Presenting the same information to humans and programs, on the other hand, will make it easy for security researchers to construct reliable signatures for the malicious campaign and quickly reduce its impact.

7   Conclusions

In this paper we pointed out how the discrepancy between the understanding of a human and a program can present both a danger (as a way for cybercriminals to escape analysis) and a maliciousness-detection opportunity at the same time. We presented two heuristics that detect cases that exemplify this situation: one directed toward textual content and one involving images, respectively countering the deception of static analyzers and of human beings.

Envisioning that these detection methods can complement existing detection tools, we have implemented a proof-of-concept detector based exclusively on these methods to discover online malicious pages. This tool alone was able to achieve a 95% precision and a 73% recall in our dataset, and was able to discover a high number of human-directed fraud pages that would otherwise be outside the detection capabilities of most traditional malware analyzers.

Acknowledgments. We would like to thank Davide Paltrinieri for his help and ABBYY for providing the OCR software.

This work was supported by the Office of Naval Research (ONR) under Grant N000140911042, the Army Research Office (ARO) under grant W911NF0910553, and Secure Business Austria. Any opinions, findings, and conclusions or recommendations expressed in this publication are those of the authors and do not necessarily reflect the views of the Office of Naval Research, the Army Research Office, or Secure Business Austria.

References

1. Anderson, D.S., Fleizach, C., Savage, S., Voelker, G.M.: Spamscatter: Characterizing Internet Scam Hosting Infrastructure. In: Proceedings of the USENIX Security Symposium (2007)
2. Barth, A., Caballero, J., Song, D.: Secure Content Sniffing for Web Browsers, or How to Stop Papers from Reviewing Themselves. In: Proceedings of the 30th IEEE Symposium on Security and Privacy. IEEE (2009)
3. Bate, R., Jin, G., Mathur, A.: In Whom We Trust: The Role of Certification Agencies in Online Drug Markets. NBER working paper 17955 (2012)
4. Bergholz, A., Paass, G., Reichartz, F., Strobel, S., Moens, M.F., Witten, B.: Detecting Known and New Salting Tricks in Unwanted Emails. In: Proceedings of the Conference on Email and Anti-Spam, CEAS (2008)
5. Chou, N., Ledesma, R., Teraguchi, Y., Mitchell, J.C.: Client-side Defense Against Web-Based Identity Theft. In: Proceedings of the Network and Distributed System Security Symposium, NDSS (2004)
6. Cova, M., Kruegel, C., Vigna, G.: Detection and Analysis of Drive-by-download Attacks and Malicious JavaScript code. In: Proceedings of the World Wide Web Conference, WWW (2010)
7. Cova, M., Leita, C., Thonnard, O., Keromytis, A.D., Dacier, M.: An Analysis of Rogue AV Campaigns. In: Jha, S., Sommer, R., Kreibich, C. (eds.) RAID 2010. LNCS, vol. 6307, pp. 442–463. Springer, Heidelberg (2010)
8. Cunningham, P., Nowlan, N., Delany, S.J., Haahr, M.: A Case-Based Approach to Spam Filtering that Can Track Concept Drift. Knowledge-Based Systems (2005)
9. Cutts, M.: Pagerank sculpting (2009), http://www.mattcutts.com/blog/pagerank-sculpting/

10. Fumera, G., Pillai, I., Roli, F.: Spam Filtering Based on the Analysis of Text Information Embedded into Images. The Journal of Machine Learning Research 7, 2699–2720 (2006)

11. Garera, S., Provos, N., Chew, M., Rubin, A.D.: A Framework for Detection and Measurement of Phishing Attacks. In: Proceedings of the ACM Workshop on Recurring Malcode, WORM (2007)

12. Google Inc.: Image publishing guidelines (2012), http://support.google.com/webmasters/bin/answer.py?hl=en&answer=114016

13. Google Inc.: Making AJAX Applications Crawable (2014), https://developers.google.com/webmasters/ajax-crawling/

14. Google Inc.: Webmaster Guidelines (2014), http://support.google.com/webmasters/bin/answer.py?hl=en&answer=35769#2

15. Hara, M., Yamada, A., Miyake, Y.: Visual Similarity-Based Phishing Detection without Victim Site Information. In: Proceedings of the IEEE Symposium on Computational Intelligence in Cyber Security (CICS), pp. 30–36. IEEE (March 2009)

16. Invernizzi, L., Benvenuti, S., Comparetti, P.M., Cova, M., Kruegel, C., Vigna, G.: EVILSEED: A Guided Approach to Finding Malicious Web Pages. In: Proceedings of the IEEE Symposium on Security and Privacy, S&P (2012)

17. Invernizzi, L., Miskovic, S., Torres, R., Saha, S., Lee, S.J., Mellia, M., Kruegel, C., Vigna, G.: Nazca: Detecting Malware Distribution in Large-Scale Networks. In: Proceedings of the Network and Distributed System Security Symposium, NDSS (2014)

18. Kapravelos, A., Shoshitaishvili, Y., Cova, M., Kruegel, C., Vigna, G.: Revolver: An Automated Approach to the Detection of Evasive Web-based Malware. In: Proceedings of the USENIX Security Symposium (2013)

19. Kirda, E., Kruegel, C.: Protecting Users Against Phishing Attacks with AntiPhish. In: Proceedings of the International Conference on Computer Software and Applications (COMPSAC), vol. 1, pp. 517–524. IEEE (2005)

20. Konte, M., Feamster, N., Jung, J.: Fast Flux Service Networks: Dynamics and Roles in Hosting Online Scams. Tech. rep., Georgia Institute of Technology and Intel Research (2008)

21. Lee, S., Kim, J.: WarningBird: Detecting Suspicious URLs in Twitter Stream. In: Proceedings of the Network and Distributed System Security Symposium, NDSS (2010)

22. Li, Z., Alrwais, S., Xie, Y., Yu, F., Wang, X.: Finding the Linchpins of the Dark Web: A Study on Topologically Dedicated Hosts on Malicious Web Infrastructures. In: Proceedings of the IEEE Symposium on Security and Privacy (S&P), pp. 112–126 (May 2013)

23. Lin, E., Greenberg, S., Trotter, E., Ma, D., Aycock, J.: Does Domain Highlighting Help People Identify Phishing Sites? In: Proceedings of the Conference on Human Factors in Computing Systems (CHI), p. 2075. ACM Press, New York (2011)

24. Lu, L., Perdisci, R., Lee, W.: SURF: Detecting and Measuring Search Poisoning Categories. In: Proceedings of the ACM Conference on Computer and Communications Security, CCS (2011)

25. Jung, J., Milito, R.A., Paxson, V.: On the Effectiveness of Techniques to Detect Phishing Sites. In: Hämmerli, B.M., Sommer, R. (eds.) DIMVA 2007. LNCS, vol. 4579, pp. 20–39. Springer, Heidelberg (2007)

26. Mcgrath, D.K., Gupta, M.: Behind Phishing: An Examination of Phisher Modi Operandi. In: Proceedings of the USENIX Workshop on Large-Scale Exploits and Emergent Threats, LEET (2008)

27. Medvet, E., Kirda, E., Kruegel, C.: Visual-Similarity-Based Phishing Detection. In: Proceedings of the International Conference on Security and Privacy in Communication Networks (SecureComm), p. 1. ACM Press, New York (2008)
28. Microsoft Corp.: Bing Webmaster Guidelines (2014), http://www.bing.com/webmaster/help/webmaster-guidelines-30fba23a
29. Neupane, A., Saxena, N., Kuruvilla, K., Georgescu, M., Kana, R.: Neural Signatures of User-Centered Security: An fMRI Study of Phishing, and Malware Warnings. In: Proceedings of the Network and Distributed System Security Symposium (NDSS). pp. 1–16 (2014)
30. Ntoulas, A., Hall, B., Najork, M., Manasse, M., Fetterly, D.: Detecting Spam Web Pages through Content Analysis. In: Proceedings of the International World Wide Web Conference (WWW), pp. 83–92 (2006)
31. Prakash, P., Kumar, M., Kompella, R.R., Gupta, M.: PhishNet: Predictive Blacklisting to Detect Phishing Attacks. In: Proceedings of the IEEE International Conference on Computer Communications (INFOCOM), pp. 1–5. IEEE (March 2010)
32. Rajab, M.A., Ballard, L., Marvrommatis, P., Provos, N., Zhao, X.: The Nocebo Effect on the Web: An Analysis of Fake Anti-Virus Distribution. In: Large-Scale Exploits and Emergent Threats, LEET (2010)
33. Rosiello, A.P.E., Kirda, E., Kruegel, C., Ferrandi, F.: A Layout-Similarity-Based Approach for Detecting Phishing Pages. In: Proceedings of the International Conference on Security and Privacy in Communication Networks, SecureComm (2007)
34. Ruzzo, W., Tompa, M.: A Linear Time Algorithm for Finding All Maximal Scoring Subsequences. In: Proceedings of the Seventh International Conference on Intelligent Systems for Molecular Biology. AAAI (1999)
35. Seifert, C., Welch, I., Komisarczuk, P.: Identification of Malicious Web Pages with Static Heuristics. In: Proceedings of the Australasian Telecommunication Networks and Applications Conference. IEEE (2008)
36. Sheng, S., Holbrook, M., Kumaraguru, P., Cranor, L., Downs, J.: Who Falls for Phish? A Demographic Analysis of Phishing Susceptibility and Effectiveness of Interventions. In: Proceedings of the Conference on Human Factors in Computing Systems (CHI), pp. 373–382 (2010)
37. Sheng, S., Magnien, B., Kumaraguru, P., Acquisti, A., Cranor, L.F., Hong, J., Nunge, E.: Anti-Phishing Phil: The Design and Evaluation of a Game That Teaches People Not to Fall for Phish. In: Proceedings of the Symposium on Usable Privacy and Security (SOUPS), pp. 88–99 (2007)
38. Sheng, S., Wardman, B., Warner, G., Cranor, L.F., Hong, J.: An Empirical Analysis of Phishing Blacklists. In: Proceedings of the Conference on Email and Anti-Spam, CEAS (2009)
39. Stone-Gross, B., Abman, R., Kemmerer, R., Kruegel, C., Steigerwald, D., Vigna, G.: The Underground Economy of Fake Antivirus Software. In: Proceedings of the Workshop on Economics of Information Security, WEIS (2011)
40. Stringhini, G., Kruegel, C., Vigna, G.: Shady Paths: Leveraging Surfing Crowds to Detect Malicious Web Pages. In: Proceedings of the ACM Conference on Computer and Communications Security, CCS (2013)
41. Symantec: Seal License Agreement (2014), https://www.symantec.com/content/en/us/about/media/repository/norton-secured-seal-license-agreement.pdf
42. Wang, D.Y., Savage, S., Voelker, G.M.: Cloak and Dagger: Dynamics of Web Search Cloaking. In: Proceedings of the ACM Conference on Computer and Communications Security (CCS), pp. 477–489 (2011)

43. Wepawet, http://wepawet.cs.ucsb.edu
44. Whittaker, C., Ryner, B., Nazif, M.: Large-Scale Automatic Classification of Phishing Pages. In: Proceedings of the Network and Distributed System Security Symposium, NDSS (2010)
45. Wu, M., Miller, R.C., Garfinkel, S.L.: Do Security Toolbars Actually Prevent Phishing Attacks? In: Proceedings of the Conference on Human Factors in Computing Systems (CHI), pp. 601–610 (2006)
46. Xiang, G., Hong, J., Rose, C.P., Cranor, L.: CANTINA+: A Feature-Rich Machine Learning Framework for Detecting Phishing Web Sites. In: ACM Transactions on Information and System Security, pp. 1–28 (2011)
47. Yandex, N.V.: Recommendations for webmasters - Common errors (2014), http://help.yandex.com/webmaster/recommendations/frequent-mistakes.xml
48. Yandex, N.V.: Recommendations for webmasters - Using graphic elements (2014), http://help.yandex.com/webmaster/recommendations/using-graphics.xml
49. Zauner, C.: Implementation and Benchmarking of Perceptual Image Hash Functions. Master's thesis, Upper Austria University of Applied Sciences, Hagenberg Campus (2010)
50. Zhang, Y., Hong, J., Cranor, L.: CANTINA: A Content-Based Approach to Detecting Phishing Web Sites. In: Proceedings of the ACM Conference on Computer and Communications Security, CCS (2007)

You Can't Be Me: Enabling Trusted Paths and User Sub-origins in Web Browsers

Enrico Budianto[1], Yaoqi Jia[1], Xinshu Dong[2], Prateek Saxena[1], and Zhenkai Liang[1]

[1] National University of Singapore
[2] Advanced Digital Sciences Center
{enricob,jiayaoqi,prateeks,liangzk}@comp.nus.edu.sg,
xinshu.dong@adsc.com.sg

Abstract. Once a web application authenticates a user, it loosely associates all resources owned by the user to the web session established. Consequently, any scripts injected into the victim web session attain unfettered access to user-owned resources, including scripts that commit malicious activities inside a web application. In this paper, we establish the first explicit notion of *user sub-origins* to defeat such attempts. Based on this notion, we propose a new solution called USERPATH to establish an end-to-end trusted path between web application users and web servers. To evaluate our solution, we implement a prototype in Chromium, and retrofit it to 20 popular web applications. USERPATH reduces the size of client-side TCB that has access to user-owned resources by 8x to 264x, with small developer effort.

Keywords: User sub-origins, trusted path, script injection attacks.

1 Introduction

Many of the web applications today, such as DropBox, Gmail and Facebook, provide user-oriented services, where users need to create their own accounts to use the service tailored to them. User-oriented web applications isolate data belonging to individual users and bind access control privileges to specific user accounts (e.g., owners or administrators). In such web applications, the authority of a user is typically represented by a web session, and the security mechanisms are centered on protecting the web session state from being accessed by attackers. In such a setting, if an attacker is able to inject scripts into the session, the scripts run with user's full authority. In this paper, we do not focus on mechanisms to prevent web application vulnerabilities from occurring. Rather, we propose mechanisms to defend against *post-attack* malicious behavior of an injected script, which we term as *post-injection script execution* (PISE) attacks. Our proposal serves as a second line of defense when existing mechanisms of script injection prevention, such as Content Security Policy [1], fail to achieve full coverage [2].

PISE attacks are the aftermath of script-injection attacks that occur in a variety of ways, such as mixed content (over HTTP) in HTTPS sessions [3], loading malicious third-party scripts [4], or via XSS attacks [5]. The threat model in PISE attacks is strong and challenging to counteract: injected scripts already run under the same origin as the web application. In this work, we focus on PISE attacks that target sensitive

A. Stavrou et al. (Eds.): RAID 2014, LNCS 8688, pp. 150–171, 2014.
© Springer International Publishing Switzerland 2014

data owned by users and mimic normal user interactions within a web application. For example, XSS worms on Facebook profiles that utilize self-XSS attacks to befriend certain users [6] or malicious extensions that stealthily steal authentication credentials and hijack user accounts [7] are some of the real-world examples.

We observe two fundamental limitations of the present web platform. First, to defeat PISE attacks, browsers need to have the notion of a *user authority* that controls access to sensitive user-owned resources. The *same-origin policy* does not support such access control. Second, there is no direct way for server-side web applications to be faithfully informed about user's interaction at the client-side. As a result, web servers cannot, for example, distinguish between web requests generated in response to legitimate user interaction versus requests generated by injected scripts, even in the presence of web sessions protection mechanisms like HTTPS. A recent line of research has proposed piecemeal defenses to mitigate some classes of PISE attacks via client-side channels [8, 9], server-side channels [10, 11], self-exfiltration [12], or using attacks that mimic user interactions to legitimize dangerous information flows [13]. However, none of them offer a comprehensive solution to prevent PISE attacks completely.

Our Solution. We propose a solution called USERPATH, which augments the present web platform with a security primitive that explicitly represents a *User* authority and establishes an end-to-end *trusted Path* between the user and the server. We introduce the first explicit notion of *user sub-origins*[1] into web applications, which are primitives that run with the authority of web application users. Our mechanism enables user sub-origins to isolate user's data and privilege-separate the code operating on it from the rest of the web origin. Thus, our mechanism tightens the authority of the web application users from web sessions to user-suborigins. To support our end-to-end system, we build a trusted path between human users and the web application server [15]. A trusted path in our work is defined as a privileged channel, which allows the server to tightly and reliably control the communication of visible content and input with the user (via the standard DOM APIs), even in the presence of malicious application code. Although this concept has recently been explored to develop new access control mechanisms on mobile and traditional operating systems [15, 16], building it for the web has only recently been investigated [9].

Our solution is easy to deploy in practice – with a small number of changes in existing browsers and web applications, USERPATH can be set up to protect users from PISE attacks. We reuse the existing web isolation primitives and minimize new abstractions added. Our solution is a 475 lines of code patched on Chromium 12. USERPATH-enabled browsers are backward-compatible with non-USERPATH-enabled websites. From the user's perspective, using a USERPATH-enabled website would be largely identical to the original site, except for verifying a colored login input box when authenticating with a password (see Section 4). As a result, USERPATH has a much lower adoption cost as compared to another recent trusted-path proposal that requires generation and uploading of SSL keys for every website [9]. Furthermore, our solution

---

[1] Recently, browsers have added support for per-page sub-origins [14] that compartmentalize contents on a web page within several sub-authorities under the same origin. The per-page sub-origin proposal offers no guarantee to defend against PISE attacks, and we complement per-page sub-origins with the additional notion of user authority and trusted path.

can also be easily deployed with modest development effort. Specifically, developers can easily retrofit web applications to use USERPATH simply by privilege-separating sensitive data and JavaScript logic on a client-side user-suborigins called UFrame. UFrame is an `iframe`-like component that isolates code under a different JavaScript context and has the ability to render tamper-proof HTML elements. Such privilege separation of JavaScript code is straightforward for developers to use, as argued in recent works [17, 18].

From a security standpoint, users no longer trust a website at the time of login if script injection vulnerabilities are present in the website. Then, how does a user login and setup an authenticated trusted path? We address this critical issue by introducing secure UI elements [16] that protect user's login credential from malicious client-side code and using a PAKE protocol [19]. A PAKE protocol is a *zero knowledge* protocol that lets two parties authenticate each other without revealing secret information (e.g., a password) through the communication channel. Having authenticated the user, USERPATH maintains isolation of sensitive resources throughout the session by resorting to user sub-origins and a trusted path.

Summary of Results. We deploy USERPATH on 20 popular open-source web applications. The evaluation demonstrates that our solution can protect user-owned data from PISE attacks in these applications with modest adoption effort (in the order of days). For each application, we label a number of data fields as sensitive, and modify the application logic to use USERPATH abstractions. We find that USERPATH eliminates the threats to user data from 325 historical security vulnerabilities in these applications, and reduces the trusted computing base (TCB) size by 8x to 264x. Finally, the performance overhead incurred by our solution is negligible for real-world applications. All case studies and the Chromium-based implementation are available online [20], and we release a video demonstrating the smooth user experience with a USERPATH-enabled browser [21].

Contributions. In summary, we make the following contributions in the paper:

- *End-to-end Solution.* Our main contribution lies in analyzing the attack model we term as PISE attacks, examining the various dimensions of attacks, and providing an end-to-end solution to defeat them. We adapt and combine some known techniques with our new ones to achieve a solution that is easy to deploy on the existing web platform. To the best of our knowledge, this is the first comprehensive defense against PISE attacks targeting user-owned resources, which is a significant subset of self-exfiltration attacks [12].
- *User Sub-Origins & Trusted Path.* We propose the first explicit notion of user sub-origins on the web. We further develop an end-to-end trusted path to eliminate PISE attacks targeting user-owned data.

2   Problem Definition

The missing notion of user sub-origins in today's web sessions gives rise to various attacks threatening web applications. We summarize such attacks and elaborate how they can occur in an existing web application.

2.1 PISE Attacks Targeting User-owned Data

Unlike in traditional OSes (e.g., UNIX), there is no built-in notion of a user authority on the present web, where users login into sites and authenticate themselves using custom password-based interfaces. Authentication of subsequent HTTP requests is performed via "bearer tokens", such as session IDs, CSRF tokens, or cookies. In the presence of script injection vulnerabilities, these tokens are prone to attacks, either via direct token stealing [22], phishing attempts [23], or session riding (e.g., fake HTTP request [24]). In this paper, we term such illegitimate accesses from malicious scripts to resources owned by benign victim users as *post-injection script execution* (PISE) attacks.

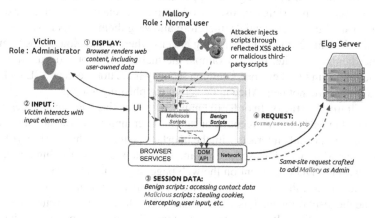

Fig. 1. Example Interactions in Elgg. Solid lines illustrate benign interactions between the user, UI elements and session data. Dashed lines illustrate the examples of PISE attacks, where an attacker injects malicious scripts into the victim's session, steals the victim's CSRF token, and performs a same-site request forgery attack to the Elgg server.

We illustrate various PISE attacks with a real-world social networking application called Elgg[2]. Elgg maintains user profiles, manages private message dispatch and blogging, and integrates itself with other social networking sites. Consider the following features available to administrators:

- *Add New User*: This is a privileged feature that can only be accessed by administrators. The administrator specifies information belonging to a particular user that is going to be added to the system. The administrator can also mark the user as a new administrator by identifying it on a checkbox element. Thereafter, this particular information is sent to the server using HTML Form submit mechanism.
- *Profile Management*: Elgg provides profile data management to maintain particular information for each user, similar to most social networking applications. In addition, there is a feature to set other users as administrators directly from their profile pages. However, this feature is privileged to an administrator. The administrator can add another user as an administrator by clicking on "Make admin" link on the user's profile page.

---

[2] http://elgg.org/

In PISE attacks, injected scripts can access user-owned resources (e.g., the state of "is admin" checkbox of a user) located at the client side and the server side, as shown in Figure 1. We systematically analyze the various channels available to PISE attacks.

At the client side, we categorize three variants of PISE attacks depending on different channels that are exposed to an attacker.

- **Display Channel Attacks.** An attacker can tamper with display elements of a web application to steal sensitive information from users. Two examples of attacks that exploit this channel are UI defacing and phishing for user credentials. In UI defacing attacks, an attacker alters the web content to mislead users. For instance, a malicious extension can change the appearance of a profile page in Facebook [6]. Besides, malicious scripts can also introduce fake UI elements (such as fake login input) to steal users' credentials, therefore allowing them to impersonate as Alice on a site O. Unlike traditional phishing attacks where a malicious website mimics another benign website, in this example the malicious scripts are running within the victim origin O. Therefore, common security indicators such as SSL lock icons and URL bars do not help Alice in detecting the phishing attempt.

- **Input Channel Attacks.** In order to tamper with sensitive data, an attacker can exploit this channel by (1) intercepting or stealing user input; or (2) launching an attack that programmatically interacts with the interface element of the web [13,16]. In the second scenario, malicious scripts can impersonate a user by forging a user interaction with the DOM element on the web page (e.g., auto-clicking the "add user" button) and mimic the user's action. Another popular attack that exploits this channel (and the display channel) is clickjacking [25], which typically runs in a different website than on Elgg. It can, for instance, load Elgg in a transparent overlay. Then underneath Elgg, it can render another malicious web page to attract users to click on the "Make admin" button in the invisible Elgg layer above. Clickjacking attacks sabotage a user's intention to interact with a UI element as intended by an attacker.

- **Session Data Channel Attacks.** Malicious scripts injected into the web page have access to arbitrary data. It can exfiltrate sensitive data, including cookies, CSRF tokens, capability-bearing URLs, and passwords, through two channels: directly to an attacker-controlled website [8] or via the victim's website itself, which is recently discussed and termed as self-exfiltration attacks by Chen et.al. [12]. Due to lack of input sanitization on Elgg's "edit page" functionality [26], cookie data can be stolen and exfiltrated using XSS attacks via a public blog entry, which is visible to the attacker. This is a confirmed security bug and has been documented as a CVE entry [27].

In addition to these three attack variants, the injected scripts have access to the network, allowing the attacker to access server-side resources of the user.

- **Network Request Channel Attacks.** Malicious scripts can craft and send HTTP requests to the server by invoking XMLHttpRequest API, or using HTML's resource tag attributes, such as a src attribute in an <img> tag. Such crafted requests can be used to perform specific operations on the server-side application. Some websites implement CSRF tokens that are sent along with HTTP requests and server-side applications verify whether the incoming requests carry expected CSRF tokens. However, secret CSRF tokens and other existing defenses for CSRF attacks, such as `Referer` and `Origin` headers [28], do not suffice for preventing requests forged by PISE attacks, as the injected scripts run in the same origin.

2.2 Insufficiency of Existing Solutions

Many existing solutions provide piecemeal defenses against PISE attacks. In Table 1, we briefly compare existing second line of defense techniques to mitigate this class of attacks. The comparison is categorized based on the four channels exposed to the attackers (Section 2.1). As Table 1 summarizes, none of them provides full protection for the four channels against malicious scripts injected into victim web sessions. We refer readers to Section 6 for a detailed comparison with previous solutions. We propose a user-based end-to-end trusted path that comprehensively protects all the four channels.

Table 1. Various Techniques for Mitigating PISE Attacks

	I^1	II^2	III^3	IV^4		I^1	II^2	III^3	IV^4
HTML5 Privilege Separation [18]			$\checkmark$		WebWallet [29]		$\checkmark$		
HTML5 Data Confinement [8]			$\checkmark$	$\checkmark$	Secure UI Toolkit [16]	$\checkmark$	$\checkmark$	$\checkmark$	
Object-Capability Sec Model [30,31]			$\checkmark$		Clickjacking Defenses [32]	$\checkmark$	$\checkmark$		
PathCutter [24]			$\checkmark$	$\checkmark$	Cryptons [9]	$\checkmark$	$\checkmark$		
Request Triggering Attribution [13]		$\checkmark$		$\checkmark$	DOMinator [33]				$\checkmark$
Adsentry [34]			$\checkmark$		Origin Bound Certificates [22]				$\checkmark$
USERPATH	$\checkmark$	$\checkmark$	$\checkmark$	$\checkmark$					

[1] Display Channel [2] Input Channel [3] Session Data Channel [4] Network Request Channel

2.3 Threat Model and Scope

We now briefly discuss the in-scope threats of our work. We consider the attacker to be a standard *web attacker* [35] that is able to exploit script injection vulnerabilities in a web application and browser's add-ons running as JavaScript (not binary plugins) [36]. All attacker payloads are client-side scripts, and we assume an uncompromised web server and web browser, as well as the underlying OS. We assume that the user is *benign*, i.e., we do not aim to prevent an attack where an authenticated user attacks the web applications within its own user authority. An HTTP parameter tampering attack, wherein Alice might attack Elgg for profit (e.g., randomly add users to increase number of friends), is such an example [37]. We also assume the security of user passwords, i.e., the users do not disclose their passwords nor use the same password for different websites. Lastly, although our approach is applicable to non-JavaScript-based attacks in concept, our discussion here precludes malicious Flash scripts or Java Applets embedded in web pages.

3 USERPATH Design and Security Properties

To protect user-owned resources in the web application from PISE attacks, we combine various techniques to protect the channels exposed to attackers (Section 3.2). Our solution requires minor changes to today's web browsers and web applications, and is easy to use for end users.

3.1   Challenges and Key Ideas

Protection for sensitive user-owned resource should cover the entire life time of web sessions, starting from user authentication to the teardown of the web session. We explain the challenges in doing so below.

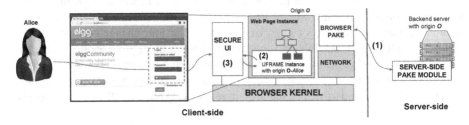

Fig. 2. Overview of USERPATH. The unshaded boxes are the contributions of our paper. A USERPATH-enabled platform has (1) server- and client-side PAKE modules to carry out PAKE protocol, (2) a web primitive called UFrame, and (3) secure UI elements.

Protecting User Credentials. Malicious scripts can exploit display channels to launch in-application phishing attacks and steal the user's password. Note that browser's security indicators (e.g., SSL lock icon, URL bar) do not help users recognize such attacks. Those security indicators operate under the assumption that a web session in an origin is trusted. Such an assumption becomes invalid with our threat model, as the attacks take place within the same session of the victim's origin. To achieve a secure authentication, our idea is to allow a web browser to render secure login elements on the web applications (Section 4). Such elements are special UI controls rendered by the browser, which can be easily verified by the user and cannot be tampered with by untrusted JavaScript code. Once users enter their credentials, leaking these credentials to an untrusted environment (a script or server) is not desirable. To address this critical problem, we employ a PAKE protocol (Figure 2 Step 1) that enables the web browser to authenticate a user to a web origin without directly exchanging credential information with the origin O.

Establishing Notion of User. After the successful authentication, another challenge is to securely establish a notion of user inside a web session. We term this step as *secure delegation* (Section 4), in which the browser creates a user sub-authority in origin O. This step constitutes a form of authority delegation on the web. To achieve this goal, the key idea is to conceptually split the web session into two partitions, one web session running under the authority of the web application origin O, the other one running under a user sub-origin O_{Alice}. USERPATH ties all sensitive resources belonging to user Alice under the sub-origin O_{Alice}, which represents the explicit notion of Alice's *sub-authority*[3] (Figure 2 Step 2). Note that code running in O_{Alice} represents the authority of Alice in O, and is more privileged than the origin O's code.

End-to-End Trusted Path. Fully protecting the four vulnerable channels is challenging with any single mechanism. Instead, we safeguard each vulnerable channel by providing the corresponding secure channel: a secure channel between the UFrame and the

---

[3] This secure delegation process is akin to executing an `su - alice` command in a UNIX-like system.

backend server, a secure channel between the UFrame and the browser kernel components, a secure visual channel, and a secure input channel – the latter two channels are
established with the web application user (Figure 2 Step 3). This constitutes an end-to-
end trusted path between the user and the server, as further discussed in Section 3.2.

3.2 USERPATH Design

Protecting User Credentials. To initiate the authentication process, USERPATH leverages the standard authentication mechanism using username and password, which can
also be extended for SSO-based authentication (see Section 3.4). The process starts with
a user Alice visiting a web page with the origin O. Alice interacts with the application
under the authority of its web origin O (Figure 5 Step A). The web application invokes
a DOM API to draw a special "credential box" (see Figure 3) for Alice to enter her
password. The origin O decides the placement and location of the credential box on the
web page and Alice needs nothing more than her usual password for this step. Unlike
prevailing password boxes where the input is directly accessible to the web page, the
data entered by Alice in the credential box will stay in the memory of the browser and
is not accessible by the application code. Therefore, it prevents attacker's scripts from
stealing the password. The `url` property of the credential box element identifies the
server-side script that handles user login.

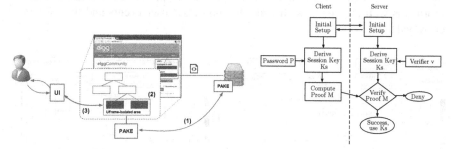

Fig. 3. A web browser displaying credential
boxes from `example.com`.

Fig. 4. The PAKE Protocol. A session
key S is derived and the server-side
PAKE verifies the message M obtained
from the client.

After Alice entered her credential information, the browser then executes a PAKE
protocol between the browser and the backend server using Alice's password as a secret, without directly exchanging Alice's password with the backend server (Figure 5
Step B). We illustrate the high-level overview of a PAKE protocol in Figure 4. In this
protocol, the server O is assumed to have gotten a verifer v which was derived from the
Alice's predefined password P. The verifier v is not a password, and cannot be used
by Alice for authentication. After Alice enters password P, the client-side PAKE sends
Alice's user information and, based on the user information, the server-side PAKE determines the corresponding verifier v. Client-side PAKE (based on user' password) and
server-side PAKE (based on verifier v) simultaneously derive a session key K_s, as well
as an evidence value M (for client-side PAKE) and M' (for server-side PAKE), according to a set of computations defined in [38]. The message M is later sent by the client to

and verified by the server-side PAKE, and vice versa for the message M'. In case of a successful authentication, the common key K_s will be used as a session key for further communications between both parties.

To allow users to distinguish the credential input element drawn by USERPATH from any other similar-looking elements rendered by malicious application code, the browser displays a rectangle of color M in its chrome area and updates the color M simultaneously around the credential box[4]. The user recognizes the authentic credential elements by a visual check. Therefore, this approach defeats any phishing attempts from malicious scripts.

Establishing Notion of User. After authentication is carried out using the PAKE protocol, USERPATH initiates the secure delegation to establish a user sub-authority O_{Alice}. USERPATH creates a UFrame to run Alice's privileged code separated from the rest of the application code within a web origin O. Unlike the temporary origin (e.g., sandboxed iframe [18]) which runs in a distinct privileged environment, the UFrame runs within the user Alice's authority with a higher privilege than any other parts in the web page. As a privileged entity, the UFrame has *one-way access* to (1) the main page's DOM via special DOM APIs including access to secure UI elements; (2) a direct secure callback channel to the browser; and (3) a dedicated XMLHttpRequest object to make HTTP requests to the backend server. USERPATH privilege-separates user-owned data from being accessed by the less-privileged application code running in O's authority, as well as separates all code that processes user events and the associated user-owned data.

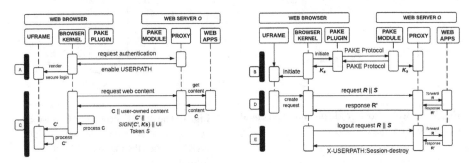

Fig. 5. Sequence of operations in a USERPATH-enabled session

So far, USERPATH ensures that the sensitive data in UFrame-protected code is not accessible to the less-privileged code (e.g., malicious JS code). But, how to make sure that the UFrame code itself is not initialized with the attacker's payload when it is fetched from the backend server? The UFrame code from the server can be hijacked by malicious scripts using a variety of ways, such as DOM clobbering [39] or prototype hijacking of XMLHttpRequest object [40]. This lets an attacker create fake

---

[4] The browser dynamically decides a foreground text color in the credential input element that has high contrast with the current background color M and randomizes it every t=5 seconds. To quantitatively measure the entropy, we set M to be randomly chosen from a palette of RGB code colors. This gives a total entropy of 24 bits.

UFrames or tamper with the original content of a UFrame. In order to securely delegate user-owned resource to the UFrame, the backend server signs the code with K_s and passes the code for the UFrame to the browser at the initialization step. Once the code is received by the browser, it checks the integrity and authenticity of the code with respect to K_s. Subsequently, the browser bootstraps the UFrame and provides a dedicated XMLHttpRequest channel to securely communicate back to the server's origin. At this point, USERPATH has established a secure **UFrame ↔ Server** channel. Note that we consider the server to be uncompromised in our threat model. If a web application developer wishes to isolate users' data better on the server side, several previous solutions such as CLAMP [10] and DIESEL [11] can be used in conjunction with USERPATH's abstractions.

Once a UFrame is initialized and executed during the web session, user-owned resources (i.e., JavaScript heap objects of the UFrame) are isolated from the less-privileged code. These sensitive user-owned resources include credit card information, sensitive images, secret key information derived from the authentication process, and other sensitive data tied to a user. To ensure compatibility with the existing web application, the users should be able to interact with (e.g., view or input into) these resources. For example, bank account number is a sensitive user-owned resource and this needs to be displayed or entered by Alice when she checks her transaction history. USERPATH introduces a set of secure DOM APIs (Table 2) to create secure input elements (e.g., textboxes, textareas) and secure display elements (e.g., images and styled-texts). Secure elements are akin to standard HTML input and display elements, except that these elements are not accessible to scripts outside the UFrame on the web origin O. For instance, only event handlers (e.g., keyboard inputs and mouse clicks) inside the UFrame code can access the secure display and input elements, and these handlers cannot be overridden by code outside the UFrame. Therefore, USERPATH establishes a secure input and visual channel to safeguard sensitive display and input elements.

End-to-End Trusted Path. Finally, a UFrame needs to communicate back to the server. The main challenge is that the server needs to disambiguate HTTP requests generated by the UFrame in response to the authentic user interaction, as opposed to fake requests generated by malicious scripts via PISE attacks. USERPATH handles this issue by creating a dedicated network channel for the UFrame code. Inside the initialized UFrame code, the server embeds a set of nonces S called *user interaction token set* (Figure 5 Step C) that can be used to generate resource access HTTP requests from client side. These tokens can only be attached by the browser kernel as a custom HTTP header X-UFRAME when the UFrame-dedicated XMLHttpRequest is invoked (Step D).

Teardown. As the user Alice logs out of O, the server invalidates the session key K_s, and sets a custom HTTP header X-USERPATH:Session-destroy in HTTP response for the log out request (Figure 5 Step E). After getting this response, the browser destroys all user interaction tokens for the session and the session key K_s. To allow session reconnection, similar to cookies, the browser caches the user interaction tokens and K_s until the user logs out. The server then redirects the request to the login page if the key and tokens expire.

Table 2. Secure DOM APIs for UFrame

Downcall API	Description	Upcall API	Description
createSecElement	Create a secure UI element	storeSecretKey	Store the key K_s that is derived from PAKE protocol
getSecElementById	Get the secure UI element's object by ID	updateUFrameCont	Update the UFrame code or data content
setSecElmAttr	Set the property of an object with the corresponding value	createContext	Create a UFrame context that runs with user privilege. It lets the UFrame access privileged APIs
getSecElmAttrVal	Get the property's value of an object	removeSecretKey	Remove the secret key K_s during teardown process
deletePAKESesKey	Delete the session key K_s from the browser kernel	removeUIToken	Remove the interaction token T during teardown process

3.3 Security Properties: Putting It Together

USERPATH enforces the following security semantics, which ensures resilience against PISE attacks.

- **P0**: **Safe Mutual Authentication & K_s Establishment.** Mutual authentication between user Alice and the server is required for web servers to securely delegate user Alice's authority O_{Alice} to client-side code within its web origin's authority O. This delegation is bootstrapped by Alice's user name and password. The secure delegation process must ensure that credential information does not leak outside Alice's authority, such as to attacker-controlled domains. After successful authentication, a session key K_s is derived. The key K_s must remain unforgeable, unguessable, and unique during the sessions.
- **P1**: **Secure Delegation.** A UFrame code that is passed from the backend server needs to be signed by K_s that is derived from mutual authentication between user and web server. Once web browser receives the content of the UFrame, it has to check the authenticity of the code with respect to K_s.
- **P2**: **Post-initialization Security of UFrame.** All sensitive data and code must be kept isolated inside a UFrame. The rest of the application code outside UFrame must not be able to access this data and code whatsoever.

   The properties P0, P1 and P2 serve as the basis for subsequent security properties P3, P4, and P5 described as follows.

- **P3**: **Secure Visual and Input Channels for Users**
   Visual channel. We reuse the standard secure visual channel that requires display, intent, spatio-temporal, and pointer integrity to ensure *distinguishability* of secure UI elements from the non-secure ones. Secure UI elements cannot be obstructed or tampered with by untrusted code. Its elements should be able to display confidential information to users and not be accessible to the non-UFrame code. This has been explored in other research works [15, 16, 32] and is not part of our contributions.
   Input Channel. All keyboard inputs to secure input elements go directly to the browser. The confidentiality and integrity of input action should not be violated by untrusted scripts. The browser should be able to distinguish genuine user interactions from those mimicked by JavaScript code.

- **P4**: **Secure Browser ↔ UFrame Channel.** A privileged UFrame can communicate to the browser directly in order to create secure UI elements or to read contents in DOM objects securely with no possibility of interception from untrusted code. The confidentiality, integrity and authenticity of such communications are maintained by the browser.
- **P5**: **Secure UFrame ↔ Server Channel.** Web server should be able to distinguish requests generated from the authentic user interaction, and those that are not. The communications between the UFrame and the server are protected in their confidentiality and integrity.

Due to space constraints, we give a more thorough example-by-example security analysis in our technical report [20].

3.4   Compatibility and Usability Implications

Our mechanism can be easily extended to handle authentication via Single-Sign On (SSO). If the server O delegates authentication to an SSO provider S, a separate HTTPS connection is established from the browser to S. Thereafter, the credential input element uses the username and password to initiate the PAKE authentication with S. Upon successful completion, the browser obtains a shared key K_s with S, which is also communicated by S to O in a separate channel. O can create a server-side representation for Alice using K_s. The browser thus creates a UFrame with the authority of $Alice@S$, which can isolate $Alice@S$ from another user.

Usability Implications. First, we assume that web application users will always check the background color of any credential-seeking elements, and only enter their passwords if the color matches that of a rectangle displayed in the browser's chrome area. Second, we rely on prior research [15,16,32] to ensure the visual, temporal and pointer integrity of a secure visual channel. Admittedly, the usability of such a scheme has not been fully evaluated; a thorough user study on its usability merits separate research (c.f., [41,42]).

4   Implementation in Chromium

We summarize the high-level abstraction of our end-to-end solution and detail how it is implemented in Chromium web browser.

Implementation Overview. We implemented UFrame and trusted path components by modifying Chromium[5], the open source version of Google Chrome. We patched Chromium version 12 by adding roughly 475 lines of code spreading over 26 files inside Chromium codebase. This does not include the logic for performing PAKE procotol, which was implemented separately by us as a plug-in. Apart from the browser, we also modified 20 PHP-based server-side applications which we discuss in Section 5.

We have released our patch to Chromium and the modified web applications on a public repository [20]. We have also released a demo video showing how USERPATH offers smooth user experience with our running example Elgg [21].

Authentication Step. As discussed in Section 3.2, once the browser identifies credential element on the HTML code, it renders this element and applies a random color on the element's background. To do so, we develop an NPAPI plug-in for the browser to render such element and update the display color in web browser's chrome bar. As the

---

[5] http://www.chromium.org/

credential element is rendered and called through privileged API, this is not accessible from web application code. To make the existing authentication process be USERPATH-compliant, developers just need to embed the plug-in into original web application's login page.

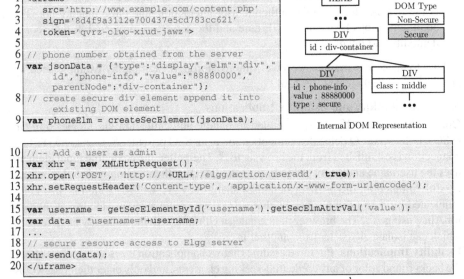

```
1  <uframe
2    src='http://www.example.com/content.php'
3    sign='8d4f9a3112e700437e5cd783cc621'
4    token='qvrz-clwo-xiud-jawz'>
5
6  // phone number obtained from the server
7  var jsonData = {"type":"display","elm":"div","
        id","phone-info","value":"88880000","
        parentNode":"div-container"};
8  // create secure div element append it into
        existing DOM element
9  var phoneElm = createSecElement(jsonData);
```

```
10  //-- Add a user as admin
11  var xhr = new XMLHttpRequest();
12  xhr.open('POST', 'http://'+URL+'/elgg/action/useradd', true);
13  xhr.setRequestHeader('Content-type', 'application/x-www-form-urlencoded');
14
15  var username = getSecElementById('username').getSecElmAttrVal('value');
16  var data = "username="+username;
17  ...
18  // secure resource access to Elgg server
19  xhr.send(data);
20  </uframe>
```

Listing 1.1. Trusted Code Running in a UFrame. This piece of code executes under the user's authority O_{Alice} to create a secure `div` element into the web page and secure HTTP request to add a user as an admin. Details elided for brevity.

Subsequently, we employ the PAKE protocol to mutually authenticate user and the backend server by integrating TLS-SRP [43] — a PAKE-based web authentication that operates at the transport layer — into USERPATH. On the web browser, we install a browser level TLS-SRP module that receives input from special credential box and carries out PAKE protocol with the specific origin O specified in `url` property of the UFrame code. The module consists of 381 C++ lines of code in total, which is roughly 2.6 MB in size. At the server side, we apply a patch to the Apache web server to handle server-side TLS-SRP authentication. This patch is available online [44].

Secure Delegation. After the authentication step finishes, the browser creates a UFrame for executing trusted JavaScript code. In this step, the browser already has a shared key K_s that can be used to secure communications with the server. Server-side web application then signs the content of the UFrame using the key K_s and sends it to the browser, embedded in a custom HTML tag named <UFRAME>. Whenever the browser encounters the UFrame content during parsing, it checks the integrity and authenticity of the UFrame code, and creates an `iframe` with a random origin $O_R = PRG(K_s)$, where $PRG(K_S)$ is a pseudorandom generator function that takes the shared key K_s as the seed.

We leverage existing mechanisms in the Chromium web browser to establish trusted paths. For ease of implementation, we modify *isolated worlds* [36], a feature provided by Chromium to separate execution context between two JavaScript code. This abstraction offers similar isolation mechanism as what iframe-based isolation with random origin provides.

Trusted Path Implementation. We use our running example in Section 2 to illustrate how we implement the trusted path execution inside a UFrame. As shown in Listing 1.1, UFrame code is purely written in JavaScript, and it has additional access to secure DOM APIs. As an example, we label contact information as a sensitive element to prevent them from being leaked to malicious code running on a web page. In Listing 1.1 line 9, a secure DOM element is created by invoking a downcall API createSecElement(). This API receives a JSON object jsonData as an input, and creates a secure display element based on data from jsonData. The object jsonData has user-owned contact information, which is sensitive data passed from the backend server to the browser. In Listing 1.1 line 10-19, we create a POST request directly from the UFrame using dedicated XMLHttpRequest to protect the client-side request to Elgg server. The data that is sent through the POST request (e.g., username, password) is obtained from user input on the secure input elements (Listing 1.1 line 15). As the XMLHttpRequest object is being called from UFrame, the browser treats the request as secure resource access to the server and appends special user interaction token for that request.

In our Chromium implementation, we make small changes in the following C++ classes: ScriptController, V8IsolatedContext and V8NodeCustom. We add a new data structure called IsolatedContextMap to maintain the relation between code running on the web page or the UFrame, represented by a context identifier. Therefore, the system can recognize the context where a JavaScript code is running by checking the data structure. Finally, we modify Chromium to mediate access from a JavaScript object to a DOM Node. The logic for mediating access to sensitive DOM element is as follows: as each element of the DOM is represented by an object, we add a special flag for every object that is created under specific privileged functions. We then modify the logic for traversing an object in a DOM tree, so that those objects with privileged flag will not be visible to the web application code running under origin O.

5   Evaluation

We deploy USERPATH on 20 open source web applications (as Table 4 shows) from 8 different categories (as Table 5 presents) including 3 frameworks (WordPress, Joomla, and Drupal). These web applications are statistically popular, built using PHP, and cover a wide range of functionalities. We evaluate our solution from four aspects – scope of vulnerabilities USERPATH can eliminate, case study of elgg, applicability to web applications & TCB reduction, and USERPATH's performance.

5.1   Scope of Vulnerabilities

We study a set of vulnerabilities in the web applications that can lead to PISE attacks. Among the 20 open source web applications that we study, there are 325 vulnerabilities on those web applications that can be exploited to launch the attacks. Most of them have been patched and recorded in the vulnerability database, but some of them are still unpatched.

Table 3. List of Vulnerabilities in 20 Open-source Web Applications. These vulnerabilities might lead to PISE Attacks

App Name & Version	Popularity Indicator	PHP # of LOC	Sensitive User Data	# of Relevant Vulnerabilities
Elgg v1.8.16	>2,800,000 downloads	114735	Private profile data and admin options (set user as admin and add new user)	3 (CVE-2012-6561: XSS, EDB-ID 17685 and 8993: XSS)
Friendica v3.2.1744	Forbes's Top 3 social network application	144555	Private contact, friend list, and message data	1 (Bug ID 0000535: Reflected XSS)
Roundcube v0.9.4	>2,400,000 downloads	109663	Address book, settings and private emails	12 (CVE-2013-5646: XSS and CVE-2009-4077: CSRF)
OpenEMR v4.1.2	Serving >30,000,000 patients	495987	Personal info, medical records, and payment	2 (ZSL-2013-5129 and 103810: XSS)
ownCloud v5.0.13	>350,000 users	337192	Contacts, export files and user share options	15 (CVE-2013-1942: XSS and CVE-2012-4753: CSRF)
HotCRP v2.61	Used by USENIX, SIGCOMM, etc.	36333	Contact information, review and privilege settings	3 (Bug ID 3f143d2: XSS)
OpenConf v5.30	Used by ACSAC, IEEE, W3C, ACM, etc.	17589	Contact info, review, edit submission and role setting	1 (CVE-2005-0407: XSS and CVE-2012-1002: XSS)
PrestaShop v1.5.6.0	Powering >150,000 online stores	250660	Personal info, credit slips, addresses and checkout info	2 (CVE-2008-6503 and CVE-2011-4544: XSS)
OpenCart v1.5.6	>250,000 downloads	93770	Account, address book and checkout information	1 (CVE-2010-1610: CSRF)
AstroSpaces v1.1.1	DZineBlog's Top 10 open social network.	6972	Profile information, private message and admin settings	1 (Bug ID 001: XSS)
Magento v1.8.0.0	Used by >200,000 business	928991	Account info, address information and checkout info	1 (CVE-2009-0541: XSS)
Zen Cart v1.5.1	>3,000,000 downloads	95381	Account, profile and checkout information	4 (CVE-2011-4567 and CVE-2012-1413: XSS)
osCommerce v2.3.3.4	>12,000 registered sites with >270,000 members	60081	Account, profile and checkout information	10 (CVE-2012-1792 and CVE-2012-2935: XSS)
StoreSprite v7.24.4.13	Incorporate 14 payment gateways	30350	Account, profile and checkout information	1 (CVE-2012-5798: XSS)
CubeCart v5.2.4	Powering thousands of online stores	11942	Account, profile and checkout information	1 (CVE-2008-1550: XSS)
WordPress v3.6	Used by >60,000,000 websites	135540	Account, contact and setting information	91 (CVE-2013-5738: XSS and CVE-2013-2205: XSS)
Joomla v3.2.0	>35,000,000 downloads	227351	Account, contact and setting information	45 (CVE-2013-3059 and CVE-2013-3267: XSS)
Drupal v7.23	>1,000,000 downloads	43835	Account, contact and setting information	126 (CVE-2012-0826: CSRF and CVE-2012-2339: XSS)
Piwigo v2.5.3	Translated into 50 languages	143144	User's management, permission, sensitive profile	4 (CVE-2013-1468: CSRF and CVE-2012-2209: XSS)
X2CRM v3.5.6	>4,500 installations across 135 countries	747261	Account, contact management & information	1 (CVE-2013-5693: XSS)

Table 3 lists our case study and summarizes the number of vulnerabilities, along with the CVE ID for the corresponding vulnerability[6]. Among those 20 web applications that we study, all of them have at least one vulnerability to a subset of PISE attacks namely XSS or CSRF attacks. Some of them even have more than ten vulnerabilities of the same attack vector. To name one of them, PrestaShop has two critical vulnerabilities. One type of vulnerability (marked by ID CVE-2008-6503) allows an attacker to inject arbitrary web scripts to the login page. The other vulnerability (marked by ID CVE-2011-4544) lets the attacker to exploit the file management process of an administrator to launch an XSS attack.

---

[6] Due to the page limit, we show the study of 8 applications from 8 different categories. For the study on all 20 applications, please check our technical report [20].

5.2   Case Study : Elgg and OpenCart

In this section, we detail our experience with real-world case studies to illustrate the steps taken for retrofitting web applications with USERPATH. We evaluate USERPATH with the following goals: (1) protecting the "add new user" feature in Elgg social network, given the presence of XSS vulnerabilities and (2) protecting the "reset password" feature in OpenCart, given a CSRF vulnerability in the web application. Based on those vulnerabilities, we thus construct four proof-of-concept attacks that tamper with the four channels discussed in Section 2.1. Due to space constraints, we describe the attacks and specify the way USERPATH prevents those attacks in our technical report [20].

Code Changes. First, we made small changes in `actions/login.php` (Elgg) and `account/login.php` (OpenCart) to let the browser render special credential boxes and initiate a TLS-SRP-based authentication with the server at their respective origins. Secondly, in the "add new user" page of Elgg, we privilege-separated the logic for displaying username, email address, password, admin flag, and a form request button into a `UFrame` section. Instead of creating those elements using HTML, the elements need to be dynamically created from within a UFrame to let them be rendered as secure elements. All the changes were made in a PHP file `forms/useradd.php`. Likewise, we protect two HTML input elements for putting in new password and a confirmation button by implementing the logic for this feature separately inside a `UFrame`. All these changes were made by modifying a file `account/password.php`. A complete set of technical changes is described in [20].

Result and Challenges. We successfully retrofitted USERPATH to Elgg and OpenCart by adding 270 and 266 lines of PHP code in their application code, respectively. The TCB size of the UFrame in the modified Elgg is 46x and 66x smaller than the size of TCB in vanilla web applications. After implementing those changes, we successfully protect the sensitive resources in the vulnerable applications from PISE attacks. We demonstrate some of the attacks in Elgg and how USERPATH defends against those through demo videos available in [21].

The main challenge of adopting USERPATH to web applications is the difficulty in locating the functionality we need to modify, because both applications were built using their own toolkit. After understanding the toolkit, the modification effort is straightforward. It took 2 days in total for us to enable USERPATH in Elgg and OpenCart.

5.3   Applicability to Web Applications and TCB Reduction

We successfully retrofit all 20 web applications to adopt USERPATH. Among these applications, we manually choose several data and operations that are sensitive to users (summarized in Table 3) and modify the PHP files where these data and operations are processed. In addition, we demonstrate the practicality of USERPATH by summarizing the adoption effort and TCB reduction of 20 retrofitted web applications in Table 4. We measure the adoption effort by the following benchmarks: number of additional code, number of modified files, and number of days spent in modifying the web application. Besides, we also measure TCB reduction by comparing the initial TCB size (i.e., the web page size) and the final TCB size after implementing USERPATH.

We find that USERPATH requires small changes to the existing web application code. Given the set of sensitive user-owned data and functionalities that we want to protect from PISE attacks, we only need to add at most 270 lines of PHP and JavaScript code

Table 4. Adoption Effort and TCB Reduction after Implementing USERPATH in 20 Open-Source Web Applications

App Name	USERPATH LOC (JS+PHP)	Original TCB (KB)	TCB after implementing USERPATH (KB)	TCB Reduction Factor	# of Modified Files	# of Days Spent
Elgg	270	414.6	9.1	46x	4	2
Friendica	176	1053.8	5.3	199x	13	1
Roundcube	96	946.0	8.0	118x	4	2
OpenEMR	141	53.6	6.6	8x	7	1.5
ownCloud	106	555.2	2.9	191x	4	1.5
HotCRP	139	184.5	4.6	40x	5	1
OpenConf	151	55.9	2.4	23x	5	1
PrestaShop	111	580.3	5.8	100x	5	1
OpenCart	266	754.8	11.5	66x	6	2
AstroSpaces	119	67.3	3.5	19x	5	1
Magento	227	987.0	11.2	88x	4	1.5
Zencart	130	241.8	6.5	37x	6	1
osCommerce	122	425.8	5.9	72x	5	1
StoreSprite	133	513.8	4.6	112x	4	1
CubeCart	118	469.2	6.2	76x	5	1
WordPress	102	308.7	3.9	79x	4	1
Joomla	87	819.3	3.1	264x	3	1
Drupal	72	199.6	2.6	77x	3	1.5
Piwigo	216	673.5	7.8	86x	6	1
X2CRM	217	1380.4	6.1	226x	10	2

into the web application, with 167 lines of code added for each web application on an average (see column "USERPATH LOC" in Table 4 for LOC of all the 20 applications). Moreover, we empirically show that we achieve the reduction of 8x to 264x in TCB for our case studies. We measure this reduction by comparing the size of final TCB (e.g., the UFrame code) with the entire web page size (see column IV in Table 4). We treat the web page size as the initial TCB size as we need to trust the entire web page in order to protect our sensitive data and operation.

We also find that modifying web applications according to USERPATH incurs relatively small burden on the developer side. On the average, given a set of sensitive user-owned resources to protect in Table 3, a developer needs to modify 6 files within 1.3 days for one web application to make it USERPATH-compliant.

5.4 Performance

The main performance factor that impact our solution include: PAKE-based secure delegation, the UFrame creation, and new secure elements introduced into DOM. As our demo video [21] shows, in our experiments with the 20 web applications, we do not observe any slowdown in user interactions with the applications. Since the login phase contains all the three factors, we measure the overhead of the login time for 20 applications from 8 different categories. Table 5 summarizes the results of the login time (averaged on 5 runs) between the click on the login button and the next page finishes loading. We can see that USERPATH introduces the negligible performance overhead to these applications. This confirms our speculation that the minimal performance overhead that might incur from USERPATH would be largely masked by the timing variances in network requests.

Table 5. Time Taken for Login without & with USERPATH (in seconds)

Category	Application Name	Time without USERPATH	Time with USERPATH	Overhead
Social Networking	Elgg	3.38	3.45	2.07%
Social Networking	Friendica	4.88	5.02	2.87%
Social Networking	AstroSpaces	0.397	0.406	2.27%
Email Application	Roundcube	7.28	7.49	2.88%
Health Information System	OpenEMR	3.238	3.338	3.09%
Conference Management System	HotCRP	1.037	1.065	2.70%
Conference Management System	OpenConf	0.173	0.176	1.73%
E-commerce Application	OpenCart	4.26	4.40	3.29%
E-commerce Application	PrestaShop	3.52	3.56	1.14%
E-commerce Application	Magento	3.02	3.07	1.66%
E-commerce Application	Zencart	1.16	1.2	2.83%
E-commerce Application	osCommerce	7.38	7.46	1.08%
E-commerce Application	StoreSprite	5.03	5.13	1.99%
E-commerce Application	CubeCart	3.05	3.09	1.31%
Content Management System	WordPress	3.708	3.777	1.86%
Content Management System	Joomla	2.74	2.81	2.55%
Content Management System	Drupal	1.56	1.62	3.44%
File Sharing System	Piwigo	1.55	1.57	1.09%
File Sharing System	ownCloud	5.2	5.36	3.08%
Customer Management System	X2CRM	9.105	9.364	2.84%

6   Related Work

In this section, we discuss recent research works that are related to our solution.

Privilege Separation. Privilege separation reduces the potential damages of compromised software components by partitioning software into different compartments. It has been widely adopted in traditional applications [45,46], web browsers [47–49], and web applications [18, 34]. View isolation implemented by PathCutter [24] separates code running in different `iframes` (views) as well as requests coming out of different views. Thus, it prevents unwanted access to data between views, either directly or indirectly via sending requests to the server. Our solution in this paper applies privilege separation using a user-centric approach. We bring in user sub-origins to the present web, and confine user data only to code delegated by the user sub-origin.

Data Confinement. Confining data in web applications has recently received attention in the research community. For instance, Roesner et al. propose ACG, which allows users to directly grant access to user-owned resources by UI interaction with such gadgets [15]. Our solution shares the similar insight as to confine user data back to user-sanctioned operations, although we face different challenges in protecting user data on the web. Unlike resources on OS, the distributed nature of the web and decoupled server-client architecture requires additional secure channels to confine user data on the web. We address such challenges by integrating TLS-SRP into web authentication to build an end-to-end trusted path from the client-side application code to the web server.

Several other works have been proposed to confine sensitive data on the web [8] or cloud platform [50]. Compared to these proposals, our solution does not confine user data according to any application-specific configuration or data propagation policies; instead, it ensures that user data only flows within user sub-origin, both at the client and the server side.

Trusted Paths.   Building trusted paths across untrusted components has practical significance today. Prior works examine potential solutions for trusted paths between user-interaction elements and software applications [41,51,52]. Similarly, Web Wallet redesigns browser's user interfaces to protect user credentials against phishing attacks [29]. The usability of trusted path proposals has been evaluated in real-world usage [42, 51]. Zhou et al. propose a hypervisor-based general-purpose trusted path design on commodity x86 computers, and present a case study on user-oriented trusted path [53].

Our solution builds an end-to-end trusted path by utilizing the existing functionality of the web browser and server. This trusted path connects the user at the client side to the server, ensuring that only user-delegated sub-origins can access protected data. Such a trusted path differs from a recent proposal on a trusted path between user keyboard inputs and the web server, where no explicit notion of users is established [9]. Moreover, compared to it, our solution requires much smaller changes to web browsers; by piggybacking on passwords for authentication, we avoid the usability challenges in requiring users to generate and upload SSL keys as in [9]. Dong et al. propose a solution to identify requests crafted by injected scripts from those triggered by user interactions [13]. We apply a similar mechanism in our solution as part of input channel protection. However, their work focuses on monitoring and diagnosing web application behavior, and does not yield a solution for protecting data in web applications.

Injection Attack Prevention.   As we discuss in this paper, injected scripts pose major threats to web applications. Previous endeavors of security researchers have devised numerous solutions to prevent or mitigate script injection, such as CSP [1], blueprint [54], DSI [55], and Noncespaces [56]. Nevertheless, in practice, it is difficult to eliminate all script injection vectors [2]. Our solution complement these solutions on script injection prevention as a second line of defense.

7   Conclusion and Acknowledgments

In this paper, we propose new abstractions to bring in the explicit notion of user suborigins into the present web and establish an end-to-end trusted path between the user and the web server. We show that our solution eliminates a large amount of PISE attacks in real-world applications, and can be integrated with today's web browsers and applications with minimal adoption cost.

Acknowledgments.   We thank the anonymous reviewers and our shepherd William Robertson for their feedback and suggested improvements for this work. We thank Kailas Patil, Atul Sadhu, Loi Luu, and Shweta Shinde for their comments on an early presentation of this work. This work is supported by the Ministry of Education, Singapore under Grant No. R-252-000-495-133. Xinshu Dong is supported by the research grant for the Human Sixth Sense Programme at the Advanced Digital Sciences Center from Singapore's Agency for Science, Technology and Research (A*STAR).

References

1. W3C: Content security policy 1.0, http://www.w3.org/TR/CSP/
2. Johns, M.: Preparedjs: Secure script-templates for javascript. In: Detection of Intrusions and Malware & Vulnerability Assessment (2013)

3. Chen, P., Nikiforakis, N., Huygens, C., Desmet, L.: A dangerous mix: Large-scale analysis of mixed-content websites. In: Information Security Conference (2013)
4. Trend Micro: New york times pushes fake av malvertisement, http://goo.gl/BtjgPc
5. Verizon: 2013 Data breach investigation report, http://www.verizonenterprise.com/DBIR/2013/
6. Enigma Group: Facebook profiles can be hijacked by chrome extensions malware, http://underurhat.com/hacking
7. Liu, L., Zhang, X., Yan, G., Chen, S.: Chrome extensions: Threat analysis and countermeasures. In: Network and Distributed System Security Symposium (2012)
8. Akhawe, D., Li, F., He, W., Saxena, P., Song, D.: Data-confined html5 applications. In: European Symposium on Research in Computer Security (2013)
9. Dong, X., Chen, Z., Siadati, H., Tople, S., Saxena, P., Liang, Z.: Protecting sensitive web content from client-side vulnerabilities with cryptons. In: Proceedings of the 20th ACM Conference on Computer and Communications Security (2013)
10. Parno, B., McCune, J.M., Wendlandt, D., Andersen, D.G., Perrig, A.: Clamp: Practical prevention of large-scale data leaks. In: IEEE Symposium on Security and Privacy (2009)
11. Felt, A.P., Finifter, M., Weinberger, J., Wagner, D.: Diesel: Applying privilege separation to database access. In: ACM Symposium on Information, Computer and Communications Security (2011)
12. Chen, E.Y., Gorbaty, S., Singhal, A., Jackson, C.: Self-exfiltration: The dangers of browser-enforced information flow control. In: Web 2.0 Security and Privacy (2012)
13. Dong, X., Patil, K., Mao, J., Liang, Z.: A comprehensive client-side behavior model for diagnosing attacks in ajax applications. In: ICECCS (2013)
14. Projects, T.C.: Per-page suborigins, http://goo.gl/PoH5pY
15. Roesner, F., Kohno, T., Moshchuk, A., Parno, B., Wang, H.J., Cowan, C.: User-driven access control: Rethinking permission granting in modern operating systems. In: Proceedings of the 2012 IEEE Symposium on Security and Privacy (2012)
16. Roesner, F., Fogarty, J., Kohno, T.: User interface toolkit mechanisms for securing interface elements. In: User Interface Software and Technology (2012)
17. Dong, X., Hu, H., Saxena, P., Liang, Z.: A quantitative evaluation of privilege separation in web browser designs. In: Crampton, J., Jajodia, S., Mayes, K. (eds.) ESORICS 2013. LNCS, vol. 8134, pp. 75–93. Springer, Heidelberg (2013)
18. Akhawe, D., Saxena, P., Song, D.: Privilege separation in html5 applications. In: USENIX Security (2012)
19. mOiwa, Y., Takagi, H., Watanabe, H., Suzuki, H.: Pake-based mutual http authentication for preventing phishing attacks. In: World Wide Web Conference (2009)
20. Budianto, E., Jia, Y.: Summary of source code modification, chromium patches, and userpath technical report, https://github.com/ebudianto/UserPath
21. Budianto, E., Jia, Y.: Url for demo video, https://github.com/ebudianto/UserPath/wiki/DEMO-Video-URLs
22. Dietz, M., Czeskis, A., Balfanz, D., Wallach, D.S.: Origin-bound certificates: A fresh approach to strong client authentication for the web. In: USENIX Security (2012)
23. Jackson, C., Simon, D.R., Tan, D.S., Barth, A.: An evaluation of extended validation and picture-in-picture phishing attacks. In: Proceedings of 1st USEC (2007)
24. Cao, Y., Yegneswaran, V., Porras, P., Chen, Y.: Pathcutter: Severing the self-propagation path of xss javascript worms in social web networks. In: Network and Distributed System Security Symposium (2012)
25. Hansen, R., Grossman, J.: Clickjacking, http://goo.gl/p7dxIC
26. YGN Ethical Hacker Group: Elgg 1.7.9 xss vulnerability, http://goo.gl/XUeqis
27. Cve-2012-6561, C.V.E.: xss vulnerability in elgg, http://goo.gl/mmW8bM

28. Barth, A., Jackson, C., Mitchell, J.C.: Robust defenses for cross-site request forgery. In: Conference on Computer and Communications Security (2008)
29. Wu, M., Miller, R.C., Little, G.: Web wallet: Preventing phishing attacks by revealing user intentions. In: Symposium on Usable Privacy and Security (2006)
30. Bhargavan, K., Delignat-Lavaud, A., Maffeis, S.: Language-based defenses against untrusted browser origins. In: USENIX Security (2013)
31. Maffeis, S., Mitchell, J.C., Taly, A.: Object capabilities and isolation of untrusted web application. In: IEEE Symposium on Security and Privacy (2010)
32. Huang, L.S., Moshchuk, A., Wang, H.J., Schechter, S., Jackson, C.: Clickjacking: attacks and defenses. In: USENIX Security (2012)
33. Zhou, Y., Evans, D.: Protecting private web content from embedded scripts. In: European Symposium on Research in Computer Security (2011)
34. Dong, X., Tran, M., Liang, Z., Jiang, X.: Adsentry: comprehensive and flexible confinement of javascript-based advertisements. In: ACSAC (2011)
35. Akhawe, D., Barth, A., Lam, P.E., Mitchell, J., Song, D.: Towards a formal foundation of web security. In: Computer Security Foundations (2010)
36. Barth, A., Felt, A.P., Saxena, P., Boodman, A.: Protecting browsers from extension vulnerabilities. In: Network and Distributed System Security Symposium (2010)
37. Bisht, P., Hinrichs, T., Skrupsky, N., Bobrowicz, R., Venkatakrishnan, V.N.: Notamper: automatic blackbox detection of parameter tampering opportunities in web applications. In: Conference on Computer and Communications Security (2010)
38. Wu, T.: The secure remote password protocol. In: Network and Distributed System Security Symposium (1998)
39. The Spanner: Dom clobbering, http://goo.gl/ZOLmal
40. pAdida, B., Barth, A., Jackson, C.: Rootkits for javascript environments. In: WOOT (2009)
41. Ye, Z.E., Smith, S.: Trusted paths for browsers. In: USENIX Security (2002)
42. Libonati, A., McCune, J.M., Reiter, M.K.: Usability testing a malware-resistant input mechanism. In: Network and Distributed System Security Symposium (2011)
43. Engler, J., Karlof, C., Shi, E., Song, D.: Is it too late for pake? In: Proceedings of Web 2.0 Security and Privacy (2009)
44. Slack, Q.: Tls-srp in apache mod_ssl, http://goo.gl/cHMoau
45. Provos, N., Friedl, M., Honeyman, P.: Preventing privilege escalation. In: USENIX Security (2003)
46. Brumley, D., Song, D.: Privtrans: automatically partitioning programs for privilege separation. In: USENIX Security (2004)
47. Grier, C., Tang, S., King, S.: Designing and implementing the op and op2 web browsers. ACM Transactions on the Web (2011)
48. Wang, H.J., Grier, C., Moshchuk, A., King, S.T., Choudhury, P., Venter, H.: The multi-principal os construction of the gazelle web browser. In: USENIX Security (2009)
49. Barth, A., Jackson, C., Reis, C., Team, T.G.C.: The security architecture of the chromium browser, http://goo.gl/BGjJqC
50. Papagiannis, I., Pietzuch, P.: Cloudfilter: practical control of sensitive data propagation to the cloud. In: Cloud Computing Security Workshop (2012)
51. Tong, T., Evans, D.: Guardroid: A trusted path for password entry. In: MoST (2013)
52. McCune, J.M., Perrig, A., Reiter, M.K.: Safe passage for passwords and other sensitive data. In: Network and Distributed System Security Symposium (2009)
53. Zhou, Z., Gligor, V.D., Newsome, J., McCune, J.M.: Building verifiable trusted path on commodity x86 computers. In: IEEE Symposium on Security and Privacy (2012)

54. Ter Louw, M., Venkatakrishnan, V.N.: Blueprint: Robust prevention of cross-site scripting attacks for existing browsers. In: IEEE Symposium on Security and Privacy (2009)
55. Nadji, Y., Saxena, P., Song, D.: Document structure integrity: A robust basis for cross-site scripting defense. In: Network and Distributed System Security Symposium (2009)
56. Gundy, M.V., Chen, H.: Noncespaces: Using randomization to enforce information flow tracking and thwart cross-site scripting attacks. In: Network and Distributed System Security Symposium (2009)

Measuring Drive-by Download Defense in Depth*

Nathaniel Boggs, Senyao Du, and Salvatore J. Stolfo

Columbia University, New York, NY
{boggs,du,sal}@cs.columbia.edu

Abstract. Defense in depth is vital as no single security product detects all of today's attacks. To design defense in depth organizations rely on best practices and isolated product reviews with no way to determine the marginal benefit of additional security products. We propose empirically testing security products' detection rates by linking multiple pieces of data such as network traffic, executable files, and an email to the attack that generated all the data. This allows us to directly compare diverse security products and to compute the increase in total detection rate gained by adding a security product to a defense in depth strategy not just its stand alone detection rate. This approach provides an automated means of evaluating risks and the security posture of alternative security architectures. We perform an experiment implementing this approach for real drive-by download attacks found in a real time email spam feed and compare over 40 security products and human click-through rates by linking email, URL, network content, and executable file attack data.

Keywords: Metrics, Defense in Depth, Drive-by Download, Measuring Security.

1 Introduction

The modern Chief Security Officer's (CSO) primary goal to secure an organization in a cost effective manner is frustrated by a lack of formal empirical data suitable for optimizing defense in depth architecture. Purchase price, maintenance costs, cost of false positives on productivity, and the costs of damages prevented by attacks blocked should all be taken into account during purchases of security products. While all these aspects of the cost of security products are important, in this work we focus on measurement of attacks blocked by various products. CSOs can follow expert knowledge codified in best practices and compliance standards such as HIPAA and PCI. This leads to deployment of many

---

* This work is sponsored in part by Air Force Office of Scientific Research (AFOSR) grant FA9550-12-1-0162 "Designing for Measurable Security." The views and conclusions contained herein are those of the authors and should not be interpreted as necessarily representing the official policies or endorsements, either expressed or implied, of AFOSR.

© Springer International Publishing Switzerland 2014

security products such as firewalls, intrusion detection systems (IDS), antivirus, web application firewalls, patch management, and others to provide defense in depth where a particular attack must evade many security products in order to be successful. Intuitively the hope is that attacks that one security product might miss will be detected by another, but such intuitive best practice assumptions often fail or are incomplete as seen in a recent quantitative study of password policy assumptions [1]

To illustrate the current ad hoc nature of defense in depth deployment, consider the following hypothetical scenarios depicted in Figure 1. Imagine an organization with security products deployed across three layers of defense: a firewall, an IDS/IPS, and host antivirus. Assume this organization suffers many attacks against its hosts which could be detected by any of these three layers. In these figures, the red squares represent attacks. For each security product consider it capable of detecting any attacks that fall within its circle. Consider two scenarios presented notionally in Figures 1A and 1B. Figure 1A illustrates the intuitive hope of defense in depth where each security product is able to detect additional attacks and few attacks are able to bypass all three. Figure 1B shows a pessimistic view where the security products only detect the same group of easily detected attacks while leaving the organization vulnerable.

Additionally, consider the scenarios in Figures 1A, 1C and 1D. In these figures, we have not only different layers of defense but consider specific products. Figure 1A represents an ideal setup, but consider an organization whose current products are as seen in Figure 1C. Once aware of the gap in coverage seen here, the organization could find a product that closes their specific gap. This is seen in Figure 1D where the organization may replace firewall 3 with firewall 2 to achieve better coverage. While similar in terms of detection rate and absolute number of attacks detected, firewall 2 and firewall 3 differ in terms of which attacks they block. Current product testing only shows per product detection rates without indication of what overlap might exist with other products.

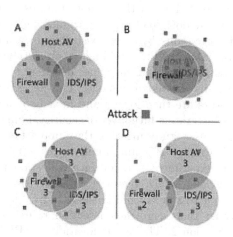

Fig. 1. Illustration of overlap and total coverage of four defense in depth deployments. Each square represents an attack. Each circle is a security product. Attacks in a circle mean that those attacks will be detected by that security product.

We address this issue by expanding the standard security product detection rate testing in two ways. First, we track not only individual security product detection rates, but also which attacks each security product detects. This allows us to take a union of the sets of attacks an arbitrary group of security products detect in order to calculate the coverage or total detection rate a set of security products have in aggregate against a set of attacks. Second, rather than testing security products against isolated pieces of attack data, we carefully record and link all data from a particular attack in its various forms so that security products from multiple layers of defense can be tested against the same attack.

This new approach to data gathering and testing could both validate the need for a new security product and give a baseline to quantitatively measure how much that security product improves the overall security posture of the organization by calculating the increase in coverage (total detection rate) after adding that product. Any inexpensive security product that is complementary to the organizations' current defense in depth becomes a good investment while expensive products that add little relative improvement could be used only to protect the most valuable of assets. Additionally, since the data sets and security products only have to be gathered and tested by one security service provider regardless of how many organizations make use of the data, this approach is scalable with costs amortized across any number of benefiting organizations.

In order to demonstrate the useful knowledge that is possible to gain from our methodology, we created a prototype system, we call Security Posture Integration and Correlation Engine (SPICE). SPICE covers four layers of security tested in near real time (within a few minutes in most cases) against real in the wild drive-by download attacks originating in widespread spam emails. To prevent biasing results by using existing known malware, we use a real time spam feed from Abusix [2] to send links to an instance of the Cuckoo Sandbox [3] honeypot driving full virtual machines designed to be vulnerable to common in the wild drive-by download exploits. The files, URLs visited, and full network packet capture are then logged and linked to the email that sent the malicious URL. We integrate a fifth layer of security, human click-through rates, into the system via a user study utilizing the same attack data allowing us to directly link the believability of spam emails to detection of the attack at other layers. While this experiment and its data collection is specific to the widespread drive-by download attack vector, we discuss applying our methodology (linking attack data across layers and tracking individual attack detection by security products rather than aggregate detection rates) to other attackers and attack vectors in Section 2. The key innovation in SPICE over existing malware collection is that we systematically and automatically link the data captured. Knowing for example which HTTP link led to which Windows PE file being loaded onto a victim machine allows us to compare a domain reputation system such as Google SafeWeb to a host or network antivirus product. We can determine that the attack would have been blocked had either successfully identified it.

This paper provides the following contributions:

1. We describe a practical methodology for calculating the coverage (total detection rate) of a group of security products deployed across many layers of security as defense in depth as well as the marginal detection rate gained by adding a new security product.

2. We apply this methodology to create SPICE, a prototype system, collecting drive-by download attacks in near real time linking emails, domain names, network traffic, and executables to each attack.
3. With this data, we test over 40 security products across many layers of defense. We report individual detection rates and delayed detections as well as the correlation and total coverage of sets of security products.
4. Using this methodology and prototype we are able to compare the results of a user study on human click through rates for actual attack emails to other security layers.
5. The data we have gathered will be provided to the research community. The linked attack components and detailed detection results may offer new research opportunities for the research community.

The remainder of this paper is organized as follows. Section 2 discusses definitions, overall approach, and the challenges facing such comprehensive measurement. Section 3 describes the SPICE system architecture. Section 4 presents detection rate, coverage, correlation results, and user study results. Section 5 discusses related work on defense in depth, drive-by downloads, measurement experiments, and best practices. Section 6 mentions future goals and directions going forward. Finally, section 7 summarizes the findings and approach.

2 Methodology

2.1 Approach

The approach for measuring defense in depth consists of a series of steps.

1. Choose a particular attack vector. This paper centers on a prototype experiment for drive-by downloads. Other potential attack vectors include web server attacks, insider attacks, data exfiltration, and so forth.
2. Find security products that are capable of detecting an attack for the chosen attack vector.
3. Set up a honeypot capable of recording all the data from the attack that each of these security products take as input. For example, ensure the honeypot can capture the network traffic to test a network IDS and executable files to test antivirus or host detectors.
4. Collect attack data and normal data if possible. In the case of testing against widespread attacks as we do with SPICE this could come from a commercial spam feed or existing honeypot. Real time in the wild data is ideal for accurately measuring existing attacks.
5. Have the honeypot record all the attacks in real time and monitor for successful attacks. Save all the data related to successful attacks and link the attack components.

6. Test each security product against appropriate attack components of the data collected and record the results. Use these results to determine which security products detected which attacks.
7. With a set of detected attacks for each security product one can answer questions such as what is the coverage (total detection rate) of a group of security products, the marginal increase in detection rate by adding each security product, and which ones detect the most difficult attacks.

This process is repeatable for each attack vector to develop a broad view of the security posture of the defenses although additional attack vector specific data collection methods would be required. The most difficult task is data collection, which in turns depends on the type of attacker an organization is interested in defending against. SPICE is as reliant as any other testing framework on good underlying data and ground truth.

2.2   Definitions

Attack: An instance of an attacker attempting to gain unauthorized access to a system. For this experiment, we more specifically define an attack as a single instance of a virtual machine in a honeypot visiting a drive-by download website and getting infected with an executable file.

Attack Cluster: A group of similar attacks presumably launched by the same attacker. For SPICE, we group attacks into attack clusters based on email contents[1].

Layer: In this work we use 'layer' to refer to all the security products deployed in a defense in depth architecture that use a particular type of data. For instance, a defense in depth architecture with regards to the drive-by download attack vector is made up of many layers such as security products operating on email content, security products operating on network traffic, etc.

2.3   Linking Attack Vector Data

We link attack data so that security products from different layers can be tested against the same attack based on whatever data that attack generates suitable for each layer. Recording and linking this data takes different forms based on the attack vector. For instance in the drive-by download scenario one would capture the spam email, the initial malicious link, the network traffic as a virtual machine visits the link and gets infected, and the files and processes loaded onto the victim machine. For web application attacks, one would capture incoming network packets, reassembled HTTP requests, server host data such as file system accesses and system calls, network traffic to the database backend, and

---

[1] We cluster emails with a similarity score greater than .8 computed between two emails' content by taking the ratio of the sum of the lengths minus the Levenshtein distance with weight two for character replacement and the sum of the lengths.

database queries linking all this data together by time window and other signatures such as IP address and process ID. For the insider threat attack vector, we could track user activity logging into each server, file transfers, host data such as file access and system calls, and outbound network traffic linking this data together by user login and machine IP address. Each security product is tested as to whether it can detect the attack through whichever piece(s) of this data it is designed to process. For example, user education would be tested on the spam email content from the attack while a network intrusion prevention system would read the network data from the same attack.

While SPICE deals only with the initial attack vector data crossing four layers of security, additional layers of security play an important role, especially against more sophisticated adversaries. The stages of an attack after initial infection such as propagation, downloading additional malicious features, and eventually data capture and exfiltration provide the potential for many more layers of security to accurately detect some stage of an attack. SPICE can incorporate these additional layers of data if additional data collection capabilities are added. The most straightforward extension would be simply to leave any infected honeypots online and observe future behaviors. This could capture any generic botnet traffic, but without exposing any sensitive data. We believe that a more sophisticated honeypot solution where attacks are run on servers with enticing but fake data such as described in [4] could be constructed. This would allow for excellent data collection and the ability to accurately test security products designed for data loss prevention or multistage infections.

2.4 Discussion of Data Sets and Adversarial Capabilities

We define each class of adversary by the additional resources/capabilities they bring to bear. While certainly not perfect, we believe that definitions along these lines provide clear means of separation and data gathering while still giving organizations a good idea of the level of sophistication of adversaries they are vulnerable to. Some of these adversaries lend themselves to easy data collection using honeypots collecting real data on the internet. Others, especially as they grow in sophistication raise the cost of in the wild collection with sparser data and the expense of fielding sophisticated honeypots. For many of these we propose approximate synthetic data set generation that while not ideal could at least provide a picture of the threat. Note that the scope of this experiment is limited to the widespread untargeted exploit kit attackers as described below.

Widespread Untargeted Exploit Kit Attackers. One drive-by download adversary class is what we term a widespread untargeted exploit kit attacker. This is an adversary that not only makes general nontargeted attacks, but does so against any email address available. A perfectly representative data set is then easily collected from honeypot emails. The only challenge in modeling such an adversary is sorting through the enormous amounts of non-harmful spam to find those spam emails that contain malicious links. These links seem to point to standard (and perhaps even outdated) exploit kits with well known exploits and mostly not so subtle executable payloads. What makes this adversary dangerous is that an organization must be prepared to deal with the attacks as they are widespread enough that they will certainly reach the organization. This is the adversary class that our experimental data set represents.

Targeted Exploit Kit Attackers. Another class of adversary is one we term as targeted exploit kit user. This adversary would still lack the innovation and/or resources to field any true zero-day exploits, but is capable of using the available attack tools to their fullest. This adversary also is capable of making targeted attacks using spear-phishing and brand new clean domains in order to compromise higher value targets. This is the level of adversary where inexpensive security products like domain reputation and email spam filtering start to fail. Classes of security products such as fully patched systems, sophisticated antivirus with whitelisting and behavioral analysis, host IDS, honey files, and data loss prevention systems become important if not necessary. Modeling this adversary class with in-the-wild data becomes difficult unless an organization has the opportunities to capture such attacks with its own honeypots for later analysis. Due to this class of adversary's reliance on existing exploit kits and available tools, we believe that a reasonable data set could be manufactured using those same tools. The challenge here is to maintain up to date copies of widely available attack tools and exploit kits especially when new exploits are added to the exploit kits before patches are widely available.

Zero-day, Insiders, and More Sophisticated Attackers. As attackers increase in sophisticated data goes from hard to collect to nearly impossible. Even if any such data becomes available, it would likely be of a historical nature and scarce. Even historical data could be interesting to test with as security products could have their updates rolled back to a date before the data was sent. Any conclusions drawn based on historical data would still be suspect as the nature of sophisticated attacks is to be fairly unique.

3   System Architecture

The Security Posture Integration and Correlation Engine (SPICE) prototype system, depicted in Figure 2 extends a traditional honeypot by carefully linking attack data across different layers in a database such that security products even from different layers of defense can all be compared. In this way, the coverage of an organization's defense in depth architecture can be evaluated. As an attack hits the honeypot, pieces of it are logged and then scanned by the appropriate security products once confirmed as malicious. As these pieces are linked, we can determine which security products detect the attack even if they run on different pieces of data linked to the same attack.

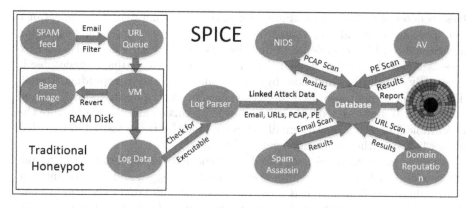

Fig. 2. An overview of SPICE. We build upon a traditional honeypot by carefully linking attack data in order to see how security products from different layers of defense overlap or complement each other.

We use an existing spam stream from spamfeed.me by Abusix [2]. It is a real-time spam feed that is captured through a large number of spam traps online. We receive 1 million emails a day. Each email is individually parsed, and all URLs from that email are then extracted and put into a database. Unfortunately, while such a feed guarantees that the emails are spam, the distribution of spam is highly skewed. Of the emails that even had links, the vast majority point to pharmaceutical spam with only a fraction of a percent serving active malicious content, handfuls per day from unique sites. We filter out links visiting only one from each domain for any twelve hour period in order to reduce the load on the VM clusters visiting each link.

To visit the URLs in emails, we use four clusters of virtual machines (VM), with 40 in each cluster that run on top of VirtualBox [5] across two physical machines. These virtual machines run off RAMdisk to minimize the impact of disk IO towards running and reverting virtual machines. Each cluster of virtual machine has its own configuration, with variations of browsers installed and its plugins such as Java, Adobe Flash, Adobe Acrobat Reader. We then validate each cluster's setup against CANVAS [6] a white hat penetration testing tool, making sure they are indeed vulnerable to existing exploits known to be targeted by exploit kits. We use Cuckoo Sandbox [3] to drive these virtual machines to visit each link logging host activity and new files created.

Each cluster has it own driver, which takes the URL feed and instructs the browser inside each machine to visit the link. We visit each URL three times per VM cluster, to compensate for the instability of the exploits. Sometimes exploits fail to infect even vulnerable machines, most likely due to poor code or nondeterministic exploit conditions. After waiting at least one minute, the VM is reverted to a clean state.

Each time, a VM visits a link the honeypot generates a log that contains a pcap file of the network traffic generated, and records details of the execution of programs in the operating system as well as new files generated. SPICE scans log files to determine if any executable files have been generated. The appearance of a new executable file is a strong indicator of an attack successfully occurring and provides a high confidence of malicious behavior, with a zero false positive rate as far as can be determined. Every successfully created new executable is eventually identified as malicious by at least one of the antivirus products tested. This classification is also used in other recent literature on drive-by download attacks [7]. If a new executable is found, we flag this as an attack and store the executable files as well as the email, pcap file, and the URLs visited during that attack linked to the attack in a central database.

We have installed three host based antivirus software programs, which scan the new files within a minute after the file has been logged and inserted into the central database. The antivirus programs rescan the files every six hours to test if new updates to the antivirus program are capable of detecting the attack. All the antivirus software is configured to update regularly. At the same time, we send the executable files to VirusTotal [8] once every 12 hours.

On top of scanning the executable files, we have the email and pcap file that are associated with the attack. We run Spam Assassin [9] on the email and Snort [10] a network IDS on the pcap file. Both of them follow the same rule for processing the incoming data: within a minute after arrival and rescans at 6 hour intervals. Spam assassin is configured to use the most up to date rules from the Internet automatically. Snort updates its rules daily from the Emerging Threats [11] public rulesets.

We also test domain reputation systems. We use the domain reputation data from four public domain blacklists to test each link that is associated with the attack to see if the domain is flagged as malicious. Whenever there is any result from the scanning system, they are added to the database for further analysis and rescanned periodically.

In order to test the efficacy of security education for users in an organization, we conducted a user study to measure the human factor in drive-by download attacks such as performed in [12]. User education has the potential to be a beneficial layer of defense as it complements almost all existing layers. If users can spot suspicious links and not click on them in the first place then the attack is thwarted. To test the likelihood of users clicking on a malicious link in the spam emails, we took one email from each of the attack clusters. After adding a unique identifier to and changing the malicious link to point to a benign web server with an unaffiliated domain name, we then sent the email to 10 randomly selected users from (anonymized) (IRB approval was received and will be cited) for each cluster resulting in a total of 360 emails sent. We send these emails from a clean account with an old nonmalicious domain for the links to evade reputation based spam filters, but content based spam filters could still affect this experiment so the results will represent more of a lower bound. If a user visited that unique link we recorded the click through and displayed a webpage detailing the study as well as warning of the dangers of clicking unknown links. By using the same attack data used by the other security products for testing, we can use this user study to see how human click-through rates overlap with other attack detection.

In the future, one could experiment with different user education techniques and by comparing their effectiveness directly against other security products one could determine whether user education is more cost effective than buying additional technical security products.

In summary, the entire list of products employed in SPICE includes:

1. One email spam detector
2. Human spam click through measurement
3. Four domain reputation systems
4. One network IDS
5. Three host antivirus programs
6. Forty antivirus engines via VirusTotal [8]

4   Results

4.1   Attack Data Collected

The 1463 virtual machines infected in the course of the five and a half week experiment cover attacks from 730 unique emails. With an average of about two infections per email out of the twelve times each link is visited (three per four virtual machine setups) we note that capturing in the wild drive-by download attacks is not reliable. The low rate of infections can be attributed to a combination of factors that make precise measurements difficult. A particular attacker may not have an effective exploit for some versions of vulnerable software. We mitigate this by confirming that in the wild exploits target the versions of vulnerable software each virtual machine setup runs. An attacker may blacklist repeat visits from the same IP or to the same unique link to thwart probing. In this case the best we can hope for is to be infected the first time. Some exploits are more reliable than others. Also, an exploit can fail or take longer to compromise a virtual machine than SPICE monitors.

Associated with these attacks are 942 distinct domains visited by virtual machines during the course of the infection and 576 unique executable files. The overlap of exactly the same files being used by attacks that started with separate emails indicates that many of these attacks are originating from the same attack campaign. In fact, most emails end up being a slight polymorphic variation of each other presumably to evade basic exact match spam filters. Once we cluster these similar emails (see Section 2.2 for details) we derive only 36 clusters. Unlike phishing emails or pharmaceutical spam, these emails' sole purpose is to get a user to visit the URL, which then launches a drive-by download attack.

In reporting successful detection of an attack cluster for a security product, we choose a pessimistic view. As launching additional attacks is inexpensive for an attacker, if a security product fails to raise at least one alert per attack in that cluster, then we claim that that security product does not detect the attack. We believe that this is the most realistic scenario since as long as one of the attacks gets through then the adversary succeeds.

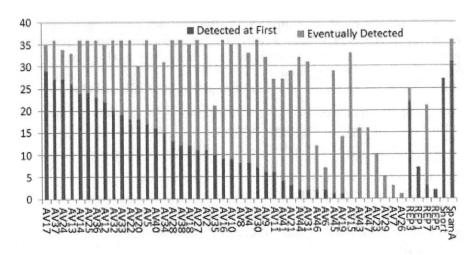

Fig. 3. Cluster detections per security product. Eventually detected attacks are ones that the product did not detect at first scan, but did detect on a later scan.

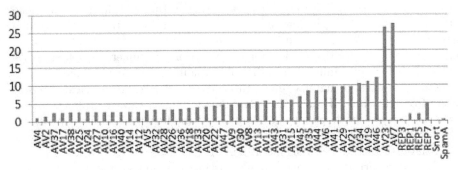

Fig. 4. Average (mean) number of days after an attack occurs that it is detected if it was not detected at first but eventually was

Clustering attacks based on email similarity yields a view untainted by repeated high volume attacks seen in Figure 3. We anonymize the commercial products in order to avoid any apparent bias or endorsement. The graph shows the number of attack clusters detected at first scan as well as those eventually detected, which is discussed further below. A wide range of individual security product effectiveness is displayed varying from products completely ineffective upon first scan to those that detect the vast majority of attack clusters. Here we see that while many security products still perform well, a need exists for multiple security products to fill gaps in coverage as no single security product detects all attacks.

4.2   Late Detections

Although the initial detection of an attack is most important and what is typically measured, we also continue to test security products over time to see if they eventually detect attacks that they initially missed. See these eventually detected attacks in Figure 3. For the initial test of each attack's appropriate data (file for antivirus, PCAP for NIDS, etc) against each security product we averaged 11.3 detected of the 36 clusters. In the weeks following the initial infection as we daily retested each attack that average eventually swelled to 27.3 detections of the 36 clusters per security product. The mean time between the attack occurring and the rescan that successfully detected previously undetected attack is 5.7 days on average for the security products we tested. This does vary significantly by secu-

Each Slice represents an attack
Each Ring repsents one layer of defense
■ Detected   Missed

Fig. 5. Graphic display of the first time each security product is tested with an attack cluster. Each concentric circle is a security product and each arc is one attack cluster. If that security product detects the attack cluster then the intersection of the circle and arc is dark otherwise it is light.

rity product as seen in Figure 4 with some security products averaging less than a day delay and others taking upwards of 25 days. This striking result confirms the need for testing to be done in real time as a significant delay can radically alter the results. The security products tested via VirusTotal may even have inflated initial detection rates as the hours delayed between capturing a new malicious file and their servers testing it could give vendors enough time to add new signatures that would not have been present during a real time attack. Based on the large number of attacks that are missed initially by security products on VirusTotal but eventually detected, we suspect that most vendors have a significant lag time in updates. While the delayed detection is certainly not ideal, this pattern of eventually detecting attacks could perhaps be leveraged into a system that saves and rescans data for an organization in order to detect what machines have been compromised in the past.

4.3   Correlation of Security Products

One of the key questions we set out to answer is whether and to what extent security products or particular defensive layers overlap i.e. do security products all tend to detect the same easy to detect attacks or do security products tend to detect separate attacks from each other. Another way to put this question is are the detection results of security products independent, or negatively or positively correlated that is do two security products, which each detect 90%

of attacks separately, together detect 99%, closer to 100%, or closer to 90% of attacks respectively. By tracking not only the detection rates, but also which attacks each security product detections even across different layers of security by linking the data each attack generates, we have the data to answer these questions for the security products tested here. We present this data in three Figures 5, 6, 7.

The first figure illustrating the correlation or overlap of the security products is Figure 5. In this figure, we show data similar to Figure 3 except that instead of each security product being a column, each security product is a concentric circle with its detection results lined up such that each arc of all the circles represents the same attack cluster. In this way rather than showing the detection rate of each security product, we can easily see which security products detect the same or different attacks. By drawing a line from outside the circle to the center, one can see which security products detected the attack represented by that arc. In order to have detected all attacks with at least one security product, one would have to choose a sufficient number of concentric circles such that any line drawn from outside the circle to its center is detected by at least one concentric circle. This visualization has its roots

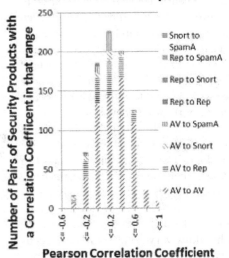

Histogram of Pearson correlation coefficient of Products pairwise

Fig. 6. Histogram of Pearson correlation coefficients of each pair of security products. A higher coefficient means that the two products overlap more.

in a common metaphor using a castle to illustrate layers of defense. Consider each security product represented by a concentric circle as a moat or castle wall and many armies (attacks) surrounding it each attacking its own section. A detection means that the particular army (attack) is unable to breach that security product.

Figure 6 uses the Pearson product-moment correlation coefficient to obtain a numerical measurement that represents the linear dependence between the attack cluster detections of a pair of security products. The coefficient is calculated for each pair of security products tested and the results are plotted as a histogram in Figure 6. The coefficient would be 1 in the case that the detection results are identical (completely overlap) and -1 if they were opposite (no overlap). On average the results show that security products tend to overlap slightly more than independent security products would. This means that by adding an average new security product to existing defense in depth we would expect it to increase the total detection rate relative to its absolute individual detection rate, but by less than if it was randomly detecting attacks at its individual detection rate. For example, if an existing security product detected 90% of attacks and one added a security product with Pearson coefficient of 0.2 with regards to the existing security product and a detection rate of 80%, one would expect slightly less than 98% combined detection rate. While skewed slightly towards positive correlations, these results show a number of negative correlations where two security products combined perform better than if their total detection probability was a simple product of their detection rates. For instance in the above example this would mean that the total detection rate would be above 98% instead.

Figure 7, also focused on the correlation of security products, graphs the number of attack clusters detected by both security products for each pair of security products versus the expected overlap in their attack cluster detection if each security product detected attacks at random based on its detection rate. Points above the line indicate a pair of security products that are more complementary than random while points below the line indicate a pair of products that overlap more than random detections. This result naturally mirrors the previous histogram of Pearson coefficients in indicating that on average security products appear to be slightly more redundant than if detections were random based on overall detection rates.

Intuitively, most products would use the same techniques and signatures making them mostly redundant, but we find that security products are only slightly redundant on aver-

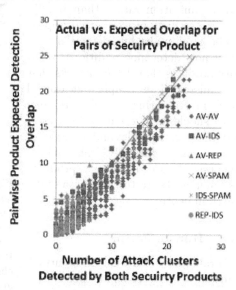

Fig. 7. Plot of the expected value of the overlap between each pair of security products if those products' detection rates were independent versus the actual overlap. Points below the line show more overlap than random.

age with many doing as well as completely independent detection mechanisms and some performing even better. While security products seem to vary greatly in their detection rates, even the less effective overall seem to occasionally detect an attack that bypasses most other security products. These results may come from a lack of attack intelligence sharing by the security industry, a wider than expected range of effective proprietary algorithms, or the challenge and chance associated with trying to detect increasingly polymorphic malware [13]. The results indicate that perhaps extensive usage of what might intuitively seem to be redundant security products could in fact significantly increase security. While using multiple inline host sensors is impractical, the results suggest that using multiple domain reputation systems and network based antivirus engines could increase the detection rate of the whole defense in depth strategy.

An advantage of SPICE is that while being able to evaluate the weaknesses of a particular security architecture, the approach also provides direction as to how to mitigate those weaknesses. The ability to find complementary security products is one of the largest contributions of SPICE. An organization rather than blindly picking security products that appear to be good in absolute detection rate, may now determine additional security products that detect attacks that are missed. This simple but crucial shift in evaluating security architecture should help organizations close existing security holes and allocate resources more efficiently. This complementary nature of security products is fundamental to the very idea of defense in depth.

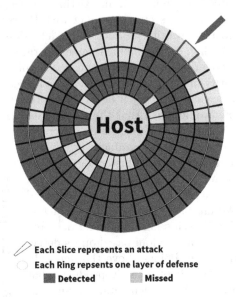

Each Slice represents an attack
Each Ring repsents one layer of defense
■ Detected   ■ Missed

Fig. 8. Graph of top AV (outer ring), top domain reputation system, Snort, Spam Assassin, and human click rate (red if at least 1 in 10 users clicked a link in the email) (inner ring). Each arc is one attack cluster. If that security product detects the attack cluster then the intersection of the circle and arc are dark otherwise it is light.

4.4 Human Factor

We ran a user study for all 36 attack clusters sending 10 emails per cluster for a total of 360 emails sent to separate users. See Section 3 for details. After three days we received click throughs on 17 of the 360 unique identifiers sent out. These hits are somewhat focused with 4 of the clusters receiving two click throughs, 20% of the users tested for those clusters. Additional education of those 5% of users who click through if effective could lead to a strong complementary layer of security. Attack clusters with emails that users fall for seem to be roughly as difficult to detect by other means. Compare the inner circle in Figure 8 with security products from other layers. The average attack is detected by about 15 security products while clusters with at least one user clicking on the link are detected by 14 security products on average. This increases slightly if we only take the clusters that at least two users clicked on the link for. From this limited study and widespread spam emails leading to drive-by downloads, we saw no significant correlation in click throughs and other security product detection of attacks. The percentage of users clicking through is lower for the study than other human factor studies [12] perhaps due to the fact that all the spam emails involved here are targeted to a general population rather than targeted to a particular organization or individual. Also note that these results likely represent a lower bound on the number of people who would click on the email as any spam filters in use by the users studied could block the email before it reached them. We took the precautions of sending from a clean source email address and having the links point to a clean domain name in order to mitigate this concern as much as possible, but the email content being that of real attack data could still trigger spam filters.

4.5 Use Case

To further illustrate the usefulness of SPICE consider a hypothetical case study based on the results. Assume a small organization with a CSO who did extensive research and deployed an antivirus and domain reputation system with the best stand-alone detection rates. In the experiment, the best stand alone detection rate for an antivirus was 29/36 attack clusters and for domain reputation 22/36. This is the current state of the art for product comparisons with both of these being best in class at least for this data set. The natural question here is what is the overlap of these two security products and do they together detect all of the attack clusters. SPICE can be used to answer this question. These two security products together managed to detect 33 of the 36 attack clusters (see the outer two circles of Figure 8). Notice that three arcs representing attacks are all light meaning that those three attack clusters went undetected by both security products.

Now assume that this hypothetical CSO wants to improve his organization's security against such widespread attacks. Considering new security products is a proper next step. The network IDS Snort [10] with the Emerging Threat rules [11] detected 27 of these same 36 attack clusters, but more importantly it detects 2 of the 3 attack clusters that were missed by the antivirus and domain reputation system. Measuring the current state of user click throughs we see users did not respond to 23/36 attack clusters including one of the three missed by both the antivirus and domain reputation system. Similarly, we can check Spam Assassin [9] an email spam detection product, which as expected considering the data set is based on widespread spam, had a strong detection rate identifying 31/36 of the attack clusters including all three that the antivirus and domain reputation system failed to detect. See Figure 8 for a visualization of all layers together. In this situation installing Spam Assassin alone covers against these attacks but also one could choose to install Snort for extra redundancy. An organization could only look at sets that already include their existing security products in order to find the next security product to deploy.

5   Related Work

Research on defense in depth often focuses on broad frameworks and the need for defense in depth without providing a specific methodology suitable for experimental measurement and evaluation of defense in depth. General themes such as the need for security products to be at least independent or multiplicative in strength and the need for measurement are repeated in many works [14] [15] [16] [17]. An argument for careful independence assumptions and goals of purposefully choosing security products that are better at detecting different classes of attacks in order to achieve higher coverage than independent security products in presented in [17]. The authors in [14] suggest measuring the attacker's cost to bypass each security product or group of security products. This approach could scale well with regards to sophisticated attackers were real attack data is scarce or outdated making direct measurement of detection rates difficult although methods of measuring such cost are still nebulous. A method for combining the detection rates of security products from all layers is presented in [15] similar to our methodology, but the authors assume each security products independent whereas, we directly measure the overlap between security products without assumptions of independence. While work on directly measuring defense in depth is rare, [18] presents a method for using attack graphs to measure firewalls combined with host vulnerability information to detect holes in a defense in depth deployment.

Drive-by downloads, the attack vector we use in the SPICE prototype system to demonstrate our methodology, is a well studied area. A number of approaches to protecting against drive-by downloads have been presented [7] [19] [20]. We use the same ground truth definition as one recent work [7] as well as its baseline comparison with VirusTotal, which we use. In future work, when we test against more sophisticated attacker data, all of these novel research approaches can be integrated into the SPICE framework as additional layers to test. Studies of using multiple antivirus security products as defense in depth have been conducted such as [21] [22] all showing benefit from combining multiple antivirus engines. These studies are limited to only one layer of defense in depth where with SPICE we expand beyond just antivirus to analyze security products across different layers. Human spam message click through has been studied before such as in [12]. We use similar mechanics with the addition of being able to link the results to other pieces of the same attack that generated the email clicked on.

Some of the most closely related work to SPICE is conducted by commercial security product testers. For example, NSS Labs [23] conducts extensive tests of security products ranging from home user anti-malware solutions to the newest corporate all-inclusive network security appliances. SPICE expands on these existing approaches. By linking the data across layers of an attack vector, we can reason about how products which operate at different layers i.e. network and host detectors complement each other. We have one set of attacks that we test all layers against at once.

The Anti-Malware Testing Standards Organization (AMTSO) [24] creates and maintains best practices for testing security products. While acknowledging the impossibility of a perfect test and evaluation, AMTSO provides guidelines and suggestions for achieving the most accurate results. We implement as much of their advice as possible including one of the most important: real time testing. In the future, we hope to implement some of their additional best practices such as the important false positive measure and running tests on bare metal machines rather than the virtual test environment we use.

Recent extensive efforts to make data more available to the research community such as Symantec's Worldwide Intelligence Network Environment (WINE) [25] and others are crucial to the repeatability of experiments and gaining of new insights into attacks. The ability to access large numbers of samples and meta data will hopefully fuel the next generation of detection algorithms. Unfortunately, such archival data sets do not lend themselves to evaluating current security products. As we see in the results, security products are much better at detecting known threats, but these threats often slip by undetected the first time seen. The data set, which we are releasing to researchers as well while suffering from the same issue of outdated samples as WINE, has one important advantage. We keep track of which samples belong to the same attack chain. Hopefully this additional metadata will help other researchers or be useful in conjunction with larger data sets such as WINE.

6 Future Work

In future work, we are actively adding additional attack vectors starting with web application attacks as discussed in Section 2.3. Also, we wish to measure how security products change over time for all attack vectors. In particular we want to see if security products that are correlated in this data set stay correlated in the first or if such correlations occur by chance or for limited time periods. We want to add software updates as a layer of security by performing studies on vulnerability life times, time to patch, and zero-day attack prevalent. With these parameters an organization could combine their patching practices with their available security products to form a set of security controls that better represents their defense in depth posture. We wish to add cost information such as false positive rates and price to security products so that sets can display total cost in addition to total detection rate. We also would like to use SPICE to test and compare how novel full class prevention security products such as BLADE [7] or virtualization layers might perform. If these security products perform up to their full potential of shutting down whole attack vectors, they may justify their high cost of user training/deployment effort. SPICE could help show how this solutions might succeed compared to multiple commercial solutions that even together suffer many weaknesses.

7 Conclusion

We presented SPICE, a novel method and framework, to measure how secure an organization is by testing real security products with real attacks. By designing additional experiments measuring all known attack vectors and security products an organization uses, we can measure how secure that organization really is. To compute this for a single organization is perhaps prohibitively expensive considering the costs associated with procuring the appropriate attacks to represent sophisticated adversaries and testing infrastructure needed to adequately test advanced security products. Fortunately, the cost can be amortized by a security services provider across a number of organizations that could benefit from the same knowledge of how their existing products complement each other and what new products could fill specific weaknesses they may have. Being able to cost effectively compare security products is crucial. Current tests give no good indication of whether a security product detects the same attacks already detected by existing products especially ones from different layers. SPICE directly measures the underlying assumption of defense in depth that security products complement each other in detecting different attacks. We provide a feasible empirical measurement of an organization's security while at the same time providing the information of which security products would most enhance that organization's security posture.

References

1. Weir, M., Aggarwal, S., Collins, M., Stern, H.: Testing metrics for password creation policies by attacking large sets of revealed passwords. In: Al-Shaer, E., Keromytis, A.D., Shmatikov, V. (eds.) ACM Conference on Computer and Communications Security, pp. 162–175. ACM (2010), http://doi.acm.org/10.1145/1866307.1866327
2. http://abusix.org
3. http://www.cuckoosandbox.org
4. Bowen, B.M., Hershkop, S., Keromytis, A.D., Stolfo, S.J.: Baiting inside attackers using decoy documents. In: Chen, Y., Dimitriou, T., Zhou, J. (eds.) SecureComm. LNCIST, vol. 19, pp. 51–70. Springer, http://dx.doi.org/10.1007/978-3-642-05284-2
5. Watson, J.: Virtualbox: Bits and bytes masquerading as machines. Linux J. 2008(166), 1 (2008)
6. http://immunityinc.com/products-canvas.shtml
7. Lu, L., Yegneswaran, V., Porras, P.A., Lee, W.: BLADE: An attack-agnostic approach for preventing drive-by malware infections. In: Al-Shaer, E., Keromytis, A.D., Shmatikov, V. (eds.) ACM Conference on Computer and Communications Security, pp. 440–450. ACM (2010), http://doi.acm.org/10.1145/1866307.1866356
8. https://www.virustotal.com/
9. http://spamassassin.apache.org/
10. Roesch, M.: Snort, intrusion detection system, http://www.snort.org
11. http://www.emergingthreats.net
12. Bowen, B., Devarajan, R., Stolfo, S.: Measuring the human factor of cyber security. In: 2011 IEEE International Conference on Technologies for Homeland Security (HST), pp. 230–235 (November 2011)
13. Song, Y., Locasto, M.E., Stavrou, A., Keromytis, A.D., Stolfo, S.J.: On the infeasibility of modeling polymorphic shellcode. In: Proceedings of the 14th ACM Conference on Computer and Communications Security, CCS 2007, pp. 541–551. ACM, New York (2007), http://doi.acm.org/10.1145/1315245.1315312

14. Stolfo, S., Bellovin, S., Evans, D.: Measuring security. IEEE Security Privacy 9(3), 60–65 (2011)
15. Cavusoglu, H., Mishra, B., Raghunathan, S.: A model for evaluating it security investments. Commun. ACM 47(7), 87–92 (2004), http://doi.acm.org/10.1145/1005817.1005828
16. Stytz, M.: Considering defense in depth for software applications. IEEE Security Privacy 2(1), 72–75 (2004)
17. Littlewood, B., Strigini, L.: Redundancy and diversity in security. In: Samarati, P., Ryan, P.Y.A., Gollmann, D., Molva, R. (eds.) ESORICS 2004. LNCS, vol. 3193, pp. 423–438. Springer, Heidelberg (2004), http://dx.doi.org/10.1007/978-3-540-30108-0_26
18. Lippmann, R., Ingols, K., Scott, C., Piwowarski, K., Kratkiewicz, K., Artz, M., Cunningham, R.: Validating and restoring defense in depth using attack graphs. In: Military Communications Conference, MILCOM 2006, pp. 1–10. IEEE (2006)
19. Cova, M., Kruegel, C., Vigna, G.: Detection and analysis of drive-by-download attacks and malicious javascript code. In: Proceedings of the 19th International Conference on World Wide Web, WWW 2010, pp. 281–290. ACM, New York (2010), http://doi.acm.org/10.1145/1772690.1772720
20. Egele, M., Wurzinger, P., Kruegel, C., Kirda, E.: Defending browsers against drive-by downloads: Mitigating heap-spraying code injection attacks. In: Flegel, U., Bruschi, D. (eds.) DIMVA 2009. LNCS, vol. 5587, pp. 88–106. Springer, Heidelberg (2009), http://dx.doi.org/10.1007/978-3-642-02918-9_6
21. Oberheide, J., Cooke, E., Jahanian, F.: CloudAV: N-version antivirus in the network cloud. In: van Oorschot, P.C. (ed.) USENIX Security Symposium, pp. 91–106. USENIX Association (2008), http://www.usenix.org/events/sec08/tech/full_papers/oberheide/oberheide.pdf
22. Gashi, I., Sobesto, B., Stankovic, V., Cukier, M.: Does malware detection improve with diverse antivirus products? An empirical study. In: Bitsch, F., Guiochet, J., Kaâniche, M. (eds.) SAFECOMP. LNCS, vol. 8153, pp. 94–105. Springer, Heidelberg (2013), http://dx.doi.org/10.1007/978-3-642-40793-2_9
23. http://www.nsslabs.com/
24. http://www.amtso.org/
25. Dumitras, T., Shou, D.: Toward a standard benchmark for computer security research: The worldwide intelligence network environment (wine). In: Proceedings of the First Workshop on Building Analysis Datasets and Gathering Experience Returns for Security, BADGERS 2011, pp. 89–96. ACM, New York (2011), http://doi.acm.org/10.1145/1978672.1978683

A Lightweight Formal Approach for Analyzing Security of Web Protocols

Apurva Kumar

IBM Research-India,
4, Block C, Vasant Kunj Institutional Area,
New Delhi, India 110070
kapurva@in.ibm.com

Abstract. Existing model checking tools for cryptographic protocol analysis have two drawbacks, when applied to present day web based protocols. Firstly, they require expertise in specialized formalisms which limits their use to a small fragment of scientific community. Secondly, they do not support common web constructs and attacks making the analysis both cumbersome as well as error-prone. In this paper, we propose a novel security analysis technique specialized for web protocols. We provide explicit support for common web mechanisms and an adversary capable of exploiting browser-based interaction. Our approach has two unique aspects. It represents the only tool built using a general purpose first-order logic based modeling language – Alloy – that can be used to analyze security of industrial strength web protocols. The other unique aspect is our use of an inference system that analyzes beliefs at honest participants to simplify the protocol model. Despite its simplicity, we demonstrate effectiveness of our approach through a case-study of SAML, where we identify a previously unknown vulnerability in its identity federation workflow.

Keywords: Security Protocols, Federated Identity, Web Security.

1   Introduction

With an increase in business transactions using resources from multiple cloud vendors, managing user identity across cloud service providers has become a common requirement. At the core of these interactions involving multiple providers are a set of web-based workflows that have emerged as de-facto standards. Identity management standards such as Security Assertion Markup Language (SAML 2.0) [13], OpenID [27] and OAuth [21] represent industry efforts in this direction. Analyzing security of such web protocols is crucial for these business transactions.

Analysis of cryptographic protocols has been an active research area in the last three decades. Analysis techniques examine a protocol's ability to establish agreement on certain data items between honest participants without revealing its secrets to an adversary. There are two contrasting styles that have been used for security protocol analysis. *Inference construction* style approaches, first

A. Stavrou et al. (Eds.): RAID 2014, LNCS 8688, pp. 192–211, 2014.
© Springer International Publishing Switzerland 2014

popularized by the Burrows, Abadi and Needham (BAN) [12] logic, attempt to use inference in specialized logics to establish required beliefs at honest participants. These approaches operate at a high abstraction level and result in efficiently computable formulations. *Attack construction* style approaches on the other hand, approach the problem from the adversary's perspective. They perform state-spaces exploration to determine whether an undesirable state – such as a secret value becoming available to an adversary – can be reached. The state machine used for representing the protocol takes into account structure of messages passing over the channel and a complex intruder model.

Both classes of approaches have their drawbacks. Despite their simplicity, interest in inference construction approaches has diminished due to soundness issues reported with published analyses. The abstraction process for converting informal protocol description into formulas of the logic – termed as idealization – is considered error-prone. Model checking approaches, apart from possible state-space blow up can be fairly complex and error-prone in usage, even for security researchers [17]. Finally, both classes of approaches have not been adapted well enough for analysis of web protocols. This can make analysis of web protocols hard as well as inaccurate.

In this paper, we describe a specialized framework for analyzing security of such web protocols. We introduce primitives representing important web mechanisms such as SSL/TLS secure channels, HTTP cookies and redirection. Our adversary model takes into account exploits specific to browser-based communication including those that employ social engineering. Unlike existing techniques, we do not use specialized model checkers or a formalism specific to security verification. Rather, we use Alloy, a general purpose first-order logic based structural modeling language. Representing protocol models in Alloy tremendously increases the accessibility of our methods to a larger community designing and developing web protocols. In our approach, we further reduce complexity of modeling web protocols, by using an inference system that performs a preliminary belief analysis. We demonstrate significant reduction in complexity of protocol modeling by using correspondence of beliefs at protocol participants. Using a combination of inference and attack construction, allows us to simplify analysis while avoiding common pitfalls associated with the use of belief logics.

To illustrate our method, we present analysis of identity management workflow used by leading protocols such as SAML and OpenID. We show that while the single sign-on flow can be considered safe, a minor variation of the flow which is used for linking user accounts across domains is flawed even when all communication is made to pass through SSL/TLS based secure channels. This is a rather surprising result, considering that SAML is one of the most analyzed web protocols. The reason for this anomaly is that existing techniques assume a standard adversary incapable of launching certain web-based attacks.

The rest of this paper is organized as follows. Background and related work discussion appears in section 2. In section 3, we present a simple extension of BAN for the web and use SAML SSO for an example analysis. We discuss soundness issues in belief logics and how we avoid them in our approach. In section 4, the generic Alloy based framework for analyzing web protocols is described. In section 5, we present a detailed analysis of SAML based identity federation. We conclude with a discussion about our contribution in section 6.

2   Background and Related Work

2.1   Formalisms for Analyzing Security

Adversary Model. The intruder model proposed by Dolev and Yao [18] in which the intruder has the ability to read, alter, encrypt, decrypt, compose and deconstruct messages is widely adopted by the cryptographic protocols community. Despite its flexibility, the Dolev-Yao model, is not ideal for the web environment due to the following reasons:

- Web protocols typically recommend or mandate usage of secure SSL/TLS communication. The assumption can result in substantial simplification of analysis.
- Dolev-Yao cannot model certain types of browser-based attacks. Clicking on a malicious link can cause an honest user to send a message to a server outside any protocol context it is aware of. The message could contain any secrets values known to the attacker and is possibly accompanied by valid cookies the user's browser has for the server's domain. This allows the attacker to mount session-fixation and cross-site request forgery (CSRF) attacks.

The adversary model we use for analyzing web protocols can be considered a variation of Dolev-Yao model in which the intruder does not have access to all messages, but at the same time has the ability to exploit browser-based communication to forge requests, manipulate redirection endpoints etc. Modeling such adversary capabilities is extremely important for proper verification of web protocols, as evidenced by our analysis of identity federation in section 5.

Multiset Rewrite Formalism. The authors of [14] attempt to formalize a standard representation of the Dolev-Yao model. The notation they use involves *facts* and *transitions*. The state transition rules are defined to describe protocol behavior as well as intruder capabilities. Facts contain a symbolic representation of messages transmitted in the protocol and the state transition rules are triggered on sending or receiving of messages. Using this formalism, the authors establish undecidability of the secrecy property for unbounded number of sessions, even with bounded message sizes, and encryption depth [19].

Applied pi Calculus Formalism. The applied pi-calculus [2] is a language for describing cryptographic protocols in terms of communication between participant processes. An adversary itself is modeled as a process and interacts with the protocol. A protocol preserves secrecy of a term if, no matter which adversarial context it is evaluated in, it will never be part of its knowledge. ProVerif [11], [8], [9] is a cryptographic protocol verifier, developed by Bruno Blanchet. The input can be specified directly as a sequence of Horn clauses or as a process in a variant of the applied pi-calculus. It is capable of evaluating reachability properties [1], correspondence properties [8] and observational equivalence [10]. Recently an add-on, WebSpi [7], that aims to make it easy to develop models for web mechanisms and protocols using Proverif has been made available.

The Strand Formalism. This formalism presents an alternative to the state space analysis by working with strand-spaces [20] which represent a graph-theoretic interpretation of the Dolev-Yao model. Several efforts have been made to automate analysis using this formalism. The most notable being the Athena tool [29]. The more recent Scyther tool [16] is also based on an extension of strand space concept.

A major drawback of above tools is that a good understanding of the protocol being modeled is not sufficient. The user also needs to be familiar with the underlying formalism. Protocol modeling using these tools is time-consuming, error-prone and requires lot of skill and practice to master [17]. In contrast, we use a general purpose modeling language such as Alloy and a generic protocol model that can be easily extended. This makes our technique approachable for protocol designers and application developers.

Modal Logics. Inference construction approaches attempt to use inference in specialized logics to establish required beliefs at protocol participants. The logic of authentication described in [12], commonly known as BAN, was one of the first successful attempts at representing and reasoning about security properties of protocols. [3] provides semantics of the logic and discusses its soundness. In [30] authors attempt to consolidate good features from earlier belief logic approaches. These logics have the advantage of being usually decidable and efficiently computable. The logics can be easily automated. In [28], a transformation of BAN logic and inference rules to first order formula is performed and theorem prover SETHEO is used for finding proofs. In [15], the authors attempt to embed BAN logic in EVES theorem prover. However, given that a real protocol has a limited number of keys, principals and messages, forward chaining approaches discussed in [23] or the model driven analysis approach in [24] are often much simpler.

2.2   Tools for Analyzing Web Protocols

Analyzing web protocols with tools having no explicit support for standard web mechanisms and a specialized adversary model can be both cumbersome as well as flawed. In [5], the authors use the SATMC tool [6], without significant changes, to analyze the SAML Single Sign-on (SSO) protocol. Not only is the multiset rewriting based formulation quite complex for a protocol of this size, use of the standard Dolev-Yao attacker without support for session-fixation or cross-site forgery attacks, results in a vulnerability not surfacing in their analysis. This vulnerability is the primary source of insecurity in the SAML identity federation protocol we analyze in section 5.

Authors of [4], model some web mechanisms using Alloy and analyze them for multiple security properties. The model in [4] is intended to capture low level properties of HTTP messages such as HTML forms, XML requests, authentication headers etc. In contrast, we model protocol entities and constructs such as users, servers, keys, messages, protocol traces etc. The higher abstraction level allows us to analyze complex web protocols. For analyzing industrial strength protocols, we propose a strategy in which the protocol model can be simplified if a prior belief logic analysis of the protocol has been conducted.

In our earlier work, [25], we explored a combination of inference and attack construction styles for security analysis. However, this preliminary work was limited in following ways:

- The Alloy model in [25] was simplistic and did not allow principals or adversary to participate in multiple sessions.
- The two styles were combined in a different way - proving of goals was performed using belief logic, while the role of Alloy was to simply verify an assumption made in the analysis. This resulted in a much more complex belief logic (rules R5-R7 in [25]), leading to soundness concerns.

In contrast, in this paper, the Alloy based method has been extended so that it no longer depends on a belief logic stage. We introduce the much needed support for multiple sessions – without which any tool for security analysis cannot be considered complete. Since goals are directly represented as assertions in the model, unlike [25], we are guaranteed a counter-example (i.e. an attack trace) if a protocol is found to be insecure. The role of the much simpler belief logic used in our work is to optionally simplify message structures when agreement about protocol parameters can be established using the inference system. Finally, in this paper, we analyze and find a flaw in SAML identity linking workflow, while in [25], security of OAuth1.0 was examined.

2.3   Overview of BAN

A formula in BAN logic [12] is constructed using operators from Table 1. P and Q range over principals. The three statements about keys and secrets represent atomic statements. X represents a BAN formula constructed using one or more BAN operators. The expression $\sharp X$ means that the message X is fresh and has not been used before the current run of the protocol. This is especially true for a nonce, a sequence number or timestamp generated with this specific purpose.

BAN defines a set of inference rules for deriving new beliefs from old ones. We describe only the most important of these rules here. The message-origin

Table 1. Operators in BAN Logic

$P \mid \equiv X$: P believes X	$P \overset{K}{\leftrightarrow} Q$: Shared key K
$P \triangleleft X$: P sees X	$\underset{K}{\longmapsto} Q$: Public key K belongs to Q
$P \mid \sim X$: P said X	$P \overset{Y}{\rightleftharpoons} Q$: Shared secret Y
$P \mid \Rightarrow X$: P controls X	$\sharp X$: Fresh X
$\{X\}_K$: X encrypted by K	$\langle X \rangle_Y$: X combined with Y

inference rule R1.2 states that if P knows that K is the public key belonging to Q and it sees a message X encrypted by the corresponding private key K^{-1}, then P is entitled to believe that Q said X. R1.1 and R1.3 are similar rules for shared keys and shared secrets, respectively.

$$\frac{P \mid\equiv P \overset{K}{\leftrightarrow} Q, P \triangleleft \{X\}_K}{P \mid\equiv Q \mid\sim X} \quad (R1.1) \qquad \frac{P \mid\equiv \overset{}{\underset{K}{\longmapsto}} Q, P \triangleleft \{X\}_{K^{-1}}}{P \mid\equiv Q \mid\sim X} \quad (R1.2)$$

$$\frac{P \mid\equiv P \overset{Y}{\rightleftharpoons} Q, P \triangleleft \langle X \rangle_Y}{P \mid\equiv Q \mid\sim X} \quad (R1.3)$$

A nonce-verification rule R2 states that, in addition if the message is known to be fresh, then P believes that Q must still believe X. Further, the *jurisdiction rule* R3 states that, if in addition, P also believes that Q is an authority on the subject of X (i.e. Q controls X), then P is entitled to believe X itself.

$$\frac{P \mid\equiv Q \mid\sim X, P \mid\equiv \sharp X}{P \mid\equiv Q \mid\equiv X} \quad (R2) \qquad \frac{P \mid\equiv Q \mid\equiv X, P \mid\equiv Q \mid\Rightarrow X}{P \mid\equiv X} \quad (R3)$$

3 Belief Logic for the Web

A potential difficulty in analyzing browser-based web protocols is the lack of identifying keys for a typical web user. Moreover, identities established are local to a security domain rather than global. In the absence of identifying keys and global identities, it is often more important to establish whether a user recently performed an action rather than knowing its identity. In section 3.1, we describe our belief logic for web, an extension of BAN. We use the logic to analyze SAML SSO in section 3.2. We discuss some pitfalls in belief logic analysis and how we avoid them in our approach in section 3.3.

3.1 Extensions to BAN

We introduce two new types of objects (sorts) to the logic: *user* and *action*. A user is defined as the client side of a secure channel which models a unilateral SSL/TLS session with server authentication. We use the channel identifier as a subscript in our notation for user. The new operators are described in Table 2. We assume *Aname* to range over function symbols representing types of user actions. A user action type has a signature of the form $\sigma_1 \times \ldots \times \sigma_n \longrightarrow action$, where $\sigma_1, \ldots \sigma_n$ are other sorts of the logic. Signing in as principal Q, represented as $SignIn(Q)$, is example of an action.

We extend BAN logic through inference rules that apply to communication over one-sided (server authentication only) SSL/TLS secure channel. R4.1 says that if a principal P (usually server) believes that a user U_C is communicating over a secure channel C, then any actions it sees over the secure channel C can be attributed to user U_C. According to R4.2, any tokens seen over a secure channel are assumed to be possessed by the user. R4.3 states that when the client side

Table 2. New operators in Extended Logic

$P \overset{A}{\leftrightarrow} U_c$: Secure channel C	$[\![X]\!]_C$: X over secure channel C
$X \rightsquigarrow Aname(v_{\sigma_1}, \ldots, v_{\sigma_n})$: X associated with action	$U_c \ni X$: User U_c possesses X
$U_c \triangleright Aname(v_{\sigma_1}, \ldots, v_{\sigma_n})$: User U_c performs action	$Pname = val$: Parameter,value

receives a statement X over a secure channel, it is entitled to believe that the server principal has recently said ($says$) X.

$$\frac{P | \equiv (P \overset{A}{\leftrightarrow} U_c), P \triangleleft [\![action]\!]_C}{P | \equiv (U_c \triangleright action)} \quad \text{(R4.1)} \qquad \frac{P | \equiv (P \overset{A}{\leftrightarrow} U_c), P \triangleleft [\![X]\!]_C}{P | \equiv (U_c \ni X)} \quad \text{(R4.2)}$$

$$\frac{U_c | \equiv (P \overset{A}{\leftrightarrow} U_c), U_c \triangleleft [\![X]\!]_C}{U_c | \equiv (P \, says \, X)} \quad \text{(R4.3)}$$

We note that soundness of rules R4.1, R4.2 follows from integrity and confidentiality properties of SSL/TLS, while R4.3 additionally uses the server authentication it provides. Eliminating man-in-the-middle attacks allows us to associate a received message with an endpoint of the secure channel, which may be a server or a user.

3.2 Example: SAML SSO

A simple example of a web-based workflow involving multiple service providers is the SAML web single sign-on (SSO) protocol shown in Figure 1. The workflow involves a web user and two web based service providers, one of which acts as the identity provider. A user requesting service S at service provider (SP) site is redirected to Identity Provider (IdP) with SAML request. After authenticating the user, IdP redirects user back to SP site with a signed SAML token having the asserted identity (Q). SP validates the token and identifies the user as Q. In the figure C1-C3 identify secure SSL/TLS channels with server authentication.

To see if agreement is reached between honest principals, C and P playing the roles of SP and IdP respectively, we idealize messages 3 (SAML request received

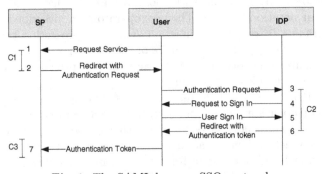

Fig. 1. The SAML browser SSO protocol

at IdP), 5 and 7 (SAML token received at SP) that convey information to C and P.

$Msg3$ $U_{C2} \rightarrow P : [\![\{auth\_req(N_{cp}, P), N_{cp}, idp = P, sp = C, cb = url_C\}_{K_c^{-1}}]\!]_{C2}$

$Msg5$ $U_{C2} \rightarrow P : [\![SignIn(Q)]\!]_{C2}$

$Msg7$ $U_{C3} \rightarrow C : [\![T, \{N_{cp}, T \leadsto SignIn(Q), idp = P, sp = C\}_{K_p^{-1}}]\!]_{C3}$ (1)

The SAML authentication request (message 3) signed by C comprises of statements about protocol roles using parameters sp, idp and callback URL (cb) to be used for redirection in step 6 (Figure 1). For brevity, we omit the argument identifying the session in our analysis and write a parameter such as $sp(N_{cp})$ simply as sp. The nonce, N_{cp} represents combination of a request identifier and a timestamp. The message is signed using the private key of service provider, C. In the idealization, we also include the term $auth\_req(N_{cp}, P)$. This allows us to additionally represent the fact that message 3 is a SAML request for P with identifier N_{cp}.

Message 5 represents a sign-in action performed at P. Message 7 represents the SAML response from identity provider containing the SAML token being received at the service provider after user is redirected back. The message signed by P, contains a token associated with the sign-in action and identifies the signed in user as Q. It also associates the information with the current session identified by N_{cp} and includes statements representing P's belief about protocol roles.

We make the following assumptions at C and P about secure channels, nonces, public keys, protocol roles and jurisdiction over parameters and actions. The first three assumptions are about the three secure channels C1-C3. The next two assumptions are about the freshness of nonce N_{cp}. These are followed by the two assumptions about public keys. The next assumption is about the protocol parameters at the service provider (C). This is followed by the assumption about C's belief in P's control over the $SignIn$ action. The final belief is about the identity provider (P) trusting the principal in the service provider role for the session for the callback (cb) parameter. In addition, we also use the following initialization rule S1 that initializes the service provider for the session as the originator of the SAML request received by an IdP.

$$C \,|\!\equiv C \stackrel{A}{\leftrightarrow} U_{C1} \qquad\qquad P \,|\!\equiv P \stackrel{A}{\leftrightarrow} U_{C2}$$

$$C \,|\!\equiv C \stackrel{A}{\leftrightarrow} U_{C3}$$

$$C \,|\!\equiv \sharp N_{cp} \qquad\qquad P \,|\!\equiv \sharp N_{cp}$$

$$C \,|\!\equiv \xmapsto{K_p} P \qquad\qquad P \,|\!\equiv \xmapsto{K_c} C$$

$$C \,|\!\equiv sp = C, idp = P, cb = url_C$$

$$C \,|\!\equiv P |\!\Rightarrow SignIn \qquad\qquad P \,|\!\equiv sp(n) |\!\Rightarrow cb(n) \quad (A1)$$

$$P \,|\!\equiv X \,|\!\sim auth\_req(n, P) \wedge P \,|\!\equiv \sharp n \;\rightarrow\; P \,|\!\equiv (sp(n) = X, idp(n) = P) \quad (S1)$$

We perform a BAN type forward chaining analysis of these messages and assumptions to evaluate beliefs at honest SP and IdP. The analysis involves simply combining facts based on rules of the logic and is detailed in Appendix A. The analysis can be easily automated using techniques such as [23], [24]. The final beliefs (including assumptions) at C and P obtained from the analysis are listed below:

$$C \mid \equiv (sp = C, idp = P) \qquad C \mid \equiv P \mid \equiv (sp = C, idp = P)$$
$$P \mid \equiv (sp = C, idp = P) \qquad P \mid \equiv C \mid \equiv (sp = C, idp = P)$$
$$P \mid \equiv (cb = url_c) \qquad P \mid \equiv U_{C2} \rhd SignIn(Q)$$
$$C \mid \equiv T \rightsquigarrow SignIn(Q) \qquad C \mid \equiv U_{C3} \ni T \qquad (2)$$

Both C and P are in agreement about the protocol roles in session identified by N_{cp}. This can be seen from the fact that their beliefs about values for variables sp, cp at the peer are consistent with their own beliefs. Further, C believes that the token corresponds to the action of signing in with login Q at P and also that the token is in possession of user U_{C3}. Are the above beliefs sufficient for C to consider user U_{C3} signed-in as Q? If not, is their a possible vulnerability in SAML SSO? These questions are answered in section 5 where we analyze a variation of this protocol which is used for linking of identities across domains.

3.3   Soundness of Belief Logic

While belief logics are credited with finding flaws in several cryptographic protocols they have also generated a fair share of controversy. In particular, the idealization step, which is required to convert informal protocol description to logical formula is error-prone. Since idealization requires representing not only what a message explicitly conveys but also what sending of the message implies (as per peer's state machine), it is possible to miss out an implication. This may result in set of beliefs derived not being maximal, but not in proving an insecure protocol correct. False positives are not the prime concern and can occur in any approach that uses abstraction (including Proverif).

A message could also be wrongly idealized by making invalid assumptions. This is far more serious and could lead to unsound analysis. This typically occurs when confidentiality of a value initially assumed as a secret, cannot be guaranteed when a message containing the value is received by a participant. This is possible, since BAN and other belief logics do not prove secrecy – they merely propagate beliefs about secrecy. A trivial case, is the Nessett example [26], in which a principal sends out a shared key encrypted by its private key – the shared key obviously cannot be considered a secret. While the idealization error is obvious and avoidable in this example, it may be fairly subtle in other cases. The Needham-Schroeder public key (NSPK) protocol is a famous example where a secret value despite being encrypted under the public key of intended recipient, cannot be used for soundly authenticating a principal.

To avoid unsound idealization, we follow a strategy that we term as *safe idealization*. We do not consider a value secret (even if it is a secret as per a principal's initial assumption), if it is communicated in a protocol message. This completely rules out use of inference rule R1.3 which relies on a supposedly secret value being received by a principal. It also means that if a shared key itself is included in a protocol message – as opposed to encrypting other terms in the message – then the assumption about it being a shared key is no longer valid and thus inference rule R1.1 cannot be triggered. This by no means implies that we cannot analyze protocols that exchange values (initially) assumed to be secrets. We simply do not use the assumption to make new authentication inferences. However, as a consequence, the restricted logic, by itself, may not be sufficient to prove protocols correct. In our approach, belief logic by itself is rarely sufficient to prove goals. The logic is used to establish agreement at honest principals about parameters in a specific run of the protocol. We use this agreement to simplify the protocol model when verifying the protocol using Alloy.

4   Generic Alloy Based Model

In this section, we describe our generic model for web protocols implemented using *Alloy* [22] - a declarative language for describing structures and a tool for exploring them. An alloy model specifies a set of constraints that apply to objects in the domain being modeled. Alloy Analyzer is a solver that takes constraints of a model and finds structures satisfying them using a SAT solver. Thus technically, it is a model-finder rather than a model-checker. A *signature* and a constraint on the signature are declared below:

```
sig S extends E {
        F: one T }
fact {
        all s:S | s.F in X }
```

It is often useful to think of Alloy as an object-oriented language, but underneath the covers S is a subset of E and F is a relation that maps each of S to a single T. Fact statements represent constraints that must always hold. Quantified expressions of the form *quantifier* s: S | F mean that constraint F holds for all, no, lone (zero or one), some (at least one) or one element(s) of S. Fact expressions that apply to a particular signature (as is the case above) can be directly appended to the signature within curly brackets. Assertions (assert {...}) are properties against which the specification needs to be checked. A check command causes the analyzer to search for a counter-example to show that the assertion does not hold. Alloy checks models of finite sizes using a specified scope which limits the maximum size of top level signatures.

4.1   Modeling Principals

The signature Process declares a set of all principals. It is extended by signatures Server and User which are (disjoint) subsets representing web service providers and end users respectively. Also declared are set of all keys (Key), asymmetric and symmetric keys (AsymKey and SymKey), instants (Time), cookies (Cookie) and values, (Value, CkValue, TkValue). A principal knows a set of keys (knownkeys) and a server principal owns a private key (ownedkey). The relations uniquecookie and uniqueval associate a Server with a unique cookie and a secret/nonce value, respectively. Minor changes in the declarations are required to represent protocols needing more than cookie, secret per server role. Constraint on uniquecookie relation ensures that cookie points to the correct server.

Listing 1.1. Modeling service providers and users

```
abstract sig Process {
 knownkeys: set Key,
 seentokens: set TkValue->Time
}
sig Time { }
sig Key { deckey : one Key }
sig AsymKey extends Key { }
sig SymKey extends Key {} {deckey = this}
sig Value { }
sig TkValue extends Value { }
sig CkValue extends Value { }

sig Cookie {
 value: one CkValue,
 server: one Server }

sig Server extends Process {
 ownedkey: one AsymKey,
 uniqueval: one TkValue,
 uniquecookie: one Cookie
} { peer != this, uniquecookie.server = this }

sig User extends Process {
 knowncookies: set Cookie->Time
} { ... }

sig HUser extends User { }

fact {
 all k: Key | k in AsymKey =>
 k.deckey in (AsymKey - k) && k.deckey.deckey = k }

fact {
 all s1,s2: Server|s1 != s2 =>
 (s1.uniqueval != s2.uniqueval) && (s1.ownedkey !=
 s2.ownedkey) && (s1.uniquecookie)!= (s2.uniquecookie)
}
```

seentokens associates a principal with a set of (value, time) pairs each indicating that a *value* was known to the principal at *time*. The relation knowncookies provides a similar association for cookies known to a user. Finally, the facts represent constraints on keys, nonces and cookies.

4.2   Protocol Messages

The signature Sent is used to declare a set of possible protocol HTTP messages. Each message has a sender and receiver principal and is associated with a time when it is transmitted. The other relations on message are a set of values (content) and a set of cookies (cookies) contained in the message. A message may also contain a redirection URL (redirectURL), if it represents an HTTP redirect.

We present a slightly simplified message structure which is sufficient for modeling all web protocols we have analyzed – though more complex structures can be easily modeled using Alloy. The message content is a concatenation of simple tokens, optionally encrypted using enckey.

```
1   sig URL { target: one Process }
2
3   sig Sent {
4     cookies: set Cookie,
5     sender: one Process,
6     receiver: one Process,
7     time: one Time,
8     content: set TkValue,
9     session: lone SessionID,
10    redirectURL: lone URL,
11    enckey: lone AsymKey
12  }{ sender in HUser =>
13    (all c: Cookie | c in cookies <=> c->time
14     in sender.knowncookies && c.server = receiver)
15    sender != receiver }
16
17  fact {
18    all p: Sent | all v: TkValue | (v in p.content
19    => (v->p.time in p.sender.seentokens) ||
20      (some q: Sent | q.receiver = p.sender && v=q.
                content
21      && p.time.ord/gte[q.time] && q.encKey = p.encKey))
22
23    all p: Sent | enckey in sender.knownkeys || some
24    q: Sent | q.receiver=p.sender && p.content=q.
              content
25      && p.time.ord/gte[q.time] && q.encKey=p.encKey
26  }
```

The constraint on Sent requires that a message sent by an honest user (HUser) shall only contain cookies that were known to the sender at the time of sending the message and were received earlier from the target of that message. The bi-implication requires that all such cookies must necessarily be included in the message. A similar restriction regarding tokens sent in a message (line 18-21) requires that either the token must have already been seen by the principal, otherwise it must have been forwarded. Similarly, an encryption key used on a message must either be known to the principal sending the message, unless the principal is forwarding a previously received message (line 23-25).

4.3 Learning Rules

The rules for a user learning new secret values or cookies are expressed as constraints appended to the User signature. The utility ordering is used to order elements of Time. The first constraint (line 3-5) implies that a pair (cookie, t) appears in knowncookies if and only if the user has seen a message containing cookie at a time ≤ t. The rule for seeing tokens says that the principal must have received a message containing that token and must possess the corresponding decryption key (line 9-11).

```
1   open util/ordering[Time] as ord
2   sig User extends Process { ...} {
3     all c: Cookie | all t: Time | (c->t in knowncookies
4       <=> some s: Sent | c in s.cookies
5       && s.receiver = this && t.ord/gte[s.time])
6   }
7
8   sig Process { ... } {
9     all v: TkValue | all t: Time | (v->t in seentokens
10      <=> some s: Sent | v in s.content && s.receiver=
          this
11      && t.ord/gte[s.time] && s.encKey.deckey in
          knownkeys)
12  }
```

4.4 Protocol Flow

The signature ProtoSeq represents all possible sequences of messages under generic and protocol specific constraints. If p and q are possible sent messages, then p->q appearing in the sequence implies that receiver of p is the sender of q. Also the timestamp on q must be the next time instant following the timestamp of p (line 3-6).

```
1   sig ProtoSeq {
2       sequence: set Sent->Sent
3   }{ all p,q: Sent | (p->q in sequence) =>
4       (q.sender = p.receiver)
5       all p,q: Sent | (p->q in sequence) =>
6       (q.time = ord/next[p.time])
7       all p: Sent | (p.receiver in HUser) && p.
          redirectURL
8       => (some q: Sent | (p->q in sequence)
9       && (q.receiver = p.redirectURL.target)
10      && (q.content = p.content)) }
```

The last generic constraint describes handling of an HTTP redirect for an honest user (HUser) (line 7-10). It specifies that if an honest user receives a redirect message, the next message in the sequence must be a message sent by this user to the target of the redirection URL. The message should include any values/tokens received in the redirect. The other constraints on protocol sequence are specific to the protocol being modeled.

4.5   Adversary Model

The intruder is simply a `User`. The redirection constraint for honest user does not apply to it. The intruder learns new values based on learning rules for tokens and can only send seen tokens (as per constraint on `Sent` discussed earlier). Communication from a dishonest to honest user (e.g. through a malicious hyperlink) is modeled as a redirect message generated by the dishonest user.

In addition, we include the possibility of dishonest servers colluding with the intruder. This is done by allowing dishonest principals to share any tokens they obtain with the attacker. This is modeled as a message from a server process representing a corrupted principal role to `User`.

5   Analyzing SAML ID Linking

The workflow we discuss here corresponds to "Federation via persistent pseudonym identifiers" described in the SAML 2.0 protocol specifications [13]. The objective of this workflow is to allow a web user to link identities across security domains. Despite being a widely deployed identity federation protocol, it does not appear to be the subject of scrutiny in a prior security analysis work. The message exchange illustrated in Figure 2 is a minor variation of the browser SSO flow discussed in section 3.2. After the user's browser is redirected back to SP and the SAML token has been validated, SP requests the user to sign-in with a local identity. Once user signs in successfully with a login R, SP links local identity R with remote principal name Q. In future, when SP sees a user carrying a SAML token from IdP asserting identity Q, it automatically signs in the user as R.

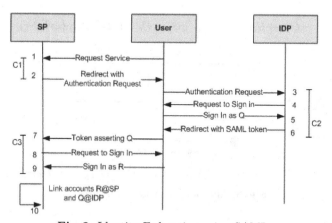

Fig. 2. Identity Federation using SAML

5.1   Mapping SAML messages to Alloy Model

The two primary protocol specific constructs to be represented are SAML request and SAML response. We introduce two signatures `SAMLRequest` and `SAMLToken`.

In the listing `consumer` and `provider` refer to principals playing SP and IdP role, respectively. We use a minor variation of Alice-Bob notation to show how SAML messages map to these signatures. The notation explicitly identifies cookies and redirection URL in HTTP headers. The principal names (C and P) and other parameter values are as per description of SAML SSO in section 3.2. In Figure 3, we show mapping of SAML request in message 2 and SAML Token in message 6 of Figure 2 against protocol specific signatures `SAMLRequest`, `SAMLToken` and the signature `Sent` from the generic model of section 4.

```
sig SAMLRequest extends TkValue {
    id: one SessionID,
    consumer: one Server,
    provider: one Server,
    callback: one URL }
sig SAMLToken extends TkValue {
    id: one SessionID,
    consumer: one Server,
    provider: one Server,
    principal: one User
}
```

We performed belief analysis of SAML SSO in section 3.2 and detailed in Appendix A. We now explore how the analysis can help us simplify our Alloy model even further. From (2), we know that C and P are in agreement about protocol roles and callback URL for the protocol session identified by N_{cp}. We represent this agreement by moving these parameters into a new signature `Session` and referring to appropriate session from `SAMLRequest` and `SAMLToken`.

$$C \longrightarrow U_{C1}: \quad \{N_{cp}, \quad C, \quad P, \quad url_c\}_{K_c^{-1}}, \{url_p, -\}$$

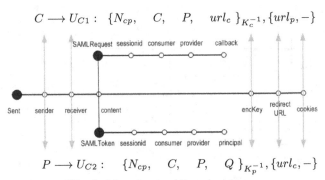

$$P \longrightarrow U_{C2}: \quad \{N_{cp}, \quad C, \quad P, \quad Q\}_{K_p^{-1}}, \{url_c, -\}$$

Fig. 3. Mapping to Alloy signatures

```
abstract sig SAMLMsg extends TkValue {
    sessionid : one SessionID
}
sig SAMLRequest extends SAMLMsg { }
sig SAMLToken extends SAMLMsg {
    subject: one User }
sig Session {
```

```
        id: one SessionID,
        consumer : one Server,
        provider : one Server,
        callback: lone URL
} { consumer != provider }
fact {
        all s1,s2: Session | s1 != s2 => s1.id != s2.
        id }
```

5.2   Specifying the Goal Constraint

The goal of ID federation is to establish at service provider that the two sign-in actions were performed by the same user. Message 9 in the identity linking workflow generates the following additional belief compared to the SSO protocol analysis of Appendix A.

$$C \mid\equiv U_{C3} \triangleright SignIn(R) \tag{A1}$$

This follows by combining assumption about channel C3 at C with message 9 using rule R4.1. We also have the belief that $P \mid\equiv U_{C2} \triangleright SignIn(Q)$ from (2). Also from belief analysis we have the beliefs at C and P that the sign in actions were performed by users who sent messages 3 and 7, respectively. To establish that they correspond to the same user, we include a field subject in the signature SAMLToken which is set by IdP (P) as the sender of message 3 (SAML request). The goal of SAML ID linking now equates to checking whether carrier of token in message 7 is indeed the subject mentioned in the token:

```
assert isSignedIn {
 all p: Sent | p.receiver in HServer && p.content
  in SAMLToken => p.content.subject = p.sender }
```

5.3   Protocol Rules

The following constraint, requires that on receipt of a SAML request with a session ID, the next message in the sequence must be a SAML token returned to the sender having the same session ID as the request and with the subject field set as the sender of the request, as discussed above in section 5.2.

```
all p: Sent | all s: Session | (p.receiver in
   HServer)
  && (p.content in SAMLRequest)
  => some q: Sent | (p->q in sequence) && (q.
     receiver
  = p.sender) && (q.content in SAMLToken) &&
  (q.content.sessionid=p.content.sessionid) &&
  (q.content.sessionid = s.id) && (q.content.
     subject
  = p.sender) && (q.redirectURL.target = s.
     consumer)
```

We also ensure, through the following rule, that a SAML token can only be generated by the identity provider for the session, and while it can be forwarded it cannot be tampered with. Since this rule ensures integrity of the SAML token, we can remove the private key encryption, without impacting security. This allows us to use an even simpler message structure than discussed in section 4.2 and further simplifies rules for learning new values and sending messages in section 4.

```
content in SAMLToken =>(some s: Session |
(content.sessionid = s.id) && (s.provider =
   sender))
|| (content->time in sender.seentokens)
```

5.4   Result of Alloy Analysis

We modeled SAML identity linking, with and without the simplification introduced due to belief logic. In both cases only messages 2, 3, 6, 7 were considered, since messages 4, 5, 8 and 9 establishing authentication have already been accounted for while specifying the goal in section 5.2. We compared the complexity of resulting models, to estimate reduction of modeling effort on the part of an analyst using our tool. The model using results from belief logic contained 25 atomic statements, compared to the base model (without simplification) having 60 atomic statements, a saving of nearly 60%.

We execute the simplified model corresponding to messages 2, 3, 6 and 7 and with message structures simplified as described above and check for the goal assertion. Alloy generates the counter-example shown in Figure 4 in less than 3 seconds on an Intel Core i5 2.4 GHz, 4 GB system for a scope up to 10 messages in a protocol sequence. We observe that the message sent by an honest user (HUser) at instant time4 contains a SAMLToken with subject as User.

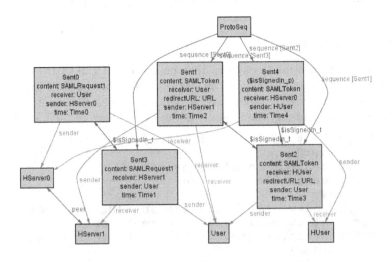

Fig. 4. Counter-example for SAML account linking

A correct execution of the protocol should have exactly four messages (corresponding to messages 2, 3, 6, 7 in Figure 2). However, the counter-example shows five messages where the first three messages (corresponding to messages 2, 3, 6) with timestamps Time0, Time1 and Time2 are exchanged with User. This is followed by a message from User to the victim (modeling following of a malicious link by HUser) and a message from HUser to Consumer containing the SAML token actually issued to User. This translates to the following attack on the SAML ID federation protocol.

Attack on SAML ID Linking. An attacker having a valid account A at IdP authenticates itself and chooses to be redirected to SP. However, instead of following the redirect request from IdP, it extracts the request parameters and induces the victim into clicking a link or submitting a form (depending on whether HTTP redirect binding or POST binding is used for the exchange). Following the link takes the victim to the SP site, unwittingly carrying the SAML token issued to the attacker. The victim has an account (say V) at the SP site and is requested to sign-in. On signing in, SP links local identity V with attacker's identity A at IdP. In future, attacker can sign-in at IdP, get redirected to SP and automatically get access to the victim's account at SP.

6 Conclusion

We propose a new method for formalizing and analyzing security of web-based protocols. The method provides native support for common web mechanisms and employs a specialized adversary model for the web environment. In this framework, web mechanisms and protocol rules are directly represented in first order logic based Alloy analyzer. To simplify analysis of medium to high complexity protocols, we propose a simplification strategy that utilizes correspondence about protocol parameters established using belief logic. We illustrate for an industrial strength protocol, that this reduces the complexity of the protocol model by 60%. We apply our methods to analyze security of the SAML account linking workflow and identify a previously unreported vulnerability.

Specialized formalisms for security verification were proposed when general purpose approaches were not up to the task. Our experience with using Alloy for security protocol modeling and analysis suggests that general purpose approaches may now be ready for the challenge. We believe that our lightweight framework could play a role in making security verification more mainstream with the eventual objective of its uptake from industry and standard bodies.

References

1. Abadi, M., Blanchet, B.: Analyzing security protocols with secrecy types and logic programs. Journal of the ACM (JACM) 52(1), 102–146 (2005)
2. Abadi, M., Fournet, C.: Mobile values, new names, and secure communication. In: Proceedings of The 28th ACM SIGPLAN-SIGACT Symposium on Principles of Programming Languages, pp. 104–115. ACM (2001)

3. Abadi, M., Tuttle, M.: A semantics for a logic of authentication. In: Proceedings of the Tenth Annual ACM Symposium on Principles of Distributed Computing, pp. 201–216. ACM (1991)
4. Akhawe, D., Barth, A., Lam, P., Mitchell, J., Song, D.: Towards a formal foundation of web security. In: Proceedings of 23rd IEEE Computer Security Foundations Symposium, pp. 290–304. IEEE (2010)
5. Armando, A., Carbone, R., Compagna, L., Cuellar, J., Tobarra, L.: Formal analysis of SAML 2.0 web browser single sign-on: Breaking the SAML-based single sign-on for Google Apps. In: Proceedings of the 6th ACM Workshop on Formal Methods in Security Engineering, pp. 1–10. ACM (2008)
6. Armando, A., Compagna, L.: SATMC: A SAT-based model checker for security protocols. In: Alferes, J.J., Leite, J. (eds.) JELIA 2004. LNCS (LNAI), vol. 3229, pp. 730–733. Springer, Heidelberg (2004)
7. Bansal, C., Bhargavan, K., Maffeis, S.: Discovering concrete attacks on website authorization by formal analysis. In: 2012 IEEE 25th Computer Security Foundations Symposium (CSF), pp. 247–262. IEEE (2012)
8. Blanchet, B.: Automatic verification of correspondences for security protocols. Journal of Computer Security 17(4), 363–434 (2009)
9. Blanchet, B.: Using Horn clauses for analyzing security protocols. Formal Models and Techniques for Analyzing Security Protocols 5, 86–111 (2011)
10. Blanchet, B., Abadi, M., Fournet, C.: Automated verification of selected equivalences for security protocols. Journal of Logic and Algebraic Programming 75(1), 3–51 (2008)
11. Blanchet, B., et al.: An efficient cryptographic protocol verifier based on Prolog rules. In: Proceedings of the 14th IEEE workshop on Computer Security Foundations, pp. 82–96 (2001)
12. Burrows, M., Abadi, M., Needham, R.: A logic of authentication. ACM Transactions on Computer Systems 8(1), 18–36 (1990)
13. Cantor, S., Kemp, I., Philpott, N., Maler, E.: Assertions and protocols for the OASIS Security Assertion Markup Language V2.0. OASIS Standard (March 2005)
14. Cervesato, I., Durgin, N.A., Lincoln, P., Mitchell, J.C., Scedrov, A.: A metanotation for protocol analysis. In: Proceedings of the 12th IEEE Computer Security Foundations Workshop, 1999, pp. 55–69. IEEE (1999)
15. Craigen, D., Saaltink, M.: Using EVES to analyze authentication protocols. Technical Report TR-96-5508-05, pp. 6–55 (1996)
16. Cremers, C.: Unbounded verification, falsification, and characterization of security protocols by pattern refinement. In: Proceedings of the 15th ACM Conference on Computer and Communications Security, pp. 119–128. ACM (2008)
17. Cremers, C.J.F., Lafourcade, P., Nadeau, P.: Comparing state spaces in automatic security protocol analysis. In: Cortier, V., Kirchner, C., Okada, M., Sakurada, H. (eds.) Formal to Practical Security. LNCS, vol. 5458, pp. 70–94. Springer, Heidelberg (2009)
18. Dolev, D., Yao, A.: On the security of public key protocols. IEEE Transactions on Information Theory 29(2), 198–208 (1983)
19. Durgin, N., Lincoln, P., Mitchell, J., Scedrov, A.: Undecidability of bounded security protocols. In: Proceedings of the Workshop on Formal Methods and Security Protocols (1999)
20. Fábrega, F., Herzog, J., Guttman, J.: Strand spaces: Why is a security protocol correct? In: Proceedings of 1998 IEEE Symposium on Research in Security and Privacy, pp. 160–171. IEEE (1998)

21. Hammer-Lahav, E., Recordon, D., Hardt, D.: The OAuth 2.0 authorization protocol. tools.ietf.org/html/ietf-oauth-v2-31, 8 (2011)
22. Jackson, D.: Alloy: A lightweight object modelling notation. ACM Transactions on Software Engineering and Methodology (TOSEM) 11(2), 256–290 (2002)
23. Kindred, D., Wing, J.: Fast, automatic checking of security protocols. In: Proceedings of 2nd Workshop on Electronic Commerce, pp. 41–52. USENIX (1996)
24. Kumar, A.: Model driven security analysis of IDaaS protocols. In: Kappel, G., Maamar, Z., Motahari-Nezhad, H.R. (eds.) ICSOC 2011. LNCS, vol. 7084, pp. 312–327. Springer, Heidelberg (2011)
25. Kumar, A.: Using automated model analysis for reasoning about security of web protocols. In: Proceedings of 28th Annual Computer Security Applications Conference, ACSAC 2012, pp. 289–298 (2012)
26. Nessett, D.: A critique of the Burrows, Abadi and Needham logic. ACM SIGOPS Operating Systems Review 24(2), 35–38 (1990)
27. Recordon, D., Reed, D.: OpenID 2.0: A platform for user-centric identity management. In: Proceedings of the Second ACM Workshop on Digital Identity Management, pp. 11–16. ACM (2006)
28. Schumann, J.: Automatic verification of cryptographic protocols with SETHEO. In: McCune, W. (ed.) CADE 1997. LNCS, vol. 1249, pp. 87–100. Springer, Heidelberg (1997)
29. Song, D., Berezin, S., Perrig, A.: Athena: A novel approach to efficient automatic security protocol analysis. Journal of Computer Security 9(1/2), 47–74 (2001)
30. Syverson, P., Van Oorschot, P.: On unifying some cryptographic protocol logics. In: Proceedings of 1994 IEEE Symposium on Research in Security and Privacy, pp. 14–28. IEEE (1994)

A   SAML SSO Belief Analysis

Table 3. Belief Logic Analysis of SAML SSO

	Analysis
Msg 3	$$\dfrac{P \vartriangleleft \{auth\_req(N_{cp}, P), N_{cp}, idp = P, sp = C, cb = url_C\}_{K_c^{-1}} \quad P \mid\equiv \xmapsto{K_c} C}{P \mid\equiv C \mid\sim (auth\_req(N_{cp}, P), N_{cp}, idp = P, sp = C, cb = url_C)} \text{ R1.1}$$ $$\dfrac{P \mid\equiv C \mid\sim auth\_req(N_{cp}, P) \quad P \mid\equiv \natural N_{cp}}{P \mid\equiv (sp = C, idp = P)} \text{ S1}$$ $$\dfrac{P \mid\equiv C \mid\sim (idp = P, sp = C, cb = url_C) \quad P \mid\equiv \natural N_{cp}}{P \mid\equiv C \mid\equiv (sp = C, idp = P, cb = url_c)} \text{ R2}$$
Msg 5	$$\dfrac{P \mid\equiv C \mid\equiv cb = url_c \quad P \mid\equiv C \mid \Rightarrow cb}{P \mid\equiv cb = url_c} \text{ R3}$$ $$\dfrac{P \mid\equiv P \overset{A}{\leftrightarrow} U_{C2} \quad P \vartriangleleft [\![SignIn(Q)]\!]_{C2}}{P \mid\equiv U_{C2} \vartriangleright SignIn(Q)} \text{ R4.1}$$
Msg 7	$$\dfrac{C \mid\equiv C \overset{A}{\leftrightarrow} U_{C3} \quad C \vartriangleleft [\![T, \ldots]\!]_{C3}}{C \mid\equiv U_{C3} \ni T} \text{ R4.2}$$ $$\dfrac{C \vartriangleleft \{N_{cp}, T \rightsquigarrow SignIn(Q), idp = P, sp = C\}_{K_p^{-1}} \quad C \mid\equiv \xmapsto{K_p} P, C \mid\equiv \natural N_{cp}}{C \mid\equiv P \mid\equiv (idp = P, sp = C, T \rightsquigarrow SignIn(Q))} \text{ R1.1R2}$$

Why Is CSP Failing? Trends and Challenges in CSP Adoption

Michael Weissbacher, Tobias Lauinger, and William Robertson

Northeastern University, Boston, USA
{mw,toby,wkr}@ccs.neu.edu

Abstract. Content Security Policy (CSP) has been proposed as a principled and robust browser security mechanism against content injection attacks such as XSS. When configured correctly, CSP renders malicious code injection and data exfiltration exceedingly difficult for attackers. However, despite the promise of these security benefits and being implemented in almost all major browsers, CSP adoption is minuscule—our measurements show that CSP is deployed in enforcement mode on only 1% of the Alexa Top 100.

In this paper, we present the results of a long-term study to determine challenges in CSP deployments that can prevent wide adoption. We performed weekly crawls of the Alexa Top 1M to measure adoption of web security headers, and find that CSP both significantly lags other security headers, and that the policies in use are often ineffective at actually preventing content injection. In addition, we evaluate the feasibility of deploying CSP from the perspective of a security-conscious website operator. We used an incremental deployment approach through CSP's report-only mode on four websites, collecting over 10M reports. Furthermore, we used semi-automated policy generation through web application crawling on a set of popular websites. We found both that automated methods do not suffice and that significant barriers exist to producing accurate results.

Finally, based on our observations, we suggest several improvements to CSP that could help to ease its adoption by the web community.

Keywords: Content Security Policy, Cross-Site Scripting, Web Security.

1   Introduction

The web as a platform for application development and distribution has evolved faster than it could be secured. Consequently, it has been plagued by numerous classes of security issues, but perhaps none are as serious as content injection attacks. Content injection, of which cross-site scripting (XSS) is the most well-known form, allows attackers to execute malicious code that appears to belong to trusted origins, to subvert the intended structure of documents, to exfiltrate sensitive user information, and to perform unauthorized actions on behalf of victims. In response, many client- and server-side defenses against content injection have been proposed, ranging from language-based auto-sanitization [17] to sandboxing of untrusted content [12] to whitelists of trusted content [11].

A. Stavrou et al. (Eds.): RAID 2014, LNCS 8688, pp. 212–233, 2014.
© Springer International Publishing Switzerland 2014

Content Security Policy (CSP) is an especially promising browser-based security framework for refining the same-origin policy (SOP), the basis of traditional web security. CSP allows developers or administrators to explicitly define, using a declarative policy language, the origins from which different classes of content can be included into a document. Policies are sent by the server in a special security header, and a browser supporting the standard is then responsible for enforcing the policy on the client. CSP provides a principled and robust mechanism for preventing the inclusion of malicious content in security-sensitive web applications. However, despite its promise and implementation in almost all major browsers, CSP is not widely used in practice—in fact, according to our measurements, it is deployed in enforcement mode by only 1% of the Alexa Top 100.

In this paper, we present the results of a long-term study to determine why this is the case. In particular, we repeatedly crawled the Alexa Top 1M to measure adoption of web security headers, and find that CSP significantly lags behind other, more narrowly-focused headers in adoption. We also find that for the small fraction of sites that have adopted CSP, it is often deployed in a manner that does not leverage the full defensive power of CSP.

In addition to our Internet-scale study, we also quantify the feasibility of incrementally deploying CSP from the perspective of a security-conscious administrator using its report-only mode at four websites. Although this is an oft-recommended practice, we find significant barriers to this approach in practice due to interactions with browser extensions and the evolution of web application structure over time.

Finally, we evaluate the feasibility of automatically generating CSP rules for web applications, again from the perspective of an administrator. We find that for websites that are well-structured and do not change significantly over time, rules can indeed by generated in a black-box fashion. However, for more complex sites such as those that make use of third-party advertising libraries in their proper site context, policy generation is significantly more difficult.

To summarize, the contributions of this paper are the following:

- We perform the first long-term analysis of CSP adoption in the wild, performing repeated crawls of the Alexa Top 1M over a 16 month period.
- We investigate challenges in adopting CSP, and why it is not deployed to its full extent even when it has been adopted.
- We evaluate the feasibility of both report-only incremental deployment and crawler-based rule generation, and show that each approach has fundamental problems.
- We suggest several avenues for enhancing CSP to ease its adoption.
- We release an open source CSP parsing and manipulation library. [1]

2   Content Security Policy

The goal of CSP is to mitigate content injection attacks against web applications directly within the browser [6, 19]. In the following, we describe CSP as it is

---

[1] https://github.com/tlauinger/csp-utils

Table 1. The types of directives supported in the current W3C standard CSP 1.0

Directive	Content Sources
default-src	All types, if not otherwise explicitly specified
script-src	JavaScript, XSLT
object-src	Plugins, such as Flash players
style-src	Styles, such as CSS
img-src	Images
media-src	Video and audio (HTML5)
frame-src	Pages displayed inside frames
font-src	Font files
connect-src	Targets of XMLHttpRequest, WebSockets

currently implemented, and briefly discuss both future extensions and the classes of attacks it is intended to prevent.

2.1   Overview of CSP

Content Security Policy is fundamentally a specification for defining policies to control where content can be loaded from, granting significant power to developers to refine the default SOP. Developers or administrators can configure web servers to include `Content-Security-Policy` headers as part of the HTTP responses issued to browsers. CSP-enabled browsers are then responsible for enforcing the policies associated with each resource.

A content security policy consists of a set of directives. Each directive corresponds to a specific type of resource, and specifies the set of origins from which resources of that type may be loaded. Table 1 explains the directive types supported in the current W3C standard CSP 1.0.[2] The scheme and port in source expressions are optional.

CSP also supports wildcards (∗) for subdomains and the port, and has additional special keywords: 'self' represents the origin of the resource, while 'none' represents an empty resource list and prevents any resource of the respective type from being loaded. The `script-src` and `style-src` directives additionally support the 'unsafe-inline' keyword, which allows inline script or CSS to be included in the HTML document rather than being loaded from an external resource. Finally, 'unsafe-eval' allows JavaScript to use string evaluation methods such as `eval()` and `setTimeout()`. If not explicitly whitelisted, CSP disables these special source types because their use is considered to be particularly unsafe. However, changing websites to remove all inline scripts can be a burden on developers, and increase page load latency by introducing additional external resources.

---

[2] The directive `script-src http://seclab.nu:80`, for instance, allows a protected website to load scripts from the host `seclab.nu` via HTTP on port 80, but blocks all scripts from other sources

CSP can operate in one of two modes: *enforcement* or *report-only*. In enforcement mode, compatible browsers block resources that violate a policy. In report-only mode, however, browsers do not enforce policies, but rather report violations that would be blocked on the developer console. Additionally, a special CSP directive (`report-uri`) can be used to instruct browsers to send violation reports to the given URI. This feature can be used to learn policies before enabling enforcement, or to monitor for unforeseen changes or attacks against a website. In this paper, we make extensive use of the report-only mode and violation reports to explore various ways to (semi-)automatically generate policies for websites.

CSP has been widely adopted by the browser manufacturers. It is supported by the current versions of almost all major browsers, including some mobile browsers. It is, however, only partially supported by Internet Explorer.

2.2 Deploying CSP

To prevent XSS attacks, disallowing inline scripts and `eval` is the core requirement to benefit from CSP. Inline scripts should be disabled to prevent the browser from inadvertently executing scripts that have been injected into the site. Eval-constructs, often abused to parse JSON strings, can be used directly by an attacker to execute arbitrary code if she controls the data source. While the `unsafe-inline` and `unsafe-eval` options allow this behavior to be enabled, their presence marginalizes the benefit of CSP.

Therefore, for version 1.0 of CSP, inline scripts should be moved to files and `eval` replaced with a safe equivalent for the corresponding task, such as `JSON.parse()` to parse JSON. Furthermore, JavaScript should be hosted on a domain that only serves static files instead of user content. This separation makes it harder for attackers to execute code in the browser. Also, external scripts should be moved to a server controlled by the website owner, reducing trust in third-party servers. The number of whitelisted sources should be kept to a minimum to increase the difficulty of data exfiltration for attackers.

In the current draft version 1.1, additional features have been introduced to safely support inline scripts as well as functionally replace the `X-Frame-Options` header. As these features are subject to change, we do not address them in this work.

2.3 Attacks Outside the Scope of CSP

CSP can prevent general content injection attacks, and in draft version 1.1 subsumes previous mechanisms such as the `X-XSS-Protection` header, which serves the narrow purpose of enabling browser XSS filters. However, it is not intended to address other web attacks such as cross-site request forgery (CSRF). More fundamentally, CSP describes which content can be loaded by source, but the order of inclusion is out of scope. Hence, even with strict rules and perfect enforcement, out-of-order inclusion can lead to undesired side effects in JavaScript applications [8]. JSONP (JSON with padding) is a mechanism to bypass SOP restrictions by including a script tag from a remote server and specifying a function to be executed once a result becomes available. Hence, whitelisted JSONP sources can be used for calls to arbitrary functions—or, if input for the callback function is not filtered, arbitrary code execution.

3 HTTP Security Headers

In this section, we describe our data collection of HTTP response headers. We collected this data in an effort to understand the landscape of security headers in the wild, particularly in regards to CSP.

3.1 Methodology

To acquire a long-term overview of CSP adoption, we performed weekly crawls of the web starting in December 2012. We crawled the front page of each site in the Alexa Top 1M most frequently visited websites. For every site x, we connected to http://x, https://x, http://www.x and https://www.x. We counted a site as using a particular header if any of the four responses served that header. However, our crawler only visited the front page of each Alexa entry. Therefore, sites that employ CSP only on subdomains or areas other than the front page were not detected in the crawl.[3] Furthermore, if the CSP rules are generated based on user agent discrimination, the collected data does not hold for all types of browsers visiting the site. We used a Firefox user agent string, updating version information over time.

Description of HTTP Security Headers

To discuss CSP in context, we provide a brief overview of the other security relevant HTTP response headers. Details about them can be found at IETF, W3C, or in the browser specifications.

Platform for Privacy Preferences (P3P) [2]. Websites can use this header to describe their privacy policy. However, it is not supported by major browsers and has not been actively developed for several years. The header is still in use as Internet Explorer blocks third-party cookies by default if no policy is present. P3P is legally binding and has been used in litigation in the past.

DNS Prefetch Control [1]. DNS prefetching is a technique for browsers to reduce latency by resolving referenced hostnames before a user follows a link. This header allows websites to override the default behavior of the browser.

XSS Protection [3]. This header can be used to enable or disable client-side heuristic XSS filtering. The reflected-xss directive of CSP 1.1 is functionally equivalent.

Content Type Options [4]. As the Content-Type header is often not set correctly, MIME type sniffing can be used to detect the actual response content

---

[3] One example is Twitter, which uses CSP for parts of their site, but not the front page.

type. The `nosniff` directive is the only option available for this header and disables MIME type sniffing, preventing possible type confusion.

Frame Options [9]. This header allows a website to restrict iframing to prevent UI redressing attacks. CSP draft 1.1 includes these features under the `frame-ancestors` directive, and may replace this header.

HTTP Strict Transport Security (HSTS) [5]. By using HSTS, websites can specify that in the future, the browser should only connect to them via a secure connection, thereby preventing SSL stripping.

Cross-Origin Resource Sharing (CORS) [7]. SOP has proven to be an obstacle for modern web applications, and has been worked around by various methods such as JSONP. CORS allows websites to operate outside the limitations of SOP by extending it, while not completely side-stepping it.

3.2   Adoption of HTTP Security Headers

To measure the popularity of CSP in contrast to other security headers, we looked at the HTTP response headers in our weekly crawls, as well as a static snapshot from the end of March 2014. For the static snapshot, we used the entire Alexa Top 1M, breaking down websites by popularity. We used a snapshot of the Top 10K to track the evolution of response headers back to December 2012.

To compare the adoption of security-related headers between different levels of site popularity, we split Table 2 into brackets. From the data, it is apparent that websites that are less popular use CSP less frequently. For instance, among the 100 most popular sites, only two used CSP (2%), while CSP was enabled for only 775 among the 900,000 least popular sites (0.00086%).

Hence, websites that are less popular use CSP less frequently. In contrast, for CORS, header usage was more evenly spread out, with all brackets between 0.7% and 2.6%.

During our crawls, we noticed that Google enabled CSP headers only occasionally. We performed an additional test of `google.com` with 1,000 requests, finding that 0.8% of the responses included CSP headers. While Google had 18 sites in the top 100, none of them issued CSP headers in the crawl of Table 2.

In Figure 1, we track the evolution of security-related headers of the Alexa Top 10K from March 2014 backwards in time to December 2012. P3P was particularly popular; however, the P3P policies served were often invalid, providing only an explanation for why the website did not support it. We observe that CSP is only slowly gaining traction over time. The main contributing factor for the fluctuation of CSP headers in the data is due to Google.

For the hosts in the Top 10K of this crawl, we identified all servers that had sent CSP rules at any point in time during our study. We found 140 sites that did so; 110 of those belonged to Google (79%).

3.3   Detailed Analysis of CSP Headers

In this part, we describe in detail how websites use CSP, whether they use CSP's reporting feature to learn policies, whether they actively enforce policies, and how effective those policies are in mitigating attacks.

Table 2. Number of websites with security-related HTTP response headers, grouped by intervals of site popularity, for the Alexa Top 1M ranking

Header / Alexa Rank	$[1 - 10^2]$	$(10^2 - 10^3]$	$(10^3 - 10^4]$	$(10^4 - 10^5]$	$(10^5 - 10^6]$
P3P	47	176	849	6,315	79,600
DNS Prefetch Control	1	0	3	40	461
XSS Protection	26	77	269	2,336	43,045
Content Type Options	10	27	172	1,995	42,150
Frame Options	43	165	581	2,747	21,746
HSTS	5	16	83	476	2,475
CORS	1	26	217	1,228	7,149
CSP	2	2	15	57	775
Any security header	66	304	1,623	11,491	132,347

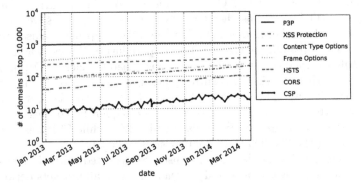

Fig. 1. Popularity of security headers in the Alexa Top 10K

Enforcement vs. Report-Only. During our crawl at the end of March, we found 815 sites in enforcement mode, 35 sites in report-only mode, and no sites that sent both types of headers. Out of the websites in enforcement mode, only 23 collected violation reports.

In the Top 10K, we observed only one site in report-only mode that later switched to enforcement. The Norwegian financial services site dnb.no started collecting reports in June 2013, and enabled enforcement in February 2014. Their enforced `default-src` directive consists of 74 sources, including the schemes `chrome-extension`, `chromeinvoke`, and `chromeinvokeimmediate`. Furthermore, `unsafe-inline` and `unsafe-eval` are both enabled. Therefore, this policy appears to provide little benefit over not using CSP at all.

We noticed that several websites use CSP to test for mixed content. Mixed content is the inclusion of unencrypted content into HTTPS sessions, which reduces the benefit of encryption. Google's sampling uses the following report-only policy: `default-src https: data:; options eval-script inline-script; report-uri /gen_204?atyp=csp`. Etsy also samples for mixed content; we found

CSP headers in nine out of 2,000 (0.45%) responses. Similarly, `hootsuite.com` tested for mixed content from April 2013 to March 2014 for all responses, but we observed no CSP headers after that.

Types of Sites Using CSP. To further understand the types of websites that use CSP, we looked for similarities in website titles. The largest portion of sites supporting CSP, 417, is due to phpMyAdmin, a PHP-based web application used to manage MySQL databases. phpMyAdmin ships with CSP enabled by default, which allows inline scripts, `eval`, and restricts sources to `'self'`. While this policy does not prevent XSS, data exfiltration is more difficult. These rules can be deployed as the software is fairly static. However, when conducting a search for phpMyAdmin and CSP, we found users having trouble including images when modifying their installations. The general solution offered was to disable CSP in the configuration rather than updating the default policy.

Ironically, on the vendors' demo site `http://demo.phpmyadmin.net/master/`, the operators tried to include Google analytics. While the Google analytics domain is whitelisted using `default-src`, it is not in the `script-src` source list. As specific directives override the `default-src` directive, the script is unintentionally blocked.

We also found 170 OwnCloud instances, which uses CSP by default from version 5.

Prevalence of Unsafe Policies. We identified several patterns in CSP policies that violate deployment best practices as described in Section 2.2. In Table 3, we summarize the observed rules in enforcement over the Alexa Top 1M from March 24th. We split at the 10K rank to discriminate between more popular websites and lower ranking ones. '*' represents either the literal asterisk, or the entire HTTP(S) scheme is whitelisted in one or more of the source lists.

On the majority of sites, `eval` and inline is enabled: eight out of 13 and 11 out of 13 in the Top 10K bracket, 700 out of 802 and 728 out of 802 in the remaining 990,000 sites. This configuration strongly reduces the benefits of CSP for XSS mitigation. Configuring asterisk or a whole scheme as a source in a directive enables data leakage to any host. Six out of 13 and 230 out of 802 websites respectively served such directives. 10 out of 13 sites in the Top 10K bracket had no `report-uri` to collect violation reports. This is surprising as CSP could be used as a warning system.

While CSP in theory can effectively mitigate XSS and data exfiltration, in practice CSP is not deployed in a way that provides these benefits.

3.4   Conclusions

While some sites use CSP as an additional layer of protection against content injection, CSP is not yet widely adopted. Furthermore, the rules observed in the wild do not leverage the full benefits of CSP. The majority of CSP-enabled websites were installations of phpMyAdmin, which ships with a weak default policy. Other recent security headers have gained far more traction than CSP, presumably due to their relative ease of deployment. That only one site in the Alexa

Table 3. Overview of enforced policies

Feature / Alexa Rank	$[1 - 10^4]$	$(10^4 - 10^6]$
unsafe-eval	8	700
unsafe-inline	11	728
script-src 'self'	12	789
no report-uri	10	782
#script-src > 10	2	33
* as source	6	230
Median #directives	6	4
Median #script sources	4	1
# CSP Policies	13	802

Top 10K switched from report-only mode to enforcement during our measurement suggests that CSP rules cannot be easily derived from collected reports. It could potentially help adoption if policies could be generated in an automated, or semi-automated, fashion.

4   CSP Violation Reports

Web browsers compatible with CSP can be configured to report back to the website whenever an activity, whether carried out or blocked, violates the site's policy. This is meant as a debugging mechanism for web operators, both to develop policies from scratch, and to be informed when an existing policy needs to be updated. Starting with a "deny all" policy in report-only mode, operators can collect information about all resources that need to be whitelisted in order for the site to function, compile a corresponding policy, and eventually switch to enforcement mode. We applied this approach to four websites and analyzed the reports that we received, gaining unexpected insights into the web ecosystem.

4.1   Background

CSP includes an optional `report-uri` directive that allows website operators to specify a sink for violation reports. It is supported in both report-only and enforcement mode of CSP. As an illustration, consider the following policy: `img-src` 'none'; `report-uri /sink.cgi`. When a user visits the URL `http://seclab.nu/test.html` and that page includes the image resource `http://seclab.nu/pic.gif`, the browser would send a report similar to the following one: `{"blocked-uri":` `"http://seclab.nu/pic.gif"`, `"violated-directive"`: `"img-src 'none'"`, `"document-uri"`: `"http://seclab.nu/test.html"`, ...}. From this report, the developer can infer that the policy entry `img-src http://seclab.nu` should be added to the policy.

4.2   Methodology

We deployed CSP on four of our own websites: two personal pages, an institutional page, and a popular analysis service. The policies we used specified empty resource lists for all supported directive types—that is, any browser activity covered by CSP was explicitly forbidden and should generate a report. We deployed the policies in report-only mode to not interfere with the normal operation of the site. Besides the additional CSP headers, the sites were not modified in any way.

During our analysis, we observed that the formats of reports sent by different browser versions varied slightly. Older Firefox versions, for instance, explicitly stated when a violation was due to the special cases 'unsafe-inline' or 'unsafe-eval' for script and style directives, as opposed to violations based on a resource URI. All recent versions of browsers, however, reported only an empty blocked-uri instead. Unfortunately, this format did not allow us to distinguish between 'unsafe-inline' and 'unsafe-eval' script violations.

In order to work around this issue, we leveraged the fact that recent browser versions supported multiple CSP headers in parallel. That is, in addition to the *regular* policy discussed above that captured any CSP event, we added two more policies that caused reports only for *eval* and *inline* violations, respectively:

```
    default-src *; script-src * 'unsafe-inline';
style-src * 'unsafe-inline'; report-uri /sink.cgi?type=eval
    default-src *; script-src * 'unsafe-eval';
style-src *; report-uri /sink.cgi?type=inline
```

We deployed all three policies and distinguished the reports we received using the type parameter in the report URI. We removed duplicate eval and inline violations that were reported for the *regular* policy (30 % on site D). Furthermore we removed some violations reported for the *eval* and *inline* policies that were in fact no eval or inline violations (1.8 % on site D). Those were triggered by a bug in older Firefox versions that did not properly execute multiple policies in parallel. Since newer Firefox versions were not affected, the user agent distributions of the original and the filtered data set were very similar. Table 4 shows the number of reports retained in the filtered data set, which is the basis for the following discussion.

From each report, we derive a policy entry that whitelists the respective violation. We extract the type, such as img-src, from the violated-directive. For *regular* violations, we append the scheme, host name and port from the blocked-uri, such as http://seclab.nu. For *inline* or *eval* violations, we append 'unsafe-inline' or 'unsafe-eval'. We generate a single policy per site by combining all entries and set default-src 'none' to block everything else.

Our approach is to generate one single policy that is general enough to cover the entire protected site. Such a site-wide policy is easier to generate than individual policies, since any similarity between pages on the same site reduces the number of violation reports necessary to generate a policy. Furthermore, site-wide policies are easier to configure; a site-wide reverse proxy could insert a static policy into HTTP responses without the need to change application code.

Table 4. Overview of the CSP violation report data sets received from our websites in early 2014, after removing inconsistent reports

Site	A	B	C	D
Type	personal	personal	institutional	service
# Reports	1.1 K	21.8 K	48.0 K	7.1 M
Median Reports/Day	9	671	2.1 K	348.5 K
# IP Addresses	78	1.6 K	1.2 K	14.4 K
Median Reports/Addr.	7	7	28	85
% Reports/Browser				
Chrome (mobile, derivatives)	46.6 (+5.4)	59.3 (+8.3)	54.3 (+3.7)	61.0 (+2.3)
Firefox (mobile, derivatives)	23.8 (+0.5)	22.2 (+0.6)	30.1 (+0.5)	30.3 (+0.2)
Safari (mobile)	5.7 (+2.3)	2.3 (+3.5)	4.1 (+3.7)	1.5 (+0.5)
Opera	0.5	0.3	0.6	1.9
Googlebot	15.1	3.1	2.0	2.1

4.3   Results

Table 5 summarizes the policies we generated for each of our sites. We verified manually each entry in the policies and found that many of the whitelisted resources were not actually intended to be included in the websites. The policy generated for site A, for instance, is `default-src 'none'; frame-src https://srv.mzcdn.com; img-src 'self' data: http://1.2.3.11; object-src http://www.ajaxcdn.org; script-src 'unsafe-eval' 'unsafe-inline' http://ajax.googleapis.com http://f.ssfiles.com http://i.bestoffersjs.info http://srv.mzcdn.com http://www.superfish.com https://www.superfish.com; style-src 'unsafe-inline'`. Yet, site A was entirely static and did not contain any script at all. The correct policy for site A would have been `default-src 'none'; img-src 'self' data:; style-src 'unsafe-inline'`. In other words, only 21 % of the policy entries generated from the received reports were legitimate.

On site D, only 2 % of the policy entries were legitimate. Furthermore, many of the legitimate entries simply enumerated all the alternative domain names of the same site (e.g., with or without the `www` subdomain), or they were due to the same resource being loaded over HTTP or HTTPS. When disregarding these details to allow for a fairer comparison, as noted in brackets in the table, the percentage of legitimate policy entries drops to only 0.8 % on site D.

Reasons for Invalid Policy Entries. We identified a number of reasons why web browsers sent CSP violation reports for resources that did not exist in the original websites. Many of these reports appeared to be caused by browser extensions that modified the DOM of the page by injecting additional resources such as scripts or images. We observed extensions for blocking advertisements, extensions injecting advertisements, price comparison toolbars, an anti-virus scanner, a notetaking plugin, and even a BitTorrent browser extension. We could auto-

Table 5. Length of policies when whitelisting all violations from the report data set (a), and with an additional filter for URL schemes of browser extensions (b). Most of the policy entries correspond to injected resources; only few are intended to be included. (In brackets, the number of unique policy entries when disregarding the protocol HTTP(S) or alternative domains, such as the www subdomain.)

Site	A	B	C	D
# Entries (a)	14	221	226	1,113
# Entries, extension filter (b)	14	212	215	1,090
Correct Subset	3 (3)	14 (9)	38 (13)	22 (9)

Table 6. Most frequent Chrome extensions observed at site D

Name	# Reports
AdBlock	38 K
AdBlock Plus	29 K
Grooveshark Downloader	9.5 K
ScriptSafe	8.8 K
DoNotTrackMe	8.2 K

matically identify some browser extensions based on violation reports because they attempted to load resource URIs that contained the `chrome-extension` or `safari-extension` schemes followed by the unique identifier of the extension. AdBlock and AdBlock Plus were the most frequent extensions for the Chrome browser (Table 6), while the most frequent Safari extension was Evernote. Yet, automatically removing these reports (and a few other unexpected schemes, such as `about` and `view-source`) accounted for fewer than 5 % of all incorrect policy entries, as shown in the second row of Table 5. The remaining browser extensions exhibited no such uniquely distinguishing features, often injecting libraries that are used not only in browser extensions but also in many websites, such as Ajax tools, Google Analytics, and resources from large content distribution networks.

When browsers send violation reports for modifications due to browser extensions, the reverse conclusion is that websites enforcing CSP can cause browser extensions to stop functioning. Some browser extensions thus intercept CSP headers and modify them in order to whitelist their own resources or disable CSP. We observed reports caused by one such extension, which were sent because the modification resulted in a semantic error. We cannot quantify how often such modifications were successful as they are not observable with our methodology.

In addition to browser extensions, "in-flight" modification of pages by ISPs or web applications such as anonymity proxies can also cause violation reports. The image loaded from `1.2.3.11` in the example above appeared to be injected by a mobile Internet provider. These examples illustrate that even when CSP violations due to browser extensions were filtered (or not reported by the browsers), other non-attack scenarios can still cause websites to receive spurious reports.

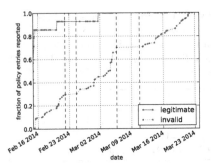
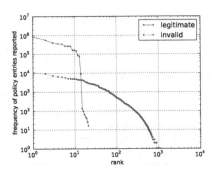

Fig. 2. Fraction of new policy entries discovered over time on site B (measurement inactive during the dashed intervals). It can take some time until all legitimate resources have been accessed at least once; in the meantime, many injected resources are reported.

Fig. 3. Frequency of legitimate and invalid violations being reported on site D. Some injected resources occurred orders of magnitude more often than legitimate resources.

Administrators who plan to generate a policy from reports submitted by their visitors' web browsers may need to manually verify a large number of policy entries in order to avoid accidentally whitelisting resources injected by browser extensions or ISPs (let alone attackers).

Time Delay Until a Policy can be Generated. On site B, it took around two weeks to receive at least one report for each valid policy entry. The last resource that was discovered was an embedded YouTube video. Another resource that was discovered relatively late was an image loaded over HTTPS instead of HTTP; all other valid policy entries could be generated within the first two days of the measurement. For the other sites, the durations were similar. In practice we expect these numbers to vary, thus website operators will need some prior knowledge about the resources used on their website so that they can decide when it is safe to switch from report-only to enforcement mode without causing any disruption. Operators could therefore be tempted to run the observation period for as long as possible in order to minimize the risk of not receiving reports for legitimate resources. However, as Figure 2 shows, the rate of newly observed, invalid policy entries remained relatively constant over time, suggesting that longer measurement periods can significantly increase the number of policy entries an operator needs to verify manually.

Report Frequency as a (Poor) Distinguishing Feature. Only about 4 % of all reports received on site D during our measurement resulted in an invalid policy entry. Hence, one might attempt to use the frequency of a report as an indicator for its validity. However, this approach would be problematic for two reasons. First, an attacker can easily influence the frequency distribution observed by the website by submitting forged reports. Second, even in the absence of attacks, resources injected into websites can be so popular that they cause reports more often than some legitimate, but infrequently accessed, resources.

Figure 3 visualizes this phenomenon. The most frequently injected resource (a script loaded from `superfish.com` for price comparison) was reported more than 22,000 times. In contrast, `connect-src 'self'`, which is used by a progress meter on the site, was reported only 9,000 times, and reports corresponding to alternative domain names of site D were received even less frequently.

4.4 Conclusions

Websites small and large observe CSP violation reports for injected resources. Even in the absence of ostensibly malicious activity, which we did not observe, the high number of injected resources complicates the process of generating a viable policy from the received reports. At the moment, this task is mostly a tedious and, from our own experience, error-prone manual process. As a semi-automated approach to filtering reports, it might be possible to generate signatures for the most common browser extensions, either manually or by leveraging the fact that an installed browser extension usually causes several violations to co-occur (based on time, IP address, and user agent signature). These signatures could be shared with the community and could be used to reduce the number of reports that need to be verified manually.

5   Semi-automated Policy Generation

An alternative approach to generating a policy from appropriately filtered and verified reports submitted by visitors is to make use of trustworthy reports only. In order to explore this approach further, we developed a proof-of-concept web crawler that generates violation reports in a controlled environment.

5.1   Methodology

Our crawler is implemented as an extension for the Chromium browser based on Site Spider, Mark II. The crawler follows at most 500 internal links on the main domain of the crawled site in a non-randomized breadth-first search. After navigating to a page, the crawler pauses for 2.5 s to load all resources of a document such as images, scripts, and external pages displayed in frames. The browser accesses the web through an instance of the Squid web proxy with an ICAP module. The proxy inserts the CSP report-only headers described in Section 4.2 and collects the resulting reports. The proxy also intercepts encrypted SSL traffic.

After crawling a site, we discarded all reports that did not match the site's main domain. These reports referred to external documents loaded in a frame and were not necessary to generate a policy for the main document. (In CSP, a document's policy does not transitively apply to nested documents loaded inside a frame.) From the remaining reports, we generated a policy as in Section 4.2.

The crawler should be considered a proof-of-concept to explore the feasibility of automatically generating policies for websites. By following only hypertext links, the crawler cannot detect violations that conditionally occur after load-time, such as clicking the "play" button in a Flash movie, or triggering JavaScript-related events. We leave ways to increase the crawler's coverage to future work.

As a potentially more targeted alternative to automated crawling, we also manually browsed websites in a fresh browser instance and used the proxy to collect reports. This process included no feedback. The goal was to cover all areas of the site and trigger as many different violations as possible by specifically exercising functionality implemented in JavaScript or browser plugins.

5.2   Evaluation

The question of whether semi-automated policy generation for websites is a suitable approach—without requiring modifications to the sites—depends on two opposing goals. First, the generated policy must not break the site. A policy generation mechanism must discover all resources being included by a site, or a superset thereof. Second, the generated policy should be as narrow as possible in order to provide the maximum safety gain. Unnecessary resources should not be allowed by the policy, and unsafe mechanisms should not be used. In the first part of this evaluation, we compare methods of collecting reports for policy generation on sites where we know that a sound policy exists. In the second part, we explore how well different site architectures work with CSP; that is, whether a sensible policy can be deployed without changing the sites.

Crawling and Manual Browsing of Our Own Sites. From the reports submitted by visitors' web browsers in Section 4.3, we know that stable policies exist for our own four sites. Indeed, the sets of policy entries generated by crawling and manual browsing as shown in the upper part of Table 7 overlap, and only a few entries were found by only one method. Especially when disregarding differences due to alternative domain names and HTTP(S), both methods performed similarly. However, neither method was perfect. The crawler discovered resources in a rather hidden portion of site B that manual browsing did not uncover. On site D, in turn, manual browsing discovered a resource inclusion that the crawler was not able to find, which was due to exercising JavaScript code when submitting content to the site. The policy entries generated from valid user-submitted reports were always a strict superset of those derived from crawling and browsing (as shown in the lower two-thirds of the table), except for site B where we found that a technical mistake had prevented CSP headers from being sent to users in a small portion of the site. We conclude that the crawler and manual browsing techniques need more refinement before they can fully replace user-submitted reports. Since both techniques are complementary, combining them could prove useful to increase coverage.

Table 7. Overlap between the sets of policy entries generated by the crawler, through manual browsing and from user-submitted reports. (In brackets, the number of common/different policy entries when disregarding alternative domain names or HTTP(S).) No method was fully reliable.

Site	A	B	C	D
crawler only	0 (0)	8 (8)	0 (0)	0 (0)
both	3 (3)	12 (9)	12 (10)	8 (7)
manual only	0 (0)	2 (0)	1 (0)	9 (2)
crawler only	0 (0)	9 (9)	0 (0)	0 (0)
both	3 (3)	11 (8)	12 (10)	8 (7)
valid user reports only	0 (0)	3 (1)	26 (3)	14 (2)
manual only	0 (0)	3 (2)	0 (0)	2 (0)
both	3 (3)	11 (7)	13 (10)	15 (9)
valid user reports only	0 (0)	3 (2)	25 (3)	7 (0)

Crawling and Manual Browsing of CSP-enabled Sites. In order to compare our crawler-generated policies to real-world policies, we generated policies for large public websites that deployed CSP in enforcement mode. As a case study, we provide more detail for Facebook and GitHub.

Our crawl included the public portion of Facebook as well as authenticated sessions. The policy generated by the crawler was a subset of Facebook's actual policy. It listed the specific subdomains of Content Distribution Networks (CDNs) observed during the crawl, whereas Facebook whitelisted all CDN subdomains with a wildcard. Furthermore, while Facebook's policy restricted only `script-src` and `connect-src`, the crawler also generated entries for `img-src`, for instance. Both issues could cause unobserved (but legitimate) behavior to be blocked and illustrate that automatically generated policies are likely to require fine-tuning using domain knowledge before they can be deployed.

On GitHub, the crawler discovered all whitelisted resources of the original policy (which did not use any wildcards, and restricted only `script-src`, `style-src`, and `object-src`). The crawler generated additional entries that were not part of GitHub's policy. Upon manual verification, we found that some resources included in GitHub's blog were not loaded due to missing policy entries. This finding illustrates the importance of monitoring enforced policies when websites evolve; regular crawls of a website could be a useful tool to help detect such changes.

Influence of Design Choices on CSP. Architectural features of a site can influence whether it is possible to deploy a meaningful policy without changing the site. Our crawls of Twitter, for instance, found a small, stable set of policy entries, while additional manual browsing discovered only one additional policy entry. Most of the resources were internal. Multimedia content included in tweets, for instance, was loaded from internal subdomains with constant names. Such an architecture makes it relatively convenient to deploy CSP without major changes. Indeed, Twitter used CSP in some subdirectories and subdomains.

Other sites such as Amazon, Google, and YouTube dynamically used explicitly named subdomains of CDNs such as `mt{2,3}.google.com`, similarly to Facebook. These subdomains appeared to be used for load balancing and could therefore be considered equivalent from a security point of view. Our crawler was not able to enumerate all these subdomains, but post-processing of the policy such as using a wildcard `*.google.com` could address the issue. A drawback of this approach is that sites such as Amazon that use external CDNs would also be whitelisting other customers' subdomains. A cleaner approach would be to use static domain names at the web application layer and address load balancing transparently at lower layers, as appears to be done by Twitter.

In the examples above, it was possible to compensate for some degree of variability in the sites by broadening the generated policy because the variability was systematic. On certain types of sites such as blogs where users are allowed to include externally hosted content, this may not be possible. The policy used by GitHub shows a possible compromise in such situations: the site allowed images to be loaded from any source and restricted only more sensitive resource types such as scripts and plugins.

Stability of Policies. A requirement to successfully deploy an enforceable policy is to predict at policy generation time the external resources that will be included when a page is rendered in a browser. A particularly unpredictable type of external content is advertising. The exact advertisement shown to a user is typically determined dynamically while the page is loading. Dynamic advertising can involve techniques such as Real-Time Bidding (RTB), where the opportunity to display an advertisement to a visitor is auctioned off in real-time, and further dynamic activity such as cookie matching between the host website and the winner of the auction. There are routinely tens to hundreds of potential bidders in RTB [16], each of whom represent a large number of actual advertisers.

In order to better understand how this dynamic activity can be reconciled with the more static requirements of CSP, we performed repeated crawls of two large websites with dynamic advertisements and counted how many new policy entries we discovered in each subsequent crawl (Table 8). Twitter, which we crawled as a control data point, remained stable and resulted in exactly the same policy in all crawls. On the BBC, the crawler discovered between 13 and 61 new policy entries in each of the follow-up crawls; the vast majority of them were scripts or other content related to advertising. On CNN, the follow-up crawls discovered only between one and four new policy entries, and only one was unambiguously related to advertising. Since both sites displayed comparable types and amounts of advertisements, the differences must be due to the way advertising was implemented. Indeed, the BBC loaded all advertisement-related resources, including RTB scripts, tracking code, and the final image being displayed, directly into the body of the main document. It would be very challenging to deploy CSP in such a scenario because it seems unfeasible to proactively determine any resource that could potentially be loaded. In contrast, CNN isolated advertisements from the main document by loading them as a separate document displayed inside an embedded frame.

Table 8. Additional policy entries discovered in repeated crawls. The high variability due to advertising on the BBC precludes CSP from being used effectively. CNN's way of including advertisement results in a relatively stable (and enforceable) policy.

Crawl number	1	2	3	4	5
BBC	285	+34	+61	+13	+53
CNN	116	+4	+2	+ 1	+1
Twitter	20	+0	+0		

This decoupling significantly eases the deployment of CSP because the main document's policy does not transitively apply to the document inside the frame. In such a deployment, it would be possible to enforce a rather strict policy for the main document and a much more permissive policy for the embedded advertisement document (or none at all). The SOP as well as the HTML5 frame sandboxing mechanism can be used to ensure that untrustworthy scripts in the frame cannot access or modify the main document.

Safety of Policies. To assess whether policies generated for a site represent any significant reduction in exposure to attacks, we checked whether the policies included "unsafe" CSP features—that is, inline script or style and calls to `eval`. Among our own sites that included JavaScript, only site B did not require `eval` privileges. Amazon, the BBC, CNN, Facebook, Google, the Huffington Post, and YouTube required all three privileges; Twitter needed inline script and style, and GitHub only inline style. These requirements may be due to code on the sites or in external libraries they include. Even though allowing inline script and `eval` reduces the effectiveness of CSP against XSS attacks, by restricting where external resources may be loaded from, CSP could still make it more difficult for attackers to include custom content such as images or to exfiltrate stolen data.

5.3   Conclusions

Neither naïve crawling nor manual browsing alone are sufficient methods to generate a content security policy for a website. In our approach, a certain amount of fine-tuning of generated policies is required for all but the simplest sites. Advanced crawling, or applying machine learning to the generated policies, could reduce the importance of manual tweaks. More complex sites may be able to use only a subset of CSP unless they adjust their architecture. Once a policy has been deployed, an additional challenge is to ensure that it is always up to date.

6   Discussion

We saw that only few websites use CSP, and those that do use it do not leverage its full benefits. For this section, we reached out to security engineers behind larger CSP deployments and summarize key points. Furthermore, we suggest several ways in which CSP adoption could be improved.

6.1   Discussions with Security Engineers

To understand implementation decisions behind real-world CSP deployments, we talked to security engineers responsible for three of the measured websites. Out of these sites, two were in the Alexa Top 200, and one in the Top 5,000. The websites used CSP in enforcement mode or report-only for testing. We summarize the key observations in an anonymized fashion.

Websites Prefer Not to Remove Inline Script. While inline script can be completely removed from websites, this represents significant effort and can lead to more roundtrips when loading the page. Engineers hope to address this issue with the nonce and hash features of CSP draft version 1.1. Hash might be more promising because documents can be distributed over CDNs more easily, whereas for nonce a new document would need to be generated for each response.

Risk of Breaking Functionality. This was manifested by disabling CSP for browser versions with problematic CSP implementations, including Chrome and Firefox. A website that is secure but not usable can harm business more than occasional XSS. For the future, reliable implementations of CSP in browsers are anticipated.

Enforcement over Extensions is Considered a Bug. CSP rule enforcement can break the functionality of browser extensions. A workaround is to whitelist popular sources. However, extensions could still be unintentionally restricted. A modification of browser implementations or the standard to not enforce rules over extensions could solve this.

6.2   Suggested Improvements

We briefly summarize approaches that could help the adoption of CSP and increase its security benefits when deployed.

Ads should be Integrated into iframes instead of the Main Site. Instead of whitelisting all possible ad networks or developing a mechanism for recursive policy adoption, ads should be moved into sandboxed iframes. This allows the main site to be protected with an effective policy, while the iframe can be more permissive, but isolated. Conflating both the site proper and ads in the same context is not necessary, since information required by ads can be passed via `postMessage` cross-window communication. However, while not widely available, alternatives such as Security Style Sheets [14] have been proposed that would allow for such separation without moving content to iframes.

More Web Applications and Frameworks should Adopt CSP. Introducing CSP to programs that are deployed widely can have a higher impact on the overall security of the web as compared to individual websites adopting CSP. As examples, phpMyAdmin and OwnCloud have adopted CSP, and Django can be configured with CSP. Most desirable would be the introduction of CSP to web frameworks, which could drastically improve adoption of CSP and the safety of the web.

Browsers Should not Enforce CSP on Extensions. As discussed in Section 4, enforcing policies on browser extensions generates many unexpected reports for websites. Websites should not be forced to whitelist extensions since the number of extensions and third-party resources included by those extensions is theoretically unbounded and cannot be predicted by application developers. Furthermore, CSP in its current form is not an adequate mechanism for websites to block potentially undesired extensions and should not be used as such.

7   Related Work

CSP was proposed by Stamm et al. [19], who provided the first implementation in the Firefox browser. Subsequently, CSP became a W3C standard [6] and was adopted by most major browsers. Other publications have addressed limitations of CSP and suggested extensions or modifications to the standard. For instance, Soel et al. [18] proposed an extension of CSP to address shortcomings in `postMessage` origin handling.

CSP was the first widely deployed browser policy framework to mitigate content injection attacks. However, it was not the first one to be suggested. SOMA (Same Origin Mutual Approval) [15] reduces the impact of XSS and CSRF by controlling information flows. Website operators need to approve content sources in a manifest file, as well as content providers need to approve websites to include their content. BEEP [11] can prevent XSS attacks with a whitelist approach for JavaScript and a DOM sandbox for possibly malicious user content. Script tags are whitelisted by hash, a feature that is also proposed in the 1.1 draft of CSP. BLUEPRINT [20] enforces restrictions on the document parse tree in the browser. Web application server components make parsing decisions and transport the DOM structure to the client. By enforcing a consistent document structure, misuse of browser rendering quirks is eliminated. CONSCRIPT [12] supports a variety of policies for JavaScript enforcement, which can be generated automatically. Static policy generation is supported for Script#, a Microsoft tool that generates JavaScript from C# code, as well as a dynamic training mode for other platforms. Weinberger et al. [21] performed an evaluation of browser-side policy enforcement systems. They concluded that security policies for HTML should be a central mechanism for preventing content injection attacks, but need more research to become effective. We performed the first study on CSP adoption in the wild, analyzing how usage has evolved in the past year on the most popular websites. Also, we investigate how report-only mode can be used to devise policies, and whether those are effective.

Currently, inline scripts are as popular with websites as they are bad for the effectiveness of CSP to prevent XSS. Bugzilla and HotCRP required substantial changes to support CSP [21], while `addons.mozilla.org` required an effort of several hours [19]. Previous work performed automatic rewriting of .NET applications to better support CSP [10]. Recent changes to the CSP draft, such as nonce and hash whitelisting of scripts, represent an approach that relieves developers of removing inline scripts while allowing for control over code. Trust relationships in external script sources have been analyzed by Nikiforakis et al. [13]. 88% of the Alexa Top 10K most visited websites included scripts from remote sources, and the most popular single library was included from 68% of the sites. An outlook on the possible future of web vulnerabilities has been summarized by Zalewski [8]. While CSP addresses a wide range of vulnerabilities, it can not prevent out-of-order execution of scripts, code reuse through JSONP interfaces, and others.

8   Conclusion

In this paper, we have presented the results of a long-term study on CSP as it is deployed on the web. We have found that CSP adoption significantly lags other web security mechanisms, and that even when it has been adopted by a site, it is often deployed in a way that negates its theoretical benefits for preventing content injection and data exfiltration attacks.

In addition, by enabling CSP at four sites, we observed that it is difficult for third parties to deploy CSP, either through incremental deployment using report-only mode or through web application crawling to semi-automatically generate policies.

CSP clearly holds great promise as a web security standard, but we can only conclude that it is difficult for most sites to deploy it to its full potential in its current form. It is our hope that the improvements we suggest here, as well as up-coming features of the 1.1 draft, will allow site operators and developers to make effective use of content security policies and result in a safer web ecosystem.

Acknowledgements. This work was supported by the Office of Naval Research (ONR) under grant N00014-12-1-0165. We would like to thank our shepherd Anil Somayaji and the anonymous reviewers for their helpful comments. Furthermore, we thank Collin Mulliner and Clemens Kolbitsch for their help in data collection.

References

1. DNS Prefetching - The Chromium Projects, http://www.chromium.org/developers/design-documents/dns-prefetching
2. The Platform for Privacy Preferences 1.0 (P3P1.0) Specification (2002), http://www.w3.org/TR/P3P/
3. IE8 Security Part IV: The XSS Filter (2008), http://blogs.msdn.com/b/ie/archive/2008/07/02/ie8-security-part-iv-the-xss-filter.aspx
4. IE8 Security Part V: Comprehensive Protection (2008), http://blogs.msdn.com/b/ie/archive/2008/07/02/ie8-security-part-v-comprehensive-protection.aspx
5. RFC 6797 - HTTP Strict Transport Security, HSTS (2012), http://tools.ietf.org/html/rfc6797
6. Content Security Policy 1.1 (2013), https://dvcs.w3.org/hg/content-security-policy/raw-file/tip/csp-specification.dev.html
7. Cross-Origin Resource Sharing, W3C Candidate Recommendation (January 29, 2013), http://www.w3.org/TR/cors/
8. Postcards from the post-XSS world (2013), http://lcamtuf.coredump.cx/postxss/
9. RFC 7034 - HTTP Header Field X-Frame-Options (2013), http://tools.ietf.org/html/rfc7034

10. Doupé, A., Cui, W., Jakubowski, M.H., Peinado, M., Kruegel, C., Vigna, G.: deDacota: Toward Preventing Server-Side XSS via Automatic Code and Data Separation. In: ACM Conference on Computer and Communications Security, CCS (2013)
11. Jim, T., Swamy, N., Hicks, M.: Defeating Script Injection Attacks with Browser-Enforced Embedded Policies. In: International Conference on World Wide Web, WWW (2007)
12. Meyerovich, L.A., Livshits, B.: ConScript: Specifying and enforcing fine-grained security policies for Javascript in the browser. In: IEEE Symposium on Security and Privacy, Oakland (2010)
13. Nikiforakis, N., Invernizzi, L., Kapravelos, A., Van Acker, S., Joosen, W., Kruegel, C., Piessens, F., Vigna, G.: You Are What You Include: Large-scale Evaluation of Remote JavaScript Inclusions. In: ACM Conference on Computer and Communications Security, CCS (2012)
14. Oda, T., Somayaji, A.: Enhancing Web Page Security with Security Style Sheets. Carleton University (2011)
15. Oda, T., Wurster, G., van Oorschot, P.C., Somayaji, A.: SOMA: Mutual Approval for Included Content in Web Pages. In: ACM Conference on Computer and Communications Security, CCS (2008)
16. Olejnik, L., Tran, M.D., Castelluccia, C.: Selling Off Privacy at Auction. In: ISOC Network and Distributed System Security Symposium (NDSS) (2014)
17. Samuel, M., Saxena, P., Song, D.: Context-Sensitive Auto-Sanitization in Web Templating Languages Using Type Qualifiers. In: ACM Conference on Computer and Communications Security, CCS (2011)
18. Son, S., Shmatikov, V.: The Postman Always Rings Twice: Attacking and Defending postMessage in HTML5 Websites. In: ISOC Network and Distributed System Security Symposium, NDSS (2013)
19. Stamm, S., Sterne, B., Markham, G.: Reining in the Web with Content Security Policy. In: International Conference on World Wide Web, WWW (2010)
20. Ter Louw, M., Venkatakrishnan, V.: BLUEPRINT: Robust Prevention of Cross-site Scripting Attacks for Existing Browsers. In: IEEE Symposium on Security and Privacy, Oakland (2009)
21. Weinberger, J., Barth, A., Song, D.: Towards Client-side HTML Security Policies. In: Workshop on Hot Topics on Security, HotSec (2011)

Synthetic Data Generation and Defense in Depth Measurement of Web Applications*

Nathaniel Boggs, Hang Zhao, Senyao Du, and Salvatore J. Stolfo

Columbia University, New York, NY
{boggs,zhao,du,sal}@cs.columbia.edu

Abstract. Measuring security controls across multiple layers of defense requires realistic data sets and repeatable experiments. However, data sets that are collected from real users often cannot be freely exchanged due to privacy and regulatory concerns. Synthetic datasets, which can be shared, have in the past had critical flaws or at best been one time collections of data focusing on a single layer or type of data. We present a framework for generating synthetic datasets with normal and attack data for web applications across multiple layers simultaneously. The framework is modular and designed for data to be easily recreated in order to vary parameters and allow for inline testing. We build a prototype data generator using the framework to generate nine datasets with data logged on four layers: network, file accesses, system calls, and database simultaneously. We then test nineteen security controls spanning all four layers to determine their sensitivity to dataset changes, compare performance even across layers, compare synthetic data to real production data, and calculate combined defense in depth performance of sets of controls.

Keywords: Metrics, Defense in Depth, Web Application Attacks, Measuring Security.

1 Introduction

To develop a science of security, at a minimum researchers need a convenient means to run repeatedable scientific experiments. To design a defense in depth security architecture, system security enginners benefit from a useful workbench to compare and place different security controls. In this work, we use security control as a broad label to include anything that hinders an attacker, including any security product, network, host, or database sensor, as well as more emphemerial controls such as user security training or corporate policies. Both goals

---

* This work is sponsored in part by Air Force Office of Scientific Research (AFOSR) grant FA9550-12-1-0162 "Designing for Measurable Security" and DARPA grant FA8650-11-C-7190 "Mission-oriented Resilient Clouds." The views and conclusions contained herein are those of the authors and should not be interpreted as necessarily representing the official policies or endorsements, either expressed or implied, of AFOSR or DARPA.

A. Stavrou et al. (Eds.): RAID 2014, LNCS 8688, pp. 234–254, 2014.
© Springer International Publishing Switzerland 2014

require tools to mearure security properties. Measuring and comparing effectiveness of security controls is a difficult task the security research community faces. Researchers usually want to repeat other experiments, so they can compute on the same dataset and verify the accuracy of the analysis to ensure that security controls are compared fairly. For experiments to be repeatable, datasets and algorithms used must be made available to others. However, legal, privacy and logistic issues often prevent data sharing. The present solution is to acquire as many security controls as possible locally, so one could test them against datasets she has access to in order to measure and compare their effectiveness. Since no single dataset could contain all the security problems to be assessed, as we learn from now famous TLS Bug[1], this approach at best provides only a partial view into the effectiveness of these security controls.

In order to gain a fuller picture of these security controls, we need quality shareable datasets. Unfortunately, anonymizing real user data is not a trivial matter[1][2].So we have to look for the alternative–Synthetic Data, data generated through using existing user models. It offers advantages besides being shareable. The forms of these data will be close, if not identical to those from real users. Less realism is traded for more precise control of different parameters, e.g. content length. By adjusting these parameters, we can find exactly what changes each security control is sensitive to. In addition, by controlling when and what attacks are introduced, we have a clear view of ground truth, whereas in real user data, attacks are hard to identify, resulting in additional unknown false negatives. In fact, even in real user data, synthetic attack data is often injected for testing, as labeling the datasets with often sparse attacks is a cumbersome and potentially inaccurate process.

In this paper, we propose a modular synthetic dataset generation framework for web applications, and a monitoring infrastructure that is capable of recording data from multiple layers, including TCP packets on the network, database queries, and even host system calls, so that security controls at different layers can be compared to each other. We call this system Wind Tunnel. By limiting the scope of Wind Tunnel to one important attack vector, remote attacks on web applications, we can better model the content and measure security controls designed to defend against it. In order to incorporate more realism in the synthetic dataset, we use publicly available content, such as known usernames, passwords, English text, and images as the fundamental data sources in Wind Tunnel. For a particular web application, we first create use cases and then drive multiple instances of Firefox via Selenium [3] based on these use cases to simulate users. Each dataset has configurable distributions for each parameter and has all the network traffic, system calls, and database queries recorded. For attack data, we write scripts using Metasploit [4], launch the attacks, and execute post-compromise data exfiltration.

With a modular design and focus on the ease of data generation, one can easily change a parameter or substitute different user content to determine how that change affects all the security controls tested. Collecting data from multiple

---

[1] http://heartbleed.com/

layers at the same time allows us to compare security controls operating at different layers directly to one another. For instance, we can determine if a web content anomaly detector and a file access sensor each detect the same attack. In later sections, we describe Wind Tunnel and how we use it to generate nine datasets representing three separate web applications, varieties of user content, changes in length parameters, and two different servers. We then test nineteen security controls at four different layers, using the results to discover what changes affect different types of security controls. We illustrate how we can compare security controls from different layers including web content anomaly detectors, database sensors, file access sensors, and more with this multilayer dataset, as well as perform analysis on how such security controls could be optimized in a defense in depth architecture by showing their overlap. Furthermore, we compare our generated data to that of a production web server dataset and another synthetic dataset published previously [5].

The remainder of the paper is layed out as follows. In Section 2, we describe our board approach. Section 3 details our implementation. All results are presented in Section 4. In Section 5, we discuss related work. Finally, we remark on future goals and conclusions in Sections 6 and 7.

2   Data Generator Framework

The goals of Wind Tunnel is to generate realistic synthetic data across multiple layers in a modular, repeatable, and automated manner. We want the synthetic data to be realistic enough that measurements of security control performance are predictive of at least relative performance of security controls on real production data. We focus on modeling web application content rather than network connection information, source reputation, volumetrics, or fine grain timing. In the future, with the modular nature of Wind Tunnel, we can integrate more sophisticated models of user behavior. By generating multiple layers of data, we can test security controls that protect against a particular attack vector regardless of the layer at which they operate. A modular framework allows individual components such as new sources of user content, new web applications, or new attacks to be quickly integrated. Rather than just generating data once, Wind Tunnel is designed to repeatedly create a dataset either for use with inline defenses that cannot be tested against a static dataset or to adjust various parameters in order to explore what effect certain changes have on various security controls.

Wind Tunnel consists of seven steps any of which can be reconfigured or expanded without having to build a whole dataset from scratch. A visual overview can be seen in Figure 1.

- Set up a web application server
- Program use cases with Selenium [3]
- Choose existing or create additional raw content data sets for user submitted content
- Create attacks and define permutations
- Start recording on server and start clients

- Launch attacks
- Test security controls against data
- Process, analyze and visualize results

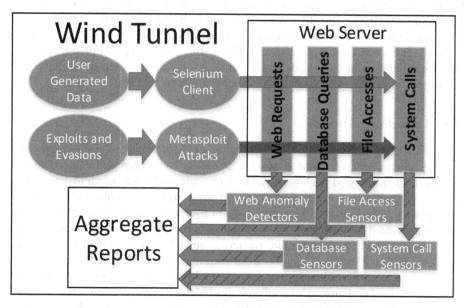

Fig. 1. Wind Tunnel System Overview

2.1   Normal Traffic Generation

Use cases in Wind Tunnel are Java code that use the Selenium library to drive a Firefox web browser to perform actions on and submit to the chosen web application that simulate a user completing some typical use of the website. These can range from simply visiting the home page to performing a complex series of actions such as logging in, page navigation, filling out and submitting a form, and uploading a file. Similar to using such tools as a testing framework, we want a variety of use cases that cover all the major functionality of the web application, especially vulnerable ones. Anytime a choice has to be made in the course of executing use cases, such as what content and how much or which image to upload, a configurable parameter is provided to the security researcher. Each use case has access to a set of usernames, image files, English text, etc. The use case can be configured to use a particular distribution of content such as using a Zipf distribution when choosing from available usernames or a normal distribution with a specific mean for choosing the number of English sentences to post in a form field. These types of distributions and their parameters can all be reconfigured. For instance, it would be important to know during evaluation if even minor changes in the average length of blog posts affects the false positive rate of a content-based anomaly detector.

We focus on modeling user submitted content as this is where web applications are typically vulnerable. Content anomaly detectors in particular are sensitive to normal data as that is what their models are built on and if that data is unrealistically regular they can have unrealistically high performance. To bring the messiness of real user data to Wind Tunnel, we reuse existing real user data from public sources. To add realism, the data should be as closely related to what the web application is expecting. For instance, any English text could also be used for usernames and password fields, but gathering samples from real world usernames and passwords and using those should add realism as character distributions are likely drastically different from standard English text.

2.2   Launching Attacks

For attack data, we leverage the Metasploit Framework [4] to use existing attacks, evasions, and payloads as well as the ability to add new attacks, evasions, and payloads as needed without having to recreate each piece of an attack chain from scratch. We take a set of attacks, evasions, and post compromise exfiltration actions and generate a Metasploit script for each permutation. Attacks can vary from already known vulnerabilities, induced zero-days where we modify a web application to be vulnerable, to actual zero-day attacks against the web application. Attacks can be chosen from common web application attacks such as SQL injection, file upload attacks, code inclusion, etc. Evasions can include simple encoding schemes, advanced polymorphic code rewrites, padding attacks and others. Post compromise data exfiltration actions can be modeled as well.

2.3   Labeling the Data

After sufficient normal data is sent to the web application server, attacks are all launched in sequence while collecting their start and end times in order to label the data. At the network layer simply launching attacks from distinct IP addresses gives an easy labeling mechanism as in this attack vector we are not modeling source IP address patterns. We take a sliding window approach and treat the system call security controls as a warning system so any alert during an attack time windows counts as a true positive while alerts during only normal traffic count as false positives. File accesses are much rarer events, and since we know what the attacks are scripted to do, compromises are much easier to label. Malicious database queries launched as part of the attacks can be labeled based on timing when launched.

3   Prototype Implementation

3.1   Dataset Generation

Web Applications. We generate data for three PHP based web applications: Wordpress, Tikiwiki, and Testlink. All of the web applications run PHP 5.3.3, and both the web application version and PHP version were selected intentionally since known vulnerabilities exist in these versions. Wordpress is a widely used platform for running personal websites or blogs. We run Wordpress 3.3 with plugins Buddypress 1.5.4 and Foxypress 0.4.2.1. Buddypress is a plugin for social networking, and Foxypress is an ecommerce plugin. Tikiwiki is an open sourced 'all in one' content management system. We use Tikiwiki version 8.3 for these experiments. Testlink version 1.9.3 is a management system for tracking software quality.

Data Sources. In general, there were five different types of data that the use cases require: text, username, password, images, and files. We use three English text corpora the nonredundant Usenet corpus [6], the Wikipedia corpus from WetburyLab [7] and post data from Stackoverflow [8]. The text data is used to fill in titles, descriptions, posts, among other text data that users send to servers. The benefits of these publicly available data sets is that the text is actual data generated by real users. This has the following implications: 1) Text that is close by tends to be contextual and related 2) the text is representative of user text in online contexts 3) data from a particular site could have different properties.

The usernames and passwords that we use during experiments are from a Stack Exchange Data Explorer [9] query for 20 thousand usernames and the Rockyou password leak file containing millions of unencrypted passwords [10]. These two data sets provided actual examples of usernames and passwords that were used historically on public websites, and provide us with representative data of both.

Images were used in file uploads and incorporated into the user generated data for many applications. Images were taken from Wiki Commons public domain images [11]. This image source provides us with a freely usable and distributable repository of images.

Some applications expect to have text files uploaded as part of a description. In general, we seed these text files with data from Stackoverflow [8]. Steps were taken to ensure that the data used in the files did not overlap with the data that was used in the user submitted text since that could result in duplication of POST data to the server.

A variety of use cases composing typical normal user behavior are created. Care is taken to ensure that any function of the application targeted by an exploit in the attack dataset has a corresponding normal use case so that an anomaly detector does not simply detect the attack because user behavior was incorrectly modeled. In the configuration file, each use case had an associated weight. When running a use case, Wind Tunnel chooses one at random with probability $\frac{\text{weight of use case}}{\text{sum of all use case weights}}$.

Data Volume. For each dataset generated we capture enough HTTP requests with user submitted parameters to be able to train the network content anomaly detection sensors, which as described in Section 3.2, require 100,000 such requests to build their models. In order to have sufficient variety of data for testing false positives, we generate data until we have at least 25% more requests with arguments. Many more HTTP requests without user arguments are sent, often three to six times as many, in the synthetic datasets depending on the web application. Each dataset generates full packet content on the order of tens of gigabytes of uncompressed PCAP files, tens of gigabytes of compressed system call logs, and gigabytes of uncompressed SQL query logs. Such data generation takes between ten and twenty-four hours to complete in our laboratory environment.

Attack Data. For attack exploits, we use four known vulnerabilities and edit the applications to add two additional vulnerabilities. We utilize a corresponding Metasploit module for three of them and build new Metasploit modules for the three that did not already have one. For TikiWiki, we use CVE-2012-0911 which is a vulnerable PHP unserialize() allowing arbitrary code execution. For Testlink, we use OSVDB 85446 [12] an arbitrary file upload vulnerability which is then called to execute arbitrary code. For Wordpress we use two vulnerabilities in the add-ons FoxyPress and BuddyPress. For FoxyPress, we use OSVDB 82652 [13] that is another arbitrary file upload vulnerability leading to arbitrary code execution. In BuddyPress we use CVE-2012-2109 a SQL injection vulnerability that we use to gain arbitrary code execution. For TikiWiki and Testlink, we add an additional SQL injection vulnerability to the login page and exploit it. We provide Metasploit modules for these last three SQL injection exploits.

We add two basic evasion techniques to these base exploits, PHP base64 encoding and normal data padding. PHP base64 encoding transform the bulk of the payload code into alphanumeric text to obscure any alerts based on strange characters or naive code patterns. Normal data padding is where we take a sample of normal traffic to the website and extract typical user submitted data to concatenate to the malicious HTTP POST data in order to fool content anomaly detection models using a straightforward mimicry attack.

Once the attack establishes a shell connection to the server, we create two scenarios of data exfiltration. Both read the web application database configuration file to obtain the database login credentials. The first simply exfiltrates the user tables with usernames and passwords while the second scenario queries the entire database table by table to represent a more noisy attacker. Metasploit establishes a reverse shell on a separate port for these later attack stages so not all of the attack is exposed to the network security controls operating on HTTP requests. Each attack script is run in its own time window.

Real Web Server Data. In order to compare the synthetic data to production user data, under institutional review board approval, we acquire network traffic to a department web server for just over six days time. In the period, we collected 156GB of HTTP traffic representing of over 1.5 million HTTP requests. A main advantage of this data is that we can calculate realistic "in the wild" false positive rates. Unfortunately this web server is not the best analogy to the individual web applications as it runs many web applications on the same server forcing the content anomaly detectors to model them all at once. While significant attack traffic is seen, most (hopefully all) of those attacks fail to compromise the server so only the initial attack request is seen whereas in the synthetic datasets all the attacks consist of multiple requests lasting over the initial compromise and data exfiltration.

Labeling Ground Truth. For the production data server, which is exposed to the internet, all manner of attack data can be mixed in so establishing ground truth becomes a difficult task. We use the same method as used in prior work [14] to label the attack data as best we can via clustering and manual inspection. Some unknown number of false negatives may certainly be present. For the synthetic data as we have control of the attacks, we are able to better label ground truth. As discussed in Section 2, as different layers will see different aspects of the attacks, we label attack data at the network layer by determining whether it came from the attack machine IP address or not. For determining whether a security control detects an attack we check for any alerts during the attack time period. This is useful as no security control can see all the aspects of the attack at different layers and even without detecting all parts of the attack at a certain layer, by alerting, a security control brings attention to the attack.

3.2   Security Controls

We acquired and installed 19 sensors across the network, file access, system call, and database layers to test against the datasets. All of the sensors in this prototype are run in offline mode testing on the data after it has been collected; however, the sensors are designed for and capable of running in real time.

Network Layer. We run six content anomaly detection (CAD) sensors operating on user submitted argument strings in HTTP GET and POST requests that they extract from reassembled TCP streams from raw network traffic. For POST requests this is all the content after the HTTP header and for GET requests this is the string following the ? in the URI and is typically made up of attribute value pairs. For instance, in a GET request like GET /index.php?username=alice HTTP/1.1, username=alice is the content modeled by the CAD systems. The six CADs used for network layer detection are Spectrogram [15], Anagram [16], and four models previously developed by Kruegel and Vigna [17] attribute length, attribute existence, attribute character distribution, and attribute tokens. All of these are implemented on top of STAND [18] a data sanitization framework to build sanitized AD models from a sliding windows of 25 submodels built on time slices of content. STAND is configured to use the content normalization developed for Spectrogram [15]. For our synthetic data sets each detection model is computed on 100,000 HTTP requests with user arguments before testing starts. For the production web server data, we use the calibrator feature of STAND described in [19] that is time aware and ended up building its models on about 3 days worth of data.

Database Layer. We run six sensors on MySQL queries captured during the data generation process. We implement five content anomaly detection sensors operating on user specified inputs in those queries using a similar approach discussed in related work [20]. For each MySQL query, we extract all user specified inputs and insert them into a list in the order they appeared in the query. Then we replace each occurrence of user input in the original query with an empty placeholder token to generate a query skeleton. Similar to the web layer detection, we use five CADs including Spectrogram, Anagram, and three models from related work [20] attribute length, attribute character distribution, and attribute tokens. For all the attribute-based sensors, models are built separately for each type of query skeleton. Attribute existence sensor is ineffective for MySQL inputs because any given query skeleton pre-defines a list of user specified inputs as well as the relative order of them.

Besides the five CAD security controls, we also implement an offline sensor on top of an open source version of GreenSQL [21], a well-known unified solution for detecting database layer intrusions. We use the source code from an open source version (1.3.0) for these experiments. While the methodology to use greensql is to integrate it along with the running database, we have extracted the part that does the rule based pattern matching on the sql commands issued in order to generate alerts. This provides us with a mechanism to compare the efficiency of an open source sensor using the same datasets, on an offline basis. We use the default rule set and compute the anomaly scores based on the number of rules being fired for each MySQL query.

File Accesses Layer. We implement a anomaly detector that monitors file system calls to detect anomalous accesses based on prior work [22]. We use Auditd [23], the default Linux auditing system, to audit file system accesses, and an unsupervised machine learning system to compute normal models for those accesses. The anomaly detection engine utilizes the Probability Anomaly Detection (PAD) algorithm [24] and trains the normal models on a selected set of features associated with each file access, namely, UID, WD (current working directory), CMD (command being executed), Syscall Number, File Name, and Frequency. PAD calculates first order and second order probability for each of the 6 features giving a total of 36 probability values for each file access entry. An alert score is then computed using a multinomial model with a hierarchical prior based on dirichlet distribution, and log probabilities are used at each step to avoid underflows [22].

System Calls Layer. We run six sensors on system calls collected during the data generation process. Due to the negative impact on system performance when training an extreme large volume of system calls, we carefully select a subset of system calls that are audited by Snare's audit facility [25,26] to train the CAD sensors. Those system calls cover the most suspicious activities at the system call level when a large set of intrusions are observed. We therefore implement five content anomaly detectors operating on system call parameter and value pairs, including Spectrogram, Anagram, attribute length, attribute character distribution, and attribute token. Similarly, the attribute existence sensor is omitted as the presence of system call arguments are predefined. For those attribute-based sensors, normal models are built separately for each unique system call.

We also experiment with an anomaly detector called Stide on system call sequences that studies the short-range correlations in system calls for each process [27,28]. The algorithm builds the normal model using short sequences of system calls of length N for each process, and store the model information in a tree structure for efficient access. Thus an intrusion is detected when unseen sequences are observed for that process within certain locality window. In these experiments, we run the detector against the entire set of collected system calls with system call length of 6 and locality window of length 20 [27,28].

4 Experiments and Results

The goals of our experiments are fourfold. We want to determine the sensitivity of each security control to various dataset changes, compare security control stand alone performance across layers, determine whether performance on synthetic datasets predicts performance on a production dataset, and analyze how total performance of security controls scales when combined together. To this end, we use Wind Tunnel to generate nine synthetic datasets with normal and attack data using various parameters described below in addition to the real user production web server dataset described in Section 3.1.

4.1 Datasets

We experiment with four changes that security controls could be sensitive to in the underlying data. First, we test the natural variance between data generation with the same configuration both on the same server and then when changing to another host machine. Second, we look at the effect of content source by running the same configuration but changing from the USENET corpus [6] to a Wikipedia corpus [7] of English text or forum post data from Stackoverflow [8]. Third, we vary the length of user content inputs by changing the distribution of the length

Table 1. Comparison of the nine generated datasets

Dataset Name	Application	Content	Length	Run
wp_usenet_base	Wordpress	USENET	Normal	host machine A
wp_usenet_base2	Wordpress	USENET	Normal	repeated on host A
wp_usenet_base3	Wordpress	USENET	Normal	repeated on host B
wp_wiki	Wordpress	Wikipedia	Normal	host machine A
wp_stack	Wordpress	Stackoverflow	Normal	host machine A
wp_usenet_short	Wordpress	USENET	Halved	host machine A
wp_usenet_long	Wordpress	USENET	Doubled	host machine A
tiki_usenet	TikiWiki	USENET	Normal	host machine A
tk_usenet	Testlink	USENET	Normal	host machine A

of English text submitted by doubling it for one dataset and halving it for another dataset. Fourth, we generate datasets with three different web applications thus changing all the use cases as well. See Table 1 for a summarized comparison of the datasets. To compare these changes in datasets, we start with a baseline dataset using the Wordpress web application with the USENET corpus of English text. Data sources and use case distribution parameters are described in Section 3.1.

In addition to the datasets generated with this prototype, we add two additional web layer only datasets in order to compare results, a private dataset from the Columbia University Computer Science (CUCS) department web server and the publicly available ISCX 2012 Intrusion Detection Dataset [5]. The CUCS web server dataset consists of over 1.5 million HTTP requests, 60 thousand of which contain user argument strings which are processed by the web layer sensors. In manually labeling the resulting alerts, 1257 attack requests are seen. From the ISCX 2012 dataset, we use only the HTTP traffic destined to the web server that is attacked with web application attacks. This leaves us with over 3 million HTTP requests, 18 thousand of which contain user argument strings processed by the web layer sensors. Of these 18 thousand, 77 are labeled malicious constituting various web application attacks.

4.2   Comparison Experiments

With 19 sensors being tested across eleven different datasets, concise summation of data is key. In Table 2, we present the area under the curve (AUC) of each receiver operating characteristic (ROC) curve for each sensor and dataset pair. Note that for the department web server dataset CUCS and the ISCX dataset that only network traffic is available so file access, host, and database sensors are not tested. Note that the low scores for database sensors are in large part due to the fact that for the Wordpress and TikiWiki attacks only one of the two exploits leaves traces in the database layer after the preprocessing normalization. This makes the maximum AUC that a database sensor can achieve for a Wordpress dataset 0.5 and 0.33 for TikiWiki. The TikiWiki SQL exploit does not function without the PHP base64 encoding leaving twice as many instances of the other exploit.

The metric AUC gives a good general first impression of the performance of a sensor in terms of its detection rate and false positive rate trade off; however, deeper analysis is often needed to fully understand a sensor's performance. At first glance, many of the host sensors appear to dramatically outperform everything else. While this is the case in terms of false positive rate, one must remember that the raw count of system calls is high compared to the number of web requests with user parameters or database queries. In practice, this means that even for a false positive rate that rounds off to zero when computing the AUC, the host sensors can still have tens of thousands of individual alerts per dataset. This turns out to be the case here for all host sensors. These high raw counts of alerts may or may not translate to high costs for running the sensors depending on what sort of alert triage approaches are deployed. See Section 4.5 for further discussion of approaches for reducing the costs of false positives.

Table 2. Area under the curve (AUC) of the receiver operating characteristic (ROC) curve for each security control and dataset pair

	ISCX 2012	CUCS	wp_usenet_base	wp_usenet_base2	wp_usenet_base3	wp_usenet_base	wp_wiki	wp_stack	wp_usenet_base	wp_usenet_short	wp_usenet_long	wp_usenet_base	tiki_usenet	tk_usenet
webAnagram	1.00	0.84	0.98	0.98	0.99	0.98	0.98	0.98	0.98	0.98	0.98	0.98	1.00	1.00
webSpectrogram		0.96	0.98	0.98	0.97	0.98	0.98	0.98	0.98	0.98	0.98	0.98	1.00	1.00
webAttCharDist	1.00	0.76	0.97	0.97	0.97	0.97	0.97	0.94	0.97	0.96	0.96	0.97	0.98	1.00
webAttExistence	1.00	0.76	0.98	0.98	0.99	0.98	0.98	0.98	0.98	0.97	0.98	0.98	0.00	0.60
webAttLength	0.98	0.81	0.32	0.51	0.39	0.32	0.40	0.45	0.32	0.38	0.41	0.32	0.99	0.97
webAttToken	1.00	0.77	0.30	0.39	0.34	0.30	0.53	0.51	0.30	0.50	0.49	0.30	0.82	0.99
mysqlAnagram			0.50	0.50	0.50	0.50	0.50	0.50	0.50	0.50	0.50	0.50	0.33	1.00
mysqlSpectrogram			0.49	0.49	0.50	0.49	0.49	0.50	0.49	0.49	0.49	0.49	0.33	1.00
mysqlAttCharDist			0.50	0.50	0.50	0.50	0.50	0.50	0.50	0.50	0.50	0.50	0.33	1.00
mysqlAttLength			0.48	0.48	0.48	0.48	0.48	0.48	0.48	0.48	0.48	0.48	0.33	0.99
mysqlAttToken			0.50	0.50	0.50	0.50	0.50	0.50	0.50	0.50	0.50	0.50	0.31	0.97
mysqlGreensql			0.50	0.50	0.50	0.50	0.50	0.50	0.50	0.50	0.50	0.50	0.33	0.70
hostAnagram			0.95	0.96	0.94	0.95	0.97	0.96	0.95	0.95	0.97	0.95	0.99	0.97
hostSpectrogram			1.00	1.00	1.00	1.00	1.00	1.00	1.00	1.00	1.00	1.00	1.00	1.00
hostAttCharDist			0.99	0.91	1.00	0.99	0.97	1.00	0.99	0.95	0.91	0.99	1.00	1.00
hostAttLength			0.97	1.00	1.00	0.97	0.96	1.00	0.97	1.00	1.00	0.97	1.00	1.00
hostAttToken			0.84	0.83	0.77	0.84	0.82	0.79	0.84	0.84	0.83	0.84	0.93	0.89
hostFileAccess			1.00	1.00	1.00	1.00	1.00	1.00	1.00	1.00	1.00	1.00	0.99	0.98
hostSyscallSeq			1.00	1.00	1.00	1.00	1.00	1.00	1.00	1.00	1.00	1.00	1.00	1.00

Sensor performance on the real world production dataset differs substantially from the synthetic datasets. Some significant portion of this difference could be due to the nature of the CUCS dataset. The CUCS server hosts many different web applications at once, whereas the synthetic datasets all model one web application. The CUCS dataset has requests for many more different individual pages instead of the handful of specific use cases we see in the synthetic datasets. Further research into different categories of real world web application servers is needed. If this noise turns out to typical, the use cases should be adapted to produce such additional variance. With Wind Tunnel, such modifications can be integrated seamlessly into the data generation process as more data becomes available describing typical usage of web applications.

Experiment with Natural Variation. For the first experiment, we generate two separate datasets against the same server with the same configuration. For these baselines we use the USENET corpus as the source of English text and generate traffic against the Wordpress web application. Additionally, we run the same configuration against a separate server running the same Wordpress application. For the most part, AUC scores of the sensors stay fairly stable across these three datasets. The host layer character distribution sensor does fluctuate due to a large amount of normal data scoring just below the scores the sensor gives to the SQL exploit attack variations. For this reason a slight change in attack scores significantly affects the number of false positives thus changing the AUC.

Experiment with Varying Content Source. To test the sensitivity of sensors to changes in the distribution of English text, we conduct a second experiment reusing the same baseline of the Wordpress application with USENET data compared to the same configuration but with Wikipedia text and StackOverflow text respectively. This change in data source seems to have little overall impact on the sensors. The most apparent effect comes in the web layer character distribution sensor which has a reduction in its AUC for the StackOverflow dataset. Rather than just a small change in attack scores raising false positives, Figure 2 suggests that the general distribution of normal data score differs for the StackOverflow dataset for this sensor. As the sensor models the portion of characters often used and rarely used perhaps the StackOverflow text has higher variance in such text patterns with its often technical forum posts referencing code.

Experiment with Varying Content Length. In the third experiment, we vary the content length when sending English text data as titles, paragraphs, posts, etc.. We halve the mean of the length distribution for short texts and double it to make the long text configuration. Any impact this change had if any is within the natural variance between data generation. Only the host layer Anagram sensor increases its AUC from short to normal to long lengths. It is correlated only to one other sensor and the

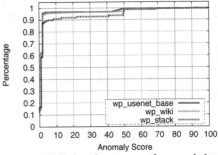

Fig. 2. CDF for the scores of normal data for web layer attribute character distribution sensor for three web applications

only negative correlation increasing AUC from long to short is the host layer attribute token sensor, which only shows change between long and normal.

Experiment with Varying Applications. Next we generate data against different web applications. We generate datasets for TikiWiki and Testlink in addition to the Wordpress baseline. As one might expect, changing the web application makes the largest impact on sensor performance out of the variations we show. As noted above, the Testlink attacks all have database level components so the database layer sensors are able to detect all attacks. The largest outlier we see occurs in this experiment in the web layer where the attribute existence sensor scores all the TikiWiki attacks as perfectly normal achieving 0 AUC. This is due to the simplistic nature of the sensor which checks whether it has seen

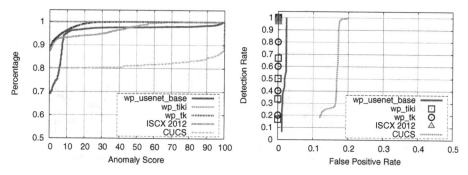

Fig. 3. CDF for the scores of normal data for web layer anagram sensor for three web application, production web server and ISCX dataset

Fig. 4. ROC curves for web layer anagram sensor for three web applications, production web server and ISCX dataset

all the variable name attributes in a request before. The TikiWiki exploits both only use attributes that are also used in normal operation so the sensor correctly performs just with a flawed detection mechanism. We also see a large increase in the performance of the web layer length and token sensors compared with their Wordpress performance.

Synthetic and Production Dataset Comparison. In order to visualize the differences in datasets, we graph the performance in detail of the web layer Anagram sensor for each separate web application that is the Wordpress, TikiWiki and Testlink datasets, the ISCX 2012 dataset, and the CUCS department web server dataset. In Figure 3, we plot the cumulative distribution of the Anagram anomaly scores for the legitimate data. For any given score (x-axis), the percentage of the normal data that scores at or below that score is given (y-axis). Note that a higher score means that Anagram describes that data as more abnormal with 100 meaning that no ngrams from the data are present in the Anagram model. This graph gives a visual representation of the distribution of the scores of the nonattack data. The CUCS department web server dataset, while sharing the pattern of a large portion of data being completely normal at score zero, has a large spike at score 100 meaning that many legitimate requests are never before seen by the Anagram model. Many of these are short searches with unique enough terms that they score high. Another large component of these score 100 legitimate requests are rarely used application features. With the model sanitization phase of STAND, requests seen only rarely in the training set are discarded to reduce model poisoning from widespread but low volume attacks.

We also plot the receiver operator characteristic (ROC) curve for Anagram across these five datasets in Figure 4. This plots the detection rate against the false positive rate for Anagram run on each dataset. Again the CUCS web server dataset is distinct as with so many legitimate requests receiving a score of 100 the false positive rate is correspondingly high. Additional use cases could be

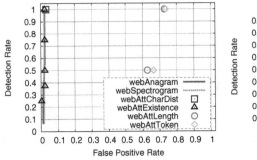

Fig. 5. ROC curves for six web layer sensors for the wordpress baseline dataset

Fig. 6. ROC curves for six database layer sensors for the wordpress baseline dataset

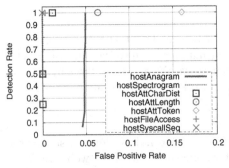

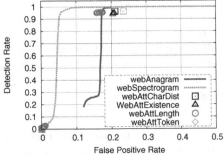

Fig. 7. ROC curves for seven host/file access layer sensors for the wordpress baseline dataset

Fig. 8. ROC curves for six web layer sensors for the production server dataset

created from this insight to model a server where some features are rarely accessed to the point where sensors have trouble modeling them. More high scoring use cases such as image uploads or short random searches could also be added. Further research into the typical use cases in production datasets from web servers with only a single web application server is needed to determine whether these patterns of high scoring alerts are typical or an artifact of the one production dataset we have.

4.3   Sensor Performance

In addition to Table 2, we present a brief sample of the results visually as ROC curves for the wp_usenet_base dataset with all 19 sensors tested as well as the web layer sensors for the CUCS web server in Figures 5, 6, 7, and 8. Note that each graph has different x-axis scales. In Figure 5, the web layer attribute length and attribute token sensors experience a large false positive rate. In Figure 6, we see plainly the effect of one of the Wordpress exploits leaving no trace in the database layer bounding all the sensors at 50% detection rate. The CUCS web server data shown in Figure 8 shows a clear winner in the Spectrogram sensor, which achieves the same detection rate at less than half of the false positive rates of the closest contender.

4.4   Correlation and Overlap between Sensors

The main advantage of Wind Tunnel is to generate, link, and test data across different layers. Rather than independent evaluation and detection rates, we can identify which sensors detect the same or different attacks regardless of layer.

We can also compute a total detection rate for any set of sensors, overlapping detections, and find sensors that add the largest marginal increase in total detection rate to a set of existing sensors. Figure 9 visually illustrates this ability. Each ring or concentric circle presents a particular sensor. Each arc represents an attack, which in this case is a particular exploit possibly permuted with various evasion techniques. Think of the circles as many walls surrounding a castle. Each attack then starts outside the walls and attacks each wall in turn proceeding directly to the center of the castle. All walls 'destroyed' are in red. Those walls that still stand (detecting the attack) are in green. The goal of the defender would be to have walls (sensors) such that no single attack knocks them all down (all red along a single arc), which would mean that each attack is detected by at least one sensor. In this figure, the bottom half shows attacks using the SQL injection exploit with the top half showing attacks

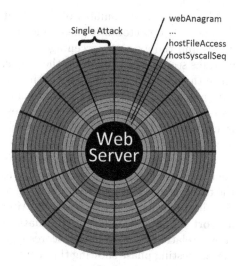

Fig. 9. Concentric circles represent each of the 19 sensors in the same order as Table 2. Each arc represents one attack permutation for the Wordpress synthetic data set. Green indicates that the attack is detected by the sensor at a false positive rate of at most 1% on the wp_usenet_base dataset.

using the file upload exploit. At this false positive rate some sensors detect all of the attacks. Also observe how certain sensors detect half and especially that some of those detect a different half than others such that those two sensors each with a 50% detection rate together would detect all the attacks. Access to this type of data instead of only a raw detection rate with little insight into how a set of sensors overlap is important for architecting defense in depth.

4.5 False Positive Analysis

In the experiments, content anomaly detectors perform quite well on user posts containing large amounts of previously unseen English text implying that these anomaly detectors are able to learn English well enough to label new English text as fairly normal. To verify that this is indeed the case, we run a stand alone version of Anagram on the raw English text sources used. The anomaly detector builds a Bloom Filter from a training set using sliding n-grams of the HTTP request (ie, if n = 5, then the first two sliding 5-grams of "abcdef" are "abcde" and "bcdef"). In Wind Tunnel, Anagram running on STAND uses n = 5. We then built a training set of posts to train the anomaly detector, and then tested it on a set of 10000 posts to see how it performed. The results are shown in Figure 10.

The graph has the number of posts that the anomaly detector is trained on for the x-axis and the average percentage of new n-grams seen in the test set on the y-axis. Since the anomaly detectors use a threshold on the percentage of new n-grams as its measure of whether or not the request is an anomaly, this tests should accurately predict how the anomaly detector will react to each data set. The graph has exponentially decaying curves with respect to the training size and more new n-grams as the number n increases as expected. After a short amount of training, the dataset shows relatively low anomaly scores during the testing phase showing that content anomaly detectors are flexible enough es-

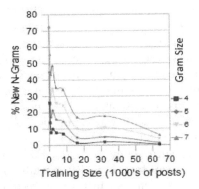

Fig. 10. Anagram training on usenet raw text data directly to test learning of English with a small sample of text

pecially at small sliding window sizes to roughly learn English.

To make sure we model data that is content anomaly detectors have trouble with, we add image upload use cases. Any compressed, random, or encrypted data is difficult for these sensors to model unlike English text. A large portion of the false positives from Anagram and Spectrogram come from such image uploads. Other common false positives we see include short high entropy strings such as session identifiers and to a lesser amount usernames and passwords.

False positive rates and counts in general best serve as a relative metric between sensors on the same dataset. Much more external data is needed in order to evaluate whether a sensor is useable at a certain false positive rate or raw false positive count. The strategy of managing false positives has a large impact on the actual cost incurred. For instance, automated methods of filtering false positives such as a shadow server [16] will have drastically lower costs than relying on a human analyst. Correlation between cooperating organizations can further filter out alerts to only require a human analyst for a small portion as previously demonstrated [14]. Even if a human analyst is required, many false positives or at least types of false positives repeat over time so an initial effort of labeling and creating filtering rules could drastically change the consequential costs. The data generated by Wind Tunnel and tested by sensors can be further filtered by any of these methods in order to provide organizations with a better idea of what costs would be incurred by any set of security controls tested.

4.6   Attack Evasion

In addition to testing the effect of variations in normal data generation, we have evasion mechanisms applied to attack data. The most targeted of these is the padding attack, which aims to bypass content anomaly detectors by appending normal data to attack content in order to reduce the score of the overall request. All the Wordpress datasets had padding attacks launched as one of their attack permutations. The effect is most seen in the two sensors Anagram and Spectrogram, which look at the full stream of user submitted data for each request without breaking it down into attribute value pairs as the other web layer sensors do. The score given to attacks with padding is significantly lower. For example Anagram goes from scoring the attacks at over 90 to scoring them in the mid 40s. Despite this, the AUC of each of these sensors suffers only by a few hundredths at most when looking at only padding attacks compared to attacks without padding. This is due to the large majority of the normal data being scored by both sensors at such low scores that lowering the threshold to still detect padding attacks does not induce too many more false positives.

5   Related Work

There have been a number of efforts to generate quality synthetic data in the past. Arguably the most famous, the 1999 DARPA dataset contained serious flaws [29]. A more recent data set from ISCX [5] attempts to address those flaws by collecting all traffic including attack traffic at once and using more recent multistage application level attacks in addition brute force and denial of service. Our focus differs in that we focus on one attack vector, web application attacks, and try to model user content whereas the ISCX data represents a broad array of attack data at only the network level and focuses on modeling volumetrics and other connection level details. The DETER testbed [30] [31] provides a secure and scalable remote test environment. The goals of the DETER project to push the state of the art of experiments in computer security are similar to ours. DETER focuses on network scaling and containment of dangerous experiments in a remotely accessible testbed. Wind Tunnel is complementary to DETER as we focus on modeling content with multilayer data collection. Wind Tunnel could be deployed in a large scale network environment such as DETER to model larger scale systems such as large cloud environments with realistic content.

Others have addressed aspects of comparing sensors and measuring defense in depth. In related work [32], the authors compare a variety of anomaly detectors against a set of real user data while injecting synthetic attack data. Such effort illustrated the need for better comparison and tests against baseline datasets. We use similar sensors in Wind Tunnel, but expand to additional layers and focus on creating shareable datasets. Others [33] suggest an empirical approach to measuring defense in depth assuming each layer is independent and combining detection rates to infer total security. A more direct measurement approach is suggested for defense in depth in prior work [34] without assuming independence between layers by linking attack data directly. This is the type of approach we utilize here, by linking attack data across layers since we have the ground truth of when attacks begin and end.

6   Future Work

The modularity of Wind Tunnel lends itself to many useful future endeavors. We hope to add more Selenium use cases, attacks, and security controls to grow the usefulness of Wind Tunnel. We plan to leverage this modularity to generate new datasets to model different usage scenarios and test various hypothesis without having to construct such experiments from scratch. In particular we wish to test inline security controls such as various server side taint tracking techniques. To support inline sensors, which will require the same dataset to be generated once for each inline security control as well as once for all the out of band security controls, we plan to add significant determinism to regenerating data sets. In order to make Wind Tunnel more usable, we plan to create a web front-end with a fully automated dataset generation process for any new use cases, web application servers, and attacks are created. The goal would be for anyone with an experiment idea to be able to add any components not currently included and then generate a dataset from that configuration. Over time this could evolve into a repository of interchangeable experiment components saving significant time and opening up more rigorous evaluation of new security controls.

7   Conclusion

We present Wind Tunnel, a framework and working prototype for generating synthetic datasets across multiple layers suitable for testing security controls defending against web application attacks regardless of the layer of data they operate on. We provide the ability to evaluate security controls not against ones of the same type, but also against security controls operating at entirely different layers. In addition, by tracking which individual attacks or attack permutations each security control detects at a certain false positive rate, we are able to compute a total detection rate for any arbitrary set of security controls. Instead of making assumptions of independence about how security control overlap, we can directly measure the overlap. The modularity of Wind Tunnel will allow future research to perform performance evaluation and comparison of new security controls against a wide array of previous research and either generate or reuse synthetic datasets, which can be widely shared. This reduces the effort required to independently setup each security control or undertake the task of generating or acquiring datasets. Our synthetic datasets, source code, and instructions for others to be able to use and expand this syetem are available for all researchers (http://ids.cs.columbia.edu/content/windtunnel).

References

1. Sweeney, L.: k-anonymity: A model for protecting privacy. International Journal of Uncertainty, Fuzziness & Knowledge-Based Systems 10(5), 557 (2002), http://ezproxy.cul.columbia.edu/login?url=http://search.ebscohost.com/login.aspx?direct=true&db=bah&AN=8584293&site=ehost-live&scope=site
2. Dwork, C.: Differential privacy. In: Bugliesi, M., Preneel, B., Sassone, V., Wegener, I. (eds.) ICALP 2006. LNCS, vol. 4052, pp. 1–12. Springer, Heidelberg (2006), http://link.springer.com/chapter/10.1007/11787006_1
3. Selenium, http://seleniumhq.org
4. Rapid 7 Open Source Projects Metasploit framework, http://www.metasploit.com/
5. Shiravi, A., Shiravi, H., Tavallaee, M., Ghorbani, A.A.: Toward developing a systematic approach to generate benchmark datasets for intrusion detection. Computers & Security 31(3), 357–374 (2012), http://dx.doi.org/10.1016/j.cose.2011.12.012
6. Shaoul, C., Westbury, C.: A reduced redundancy usenet corpus (2005–2011), http://www.psych.ualberta.ca/~westburylab/downloads/westburylab.wikicorp.download.html (2013)
7. Shaoul, C., Westbury, C.: The westbury lab wikipedia corpus (2010), http://www.psych.ualberta.ca/~westburylab/downloads/westburylab.wikicorp.download.html
8. Stack exchange data dump, https://archive.org/details/stackexchange
9. Stack exchange data explorer, http://data.stackexchange.com/
10. Skull security wiki rockyou password file, https://wiki.skullsecurity.org/Passwords
11. Wikimedia commons public domain images (2013), http://commons.wikimedia.org/wiki/Category:PD-user
12. OSVDB, Testlink... arbitrary file upload weakness (2012), http://osvdb.org/show/osvdb/85446
13. OSVDB, Foxypress plugin for wordpress.. file upload php code execution (2012), http://osvdb.org/show/osvdb/82652
14. Boggs, N., Hiremagalore, S., Stavrou, A., Stolfo, S.J.: Cross-domain collaborative anomaly detection: So far yet so close. In: Sommer, R., Balzarotti, D., Maier, G. (eds.) RAID 2011. LNCS, vol. 6961, pp. 142–160. Springer, Heidelberg (2011), http://dx.doi.org/10.1007/978-3-642-23644-0_8
15. Song, Y., Keromytis, A.D., Stolfo, S.J.: Spectrogram: A mixture-of-markov-chains model for anomaly detection in web traffic. In: NDSS 2009: Proceedings of the 16th Annual Network and Distributed System Security Symposium (2009)
16. Wang, K., Parekh, J.J., Stolfo, S.J.: Anagram: A Content Anomaly Detector Resistant to Mimicry Attack. In: Symposium on Recent Advances in Intrusion Detection, Hamburg, Germany (2006)
17. Kruegel, C., Vigna, G.: Anomaly Detection of Web-based Attacks. In: ACM Conference on Computer and Communication Security, Washington, D.C (2003)

18. Cretu, G., Stavrou, A., Locasto, M., Stolfo, S., Keromytis, A.: Casting out demons: Sanitizing training data for anomaly sensors. In: IEEE Symposium on Security and Privacy, SP 2008, pp. 81–95 (May 2008)

19. Cretu-Ciocarlie, G.F., Stavrou, A., Locasto, M.E., Stolfo, S.J.: Adaptive Anomaly Detection via Self-Calibration and Dynamic Updating. In: Kirda, E., Jha, S., Balzarotti, D. (eds.) RAID 2009. LNCS, vol. 5758, pp. 41–60. Springer, Heidelberg (2009)

20. Valeur, F., Mutz, D., Vigna, G.: A learning-based approach to the detection of sql attacks. In: Julisch, K., Kruegel, C. (eds.) DIMVA 2005. LNCS, vol. 3548, pp. 123–140. Springer, Heidelberg (2005)

21. Greensql opensource database firewall, http://www.greensql.net/download-dot-net

22. Stolfo, S.J., Apap, F., Eskin, E., Heller, K., Honig, A., Svore, K.: A comparative evaluation of two algorithms for windows registry anomaly detection. Journal of Computer Security, 659–693 (2005)

23. The linux audit daemon, http://linux.die.net/man/8/auditd

24. Eskin, E.: Anomaly detection over noisy data using learned probability distributions. In: Proceedings of the International Conference on Machine Learning, pp. 255–262. Morgan Kaufmann (2000)

25. Mutz, D., Valeur, F., Vigna, G., Kruegel, C.: Anomalous system call detection. ACM Trans. Inf. Syst. Secur. 9(1), 61–93 (2006), http://doi.acm.org/10.1145/1127345.1127348

26. System intrusion analysis & reporting environment(snare) for linux, http://www.intersectalliance.com/projects/snare/.

27. Forrest, S., Hofmeyr, S.A., Somayaji, A., Longstaff, T.A.: A sense of self for unix processes. In: Proceedings of the 1996 IEEE Symposium on Security and Privacy, SP 1996. IEEE Computer Society, Washington, DC (1996), http://dl.acm.org/citation.cfm?id=525080.884258

28. Sequence-based intrusion detection, http://www.cs.unm.edu/~immsec/systemcalls.htm

29. Tavallaee, M., Bagheri, E., Lu, W., Ghorbani, A.A.: A detailed analysis of the kdd cup 99 data set. In: Proceedings of the Second IEEE International Conference on Computational Intelligence for Security and Defense Applications, CISDA 2009, pp. 53–58. IEEE Press, Piscataway (2009), http://dl.acm.org/citation.cfm?id=1736481.1736489

30. The DETER testbed: Overview (August 2004), http://www.isi.edu/deter/docs/testbed.overview.pdf

31. Benzel, T., Braden, R., Kim, D., Neuman, C., Joseph, A.D., Sklower, K.: Experience with deter: A testbed for security research. In: TRIDENTCOM. IEEE (2006)

32. Ingham, K.L., Inoue, H.: Comparing anomaly detection techniques for http. In: Kruegel, C., Lippmann, R., Clark, A. (eds.) RAID 2007. LNCS, vol. 4637, pp. 42–62. Springer, Heidelberg (2007), http://dx.doi.org/10.1007/978-3-540-74320-0_3

33. Cavusoglu, H., Mishra, B., Raghunathan, S.: A model for evaluating it security investments. Commun. ACM 47(7), 87–92 (2004), http://doi.acm.org/10.1145/1005817.1005828

34. Boggs, N.G., Stolfo, S.: Aldr: A new metric for measuring effective layering of defenses. In: Fifth Layered Assurance Workshop (LAW 2011), Orlando, Florida, December 5-6 (2011)

A Comparative Evaluation of Implicit Authentication Schemes

Hassan Khan, Aaron Atwater, and Urs Hengartner

Cheriton School of Computer Science
University of Waterloo
Waterloo, ON, Canada
{h37khan,aatwater,urs.hengartner}@uwaterloo.ca

Abstract. Implicit authentication (IA) schemes use behavioural biometrics to continuously and transparently authenticate mobile device users. Several IA schemes have been proposed by researchers which employ different behavioural features and provide reasonable detection accuracy. While these schemes work in principle, it is difficult to comprehend from these individual efforts which schemes work best (in terms of detection accuracy, detection delay and processing complexity) under different operating conditions (in terms of attack scenarios and availability of training and classification data). Furthermore, it is critical to evaluate these schemes on unbiased, real-world datasets to determine their efficacy in realistic operating conditions. In this paper, we evaluate six diverse IA schemes on four independently collected datasets from over 300 participants. We first evaluate these schemes in terms of: accuracy; training time and delay on real-world datasets; detection delay; processing and memory complexity for feature extraction, training and classification operations; vulnerability to mimicry attacks; and deployment issues on mobile platforms. We also leverage our real-world device usage traces to determine the proportion of time these schemes are able to afford protection to device owners. Based on our evaluations, we identify: 1) promising IA schemes with high detection accuracy, low performance overhead, and near real-time detection delays, 2) common pitfalls in contemporary IA evaluation methodology, and 3) open challenges for IA research. Finally, we provide an open source implementation of the IA schemes evaluated in this work that can be used for performance benchmarking by future IA research.

1 Introduction

Smartphones are strongly tied to their owners' identity and contain personal data. In order to protect this data from unauthorized access, smartphones are equipped with authentication mechanisms including PINs, pass-locks, and facial and fingerprint recognition systems. These authentication mechanisms provide traditional all-or-nothing access control. However, smartphone use is characterized by short and frequent sessions, and PIN entry for every short session is inconvenient for users [18]. Furthermore, the all-or-nothing access approach is

A. Stavrou et al. (Eds.): RAID 2014, LNCS 8688, pp. 255–275, 2014.
© Springer International Publishing Switzerland 2014

unsuitable for smartphones where 40% of frequently accessed apps do not contain personal data [18]. Due to these usability issues, 50% of smartphone owners do not configure a pass-lock on their devices [29]. In addition to usability issues, pass-locks have been subject to shoulder surfing attacks and operating system flaws [40]. The facial and fingerprint recognition systems on modern high-end devices have also been shown to be vulnerable [1,30]. These security and usability limitations of primary authentication mechanisms have prompted researchers to develop behaviour-based methods of recognizing and validating the identity of smartphone users. These behaviour-based authentication methods are known as implicit authentication (IA) schemes, which authenticate a user by using distinctive, measurable patterns of device use that are gathered from the device user without requiring deliberate actions [9]. IA schemes can be used as a secondary line of defense in multiple scenarios. For example, they might be used by enterprise or banking apps to ensure that a user's password has not been compromised. Alternatively, they provide a middle ground for the smartphone owners who do not employ pass-locks on their devices due to usability issues.

To provide IA support on smartphones, a variety of behaviour-based classifiers have been proposed [8,10,11,12,13,15,24,26,34,35,42]. Many of these behavioural classifiers have reasonably high accuracy rates, low performance overhead and reasonable detection delay. While these results appear to stand on their own, it is often difficult to compare different proposals. For example, some IA schemes based on touchscreen input behaviour [11,42] provide exceptional accuracies when they are evaluated on datasets collected by those individual efforts. However, Feng et al. [12] showed that on data collected in an uncontrolled environment, the accuracy of these approaches reduces significantly. Similarly, due to the unavailability of real-world datasets, it is not possible for these individual research efforts to accurately report the training and detection delay in an uncontrolled environment. Finally, a majority of existing IA proposals fall short of providing performance benchmarks (in terms of CPU and memory overhead) on smartphones. Consequently, it is difficult to understand the impact on user experience due to overhead on power-constrained smartphones by these schemes.

In addition to unreported performance numbers (in terms of detection delay and computational cost), many IA schemes use behavioural features, for which it is non-trivial to estimate the frequency or availability of such data. For example, characterizing a device owner's gait may be a useful discriminative tool for authentication, but is not useful if the device owner is stationary most of the time. Therefore, there is a need not only for datasets that allow IA schemes' evaluation in realistic scenarios, but an analysis of real-world behavioural patterns that may influence the appropriateness of deploying one scheme over another.

In this paper, we evaluate and compare six IA schemes using four independently collected datasets from multiple geographic locations, comprising over 300 participants. The objectives of this study are: 1) to quantify and compare the accuracies of these IA schemes on independently collected datasets from uncontrolled environments, 2) to use real-world traces to measure training and detection delays for these IA schemes, 3) to determine the performance overhead of these IA schemes on mobile devices, 4) to determine the frequency of data availability for different behavioural features employed by these IA schemes, 5) to identify key research challenges in IA research, and 6) to release open source implementations of these IA schemes for performance benchmarking.

The IA schemes evaluated in this work use diverse behavioural biometrics including touchscreen input behaviour, keystroke patterns, gait patterns, call and text patterns, browser history, and location patterns. Some also combine touchscreen input behaviour with a device's micro-movements as a reaction to touch input and context information, respectively. Some of these IA schemes employ machine learning while others employ statistical measures for classification purposes. This diversity allows us to better scrutinize different aspects of these individual IA schemes and determine research challenges and best practices.

We evaluate these IA schemes on eight criteria: 1) accuracy, 2) data availability, 3) training delay, 4) detection delay, 5) CPU and memory overhead, 6) uniqueness of behavioural features, 7) vulnerability to mimicry attacks, and 8) deployment issues on mobile platforms. Our results show that while the majority of IA schemes provide reasonable accuracy with low detection delay, IA schemes based on touchscreen input behaviour outperform others by providing near real-time misuse detection with high accuracy. We find that some IA schemes perform well in terms of detection accuracy but frequently do not have enough data available for classification. We recommend choosing complementary sources of features to mitigate this problem and also to aid in preventing mimicry attacks. Finally, we release[1] our open source implementations of the six IA schemes evaluated in this paper.

2   Related Work and Background

In this section, we discuss related work and provide a brief description of the six IA schemes evaluated in this paper.

2.1   Related Work

Various IA schemes have been proposed as secondary authentication mechanisms to complement primary authentication mechanisms (such as PINs and passlocks). These schemes employ a variety of behavioural features including a user's location patterns [38], call/text patterns [35], keystroke patterns [8,13,26], proximity to known devices [21], gait patterns [14,17,27,28], and touchscreen input behaviour [10,11,12,15,24,34,42]. Furthermore, some authors have proposed combining behavioural features and contextual information from multiple sources [4,29,35]. While these research efforts demonstrate that these IA schemes and behavioural features work in principle, we provide a comparative evaluation of these schemes on independently collected datasets across a more comprehensive evaluation criteria than the original papers.

---

[1] https://crysp.uwaterloo.ca/software/ia/

To the best of our knowledge, a comparative evaluation of different IA schemes has not been performed yet. Serwadda et al. [33] perform a benchmark evaluation of three touch-based IA schemes using ten classification algorithms to evaluate which classifiers work best. While their analysis provides interesting insights, we aim to provide a comparative evaluation of IA schemes that employ different behavioural features. Furthermore, except [12] and [34], none of the other authors have provided a comparison with other schemes. We believe this is due to the effort required to implement another scheme and to collect data to perform empirical evaluations. Therefore, in addition to providing a comparative evaluation of IA schemes, by making the implementation and datasets publicly available, we will enable future researchers to quantify the efficacy of their approach with other related schemes. Finally, our findings will also provide better insights to researchers who are designing generic IA frameworks [7,9].

2.2   Implicit Authentication Schemes

For comparative evaluation, our goal is to compare IA schemes that rely on different behavioural features. To this end, we chose an IA scheme based on call/text/URL history and location [35], an IA scheme based on gait patterns [14], an IA scheme based on touch input behaviour [15], an IA scheme based on keystroke behaviour [13], an IA scheme based on touch and micro-movement behaviour [4], and an IA scheme based on touch behaviour and user context [12].

Before describing these IA schemes, we define some terms that are used throughout this paper. A *true accept* (TA) is when an access attempt by a legitimate user is granted; a *false reject* (FR) is when an access attempt by a legitimate user is rejected by the IA scheme. A *true reject* (TR) is when an access attempt by an adversary is rejected; a *false accept* (FA) is when an access attempt by an adversary is granted by the IA scheme. *Equal Error Rate* (EER) is the operating point where the rate of true accepts is equal to the rate of true rejects. In this work, *accuracy* is defined as $\frac{TA+TR}{TA+FA+TR+FR}$. We now provide a brief description of the IA schemes evaluated in this paper; interested readers are referred to the original papers for full descriptions of the respective methods.

Shi et al. IA Scheme (Shi-IA) [35]. Shi et al. [35] propose an IA scheme that uses good and bad events to determine an authentication score for a user. Good/habitual behaviour is determined by a phone call/text to a known number, a visit to a familiar website, and presence at habitual locations around a certain time-of-day. Similarly, bad behaviour is a phone call/text to an unknown number, a visit to an unfamiliar website, and presence at previously unseen locations. Passage of time since the last good event is also treated as a negative event and results in gradual decay of the authentication score. For empirical evaluations, the authors used data gathered from 50 participants, trained on 2 weeks of their usage data and evaluated on the remaining data. Their results indicate that 95% of the time an adversary can be detected using 16 or fewer usages of the devices with negligible false rejects (1 in 165). We choose Shi-IA for empirical evaluations because of the unique feature set it employs for IA.

Gait Pattern for User Identification (Gait-IA) [14]. Various authors have proposed using gait patterns for user identification on smartphones [14,17,27,28]. We chose Frank et al. [14] for empirical evaluations as the authors have made their implementation and dataset publicly available, making it easier to reproduce their results for verification purposes. Furthermore, they report significantly higher accuracy than other gait pattern based schemes. We also note that Frank et al. only propose employing gait patterns for user identification and not for IA; nevertheless, we evaluate whether gait behaviour can be used to effectively implicitly authenticate a user.

Frank et al. propose a time-delay embedding approach to gait recognition. Time-delay embedding is employed to reconstruct the state of an unknown dynamical system from observations of that system taken over time. The authors first extract features using time-delay embeddings and then perform noise-reduction over those features using principal component analysis (PCA) [20] on a short embedding of training data. PCA produces a projection from the time-delay embedding space to a lower dimension model space. These resulting features are then employed in an ANN classifier [2]. Empirical evaluation on walking data from 25 individuals (with the device in the front trouser pocket) resulted in 100% detection accuracy.

Touchalytics [15]. Touchscreen input behaviour has been widely investigated for IA [10,11,15,24,34,42]. For our empirical evaluations, we choose Touchalytics as the authors have made their implementation and dataset publicly available. Touchalytics, is an IA scheme that relies on the finger movement patterns of users on the touchscreen of their smartphone. Touchalytics uses data generated as a result of a user's normal interaction with the touchscreen and does not require him to perform special gestures. It operates by first recording the raw touch data and then extracting 31 features from the raw data. These features capture the user behaviour in terms of the touch location on the screen, the length, direction and duration of a swipe, the velocity and acceleration of a swipe, and the finger pressure and the area covered by a swipe. The extracted features are then used to classify a user using an SVM or kNN classifier. The authors evaluate their approach on a dataset of 41 participants and show that their approach is able to provide an EER of $\leq 3\%$ by using a window size of 13 swipes.

Keystroke Behaviour-Based IA Scheme (Keystroke-IA) [13]. Various classifiers have been proposed that use keystroke behaviour to implicitly authenticate the device owners [8,13,26]. Some keystroke classifiers [8,26] use two features — inter-stroke delay and key holding time (time elapsed between a key press and the corresponding key release event). Furthermore, these classifiers have been tested on multiplexed numeric keypads. In a recent paper [13], the authors employ an additional feature – touch pressure – to provide IA for virtual keypads on modern smartphones. Empirical evaluations on data collected from 40 users and a window size of 15 keystrokes provide an EER of $\leq 10\%$, $\leq 20\%$ and $\leq 5\%$ for J48, Random Forrest and Bayesian classifiers, respectively.

SilentSense [4]. We choose SilentSense as a candidate IA scheme for our evaluations because of the unique feature set that it uses and because of its high detection accuracy ($\sim$ 100%). The authors of SilentSense [4] observe that a combination of the touch input behaviour and the corresponding reaction of a smartphone (micro-movement) can be used to create a more robust model of a user's behaviour. SilentSense operates by combining interacting features from touch behaviour (such as pressure, area, duration, and position) for different touch actions (including fling, scroll, and tap) with the reaction of device features (like acceleration and rotation) to model user behaviour. For the scenarios where the user is walking, the micro-movement patterns are perturbed, since the sensory data generated during walking will skew the sensory data generated due to the reaction of the device to touchscreen interactions. To deal with the walking scenario, the authors extract four features including: (1) vertical displacement of each step; (2) current step frequency; (3) mean horizontal acceleration for each step; and (4) standard deviation of vertical acceleration for each step. They evaluate their approach on a dataset containing data from 10 users and 90 guests. Their evaluations show that by using an SVM classifier, they are able to achieve an EER of $\leq 1\%$ by using a window of three touch strokes.

Context-Aware Touch Behaviour-Based IA Scheme (TIPS) [12]. Feng et al. [12] demonstrate that the EER of a classifier based on touch screen input behaviour reaches up to 40% when it is evaluated on data from multiple applications in an uncontrolled environment. The authors argue that this accuracy degradation is due to variations in usage behaviour. For example, data generated for the same user for different device holding patterns (left hand vs. right hand); for different mobility patterns (stationary vs. walking); and for different applications (maps vs. browser) is different enough to cause accuracy degradation. To mitigate this degradation, the authors propose a multi-stage filtering hierarchy consisting of four levels: (1) foreground application; (2) direction of swipe; (3) swipe length; and (4) swipe curvature. During the one week training period, the prototype of their scheme collected 2000 gestures from 23 smartphone users. After generating the templates by performing multi-stage filtering, the authors were able to achieve an EER of $\leq 10\%$ using a window of eight swipes. Despite the fact that TIPS uses similar features to Touchalytics [15], we choose TIPS for performance evaluation in order to evaluate the impact of intelligent use of contextual information to increase the accuracy of existing IA schemes.

3   Evaluation Datasets

For the empirical evaluation of the IA schemes, we use real-world and unbiased datasets that capture the natural behaviour of the participants. We use two real-world data sets that broadly capture data from devices while users are using them (e.g., location, wireless connections including network, bluetooth and WiFi, contacts, battery status, call logs, text logs, phone orientation, gyroscope and accelerometer readings, and running apps). These datasets are used

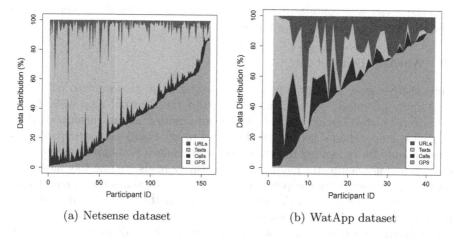

(a) Netsense dataset   (b) WatApp dataset

Fig. 1. Distribution of URL, text, call and GPS records collected from different participants in the Netsense and WatApp datasets, sorted by fraction of GPS data. Percentages are derived from the number of discrete events collected from each participant.

to evaluate Shi-IA and Gait-IA. However, these datasets do not include touch or keystroke data. We therefore use a third real-world dataset that captures swipe data and use it for evaluating Touchalytics, SilentSense and TIPS. Ideally we would gather day-to-day freehand keyboard input from participants. For privacy reasons, however, we cannot use a user's real-world communications for keystroke data. We therefore have users type predefined email and SMS strings to evaluate Keystroke-IA. In this section, we provide data collection goals, experimental design, and the process used for collecting the four evaluation datasets.

3.1 Netsense Dataset [37]

University of Notre Dame researchers created the Netsense dataset by providing 200 first-year Notre Dame students with Android smartphones. These devices were modified to log many events including contacts, texts, voice calls, Wi-Fi scanning results and current access point, Bluetooth scanning results and connections, browser history, running apps, battery status, location, email, and port traffic. While the purpose of their study was to understand social ties, many of these features overlap with the features used by researchers for IA [35].

Data Statistics. We contacted Striegel et al. [37] to request a chunk of their dataset. They provided us with data that they logged between 2012-11-01 09:34:35 and 2012-11-30 12:49:50. This chunk of the dataset contained data belonging to 158 participants. For our study, we extract the location, call history, text history and browser history data. For these users, we extract 125846, 15003, 244627 and 4817 location events, call events, text events and webpage access events, respectively. The data distribution across participants is plotted in Fig. 1(a). We note that this dataset is not labeled (i.e., there is no way to label the data for instances when the device was voluntarily given to someone for use by the owner or when it was deliberately misused by a non-owner).

3.2 WatApp Dataset

While the Netsense dataset is useful for our study, we also want to collect labeled data. Therefore, we instrument WatApp[2] (an Android App widely used by University of Waterloo students to get information about current weather, searchable maps, class schedules, and events) to log events on participants' devices. In addition to logging the same data as Netsense, WatApp logs gyroscope readings and accelerometer readings. The sensitive fields are one-way hashed to preserve the privacy of participants. Furthermore, to establish the ground truth, we ask participants to label the intervals for which they are *absolutely certain* that the device was in their possession.

To advertise for participants, we used our university-wide mailing list to advertise for people who would be interested in a study on "Mobile Misuse Detection". Participants were expected to install WatApp on their smartphones for ten weeks. Participants had the option to opt-out any time they wanted by disabling the data collection mode. Furthermore, if they wanted WatApp to not log data, they were provided with the option to pause data collection for an indefinite amount of time. We paid the participants $5 for each week of participation (up to $50 in total for ten weeks of participation).

Data Statistics. Our application was downloaded and installed by 74 participants and 42 of those participants completed the study. In total, we logged 1371908 events over ten weeks. For 42 users, we extracted 121525, 15962, 28958 and 36178 location events, call events, text events and webpage access events, respectively. Data distribution across participants is plotted in Fig. 1(b).

3.3 Touchscreen Input Dataset

Our goal is to collect a dataset that captures the natural behaviour of the participants when they use the touchscreens of their smartphones. We do not want the participants to perform predefined tasks. We also want to study touchscreen input behaviour across a diverse set of applications. Therefore, to capture data that satisfies our data collection goals, we instrument four Android apps: a browser app[3], a maps/ navigation app[4], a launcher app[5] and a comic viewer app[6]. The apps that we choose belong to diverse categories and help us in understanding user behaviour across different apps. To advertise for participants, we used our university-wide mailing list for people who would be interested in a study on smartphones apps. Participants were expected to install these apps on their

---

[2] http://play.google.com/store/apps/details?id=watapp.main

[3] http://code.google.com/p/zirco-browser/

[4] http://code.google.com/p/osmand/

[5] http://code.google.com/p/android-launcher-plus/

[6] http://code.google.com/p/andcomics/

Table 1. Statistics of touch points dataset

App.	Num. of touchpoints	Num. of Swipes	Sessions	Mean (Median) swipes per session
Launcher	642442	19740	4417	4.46 (2)
Browser	1164011	20139	826	24.3 (16)
Maps	236878	4664	365	12.7 (8)
Comics	445538	8928	272	32.8 (16)
Total	**2488869**	**53471**	**5880**	**9.09**

smartphones for ten weeks. We did not ask the participants to explicitly perform any tasks and participants were to use these apps as per their needs. This allowed us to capture participants' *in the wild* behaviour. We paid the participants $5 for each week of participation (up to $50 in total for ten weeks of participation).

For data collection, every time a participant interacts with the touchscreen on one of the provided applications, we record: 1) time stamp in milliseconds; 2) x and y co-ordinates of the touch point, 3) finger pressure on the screen; 4) area covered by the finger on the screen; 5) values from the accelerometer sensor; 6) finger orientation; 7) screen's orientation; 8) smartphone's orientation sensor's value (roll, pitch and azimuth); and 9) accelerometer sensor values. These values are temporarily stored on the participant's device and then batch transmitted to a server. Before every data transmission, we establish the ground truth (only the participant used the applications) by asking the participants to label the intervals for which they are *absolutely certain* that the device was in their possession.

Data Statistics. Our applications were downloaded and used by 61 participants. In total, we logged about 2.49 million touch points comprising over 53,000 swipes in ten weeks. The details of swipes, their distribution across applications and distribution across user sessions is provided in Table 1.

3.4 Keystroke Dataset

We want to collect keystrokes of participants during their normal usage sessions; however, this is difficult in a privacy preserving manner. Therefore we present users with text strings that are used in everyday communication. To this end, we choose text strings from existing publicly available SMS [6] and email corpora [23]. We develop an Android app that presents a participant with each string of data that they are expected to input using the virtual keypad on their smartphone. Once a user inputs all the strings, the logged keystroke data is transmitted to our server. To advertise for participants, we used our university-wide mailing list for people who would be interested in a study on "The need for Auto-complete and Auto-correct on Smartphones". To avoid any bias, we do not tell participants about the real purpose of this study before the conclusion of the study. Finally, we do not restrict the participants to complete the study in a limited number of sessions nor ask them to complete it in a lab. We paid $10 to each participant for completing this study.

Data Statistics. We presented participants with 13 strings. These strings contained 43 words and 268 characters in total. We required every participant to input each string four times to collect 1072 keystrokes from each participant. Our application was installed and used by 40 participants. The mean time taken to complete the study was eight minutes.

4   Comparative Evaluation

In this section, we first discuss our experimental setup and then provide the results of our evaluations.

4.1   Evaluation Setup

While most of the evaluation metrics that we use are independent of the underlying implementation language, we wish to measure processing complexity on real Android devices. By using Java as our implementation platform, we are able to measure these statistics easily. Therefore, despite the availability of Matlab source code for Touchalytics [15], we re-implement it in Java. We re-use the publicly available C++ implementation of Gait-IA [14] via the Android Native Development Kit. We note that evaluating the Gait-IA scheme as a native app will result in relatively better results for processing overhead metrics. For the evaluation of other metrics, we used automated scripts on a desktop machine

For our evaluations, we use the recommended parameter values of IA schemes from their original papers. If a paper does not specify a recommended value (e.g., the decay parameter for Shi-IA), we first evaluate the proposed scheme while keeping the classifier threshold to a constant value to determine the best operating point of the tuning parameter for which a recommended value is not provided. To evaluate Shi-IA, we use the Netsense and WatApp datasets. For Gait-IA, we use sensor readings from the WatApp dataset. Keystroke-IA uses the Keystroke dataset for training and classification purposes. Finally, the Touchalytics, SilentSense and TIPS schemes all use the Touchscreen Input dataset.

We construct non-overlapping training and test sets for each of the participants, using negative instances from other users. In practice, it is recommended that IA classifiers come prepackaged with such data to be used as negative instances, allowing robust classifiers to be trained on-device. In our work, the negative training sets of a user for the Keystroke and Touch datasets are constructed by employing usage data from 20 other users. For the Netsense and WatApp datasets, we use one day of data from 14 other users to construct two weeks of negative test data. Frank et al. [14] recommend using a continuous block for training their classifier; consequently, we employ the largest single block of continuous data for training. For Touchalytics, Keystroke-IA, and SilentSense, we use half of the data for training, and the remaining data for testing. In the case of TIPS, we use a 30/70 ratio for training and testing, respectively. This variation in partition ratios is due to us following the convention established in the respective original papers, and due to the heterogeneity of the different types of data used by the different schemes in this work.

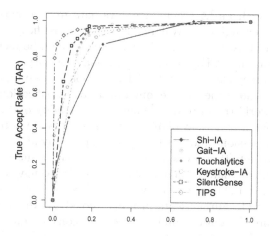

Fig. 2. Accuracy evaluation of the six IA schemes evaluated in this work

4.2 Evaluation Results

Accuracy Evaluation. The accuracy of an IA scheme is its most critical evaluation metric. Ideally, the scheme should have no false rejects (for a seamless user experience of the device owner) and 100% true reject rate (to detect and prevent misuse by an adversary). To understand the accuracy of these classifiers, we plot the ROC curve using the True Accept Rate (TAR) and the False Accept Rate (FAR). To understand the trade-off between TAR and FAR, we threshold the authentication score. Thresholding of Shi-IA is performed over the computed authentication score. Gait-IA and Touchalytics, which use ANN [2] and k-NN for classification, are thresholded over the distance function score and over k, respectively. Keystroke-IA implementation uses a Bayesian Network classifier [16] and is thresholded over the p score. Our implementation of SilentSense uses LIB-SVM [5] with a gaussian radial-basis function (rbf) as kernel. For thresholding, we tune the γ and C parameters to rbf. TIPS uses Dynamic Time Warping [3] to compute a similarity score and we threshold the similarity score. The results of the accuracy evaluation, averaged across all users, for the six classifiers are provided in Fig. 2.

As shown, the TIPS scheme outperforms the others in almost all cases. In particular, it is able to achieve a TAR of 79% with a FAR of only 0.43%. TIPS and SilentSense together Pareto dominate all other schemes when the FAR is under 25%. Shi-IA generally underperforms the other schemes, although it has the distinction of being the only IA scheme to achieve a TAR of 100% with a FAR of less then 100% (specifically, 71%). Empirically, this may be due to the fact that Shi-IA uses location information as a discriminator, while the datasets are mostly taken from students living in tightly grouped geographic areas. Consequently, these results may be different for other types of users (e.g., people who travel often). This phenomenon is discussed further in Section 5.

Data Availability. If an IA scheme employs data from a behavioural source that does not have enough data available to make a classification decision for a significant number of usage sessions, the IA scheme would be ineffective despite its high detection accuracy. For example, while Gait-IA outperforms Keystroke-IA in terms of accuracy (see Fig. 2), Gait-IA will not be useful if the device user is stationary and is not generating enough data for classification purposes. We leverage our real-world traces to determine the availability of data for these IA schemes. To compute the data availability we assume that IA is to be performed only once during a session (and not performed repeatedly after a predefined interval of time). We note that an IA scheme may save past authentication scores and re-use them in case data is unavailable (e.g., Gait-IA may compute authentication score prior to the device usage when accelerometer data is available and then reuse this score to authenticate future sessions). However, for a fair comparison, to compute the data availability we only consider data that has been generated during a device usage session.

From the Netsense and WatApp datasets, we calculate the total number of usage sessions (delimited by screen-on events) and the sessions in which enough behavioural features are available to perform a classification decision for Shi-IA, Gait-IA and Keystroke-IA. For keystroke availability, exact keystroke data is not available and so we assume enough data is available whenever the keyboard is displayed on the screen during the session; note that this will lead to some overreporting of keystroke data availability for insufficient data. Since the Netsense and Watapp datasets do not log touchscreen interactions, for Touchalytics, SilentSense and TIPS, we report data availability against the four apps used in the touchscreen input dataset. This will also result in some overreporting of data availability; however, since touchscreen interaction is the primary input mechanism on modern devices, we expect our results to hold for other apps.

As seen in Fig. 3, data derived from touchscreen interaction is almost always available, so IA schemes making use of it are thus most likely to be usable. SilentSense additionally makes use of accelerometer data; when the device is resting on a stable surface this data will not be as meaningful as when the device is being held, but it is still available for training and classification. Availability of data for Shi-IA is highly dependent upon the users' context and is discussed further in Section 5. Gait information was generally the most difficult to find, with enough information available in only 13.1% of sessions.

Training Delay. An IA scheme that could employ data from a few sessions to robustly train itself would be highly desirable. While the IA scheme may explicitly request a user to provide training data (for example, a keystroke classifier asks a user to input a set of strings), most of the existing schemes rely on collecting data during normal usage for training purposes. We utilize the datasets as described in Section 4.1 to determine the training delay for each of the six schemes evaluated in this work. To measure training delay, we set all the tuning parameters including the classification threshold to a constant value and then train the classifier by incrementally increasing the size of training data to the

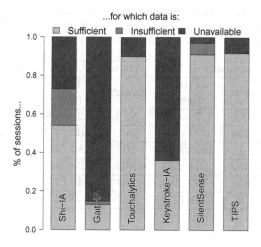

Fig. 3. Data availability on real-world datasets

classifier. For IA schemes that employ classifiers that require negative training instances (e.g., Touchalytics, SilentSense), we use equal amounts of out-of-class training instances from 20 out-of-class sources. For every training session, we measure the accuracy of the classifier by running it on the test dataset. Using this process, we find the minimum number of events and the amount of time required to collect these events to obtain an accuracy of $\geq 70\%$, $\geq 80\%$, and $\geq 90\%$. These results are provided in Table 2.

Training delays are closely correlated with data availability rates. When gait information is available—which is frequently not the case, as discussed previously—Gait-IA takes the least amount of time to accumulate enough information to train a model with high accuracy. Touchalytics and SilentSense take only a few minutes extra, as touch input is a frequent event. Keystroke-IA data takes longer as high accuracy requires the user to type strings that cover a fair amount of the bigram space (as the training data is derived from interstroke timings). The TIPS scheme, despite having the best TAR and FAR overall, requires approximately one hour of data collection to achieve $\geq 90\%$ accuracy. Shi-IA requires several weeks' worth of data, as it relies on user behaviour patterns repeating over large periods of time.

Detection Delay. While the data availability metric determines whether enough data is available across sessions, we evaluate detection delay for these IA schemes to measure the sensitivity of these schemes to misuse attempts. Ideally, we would like the detection delay to be as low as possible to prevent the adversary from accessing confidential data on the device. We measure detection delay in terms of time elapsed from the start of misuse to the time when the IA scheme detects the misuse. For detection delay evaluation, we play back negative instances and look for those that are correctly classified as true rejects by the IA scheme (i.e., we ignore data that results in false accepts).

Table 2. Minimum training delay to achieve accuracy rates of $\geq 70\%$, $\geq 80\%$, $\geq 90\%$. 95% confidence intervals are provided in parentheses. Note that Shi-IA uses the contents of logs as a whole and as such has no concept of an "event".

	Accuracy $\geq 70\%$		Accuracy $\geq 80\%$		Accuracy $\geq 90\%$	
	Events	Time (sec)	Events	Time (sec)	Events	Time (sec)
Shi-IA	N/A	1.7 weeks	N/A	3.2 weeks	N/A	N/A
Gait-IA	1434	159 (32)	1832	205 (47)	2338	287 (59)
Touchalytics	67	106 (9.96)	165	280 (30)	275	464 (49)
Keystroke-IA	1352	594 (55)	2028	839 (108)	3380	1101 (360)
SilentSense	86	139 (14)	204	346 (36)	272	460 (49)
TIPS	738	1391 (224)	1295	2443 (378)	1611	3034 (445)

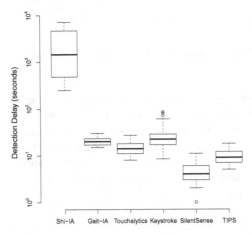

Fig. 4. Detection delay for true rejects (note log scale)

The detection delay results are shown in Fig. 4. SilentSense generally detects non-owners the fastest, in the range of 2-11 seconds. Other schemes generally detect non-owners in less than 30 seconds, with the exception of Shi-IA. Shi-IA takes more than 15 minutes on average before enough data is available for it to reject a non-owner from the device. This result is significantly longer than the average session length, and a malicious user would likely be able to export data from the device before even realizing that an IA scheme is in use.

Processing Complexity. Since the target for these IA schemes is mobile platforms, it is critical for the IA schemes to have low processing complexity. For complexity evaluations, we measure the performance overhead in terms of elapsed CPU time and heap size of the IA scheme for feature collection, training and classification operations. We divide the performance overhead into these operations to distinguish the one-time (training) and run-time (feature collection and

Table 3. Performance evaluation of the IA schemes evaluated in this work. 95% confidence intervals are provided in parentheses. N1: Nexus 1 and N4: Nexus 4.

		CPU (ms)				Heap(kB)
		Init.	Feat. Extraction	Training	Classification	Runtime
N1	Keystroke-IA	21 (2.08)	<1 ($\simeq$0)	<1 ($\simeq$0)	0.2 ($\simeq$0)	3.2 (0.19)
	Touchalytics	5 (0.27)	0.27 ($\simeq$0)	65 (2.16)	1.7 ($\simeq$0)	59.1 (1.43)
	SilentSense	1162 (81)	0.75 ($\simeq$0)	10384 (91)	0.12 ($\simeq$0)	18.3 (1.14)
	Shi-IA	677 (26)	1758 (31)	13053 (87)	58 (4)	790 (6)
	Gait-IA	5 (0.15)	7 (0.24)	764 (42)	93 (7)	9532 (81)
	TIPS	5 (0.18)	0.23 ($\simeq$0)	35 ($\simeq$1.4)	1.12 ($\simeq$0)	92 (2.2)
N4	Keystroke-IA	12 (0.95)	<1 ($\simeq$0)	<1 ($\simeq$0)	0.05 ($\simeq$0)	2.9 (0.13)
	Touchalytics	3 (0.27)	0.05 ($\simeq$0)	15 (0.5)	1.08 ($\simeq$0)	67 (5.59)
	SilentSense	972 (67)	0.55 ($\simeq$0)	5937 (329)	0.07 ($\simeq$0)	21 (0.68)
	Shi-IA	575 (24)	1406 (22)	10964 (74)	51 (3)	817 (5)
	Gait-IA	4 (0.1)	5 (0.13)	522 (31)	75 (6.8)	9775 (94)
	TIPS	3 (0.18)	0.03 ($\simeq$0)	8.2 ($\simeq$0.86)	0.73 ($\simeq$0)	96.4 (2.5)

classification) costs. An efficient IA scheme would have a reasonable one-time cost and minimal run-time cost.

For execution time calculation, we choose an HTC Nexus 1 and an LG Nexus 4. The Nexus 1 has Android OS v2.1 on a 1GHz processor with 512MB of RAM. The Nexus 4 has Android OS v4.2 on a Quad-core 1.5GHz processor with 2GB of RAM. Execution time results for both devices are provided in Table 3.

The Nexus 4 generally performs operations faster than the Nexus 1, but with marginally higher memory overhead. In our experience, these small differences are generally due to changes in the Android API. SilentSense initialization and training take several seconds due to the SVM classifier used; it also loads negative instances from disk at initializaton. Shi-IA takes 1-2 seconds to extract features from data as it must make a GPS request and also filter call, SMS, and browser logs. All schemes are able to perform classification in tens of milliseconds in the worst case.

Uniqueness of Behavioural Features. Jain et al. [19] list distinctiveness as one of the key properties of a biometric-based authentication system, which requires any two persons to be sufficiently different in terms of the characteristics measured. While the presence of false accepts in Fig. 2 indicates that none of the behavioural features employed in the IA schemes evaluated in this work are distinct, nevertheless they should provide sufficient discriminatory information among a *sufficiently* large set of users to provide an acceptable FAR. To gain insight into this, we simulate N non-owners attempting to access a protected device, and measure the rate at which someone is able to successfully bypass IA. By varying the number N, we gain some sense of the device owner's uniqueness

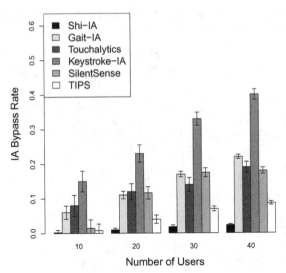

Fig. 5. Relationship between IA bypass rate and number of users

in a crowd of that size. For each value of N, this simulation is run using 4-fold cross-validation for each user and the results are averaged.

Fig. 5 shows the results from this simulation. All of the IA schemes tested appear to exhibit similar growth patterns in IA bypass rate as the number of users increases. While TIPS and Shi-IA exhibit the most uniqueness overall, SilentSense is also quite resilient when faced with 10 or fewer adversaries. Keystroke-IA does not appear to be distinctive even in scenarios with few nonowners present, suggesting that it would be wise to pair these features with other, non-keystroke-derived attributes when creating IA schemes.

Vulnerability to Mimicry Attacks. While a detailed analysis of vulnerability to mimicry attacks is beyond the scope of this paper, in this section we consider the informed adversary threat scenario. An uninformed adversary may be a curious stranger/thief who found/stole a device, while an informed adversary might be an inquisitive friend, co-worker, or family member. The difference between these two types of adversary is that the latter may have additional knowledge about the behaviour of the victim (for example, he may know that the victim always uses his right hand for swiping). Based on the informed adversary scenario, we consider how effortlessly such an adversary can defeat an IA scheme. Interested readers are referred to [31,32] on advanced automated mimicry attack scenarios for touch- and keystroke-based IA schemes.

We argue that in accordance with Kerckhoffs's principle, the IA mechanism (including its features and computation of anomaly score) is public knowledge but feature values for individual users are secret. Consequently, if an adversary can estimate the feature values for an IA scheme easily and mimic those feature values, he can steal data from the device. From the approaches that we evaluate,

Shi-IA is the most vulnerable to mimicry attacks. Even an uninformed adversary can scan the device for call/text logs and browser history and then mimic it to ensure that the device does not lock him out. An informed adversary would attempt to stay in the same vicinity as the device owner to get an even better authentication score.

Other IA schemes evaluated in this work are more difficult to mimic. Some of the schemes rely on features that may be estimated by an informed adversary. For example, in Touchalytics, an adversary may be able to approximate the start and end co-ordinates for swipes. Similarly, for SilentSense, the adversary may be able to coarsely estimate the amount of action force by looking at the reaction of the device. While the aforementioned features for their respective IA schemes are relatively easy to estimate by an informed adversary, most of the features used by these schemes are hidden (not measurable by a naked eye). For example, the touch width of a swipe is hidden to a surveilling adversary. Similarly, the key release time for keystroke classifier are difficult to approximate without special equipment.

A more serious attack surface for these IA schemes exists in that many of the features employed by these schemes can be collected by any app without requiring any special Android permissions (except Shi-IA, which requires the permissions mentioned in § 4.2). Consequently, an adversary might persuade the victim to install a Trojan app on his device in order to log his behaviour. The adversary can then train himself to mimic the victim. Tey et al. [39] mounted this attack on a keystroke-based authentication scheme for traditional keyboards. They demonstrated that by using a carefully designed user interface, they were able to train participants of their study to achieve an average FAR of 63%. It is possible that similar active attacks could be mounted on touch-, keystroke- and gait-based IA schemes, which is an area that needs further study.

Ease of Deployment on Mobile Platform. Finally, we look at the deployment related issues for these IA schemes on the popular iOS and Android platforms. We understand that sufficient changes might be introduced by the OS providers in future versions to mitigate the deployment limitations of these IA schemes; nevertheless, we provide an overview of the deployment issues on contemporary mobile platforms.

The features used by Gait-IA can be collected without requiring any permissions. Features employed by Shi-IA can be collected using non-root permissions. More specifically, on Android five permissions including ACCESS_FINE_LOCATION, READ_SMS, READ_CALL_LOG, READ_HISTORY_BOOKMARKS and READ_CONTACTS can be used to implement Shi-IA. Feature extraction for touch- and keystroke-based classifiers is more complicated. Due to security and privacy concerns, iOS and Android only allows a foreground app to receive input events (touch and keystroke events). Therefore, IA schemes that employ these features including [4,12,13,15] can only be deployed either on rooted devices or deployed per app instance [22].

5   Discussion and Open Challenges

This section discusses guidelines for creating implicit authentication schemes that we derive from the data collection process, the results in Section 4, and our experience in implementing the schemes on Android devices.

Practical Implicit Authentication Is Possible with Low Overhead and in Near-real-time. Our results on Nexus 1 and Nexus 4 devices given in Table 3 show there are IA schemes that can run feature extraction and classification in only milliseconds. Even the worst case training scenarios take only ten seconds, which is performed one-time only and can be done in a background thread. In terms of accuracy, touch behaviour-based approaches provide $\geq 90\%$ true accepts with $\leq 10\%$ false accepts and are a good candidate for secondary authentication. Finally, in case of misuse by non-owner, the majority of these implicit authentication schemes are able to detect misuse in under 30 seconds.

Features Should be Chosen in a Complementary and Context-aware Manner. Sources for behavioural features must be chosen carefully, and take the intended deployment context into account. Touch-based data is almost always available (Fig. 3) but should be augmented with a secondary source (such as keystrokes) for better coverage. Taking into account user context information – e.g. whether the user is walking or stationary, which app the user is interacting with – is important for classifying data from onboard sensors (TIPS), but does not necessarily make a good discriminator by itself (Shi-IA). No individual source of behavioural data provides a silver bullet for IA.

Devices May Not Need to Be Rooted to Make Use of IA. Android does not allow background applications to gather input events (touch and key input events) due to security concerns. Therefore, IA schemes that rely on input events (e.g. touch- and keystroke-based schemes) require root privileges on the device in order to collect data. On the other hand, Shi-IA and Gait-IA do not require root privileges and only require Android permissions. Input event data can be collected by individual apps without any additional permissions, which opens the door for IA protection at the app level instead of at the device level [22]. For example, enterprises can bundle IA schemes within their apps to protect confidentiality of their corporate data. While providing IA at the app level mitigates the restrictions imposed by Android, it also imposes significant development overhead. All of these are open questions that should be considered when proposing any new IA scheme.

Using a Realistic Threat Model and Evaluating in an Uncontrolled Environment Is Necessary When Evaluating an IA Scheme. Some IA proposals are accompanied by unrealistic evaluations, by having users perform a repeated task in a lab setting to generate data. When these schemes are then applied in real-world settings, the assumptions made in the lab may prove false and the scheme's performance will suffer accordingly. Feng et al. [12] demonstrate that on real-world datasets, many existing touch-based IA schemes have significantly higher EER than reported in the original papers. Our findings are similar for the IA schemes that had their datasets publicly available [14,15].

Furthermore, a recent Symantec study finds that 68% of non-owners who attempted to access private data on an unguarded smartphone did so on the spot, which would make location filtering an unhelpful IA feature [41]. A similar study by Lookout-Sprint [25] found that 44% of users were primarily concerned with their devices being accessed by family and friends, as opposed to strangers. Since such adversaries may have multiple overlapping features (e.g., location and contacts), IA schemes that rely in such features will not be very effective. Therefore, it is critical to provide protection against a realistic threat model that captures these security and privacy concerns of smartphone users.

Mimicry Attacks On IA Schemes Are Possible. In addition to the natural collisions of behaviour we showed in Fig. 5, some researchers have shown deliberately trained attacks on swipes and keystroke input [31,32]. We argue that implicit authentication (i) should be used as a secondary authentication mechanism complementing primary authentication mechanisms, and (ii) should use behavioural features from multiple sources. Using multiple types of characteristics greatly increases the difficulty of building devices that mimic natural human behaviour, and adds dimensions to the complexity of training users to fool behavioural models [36].

6   Conclusion

In this paper we provided a comparative evaluation of six IA schemes that employ different behavioural features. Our empirical evaluations show that IA can be performed with reasonable accuracy and low complexity with acceptable detection delay on contemporary mobile devices. More specifically, our evaluations show that in addition to adequate data availability for training and classification, touch behaviour-based IA schemes outperform other schemes in terms of accuracy and detection delay. We also analyzed real-world traces to show that while keystroke- and gait-based IA schemes provide reasonable performance, there was not enough data available for a significant proportion of sessions to make a classification decision. In terms of evaluation of IA schemes by the research community, our findings emphasize the need for evaluation on uncontrolled datasets and a more realistic threat model. We have made our implementations publicly available to further research in the IA domain.

Acknowledgements. We thank Tao Wang, Sarah Harvey, the anonymous reviewers and our shepherd, Alina Oprea, for their helpful comments. We thank Aaron Striegel, Mario Frank, Jordan Frank and Shu Liu for providing sourcecode of classifiers and datasets. We also thank Google and NSERC for their support.

References

1. Android Authority: Android face unlock hacked (March 2014),
   http://androidauthority.com/android-jelly-bean-face-unlock-
   blink-hacking-105556/

2. Arya, S., Mount, D.M., Netanyahu, N.S., Silverman, R., Wu, A.Y.: An optimal algorithm for approximate nearest neighbor searching fixed dimensions. Journal of the ACM (JACM) 45(6) (1998)
3. Berndt, D.J., Clifford, J.: Using dynamic time warping to find patterns in time series. In: KDD Workshop, vol. 10 (1994)
4. Bo, C., Zhang, L., Li, X.Y., Huang, Q., Wang, Y.: Silentsense: silent user identification via touch and movement behavioral biometrics. In: MobiCom. ACM (2013)
5. Chang, C.C., Lin, C.J.: Libsvm: A library for support vector machines. ACM TIST 2(3) (2011)
6. Chen, T., Kan, M.-Y.: Creating a live, public short message service corpus: The nus sms corpus. Language Resources and Evaluation 47(2), 299–335 (2013)
7. Clarke, N., Karatzouni, S., Furnell, S.: Flexible and transparent user authentication for mobile devices. In: Gritzalis, D., Lopez, J. (eds.) SEC 2009. IFIP AICT, vol. 297, pp. 1–12. Springer, Heidelberg (2009)
8. Clarke, N.L., Furnell, S.: Authenticating mobile phone users using keystroke analysis. International Journal of Information Security 6(1) (2007)
9. Crawford, H., Renaud, K., Storer, T.: A framework for continuous, transparent mobile device authentication. Elsevier Computers & Security 39 (2013)
10. De Luca, A., Hang, A., Brudy, F., Lindner, C., Hussmann, H.: Touch me once and i know it's you!: implicit authentication based on touch screen patterns. In: CHI. ACM (2012)
11. Feng, T., Liu, Z., Kwon, K.A., Shi, W., Carbunar, B., Jiang, Y., Nguyen, N.: Continuous mobile authentication using touchscreen gestures. In: HST. IEEE (2012)
12. Feng, T., Yang, J., Yan, Z., Tapia, E.M., Shi, W.: Tips: Context-aware implicit user identification using touch screen in uncontrolled environments. In: HotMobile. ACM (2014)
13. Feng, T., Zhao, X., Carbunar, B., Shi, W.: Continuous mobile authentication using virtual key typing biometrics. In: TrustCom. IEEE (2013)
14. Frank, J., Mannor, S., Precup, D.: Activity and gait recognition with time-delay embeddings. In: AAAI (2010)
15. Frank, M., Biedert, R., Ma, E., Martinovic, I., Song, D.: Touchalytics: On the applicability of touchscreen input as a behavioral biometric for continuous authentication. IEEE TIFS 8(1) (2013)
16. Friedman, N., Geiger, D., Goldszmidt, M.: Bayesian network classifiers. Machine Learning 29(2-3) (1997)
17. Gafurov, D., Helkala, K., Søndrol, T.: Biometric gait authentication using accelerometer sensor. Journal of Computers 1(7) (2006)
18. Hayashi, E., Riva, O., Strauss, K., Brush, A., Schechter, S.: Goldilocks and the two mobile devices: Going beyond all-or-nothing access to a device's applications. In: SOUPS. ACM (2012)
19. Jain, A.K., Ross, A., Prabhakar, S.: An introduction to biometric recognition. IEEE Transactions on Circuits and Systems for Video Technology 14(1) (2004)
20. Jolliffe, I.: Principal component analysis. Wiley Online Library (2005)
21. Kalamandeen, A., Scannell, A., de Lara, E., Sheth, A., LaMarca, A.: Ensemble: Cooperative proximity-based authentication. In: MobiSys. ACM (2010)
22. Khan, H., Hengartner, U.: Towards application-centric implicit authentication on smartphones. In: HotMobile. ACM (2014)
23. Klimt, B., Yang, Y.: Introducing the enron corpus. In: CEAS (2004)
24. Li, L., Zhao, X., Xue, G.: Unobservable reauthentication for smart phones. In: NDSS (2013)

25. Lookout Blog: Sprint-lookout mobile behavior survey (March 2014), `http://blog.lookout.com/blog/2013/10/21`

26. Maiorana, E., Campisi, P., González-Carballo, N., Neri, A.: Keystroke dynamics authentication for mobile phones. In: SAC. ACM (2011)

27. Mantyjarvi, J., Lindholm, M., Vildjiounaite, E., Makela, S.M., Ailisto, H.: Identifying users of portable devices from gait pattern with accelerometers. In: ICASSP 2005. IEEE (2005)

28. Muaaz, M., Mayrhofer, R.: An analysis of different approaches to gait recognition using cell phone based accelerometers. In: MoMM. ACM (2013)

29. Riva, O., Qin, C., Strauss, K., Lymberopoulos, D.: Progressive authentication: deciding when to authenticate on mobile phones. In: USENIX Security (2012)

30. Schneier on Security: Apple iphone fingerprint reader hacked (March 2014), `http://schneier.com/blog/archives/2013/09/apples_iphone_f.html`

31. Serwadda, A., Phoha, V.V.: Examining a large keystroke biometrics dataset for statistical-attack openings. ACM TISSEC 16(2) (2013)

32. Serwadda, A., Phoha, V.V.: When kids' toys breach mobile phone security. In: CCS. ACM (2013)

33. Serwadda, A., Phoha, V.V., Wang, Z.: Which verifiers work?: A benchmark evaluation of touch-based authentication algorithms. In: BTAS. IEEE (2013)

34. Shahzad, M., Liu, A.X., Samuel, A.: Secure unlocking of mobile touch screen devices by simple gestures: you can see it but you can not do it. In: MobiCom. ACM (2013)

35. Shi, E., Niu, Y., Jakobsson, M., Chow, R.: Implicit authentication through learning user behavior. In: Burmester, M., Tsudik, G., Magliveras, S., Ilić, I. (eds.) ISC 2010. LNCS, vol. 6531, pp. 99–113. Springer, Heidelberg (2011)

36. Shrestha, B., Saxena, N., Truong, H.T.T., Asokan, N.: Drone to the rescue: Relay-resilient authentication using ambient multi-sensing. In: Financial Cryptography and Data Security (2014)

37. Striegel, A., Liu, S., Meng, L., Poellabauer, C., Hachen, D., Lizardo, O.: Lessons learned from the netsense smartphone study. In: HotPlanet. ACM (2013)

38. Studer, A., Perrig, A.: Mobile user location-specific encryption (mule): Using your office as your password. In: Wi'Sec. ACM (2010)

39. Tey, C.M., Gupta, P., Gao, D.: I can be you: Questioning the use of keystroke dynamics as biometrics. In: NDSS (2013)

40. Threatpost: Samsung android lockscreen bypass (March 2014), `http://threatpost.com/lock-screen-bypass-flaw-found-samsung-androids-030413/77580`

41. Wright, S.: Symantec honey stick project. Symantec Corporation (March 2012)

42. Zhao, X., Feng, T., Shi, W.: Continuous mobile authentication using a novel graphic touch gesture feature. In: BTAS. IEEE (2013)

Protecting Web-Based Single Sign-on Protocols against Relying Party Impersonation Attacks through a Dedicated Bi-directional Authenticated Secure Channel

Yinzhi Cao[1], Yan Shoshitaishvili[2], Kevin Borgolte[2],
Christopher Kruegel[2], Giovanni Vigna[2], and Yan Chen[1]

[1] Northwestern University
{yinzhi.cao@eecs,ychen@cs}.northwestern.edu
[2] University of California, Santa Barbara
{yans,kevinbo,chris,vigna}@cs.ucsb.edu

Abstract. Web-based single sign-on describes a class of protocols where a user signs into a web site with the authentication provided as a service by a third party. In exchange for the increased complexity of the authentication procedure, SSO makes it convenient for users to authenticate themselves to many different web sites (*relying parties*), using just a single account at an *identity provider* such as Facebook or Google.

Single sign-on (SSO) protocols, however, are not immune to vulnerabilities. Recent research introduced several attacks against existing SSO protocols, and further work showed that these problems are prevalent: 6.5% of the investigated relying parties were vulnerable to impersonation attacks, which can lead to account compromises and privacy breaches. Prior work used formal verification methods to identify vulnerabilities in SSO protocols or leveraged invariances of SSO interaction traces to identify logic flaws. No prior work, however, systematically studied the actual root cause of impersonation attacks against the relying party.

In this paper, we systematically examine existing SSO protocols and determine the root cause of the aforementioned vulnerabilities: the design of the communication channel between the relying party and the identity provider, which, depending on the protocol and implementation, suffers from being a one-way communication protocol, or from a lack of authentication. We (a) systematically study the weakness responsible for the vulnerabilities in existing protocols that allow impersonation attacks against the relying party, (b) introduce a dedicated, authenticated, bi-directional, secure channel that does not suffer from those shortcomings, (c) formally verify the authentication property of this channel using a well-known cryptographic protocol verifier (ProVerif), and (d) evaluate the practicality of a prototype implementation of our protocol.

Ultimately, to support a smooth and painless transition from existing SSO protocols, we introduce a proxy setup in which our channel can be used to secure existing SSO protocols from impersonation attacks. Furthermore, to demonstrate the flexibility of our approach, we design two different SSO protocols: an OAuth-like and an OpenID-like protocol.

A. Stavrou et al. (Eds.): RAID 2014, LNCS 8688, pp. 276–298, 2014.
© Springer International Publishing Switzerland 2014

1   Introduction

The proliferation of web applications on the Internet has led to a sharp increase in the number of accounts (and corresponding credentials) that a web user has to create and remember. Inconveniences stemming from having to keep track of the accounts, and the tendency of web sites to suffer from security breaches, in which user credentials are exposed, has resulted in a recent push to adopt *single sign-on* (SSO) systems more widely[1]. As the name implies, these systems help reduce the large amount of account credentials a web user has to keep track of, by replacing these credentials with a single identity with which she can authenticate herself at many different web sites.

SSO systems allow users to sign into a web site (the *Relying Party*, or RP), such as StackOverflow, with authentication provided by a third party (the *Identity Provider*, or IdP), like Facebook or Google. While this greatly increases the convenience for both the users and the web site operators, it also brings new opportunities for attackers. A recent analysis of web-based SSO protocols by Wang et al. [33] identified five vulnerabilities in which a malicious attacker can impersonate a benign RP or intercept the communication between a benign RP and the IdP, leading to a compromise of the user's account's security. In fact, further research by Sun et al. [28] shows that 6.5% of RPs[2] are vulnerable to such impersonation attacks.

To understand SSO vulnerabilities better, formal security analysis has been carried out for existing SSO protocols. For example, AuthScan by Bai et al. [13] extracts the protocol specification from a SSO implementation and verifies the retrieved specification using formal analysis. On the other hand, ExplicatingSDK by Wang et al. [34] leverages formal analysis combined with a semantic model to identify hidden assumptions in the designs of the software development kits that are the foundation of many SSO implementations. Similarly, InteGuard by Xing et al. [35] correlates program invariants, to identify and mitigate logic flaws in SSO specifications, through a proxy situated between the user and the IdP. However, none of these prior approaches identified the actual root cause for vulnerabilities in SSO protocols that allow impersonation attacks, i.e., why these flaws exist in the current protocols in the first place. In this paper, we examined the design of existing SSO protocols and determined that the root cause of the aforementioned vulnerabilities lies in the broken design of the communication channel between the RP and the IdP. Depending on the protocol implementation, this channel either suffers from being a one-way communication protocol, or from a lack of authentication. This untrustworthy channel, in turn, makes existing protocols prone to impersonation attacks. Therefore, we propose to use a secure, authenticated, bi-directional channel between the RP and the IdP to prevent these attacks, by eliminating the root cause.

It is important to realize that the attacks discussed in this paper are not just theoretical. In fact, the vulnerabilities present in these protocols are currently

---

[1] Clearly, using the same credentials on multiple web sites is not viable solution if data might leaked or a privacy breach might occur.

[2] The original text states "we also found that 13% of RPs use a proxy service from Gigya, and half of them are vulnerable to an impersonation attack."

being used by attackers to subvert authentication via SSO. Real-world, high-profile attacks have been carried out in the past on extremely popular web sites. One such example is last year's attack on the SSO communication between the web site of the New York Times (the 38th most popular web site in the US; henceforth NYTimes), acting as the RP, and Facebook, acting as the IdP [33]. In this case, attackers exploited weaknesses in the design of current web-based SSO protocols that allowed them to access a victim's account with the same privileges that the victim had given to the NYTimes, including access to private user data and, in some cases, the ability to post messages on the user's behalf. Similar attacks have also been carried out against the communication between Facebook and Zoho.com, the JanRain wrapping layer over Google's SSO implementation, and other web sites that rely on SSO protocols [33].

This makes the solutions presented in this paper not just *theoretically interesting*, but actually *practically relevant* in solving a pressing problem in the area of user authentication, privacy, and web security.

Additionally, to support a smooth transition from existing systems, i.e., to give time for our design to be adopted, we introduce a *proxy* that can be deployed by web sites' operators (RPs in the current model) to secure existing, insecure SSO protocols. We are confident that our proxy design will ease the adoption of our secure SSO protocol and mitigate current vulnerabilities.

In this paper, we make the following technical contributions:

- *Dedicated, Bi-directional, Authenticated, Secure Channel.* Utilizing an existing in-browser communication channel, we establish a dedicated, bi-directional, authenticated, secure channel between the RP and the IdP. Leveraging public-key cryptography, an RP and an IdP authenticate each other and share a common secret, i.e., the session key. All further communication between the RP and the IdP is then encrypted with the session key and is kept secret from eavesdroppers.

- *Flexible SSO Protocol over the Secure Channel.* The aforementioned secure channel provides flexibility for SSO protocol designers. Specifically, our channel design provides a secure platform for customization by protocol architects. We discuss possible implementations of the most popular SSO protocol designs: an OAuth-like and an OpenID-like protocol, both build upon our channel design. In contrast, existing, verified protocols, such as the Secure Electronic Transaction (SET) [8] protocol, do not allow any further customization and require customers and users to strictly follow the protocol specification at hand.

- *Formal Verification of the Channel.* We formally verify the correctness and the security properties of our channel design with the cryptographic protocol verifier ProVerif by Blanchet [6] to ensure that the security guarantees hold in our respective threat model.

- *Performance Evaluation.* We evaluate a prototype implementation of our secure channel design. In our evaluation (Section 6), we show that the overhead our approach introduces is only about 650ms of initial latency (given a network delay of 50ms to reflect the latency observed at standard, residential Internet connections), i.e., a one-time authentication overhead of 650ms incurred at the beginning of each authentication session, which we believe is acceptable for the security guarantees it provides. In addition, we provide a detailed breakdown of the latency of each step of our SSO protocol implementation.

- *Gradual Deployment.* Apart from our clean-slate design, which must be deployed by the IdP, we introduce a proxy that acts as a "fourth-party" IdP. This proxy accommodates and protects existing SSO protocols and, thus, allows for a smooth and painless transition from existing SSO protocols to our more secure one. Aiming for broad adoption and a general solution, we designed our proxy so that it can be deployed by a legacy RP or a legacy IdP. From the viewpoint of a legacy IdP, our proxy acts as an RP retrieving users' information in a controlled, secure environment; from the viewpoint of the legacy RP, it acts an IdP relaying the users' information it retrieved from the real IdP. To guarantee the various security properties that must hold to ensure protection against impersonation attacks with respect to the threat model, we formally verify the design of our proxy with ProVerif.

2   Threat Model

In this section, we introduce several key concepts relating to web-based SSO protocols and present several known attacks against current protocols and their implementations. For completeness, and to provide a better understanding of the threat model, we discuss attacks that are in the scope of this paper, as well as attacks that are out of scope.

2.1   Concepts

Generally, three entities are involved in an instance of a SSO protocol. The three participating parties are:

- *Identity Provider (IdP).* The identity provider serves as a centralized identification service for its users. Some examples of such identity parties are OpenID [5], Facebook Connect [19], and Google's single sign-on implementation. Additionally, there also exist aggregation services, such as JanRain Engage [2], which handle SSO services for a set of multiple IdPs. Special to the latter case, both JanRain Engage and the original IdP act as IdPs.
- *Relying Party (RP).* The relying party is a web site that uses the services an IdP provides to authenticate its users. The way users are authenticated differs between protocols: for an OpenID-like service, the RP acquires the user's identity with the IdP's signature; alternatively, for an OAuth-like service, the RP acquires a token or key from the user (who interacts with the IdP), which can then be used to fetch additional information from the IdP (e.g., to verify personal information or the identity of the user).
- *User.* The user is a client of both the IdP and the RP. The user maintains a SSO identity on the IdP's web site (e.g., an account with the IdP) and uses this identity to authenticate to different RPs. It is important to note that in our threat model, users are benign; in other words, we do not consider attacks initiated from the user's browser, and we require that the same-origin policy is enforced in the user's web browser.

Listing 1.1. Example of a HTTP request from the RP to the IdP. Here, a malicious RP can initiate the communication by using a benign RP's app_id or intercept the communication by changing the redirection_url or next_url parameter.

```
GET https://www.idp.com/login?app_id=****
    &redirection_url=https://www.idp.com/granter?
    next_url=https://www.rp.com/login
Host: www.idp.com
Referer: https://www.rp.com/login
Cookie: ****
```

2.2 In-scope Attacks

Recent research by Wang et al. [33] identified many vulnerabilities allowing *identity impersonation attacks* in SSO protocols, i.e., attacks where an adversary manages to spoof the identity of parties involved in the execution of the SSO protocol. In our threat model, we only consider the case where an attacker is able to impersonate the RP in an attempt to obtain a user's private information. In fact, these attacks account for five of the eight confirmed attacks on SSO protocols identified by Wang et al. [33] and are the most critical. The remaining three cases are out-of-scope, and we discuss the reason for this decision in more detail later on (Section 2.3). The five attacks that are in-scope can be classified into two categories:

- *A malicious RP initiates the attack.* In this case, as in the vulnerability between the New York Times (NYTimes) and Facebook, a malicious web site pretends to be the NYTimes and initiates the SSO process, i.e., an attacker simply sends a request using the application ID of the NYTimes (app_id in Listing 1.1) to spoof the identity of the NYTimes.
- *A benign RP initiates the request, but a malicious RP receives the response.* Here, as in a vulnerability found in the interaction between Zoho.com and Facebook, Zoho.com initiates the communication to Facebook, but a malicious party receives the response from Facebook, i.e., an attacker can change the `redirection_url` or the `next_url` in Listing 1.1 to receive the response that contains the token to access the user's information.

2.3 Out-of-scope Attacks

Since SSO protocols are a very broad topic, some categories of attacks are out-of-scope for this paper. Here, we list the attacks that we deem out-of-scope, and we argue why we decided to not take them into account. Generally, many of the attacks listed can already be mitigated leveraging prior work and we list them simply for completeness.

- *Social engineering, e.g. phishing.* We consider social-engineering attacks, such as the phishing of a user's credentials, to be out-of-scope because, in our opinion, the prevention of social-engineering attacks is more of an educational or user-interface issue than it is a protocol issue.
- *Compromised or vulnerable RP.* Bhargavan et al. [15] consider that an RP might be compromised and propose defensive JavaScript techniques to prevent untrusted browser origins. On the contrary, in our threat model, we assume that a benign RP remains integral and uncompromised. The communication

channel between the benign RP and the IdP on the other hand is vulnerable as to that a malicious RP can control the channel fully. We exclude vulnerabilities related to such a compromised or vulnerable RP from our threat model because the user's information can already be obtained at the RP, and because we argue it is more of a secure deployment rather than protocol issue.

- *Malicious browser.* Some of the discovered attacks occur inside of the attacker's browser. For example, in an attack involving Google ID [33], the adversary is able to log into a user's account from his own machine because the RP does not check whether the email field is signed by the IdP. Those attacks cannot be prevented on a protocol level, and, therefore, they are out of scope.
- *Implementation issues.* Some of the discovered attacks exist because the RP and the IdP interpret the protocol or its specification differently. For example, in a vulnerability involving PayPal [33], the RP (PayPal) and IdP (Google) treat a data type differently.
- *Privacy leaks.* Uruena et al. [32] identify possible privacy leaks to third party providers (such as advertisers and corresponding industries) in the OpenID protocol.

Generally, we consider these attacks as out-of-scope because they are due to a user error, an implementation error (specific to improperly-implemented RPs or IdPs; potentially the result of poor documentation), or do not involve any communication between the RP and the IdP. In this paper, we solely focus on protocol level attacks.

3   Revisiting Existing SSO Designs and Attacks

To identify the root cause of the identity impersonation attacks, as defined by Wang et al. [33], it is critical to understand some main aspects of existing SSO protocol designs, especially the communication protocol between the RP and the IdP. Wang et al. [33] abstracted this communication by introducing the concept of a *browser-relayed message* (BRM), which describes a request from an IdP or an RP, to the RP or the IdP respectively, together with the resulting response. While this abstraction is already helpful for identifying vulnerabilities, it does not capture the root cause of many vulnerabilities in existing SSO protocol designs and leaves the communication unnecessarily complex. Instead, we abstract the protocol differently: the RP simply communicates with the IdP through an established channel. In this context, only two questions remain: (*i*) what is the identity of the parties involved (authenticity), and (*ii*) how do these parties communicate to achieve confidentiality and integrity?

3.1   Identity

As said, three parties are involved in a SSO instance. Understanding how each party is identified by the other parties is a prerequisite to analyze the root cause of impersonation attacks.

- *IdP.* The IdP is generally identified by its web origin, i.e., <scheme, host, port>.
- *User.* The user is identified by a unique identifier, such as their username or email address. While the identification of users can cause some confusion in an SSO protocol, attacks resulting from this confusion are out-of-scope because

they are implementation or documentation errors. In this paper, we assume that there exists a correct and unique identifier for each user.

- *RP.* The identity of an RP can vary according to protocols imposed by different IdPs, but is a unique identifier nonetheless. For example, Facebook Connect uses the identifier "app_id" to identify an RP, while JanRain chose to adopt "AppName" and "settingsHandle" as the RP's identifier [33].

Recent attacks show that the identity of a benign RP might be easily forgeable by a malicious RP. For instance, in the example involving Facebook and the NYTimes [33], the malicious RP spoofed/forged the identifier of the NYTimes. Because of this, we require an unforgeable identifier to represent the identity of an RP. In the same spirit as for the IdP, one can use the web origin as tracked by the client browser. Since web origin tracking is already a basic security property that is enforced by all modern browsers, it is very hard for a malicious RP to forge it[3].

3.2   Communication between the RP and the IdP

Simply equipping the RP with an unforgeable identifier, however, does not mitigate existing vulnerabilities. During the execution of an SSO protocol, one must verify the identity of the RP at every step. To detail the problems caused by this, we carefully re-examine the communication between the RP and the IdP via a client's browser in existing protocols. We classify those interactions into two main categories: HTTP(s) requests to a third-party server and an in-browser communication channel.

HTTP(s) Requests to a Third-Party Server. In the first category, comprising of OpenID, Security Assertion Markup Language (SAML) [9], and AAuth [31], the RP and the IdP communicate with each other via HTTP(s) requests. The process of an RP trying to connect to an IdP is as follows. First, the RP's JavaScript code -running in the client's browser- sends a request to the RP. The RP sends a response containing an HTTP 3xx redirection (or, alternatively, some kind of other redirection, for instance, via automatic form submission) to the client. Based on this redirection, the RP's code in the client browser sends a request to the IdP. Finally, the browser communicates with the IdP and completes the authentication process.

The problem: The interaction via third-party HTTP(s) requests is a one-way channel, i.e., after an RP talks to an IdP, the IdP cannot send a response back. In order to actually receive a response, the RP needs to tell the IdP where to forward the client's browser upon authentication. Generally, this is done by utilizing a parameter in the request, such as the next_url parameter in Listing 1.1. The issue here is that this parameter can be modified by an attacker, and, in turn, can lead to an identity impersonation attack. To mitigate this vulnerability, a bi-directional communication channel is necessary.

In-browser Communication Channel. The second category describes protocols that communicate via an in-browser communication channel. This includes

---

[3] Impossible to forge, if web origin and its tracking is correctly implemented by the browser and configured properly by the web site operator, i.e., according to RFC6454

Facebook Connect[4] [19] and other protocols in which the RP and the IdP use JavaScript in the client's browser to communicate with each other. The different parties might communicate with each other through a number of mechanisms, such as postMessage [14], URI fragments [14], or even Flash objects [33].

The problem: Two issues remain with this approach. First, the in-browser communication channel is an undedicated, bi-directional channel without proper authentication. For each message exchanged between the RP and the IdP, the origin needs to be verified independently. Recent work has established that this verification step is frequently forgotten by developers [21, 27]. The omission of this crucial verification step can make the protocol vulnerable to impersonation attacks. For instance, Hanna et al. [21] determined that two prominent SSO protocols, Facebook Connect and Google Friend Connect, exhibit this problem. Further, Son et al. [27] identified 85 popular web sites that were using the postMessage API incorrectly. This demonstrates the requirement for a dedicated channel with built-in authentication for the RP-IdP communication. Second, the in-browser communication channel is insecure. In the vulnerability between Facebook and NYTimes [33], attackers exploited this fact to eavesdrop on the in-browser communication between the IdP and the RP and intercept users' access tokens while the authentication was taking place. Once the attacker obtains this access token, he can successfully impersonate the NYTimes to Facebook. Here, the channel's insecurity was introduced by the use of Flash objects. However, even if the communication channel would be changed from Flash objects to postMessage, the vulnerability would remain, as demonstrated by Barth et al. [14] and Yang et al. [36]. Furthermore, Cao et al. [17] show that the postMessage vulnerability originally proposed by Barth et al. still exists in modern browsers for requests from the same domain, such as different blogs or applications hosted under that same domain.

To mitigate all these threats, a *dedicated, bi-directional, secure channel with authentication* is required. In the next section, we discuss the steps involved in establishing such a channel.

4   Design

In the previous section, we argued for the necessity of a new, dedicated, bi-directional, secure channel between the IdP and the RP, along with a new approach to verify the identity of the RP. Following, we discuss the design of our SSO protocol, which addresses the shortcomings of prior protocol designs. We introduce two solutions: a clean-slate redesign and a legacy-compatible proxy. The clean-slate design (Section 4.1) must be deployed by the IdP as a new SSO service; the proxy design (Section 4.2) serves as a "fourth-party" IdP and is designed to be deployed by an RP that wants to protect its users from RP impersonation attacks on legacy SSO services, while still supporting authentication through existing, but insecure services.

4.1   IdP Deployment – Clean-slate Design

The core requirements of our clean-slate design of SSO are (i) the use of the web origin as an RP and IdP identifier, and (ii) the use of a dedicated, secure,

---

[4] Facebook Connect mixes the usage of HTTPS requests to a third-party server and an in-browser communication channel.

bi-directional channel with authentication for all communication between the RP and the IdP (Section 3).

Identity Design. In our protocol, the identity of the RP is its web origin. There are two alternatives for choosing this identity:

- *Web Origin is defined by the RP.* If the RP has its own web origin, such as the NYTimes, the RP can simply define a sub-domain for its SSO communication. For example, the NYTimes could make use of *facebookconnect.nytimes.com* for all communication with Facebook Connect to authenticate users through SSO.
- *Web Origin is provided by the IdP.* If the RP does not have a web origin, such as in the case of an application designed by a third-party web developer, the RP can adopt a sub-domain origin of the IdP (for example, *application1.connect.facebook.com*) as its identity for communication with Facebook during the authentication of users through SSO.

In both cases, the RP can leverage the sandbox tag defined in HTML5 to ensure proper isolation of the web origin.

Communication Channel. Next, we will detail the life-cycle of a bi-directional, authenticated, secure communication channel over the following three steps: (i) establishing the channel, (ii) using the channel to communicate securely, and (iii) destroying the channel.

Establishing the Channel: Handshake Protocol. To establish a secure communication channel between the RP and the IdP, JavaScript first creates a secure socket that listens to connections from a given web origin (for example, the web origin belonging to the RP), optionally specifying a target window (such as *parent*), as shown in Listing 1.2. When the RP's web page is loaded, its JavaScript connects to the socket created by the IdP by specifying the target window (*e.g.*, a reference to an inline frame) and the target origin (*i.e.*, the IdP's web origin), c.f., Listing 1.2, line 11-14).

Listing 1.2. JavaScript Primitive for the Channel

```
 1 parameters = {
 2  mWindow: parent , // optional when listening
 3  mOrigin: IdP/RP Origin ,
 4  onMessage: function(m) { /* receiving message callback */ }
 5  onConnect: function() { /* creating channel callback */ }
 6  onDestroy: function() { /* destroying channel callback */ }
 7 }
 8 // Listening to a channel
 9 var socket = new SecureSocket();
10 socket.listen(parameters)
11 // Creating a channel
12 var iframe = document.getElementById("myid");
13 var socket = new SecureSocket();
14 socket.connect(parameters)
```

The handshake protocol establishes the secure channel between the RP and the IdP, by exchanging their keys. The process includes the following five steps:

1. The RP verifies the identity of the IdP and sends its public key (PK_RP) to the IdP.
2. Upon receipt of the public key from the RP, the IdP verifies the identity (web origin) of the RP.
3. The IdP generates a session key (SK), encrypts it with the public key from the RP, and sends the encrypted session key and an encrypted partial channel number (PK_RP(N_IdP)) to the RP.
4. The RP decrypts the session key and partial channel number using its own private key and responds with an encrypted partial channel number (SK(N_RP)). This channel number, and the channel number generated by the IdP in (3) are then stored by the browser as an index to look up the session key.
5. With both parts of the channel number, the RP and the IdP can communicate with each other. Both N_IdP and N_RP are needed to send a message, and each message consists of a ControlByte (later used to determine the status of the channel) and the message content, encrypted with the session key.

In the aforementioned steps, N_IdP and N_RP are used to look up the session key by both the RP and the IdP, and the ControlByte is used to determine the status of the current channel, such as whether it has been destroyed. During the negotiation period, both partial channel numbers (N_IdP and N_RP) are encrypted and protected. Later on, N_IdP and N_RP are not encrypted, and thus easily modifiable. If an attacker modifies N_IdP or N_RP, however, a different session key and message handler will be used to process the message, and, in turn, it will result in the message being delivered to an incorrect channel. In the absence of the correct keys, an entity listening on this channel will be unable to decrypt the message and fail.

Use of the Channel: Sending Messages (Figure 1). After the channel is created, messages can be sent. When either side wants to send a message, it calls the JavaScript primitive *socket.sendMessage(msg)*, which divides the input message into small chunks (to fit the key size), appends the control byte to indicate the status of current channel, encrypts all the divided chunks with the shared session key, and appends N_IdP+N_RP to the result. This message is then sent via the in-browser communication channel, which ensures the delivery of the message.

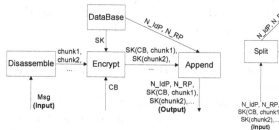
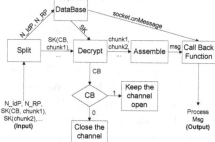

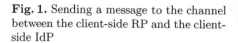

Fig. 1. Sending a message to the channel between the client-side RP and the client-side IdP

Fig. 2. Receiving a message from the channel between the client-side RP and the client-side IdP

Use of the Channel: Receiving Messages (Figure 2). When a message is sent by one of the parties, the system first uses the N_IdP and N_RP to retrieve the session key and socket from the browser. The session key is used to decrypt the encrypted message chunks and the ControlByte. These chunks are then stitched back together accordingly and delivered to the processing function on the other end of the corresponding socket.

Destroying a Channel: Releasing Resources.   In the process of destroying a channel, *socket.close()* is called. When either the IdP or RP calls the close method, the other side is notified and must close the channel as well.

For example, if the RP wants to close the channel during the communication, it sends a message with the ControlByte set to 0. When the IdP receives this message, it sends an equivalent response (with the ControlByte of 0) and releases resources such as the channel number, session key, and socket. After the RP receives the response message, it also releases its resources. This is a process analogous to the closing handshake of a TCP network socket.

SSO Protocol over the Channel. Our secure communication channel between the RP and IdP can now be used in the design of a secure SSO protocol. Traditionally, SSO is classified into two categories: OAuth-like protocols for authorization and OpenID-like protocols for authentication. In the former, the RP asks the IdP for an access token to fetch a user's information from the IdP; in the latter, the RP asks the IdP to verify the identity of a user. We describe both paradigms in the context of our secure channel.

OAuth-like Protocol:
1. Client-side JavaScript code served by the RP initiates a connection with the JavaScript code served by the IdP by establishing the secure channel.
2. The RP JavaScript requests a token, which can be used to access a user's data, from the IdP JavaScript.
3. The IdP authenticates the user, usually by having them log into the IdP's service.
4. When the user authenticates successfully, the IdP asks the user for permission to allow the RP to access their information.
5. If permission is granted, the IdP then sends the token to the IdP JavaScript, which forwards the token to the RP JavaScript.
6. The RP JavaScript sends the token to the RP server, which then uses that token to request the user's information from the IdP service.

OpenID-like Protocol:
1. JavaScript served by the RP establishes a secure channel to JavaScript served by the IdP through our protocol.
2. The RP JavaScript asks the IdP JavaScript to authenticate the user.
3. The IdP server authenticates the user, usually by having them log into the IdP service.
4. Upon successful authentication, the IdP server sends an authentication proof (typically a token encrypted or signed with the IdP's private key) to the IdP JavaScript.
5. The IdP JavaScript relays the authentication proof to the RP JavaScript.
6. The RP JavaScript relays the authentication proof to the RP server.

4.2 RP Deployment – Proxy Design

Many existing, unprotected protocol SSO implementations are currently deployed, and migrating them to our secure design will take time since it requires manual development effort. To assist in securing these legacy implementations, we introduce a proxy that integrates them into our design, and allows for a seamless transition.

The proxy mediates the communication between an RP and the IdP (Figure 3). It acts as a legacy RP to the legacy IdP, authenticating against it like any other currently deployed RP, but with sufficient isolation to protect it from identity impersonation attacks. Additionally, this proxy acts as a secure IdP to the RP using our secure protocol.

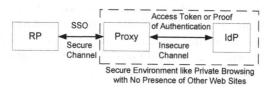

Fig. 3. Overview of the proxy design. The secure RP is talking to our proxy through the secure channel, and our proxy is talking to the legacy IdP using a legacy SSO protocol, but contained in a secure, controlled environment.

Communication with the Legacy IdP. To communicate with the legacy IdP, the proxy needs to act as a legacy RP. For the IdPs of most existing SSO implementations (for example, Facebook Connect), we must register an application for each user, and keep the application ID secret from attackers to avoid any impersonation attacks. Specifically, only the legacy IdP and our proxy must know the application ID.

After registering an application with the IdP, the proxy authenticates normally with the IdP and acquires the access token (for an OAuth-like protocol) or proof of authentication (for an OpenID-like protocol). Since these tokens incorporate the *privileges* that an RP has over the authenticating user's account, and since some subset of these privileges will be ultimately used by the secure RPs that communicate through our proxy, the proxy must request the total set of permissions that will be needed by all the secure RPs. To accommodate different privileges levels, the proxy stores this confidential information inside its own database on the proxy server side.

Since the communication with the legacy IdP takes place using an insecure SSO implementation, the process should ideally be done in private browsing mode on a secure machine with no other web sites open. This is to prevent details such as the application ID of the proxy from being leaked to potential attackers.

Communication with the Secure RP. After the initial setup, the secure RP communicates only with our proxy, instead of the legacy IdP. Communication between the RP and our proxy is done over the secure channel (Section 4.1). We first authenticate the user, and then, for OAuth-like protocols, generate our own token for the RP with a corresponding subset of the privileges granted to us by the legacy IdP. For OpenID-like protocols, the proxy can simply forward the authentication proof directly to the RP.

Fetching the User's Information. In an OAuth-like protocol, when the RP asks for the user's information using the token issued by us, the proxy sends a request for this information to the legacy IdP with the token issued by that legacy IdP. When the legacy IdP returns the requested information, the proxy forwards the information to the RP.

5   Implementation

In this section, we present the implementation details of our system. First, we introduce the implementation of our clean-slate design (Section 5.1). We implemented the authenticated, bi-directional, secure channel as a layer on top of the existing *postMessage* channel available in modern browsers, and then leveraged this channel to implement our SSO protocol. Next, we discuss a prototype implementation of our proxy design (Section 5.2).

5.1   IdP Deployment

Our implementation of the clean-slate design is very lightweight: it consists of only 252 lines of JavaScript code (excluding external libraries), 264 lines of HTML code, and 243 lines of PHP code. The bi-directional secure channel with authentication is implemented exclusively in JavaScript; the RP-side and IdP-side code is implemented in HTML and PHP.

Our JavaScript implementation of the secure channel uses two external libraries, the JavaScript Cryptography Toolkit [3] and the Stanford JavaScript Crypto Library [10], both for cryptographic purposes. The former is used for public and private key generation and asymmetric encryption and decryption; the latter is used for session key generation and symmetric encryption and decryption. The public and private keys in the implementation are 512 bits, and the session key is 128 bits. However, these are implementation details, and can be modified to address different security requirements. As mentioned before, we implemented the protocol by adding our security layer on top of the *postMessage* functionality available in modern browsers, which provides a reliable, but insecure, communication channel that guarantees in-order delivery of messages.

We use a socket pool for session tracking. For each incoming message, the system looks in the socket pool for a channel with the corresponding N_IdP and N_RP and, if one is found, fetches the socket and session key. Otherwise, a new socket is created (Section 4.1), and kept track of in the socket pool.

To evaluate the practicality of our design, we created reference IdP and RP implementations. A login interface for the IdP prompts the user to input his username and password. The IdP's server-side code looks up the credentials in a database and, if the username and password match, it generates an access token and transfers the token to the IdP JavaScript. Since the authentication process involves multiple server-side pages, we load an iframe to embed the authentication process and communicate with the RP. This iframe talks to the IdP iframe, which is responsible for authentication through another secure channel.

5.2 Proxy RP Deployment

To demonstrate the feasibility of our proxy design, we implemented a prototype RP that authenticates against Facebook through our proxy. The proxy process works as follows: first, a user who wants to authenticate via SSO through our proxy needs to register on our site. We enable the Facebook developer account for that user and let the user register a Facebook application under his account. This process is manual since it involves solving a simple captcha and acknowledging the terms of service, but could theoretically be automated if endorsed by Facebook. The user then provides the proxy's application's ID and secret key, so that the proxy can act as the application. While technically not necessary, we use the user's account to register an application because it lets the user maintain full control over the application, and the overall security is tied to the user's account. The whole process is done only once per user, as would happen when installing a normal application. A similar system can be implemented for Google's SSO implementation, which also adopts a user application key and secret to authenticate an application. In the OAuth case, the user will then grant the proxy permissions to access his/her user data. As mentioned previously, these permissions are a superset of those that the proxy can provide to an RP.

Afterwards, when a user visits an RP supported by our proxy, the SSO process will be the same as with the clean-slate design in the IdP deployment. We use Facebook's SDK [1], safely isolated from the RP, on the server-side to fetch the user's data and forward them to the RP.

There are, however, some implementation concerns unique to the proxy deployment:

Secrecy of the Legacy IdP Application ID. To guarantee the security of the proxy design, the application ID used by the proxy to identify itself at the legacy IdP must remain secret. In the case of the legacy IdP being Facebook Connect, we take two measures to ensure this secrecy. First, we register a unique Facebook application ID for each user. This is done so that an attacker cannot learn the application ID by using the proxy service himself. Second, certain legacy IdPs, such as Facebook, provide a sandbox mode [7] for developer use. This sandbox mode isolates the application from all users except for the developer. In our case, the "developer" is the user of the proxy implementation, and this functionality allows us to keep the application ID secret.

Legacy IdP Terms of Service. When implementing the proxy design, care must be taken to avoid violating the legacy IdP's terms of service. We have reviewed Facebook's terms of service and determined that encouraging every user to enable Facebook Developer Mode is acceptable. Additionally, we made the legacy IdP portion of the proxy as lightweight as possible to avoid putting any significant load on Facebook's infrastructure.

Legacy IdP Access Token Expiration. Tokens acquired from legacy IdPs, such as Facebook Connect, have an expiration time past which they cease granting access to a user's data. For Facebook Connect, this expiration is 60 days from the token's issuance time. After these 60 days, a reacquisition of the token by our proxy has to occur. This requires the user to repeat the initial setup process, which should be done in a private browsing mode to guarantee security. Tokens granted by the proxy to the RP do not expire in the current implementation, but introducing the functionality is straight-forwarding and requires only some engineering effort.

6   Evaluation

To evaluate our design, we first formally verify the channel (Section 6.1). Following, we empirically examine existing vulnerabilities (Section 6.2). Finally, we study the performance of our implementation to show that our protocol incurs only a reasonable overhead for the security guarantees it provides (Section 6.3).

6.1   Formal Protocol Verification

We verify the correctness of our protocol with ProVerif [6, 16], an automatic cryptographic protocol verifier based on the Dolev-Yao model [18]. ProVerif can prove properties including secrecy, authentication, strong secrecy, and equivalences of a protocol. For our formal verification, we require only the former two properties.

Channel Verification. We model the channel and the attacker, and then verify the channel using the attacker model.
Channel Model. Using ProVerif, we model our secure channel by using two processes and one free channel according to our threat model (Section 2). These two processes model the client-side and the server-side. The free channel, exposed to the attacker by definition, is used to communicate between the client and the server.

First, the RP sends its public key to the IdP. Second, the server verifies the web origin (defined as a bitstring transmitted together with the public key in the first step). This happens because browsers always send the web origin as part of a message via the postMessage functionality. If the origin matches, we generate a symmetric session key. Following, on the IdP side, the session key and partial channel number N_IdP are generated and encrypted. After receiving the encrypted session key, the RP decrypts the message. It then encrypts its own, generated partial channel number N_RP with the session key. In the end, the IdP can send messages securely by encrypting messages with the session key and appending N_IdP and N_RP.
Attacker Model. In ProVerif, an attacker in the context of a secure channel is an active and passive adversary who is capable of sending messages to either party and also capable of eavesdropping on messages sent across the channel.
Results. After modeling the channel and attacker, ProVerif determined that an attacker would be unable to obtain the plaintext of an encrypted message sent over the secure channel. To further validate this assessment, we introduced an intentional vulnerability into the protocol and verified that ProVerif was able to produce a valid attack scenario in which the adversary was able to read the message in the clear.

For this vulnerability, we simply removed the origin check, of the RP, that is performed by the IdP. Once removed, ProVerif produced a counterexample showing the attack scenario. The produced attack works as follows: a malicious

RP directly sends its own PK_RP to the IdP, and, in turn, acquires the session key SK and channel number N_IdP. Since the IdP does not verify the RP's identity, the malicious RP can impersonate the legitimate RP and talk to the IdP as if it is the legitimate RP.

SSO Protocol Verification. We model the SSO protocol and the attacker in ProVerif, and we verify its security guarantees in respect to our threat model.
SSO Protocol Model. We model the SSO protocol with two secure channels and three processes. The three processes represent the client-side RP, the client-side IdP and the server-side IdP. The client-side RP and the client-side IdP communicate with each other over the secure channel (Section 6.1). The client-side IdP and the server-side IdP communicate through HTTPS, a well-known secure channel.
Attacker Model. In respect to our threat-model, attackers are either network attackers or web attackers, as defined by Akhawe et al [11]. A network attacker is a passive adversary capable of eavesdropping on the network traffic, while a web attacker can also control malicious web sites and clients.
Results. Both channels are verified as secure with properly authenticated peers. Because of this, an attacker cannot acquire any useful information from either channel. ProVerif confirms this result.

Proxy Design Verification. To validate our proxy design, we model and verify the proxy in ProVerif.
Proxy Design Model. We model the proxy design with one secure channel, one insecure channel, and three processes. These three processes correspond to the RP, our proxy (the new, secure, fourth-party IdP), and the real, legacy IdP. The channel between the RP and our proxy is secure (as established in Section 6.1), and the channel between our proxy and the legacy IdP is insecure.
Attacker Model. The attacker model follows the attacker model definition from the Channel Verification (Section 6.1).
Results. Since all communication of our proxy and the real IdP occurs over insecure channel, a malicious RP can intercept any ongoing communication. Unsurprisingly, ProVerif yields that the information transmitted over the channel between our proxy and the real IdP can be obtained by an attacker. Thus, as discussed in Section 4.2, it is crucial that we need to keep the identity of our proxy at the real IdP confidential (to prevent impersonation attacks on the proxy) and that the initial setup, during which communication between the proxy and the real IdP occurs, is performed in a secure environment, such as in private browsing mode with no other web sites open to which information of the proxy might leak.

6.2   Security Analysis

Following, we study several existing RP impersonation vulnerabilities [33] and show how our design mitigates such vulnerabilities effectively.

Facebook and NYTimes. The first vulnerability we discuss was found in the interaction between the NYTimes as the RP and Facebook as the IdP. In this vulnerability, a malicious RP impersonates the NYTimes by spoofing its app_id. In turn, Facebook continues to authenticate the user and generate an access token that is supposed to be delivered to the NYTimes. However, due to nature of cross-domain communication in Adobe Flash, i.e., its "unpredictability" [4], the in-browser channel can be eavesdropped on and the access token is being leaked to the malicious RP, the actual initiator of the authentication request.

Mitigation.   The vulnerability has two major components: a malicious RP impersonating the NYTimes and the insecure communication channel between the NYTimes and Facebook. Both vulnerabilities are mitigated in our protocol by design. First, we leverage web origins to verify the identity of the RP, thus a malicious RP cannot impersonate the NYTimes. Second, the communication channel between the NYTimes and Facebook is over a secure channel with authentication, therefore, even if a malicious RP would acquire the messages transmitted, it cannot easily decrypt and retrieve the clear message.

JanRain Wrapping GoogleID. A second interesting vulnerability was found in how JanRain wraps GoogleID [33]. Here, a malicious RP registers itself with JanRain. Initially, the malicious RP initiates the communication. Then, once JanRain redirects the communication to Google, the malicious RP impersonates the victim RP and sets the return URL to its own URL. Since Google is using the HTTP redirection method (c.f., Section 3.2) to communicate with the RP, confidential information will be leaked to the malicious RP.

Mitigation.   In our design, when the RP talks to the IdP, all communication occurs over a bi-directional secure channel. As such, when the real RP talks to the IdP, the IdP will respond to the original, legitimate RP rather than to a different, malicious RP. Thus, the vulnerability is mitigated by design.

Facebook and Zoho. Similar to the vulnerability found in how JanRain wraps GoogleID, a vulnerability in the use of HTTP redirection was discovered between Facebook and Zoho.com [33]. To exploit this vulnerability, after receiving the authorization code from the `redirect_url` of Zoho, the attacker sends a request to Zoho and sets the `service_url` to a malicious URL. Zoho fails the SSO, but still redirects the user to the malicious URL.

Mitigation.   The root cause of this vulnerability is very similar to 2). Since our protocol leverages a bi-directional secure channel, a return URL is not required in our design, thus preventing this vulnerability by design.

JanRain Wrapping Facebook. In this vulnerability, JanRain wraps Facebook as the IdP [33]. Here, *sears.com* incorrectly set its whitelist to **.sears.com* rather than to the more restrictive *rp.sears.com*, thus exposing it to an attack similar to the *document.domain* attack by Singh et al. [26].

Mitigation.   Since our design specifically uses web origins as the identity of the RP, the concept of a whitelist is irrelevant, thus preventing the misconfiguration of any such whitelist by design.

Facebook Legacy Canvas Auth. Lastly, a third vulnerability that allows *IdP* impersonation rather than *RP* impersonation was discovered in how Facebook is being used as the IdP. In this case, the vulnerability lies in in the fact that, for Facebook's legacy canvas authentication [33], the generated signature is not properly verified by a Facebook app (specifically, *FarmVille.com*). Because of this, the RP renders itself vulnerable to IdP impersonation attacks, leading to arbitrary user impersonation attacks and resulting leaks of private or confidential user data.

Mitigation. Since we transmit every message in an established secure channel that provides authentication, it is not necessary for the RP to verify any signature itself. For this reason, it reduces the risk of missing or omitted signature verification steps and preventing the impersonation attacks that might arise.

6.3 Performance Analysis

Environment and Methodology. Our client-side experiment was performed on a 2.67GHz Intel(R) i7 CPU with four physical cores and 8GB of memory running Ubuntu 13.04 64-bit. The browser at the client-side was Firefox 22.0 in the 32-bit version. The RP server was deployed on a CentOS 64-bit server with a 2.50GHz Intel(R) Xeon(R) CPU with eight physical cores and 16GB memory. The IdP server was deployed on a CentOS 64-bit server with a 2.80GHz Intel(R) Xeon(R) CPU with four cores and 16GB memory. The average round-trip network latency between the client and the two servers was measured to be about 50ms.

To measure the delay of each step of the secure channel and an instantiation of our SSO protocol, we make use of the JavaScript primitive *Date()* and subtract the monitored value at start and end points to calculate the delay. Each experiment was repeated ten times to calculate the average delay and to account for outliers and deviations.

Table 1. Breakdown of the authentication performance of our prototype implementation

Operation	Delay
(1) Creating the Channel between RP and IdP	164±11ms
(2) Creating IdP Iframe	57±3ms
(3) Sending the First Message from RP to IdP	32±2ms
(4) Creating IdP Iframe for Authentication	57±3ms
(5) Creating the Second Channel inside IdP	165±11ms
(6) Authenticating the User	56±4ms
(7) Getting the User's Permission	57±3ms
(8) Sending the Token inside IdP Iframe	32±2ms
(9) Sending the Token to RP	33±2ms
Total	653±21ms

Note: Step (2), (4), (6) and (7) are extremely depended on the network latency.

Performance of SSO Implementation. We measure the performance of our prototype implementation of our SSO protocol. The results are shown in Table 1 and they are divided into three categories: channel creation, network delay, and message passing. (1) and (5) correspond to channel creation, which takes about 164ms. (2), (4), (6) and (7) are almost exclusively driven by the network delay. (2) and (4) are to fetch content from the IdP, and (6) and (7) are used to communicate with the IdP. In the end, (3), (8), and (9) are used to communicate between iframes within the browser through our established secure channel, which is about 32ms.

Overall, the total overhead of our prototype implementation is only 653ms, i.e., acceptable from a user's perspective given the strong security guarantees of our SSO protocol.

7   Related Work

We present related work that looks for vulnerabilities in existing SSO protocol designs and work investigating protection mechanisms for existing SSO protocols.

7.1   Vulnerability Identification

Much research has been carried out to identify vulnerabilities in existing SSO protocols. The work falls into three types: manual to mostly manual analysis, automatic analysis, and user studies.

Table 2. Comparison and positioning of our work with related work

	Deployment at	Protecting	Preventing Impersonation Attacks	Proactive Deployment
InteGuard [35]	IdP and Gateway	IdP users and in-network devices	✓	✗
AUTHSCAN [13]	IdP	IdP users	✓	✗
Explicating SDKs [34]	IdP	IdP users	✓	✗
Defensive JavaScript [15]	IdP and RP	IdP and RP users	✗	✓
Our Work	IdP and RP	IdP and RP users	✓	✓

- *Manual analysis to mostly manual analysis.* Wang et al. [33] propose a browser relay message analyzer and identify eight vulnerabilities in protocol implementations through by manually analyzing them. Sun et al. [28] perform an empirical study to identify vulnerabilities in three major OAuth identity providers (IdP) (Facebook, Microsoft, and Google). Uruena et al. [32] manually identify privacy leaks in SSO protocols, which are beyond the scope of the paper, and they propose short-term and long-term solutions. Pfitzmann et al. [25] empirically analyze SSO protocols and identify several vulnerabilities.
- *Automatic Analysis.* Bai et al. [13] introduce AUTHSCAN, a tool that automatically extracts a specification from SSO implementation and identifies vulnerabilities from the extracted specification through formal analysis. Similarly, Explicating SDKs by Wang et al. [34] extracts the underlying assumptions of SSO protocols from their respective SDKs and detects corresponding vulnerability patterns. On the other hand, Armando et al. [12] formally analyze the SAML 2.0 protocol and identify vulnerabilities in the protocol. Lastly, much work based on formal analysis [20, 22–24] has been carried out focusing on the Facebook Connect protocol, SAML, and OAuth respectively.
- *User Studies.* A different categories of vulnerabilities, namely denial of service, such as single point-of-failure related issues, have been highlighted by Sun et al. [30] in an empirical user study to gauge the reaction and opinion on SSO protocols by its respective users. Overall, their study shows that 26% of users express concerns about denial of service attacks on the identity provider, i.e., concerns about attacks preventing them from authenticating to the RP.

7.2   Defense Mechanism

InteGuard [35] describes a proxy in between the client's browser and the IdP. InteGuard extracts a set of invariant relations among HTTP messages it observes and deduces their relation to the security of the protocol. Due to its nature, InteGuard is deployed at the server-side together with a server's load balancer or as process at client's browser. Defensive JavaScript [15] on the other hand is a subset of the JavaScript language that guarantees that scripts integrity is being kept even in an adversarial environment. Alternatively, an OpenIDemail enabled browser [29] modifies the client browser to support OpenID natively and hides the OpenID identifiers from users by using their existing email accounts.

Prior work compares to our protocol as follows:

– *Deployment by the IdP.* All existing approaches can be deployed by the IdP. However, except for Defensive JavaScript [15], they reactively identify and mitigate vulnerabilities in existing and deployed SSO implementations. Instead, our framework proactively mitigates those vulnerabilities from the start by addressing the root cause (analogously to how memory-safe languages address the root cause of memory corruption vulnerabilities). It is important to note that Defensive JavaScript [15] is complementary to our approach. First, it uses a different threat model than we do, i.e., a benign RP might be compromised. In our threat model, however, a benign RP must remain uncompromised. Second, while the communication is secured in our protocol, in the case of Defensive JavaScript the communication between the RP and the IdP remains vulnerable. Thus, a malicious party can sniff or modify messages, as in the case of the NYTimes and Facebook [33] attack.

– *Deployment by non-IdP.* InteGuard [35] can also be deployed by the other entities, essentially acting as a gateway or firewall, thus protecting a set of physical machines with different users behind it. For example, if InteGuard would be deployed at a university, it protects all machines at the university, but a student connecting to a RP from home would not be protected. In contrast, our protocol protects users regardless of where they are connecting from.

Alternatively, in the case of OpenIDemail, a compatible browser [29] must be used by the user, which is generally considered an impractical burden to the user, and hard to enforce on a large scale. Our design, regardless of its actual deployment scenario, does not require any such modification to the user's browser.

8   Conclusion

In this paper, rather than identifying individual vulnerabilities in SSO protocols, we determined the root cause of why RP impersonation attacks exist: an undedicated, insecure, one-way channel between the RP and the IdP. Based on our findings, we propose to abandon simple HTTP redirection or the raw in-browser communication channel currently used when designing SSO protocols. Instead, a dedicated bi-directional secure channel is needed that can be built on top of existing, in-browser communication channels.

We introduced a technique to establish such a channel securely, proposed a SSO protocol that uses a channel established with our method, and verified the correctness of our protocol formally with ProVerif [6], which was unable to create an attack scenarios in respect to our threat model. Additionally, we provide an example of a vulnerability introduced into the protocol deliberately, for which ProVerif identified the vulnerability correctly and generated a valid attack scenario.

In addition to our clean-slate and secure SSO protocol design, we detailed a proxy that allows and supports a smooth transition from existing SSO protocols to our new and secure protocol. The design of this proxy is formally verified in respect to our threat model.

Finally, we evaluated the performance and overhead of our SSO protocol implementation. With an overall small latency overhead of about 650ms, and a clear bottleneck in our prototype implementation in the generation of the private and public key that can be remedied with some engineering effort, our new SSO protocol proves to have a clearly acceptable overhead given its strong security guarantees.

Acknowledgment. This material is based upon work supported by the Department of Homeland Security under grant 2009-ST-061-CI0001; the National Science Foundation under grants CNS-0845559, CNS-0905537, CNS-1116967, and CNS-1255546; by the Office of Naval Research through grants N00014-09-1-1042, and N00014-12-1-0165; by the Army Research Office under grant W911NF-09-1-0553; and Secure Business Austria. This work is also sponsored by DARPA under agreement number FA8750-12-2-0101 and N66001-13-2-4039. The U.S. Government is authorized to reproduce and distribute reprints for Governmental purposes notwithstanding any copyright notation thereon.

The views and conclusions contained herein are those of the authors and should not be interpreted as necessarily representing the official policies or endorsements, either expressed or implied, of DARPA or the U.S. Government.

References

1. Getting started with the facebook sdk for php, https://developers.facebook.com/docs/php/gettingstarted/
2. JanRain Engage, http://janrain.com/products/engage/
3. JavaScript Cryptography Toolkit, http://ats.oka.nu/titaniumcore/js/crypto/readme.txt
4. LocalConnection, http://help.adobe.com/en_US/FlashPlatform/reference/actionscript/3/flash/net/LocalConnection.html
5. OpenID, http://openid.net/
6. ProVerif: Cryptographic protocol verifier in the formal model, http://prosecco.gforge.inria.fr/personal/bblanche/proverif/
7. Sandbox mode of facebook application, https://developers.facebook.com/docs/ApplicationSecurity/
8. Secure electronic transaction, http://goo.gl/2SpMbF
9. Security assertion markup language, http://en.wikipedia.org/wiki/Security_Assertion_Markup_Language
10. The Stanford Javascript Crypto Library, http://crypto.stanford.edu/sjcl/
11. Akhawe, D., Barth, A., Lam, P.E., Mitchell, J.C., Song, D.: Towards a formal foundation of web security. In: CSF (2010)

12. Armando, A., Carbone, R., Compagna, L., Cuellar, J., Tobarra, L.: Formal analysis of saml 2.0 web browser single sign-on: Breaking the saml-based single sign-on for google apps. In: FMSE: The ACM Workshop on Formal Methods in Security Engineering (2008)
13. Bai, G., Lei, J., Meng, G., Venkatraman, S.S., Saxena, P., Sun, J., Liu, Y., Dong, J.S.: AUTHSCAN: Automatic Extraction of Web Authentication Protocols from Implementations. In: NDSS (2013)
14. Barth, A., Jackson, C., Mitchell, J.C.: Securing frame communication in browsers. In: USENIX Security Symposium (2008)
15. Bhargavan, K., Delignat-Lavaud, A., Maffeis, S.: Language-based defenses against untrusted browser origins. In: USENIX Security Symposium (2013)
16. Blanchet, B.: An efficient cryptographic protocol verifier based on prolog rules. In: CSFW (2001)
17. Cao, Y., Rastogi, V., Li, Z., Chen, Y., Moshchuk, A.: Redefining web browser principals with a configurable origin policy. In: DSN (2013)
18. Dolev, D., Yao, A.C.: On the security of public key protocols. Tech. rep., Stanford, CA, USA (1981)
19. Facebook. Facebook connect, http://goo.gl/ZUyBXF
20. Gro, T.: Security Analysis of the SAML Single Sign-on Browser/Artifact Profile. In: ACSAC (2003)
21. Hanna, S., Shin, R., Akhawe, D., Saxena, P., Boehm, A., Song, D.: The emperor's new APIs: On the (in)secure usage of new client-side primitives. In: W2SP (2010)
22. Hansen, S.M., Skriver, J., Nielson, H.R.: Using static analysis to validate the saml single sign-on protocol. In: WITS: The Workshop on Issues in the Theory of Security (2005)
23. Miculan, M., Urban, C.: Formal Analysis of Facebook Connect Single Sign-On Authentication Protocol. In: SOFSEM (2011)
24. Pai, S., Sharma, Y., Kumar, S., Pai, R.M., Singh, S.: Formal verification of oauth 2.0 using alloy framework. In: CSNT: The International Conference on Communication Systems and Network Technologies (2011)
25. Pfitzmann, B., Waidner, M.: Analysis of liberty single-sign-on with enabled clients. IEEE Internet Computing 7(6), 38–44 (2003)
26. Singh, K., Moshchuk, A., Wang, H., Lee, W.: On the Incoherencies in Web Browser Access Control Policies. In: SP: IEEE Symposium on Security and Privacy (2010)
27. Son, S., Shmatikov, V.: The Postman Always Rings Twice: Attacking and Defending postMessage in HTML5 Websites. In: NDSS (2013)
28. Sun, S.-T., Beznosov, K.: The devil is in the (implementation) details: An empirical analysis of oauth sso systems. In: CCS (2012)
29. Sun, S.-T., Hawkey, K., Beznosov, K.: OpenIDemail enabled browser: towards fixing the broken web single sign-on triangle. In: DIM (2010)
30. Sun, S.-T., Pospisil, E., Muslukhov, I., Dindar, N., Hawkey, K., Beznosov, K.: What makes users refuse web single sign-on?: An empirical investigation of openid. In: SOUPS (2011)
31. Tassanaviboon, A., Gong, G.: Oauth and abe based authorization in semi-trusted cloud computing: aauth. In: DataCloud-SC: The International Workshop on Data Intensive Computing in the Clouds (2011)
32. Urueña, M., Muñoz, A., Larrabeiti, D.: Analysis of privacy vulnerabilities in single sign-on mechanisms for multimedia websites. Multimedia Tools and Applications (2012)
33. Wang, R., Chen, S., Wang, X.: Signing me onto your accounts through facebook and google: A traffic-guided security study of commercially deployed single-sign-on web services. In: IEEE Symposium on Security and Privacy (2012)

34. Wang, R., Zhou, Y., Chen, S., Qadeer, S., Evans, D., Gurevich, Y.: Explicating sdks: Uncovering assumptions underlying secure authentication and authorization. In: USENIX Security Symposium (2013)
35. Xing, L., Chen, Y., Wang, X., Chen, S.: InteGuard: Toward Automatic Protection of Third-party web service integrations. In: NDSS (2013)
36. Yang, E.Z., Stefan, D., Mitchell, J., Mazieres, D., Marchenko, P., Karp, B.: Toward principled browser security. In: HotOS (2013)

Wait a Minute! A fast, Cross-VM Attack on AES

Gorka Irazoqui, Mehmet Sinan Inci, Thomas Eisenbarth, and Berk Sunar

Worcester Polytechnic Institute, Worcester, MA, USA
{girazoki,msinci,teisenbarth,sunar}@wpi.edu

Abstract. In cloud computing, efficiencies are reaped by resource sharing such as co-location of computation and deduplication of data. This work exploits resource sharing in virtualization software to build a powerful cache-based attack on AES. We demonstrate the vulnerability by mounting Cross-VM *Flush+Reload* cache attacks in VMware VMs to recover the keys of an AES implementation of OpenSSL 1.0.1 running inside the victim VM. Furthermore, the attack works in a *realistic setting* where different VMs are located on separate cores. The modified *flush+reload* attack we present, takes only in the order of seconds to minutes to succeed in a cross-VM setting. Therefore long term co-location, as required by other fine grain attacks in the literature, are not needed. The results of this study show that there is a great security risk to OpenSSL AES implementation running on VMware cloud services when the deduplication is not disabled.

Keywords: Cross-VM, memory deduplication, flush+reload, cache attacks.

1 Introduction

In recent years we witnessed mass adoption of cloud based storage and compute systems such as Dropbox, Amazon EC2 and Microsoft Azure. Rather than acquiring and maintaining expensive workstations, clusters or servers, businesses can simply rent them from cloud service providers at the time of need. However, as with any new technology, cloud systems also come with problems of their own, namely co-residency data leakage problems. The data leakage problem is an indirect outcome of cloud's temperament. By definition a cloud system allows multiple users to share the same physical machine rather than assigning a dedicated machine to every user. Co-residency keeps the number of physical machines needed and the operating costs such as maintenance, electricity and cooling low but at a price. In cloud systems, different users run their virtual machines (VM) on the same physical machine separated only by a virtualization layer provided by a virtual machine manager (VMM) and supervised by a hypervisor. In theory *sandboxing* enforced by the VMM should suffice to completely isolate VMs from each other, but as elegantly stated many times: *"In theory there is no difference between theory and practice. But in practice, there is."*

A serious security problem that threatens VM isolation, stems from the fact that people are using software libraries that are designed to run on single-user

A. Stavrou et al. (Eds.): RAID 2014, LNCS 8688, pp. 299–319, 2014.
© Springer International Publishing Switzerland 2014

servers and not on shared cloud hardwares and VM stacks. For privacy critical data, especially cryptographic data, this gives rise to a blind spot where things may go wrong. Even though classical implementation attacks targeting cryptosystems featuring RSA and AES have been studied extensively, so far there has been little discussion about safe implementation of cryptosystems on cloud systems. For instance, implementation attacks on AES implementations, as proposed by Bernstein [8] and later [9,13], use the timing difference of cache accesses to recover the secret key. A more recent study by Gullasch et.al [13] applies *Flush+Reload* attack between AES memory accesses. The attack recovers the key with as less as 100 encryptions. Even though these aforementioned methods have been implemented and the vulnerabilities are public, most cryptographic libraries still use vulnerable and unpatched implementations. Considering the level of access an adversary will have on a virtual machine, any of these attacks and many novel attacks can and will be realized on the cloud.

Another feature that can break process isolation or VM isolation is deduplication. Its exploitability has been shown in several studies. In 2011, Suzaki et al. [24] exploited an OS-optimization, namely Kernel Samepage Merging (KSM), to recover user data and subsequently identify a user from a co-located VM in a Linux Kernel-based Virtual Machine (KVM) [2] setting. In this study, authors were able to exploit the side-channel leakage to establish a covert communication channel between VMs and used this channel to detect co-residency with a target VM. Also in 2011 Suzaki et al. [23] exploited the same memory deduplication feature to detect processes like `sshd`, `apache2`, `IE6` and `Firefox` running on co-resident VM. The significance of this study is that not only it is possible to exploit the memory deduplication to detect the existence of a VM, but one can also detect the processes running on the target VM. This leads to cipher specific attacks and information thefts, as demonstrated by Suzaki et al. in [22]. In this latest study, the authors were able to detect security precautions such as antivirus software running on the co-resident target VM. Even though these studies paved the way for cross-VM process detection and shed light on vulnerabilities enabled by memory deduplication, a concrete attack recovering cryptographic keys has yet to be shown.

In [31] Weiß et al. for the first time presented a traditional cache timing attack on AES running inside a L4Re VM on an ARM Cortex-A8 single-core CPU with a `Fiasco.OC` microkernel. The attack is realized using Bernstein's correlation attack and targets several popular AES implementations including the one in `OpenSSL` [26]. The significance of this work is that it showed the possibility of extracting even finer grain information (AES vs. ElGamal keys in [34]) from a co-located VM. Recently, Irazoqui et al. [15] used Bernstein's attack to partially recover an AES key from a cross-VM attack running in XEN and VMware. While that work is the first one to show that fine-grain side-channel attacks can be mounted in cloud-like environments, the present attack is more efficient since it needs much less encryptions.

Our Contribution

In this work, we show a novel cache-based side-channel attack on AES that—by employing the *Flush+Reload* technique—enables, for the first time, a *practical* full key recovery attack across virtual machine boundaries in a *realistic* cloud-like server setting. The attack takes advantage of deduplication mechanism called the Transparent Page Sharing which is employed by VMware virtualization engine and is the focus of this work. The attack works well across cores, i.e. it works well in a high-end server with multiple cores scenario that is commonly found in cloud systems. The attack is, compared to [13], minimally invasive, significantly reducing requirements on the adversary: memory accesses are minimal and the accesses do not need to interrupt the victim process' execution. This also means that the attack is hardly detectable by the victim. Last but not least, the attack is lightning fast: we show that, when running in a realistic scenario where an encryption server is attacked, the whole key is recovered in less than 10 seconds in non-virtualized setting (i.e. using a spy process) even across cores, and in less than a minute in virtualized setting across VM boundaries.

In summary, this work

- shows for the first time that deduplication enables fine grain cross-VM attacks;
- introduces a new *Flush+Reload*-based attack that does not require interrupting the victim after each encryption round;
- presents the first *practical* cross-VM attack on AES; the attack is generic and can be adapted to any table-based block ciphers.

Since the presented attack is minimally invasive, it is very hard to detect. Finally, we also show that these attacks can be prevented without too much overhead.

After reviewing additional related work in Section 2 we detail on existing cache-based side-channel attacks in Section 3 and on memory deduplication in Section 4. The proposed attack is introduced in Section 5. Results are presented in Section 6. Before concluding in Section 8 we discuss possible countermeasures in Section 7.

2   Related Work

The first consideration of cache memory as a covert channel to extract sensitive information was mentioned by Hu [14]. Later in 1998 Kesley et al. [16] mentioned the possiblity of applying the cache as a resource to perform attacks based on cache hit ratio. One theoretical example of cache attacks was studied later in 2002 by Page [20]. One year later, Tsunoo et al. [27] investigated timing side channel attacks due to internal table look up operations in the cipher that affect the cache behavior. Over the last decade, a great number of research has been done in the field of cache-based side-channel attacks. One of the studies is the time driven attack that was done by Bernstein when he observed that non-constant time implementations of cryptographic algorithms leak sensitive information in terms of time which can be used to extract the secret key [8]. His target was the OpenSSL implementation of the cryptographic algorithm AES. Neve further analyzes Bernstein's attack and the causes for observed timing variations in his PhD thesis [17]. Bonneau and Mironov's study [9] shows how to exploit cache collisions in AES as a source for time leakage.

Trace driven attacks were investigated by Osvik et al. [19] where they tried the *prime and probe* attack on AES. In the aforementioned study, a *spy process* fills the cache with attacker's own data and then waits for the victim to run the encryption. When the encryption is finished, the attacker tries to access her own data and measures the access time to see which cache lines have been evicted from the cache. Then, comparing the access times with the reference ones, attacker discovers which cache lines were used. In the same study, authors also analyze *evict+time* method that consists of triggering two encryptions of the same plaintext and accessing some cache lines after the first encryption to see which lines are again loaded by the second encryption. In the same line, Acıiçmez and Koç [5] investigated a collision timing attack in the first and the second round of AES. Also, in another study done by Gullasch et al. [13] *flush+reload* is used to attack AES encryption by blocking the execution of AES after each memory access.

Even though AES is a popular target for side-channel cache attacks, it is not the only target. Acıiçmez in [4] was the first one discovering that the instruction cache as well as the data cache leaked information when performing RSA encryption. Brumley and Boneh performed a practical attack against RSA in [10]. Later Chen et al. developed the trace driven instruction cache attacks on RSA. Finally Yarom et al. were the first ones proposing a *flush+reload* attack on RSA using the instruction cache [33]. Finally, again Yarom et al. used the *Flush+Reload* technique to recover the secret key from a ECDSA signature algorithm [32].

In a cloud environment, several studies have been conducted with the aim of breaking the isolation between co-located VMs to perform side-channel attacks. In 2009, Ristenpart et al. [21] demonstrated that it is possible to solve the co-location problem in the cloud environment and extract sensitive data from a targeted VM. In the study, Amazon's EC2 servers were targeted and using their IP addresses provided by Amazon, VMs were mapped to various types of cloud instances. Using a large set of IP-instance type matches and some network delay timing measurements, they were able to identify where a particular target VM is likely to reside, and then instantiate new VMs until one becomes co-resident with the target VM. Along with the placement information, they exploited Amazon EC2's sequential placement policy and were able to co-locate two VMs on a single physical machine with 8% probability. Even further, the authors show how cache contention between co-located Xen VMs may be exploited to deduce keystrokes with high success probability. By solving the co-location problem, this initial result fueled further research in Cross-VM side-channel attacks.

After solving the co-location problem, stealing fine grain secret information from a target turns into an ordinary side-channel cache attack. In 2012, Zhang et al. [34] presented an access-driven side-channel attack implemented across Xen VMs that manages to extract fine-grain information from a victim VM.

In the study, authors managed to recover an ElGamal decryption key from a victim VM using a cache timing attack. The significance of this work, is that for the first time the authors were able to extract *fine grain* information across VMs—in contrast to the earlier work of Ristenpart et al. [21] who managed to extract keystroke patterns. Later, Yarom et al. in [33] suggested that their attack could be used in a virtualized environment but they never tried it in a real cloud environment. Again, for the AES case, Weiss et al. used Bernstein's attack on an ARM system in a virtualized environment to extract information about AES encryption keys [31].

Finally in 2014 Irazoqui et al. [15] implemented Bernstein's attack for the first time in a virtualized environment where Xen and VMware VMMs with cross-VM setting were used. In the study, authors were able to recover AES secret key from co-resident VM running AES encryption using the timing difference between cache line accesses. The downside of the attack was that average of 2^{29} encryption samples were needed for the attack to work which takes about 4-5 hours on a modern Core i5 platform.

3   Cache-Based Side-Channel Attacks

In this work we demonstrate a fine-grain cross-VM attack that one might use in the real world. We not only want the attack to allow us to recover fine-grain information, but also work in a reasonable amount of time, with assumptions one can fulfill rather easily on cloud systems. Since Bernstein's attack [8] numerous trace-driven, access-driven and time-driven attacks have been introduced mainly targeting AES implementations. We will employ a new variant: **the flush and reload attack** on AES. In what follows we explain the basics of cache side-channel attacks, and briefly review the many cache side-channel attacks that have been used to attack AES.

Cache Architecture. The cache architecture consists of a hierarchy of memory components located between the CPU cores and the RAM. The purpose of the cache is to reduce the average access time to the main memory by exploiting locality principles. When the CPU needs to fetch data from memory, it queries the cache memory first to check if the data is in the cache. If it is, then it can be accessed with much smaller delay and in this case it is said that a cache *hit* has occurred. When the data is not present in the cache, it needs to be fetched from a higher-level cache or even from main memory. This results in greater delays. This case is referred to as a cache *miss*. When a cache miss occurs, the CPU retrieves the data from the memory and a copy is stored in the cache. The CPU loads bigger blocks of data, including data in nearby locations, to take advantage of *spatial locality*. Loading the whole block of data improves the execution performance because values stored in nearby locations to the originally accessed data are likely to be accessed.

The cache is organized into fixed sized *cache lines*, e.g of l bytes each. A cache line represents the partitions of the data that can be retrieved or written at a time when accessing the cache. When an entry of a table stored in memory is accessed for the first time, the memory line containing the retrieved data is loaded into the cache. If the process tries to access to the same data from the same memory line again, the access time will be significantly lower, i.e. a cache hit occurs. Therefore—for a cryptographic process—the encryption *time* depends directly on the accessed table positions, which in turn depend on the secret internal state of the cipher. This timing information can be exploited to gain information about the secret key that is being used in the encryption. Also, in case that there are no empty (invalid) cache lines available, one of the data bearing lines gets reallocated to open up space for the the incoming line. Therefore, cache lines that are not recently accessed are *evicted* from cache.

Exploiting Cache Timing Information. Up until this point, we established that a cache miss takes more time to be processed than a cache hit. Using the resulting *state-dependent* timing information, an attacker can obtain sensitive information from an encryption process and use this information to recover information about the secret key, eventually resulting in a full key recovery. The runtime of a fast software implementation of a cipher like AES [18] often heavily depends on the speed at which table look ups are performed. A popular implementation style for the AES is the T table implementation of AES [11] which combines the SubBytes, ShiftRows and MixColumns operations into one single table look up per state byte, along with XOR operations. This operation is called the *TableLookUp* operation. The advantage of this implementation style is that it allows the computation of one round using only table look-ups and XOR operations which is much faster than performing the actual finite-field arithmetic and logic operations. Compared to using standard S-boxes, T table based implementations use more memory, but the encryption time is significantly reduced, especially on 32-bit CPUs. For this reason, *almost all* of the current software implementations of the AES encryption for high-performance CPUs are T table implementations.

Note that the index of the loaded table entry is determined by a byte of the cipher state. Hence, information on which table values have been loaded into cache can reveal information about the secret state of AES. Such information can be retrieved by monitoring the cache directly, as done in *trace-driven* cache attacks. Similar information can also be learned by observing the timing behavior of multiple AES executions over time, as done in *time-driven* cache attacks. Finally, there are *access driven* cache attacks, which require the attacker to learn which cache lines have been accessed (like trace-driven attacks), but (like timing-driven attacks) do not require detailed knowledge on when and in what order the data was accessed. So the difference between these classes of attacks is the attacker's access capabilities:

- **Time driven attacks** are the least restrictive type with the only assumption that the attacker can observe the aggregated timing profile of a full execution of a target cipher.
- **Trace driven** attacks assume the attacker has access to the cache profile when the targeted program is running.
- **Access driven** attacks assume only to know which sets of the cache have been accessed during the execution of a program.

The attacks presented in this paper belong to a sub-class of *access-driven* cache attacks, which we discuss next.

3.1   The Flush+Reload Technique

The *Flush+Reload* attack is a powerful cache-based side-channel attack technique first proposed in [13], but was first named in [33]. It can be classified as an access driven cache attack. It usually employs a spy process to ascertain if specific cache lines have been accessed or not by the code under attack. Gullasch et al. [13] first used this spy process on AES, although the authors did not brand their attack as *Flush+Reload* at the time. Here we briefly explain how *Flush+Reload* works. The attack is carried out by a spy process which works in 3 stages:

Flushing stage: In this stage, the attacker uses the `clflush` command to flush the desired memory lines from the cache hence make sure that they have to be retrieved from the main memory next time they need to be accessed. We have to remark here that the `clflush` command does not only flush the memory line from the cache hierarchy of the corresponding working core, but it flushes from all the caches of all the cores in the PC. This is an important point: if it only flushed the corresponding core's caches, the attack would only work if the attacker and victim's processes were co-residing on the same core. This would have required a much stronger assumption than just being in the same physical machine.

Target accessing stage: In this stage the attacker waits until the target runs a fragment of code, which might use the memory lines that have been flushed in the first stage.

Reloading stage: In this stage the attacker reloads again the previously flushed memory lines and measures the time it takes to reload. Depending on the reloading time, the attacker decides whether the victim accessed the memory line in which case the memory line would be present in the cache or if the victim did not access the corresponding memory line in which case the memory line will not be present in the cache. The timing difference between a cache hit and a cache miss makes the aforementioned access easily detectable by the attacker.

The fact that the attacker and the victim processes do not reside on the same core is not a problem for the *Flush+Reload* attack because even though there can exist some isolation at various levels of the cache, in most systems there is some level shared between all the cores present in the physical machine. Therefore, through this shared level of cache (typically the L3 cache), one can still distinguish between accesses to the main memory.

4   Memory Deduplication

Memory deduplication is an optimization technique that was originally introduced to improve the memory utilization of VMMs. It later found its way into common non-virtualized OSs as well. Deduplication works by recognizing processes (or VMs) that place the same data in memory. This frequently happens when two processes use the same shared libraries. The deduplication feature eliminates multiple copies from memory and allows the data to be shared between users and processes. This method is especially effective in virtual machine environments where multiple guest OSs co-reside on the same physical machine and share the physical memory. Consequently, variations of memory deduplication technology are now implemented in both the VMware [28,29] and the KVM [3] VMMs. Since KVM converts linux kernel into a hypervisor, it directly uses KSM as page sharing technique, whereas VMware uses what is called Transparent Page Sharing(TPS). Although they have different names, their mechanism is very similar; the hypervisor looks for identical pages between VMs and when it finds a collision, it merges them into one single page.

Even though the deduplication optimization method saves memory and thus allows more virtual machines to run on the host system, it also opens door to side-channel attacks. While the data in the cache cannot be modified or corrupted by an adversary, parallel access rights can be exploited to reveal secret information about processes executing in the target VM. Also, an adversary can *prime* the cache and wait for the victim to access some of this primed data. The accessed/replaced cache data reveals information about the victims behavior. In this study, we will focus on the Linux implementation of Kernel Samepage Merging (KSM) memory deduplication feature and on TPS mechanism implemented by VMware.

4.1   KSM (Kernel Same-page Merging)

KSM is the Linux memory deduplication feature implementation that first appeared in Linux kernel version 2.6.32 [3]. In this implementation, KSM kernel daemon ksmd, scans the user memory for potential pages to be shared among users [7]. Also, since it would be CPU intensive and time consuming, instead of scanning the whole memory continuously, KSM scans only the potential candidates and creates signatures for these pages. These signatures are kept in the deduplication table. When two or more pages with the same signature are found, they are cross-checked completely to determine if they are identical. To create signatures, the KSM scans the memory at 20 msec intervals and at best only scans the 25% of the potential memory pages at a time. This is why any memory disclosure attack, including ours, has to wait for a certain time before the deduplication takes effect upon which the attack can be performed. During the memory search, the KSM analyzes three types of memory pages [25];

- **Volatile Pages**: Where the contents of the memory change frequently and should not be considered as a candidate for memory sharing.
- **Unshared Pages**: Candidate pages for deduplication where are the areas that the *madvise* system call advises to the ksmd to be likely candidates for merging.
- **Shared Pages**: Deduplicated pages that are shared between users or processes.

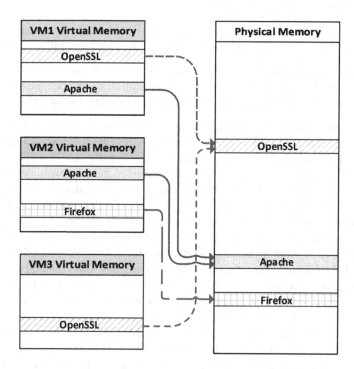

Fig. 1. Memory Deduplication Feature

When a duplicate page signature is found among candidates and the contents are cross-checked, ksmd automatically tags one of the duplicate pages with copy-on-write (COW) tag and shares it between the processes/users while the other copy is eliminated. Experimental implementations [3] show that using this method, it is possible to run over 50 Windows XP VMs with 1GB of RAM each on a physical machine with just 16GB of RAM. As a result of this, the power consumption and system cost is significantly reduced for systems with multiple users.

5 CFS-free Flush+Reload Attack on AES

In this section we will describe the principles of our *Flush+Reload* attack on the C-implementation of AES in OpenSSL. In [13] Gullasch et al. described a *Flush+Reload* attack on AES implementation of the OpenSSL library. However in this study, we are going to use the *Flush+Reload* method with some modifications that from our point of view, have clear advantages over [13]. Prior to the comparison with other cache side channel attacks, a detailed explanation of our *Flush+Reload* spy process is given along with the attack steps. We consider two scenarios: the attack as a spy process running in the same OS instance as the victim (as done in [13]), and the attack running as a cross-VM attack in a virtualized environment.

5.1 Description of the Attack

As in prior *Flush+Reload* attacks, we assume that the adversary can monitor accesses to a given cache line. However, unlike the attack in [13], this attack

- only requires the monitoring of a *single* memory line; and
- flushing can be done before encryption, reloading after encryption, i.e. the adversary does not need to interfere with or interrupt the attacked process.

More concretely, the Linux kernel features a completely fair scheduler which tries to evenly distribute CPU time to processes. Gullasch et al. [13] exploited Completely Fair Scheduler (CFS) [1], by overloading the CPU while a victim AES encryption process is running. They managed to gain control over the CPU and suspend the AES process thereby gaining an opportunity to monitor cache accesses of the victim process. Our attack is agnostic to CFS and does not require time consuming overloading steps to gain access to the cache.

We assume the adversary monitors accesses to a single line of one of the T tables of an AES implementation, preferably a T table that is used in the last round of AES. Without loss of generality, let's assume the adversary monitors the memory line corresponding to the first positions of table T, where T is the lookup table applied to the targeted state byte s_i, where s_i is the i-th byte of the AES state before the last round. Let's also assume that a memory line can hold n T table values, e.g, the first n T table positions for our case. If s_i is equal to one of the indices of the monitored T table entries in the memory line (i.e. $s_i \in \{0, \ldots, n\}$ if the memory line contains the first n T table entries) then the monitored memory line will with very high probability be present in the cache (since it has been accessed by the encryption process). However, if s_i takes different values, the monitored memory line is not loaded in this step. Nevertheless, since each T table is accessed l times (for AES-128 in OpenSSL, $l = 40$ per T_j), there is still a probability that the memory line was loaded by any of the other accesses. In both cases, all that happens after the T table lookup is a possible reordering of bytes (due to AES's Shift_Rows), followed by the last round key addition. Since the last round key is always the same for s_i, the n values are mapped to n specific and constant ciphertext byte values. This means that for n out of 256 ciphertext values, the monitored memory line will *always* have been loaded by the AES operation, while for the remaining $256 - n$ values the probability of having been reloaded is smaller. In fact, the probability that the specific T table memory line i has not been accessed by the encryption process is given as:

$$\Pr\left[\text{no access to } T[i]\right] = \left(1 - \frac{t}{256}\right)^l$$

Here, l is the number of accesses to the specific T table. For OpenSSL 1.0.1 AES-128 we have $l = 40$. If we assume that each memory line can hold $t = 8$ entries per cache line, we have $\Pr\left[\text{no access to } T[i]\right] = 28\%$. Therefore it is easily distinguishable whether the memory line is accessed or not. Indeed, this turns out to be the case as confirmed by our experiments.

Algorithm 1. Recovery algorithm for key byte k_0

Input : X_0 //Reload vector for ciphertext byte 0

Output: k_0 //Correct key byte 0

forall $x_j \in X_0$ do
  //Threshold for values with low reload counter.
  if $x_j < Low\_counter\_threshold$ then
    for $s = 0$ to n do
      //xor with each value of the targeted T table memory line
      $K_0[j \oplus T[s]]$++;
    end
  end
end
return $\mathrm{argmax}_k(K_0[k])$;

In order to distinguish the two cases, all that is necessary is to measure the timing for the *reload* of the targeted memory line. If the line was accessed by the AES encryption, the reload is quick; else it takes more time. Based on a threshold that we will empirically choose from our measurements, we expect to distinguish main memory accesses from L3 cache accesses. For each possible value of the ciphertext byte c_i we count how often either case occurs. Now, for n ciphertext values (the ones corresponding to the monitored T table memory line) the memory line has always been reloaded by AES, i.e. the reload counter is (close to) zero. These n ciphertext values are related to the state as follows:

$$c_i = k_i \oplus T\left[s_{[i]}\right] \tag{1}$$

where the $s_{[i]}$ can take n consecutive values. Note that Eq. (1) describes the last round of AES. The brackets in the index of the state byte $s_{[i]}$ indicate the reordering due to the Shift_Rows operation. For the other values of c_i, the reload counter is significantly higher. Given the n values of c_i with a low reload counter, we can solve Eq. (1) for the key byte k_i, since the indices $s_{[i]}$ as well as the table output values $T\left[s_{[i]}\right]$ are known for the monitored memory line. In fact, we get n possible key candidates for each c_i with a zero reload counter. The correct key is the only one that all n valid values for c_i have in common.

A general description of the key recovery algorithm is given in Algorithm 1, where key byte number 0 is recovered from the ciphertext values corresponding to n low reload counter values that were recovered from the measurements. Again, n is the number of T table positions that a memory line holds. The *reload vector* $X_i = [x(0), x(1), \ldots, x(255)]$ holds the reload counter values $x(j)$ for each ciphertext value $c_i = j$. Finally K_0 is the vector that, for each key byte candidate k, tracks the number of appearances in the key recovery step.

Example Assume that the memory line can hold $n = 4$ T table values and we want to recover key byte k_0. There are four ciphertext values detected with a low reload counter. Assume further that each c_0 has been xored with the T table values of the monitored memory line (the first 4 if we are working with the first positions), giving $k_0^{(i)} = c_0^i \oplus T[s_{[0]}]$. For each of the four possibilities of c_0, there are $n = 4$ possible solutions for k_0. If the results are the following:

$$k_0^{(0)} \begin{cases} 43 \\ ba \\ 91 \\ 17 \end{cases} k_0^{(1)} \begin{cases} 8b \\ 91 \\ f3 \\ 66 \end{cases} k_0^{(2)} \begin{cases} 91 \\ 45 \\ 22 \\ af \end{cases} k_0^{(3)} \begin{cases} cd \\ 02 \\ 51 \\ 91 \end{cases}$$

And since there is only one common solution between all of them, which is 91, we deduce that the correct key value is $k_0 = 91$. This also means that $K_0[91] = 4$, since $k = 91$ appeared four times as possible key candidate in the key recovery step.

Note that this is a *generic attack* that would apply virtually to any table-based block cipher implementation. That is, our attack can easily be adapted to other block ciphers as long as their last round consists of a table look-up with a subsequent key addition.

5.2 Recovering the Full Key

To recover the full key, the attack is expanded to all tables used in the last round, e.g. the 4 T tables of AES in `OpenSSL 1.0.1`. For each ciphertext byte it is known which T table is used in the final round of the encryption. This means that the above attack can be repeated on each byte, by simply analyzing the collecting ciphertexts and their timings for each of the ciphertext bytes individually. As before, the timings are profiled according to the value that each ciphertext byte c_i takes in each of the encryptions, and are stored in a ciphertext byte vector. The attack process is described in Algorithm 2. In a nutshell, the algorithm monitors the first T table memory line of all used tables and hence stores four reload values per observed ciphertext. Note that, this is a *known ciphertext attack* and therefore all that is needed is a flush of one memory line before one encryption. There is no need for the attacker to gain access to plaintexts.

Finally the attacker should apply Algorithm 1 to each of the obtained ciphertext reload vectors. Recall that each ciphertext reload vector uses a different T table, so the right corresponding T table should be applied in the key recovery algorithm.

Performing the Attack. In the following we provide the details about the process followed during the attack.

Step 1: Acquire information about the offset of T tables. The attacker has to know the offset of the T tables with respect to the beginning of the library. With that information, the attacker can refer and point to any memory line that holds T table values even when the ASLR is activated. This means that some reverse engineering work has to be done prior to the attack. This can be done in a debugging step where the offset of the addresses of the four T tables are recovered.

Algorithm 2. Flush and reload algorithm extended to 16 ciphertext bytes

---

Input   : $T0_0, T1_0, T2_0, T3_0$ //Addresses of each T table

Output: $X_0, X_1, ... X_{15}$ //Reload vectors for ciphertext bytes
                                 //Each X_k holds 256 counter values

while *iteration < total number of measurements* **do**
$\quad$ clflush($T0_0, T1_0, T2_0, T3_0$);   //Flush data to the main memory
$\quad$ ciphertext=Encryption(plaintext); //No need to store plaintext!
$\quad$ **for** $i \leftarrow T0_0$ **to** $T3_0$ **do**
$\quad\quad$ time=Reload(i);
$\quad\quad$ **if** *time > AccessThreshold* **then**
$\quad\quad\quad$ Addcounter(T_i, X_i);   //Increase counter of X_i using T_i
$\quad\quad$ **end**
$\quad$ **end**
end
return $X_0, X_1, \ldots, X_{15}$

Step 2: Collect Measurements. In this step, the attacker requests encryptions and applies *Flush+Reload* between each encryption. The information gained, i.e. Ti_0 was accessed or not, is stored together with the observed ciphertext. The attacker needs to observe several encryptions to get rid of the noise and to be able to recover the key. Note that, while the reload step must be performed and timed by the attacker, the flush might be performed by other processes running in the victim OS.

Step 3: Key recovery. In this final step, the attacker uses the collected measurements and his knowledge about the public T tables to recover the key. From this information, the attacker applies the steps detailed in Section 5.1 to recover the individual bytes of the key.

5.3   Attack Scenario 1: Spy Process

In this first scenario we will attack an encryption server running in the same OS as the spy process. The encryption server just receives encryption requests, encrypts a plaintext and sends the ciphertext back to the client. The server and the client are running on different cores. Thus, the attack consists in distinguishing accesses from the last level of cache, i.e. L3 cache, which is shared across cores. and the main memory. Clearly, if the attacker is able to distinguish accesses between last level of cache and main memory, it will be able to distinguish between L1 and main memory accesses whenever server and client co-reside in the same core. In this scenario, both the attacker and victim are using the same shared library. The KSM is responsible for merging those pages into one unified shared page. Therefore, the victim and attacker processes are linked through the KSM deduplication feature.

Our attack works as described in the previous section. First the attacker discovers the offset of the addresses of the T tables with respect to the begining of the library. Next, it issues encryption requests to the server, and receives the corresponding ciphertext. After each encryption, the attacker checks with the *Flush+Reload* technique whether the chosen T table values have been accessed. Once enough measurements have been acquired, the key recovery step is performed. As we will see in our results section, the whole process takes less than half a minute.

Our attack significantly improves on previous cache side-channel attacks such as *evict + time* or *prime and probe* [19]. Both attacks were based on spy processes targeting the L1 cache. A clear advantage of our attack is that —since it is targeting the last shared level cache— it works across cores. Of course both *evict + time* or *prime and probe* attacks can be applied to the last level of cache, but their performance would be significantly reduced in cross-core setting, due to the large number of evictions/probings that are needed for a successful attack.

A more realistic attack scenario was proposed earlier by Bernstein [8] where the attacker targets an encryption server. Our attack similarly works under a realistic scenario. However. unlike Bernstein's attack [8], our attack does not require a profiling phase that involves access to an identical implementation with a known-key. Finally, with respect to the previous *Flush+Reload* attack in AES, our attack does not need to interrupt the AES execution of the encryption server. We will compare different attacks according to the number of encryptions needed in Section 6.1.

5.4   Attack Scenario 2: Cross-VM Attack

In our second scenario the victim process is running in one virtual machine and the attacker in another one but on the same machine possibly on different cores. For the purposes of this study it is assumed that the co-location problem has been solved using the methods proposed in [21], ensuring the attacker and the victim are running on the same physical machine. The attack exploits memory overcommitment features that some VMMs such as VMware provide. In particular, we focus in memory deduplication. The VMM will search periodically for identical pages across VMs to merge both pages into a single page in the memory. Once this is done (without the intervention of the attacker) both the victim and the attacker will access the same portion of the physical memory enabling the attack. The attack process is the same as in Scenario 1. Moreover, we later show that the key is recovered in less than a minute, which makes the attack quite *practical*.

We discussed the improvements of our attack over previous proposals in the previous scenario except the most important one: We believe that the `evict+time`, `prime and probe` and time collision attacks will be rather difficult to carry out in real cloud environment. The first two are targeting the L1 cache, which is not shared across cores. The attacker would have to be in the same core as the victim, which is a much stronger assumption than being just in the same physical machine. Both `evict+time` and `prime and probe` could be applied to work with the L3 cache, but the noise and the amount of measurements would need to be drastically increased. Even further, due the increasing amount of source noises present in a cloud scenario (more layers, network latency) both `evict+time` and time collision attacks would be hard to perform. Finally, targeting the CFS [13] to evict the victim process, requires for the attacker's code to run in the same OS, which will certainly not be possible in a virtualized environment.

6   Experiment Setup and Results

We present results for both a spy process within the native machine as well as the cross-VM scenario. The target process is executed in Ubuntu 12.04 64 bits, kernel version 3.4, using the C-implementation of AES in `OpenSSL 1.0.1f` for encryption. This is used when `OpenSSL` is configured with `no-asm` and `no-hw` option. We want to remark that this *is not* the default option in the installation of `OpenSSL` in most of the products. All experiments were performed on a machine featuring an Intel i5-3320M four core clocked at 3.2GHz. The Core i5 has a three-level cache architecture: The L1 cache is 8-way associative, with 2^{15} bytes of size and a cache line size of 64 bytes. The level-2 cache is 8-way associative as well, with a cache line width of 64 bytes and a total size of 2^{18} bytes. The level-3 cache is 12-way associative with a total size of 2^{22} bytes and 64 bytes cache line size. It is important to note that each core has private L1 and L2 caches, but the L3 cache is shared among all cores. Together with the deduplication performed by the VMM, the shared L3 cache allows the adversary to learn about data accesses by the victim process.

The *attack scenario* is as follows: the victim process is an encryption server handling encryption requests through a socket connection and sends back the ciphertext, similar to Bernstein's setup in [8]. But unlike Bernstein's attack, where packages of at least 400 bytes were sent to deal with the noise, our server only receives packages of 16 bytes (the plaintext). The encryption key used by the the server is unknown to the attacker. The attack process sends encryption queries to the victim process. All measurements such as timing measurements of the reload step are done on the attacker side. The server uses `OpenSSL 1.0.1f` for the AES encryption. In our setup, each cache line holds 16 T table values, which results in a 7.6% probability for not accessing a memory line per encryption. All given attack results target only the first cache line of each T table, i.e. the first 16 values of each T table for flush and reload. Note that in the attack any memory line of the T table would work equally well. Both native and cross-VM attacks establish the threshold for selecting the correct ciphertext candidates for the working T table line by selecting those values which are below half of the average of overall timings for each ciphertext value. This is an empirical threshold that we set up after running some experiments as follows

$$\text{threshold} = \sum_{i=0}^{256} \frac{t_i}{2 \cdot 256} .$$

Spy Process Attack Setup: The attack process runs in the same OS as the victim process. The communication between the processes is carried out via

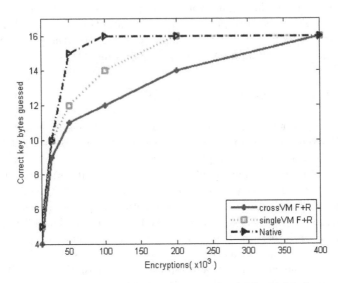

Fig. 2. Number of correct key bytes guessed of the AES-128 bit key vs. number of encryption requests. Even 50.000 encryptions (i.e. less than 5 seconds of interaction) result in significant security degradation in both the native machine as well as the cross-VM attack scenario.

localhost connection and measures timing using Read Time-Stamp Counters (`rdtsc`). The attack is set up to work across cores; the encryption server is running in a different core than the attacker. We believe that distinguishing between L3 and main memory accesses will be more susceptible to noise than distinguishing between L1 cache accesses and main memory accesses. Therefore while working with the L3 cache gives us a more realistic setting, it also makes the attack more challenging.

Cross-VM Attack Setup: In this attack we use VMware ESXI 5.5.0 build number 1623387 running Ubuntu 12.04 64-bits guest OSs. We know that VMware implements TPS with large pages (2 MB) or small pages (4 KB). We decided to use the later one, since it seems to be the default for most systems. Furthermore, as stated in [28], even if the large page sharing is selected, the VMM will still look for identical small pages to share. For the attack we used two virtual machines, one for the victim and one for the attacker. The communication between them is carried out over the local IP connection.

The results are presented in Figure 2 which plots the number of correctly recovered key bytes over the number of timed encryptions. The dash-dotted line shows that the spy-process scenario completely recovers the key after only 2^{17} encryptions. Prior to moving to the cross-VM scenario, a single VM scenario was performed to gauge the impact of using VMs. The dotted line shows that due to the noise introduced by virtualization we need to nearly double the number of encryptions to match the key recovery performance of the native case. The solid line gives the result for the cross-VM attack: 2^{19} observations are sufficient for stable full key recovery. The difference might be due to cpuid like instructions which are emulated by the hipervisor, therefore introducing more noise to the attack. In the worst case, both the native spy process and the single VM attack took around 25 seconds (for 400.000 encryptions). We believe that this is due to communication via the localhost connection. However when we perform a cross-VM attack it takes roughly twice as much time as in the previous cases. In this case we are performing the communication via local IPs that have to reach the router, which is believed to add the additional delay. This means that *all of the described attacks —even in the cross VM scenario— completely recover the key in less than one minute!*

6.1   Comparison to other Attacks

Next we compare the most commonly implemented cache-based side-channel attacks to the proposed attack. Results are shown in Table 1. It is difficult to compare the attacks, since most of them have been run on different platforms. Many of the prior attacks target OpenSSL's 0.9.8 version of AES. Most of these attacks exploit the fact that AES has a separate T Table for the last round, significantly reducing the noise introduced by cache miss accesses. Hence, attacks on OpenSSL0.9.8's AES usually succeed much faster, a trend confirmed by our attack results. Note that our attack, together with [6] and [15] are the only ones that have been run on a 64 bit processor. Moreover, we assume that due to undocumented internal states and advanced features such as hardware prefetchers, implementation on a 64 bit processor will add more noise than older platforms running the attack. With respect to the number of encryptions, we observe that the proposed attack has significant improvements over most of the previous attacks.

Spy Process in Native OS: Even though our attack runs in a noisier environment than Bernstein's attack, *evict and time*, and cache timing collision attacks, it shows better performance. Only *prime and probe* and *Flush+Reload* using CFS show either comparable or better performance. The proposed attack has better performance than *prime and probe* even though their measurements were performed with the attack and the encryption being run as one unique process. The *Flush+Reload* attack in [13] exploits a much stronger leakage, which requires that attacker **to interrupt the target AES between rounds** (an unrealistic assumption). Furthermore, *Flush+Reload* with CFS needs to monitor the entire T tables, while our attack only needs to monitor a single line of the cache, making the attack much more lightweight and subtle.

Cross-VM Attack: So far there is only one publication that has analyzed cache-based leakage across VMs for AES [15]. Our proposed attack shows dramatic improvements over [15], which needs 2^{29} encryptions (hours of run time) for a partial recovery of the key. Our attack only needs 2^{19} encryptions to recover the full key. Thus, while the attack presented in [15] needs to interact with the target

Table 1. Comparison of cache side-channel attack techniques against AES

Attack	Platform	Methodology	OpenSSL	Traces
Spy-Process based Attacks:				
Collision timing [9]	Pentium 4E	Time measurement	0.9.8a	300.000
Prime+probe [19]	Pentium 4E	L1 cache prime-probing	0.9.8a	16.000
Evict+time [19]	Athlon 64	L1 cache evicting	0.9.8a	500.000
Flush+reload (CFS) [13]	Pentium M	*Flush+reload* w/CFS	0.9.8m	100
Our attack	i5-3320M	L3 cache *Flush+reload*	0.9.8a	8.000
Bernstein [6]	Core2Duo	Time measurement	1.0.1c	2^{22}
Our attack	i5-3320M	L3 cache *Flush+reload*	1.0.1f	100.000
Cross-VM Attacks:				
Bernstein [15][1]	i5-3320M	Time measurement	1.0.1f	2^{30}
Our attack(VMware)	i5-3320M	L3 cache *Flush+reload*	1.0.1f[2]	400.000

[1] Only parts of the key were recovered, not the whole key.

[2] The AES implementation was not updated for the recently released OpenSSL 1.0.1g and 1.0.2 beta versions. So the results for those libraries are identical.

for several hours, our attack succeeds in under a minute and recovers the entire key. Note that, the CFS enabled *Flush+Reload* attack in [13] will not work in the cross-VM setting, since the attacker has no control over victim OS's CFS.

7   Countermeasures

AES-NI: Using AES-NI instructions solves the cache-access leakage for AES. In this case the AES encryption does not use the memory but it uses specific hardware instructions, avoiding the possibility of implementing a cache-based side-channel attack completely. However, AES is not the only symmetric cipher in use nowadays: the problem remains for other encryption algorithms for which hardware acceleration is not provided.

Cache Prefetching: Prefetching the T tables (or other table-based look-ups for other ciphers) prior to each AES round execution can mitigate the problem of using them as a source for side-channel attacks. An attacker cannot observe differences between access times if all T table values reside in the cache before the execution. However, since T tables have a total size of 4KB, this would require to fill a large portion of the cache. The prefetching also takes time, and this would increase the encryption time for AES. OpenSSL provides an assembly version of AES that uses this technique (among others like bit slicing and vector permutation) to avoid having cache leakage due to T table accesses.

Cache Flushing: Flushing each of the T table values after the AES execution will have the similar consequences as prefetching them before the execution [15].

When the attacker wants to decide whether a line has been accessed, he will find that the T tables are in the memory and therefore, he will not see any time differences. Again this implies a higher execution time. With such a counter-measure the only possibility left to the attacker is to block the AES execution during some of its rounds (as done in [13]). Hence, this would mitigate cross-VM attacks and require a more advanced attacker than we considered for our attack.

Restricting the Deduplication: Disabling the deduplication would make the attack impossible in the cloud however memory deduplication is highly per-formance beneficial, especially in cloud where multiple users share the same hardware. This is why we believe that the system designers should restrict the deduplication mechanism rather then completely disabling it. The `madvise` [12] system call that manages the deduplication process scans only selected portions of the memory. One can exploit this feature and limit the resource sharing be-tween VMs. This limitation can either be on hardware or software level. As suggested by Wang and Lee [30] the OS can enforce a smart process scheduling method to protect critical processes with sensitive data and make sure that they are never shared between VMs.

8   Conclusion

Flush+Reload in **AES: A New Fine Grain Attack:** Our experiments show that if applied in a clever way, *Flush+Reload* is a fine grain attack on AES and can recover the whole key. Furthermore, the attack can be applied to any block cipher that uses a T table based implementation. The attack has to take advantage of deduplication so that victim and attacker share the same memory.

Making The Attack Feasible in The Cloud: We not only performed the attack in native machine, but also in a cloud-like cross-VM scenario. Although there is more noise in the latter scenario, the attack recovers the key with just 400.000 encryptions. In this case, the attacker has to take advantage of some memory sharing mechanism (such as TPS in VMware).

Lightning-Fast Attack: Even in the worst case scenario (cross-VM) the attack succeeds in less than a minute. To the best of our knowledge, no faster attack has been implemented against AES in a *realistic* cloud-like setting. This also means that just one minute of co-location with the encryption server suffices to recover the key.

Acknowledgments. This work is supported by the National Science Founda-tion, under grant CNS-1318919 and CNS-1314770. We would like to thank the anonymous reviewers of RAID 2014 for their helpful comments, in particular for pointing out that disabling the ASLR on the attacker's side is not needed. We would like to thank Dan Bernstein for his helpful comments on the related work and history of cache attacks as well as Huzaifa Sidhpurwala for pointing out the partially protected assembly implementations of AES in OpenSSL.

References

1. CFS Scheduler (April 2014), https://www.kernel.org/doc/Documentation/scheduler/sched-design-CFS.txt
2. Kernel Based Virtual Machine (April 2014), http://www.linux-kvm.org/page/Main_Page
3. Kernel Samepage Merging (April 2014), http://kernelnewbies.org/Linux_2_6_32#head-d3f32e41df508090810388a57efce73f52660ccb/
4. Acıiçmez, O.: Yet Another MicroArchitectural Attack: Exploiting I-Cache. In: Proceedings of the 2007 ACM Workshop on Computer Security Architecture, CSAW 2007, pp. 11–18. ACM, New York (2007)
5. Acıiçmez, O., Koç, Ç.K.: Trace-driven cache attacks on AES (short paper). In: Ning, P., Qing, S., Li, N. (eds.) ICICS 2006. LNCS, vol. 4307, pp. 112–121. Springer, Heidelberg (2006)
6. Aly, H., ElGayyar, M.: Attacking AES Using Bernstein's Attack on Modern Processors. In: Youssef, A., Nitaj, A., Hassanien, A.E. (eds.) AFRICACRYPT 2013. LNCS, vol. 7918, pp. 127–139. Springer, Heidelberg (2013)
7. Arcangeli, A., Eidus, I., Wright, C.: Increasing memory density by using KSM. In: Proceedings of the Linux Symposium, pp. 19–28 (2009)
8. Bernstein, D.J.: Cache-timing attacks on AES (2004), http://cr.yp.to/papers.html#cachetiming
9. Bonneau, J., Mironov, I.: Cache-Collision Timing Attacks against AES. In: Goubin, L., Matsui, M. (eds.) CHES 2006. LNCS, vol. 4249, pp. 201–215. Springer, Heidelberg (2006)
10. Brumley, D., Boneh, D.: Remote Timing Attacks are Practical. In: Proceedings of the 12th USENIX Security Symposium, pp. 1–14 (2003)
11. Daemen, J., Rijmen, V.: The Design of Rijndael. Springer (2002)
12. Eidus, I., Dickins, H.: How to use the Kernel Samepage Merging feature (November 2009), https://www.kernel.org/doc/Documentation/vm/ksm.txt
13. Gullasch, D., Bangerter, E., Krenn, S.: Cache Games – Bringing Access-Based Cache Attacks on AES to Practice. In: IEEE Symposium on Security and Privacy, pp. 490–505 (2011)
14. Hu, W.-M.: Lattice scheduling and covert channels. In: Proceedings of the 1992 IEEE Symposium on Security and Privacy, SP 1992, p. 52. IEEE Computer Society, Washington, DC (1992)
15. Irazoqui, G., Inci, M.S., Eisenbarth, T., Sunar, B.: Fine grain Cross-VM Attacks on Xen and VMware are possible, https://eprint.iacr.org/2014/248.pdf
16. Kelsey, J., Schneier, B., Wagner, D., Hall, C.: Side Channel Cryptanalysis of Product Ciphers. J. Comput. Secur. 8(2,3), 141–158 (2000)
17. Neve, M.: Cache-based Vulnerabilities and SPAM analysis. Doctor thesis, UCL (2006)
18. National Institute of Standards and Technology. Advanced Encryption Standard. NIST FIPS PUB 197 (2001)
19. Osvik, D.A., Shamir, A., Tromer, E.: Cache Attacks and Countermeasures: The Case of AES. In: Pointcheval, D. (ed.) CT-RSA 2006. LNCS, vol. 3860, pp. 1–20. Springer, Heidelberg (2006)
20. Page, D.: Theoretical Use of Cache Memory as a Cryptanalytic Side-Channel (2002)
21. Ristenpart, T., Tromer, E., Shacham, H., Savage, S.: Hey, You, Get off of My Cloud: Exploring Information Leakage in Third-party Compute Clouds. In: Proceedings of the 16th ACM Conference on Computer and Communications Security, CCS 2009, pp. 199–212. ACM, New York (2009)

22. Suzaki, K., Iijima, K., Toshiki, Y., Artho, C.: Implementation of a Memory Disclosure Attack on Memory Deduplication of Virtual Machines. Communications and Computer Sciences 96(1), 215–224 (2013)
23. Suzaki, K., Iijima, K., Yagi, T., Artho, C.: Memory deduplication as a threat to the guest OS. In: Proceedings of the Fourth European Workshop on System Security, p. 1. ACM (2011)
24. Suzaki, K., Iijima, K., Yagi, T., Artho, C.: Software side channel attack on memory deduplication. SOSP POSTER (2011)
25. Suzaki, K., Iijima, K., Yagi, T., Artho, C.: Effects of Memory Randomization, Sanitization and Page Cache on Memory Deduplication
26. The OpenSSL Project. OpenSSL: The open source toolkit for SSL/TLS (April 2003), http://www.openssl.org
27. Tsunoo, Y., Saito, T., Suzaki, T., Shigeri, M., Miyauchi, H.: Cryptanalysis of DES implemented on computers with cache. In: Walter, C.D., Koç, Ç.K., Paar, C. (eds.) CHES 2003. LNCS, vol. 2779, pp. 62–76. Springer, Heidelberg (2003)
28. VMware. Understanding Memory Resource Management in VMware vSphere 5.0, http://www.vmware.com/files/pdf/mem_mgmt_perf_vsphere5.pdf
29. Waldspurger, C.A.: Memory resource management in VMware ESX server. ACM SIGOPS Operating Systems Review 36(SI), 181–194 (2002)
30. Wang, Z., Lee, R.B.: Covert and side channels due to processor architecture. In: 22nd Annual Computer Security Applications Conference, ACSAC 2006, pp. 473–482. IEEE (2006)
31. Weiß, M., Heinz, B., Stumpf, F.: A Cache Timing Attack on AES in Virtualization Environments. In: Keromytis, A.D. (ed.) FC 2012. LNCS, vol. 7397, pp. 314–328. Springer, Heidelberg (2012)
32. Yarom, Y., Benger, N.: Recovering OpenSSL ECDSA Nonces Using the FLUSH+RELOAD Cache Side-channel Attack. Cryptology ePrint Archive, Report 2014/140 (2014), http://eprint.iacr.org/
33. Yarom, Y., Falkner, K.E.: Flush+Reload: a High Resolution, Low Noise, L3 Cache Side-Channel Attack. IACR Cryptology ePrint Archive, 448 (2013)
34. Zhang, Y., Juels, A., Reiter, M.K., Ristenpart, T.: Cross-VM Side Channels and Their Use to Extract Private Keys. In: Proceedings of the 2012 ACM Conference on Computer and Communications Security, CCS 2012, pp. 305–316. ACM, New York (2012)

Count Me In: Viable Distributed Summary Statistics for Securing High-Speed Networks

Johanna Amann[1], Seth Hall[1,2], and Robin Sommer[1,2]

[1] International Computer Science Institute
[2] Lawrence Berkeley National Laboratory

Abstract. Summary statistics represent a key primitive for profiling and protecting operational networks. Many network operators routinely measure properties such as throughput, traffic mix, and heavy hitters. Likewise, security monitoring often deploys statistical anomaly detectors that trigger, e.g., when a source scans the local IP address range, or exceeds a threshold of failed login attempts. Traditionally, a diverse set of tools is used for such computations, each typically hard-coding either the features it operates on or the specific calculations it performs, or both. In this work we present a novel framework for calculating a wide array of summary statistics in real-time, independent of the underlying data, and potentially aggregated from independent monitoring points. We focus on providing a transparent, extensible, easy-to-use interface and implement our design on top of an open-source network monitoring system. We demonstrate a set of example applications for profiling and statistical anomaly detection that would traditionally require significant effort and different tools to compute. We have released our implementation under BSD license and report experiences from real-world deployments in large-scale network environments.

1 Introduction

Researchers and operators alike routinely measure statistical properties of network traffic, such as throughput, traffic mix, and "heavy hitters"; both for traffic profiling and control, as well as for specific security purposes when aiming to spot activity that "doesn't look right". For the latter, statistical anomaly detection proves particularly valuable by reporting activity that exceeds levels one would normally expect so see, such as during port and address scans, login brute-forcing, and application-layer vulnerability probing. Traditionally, we find a diverse set of approaches in use for implementing such monitoring, typically limited to traffic features readily available in existing data sets such as NetFlow records, SNMP counters, IDS output, or system logs; and often implemented in the form of ad-hoc shell scripts processing files offline in batches. While conceptually most profiling and anomaly detection tasks leverage just a rather small set of statistical primitives, existing approaches tend to hard-code either the feature set they operate on or the specific computation they perform; and regularly both. Consequently, sites find it challenging to later adapt a setup to changes in

A. Stavrou et al. (Eds.): RAID 2014, LNCS 8688, pp. 320–340, 2014.
© Springer International Publishing Switzerland 2014

requirements, miss out on opportunities for reuse in different settings, and see little incentive to optimize an implementation for performance.

In this work we present a novel *summary statistics framework* that facilitates a wide array of typical profiling tasks and security applications. Our system processes high-volume packet streams in real-time, operates transparently on arbitrary features extracted from all levels of the protocol stack, and aggregates results across independent monitoring points distributed across a network. We focus on providing a transparent, easy-to-use user interface that, in particular, hides the communication in distributed setups behind a simple, intent-based API. We target operational deployment in large-scale network environments, with link capacities of 10 GE and beyond; and we implement our design on top of an existing open-source network monitoring system that is regularly deployed in such settings. Our implementation includes a set of probabilistic data structures to support memory-efficient operation, as well as a plugin interface that allows users to extend the supplied range of statistical primitives. We demonstrate a number of real-world example security applications, including computation of traffic matrices, detection of IP scans and SQL injection, and real-time "top-k" measurements to determine, e.g., the most frequent hosts, HTTP destinations, or DNS requests. We furthermore interface the latter to a browser-based visualization library that renders the current "heavy hitters" in real-time for immediate inspection. We evaluate our system in terms of the overhead it imposes on the underlying network monitor with regards to CPU, memory, and inter-node communication; and we find it to scale well in realistic settings. We have released our implementation as open-source software under a BSD-license as part of the recent release of the underlying network monitor. It is in deployment now at a broad range of sites, where it helps operations to protect their networks.

We structure the remainder of this paper as follows. §2 presents the motivation and design of the summary statistics framework, and §3 describes our implementation. §4 demonstrates a number of real-world example applications, along with experiences from operational deployments. In §5 we asses performance characteristics. §6 discusses related work, and we conclude in §7.

2   Design

Our work introduces a novel summary statistics framework that offers a flexible platform to compute a wide variety of summary statistics in large-scale operational network environments. In the following we first review the underlying motivation and then walk through a number of design aspects for the framework.

2.1   Motivation

While summary statistics constitute a crucial ingredient for many operational network monitoring tasks, existing implementations generally cater to a specific application or setting (see §6). Our framework instead aims to enable users to define their *own* statistics, with no limitation on what input or computation to use. The challenge with this approach lies in designing a system that provides such flexibility while also offering the efficiency required to accommodate large-scale deployment in high-performance settings.

To illustrate our motivation, consider the task of counting. Researchers and operators alike tend to ask questions about their networks such as "How many local IP addresses do we see?", "What system produces the most traffic?", "What are the prevalent application protocols?", and "Is there any host unsuccessfully querying a large number of DNS names?". Traditionally, answering such questions requires using a variety of different tools. While conceptually these questions all come down to counting features, they process conceptually quite different information, from packet-level information like IP addresses to complex application-layer attributes such as rejected DNS requests. Our goal is to unify the computing of such results within a single system that decouples feature extraction from the statistical infrastructure, providing users with a platform for answering a wide range of their questions.

From experience with research and operations, we identify two overall types of applications that network-based statistics tend to support: *(i) network profiling* aims to answer questions as sketched above for characterizing ongoing activity; and *(ii) statistical anomaly detection* identifies situations where observed features exceed an expected range, potentially leading to a security incident. Regarding the former, while the range of possible profiling tasks is large, most consist of a rather small set of computational primitives, such as summation and aggregation of values, standard set operations, computing simple measures such as maximum and average, and also sorting. Turning to statistical anomaly detection, one typically finds conceptually simple measures deployed operationally; often just straight-forward threshold schemes that trigger when activity exceeds a predetermined value or ratio. The most common application is scan detection, which finds hosts probing the local network by spotting an excessive number of failed attempts. While traditionally scan detection refers to IP address or TCP/UDP port probing, the concept extends to application-layer features as well, including probing web servers with requests, email servers with destination addresses, DNS servers with lookups, and also probing for vulnerable systems by trying application-layer exploits. While many monitoring systems support profiling and/or statistical anomaly detection, their implementations typically hardcode either the feature set they operate on or the specific calculation they perform.

2.2 Objectives

We identify the following objectives for our summary statistics framework.

Simple, Yet Flexible User Interface. The interface that the framework exposes to the user should be easy to understand and use, yet sufficiently flexible to support computation of a wide range of target statistics.

Data Agnostic. The framework should be data agnostic and avoid imposing any constraints on the features it operates on.

Extensibility. The available statistical functionality should be adaptable and extensible to computations not supported out-of-the-box.

Real-Time Operation. The framework should process input in real-time and provide results, including alarms, as quickly as possible.

Scalability. The framework needs to scale to large networks, including support for multiple traffic sources for either distributed monitoring or load-balancing purposes.

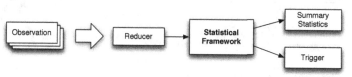

Fig. 1. Basic Architecture

2.3 Architecture

Figure 1 summarizes the summary statistics framework's high-level architecture. It *observes* a stream of tuples $(key, value)$ in which in general both *key* and *value* represent features derived in real-time from the incoming network traffic. As it processes the stream, the summary statistics framework continuously *reduces* each key's values to an aggregate result. The framework also continuously evaluates a *predicate* on these aggregates to flag specific situations by executing corresponding *triggers*. Finally, at the end of a measurement interval, the framework reports the final *summary statistics* to the user in the form of (key, agg) pairs where *agg* is the final aggregate value for that key.

As one application example consider a simple TCP scan detector. Observations might take the form of tuples (s, d) representing failed connection attempts from a source address s to a destination address d. A reducer *Unique* would compute the number of unique destinations d for each source s, and a predicate *Threshold* would flag if that exceeds a specified limit by executing a *ScanAlarm* trigger that reports an alarm. As another example, if one wanted to compute the most popular DNS names overall, the observation values would be query names extracted from DNS traffic. One would then aggregate all values into a single global result by fixing the observation key to a static value, and deploy a "top-k" reducer that computes the k most frequently seen values among its inputs.

The summary statistics framework supports deployment in settings where the traffic is not just monitored by a single process, yet with sets of physically separated monitors, as long as the instances see disjunct packet streams. This could be at different ingress points of a large network, or in a cluster setting where a load-balancer splits up the overall traffic to sent individual slices to separate monitoring backends (as, e.g., in [25]). In such a setting the summary statistics framework computes results transparently for the overall traffic aggregate, similar to what a single instance would produce if it were seeing all the traffic at one location. To accommodate such settings, we extend the basic architecture into a distributed setup in which independent sensors reduce values locally first, and then at the end of a measurement interval forward their results to a master server that merges them into global aggregates. That server then also evaluates

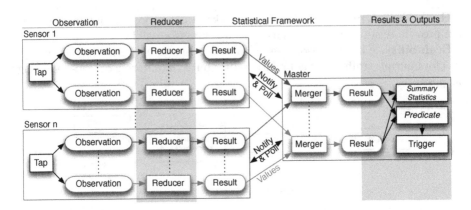

Fig. 2. Distributed Architecture

the predicates and executes the trigger. Figure 2 illustrates the distributed setting. As the reduced intermediary results will typically be small in volume, the architecture scales well with increasing numbers of sensors.

As one additional ingredient to the distributed operation, we add *result polling* that allows the server to request intermediary results from the sensors on demand. Normally, the server would evaluate predicates only at the end of a measurement interval once it has received all the local results. As that however might introduce a potentially significant delay until triggers execute, we introduce two additional optimizations. First, we allow the server to poll sensors for their current values on demand, even before the end of the measurement interval. It can then already evaluate the predicate on the received intermediate values. Polling alone however would not reduce trigger latencies sufficiently without also causing significant communication overhead. Hence, we furthermore provide the sensors with a notification mechanism to signal that their intermediate local values have changed sufficiently to warrant requesting an update. For example, for a threshold computation a sensor could notify the server once it has observed 20% of the specified limit locally, with the assumption that other sensors are likely seeing similar activity and, hence, globally the threshold might have been crossed. Upon receiving the notification, the server polls all the sensors, executes the predicate, and runs the trigger if applicable.

2.4 Reducers

We conclude this section by examining the properties of reducers in more detail, as they have to satisfy a number of requirements to fit with the framework's operation. Recall that a reducer processes $(key, value)$ pairs, aggregating them into outputs (key, agg) where agg is an aggregate of all of key's value as determined by the reducer's computation. In the following we first look at constraints we impose on reducers, and then present a set of examples that satisfy these requirements and all come with our implementation.

Composable Results. As a crucial property for reducers in the distributed setting, we require *composability*, i.e., support for aggregating the sensor's local results at the server-side. As a simple example, a reducer adding up numerical observations is trivially composable: the global sum is the total of the local results. This constraint can however be challenging to satisfy for other operations, even if conceptually simple. For instance, when sampling input randomly, deciding which samples to choose during merging without biasing the result is non-trivial.

Constant Memory Size. When processing observations reducers typically have to keep internal state during the measurement interval (e.g., the sum of all values so far). However, to reliably support computing statistics on arbitrary input volumes we require a constant bound on the amount of memory a reducer maintains. Due to this restriction, our framework can, e.g., not compute the *median* across observations.

Meaningful Intermediary Results. To support arbitrary measurement intervals as well as continuous predicate evaluation, a reducer's intermediary values must be meaningful on their own at any time. This is again obviously the case for a sum, which always reflects the current total; but less so for some of the more complex data structures.

Summation, Average, Deviation, Variance, Maximum, Minimum. These standard statistical measures are frequently used for traffic measurement tasks. They all support a stream-based calculation model where the reducer holds just the current result reflecting all observations seen so far, updating it when a new observation comes in.

Unique. Determining the number of unique observations proves highly useful for many network-oriented measurement tasks. However, a naive set-based implementation would have a memory requirement of $O(n)$ with n representing the number of observations, rendering it infeasible to use. Instead, we use a probabilistic version based on the HyperLogLog data structure (HLL; [10]). HLL provides approximate results with well-defined error margins. It uses $O(1)$ memory, is composable, and provides meaningful intermediary results.

Top-k. Finding the top-k "heavy hitters" represents another common task. However, similar to *Unique*, a naive implementation requires $O(n)$ memory, with n the number of observations. We thus likewise choose a probabilistic version instead: Metwally et al's algorithm [17], which in addition also provides estimates on the number of times specific elements were seen. Just as HLL, the algorithm satisfies all our constraints, including composability (see [5]).

Sampler. For many applications it is not only interesting to know the final result itself yet also to receive with it a sample of individual contributing values (e.g., when seeing an unusually high number of DNS requests from a single source, seeing a few example requests can prove illuminating). We support that by providing a "Sample" reducer that maintains a fixed number of k uniformly distributed samples taken out of the complete observation stream. By using reservoir sampling [26], we are able to satisfy all our constraints.

2.5   Comparison with MapReduce

It is no accident that our model, and terminology, shares similarities with MapReduce [6]. They both operate in similar phases. The "Map" step of MapReduce corresponds to taking observations in our model; in either approach, input data maps to a key and a value. The "Reduce" step of MapReduce is equivalent to our server-side merging of results computed locally at the sensors. What we call a "reducer" indeed corresponds to a "combiner" in a refinement of the MapReduce model: combiner functions merge partial results before data gets forwarded [6]. The underlying reason for this naming difference is that in our design the main part of the data reduction does indeed occur already on the sensor nodes.

One difference between the two models concerns the input side. While either approach assumes suitably pre-split sets of input, MapReduce does not tie them to a specific compute node. In our model, by tapping disjunct packet sources yet not further dividing up their inputs, we implicitly link each source with one specific sensor that processes it. While this remains less flexible, it provides a significant performance advantage by effectively leveraging the network itself for partitioning input appropriately, either indirectly by virtue of its structure (in the case of tapping different physical locations), or directly via a front-end load-balancer (in the case of a cluster setup [25]). In either case we avoid the—potentially prohibitive—performance penalty of redistributing traffic within the summary statistics framework.

Overall, we emphasize that the two approaches share significant similarities. As such, we do not consider our framework's abstract computational model the primary contribution of this work, yet rather its integration into an efficient, deployable system that provides a transparent, simple-to-use API to the user.

3   Implementation

We implement our design of the summary statistics framework on top of the Bro network monitoring platform [3,19]. Bro aligns well with our objectives as it *(i)* provides the user with the necessary flexibility through its Turing-complete scripting language; *(ii)* extracts a wide range of features from network traffic to measure; and *(iii)* supports distributed operation in cluster setups. We implement the summary statistics framework completely within Bro's scripting language, with no changes to the system's C++ core for the general functionality. As the only extension to Bro's internals, we add support for the probabilistic data structures that some of the reducers deploy. Our implementation comes with pre-written analysis scripts that leverage its capabilities for detection of, e.g., host and port scans, traceroutes, and SQL injection attacks. In the following, we discuss our implementation in terms of its user interface (§3.1), cluster integration (§3.2), and computation plugins (§3.3) that reducers can leverage.

3.1 User Interface

The user interface of the summary statistics framework exposes a set of public functions in Bro's scripting language. In the following, we briefly sketch the main functionality available to users. As a simple example we assume the setting of a small network site that aims to track the number of connections that each local host initiates to external destinations, recording them into a log file on a hourly basis.

Measuring. Setting up the analysis requires two steps: *(i)* feeding all outgoing connections into the summary statistics framework as observations, and *(ii)* defining a corresponding summary statistic that aggregates connections by their originator addresses. For the former, the framework provides the observe() function, which injects a key/value pair into an observation stream. The framework supports an arbitrary number of independent streams and identifies them by user-chosen names. For the example application we hook into Bro's connection processing and pass on every connection attempt originating from a local host:[1]

```
event connection_attempt(c: connection) {
  [... return if connection does not originate from the local network ... ]
  SumStats::observe(
    stream  = "host-conn-attempts";   # Name of observation stream
    key     = c.originator;           # Observation key (IP address)
    value   = 1;                      # Observation value ("one attempt")
  );
}
```

For the second step we first define a reducer that adds up connection attempts:

```
local r1: SumStats::Reducer = [
  stream = "host-conn-attempts";    # Name of observation stream
  apply  = SumStats::SUM;           # Reducer plugin to use
];
```

Here, we link the reducer to the observation stream to process, *host-conn-attempts*, and specify *Summation* as the statistical operation to apply to the incoming values. For a list of currently supported operations, see §2.4; users can add further ones by supplying custom plugins (see §3.3).

Next, we define the actual summary statistic by calling the framework's create() function. In its simplest form, the function takes just four parameters:

```
SumStats::create(
  name         = "local-origins";    # Name of the summary statistic
  epoch        = 1 hour;             # Measurement interval (epoch)
  reducers     = set(r1);            # Set of reducers to deploy
  epoch_result = epoch_func;         # End of epoch callback function
);
```

---

[1] In this and later examples we simplify Bro's syntax for better readability.

With that, the summary statistic configuration is complete. During runtime, Bro will now call the `epoch_result` function each hour and provide it with the number of outgoing connections per local host. The function can process the data arbitrarily, such as by logging the information into a file.

Thresholding. We now extend the previous example to report hosts that exceed a predefined threshold of connection attempts. Here, our implementation deviates slightly from the discussion in §2. While the design provides for a generic *predicate* to check for arbitrary conditions while a computation is in progress, our implementation currently hardcodes threshold checks as the only available option. In our experience, thresholding represents the dominant application. By specifically targeting it, we can simplify both the interface (making it more intuitive for users) and the implementation (reducing complexity in the distributed setting). However, there's no conceptual limitation that would prevent us from adding the more general case in the future.

Adding a threshold check to the previous example involves passing three more parameters to the `create()` call: a function that retrieves the current measurement value for a key, a numerical threshold to compare that value with, and the trigger function to execute when the value exceeds the threshold:

```
SumStats::create(
    [...]
    threshold        = 10000.0;       # Threshold value
    threshold_val    = val_func;      # Retrieve current value
    threshold_crossed = crossed_func; # Alarm.
);
```

The `val_func` receives a key and the current intermediate reducer values for this key. It uses them to return the value to be checked against the threshold.

```
function val_func(key, val) : double {
    return val["host-conn-attempts"].sum;
}
```

In this example, `val_func` simply returns the current number of connection attempts for a host.[2] However, the function could be more complex than that. In our application, one could for example instead implement a threshold relative to the number of successful connections. For that one would add a second observation stream, say `host-conn-successes`, along with a corresponding reducer `r2` added to the `create()` call. This modified `val_func` would then calculate percentages:

```
function val_func(key, val) : double {
    return val["host-conn-attempts"].sum / val["host-conn-successes"].sum;
}
```

---

[2] As the code suggests, the state is maintained in a number of nested table structures (hash maps) indexed by the measurements.

For completeness, we conclude the example by showing the trigger function that turns an exceeded threshold into an alarm via Bro's provided `NOTICE` function:

```
function crossed_func(key, val) {
  NOTICE("Host %s exceeded conn threshold: %d conn attempts", key, val);
}
```

3.2   Cluster Integration

As discussed in §2.3, the summary statistics framework targets deployment in distributed settings where a set of local vantage points contribute to a global measurement. Bro supports distributed setups through *clustering* [25]. In a Bro cluster, a set of worker nodes examines independent traffic streams and share their results through a central manager node. Each node might either monitor a physically separate point in a network or, more commonly, contribute to analyzing a single high-speed link by analyzing a smaller traffic slice that a front-end load-balancer assigns to it. Typically such load-balancing operates on a per-flow basis and, hence, satisfies our design constraint of requiring disjunct input streams in distributed summary statistics framework deployments.

Our Bro implementation closely follows the distributed design presented in §2.3, including the optimized notification/polling scheme for timely trigger execution. We put particular emphasis on hiding the increased complexity of the distributed setting from the user: the framework uses the same API for both single-instance and distributed setups; user-supplied script code works transparently in either setting. In particular, users do not need to specify which parts of their code executes where; the summary statistics framework automatically runs the respective functionality on the correct nodes (i.e., extracting observations and processing reducers on the workers; executing aggregation, thresholding, and triggers on the manager).

3.3   Computation Plugins

The framework includes support for a number of computations for reducers to deploy. Their implementations use a generic plugin interface that also allows users to add further schemes of their own. Each computation plugin implements two functions: one for adding a new observation, and one for merging computation state from different nodes; either function has also access to the time range that a observation stream spans and may include that into its calculations. As an example, we show the implementation of the *Minimum*[3]:

---

[3] The actual implementation is slightly more verbose to deal with corner cases like undefined values. We also again simplify the syntax to match previous examples. Finally, we omit the definition of the state's `min` attribute, which extends a predefined data type to add plugin-specific storage that maintains the current value.

```
# Update current minimum.
function add(key, val, state) {
  if ( val < state.min )
    state.min = val;
}

# Aggregate two values by taking the smaller.
function aggregate(out, in1, in2) {
  out.min = (in1.min < in2.min) ? in1.min : in2.min;
}
```

In addition to *Minimum*, our implementation also provides plugins for *Maximum, Sum, Average, Standard Deviation* and *Variance, Top-k), Unique,* and Sampling (see §2.4).

4   Applications and Deployment

In this section we demonstrate the summary statistics framework's capabilities with a set of example applications. The first four (scan detector in §4.1, brute-force login detector in §4.2, SQL injection detector in §4.3, traceroute detector in §4.4) ship with Bro since version 2.2, and many network sites use them operationally now. We furthermore discuss three measurement tasks (traffic matrix in §4.6, top-k in §4.5, visualization in §4.7) that we ran experimentally in production environments. For these we make the corresponding (short) implementation scripts available in a separate repository [2].

Note that these are only example applications demonstrating the capabilities of the framework. In practice, operators will evaluate the suitability of the summary statistics framework for their tasks and implement their own scripts as appropiate.

4.1   Scan Detection

Detecting port and address scans constitutes an important capability for security operations. We implemented a corresponding scan detector as a Bro script on top of the summary statistics framework. The script tracks the number of unique ports and destination addresses that each source IP attempts to connect to, generating alarms when they exceed, by default, 15 or 25 attempts within a 5 minute interval, respectively. Users can easily adjust either threshold, as well as the time interval. The script is about 160 lines long, with the bulk representing logic for connection processing and customization functionality. The core of the script consists of just two pairs of function calls setting up the summary statistics and feeding in observations. In particular, there is no need for code to deal with distributed Bro setups. For comparison, older Bro versions used to ship with a manually written, complex scan detection script that consisted of over 600 lines of script code, with most of that focusing on maintaining the necessary counters inside nested hash tables.

Indiana University (IU) has been running versions of our new scan detector script for more than 9 months on their 49-node Bro cluster, monitoring the site's 10 GE upstream link. Their total traffic (incoming and outgoing) peaks at about 13 Gb/s on workdays and generally averages at about 5 Gb/s. Figures 3 and 4 show the number of incoming scans to different destination addresses by time and by weekday, respectively, for subinterval of that time, as identified by our detector. At peak times, there are more than 290 unique external IP addresses conducting scans of the network each hour. In total, IU encountered 33,452 scanners from 2014-02-19 to 2014-03-20. The network operators use the script's output to automatically block external scanners at the border router in near-real time. Note that due to this automated blocking, with blocks often being triggered before the end of a monitoring interval, the numbers in this section represent a lower bound.

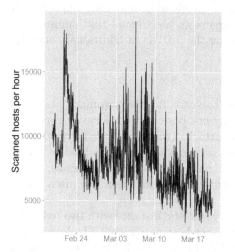

Fig. 3. Incoming address scans per hour from 2014-02-19 to 2014-03-20 at IU

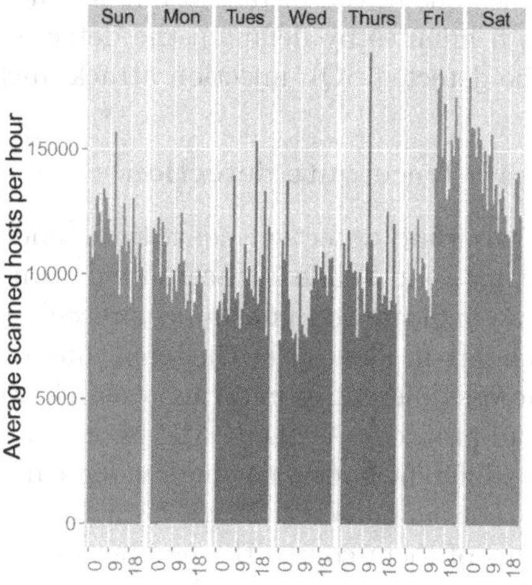

Fig. 4. Aggregate count of incoming addr. scans from 2014-02-19 to 2014-03-20 at IU.

4.2   Brute-force Login Detection

A common type of attack concerns brute-forcing accounts by trying a large number of username and password combinations. We implemented scripts to detect such attacks for the FTP and SSH protocols. For FTP, the script counts the number of failed FTP authentication attempts and generates an alarm when it sees more than, by default, 20 attempts from a specific source to a particular destination host within 15 minutes. For SSH, Bro provides a heuristic that determines if a login succeeded or failed, based on the volume of data exchanged as well as the number of packets seen during the session. Our script counts the number of times this heuristic reports a successful login and triggers an alarm when that number exceeds 30 in a 30 minute interval. A number of sites, including Indiana University, are currently running the brute-force detection scripts in their production setups.

4.3 SQL Injection Detection

We also created script for detecting automated SQL injection attacks, using a similar thresholding approach as above. When targeting a web server, attackers often iterate through a large library of canned injection URIs within a short time frame. To detect this kind of attack, we first wrote a regular expression that matches typical injection URIs (e.g., `/site.php?site=5' and 1=1 and ''='`).[4] We then set up two summary statistic instances. Both count the number of times the regular expression matches. For the first instance, the key is the source IP address while for the second we use the destination address. In other words, the first identifies attack sources (independent of how many victims each targets), and the second reports servers under attack (independent of the number of their attackers). In addition, both summary statistic instances also apply an additional *Sample* reducer, which keeps 5 URIs that have matched the regular expression. Once one of the instances hits a configured threshold of matching requests (50 in 5 minutes by default), the detector triggers an alert email that summarizes the detected SQL injection attack, including the 5 URIs as additional context.

4.4 Traceroute detection

Traceroute detection constitutes another use-case for the summary statistics framework. While a traceroute does usually not pose a direct security threat, it may indicate reconnaissance preceding an attack. Traceroutes are however challenging to identify in clustered monitoring setups where traffic is load-balanced across different monitoring systems according to its 5-tuple of addresses, ports, and protocol. As the ICMP packets belonging to one execution will often arrive at different nodes, no single node can spot it by itself.

For our detector, we use a single summary statistic instance with two reducers. One of them counts the number of packets per host pair with TTLs lower than 10. The second counts the number of ICMP Time Exceeded messages relating to the same hosts.

We consider a traceroute to be in progress if we see at least one low-TTL packet between a pair of hosts along with at least three matching ICMP Time Exceeded messages. Leveraging the summary statistics framework allows to define such a logic at a semantic level with a single if-statement, without needing to consider the underlying traffic splitting any further. We validated this scheme by running it on the Bro cluster of the National Center for Supercomputing Applications at the University of Illinois, manually executing traceroutes and sampling the corresponding reports during normal operation. Ignoring our own activity, the large number of otherwise incoming traceroutes we saw (more than 2,000 a day) surprised us. Many of them turned out to be targeting a local content management system.

---

[4] This turns out harder than it sounds: We have developed, and continuously refined, this regular expression for more than 5 years now by regularly evaluating network traffic and adding new cases as we discovered them. The expression has a size of more than 1,500 characters today.

4.5   Top-k

As examples of "top-k" measurements, we wrote a script that tracks *(i)* the top-10 source and destination hosts exhibiting the most established TCP connections; *(ii)* the top-10 second-level domains in DNS queries; and *(iii)* the top-10 `Host` header values present in HTTP requests.[5] We consider only outgoing traffic and calculate rankings over both 10-minute and 1-hour intervals.

Table 1. Top-10 outgoing DNS 2nd-level lookups and HTTP Host values (19-3-2014, 15:15–16:15)

DNS domain	Upper bound	ϵ	HTTP host	Upper bound	ϵ
.akamai.net	276,592	0	b.scorecardresearch.com	123,293	0
.akamaiedge.net	185,150	0	www.google-analytics.com	111,760	0
.berkeley.edu	158,938	0	pagead2.googlesyndication.com	87,539	0
.amazonaws.com	148,584	0	ib.adnxs.com	77,521	0
.google.com	137,474	0	ad.doubleclick.net	72,156	0
.akadns.net	135,519	0	pixel.quantserve.com	70,284	0
.yuerengu.com.cn	92,210	0	www.google.com	62,996	0
.cloudfront.net	60,234	0	i1.ytimg.com	59,607	0
.spameatingmonkey.net	57,089	142	googleads.g.doubleclick.net	56,673	0
.ustiming.org	38,108	719	setiboincdata.ssl.berkeley.edu	56,513	0
Total DNS req. (exact)	4,220,837		Total HTTP requests (exact)	10,985,712	

For demonstration purposes we ran this script on a 28-node Bro research cluster operating at the University of California, Berkeley; monitoring the campus' 2x10 GE uplink connections [25]. Daytime volume averages between 3-4 Gb/s total. Table 1 shows a snapshot of the 1-hour DNS/HTTP statistics from an early Monday afternoon. Recall that the top-k calculation uses a probabilistic data structure and, hence, the results represent estimates. The table includes what the algorithm reported as upper bounds for the number of times it encountered each value. In addition, the table also shows the corresponding uncertainty ϵ; subtracting ϵ from the upper bound gives the lower bound. This means that, e.g., a DNS request for `.ustiming.org` was encountered between 37,389 and 38,108 times. We see that generally the error rates remain very low, considering the large amount of traffic with high numbers of unique DNS domains and HTTP hosts (154,859 and 100,269, respectively, during the shown time interval; calculated independently from logs). For these measurements, we configured the probabilistic algorithm to keep at most 1,000 different values in memory for each summary statistic at any point of time.

---

[5] The `Host` headers provides an application-level view of popular web sites, vs. just looking at IP addresses. Web site addresses have become quite meaningless today with many services running on generic cloud infrastructure.

4.6 Traffic Matrix

The summary statistics framework can also be used to compute traffic matrices, such as for breaking down overall volume by subnets. To demonstrate this, we created a small Bro script which sets up a single summary statistics framework instance using two reducers tracking the volume of incoming and outgoing traffic by source, respectively. Additionally, the reducers define a key normalization function, which maps the source address of each individual observation to the containing /24 network in which the host resides. We deployed the top-k script on the Berkeley research cluster discussed in §4.5. Table 2 shows the output for the 5 (anonymized) subnets with the largest amount of total traffic during the observed one-hour period, out of 502 unique local subnets encountered.

4.7 Real-Time Visualization

As our final application, we extended the previous "top-k" setup to visualize the results in real-time. See Fig. 5 for a screenshot. Internally, the extended Bro script uses the intermediate value update mechanism of the summary statistics framework to get current values every 15 seconds. It then sends the aggregated valued to Bro's logging framework, which supports a number of different output formats including TSV files and databases. For this application, we added support for Apache's ActiveMQ message queuing framework so that Bro can send the values directly to an ActiveMQ server. We created an HTML page that uses JavaScript for visualizing the values via a persistent WebSocket connection. After each update, the value changes are immediately reflected in the browser window.

	Bytes		
Subnet	In	Out	Total
UCB Subnet A	124G	56.0G	180G
UCB Subnet B	123G	22.7G	146G
UCB Subnet C	39.7G	48.1G	87.9G
UCB Subnet D	23.3G	2.15G	25.5G
UCB Subnet E	18.6G	1.19G	19.8G

Table 2. UCB Top-5 local subnets by total traffic (28-3-2014, 11:41–12:41)

Fig. 5. Screenshot top-10 HTTP hosts (by headers) live visualization (4-4-2014, 9:28)

5 Evaluation

In this section we evaluate the overhead introduced by the summary statistics framework in terms of computation, memory, and communication. Our objective concerns ensuring that the implementation provides the performance necessary to operate in large-scale distributed environments. We focus on two applications: *Top-k* (§4.5), as the most resource-intensive application; and *scan detection* (§4.1), which stresses the inter-node communication the most.

5.1 Correctness

We first briefly double-check correctness of the summary statistics framework's calculations. While not directly an issue for the simpler calculations, the probabilistic data structures by design introduce errors into their results, along with worst-case bounds derived from their mathematical foundation. In Table 1, we show top-k results along with their error margins for a 1-hour measurement period in a large-scale cluster setup (see §4.5). We cross-check the reported numbers by calculating the actual top-k lists offline out of the log files that the Bro cluster produced during the same execution. We find that despite using the memory-efficient probabilistic data structure: *(i)* the summary statistics framework correctly identifies all entries in the right order in all but two cases, and *(ii)* all the actual values indeed fall within the given error margin. Regarding the former, the two exceptions concern the top sources. During our measurement the counts for 8 of the top 10 IP addresses were very close to each other. In both cases, the reported uncertainty ϵ (see §4.5) was greater than the difference to the next values. Hence, a user can indeed conclude from the numbers that while the reported ordering might not be fully correct, it must be closely matching the actual activity.

5.2 Computational Overhead

Internally, the summary statistics framework is a complex module consisting of several hundred lines of Bro script code for the basic framework, separate scripts for the plugins, and low-level core support for the probabilistic data structures. For evaluating the computational overhead that this extension introduces, we captured a packet trace of about 20-minutes at the Internet uplink of UC Berkeley (see §4.6). To keep the volume manageable we recorded just a subset of the total traffic, corresponding to what one node of the Bro research cluster processes (i.e., $\frac{1}{28}$ of all flows).[6] The resulting trace includes 19.8 M packets and 516 K flows, at a total volume of about 15 GB.

We measure CPU load with three different configurations: *(i)* Bro's default setup with the summary statistics framework disabled; *(ii)* enabling the scan detector from §4.1; and *(iii)* enabling the top-k script from §4.5; For each configuration, we measure CPU utilization per 1 sec trace interval. The trace is replayed using the *pseudo-realtime* mode [23] of Bro, which was created to facilitate the realistic playback of packet-traces.

---

[6] In other words, we assess the performance overhead for one worker node. We do not examine the CPU overhead of the manager node merging the data structures as that system is typically not CPU-bound and has sufficient head-room for additional operations.

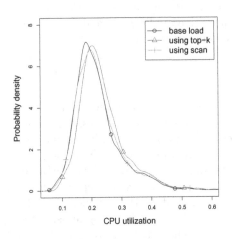
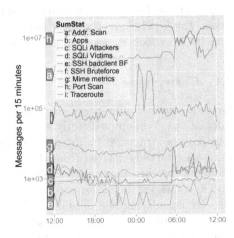

Fig. 6. Single node CPU load comparison   **Fig. 7.** Exchanged messages per sumstat

Figure 6 shows a corresponding probability density for the three configurations.[7] We see that while using the summary statistics framework imposes overhead, it remains small for scan detection (0.4 percentage points more). The difference with the top-k script (1.6 percentage points more) is more noticeable due to the increased cost per observation that the more expensive maintenance of the probabilistic data structure entails. In either case, we deem the overhead low, relative to the input volume.

5.3   Memory Overhead

We next analyze the memory overhead introduced by the summary statistics framework. For this we follow the same approach as for CPU, measuring memory usage while running Bro repeatedly on the same input trace with the same three configurations. In all cases, we find the memory overhead imposed by the summary statistics framework reasonable. Even there the mean overhead is only about 6.7% (max. 179MB) in comparison to the baseline of a standard Bro setup.

5.4   Communication Overhead

Finally, we examine the communication overhead the summary statistics framework incurs in cluster operation. We add a script to the Bro manager node that logs all incoming and outgoing messages triggered by the summary statistics framework. For each message we output its timestamp and further meta-information for identifying its origin (e.g., the name of the reducer and the exact type of the message). We ran this measurement live for 24 hours on a 57-node Bro cluster of a

---

[7] The measurement was done in a single-system Bro setup. However, we repeated it in cluster setup with a separate manager process, with similar results.

medium-sized research organization that we have access to. The cluster monitors uplink traffic averaging at about 1 Gb/s during day-time hours. The setup used the full set of standard summary statistic scripts that come with a standard Bro installation, including detecting scans, traceroutes, SQL injection attacks, and SSH bruteforcing; as well as using two custom scripts to measure MIME statistics and traffic volume to several large sites (Google, Facebook, etc.).

Figure 7 shows a breakdown of the different summary statistics and the message overhead each caused. We find the scan detector responsible for most of the exchanged messages, due to the large number of incoming connections that it needs to classify. In total, the nodes exchanged 1,930,564,662 messages, with about half of them going from the manager to the worker nodes. This is due to the manager always initiating the exchange of values (i.e., even after a worker's notification, it is the manager that then polls for updates). This means that each node sends about 399.03 messages per second each way. Messages relating to the intermediary updates constitute 0.40% of the overall communication. 69,810 times a worker node notifies the manager that it should request updates. In 27,704, or 39.68%, of these cases, the manager chooses to ignore that request (an optimization that our implementation applies to limit simultaneously outstanding key updates for the case where a set of keys triggers many notifications in short succession; by default, the framework limits the number of simultaneously running updates to 10 per summary statistic). In 15.98% of the cases that the request is accepted by the manager, the target threshold has indeed been crossed, and hence the manager alarms after aggregating the individual values.

Overall, we deem the level of communication realistic for such large-scale, high-volume settings; and clearly within what Bro's communication system is able to handle [23]. This conclusion is supported by the Indiana University setup, which is running the scan detector in operations (§4.1). We note that scan detection represents pretty much the worst case for a distributed monitoring setup as one needs to continuously correlate activity about many addresses across all nodes in a timely manner. While we have not yet performed a more systematic sensitivity analysis, we expect that we could further reduce the messages exchanged by tuning the specifics of the update mechanism.

6   Related Work

Our design and implementation represent a generic framework that supports a wide spectrum of network-based summary statistics. We are not aware of any system that provides similar flexibility with an easy-to-use interface, suitable for real-time processing in distributed deployments.

Summary statistics are widely used throughout the networking and security communities, both in research and operations. To give just a few examples of research efforts presenting applications and/or corresponding data structures, the literature includes work on finding port scanners in backbones [24], efficiently counting the number of network flows in high-speed environments [16,9], detecting attacks against routers [1], computing real-time traffic summaries [15], or identifying elephant flows [8]. However, all of these efforts remain specific to their particular target application, while our work provides a framework on top of which one can implement such analyses.

In operations, appliances from companies like SonicWall and Palo Alto Networks compute traffic summaries and break-downs, however they hardwire the analysis performed. Several open-source utilities can apply statistical computations to network traffic, in particular NetFlow-based toolsets like *SILK* [22] and *flow-tools* [11]. However, they remain restricted to the abstractions their input format provides, are intended mainly for offline/batch usage, and do not provide the flexibility of performing arbitrary computations. Splunk can compute top-k-style statistics flexibly on different features, yet its input remains limited to externally produced log files.

For intrusion detection, Denning pioneered statistical monitoring in her seminal work on the host-based IDES system [7]. Today, scan detectors come with virtually any IDS, including open-source systems such as Snort [21]. Older versions of Bro [19] used to come with four fully separate scan detector implementations, all targeting different traffic features and/or threshold schemes. Our summary statistics framework supports all four directly within its unified API. We refer to, e.g., [18,12] for a broader overview of statistical anomaly detection (as well as other approaches). We note that while we limit our summary statistics framework implementation to threshold-based schemes for now, conceptually it could support further statistical approaches as well.

Cohen et al. [4] present an abstract framework for weighted sampling in distributed settings. It is similar in intent to our work, however, it only considers the case of sampling, and evaluates optimal algorithms for this setting. Peng et al. [20] uses a cumulative sum algorithm to collect statistics at nodes and share information using a machine learning algorithm. In contrast to our work, their usage scenario is limited to cumulative sums and their evaluation focuses on optimizing detection delays and bandwidth, not on providing a generally usable framework for distributed summary statistics.

We use a set of probabilistic data structures to efficiently compute statistics that traditionally would be very resource intensive to maintain on large inputs. We choose data structures that satisfy our constraints (see §2.4), yet note that there are further candidates. For example, there are extensions available for the HyperLogLog algorithm that we use [10]: Kane et al. [14] propose an algorithm with an even lower memory overhead; it however remains complex and seems impractical to implement [13]. Heule et al. likewise propose a series of improvements to HyperLogLog [13]. As our main contributions concerns the framework itself—not individual computations—we do not further explore such alternatives, though may do so in the future if the current implementation ever turned out to represent a bottleneck.

7   Conclusion

In this work, we present the design and implementation of a novel *summary statistics framework* for network monitoring. As one of its key features, the framework supports computing statistics on arbitrary keys, such as IP addresses, DNS labels, or HTTP server names. Furthermore, our design specifically targets distributed deployment, and can thus be used in environments where sensors are either scattered over independent tapping points, or jointly process a high-volume link in a load-balancing setup. We assess the feasibility of our approach by implementing the summary statistics framework on top of the open-source Bro network monitor, and showcase a set of example applications in realistic large-scale settings.

Overall, we consider the summary statistics framework an extensible platform that enables research and operators to measure and quantify characteristics of their network traffic, with much less effort than they would traditionally require in particular in the distributed setup. Using the summary statistics framework, users can implement powerful statistical measurements in just a handful lines of code, and immediately deploy them for real-time processing.

Acknowledgments. We would like to thank for their collaboration Keith Lehigh and Indiana University; Aashish Sharma and the Lawrence Berkeley National Laboratory; Justin Azoff and the National Center for Supercomputing Applications at the University of Illinois; as well as further unnamed organisations that have operated early versions of the framework. This work was supported by the US National Science Foundation under grants OCI-1032889 and ACI-1348077; by the U.S. Army Research Laboratory and the U.S. Army Research Office under MURI grant No. W911NF-09-1-0553; and by a fellowship within the Postdoc-Programme of the German Academic Exchange Service (DAAD). Any opinions, findings, and conclusions or recommendations expressed in this material are those of the authors or originators, and do not necessarily reflect the views of the NSF, the ARL/ARO, or the DAAD, respectively.

References

1. Barman, D., Satapathy, P., Ciardo, G.: Detecting Attacks in Routers using Sketches. In: Workshop on High Performance Switching and Routing, HPSR (2007)
2. Bro SumStat Scripts & Repos, http://www.icir.org/johanna/sumstats
3. Bro Network Security Monitor Web Site, http://www.bro.org
4. Cohen, E., Duffield, N., Kaplan, H., Lund, C., Thorup, M.: Composable, Scalable, and Accurate Weight Summarization of Unaggregated Data Sets. Proc. VLDB Endow. 2(1) (August 2009)
5. Das, S., Antony, S., Agrawal, D., El Abbadi, A.: Thread Cooperation in Multicore Architectures for Frequency Counting over Multiple Data Streams. Proc. VLDB Endow. 2(1) (August 2009)
6. Dean, J., Ghemawat, S.: MapReduce: Simplified Data Processing on Large Clusters. Commun. ACM 51(1) (January 2008)
7. Denning, D.E.: An Intrusion-Detection Model. IEEE TSE 13(2) (February 1987)
8. Estan, C., Varghese, G.: New Directions in Traffic Measurement and Accounting: Focusing on the Elephants, ignoring the Mice. ACM Trans. Comput. Syst. 21(3) (August 2003)
9. Estan, C., Varghese, G., Fisk, M.: Bitmap Algorithms for Counting Active Flows on High-Speed Links. IEEE/ACM Trans. Netw. 14(5) (October 2006)

10. Flajolet, P., Fusy, É., Gandouet, O., et al.: Hyperloglog: The Analysis of a Near-Optimal Cardinality Estimation Algorithm. In: Proc. of the International Conference of Analysis of Algorithms, AFOA (2007)
11. Flow-tools information, http://www.splintered.net/sw/flow-tools
12. Garcia-Teodoro, P., Díaz-Verdejo, J.E., Maciá-Fernández, G., Vzquez, E.: Anomaly-Based Network Intrusion Detection: Techniques, Systems and Challenges. Computers & Security 28(1-2) (2009)
13. Heule, S., Nunkesser, M., Hall, A.: HyperLogLog in Practice: Algorithmic Engineering of a State of The Art Cardinality Estimation Algorithm. In: Proc. EDBT (2013)
14. Kane, D.M., Nelson, J., Woodruff, D.P.: An Optimal Algorithm for the Distinct Elements Problem. In: Proceedings ACM PODS (2010)
15. Keys, K., Moore, D., Estan, C.: A Robust System for Accurate Real-Time Summaries of Internet Traffic. In: Proc. SIGMETRICS (2005)
16. Kim, H.A., O'Hallaron, D.R.: Counting Network Flows in Real Time. In: Proc. IEEE Global Telecommunications Conference, vol. 7 (2003)
17. Metwally, A., Agrawal, D., El Abbadi, A.: Efficient Computation of Frequent and Top-k Elements in Data Streams. In: Proc. ICDT (2005)
18. Patcha, A., Park, J.M.: An Overview of Anomaly Detection Techniques: Existing Solutions and Latest Technological Trends. Computer Networks 51(12) (2007)
19. Paxson, V.: Bro: A System for Detecting Network Intruders in Real-Time. Computer Networks 31(23-24) (1999)
20. Peng, T., Leckie, C., Ramamohanarao, K.: Information Sharing for Distributed Intrusion Detection Systems. Journal of Network and Computer Applications 30(3) (August 2007)
21. Roesch, M.: Snort: Lightweight Intrusion Detection for Networks. In: LISA (1999)
22. SILK   –   System   for   Internet-Level   Knowledge, http://tools.netsa.cert.org/silk/
23. Sommer, R., Paxson, V.: Exploiting Independent State For Network Intrusion Detection. In: ACSAC (2005)
24. Sridharan, A., Ye, T.: Tracking Port Scanners on the IP Backbone. In: Proc. Workshop on Large Scale Attack Defense, LSAD (2007)
25. Vallentin, M., Sommer, R., Lee, J., Leres, C., Paxson, V., Tierney, B.: The NIDS Cluster: Scalable, Stateful Network Intrusion Detection on Commodity Hardware. In: Kruegel, C., Lippmann, R., Clark, A. (eds.) RAID 2007. LNCS, vol. 4637, pp. 107–126. Springer, Heidelberg (2007)
26. Vitter, J.S.: Random Sampling with a Reservoir. ACM TOMS 11(1) (March 1985)

Formal Analysis of Security Procedures in LTE - A Feasibility Study

Noomene Ben Henda and Karl Norrman

Ericsson Research Stockholm, Färögatan 6 16480, Sweden
{noamen.ben.henda,karl.norrman}@ericsson.com

Abstract. The only part of the Long Term Evolution (LTE) security standard that has been formally analyzed is the Authentication and Key Agreement (AKA) procedure. It is not clear how well existing security related verification tools can handle other types of procedures. In this work, we use ProVerif to analyze the procedures related to session management and mobility. Our analysis has shown that most of the secrecy and agreement properties hold which was expected. However, we had difficulties proving stronger injective agreement properties.

Keywords: Formal verification, Telecom, LTE, security.

1 Introduction

Background. Long Term Evolution (LTE), a 4th Generation (4G) mobile communication system, is the most recent standard developed by the 3rd Generation Partnership Project (3GPP) [1]. Among the objectives of LTE is to provide higher data rates, enhanced quality of service and equal or better security compared to previous generations [1] (TS 22.278). One such improvement is that LTE introduces very granular key separation. LTE mandates the use of different session keys for specific protocols and purposes between the terminal and the nodes in the network. Those keys are organized in a hierarchy (see Fig. 1b). At the root of the hierarchy is a key that is shared between the Home Subscriber Server (HSS) (see Fig. 1a) and the terminal, or User Equipment (UE) in the 3GPP specifications, where it is securely kept in a smartcard. During initial attachment of the UE to the network, mutual authentication between them is achieved by running the Authentication and Key Agreement protocol (AKA) [1] (TS 33.401). The authentication is based on the root key. The other keys are subsequently derived from keys that are closer to the root in the hierarchy than themselves.

Each key in the hierarchy is shared between the UE and a particular node in the network. For example the K_{ASME} key is shared with the Mobility Management Entity (MME); the K_{eNB} key is shared with the Evolved Node B (eNB). The LTE standard defines specific procedures for the establishment of each key. For instance, the K_{ASME} key is established by the AKA protocol which runs between the UE and the HSS, and then provisioned to the target MME node.

A. Stavrou et al. (Eds.): RAID 2014, LNCS 8688, pp. 341–361, 2014.
© Springer International Publishing Switzerland 2014

The K_{eNB} is initially established by a combination of procedures involving the MME, eNB, and the UE. The UE and MME use the K_{ASME} to agree on a K_{eNB}. The MME then provides this key to the eNB which finally activates the security between the UE and the eNB based on the K_{eNB}. Key establishment procedures like these typically have to satisfy at least the following security properties: *agreement*, *secrecy* and *freshness*. Agreement is the property that guarantees that the involved parties obtain the same key at the end of the run; otherwise, the key would be useless. Secrecy guarantees that no one, other that the involved parties (who are assumed to not leak the key to outsiders), has the key. If secrecy is not guaranteed, confidentiality protection, among other cryptographically based services, is not achievable. The last property of freshness prevents key re-use and thus, for example, situations were a plain text is encrypted twice using the same key.

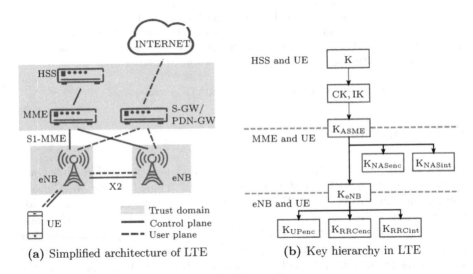

(a) Simplified architecture of LTE   (b) Key hierarchy in LTE

Fig. 1. LTE overview

In a running system, the key establishment procedures and procedures making use of the keys can be interleaved, repeated and run simultaneously by several UEs and network nodes. They can as well be used as building blocks in more complex compound procedures such as the ones handling mobility. The security procedures are dependent on each other. For instance, the establishment of a K_{eNB} key requires the existence of a K_{ASME} key and thus any procedure using the K_{eNB} cannot be executed in a pure LTE system unless an AKA run has taken place earlier. The procedures might also rely on other type of context information, such as message counters and global parameters of the system. State-based formal verification tools like SPIN [18] can model this context information and capture the effect of reruns and interleaving. However state-based approaches are not effective to model cryptographic functions that usually rely on advanced computations. Other symbolic approaches that abstract away the implementation details of cryptographic primitives have been more effective. In general, formal analysis of security protocols is usually done against the symbolic Dolev-Yao intruder (or attacker) model [16]. In this model, the attacker has full control of the communication medium. In addition, cryptography is assumed perfect so that the attacker cannot decrypt messages unless he has the required key, hash functions are collision free, etc.

Contribution. In this paper, we present our work with ProVerif [8] which we used to model and verify security properties of different key establishment procedures in LTE. This work is part of a feasibility study whose aim is to bring and put to use tools like ProVerif in an industrial context such as that of the 3GPP standardization process. Our main contribution consists in providing formal models of the LTE protocols in the input language of the ProVerif. Our implementation preserves the trust model of 3GPP. Furthermore, to the best of our knowledge, the security procedures related to mobility and session management have not been previously subject to formal analysis. Another contribution consists in showing how to model and verify different security properties. Our analysis results confirm all secrecy and most of the weak agreement properties. However, stronger agreement properties are more challenging to prove, for several reasons that we later discuss and explain. Our analysis approach using ProVerif is simple and generic and thus can be easily adapted to other case studies.

Related Work. Although LTE security has received much scrutiny during the design process, it has been less studied in the research community. In particular, the research community has mainly focused on analyzing AKA [29,28,17,30], which is largely the same authentication and key agreement protocol used for Wideband Code Division Multiplex Access (WCDMA), a 3G access. AKA as used in WCDMA was formally analyzed using BAN logic in [1] (TS 33.902). AKA is re-used exactly as is in LTE to boot strap the key hierarchy. Therefore, all analysis results on AKA as used in WCDMA carries over to LTE. A study of privacy aspects of WCDMA is presented in [5]. Although it does not study LTE, it looks at other procedures than AKA, namely the paging procedure. The study in [24] contains an analysis of a proposed, but not standardized, system for handovers between different types of radio access systems. It does not provide any analysis of LTE itself.

Research on formal verification of security protocols has been ongoing for two decades. Current state of the art tools like Scyther [13] and ProVerif can verify protocols for unbounded number of sessions and agents. Case studies by Scyther include the analysis of the Naxos protocol [14] and the IPsec exchange protocols IKEv1 and IKEv2 [15]. Other applications include the analysis of the privacy and key management protocol [27] and the handover schemes [26] in WiMAX networks. Case studies by ProVerif include the analysis the Bluetooth device pairing protocol [19], the just-fast-keying protocol [3], a secure file sharing protocol [9], authentication in 3G where both GSM and WCDMA access is used [28], and the privacy study on WCDMA mentioned earlier [5]. We note that [28] does not contain any analysis of mobility between radio access networks, but rather considers the case of authentication over the GSM/EDGE access network, when used to access a 3G network. There is a long list of similar tools from which we cite the following ones: The Tamarin tool [23] has been used for the verification of group key agreement protocols [25]. The AVISPA [6] has been used for the analysis of key management in hierarchical group protocols [12]. Other relevant tools are NRL [22], LySa [11] and Casper [21].

Outline. In the next section, we give an overview of the LTE architecture to put in context the protocol models we provide. In Section 3, we describe ProVerif and use AKA as an example illustrating our modeling approach. In Section 4, we describe the security procedures related to session management, provide the corresponding formal models and discuss the verification results. In Section 5, we present our work on security procedures in mobility events. Finally in Section 6, we conclude by a summary discussions and future work. For shortage of space, the full versions of the models that can be used to reproduce our results are not included. They are available on demand. In the description of the LTE procedures, many aspects not related to security have been omitted and thus we refer to [1] for the detailed specifications.

2   Overview of LTE

LTE provides 4G mobile broadband access service to terminals. More precisely, the service consists of providing a terminal with IP connectivity using a stable IP address, while the terminal moves throughout the LTE network.

2.1   Architecture

LTE [1] (TS 23.401) consists of a Radio Access Network (RAN) and a core network (see Fig. 1a). The radio access network consists of a set of base stations, the eNBs. The terminals connect to the eNB via the radio air interface. The eNB is connected to two nodes in the core network: the MME and the Serving Gateway (S-GW). The first node (MME) handles the control plane traffic for mobile terminals connected to the eNB. The control plane for a terminal is used to manage the terminal sessions, mobility and security. The second node (S-GW) handles the user plane traffic to and from the internet, and other operator services. Subscriber information such as authentication credentials, location, subscription preferences, etc. is kept in the HSS.

2.2   Trust Model

During the security design in 3GPP a trust model for the network is assumed. More precisely, the network is divided into two main types of trust domains: the core network trust domain, and the RAN one. The standards have a more granular concept of trust domains, but these two are sufficient for the protocols considered in this paper. The data traffic flows between nodes in different domains over an IP transport network.

The core network domain, which contains nodes like the HSS, MME, S-GW, etc. is assumed to be a physically secure one. This means that attackers do not have access to nodes in this domain other than what can be obtained remotely via the network interfaces of the nodes.

The RAN trust domain contains only the eNBs. Since such nodes may be deployed in physically insecure locations, such as on the wall of a shopping mall, or in a hotel corridor, etc. the security model in LTE is built to handle the situation where the eNBs are deployed in untrusted locations. In the standard [1] (TS 33.401), it is required that each eNB implements its security processing inside a secure environment. The purpose is to prevent attackers to gain access to any data in the eNB by physically tampering with the device. Furthermore, the IP transport network that connects nodes across different domains is to be protected using IPsec [1] (TS 33.210) unless it can be trusted.

2.3   Session and Mobility Management

The terminal maintains two control connections with the network, one with the MME managed by the Non Access Stratum (NAS) protocol, and one with the eNB managed using the Radio Resource Control (RRC) protocol. The MME keeps track of the terminal location even when it is idle, i.e., it is not exchanging user plane data. The location is defined by an area served by possibly several eNBs. The terminal keeps the MME updated of any area changes as it moves.

In case of incoming data, the MME pages the terminal on all eNBs in its last known area. In response to the paging, the terminal requests a user plane data connection from the MME. It is only then that the eNB, which the terminal uses to access the network, becomes aware of the terminal presence. The MME provides the eNB with initial state information to communicate with the terminal. The terminal can then become active sending and receiving data. Afterwards, it can become idle again. In such case, the serving eNB releases all the associated resources and is no longer aware of the terminal's presence.

2.4   Key Hierarchy

Once security is activated, the NAS protocol between the terminal and the MME becomes both integrity protected and encrypted. The same holds for the RRC protocol between the terminal and the eNB. The user plane traffic is encrypted in two hops. First the radio link between the terminal and the eNB is encrypted. The eNB terminates the encryption of uplink traffic inside its secure environment and forwards it to the S-GW through an IPsec tunnel. Downlink traffic is handled in a similar manner.

Security for NAS, RRC and user plane traffic relies on separate encryption and integrity session keys (see Fig. 1b). The keys for protecting RRC and user plane traffic are derived from the K_{eNB} which in turn, is derived from the K_{ASME}. The keys for the NAS protocol are also derived from the K_{ASME} key.

2.5   Initial Key Establishment

At start up, the terminal needs to register with the network. This is achieved by the attach procedure. In connection to the attach procedure, the terminal and network also run an AKA procedure. The outcome of AKA is the establishment of the K_{ASME} session key between the terminal and the serving MME.

Figure 2 contains a simplified chart of the message exchange related to AKA and that we briefly explain as follows: First, the UE sends its identifier IMSI and security capabilities to the MME in an attach request. The MME then stores the capabilities and forwards the IMSI to the HSS. The HSS uses the identifier to retrieve the secret subscriber key K, generates a nonce RAND and computes the K_{ASME} key together with other authentication parameters. The authentication data is then sent to the MME which uses it to authenticate the UE.

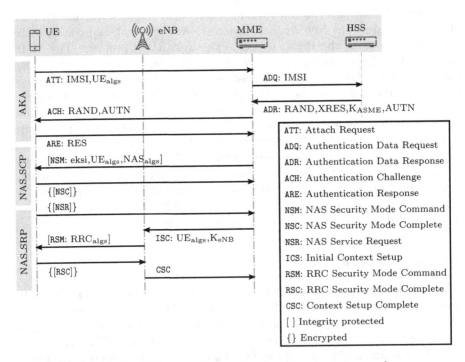

Fig. 2. AKA, NAS security control and service request procedures

3   ProVerif Overview

Before we present our work with the security procedures, we first describe ProVerif, the tool we use. We will be using AKA as a supporting example to show how protocols can be modeled and analyzed with it.

3.1   ProVerif

The tool takes formal models of the protocols together with a set of security properties as input. The input language is a typed variant of the applied pi calculus [4]. In this language, messages are modeled as terms. Relationships between cryptographic primitives are captured by rewrite rules or an equational theory. The complete specification can be found in the user manual [10].

ProVerif can prove reachability properties and correspondence assertions [7]. Reachability properties allow checking which information is in the possession of the attacker, i.e. secrecy. Correspondence properties are of the form "if some event is executed, then another event has previously been executed", and can be used for checking various types of authentication [20].

3.2   Input Language

Figure 3 shows an AKA model in the ProVerif language. In general, a protocol model can be divided in three parts: the declarations (lines 1-9), the process macros (10-31) and the main process (32). The declarations include the user types, the functions that describe the cryptographic primitives, and the security properties. The process macros consist of sub-process definitions. Each sub-process is a sequence of events. Finally, the main process is defined using those macros. In this particular example, it is defined as the parallel composition (denoted by |) of the unbounded replication (denoted by !) of three process macros representing a UE (line 10), an MME (18) and an HSS (24) node.

Declarations. Besides the built-in types: *channel*, *bitstring* and *bool*; additional user types can be declared as in line 2. Free names are introduced as in line 1 where two channels with names **pubch** and **secch** are declared. Free names are by default accessible to the attacker unless qualified by [**secret**]. In the example, the private channel is used for secure communication such as within a trusted domain or over an IPsec tunnel.

Constructors are functions used to build terms. They are declared by specifying their names, the types of the arguments and the return value (see lines 4-7). By default, functions are one-way; that is, the attacker cannot derive the arguments from the return value, unless qualified by [**data**] . Destructors (line 8) are special functions that are used to manipulate terms. Combined together, constructors and destructors are used to capture the relationship between cryptographic primitives. In the model of Fig. 3, the first three declared functions are used to derive the authentication parameters in the HSS process (lines 28-30). The last two are used to model a shared key encryption and decryption scheme.

```
1   free pubch: channel. free secch: channel [private].
2   type key. type id. type msgheader.
3   const ATT, ADR, ADQ, ACH, ARE: msgheader.
4   fun kdf(bitstring, key): key.
5   fun autn(bitstring, key): bitstring.
6   fun res(bitstring, key): bitstring.
7   fun senc(bitstring, key): bitstring.
8   reduc forall x: bitstring, y: key; sdec(senc(x, y), y) = x.
9   table db(id, key).
10  let UE() =
11      new imsi: id; new k: key;(* key provisionning *)
12      insert db(imsi, k);(* key activation *)
13      out(pubch, (ATT, imsi));(* attach request *)
14      in(pubch, (=ACH, r: bitstring, a: bitstring));
15      if a = autn(r, k) then
16          let kasme: key = kdf(r, k) in
17          out(pubch, (ARE, res(r, k))).(* authentication response *)
18  let MME() =
19      in(pubch, (=ATT, imsi: id));
20      out(secch, (ADQ, imsi));(* authentication data request *)
21      in(secch, (=ADR, kasme: key, a: bitstring, xr: bitstring, n: bitstring));
22      out(pubch, (ACH, n, a));(* authentication request *)
23      in(pubch, (=ARE, =xr)).
24  let HSS() =
25      in(secch, (=ADQ, imsi: id));(* authentication data request *)
26      new n: bitstring;
27      get db(=imsi, k: key) in
28      let kasme: key = kdf(n, k) in
29      let a: bitstring = autn(n, k) in
30      let r: bitstring = res(n, k) in
31      out(secch, (ADR, kasme, a, r, n)).(* authentication data response *)
32  process ((!UE()) | (!MME()) | (!HSS()))
```

Fig. 3. AKA model

Constants (line 3) are 0-arity functions that together with types can be used to improve the clarity of the model and can help reducing the number of valid traces during the analysis. This is also common behavior of implementations, i.e., a protocol implementation typically reject messages of unexpected types. In addition, we use the constants to identify the different exchanged messages so that they can be easily mapped in the corresponding chart (Fig. 2).

The language provides support for tables for persistent storage. In line 9, a table modeling the subscriber database is declared. Lines 11-12 model the process of registering a new subscriber; and line 27 models the process of retrieving the pre-shared secret key of a subscriber (variable k) given its identity (imsi).

Process Macros. Messages are represented by terms. A term can be a name, a variable, a tuple of terms, a constructor or destructor application. In addition, the language has support for some common Boolean functions $(=, \&\&, ||, <>)$ that use the infix notation. Pattern matching is used for term evaluation of message inputs. The pattern $x : t$ matches any term of type t and binds it to x. For a term M, the pattern $= M$ matches any term N such that $M = N$. A pattern tuple $(T_1, T_2, \ldots, T_n)$ matches any term tuple $(M_1, M_2, \ldots, M_n)$ where pattern matching is applyed recursively to each term M_i against pattern T_i. For example, the pattern $(= \texttt{ATT}, \texttt{imsi} : \texttt{id})$ in line 19 matches any term pair where the first one is the constant ATT and the second one is of type id.

Processes are defined as sequences of events. The name restriction event (line 26) creates a fresh name of a specific type and binds it inside the following events. The communication event **out**$(M, N); P$ (13), sends the term N on channel M and continue as the process P. The communication event **in**$(M, T); P$ (25), awaits a message matching pattern T on channel M and continues as P. The conditional **if** M **else** P **then** Q (15) continues as the process P if the term M evaluates to *true*, continues as the process Q if M evaluates to another value, or stops if M evaluation fails. The statement **let** $T = M$ **in** P **else** Q (28) tries to match the term M with pattern T, continues as the process P if there is a match, or continues as the process Q otherwise.

3.3   Security Properties

Security properties are declared with the keyword **query**. In our example of AKA, one of the goals is to establish the shared session key K_{ASME} between the MME and the UE. In order to check this, we consider the following properties.

```
1    event ueReachable(). event mmeReachable(). event hssReachable().
2    query event(mmeReachable()); event(hssReachable()); event(ueReachable()).
3    free secret: bitstring [private].
4    query attacker(secret).
5    event ueRunning(key). event ueCommit(key). event mmeRunning(key). event
        mmeCommit(key).
6    query k: key; event(ueCommit(k)) ==> event(mmeRunning(k)).
7    query k: key; event(mmeCommit(k)) ==> event(ueRunning(k)).
8    query k: key; inj-event(ueCommit(k)) ==> inj-event(mmeRunning(k)).
9    query k: key; inj-event(mmeCommit(k)) ==> inj-event(ueRunning(k)).
```

The first two declarations are used for sanity checks. The "reachability" events of line 1 are intended to be executed each at the end of the corresponding process macro. Events are special extension to the process grammar that do neither affect the attacker knowledge, nor the execution of the processes. When analyzing the query of line 2, ProVerif attempts to falsify its claims by generating traces that reach those events. This is useful to check that the processes can be fully executed and that there are no blocking events for example due to a constantly failing pattern matching. The declarations in lines 3-4 are used to check secrecy of the established key. The **attacker** (line 4) is a built-in predicate that can be used to check which terms are compromised.

The last declarations are correspondence assertions used for checking mutual agreement between the UE and the MME on the key. The syntax to query a basic correspondence assertion uses the **event** keyword (lines 5-7). Correspondence assertions where a one-to-one mapping is required between events, use the **inj-event** keyword instead. In our case, we recall Lowe's definitions of weak and injective agreement [20] and use the special "running" and "commit" events declared in line 5 together with the correspondence assertions of lines 6-7 to check for agreement on the established key between the MME and UE processes. In general, a commit event is added in the end of each "responder" process, to which another "initiator" process is trying to authenticate. Then for each commit, a running event is added in the "initiator" process before the last send operation.

3.4   Analysis and Discussion

ProVerif is able to solve all the properties except one of the reachability queries of line 2 and the injective correspondence assertion query of line 9. The remaining queries are solved as expected. More precisely, the correspondence and secrecy ones are proved to hold and the reachability queries are falsified.

The unresolved reachability query can be solved by restricting the attacker model. This is can be done by a special feature of ProVerif for setting internal configuration parameters. One of those parameters representing the attacker capability can be set to either *passive* or *active* directly in the model. Setting the attacker to passive has the effect of reducing the number of traces (improving the chances for termination) but the analysis is no longer sound. This is not a problem for reachability because a trace that reaches the target event in the restricted model is also valid in the non restricted one. ProVerif is then able to solve the unanswered reachability claim. Another way for achieving the same effect consists in declaring all communication channels as private. Intuitively, the goal is to check whether the protocol can be run at all in a secure environment by honest agents.

For the unresolved correspondence assertion, while further experimenting with the model we observed the following. When strengthening the claim by including an additional `id` parameter (see below), executing the corresponding commit and running events with the additional argument set to the `imsi`, and setting the attacker model to passive, then ProVerif is able to find an attack trace even for the corresponding non-injective assertion.

query i : id , k : key ; **event**(mmeCommit(i , k)) $\implies$ **event**(ueRunning(i , k)).

The attack trace is due to the ProVerif approximation [8]. In the following we describe intuitively the effects of this approximation. First, a send operation on private channels is never blocking even in case of none matching operation. This does not correctly model communication in the real system as it might be reliable (for example transport over TCP). Second, the private channel is a shared broadcast one. In our case, this is problematic as what is really needed is a tunnel-like model of communication that simulates peer-to-peer (secure) channels. The model provided by ProVerif is too broad allowing even honest agents to read and use messages not destined to them. Therefore, false attack traces sometimes appear.

4   Session Management

We consider now the procedures that take place after the terminal and MME have established the K_{ASME} by AKA (see Fig. 2). Observe that the terminal has also informed the MME about which security capabilities it supports (the ATT message). The security capabilities include lists of encryption and integrity protection algorithms that the terminal supports. As a consequence, when analyzed separately, some initialization steps are needed in the protocol models in order to set up the required security context assumed to be established by AKA.

4.1   NAS Security

NAS security is enabled by a simple request-response procedure [1] (TS 24.301) that we refer to as the NAS Security Control Procedure NAS_SCP (see Fig. 2). The procedure is initiated by the MME sending a security mode command message (NSM) to the terminal. This message indicates the security algorithms chosen by the MME. The message includes a special identifier eksi indicating which K_{ASME} to use as the basis for the key derivation. For various reasons there may be more than one K_{ASME} known simultaneously to the terminal and network [1] (TS 33.401). The message also contains the list of security capabilities provided earlier by the terminal.

In response, the terminal verifies that the received security capabilities are consistent with what the terminal supports. If the verification fails, the terminal rejects the command thus preventing bidding-down attacks. If the verification succeeds, the terminal sends an encrypted and integrity protected completion message (NSC). All NAS messages are protected from replay attacks by inclusion of a sequence number (omitted in our models).

Model Description. Figure 4 shows a ProVerif model of the NAS_SCP protocol. Compared to the AKA model, the novelty in the declaration part consists in the use of predicates and clauses to model capability sets (lines 6-9). Predicates are declared like constructors and clauses are needed in order to define the meaning of the predicates. In our case, we declare a capability set constructor together with a constant representing the empty set in line 6. Then we use the predicate of line 7 to model the set membership test function which is defined below in the clauses of lines 8-9.

Furthermore, the functions used for the shared encryption scheme (lines 4-5) have been modified in order to take into account an additional parameter representing the algorithm to be used.

The main process executes some initialization events then expands and forks in parallel unbounded number of sessions of two process macros representing a UE (line 13) and an MME (20). The initialization steps consist in creating a capability set of two arbitrary algorithms (lines 31-32), disclosing it to the attacker (33), and finally creating a secret K_{ASME} key (34). The key is supposed to have been created earlier during an AKA run, while the capabilities should have been sent by the UE at startup in an attach request. Both parameters are used as input arguments to the process macros.

The use of predicates is illustrated in line 23. This particular event binds the variable a : alg to a value that satisfies the predicate mem(a, uecaps) in the rest of the process. Intuitively, this models the MME choosing an algorithm among the ones supported by the UE. During the analysis ProVerif considers all possible choices.

Analysis and Discussion. The goal of NAS_SCP is to establish the encryption and integrity keys, K_{NASenc} and K_{NASint}, that are to be used for the NAS

```
1   free pubch: channel. free secch: channel [private].
2   type key.type alg. type caps. type id. type msgheader.
3   const NSM, NSC: msgheader. const NASINT, NASENC: bitstring.
4   fun psenc(alg, bitstring, key): bitstring.
5   reduc forall a: alg, x: bitstring, y: key; psdec(a, psenc(a, x, y), y) = x.
6   fun consset(alg, caps): caps [data]. const emptyset: caps.
7   pred mem(alg, caps).
8   clauses forall x: alg, y: caps; mem(x, consset(x, y));
9            forall x: alg, y: caps, z: alg; mem(x, y) -> mem(x, consset(z, y)).
10  fun kdf(bitstring, key): key. fun ksi(key): id.
11  fun pmac(alg, bitstring, key): bitstring.
12  free secret: bitstring [private].
13  let UE(uecaps: caps, kasme: key) =
14      in(pubch, (=NSM, =ksi(kasme), =uecaps, a: alg, nasmac: bitstring));
15      let knasint: key = kdf(NASINT, kasme) in
16      if mem(a, uecaps) && nasmac = pmac(a, (NSM, ksi(kasme), uecaps, a),
            knasint) then
17          let knasenc: key = kdf(NASENC, kasme) in
18          let msg: bitstring = (secret, pmac(a, (NSC, secret), knasint)) in
19          out(pubch, (NSC, psenc(a, msg, knasenc))).(* security mode complete *)
20  let MME(uecaps: caps, kasme: key) =
21      let eksi: id = ksi(kasme) in
22      let knasint: key = kdf(NASINT, kasme) in (* integrity protection *)
23      let a: alg suchthat mem(a, uecaps) in
24      let nasmac: bitstring = pmac(a, (NSM, eksi, uecaps, a), knasint) in
25      out(pubch, (NSM, eksi, uecaps, a, nasmac));(* security mode command *)
26      in(pubch, (=NSC, payload: bitstring));
27      let knasenc: key = kdf(NASENC, kasme) in (* confidentiality *)
28      let (=secret, nasmacr: bitstring) = psdec(a, payload, knasenc) in
29      if nasmacr = pmac(a, (NSC, secret), knasint) then 0.
30  process
31          new a1: alg; new a2: alg;
32          let uecaps = consset(a1, consset(a2, emptyset)) in
33          out(pubch, uecaps);
34          new kasme: key;
35          ((!UE(uecaps, kasme)) | (!MME(uecaps, kasme)))
```

Fig. 4. NAS security establishment model

protocol between the UE and the MME. In addition to the secrecy and sanity queries, we consider the following correspondence assertions in order to check agreement on the established keys and the chosen algorithm.

```
event ueRunning(alg, key, key). event ueCommit(alg, key, key).
event mmeRunning(alg, key, key). event mmeCommit(alg, key, key).
query a: alg, k1: key, k2: key;
    event(mmeCommit(a, k1, k2)) ==> event(ueRunning(a, k1, k2)).
query a: alg, k1: key, k2: key;
    inj-event(mmeCommit(a, k1, k2)) ==> inj-event(ueRunning(a, k1, k2)).
query a: alg, k1: key, k2: key;
    event(ueCommit(a, k1, k2)) ==> event(mmeRunning(a, k1, k2)).
query a: alg, k1: key, k2: key;
    inj-event(ueCommit(a, k1, k2)) ==> inj-event(mmeRunning(a, k1, k2)).
```

ProVerif is able to solve all the properties. The reachability queries are all falsified. The secrecy query and the basic correspondence assertions are proven to hold. However ProVerif reports attack traces on the injective assertions. This is not surprising as there is nothing in the protocol model that binds the runs to unique names (no creation of fresh names within the replicated processes). In fact the traces show that the attacker can falsify injection simply by duplicating and dropping messages to obtain a run between multiple parallel instances of MMEs against a single session of a UE and viceversa.

Modifying the model by moving the K_{ASME} key creation within the UE process and making the MME process read the key from a table leads to ProVerif proving that one of the direction holds. Intuitively, in the new model each run of the UE process is bound to a unique fresh key. Observe that this is a different system model since each replication of UE represents a new device rather than just a rerun of the same one. Furthermore, ProVerif is still able to report an attack trace for the other direction. This is expected as the modifications cannot prevent running in parallel multiple instances of MMEs that use the same K_{ASME} key and that can be matched against a single UE session. Since the K_{ASME} can only be present in one MME at a time, namely the one in which the UE is registered, it is not possible that two well behaved MMEs would be running NAS_SCP procedures simultaneously. Neither would a well behaved MME run two NAS_SCP procedures simultaneously by itself.

In fact well behaved agents would run the procedures sequentially. This we could not express in ProVerif. Even if we can express this sequential behavior, the injective agreement property will not hold. More precisely, assume the MME has sent two security mode command messages in separate sequential sessions, then it will not be able to distinguish to which session a reply belongs. This is because there is no information in the messages that tie them together, like for example a transaction identifier. It should be pointed out, that if an MME sends the same information repeatedly in different sessions, then regardless of which reply reaches the MME, the outcome of the whole procedure (algorithm negotiation and necessary key derivation) will be the same. From this perspective, injective agreement may not be necessary for this particular procedure.

4.2 RRC Security

Establishment of RRC security is achieved as follows: First, in order to send or receive data, the terminal needs to establish bearers to carry it. This is achieved by running a NAS Service Request Procedure with the network [1] (TS 24.301) and to which we refer by NAS_SRP (see Fig. 2). The terminal initiates the procedure by sending a service request (NSR) to the MME via the eNB. The radio channel between the UE and the eNB is not secured at this point, but this is not a problem since the NAS protocol provides its own security.

Upon reception of the request, the MME derives a K_{eNB} from the currently active K_{ASME} and the message sequence number associated with the NAS message. The latter parameter ensures that a fresh key is generated every time the procedure is run. This is necessary to prevent key stream re-use and replay attacks against the RRC protocol. The MME transfers the K_{eNB} together with the terminal's security capabilities to the eNB. The eNB sends a command message (RSM) to the terminal. This command includes the chosen algorithms and is integrity protected to prevent modification of the algorithm selection [1](TS 36.331). When the terminal receives the command, it derives the necessary keys and replies to the eNB with an encrypted and integrity protected completion message (RSC). From this point on, all RRC messages are integrity protected and encrypted, and all user plane traffic is encrypted.

Model and Analysis. A ProVerif model of the NAS_SRP is provided in Fig. 5. The declaration part has been removed as it is identical to that of the NAS_SCP model (see Fig. 4) except for some of the message headers and the constants used in the key derivation function, easily found in the model.

```
1   let UE(uecaps: caps, kasme: key) =
2       new nasulcount: bitstring; out(pubch, nasulcount);
3       out(secch, (NSR, nasulcount)); (* initial service request *)
4       in(pubch, (=RSM, a: alg, rrcmac: bitstring));
5       let kenb: key = kdf(nasulcount, kasme) in
6       let krrcint: key = kdf(RRCINT, kenb) in
7       if mem(a, uecaps) && rrcmac = pmac(a, (RSM, a), krrcint) then
8           let krrcenc: key = kdf(RRCENC, kenb) in
9           out(pubch, (RSC, psenc(a, (secret, pmac(a, (RSC, secret), krrcint)),
                krrcenc))).
10  let MME(uecaps: caps, kasme: key) =
11      in(secch, (=NSR, nasulcount));
12      let kenb: key = kdf(nasulcount, kasme) in
13      out(secch, (ISC, uecaps, kenb)); (* initial context setup *)
14      in(secch, =CSC).
15  let eNodeB() =
16      in(secch, (=ISC, uecaps: caps, kenb: key));
17      let krrcint: key = kdf(RRCINT, kenb) in (* integrity protection *)
18      let a: alg suchthat mem(a, uecaps) in
19      let rrcmac: bitstring = pmac(a, (RSM, a), krrcint) in
20      out(pubch, (RSM, a, rrcmac)); (* security mode command *)
21      let krrcenc: key = kdf(RRCENC, kenb) in (* confidentiality *)
22      in(pubch, (=RSC, payload: bitstring)); (* security mode complete *)
23      let (=secret, rrcmacr: bitstring) = psdec(a, payload, krrcenc) in
24      if rrcmacr = pmac(a, (RSC, secret), krrcint) then
25          out(secch, CSC). (* initial context setup response *)
26  process
27      ...
28      ((!UE(uecaps, kasme)) | (!eNodeB()) | (!MME(uecaps, kasme)))
```

Fig. 5. RRC security establishment model

The main process (line 26) executes some initialization steps then forks in parallel an unbounded number of sessions of three processes representing an UE (1), an MME (10) and an eNB (15) node. The initialization steps (omitted in the figure) are required to set up the parameters established earlier which are the user capabilities and the K_{ASME} key in a similar manner to how it is done in the model of Fig. 4. The additional in the model parameter denoted by nasulcount represents the NAS protocol message counter. This counter is used for deriving the K_{eNB} key (lines 5 and 12) that is to be provisioned to the eNB (13 and 16). It is incremented for each message exchange between the UE and MME. For example, this would be the effect of the send and matching receive operations of lines 3 and 11.

We model the counter by a fresh variable that we disclose (line 2) and make sure that it is synchronized by including it in the first NAS message (line 11). According to the specification [1](TS 33.401), when the counter, which is bounded, is about to wrap around then a new AKA run can be triggered in order to generate a new K_{ASME} key and thus preventing a K_{eNB} key reuse.

For the security properties, we consider the secrecy and sanity queries in a similar manner to the previous models. For the correspondence assertions, we focus on the agreement on the established K_{eNB} key and the chosen algorithm between the UE and the eNB. ProVerif solves all the queries as expected except one of the injective correspondence assertions (see Table 1).

5 Mobility Management

An eNB may detect that another eNB is better suited to serve an active terminal, for example because of better radio conditions. The source or serving eNB (denoted by S-eNB) hands over the terminal to the target eNB (denoted by T-eNB). There are two compound procedures to perform a handover. The first is a core network assisted handover that is called S1 handover (HO_S1). The second is a handover without core network assistance called X2 handover (HO_X2). The names come from the primary network interfaces used during the execution of the handovers.

5.1 X2 Handover

Handovers can be performed after the terminal has completed all necessary procedures so that RRC and NAS security has been activated. The X2 handover (Fig. 6) is initiated by the S-eNB calculating a K^*_{eNB} key from the currently active K_{eNB} and sending it together with the terminal security capabilities to the T-eNB in a handover request message (REQ). The T-eNB replies with the required configuration information for the terminal connection. This information includes the chosen algorithms that the T-eNB and the terminal shall use (CMD). The S-eNB then forwards the reply to the terminal, which confirms the handover with a completion message (CPL). In the last step, the T-eNB retrieves a new key called the Next Hop key (NH) from the MME. The NH which is derived from the K_{ASME} is to be used as a basis for the K^*_{eNB} calculation in the next handover event [1] (TS 33.401).

5.2 S1 Handover

In an S1 handover (Fig. 7), the S-eNB and target T-eNB are not directly connected. Instead, the S-eNB sends a handover required message (RQD) to the MME containing the security capabilities of the terminal. The MME then derives the NH key and sends it to the target node, together with the UE capabilities. The T-eNB uses the NH key to derive the K_{eNB} for communication with the terminal, and sends a handover command (CMD) containing the chosen algorithms to the source node. Finally, the S-eNB forwards the message to the terminal which replies to the T-eNB by a handover completed message (CPL).

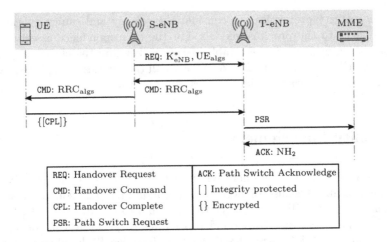

Fig. 6. X2 handover

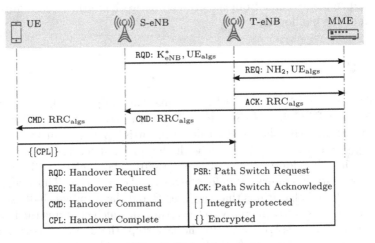

Fig. 7. S1 handover

5.3 Formal Models and Analysis

Both handover procedures involve four agents: a UE, a source S-eNB, a target T-eNB and an MME. The procedures are very similar but provide slightly different security guarantees. The ProVerif models of the protocols are provided in Fig. 8 and Fig. 9. The declaration parts have been omitted as they are very similar to previous models except for some types and constants.

In the model of X2 handover (Fig. 8), the main process performs the required initialization steps and forks unbounded sessions of the processes defined in lines 1, 6, 9 and 12 representing respectively a UE, an MME, a S-eNB and a T-eNB. The initialization steps include defining the UE capabilities (lines 22-24), the K_{ASME} key shared between the UE and the MME (25), and the K_{eNB}

```
1   let UE(uecaps: caps, kenb: key, cellid: bitstring) =
2       in(secch, (=CMD, a: alg));
3       if mem(a, uecaps) then
4           let kenbstar: key = kdf(cellid, kenb) in
5           out(pubch, (CPL, senc((a, mac((CPL, a), kenbstar)), kenbstar))).
6   let MME(nh_2: key) =
7       in(secch, =PSR);
8       out(secch, (ACK, nh_2)).
9   let SeNodeB(uecaps: caps, kenb: key, cellid: bitstring) =
10      let kenbstar: key = kdf(cellid, kenb) in
11      out(secch, (REQ, kenbstar, uecaps)).
12  let TeNodeB() =
13      in(secch, (=REQ, kenbstar: key, uecaps: caps));
14      let a: alg suchthat mem(a, uecaps) in
15      out(secch, (CMD, a));
16      in(pubch, (=CPL, msg: bitstring));
17      let (=a, rrcmac: bitstring) = sdec(msg, kenbstar) in
18      if rrcmac = mac((CPL, a), kenbstar) then
19          out(secch, PSR);
20          in(secch, (=ACK, nh_2: key)).
21  process
22          new a1: alg; new a2: alg;
23          let uecaps = consset(a1, consset(a2, emptyset)) in
24          out(pubch, uecaps);
25          new kasme: key; new nasulcount: bitstring; out(pubch, nasulcount);
26          let kenb: key = kdf(nasulcount, kasme) in
27          let nh_1: key = kdf(tobitstring(kenb), kasme) in
28          let nh_2: key = kdf(tobitstring(nh_1), kasme) in
29          new cellid: bitstring; out(pubch, cellid);
30          ( (!UE(uecaps, kenb, cellid)) | (!SeNodeB(uecaps, kenb, cellid)) |
31          (!TeNodeB()) | (!MME(nh_2)) )
```

Fig. 8. X2 handover model

shared between the UE and the S-eNB (26). The remaining additional steps are needed to establish some parameters required for deriving the current and future handover keys such as the next hop key (27-28) and the cell identifier for the T-eNB (29).

The model of S1 handover (Fig. 9) requires almost the same initialization steps (omitted here) except that the additional cell identifier `cellid` parameter of HO_X2 is no longer needed. The main difference between the models is in the MME role. In HO_S1, it is the MME that computes the key to be used in the T-eNB which is NH_2. However, in HO_X2 it is the S-eNB that computes the target's key which is the K^*_{eNB}. In addition, the MME provides its key (NH_2) in the last steps of the protocols (lines 7-8 and 20-21) for use in the next handover.

In both handover models, we consider the same type of sanity queries in order to check correctness. Recall that such queries are for special reachability events executed at each end of the process macros. ProVerif is not able to prove all of them. Nevertheless, the attack traces of the queries that ProVerif was able to falsify, show that the reachability events for the unresolved queries are executed as well. For the correspondence assertions, the aim is to prove agreement on the received handover key (K^*_{eNB} or NH_2) and the chosen algorithm between the UE and the T-eNB. ProVerif is able to prove all the assertions for the HO_X2 model

```
1   let UE(uecaps: caps, nh_2: key) =
2       in(secch, (=CMD, a: alg));
3       if mem(a, uecaps) then
4           out(pubch, (CPL, senc((a, mac((CPL, a), nh_2)), nh_2))).
5   let MME(uecaps: caps, nh_2: key) =
6       in(secch, =RQD);
7       out(secch, (ACK, nh_2, uecaps)).
8   let SeNodeB(kenb: key) =
9       out(secch, RQD).
10  let TeNodeB() =
11      in(secch, (=ACK, nh_2: key, uecaps: caps));
12      let a: alg suchthat mem(a, uecaps) in
13      out(secch, (CMD, a));
14      in(pubch, (=CPL, msg: bitstring));
15      let (=a, rrcmac: bitstring) = sdec(msg, nh_2) in
16      if rrcmac = mac((CPL, a), nh_2) then 0.
17  process
18              ...
19          ( (!UE(uecaps, nh_2)) | (!SeNodeB(kenb)) |
20            (!TeNodeB()) | (!MME(uecaps, nh_2)) )
```

Fig. 9. S1 handover model

Table 1. Analysis Results

Property	AKA	NAS_SCP	NAS_SRP	HO_X2	HO_S1
secrecy	true	true	true	true	true
weak-agree UE $\Longrightarrow$ ...	true	true	true	true	true
weak-agree ... $\Longrightarrow$ UE	true	true	true	true	true
inj-agree UE $\Longrightarrow$ ...	true	false	true	true	unresolved
inj-agree ... $\Longrightarrow$ UE	unresolved	false	unresolved	unresolved	unresolved

except one (see Table 1). For the HO_S1 model, ProVerif is unable to prove the injective assertions, but proves the basic ones.

6   Conclusion

We have presented our work on security protocols in LTE. We have used ProVerif to formalize and verify the protocols. Our analysis has shown that all the secrecy and weak agreement properties hold which was expected. However, we had difficulties proving stronger agreement properties. All our results are summarized in Table 1. To the best of our knowledge, the security command procedures and handover procedures have not been previously analyzed in this manner. During the modeling process, our aim was to remain as faithful as possible to the 3GPP specifications [1] of the protocols and their trust model. One important aspect that is lacking in ProVerif is the support for modeling local state information. As we explain later, support for that would relieve protocol designers from the common and tedious tasks of ensuring uniqueness of inputs to key derivations functions.

ProVerif verifies the models in the order of seconds on a regular laptop and the runtime is hence adequate for practical use. The concepts of the ProVerif input language matches the concepts used in the 3GPP specifications. Therefore, constructing the models does not take any significant time assuming familiarity with ProVerif and the system under study.

Future Work. We have been experimenting with other formal verification tools. For this first work, we thought that ProVerif offers a good compromise for ease of use and expressiveness of the input language. Nevertheless, we are planning to conduct a more thorough evaluation and comparison of similar tools. Furthermore, we believe that in an industrial context, such as for proposals to standardization processes, several tools should be used in combination in order to overcome their shortcomings. This does not necessarily mean that a process as defined by a standardization organization must formally mandate the use of such tools. In fact, as we explain below, there are few aspects in the protocols that we could not handle properly with ProVerif.

In general, freshness is achieved by guaranteeing uniqueness of the derived keys in each session. This can be implemented by using nonces, like in AKA for the derivation of the K_{ASME} key. However, all the derivation of lower level keys rely on other protocol parameters such as counters, cell identifiers, etc. Counters are part of the protocol state that is continuously being updated. We believe that any issue in the considered protocols would be most likely related to this aspect, especially when different protocols are interleaved and used arbitrarily in other more complex compound procedures. State-based formal verification tools can be better suited to model check such features. However in order to improve efficiency of such (usually exhaustive) state search, one can assume a weaker attacker model. As a future work, we are investigating to which extent the attacker model can be simplified and still be able to find attacks.

Other continuations of this work include performing similar analysis of the protocols for inter-operability between LTE and other types of radio access networks (GSM and WCDMA), and updating our models to handle different scenarios. For example, in the AKA model of Fig. 3, each run of the UE process represents a new device because in every run, a new fresh pair of IMSI, K is created and used. The model can be changed by adding another similar UE process which instead, gets the pair from the table being filled by the original process. This is how one can model arbitrary reruns of AKA by the same UE. In addition, the mobility models can be enhanced to include multi hop handovers. This can be used to verify further security properties, e.g. two hop forward security.

References

1. 3GPP The Mobile Broadband Standard, http://www.3gpp.org/specifications/
2. 10th Computer Security Foundations Workshop (CSFW 1997), Rockport, Massachusetts, USA, June 10-12. IEEE Computer Society (1997)
3. Abadi, M., Blanchet, B., Fournet, C.: Just Fast Keying in the Pi Calculus. In: Schmidt, D. (ed.) ESOP 2004. LNCS, vol. 2986, pp. 340–354. Springer, Heidelberg (2004)

4. Abadi, M., Fournet, C.: Mobile values, new names, and secure communication. In: Hankin, C., Schmidt, D. (eds.) POPL, pp. 104–115. ACM (2001)

5. Arapinis, M., Mancini, L.I., Ritter, E., Ryan, M., Golde, N., Redon, K., Borgaonkar, R.: New privacy issues in mobile telephony: fix and verification. In: Yu, T., Danezis, G., Gligor, V.D. (eds.) ACM Conference on Computer and Communications Security, pp. 205–216. ACM (2012)

6. Armando, A., et al.: The AVISPA Tool for the Automated Validation of Internet Security Protocols and Applications. In: Etessami, K., Rajamani, S.K. (eds.) CAV 2005. LNCS, vol. 3576, pp. 281–285. Springer, Heidelberg (2005)

7. Blanchet, B.: Automatic verification of correspondences for security protocols

8. Blanchet, B.: An Efficient Cryptographic Protocol Verifier Based on Prolog Rules. In: CSFW, pp. 82–96. IEEE Computer Society (2001)

9. Blanchet, B., Chaudhuri, A.: Automated Formal Analysis of a Protocol for Secure File Sharing on Untrusted Storage. In: IEEE Symposium on Security and Privacy, pp. 417–431. IEEE Computer Society (2008)

10. Blanchet, B., Smyth, B., Cheval, V.: ProVerif 1.88: Automatic Cryptographic Protocol Verifier, User Manual and Tutorial

11. Bodei, C., Buchholtz, M., Degano, P., Nielson, F., Nielson, H.R.: Automatic validation of protocol narration

12. Bouassida, M.S., Chridi, N., Chrisment, I., Festor, O., Vigneron, L.: Automated verification of a key management architecture for hierarchical group protocols. Annales des Télécommunications 62(11-12), 1365–1387 (2007)

13. Cremers, C.J.F.: The Scyther Tool: Verification, Falsification, and Analysis of Security Protocols. In: Gupta, A., Malik, S. (eds.) CAV 2008. LNCS, vol. 5123, pp. 414–418. Springer, Heidelberg (2008)

14. Cremers, C.J.F.: Session-state Reveal Is Stronger Than Ephemeral Key Reveal: Attacking the NAXOS Authenticated Key Exchange Protocol. In: Abdalla, M., Pointcheval, D., Fouque, P.-A., Vergnaud, D. (eds.) ACNS 2009. LNCS, vol. 5536, pp. 20–33. Springer, Heidelberg (2009)

15. Cremers, C.: Key Exchange in IPsec Revisited: Formal Analysis of IKEv1 and IKEv2. In: Atluri, V., Diaz, C. (eds.) ESORICS 2011. LNCS, vol. 6879, pp. 315–334. Springer, Heidelberg (2011)

16. Dolev, D., Yao, A.C.-C.: On the security of public key protocols. IEEE Transactions on Information Theory 29(2), 198–207 (1983)

17. Fang, J., Jiang, R.: An analysis and improvement of 3GPP SAE AKA protocol based on strand space model. In: 2010 2nd IEEE International Conference on Network Infrastructure and Digital Content, pp. 789–793 (September 2010)

18. Holzmann, G.J.: The Model Checker SPIN. IEEE Trans. Software Eng. 23(5), 279–295 (1997)

19. Jakobsson, M., Wetzel, S.: Security Weaknesses in Bluetooth. In: Naccache, D. (ed.) CT-RSA 2001. LNCS, vol. 2020, pp. 176–191. Springer, Heidelberg (2001)

20. Lowe, G.: A Hierarchy of Authentication Specification. In: CSFW [2], pp. 31–44

21. Lowe, G.: Casper: A Compiler for the Analysis of Security Protocols. In: CSFW [2], pp. 18–30

22. Meadows, C.: The NRL Protocol Analyzer: An Overview. J. Log. Program. 26(2), 113–131 (1996)

23. Meier, S., Schmidt, B., Cremers, C., Basin, D.: The TAMARIN Prover for the Symbolic Analysis of Security Protocols. In: Sharygina, N., Veith, H. (eds.) CAV 2013. LNCS, vol. 8044, pp. 696–701. Springer, Heidelberg (2013)

24. Qachri, N., Markowitch, O., Dricot, J.-M.: A formally Verififed Protocol for Secure Vertical Handovers in 4G Heterogeneous Networks. International Journal of Security and Its Applications 7(6) (2013)
25. Schmidt, B., Sasse, R., Basin, D.: Automated Verification of Group Key Agreement Protocols. In: IEEE Symposium on Security and Privacy (to appear, 2014)
26. Taha, A.M., Abdel-Hamid, A.T., Tahar, S.: Formal analysis of the handover schemes in mobile WiMAX networks. In: IFIP International Conference on Wireless and Optical Communications Networks, WOCN 2009, pp. 1–5 (April 2009)
27. Taha, A.M., Abdel-Hamid, A.T., Tahar, S.: Formal Verification of IEEE 802.16 Security Sublayer Using Scyther Tool. In: International Conference on Network and Service Security, N2S 2009, pp. 1–5 (June 2009)
28. Tang, C., Naumann, D.A., Wetzel, S.: Symbolic Analysis for Security of Roaming Protocols in Mobile Networks - (Extended Abstract). In: Rajarajan, M., Piper, F., Wang, H., Kesidis, G. (eds.) SecureComm. LNICST, vol. 96, pp. 480–490. Springer (2011)
29. Tsay, J.-K., Mjølsnes, S.F.: A Vulnerability in the UMTS and LTE Authentication and Key Agreement Protocols. In: Kotenko, I., Skormin, V. (eds.) MMM-ACNS 2012. LNCS, vol. 7531, pp. 65–76. Springer, Heidelberg (2012)
30. Zhang, M., Fang, Y.: Security analysis and enhancements of 3gpp authentication and key agreement protocol

Run Away If You Can:

Persistent Jamming Attacks against Channel Hopping Wi-Fi Devices in Dense Networks

Il-Gu Lee, Hyunwoo Choi, Yongdae Kim, Seungwon Shin, and Myungchul Kim

Graduate School of Information Security
Korea Advanced Institute of Science and Technology (KAIST)
291 Daehak-ro, Yuseong-gu, Daejeon, Republic of Korea 305-701
{iglee9,zemisolsol,yongdaek,claude,mck}@kaist.ac.kr

Abstract. Wireless local area networks (WLANs) can adopt channel hopping technologies in order to avoid unintentional interferences such as radars or microwaves, which function as proactive jamming signals. Even though channel hopping technologies are effective against proactive types of jamming, it has been reported that reactive jammers could attack the targets through scanning busy channels. In this paper, we demonstrate that reactive jamming is only effective against channel hopping Wi-Fi devices in non-dense networks and that it is not effective in dense networks. Then, we propose a new jamming attack called *"persistent jamming"*, which is a modified reactive jamming that is effective in dense networks. The proposed persistent jamming attack can track a device that switches channels using the following two features, and it can attack the specific target or a target group of devices. The first feature is that the proposed attack can use the partial association ID (PAID), which is included for power saving in the IEEE 802.11ac/af/ah frame headers, to track and jam the targets. The second feature is that it is possible to attack persistently based on device fingerprints in IEEE 802.11a/b/g/n legacy devices. Our evaluation results demonstrate that the proposed persistent jamming can improve the attack efficiency by approximately 80% in dense networks compared with the reactive jamming scheme, and it can also shut down the communication link of the target nodes using 20 dBm of jamming power and a 125 ms response time.

Keywords: WLAN, jamming, channel hopping, device tracking, ID, fingerprint, security.

1 Introduction

Wireless local area network (WLAN) technologies are an essential feature of everyday life because they are used in home networking, smart mobile devices, network infrastructure, and much more. These applications require very high throughput and long service coverage. In order to meet these demands of the users, WLAN technologies have been evolving to use wider channel bandwidths for IEEE 802.11n/ac [2,4] in the 2.4/5 GHz industry science and medical (ISM) band, and they support lower receiver sensitivity for a wider range of up to approximately 1 km for IEEE 802.11af/ah in the TV white space or sub-1 GHz frequencies [5,6]. As more and more wireless devices are connected and wireless access points (APs) are densely deployed in the scarce frequency spectrum and

A. Stavrou et al. (Eds.): RAID 2014, LNCS 8688, pp. 362–383, 2014.
© Springer International Publishing Switzerland 2014

in the limited region, the failure probability of packet transmissions is expected to increase due to interference from other devices and jammers. Because the 2.4 GHz band is already congested and the 5 GHz band will be congested soon [15], the wireless environment may suffer severe interference from unintentional jammers and intentional jammers [9, 17].

Recent studies have demonstrated that various proactive jamming methods such as constant, random, and deceptive jamming can be launched easily in wireless networks [10, 26]. Meanwhile, in order to manage jamming attacks, wireless nodes can adopt a channel hopping scheme through which nodes can switch their channel frequencies as required in order to improve the link quality [10, 28, 29]. If a certain channel is not available due to jamming signals, the wireless nodes switch channels to another idle channel according to the channel hopping protocol; consequently, the wireless nodes can avoid proactive jamming attacks. In the literature, several studies have proposed a smart jamming scheme called "reactive jamming" for efficient jamming attacks [10, 26]. The reactive jammer, which is the most popularly discussed method for disturbing channel hopping nodes, investigates a busy channel in order to identify a channel-hopped node and begins emitting a jamming signal as soon as it senses activity on that channel because the shared nature of the wireless medium allows adversaries to easily monitor the communications between wireless devices. Therefore, even though the target nodes have switched to another channel due to the jamming signal, the jammer can switch to the target node's new channel and attack again. However, the reactive jamming schemes assume that attackers can locate a channel-hopped target because the network is not dense [10, 26, 28, 29]. If there are multiple devices using different channels, the challenging question to the adversary is how to determine which channel is being used by the target device.

Our contribution In this paper, we first demonstrate that the existing jamming attacks are not effective against channel hopping devices in dense networks. Because there are multiple nodes in the channel in dense networks, a conventional jammer cannot identify the target node's channel among the multiple candidates due to the lack of channel awareness and device information. In this situation, the only way to disturb a specific node's communication is to emit a jamming signal to all busy channels and, consequently, the detection possibility of the jamming attack increases and the jamming efficacy decreases in terms of the attacker's cost and attacking damage. For this reason, a jamming attack in a dense network is considered extremely difficult. Despite the limitations, in order to stop this, in this paper we propose a new jamming method called "persistent jamming", which is a novel attack in the form of modified reactive jamming. Moreover, we demonstrate that identifying a channel hopping device and launching a jamming attack in a dense network are feasible. Based on the observation that the partial association identification (PAID) and device fingerprints can be used to identify channel hopping devices in dense networks, the attacker can persistently track and jam target devices. Our evaluation results demonstrate that persistent jamming using the PAID and device fingerprint detection can improve the attack efficiency by approximately 80% in dense networks compared with the reactive jamming scheme, and it can continuously degrade the throughput to close to zero against channel hopping target devices in order that the communication link is disconnected with a 20 dBm jamming power and 125 ms response time.

Our work provides the following three key contributions.

- This is the first investigation of the limitations of the unprotected PHY header that is identified using PAID and fingerprints extracted from the frame header in order to track a target device or a target group of devices, and to examine the feasibility of persistent jamming.
- Persistent jamming is experimentally evaluated in a field programmable gate array (FPGA) prototype that was designed and verified for commercialization as an IEEE 802.11n/ac Wi-Fi chipset.
- The proposed attack is also implemented and evaluated in a cycle true and bit true emulation platform in order to demonstrate its feasibility and performance in a dense network.

The remainder of the paper is organized as follows. In Section 2, we present the related work on the jamming attack and mitigation. In Section 3, we overview the WLAN frame format to discuss the security implications of frame headers, and propose the persistent jamming attack based on the security limitations of frame headers. In Section 4, we present the experimental setup and demonstrate the evaluation results. In Section 5, we recommend security remedies. The paper is concluded in Section 6.

2   Related Work

In this section, we present the related literature on jamming attack and mitigation.

2.1   Jamming Attack

Wireless LAN networks are highly sensitive to incidental and intentional interferences because they use a carrier sense multiple access with collision avoidance (CSMA/CA) mechanism and an orthogonal frequency division multiplexing (OFDM) modulation. IEEE 802.11-based WLAN devices defer access to a channel if the channel is busy at the transmitter or if it cannot decode the distorted OFDM modulated symbols at the receiver when the interference exceeds a specified tolerance level. Interference occurs when a node transmits a signal without verifying whether another node is accessing the same channel through increasing the clear channel assessment (CCA) threshold. In this way, the malicious node achieves its goal by degrading the signal quality at legitimate receivers or by disabling channel access at legitimate transmitters to disrupt the communication link or shut down legitimate devices. Thus, the availability of the wireless network is subverted easily through jamming attacks, which easily allow an attacker to disturb the wireless devices'communications through emitting electromagnetic signals in the wireless medium. Recently, increasing jamming attacks have been reported because attackers can easily disrupt wireless communications networks using commercial jamming devices and easily modified commercial products [8, 10, 17, 26].

There are two types of jammers: proactive jammers and reactive jammers. The proactive jammers have three forms: constant, random, and deceptive [10].

As their names imply, the constant jammer and random jammer emit a constant jamming signal continuously and jamming signals at random times, respectively, while the deceptive jammer injects decodable packets into the channel. Proactive jammers are the most prevalent jamming form due to their easy implementation that attempts to emit jamming signals irrespective of the traffic pattern in the channel, but they are inefficient in terms of attacking damage, detection probability, and energy efficiency due to the lack of channel awareness. In contrast, reactive jammers only emit a jamming signal if the channel is busy. If there is no traffic in the current channel, the reactive jammer waits and senses the channel for a predetermined time, and then switches to a busy channel and continues to jam. It is a more effective jamming attack even though the implementation is relatively complicated. This channel awareness allows for efficient jamming because it must transmit short jamming signals in a timely manner. The authors of [26] developed a software-defined reactive jammer prototype and demonstrated that a real-time reactive jammer is feasible and a serious threat to WLAN services. However, previous studies on the reactive jammer assuming non-dense networks [10, 17, 26] are limited because it has a low attack success rate when the target device switches to a different channel in a dense network because conventional jammers cannot differentiate a specific device or target group of devices from multiple candidates. In this paper, we focus on a realistic environment, i.e. a dense network, in which there are multiple devices using different channels and, in Section 5, we experimentally demonstrate that the existing reactive jamming is not effective in dense networks.

2.2 Jamming Mitigation

Traditionally, channel hopping and link adaptation techniques have been developed as solutions that mitigate the effect of jamming [1, 14, 16, 19, 22, 23, 31]. Channel hopping techniques attempt to avoid jammed channels through changing the channel among the orthogonally available channel bands. There are three types of channel hopping schemes: proactive, reactive, and passive. A pair of nodes using proactive channel hopping has a hopping sequence that periodically changes [14]. In a reactive channel hopping scheme, a node only switches to a different channel if it detects the presence of jamming signal [1, 16, 19, 23]. If a coordinator or pair of nodes decides to switch channels, all other nodes in the network switch channels as well. Consequently, the proactive channel hopping schemes are fast, but they are not used in WLANs due to their inefficiency and complexity, whereas reactive channel hopping schemes are slow but are used in WLAN products. In some commercial devices, passive-type channel hopping using firmware enables users to switch channels [24], and users can switch channels manually if the link is disconnected. However, passive channel hopping schemes require much longer to avoid interference and could worsen the situation. In addition, the IEEE 802.11h standard defines the dynamic frequency selection (DFS) mechanism in order to avoid interference from radars and other WLAN devices [3]. The DFS mechanism allows an AP and its associated stations to dynamically switch to another channel in order to avoid interference.

Link adaptation techniques can be used to improve link quality in order to compete with dynamically varying interference [22, 24, 31]. A node can mitigate the jamming effect in order to cause the link to be more robust using link adaptation schemes such as transmit power control (TPC), modulation and coding scheme (MCS) control, and CCA threshold control. Link adaptation schemes can be effective against jammers that follow the equivalent isotropically radiated power (EIRP) regulations determined by the Federal Communications Commission (FCC), but a malicious jammer may transmit signals without considering the transmit power limitations and emit radio interference with external power amplifiers even if the output is saturated. Therefore, typical legitimate nodes first attempt to adapt the link through controlling the system parameters, and then they switch channels if the error rate or link quality does not meet the system requirements.

In order to mitigate jamming attacks, the authors in [10] and [28] proposed a series of basic detection methods based on the PHY layer. The basic concept of detecting the jamming attacks was simple: the presence of jamming radio signals at the receiver can affect the received signal strength. In addition, there have been several studies on jamming effect analyses and interference mitigation methods [16,23,24]. The authors analyzed the jamming effects on WLAN systems and presented the TPC and rate control as competition against jammers. In order to achieve this, they presented a smart jammer model that scans the entire spectrum of channels, locates a busy channel, and attacks again. However, in highly dense networks and congested spectra, the attacker cannot identify specific target nodes or a target group because there are numerous candidates, and the busy state does not guarantee that the target devices will be in the channel. Thus, the attacker cannot continue to attack the target devices in dense networks.

3   Our Persistent Jamming Attack

This section introduces the tracking approaches of PHY PAID and device fingerprint to trace the channel hopping target nodes that hop channels while communicating with the AP in order to avoid jamming attacks. We review the frame format and depict the limitations from a security perspective in Section 3.1. In Sections 3.2 and 3.3, we describe the persistent jamming attack mechanism that includes the tracking and jamming techniques using PAID and device fingerprints such as SNR and timing offset.

3.1   Security Limitations

As shown in Figure 1, even though a target node switches to another channel in order to avoid jamming attacks, a persistent jammer can identify the target node's channel frequency based on the frame header information: the ID information in the signal field and the device fingerprint from the preamble. Then, the attacker can use this information to attack more effectively in ways such as tracking and jamming target devices, or jamming at a specific time or frequency. Therefore, through capturing a single packet and examining its header, an adversary can determine the existence of the target in a channel.

The frame header information is becoming more important because modern wireless communication systems have been designed to support advanced transmission techniques for high throughput, high energy efficiency, and quality of service (QoS). Therefore, frame headers include more information for wireless connectivity in the evolving Wi-Fi standards. Frame headers are transmitted using binary phase shift keying (BPSK) modulation and the lowest rate transmission mode (6 Mbps) in order to ensure reliable reception. However, frame headers do not have protection mechanisms, but the data payload is protected by security protocols and encryption techniques. The encrypted data payload uses cryptography to protect the data against eavesdropping, tampering, forging, and other security attacks. Even if the frame is intercepted, the encryption causes the data payload to be unusable. However, the unencrypted header that contains the PAID and device fingerprint is not protected: if the channel frequency of a transmitted packet is tracked, an adversary can easily jam the link to prevent communication. This is a significant threat to wireless device users because the channel frequency usage is important privacy information in a wireless network, and this data can be tracked and jammed by an attacker.

Figure 1 presents the frame structure of the IEEE 802.11ac standard specified in [4]. A frame contains a header, payload, frame check sequence (FCS), and padding/tails. The frame header consists of a preamble, signal fields, service field, and medium access control (MAC) header. The PHY frame header is used in the signal detection, timing acquisition, and signal decoding information, and the MAC frame header includes the address information and control signals. The frame body field contains variable length data information which can be encrypted. The L-STF is used for carrier sensing, gain control, and coarse frequency acquisition; the L-LTF is used for fine frequency acquisition and channel estimation. The signal fields convey information about the rate, length, and transmission mode for the receiver to decode the remainder of the received frame. The VHT-STF is used for fine gain control, and the VHT-LTF is used for channel estimation of the VHT frames. The VHT-SIG-B is used for user-specific information in multi-user transmissions. The service field is originally used to initialize the descrambler. In the data fields, the receiver decodes the incoming symbols and tracks phase errors using pilots. Any receiver can detect the PAID included in the VHT-SIG-A or extract the device fingerprint from the STFs and LTFs because the frame header is not protected. In the IEEE 802.11ac/ah/af standard, the PAID in the physical (PHY) layer header is adopted in order to improve the power efficiency for a specific user's device. The PAID information is

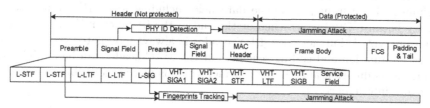

Fig. 1. IEEE 802.11ac WLAN frame structure and persistent jamming attack

a good indicator for identifying a specific node, but there is no PAID information in legacy frames such as IEEE 802.11a/b/g/n. Therefore, we use both PAID and fingerprint detection for our persistent jamming in this paper. Through utilizing the PAID information in the frame header, a persistent jammer is able to detect the changed channel if it has captured the PAID information in previously attacked channels. If there is no device that supports power saving using PAID, an attacker can track and jam a specific target or a group of target devices through analyzing the physical characteristics from the frame header information and using the device fingerprints.

3.2 ID Detection

Because WLAN devices use a contention-based channel access scheme, the preamble and signal field should be detected and decoded by all nodes in the network in order to appropriately defer access to a channel. Based on the CSMA/CA protocol, each device must listen to the channel in order to determine whether it should decode the incoming packet. Although several MAC level power saving schemes exist, they are not designed for the awake mode and they improve power efficiency through increasing the sleep period. In many consumer electronics, it is expected that an active mode device has fewer changes in the sleep mode in order to maintain an awake state that supports QoS. Therefore, the IEEE 802.11ac/af/ah standard defines the physical layer header information in order to determine whether or not to listen and decode an incoming data packet. The physical layer header information for power saving is called PAID, and it is used to identify the intended receiver so that non-intended receivers can avoid unnecessary signal processing for the remainder of the packet and to allow micro-sleeps for physical layer power saving. In order that devices in the same or overlapped basic service sets (BSSs) can avoid having the same PAID and to maximize the power saving efficiency, the PAID is determined by the device's PAID using an offset based on the AP's BSSID with which the device is associated. The additional offset minimizes the probability of the same ID use among OBSSs. Therefore, the PAID in the signal field can be used to identify the destination of the packet for any node in the wireless network. If the frame includes the ID information, it is much easier to identify the target node than the device fingerprint detection because the false positive detection rate of the ID is as low as the error rate of signal field, which is modulated using the BPSK and 1/2 code rate, as described in Section 4.1. As an alternative approach, MAC IDs such as address or SSID can be utilized. The PHY signal field has its own cyclic redundancy check (CRC) so that the receiver can use it reliably at the beginning of the frame, while the data field including MAC ID requires long latency because CRC is attached at the end of the frame even if the MAC ID is not encrypted. Furthermore, PHY header is always modulated by the most robust modulation and coding scheme, but the MAC header can be modulated by higher modulation and coding scheme, which is more susceptible to channel noise and interference.

3.3   Fingerprint Detection

Wireless fingerprinting techniques have typically been investigated for device localization [11, 12, 32]. Location fingerprinting uses deterministic and probabilistic methods for static estimation in order to determine the position using the device's physical characteristics such as the received signal strength indicator (RSSI) and clock jitter. The wireless fingerprinting techniques can be applied in location-based services or to improve the system security level. However, malicious uses of device fingerprints have not been investigated, particularly regarding jamming attacks. In this paper, we first demonstrate that a wireless device can be tracked and attacked persistently if an adversary can extract fingerprints from any frames in the wireless channel. The attacker can track the target device based on the device fingerprints generated using a unique circuit design. An electronic fingerprint or radio channel fingerprint enables the identification of a wireless device using its unique characteristics. An attacker is able to extract and analyze the physical characteristics from the PHY header, such as timing offset, RSSI, signal-to-noise ratio (SNR), and error vector magnitude (EVM); then, it can track and jam a target device using the fingerprints. In this paper, we describe how to extract the SNR and timing offset from these fingerprints in order to demonstrate the feasibility of device tracking. Although any fingerprints can be used for persistent jamming, we demonstrate the feasibility of the attack using the SNR adjusted by the EVM or timing offset assisted by both preamble and pilots due to high accuracy of estimation and reusability of the existing circuits in WLAN devices. Furthermore, in order to improve the uniqueness, we combine two different physical fingerprints, and evaluate them in Section 4.1. In a highly dense network, if higher uniqueness of physical fingerprints is required, we can combine a set of physical fingerprints.

SNR Estimation. As a signal quality indicator in a typical WLAN indoor wireless channel, the SNR can be an important factor in link adaptation based on the transmission signal quality and channel propagation loss in the received signal. An attacker can also use the measured SNR with the captured frame to determine whether a specific device uses the channel frequency in a typical indoor channel. The long training field is 8 μs in length and is composed of two identical 3.2 μs symbols. As a result of the symbol repetition, this long training field can be used to estimate the SNR [30]. The receiver extracts the two long training samples before the fast Fourier transform (FFT) processing in order to estimate the received signal quality including the transmitter/receiver impairments and channel propagation loss. In order to calculate the noise power, the samples from the first long training symbol are subtracted from the samples of the second symbol. Moreover, the two symbols are averaged in order to calculate the signal power. With the noise and signal powers, the receiver can calculate the SNR for the received frame.

The EVM is an error vector magnitude, which is a measurement to calculate distance between the received sample points and the ideal locations. The EVM can be calculated in the frequency domain using a more complicated calculation after estimating the channel response and decoding the signal field, while the

SNR can be calculated in the time domain using a simple calculation with two long training symbols [2,4,18]. The SNR typically has a linear relationship with the EVM [21]. In addition, the EVM allows the receiver to further analyze the characteristics through observing noise patterns in the frequency and time domains as a different form of SNR representation. The EVM is more useful in analyzing digitally modulated signals because the receiver can use the long data payload or pilot subcarriers to measure the signal quality, even though it requires more multipliers and adders to calculate the values of higher modulations. The EVM is a good indicator for relating the analog impairment to the device fingerprints. Through calculating the average EVM for every symbol over the subcarrier indexes of a signal field or the pilot subcarriers during one packet, the attacker can identify the device using the fingerprints. Consequently, the attacker can adjust the SNR calculated at the preamble using the pilots' EVM until the end of the frame.

Timing Offset Estimation. The sampling timing offset results from the oscillator difference between the transmitter and receiver. In the frequency domain, the phase rotation increases as time passes and the amount of phase rotation increases as the frequency increases, which is the same as in the sampling phase error. The IEEE 802.11 standard limits the timing offset to less than $+/-20$ ppm for WLAN devices. According to the Fourier transform properties, the time shift of the time domain signal has a phase rotation in the frequency domain representation of the signal, where the amount of phase rotation increases as the frequency increases. Thus, the timing offset estimator is derived using the least square rule [20]. In the derivation, the amount of sampling phase error is assumed to be small in order that the exponential term can be approximated using the linear function of the phase error. The accuracy of the estimator can be improved through using more subcarriers in multiple symbols.

Furthermore, because the carrier frequency and sampling frequency in wireless communications systems are driven by a common clock source, the frequency offset estimation result can be used to estimate the timing offset in order to improve the estimation accuracy [13]. The carrier frequency offset (CFO) is the carrier frequency difference between the transmitter and receiver. The phase rotation between two samples in repetitive training symbols separated by a time delay allows the receiver to calculate an accurate estimate of the carrier frequency offset. In WLAN systems, two preamble structures are supported, i.e. short and long preambles. The short preamble consists of 10 repetitions of the same symbol with a duration of 0.8 μs. The long preamble has two repeated symbols with a symbol period of 3.2 μs. Because the symbols are repeated, the phase rotation between two successive symbols can be estimated without knowing the channel response. The CFO is estimated twice using the short and long preambles. The initial coarse CFO is estimated using the short training field, and then the residual fine CFO is estimated using the long training field. The initial value in the timing offset estimator can be appropriately assigned using the CFO estimation, which is calculated using the preamble in advance. Then, the timing offset is adjusted using the phase offsets of the pilot tones in the data.

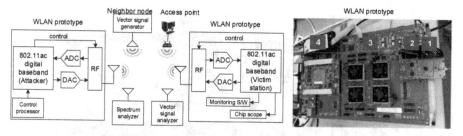

Fig. 2. Experimental setup for the prototype system

4   Implementation and Evaluation of Our Proposed Attack

In this section, we describe the experimental setup for the prototype and emulation for our proposed attack. The prototype is used for realistic experiments in the laboratory, and the emulation environment is used for multiple BSSs. Then, we present the experimental results and discuss their implications.

4.1   Real World Experiment

Experimental Setup. As shown in Figure 2, the experimental setup consisted of two WLAN prototypes, a commercial AP, a vector signal generator (VSG), a vector signal analyzer (VSA), and a spectrum analyzer. The FPGA prototypes satisfy the functionalities and performance requirements of the IEEE 802.11ac standard. One prototype is an attacker that performs a programmed jamming attack using a software controller, and the other prototype is a target node that communicates with the commercial AP. The performances and functionalities can be observed through monitoring software and a chip scope. The target node and AP communicate on channel 44. If the packet error count is larger than a predetermined threshold due to interference, they switch to channel 60. The VSG functions as a neighbor node that sends IEEE 802.11ac compliant frames in channel 52. A spectrum analyzer is used to monitor the full span spectrum in the ISM bands, and the VSA is used to analyze the signal characteristics and its effect. The image in the right of Figure 2 also illustrates the developed WLAN prototype, which consists of (1) MAX2829 RF IC, (2) analog device AD9780 digital-to-analog converter (DAC), Texas Instruments ADS4249 ADC, (3) four Xilinx Virtex6 FPGAs, and (4) an ARM Cortex-A5 processor. The four FPGAs are programmed for functionalities in the IEEE 802.11n/ac system, which has been verified with commercial products to meet the Wi-Fi certification requirements. The developed WLAN prototype can be utilized for a persistent jamming attack, and if the hardware of the other WLAN products supports functionalities for IEEE 802.11ac, such hardware can be used for the proposed attack. In order to reduce development cost, an universal software radio peripheral (USRP) can be used to develop the WLAN prototype as an alternative to the FPGAs.

This prototype was developed in order to verify the functionality and performance of the digital baseband PHY/MAC system before taping for silicon. The circuits targeted in the prototype were designed to support IEEE 802.11a/g/n/ac with a single antenna and to support a high data rate of up to 433 Mbps in the

Fig. 3. Experimental setup: (a) overall test configuration and (b) jammer

2.4 GHz and 5 GHz ISM bands. The RF IC is connected to the digital baseband through the ADC and DAC ICs operating at a 160 MHz sampling rate. The digital baseband controls the RF transceiver, which changes the system parameters including the TX/RX mode, gain, channel frequency, and filter mode through external pins or a serial-to-parallel interface (SPI).

Evaluation Results. All test results were measured in a laboratory environment. The experimental setup consisted of two FPGA boards: one was an attacker and the other was a target node. Figure 3 illustrates the experimental setup for the throughput measurement at the target node when the attacker used different jamming schemes: reactive and persistent jamming. Figure 3(a) illustrates the configuration of the jammer, neighbor node, target node, and access point, and Figure 3(b) illustrates the FPGA prototype

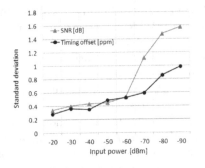

Fig. 4. Wired test: standard deviation of device fingerprints

(jammer) and vector signal generator (neighbor node). There is a target node and an AP that communicate in channel 44 or channel 60 using channel hopping in order to avoid jamming signals. They control the transmission rate using link adaptation to mitigate channel variations and jamming effects. In channel 52, a neighbor node periodically sends packets, which are generated by a vector signal generator. The jammer is implemented on the FPGA prototype through setting a high level CCA threshold in order to ignore other nodes'transmissions, and the jammer generates a jamming signal based on a jamming strategy: a reactive or a persistent jamming scheme.

Figure 4 presents the standard deviation of the measured fingerprints in the wired tests. When the input power was larger than 60 dBm, the standard deviation was less than 0.6 dB or 0.6 ppm for short distances. Small incoming signals from 60 dBm to 90 dBm had an accuracy of less than 1.6 dB or 1 ppm over long distances. Therefore, the digital baseband could estimate the SNR and timing offset as accurately as 1.6 dB and 1 ppm using preambles in the physical

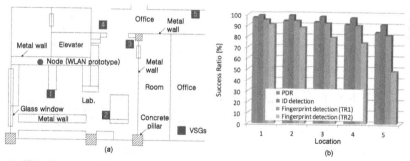

Fig. 5. Wireless test: (a) wireless measurement conditions and (b) detection success ratio vs. location

layer header for the full dynamic range. The SNR-based fingerprinting method is particularly effective for indoor channels because it is not significantly affected by multipath propagation. Furthermore, the accuracy is generally adequate for most indoor wireless applications but could be reduced through temporary physical obstructions or deviations in the radiation pattern of the target device. In low input power regions, the timing offset-based fingerprinting method has the potential to achieve higher accuracy than the SNR-based fingerprint method because the SNR and EVM are influenced more by various noise sources at the receiver in low input power regions.

Figure 5(a) depicts the experimental setup used to measure the detection success ratio of the PAID and fingerprints in wireless conditions. We measured the standard deviation of the SNR and timing offset in wired and wireless conditions. First, we tested the standard deviation in wired conditions using RF coaxial cables and RF attenuators. The VSG transmitted signals with an 8 ppm timing offset and various power levels from the vector signal generator, and the jammer measured the timing offset and SNR based on the received preambles. A Litepoint IQxel vector signal generator was used to create all packets, which were modulated and coded using MCS0 (BPSK and R $= 1/2$) and were transmitted in the 40 MHz bandwidth. The wired test enabled full control of the channel conditions and precise control while monitoring the results. Then, we performed a wireless test at different locations. We measured the detection success ratio in five different locations in order to include various wireless indoor channel and interference effects. The proposed jammer was located where the packet delivery ratio (PDR) and detection success ratio (DSR) of the PAID and device fingerprints on the SNR and timing offset could be measured. Locations 1 and 2 had line-of-sight (LOS) conditions, while Locations 3, 4, and 5 had non-line-of-sight (NLOS) conditions. The fingerprints were measured in root mean square (RMS) values and the standard deviation of over 100 packets.

As shown in Figure 5(b), we also measured the detection success ratio of the transmitted packet from different wireless conditions. The results demonstrated that the ID detection success ratio was higher than 90% for all locations, and the fingerprint detection success ratio was higher than 80% for all locations. The fingerprint detection performance was also related to the detection threshold.

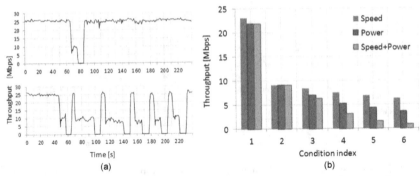

Fig. 6. (a) A throughput measurement at target node for jamming attack reactive jammr (upper), and persistent jammer (lower), and (b) jamming efficacy: throughput vs. speed and power

Two thresholds were used: Threshold 1 (TR1) had a 2 dB SNR and 1 ppm timing offset threshold, and Threshold 2 (TR2) had a 4 dB SNR and 2 ppm timing offset threshold. We observed that there was a trade-off related to the threshold between the detection success ratio and false positive detection ratio. If the threshold was large, the persistent jammer's detection was more frequent. However, the false positive detection probability also increased. In contrast, if the threshold was small, the misdetection probability was higher. The TR1 and TR2 were selected as optimal threshold sets for accurate detection and fast detection in order to cover the full dynamic range of the WLAN, respectively. A fundamental limitation of the accuracy that could be attained when measuring fingerprints resulted from the random noise and fading effects. However, if the distorted packet was filtered and adjusted by EVM and timing offset from pilots at the receiver, the SNR and timing offset measurement directly reflect the signal quality determined using a unique device. Furthermore, the PHY-based ID and fingerprint detection was faster than MAC-based schemes.

We compared the jamming effectiveness of the persistent jamming attack with a reactive jamming attack through observing the throughput at the target node. As shown in Figure 6(a), the reactive jammer succeeded in its first attack on the target node within approximately 65 seconds (above) and 45 seconds (below). After the target node switched to a different channel, the reactive jammer could not attack it because the reactive jammer attacked channel 52 rather than channel 60. In contrast, the persistent jammer switched to the target device's channels. As a result, the measured throughput was continuously degraded even though the target node switched channels. In order to evaluate the efficacy of the jamming schemes over the attacker's capability, different response times and transmit powers were used as described in Table 1. In this table, (x,y) refers to the condition with x second response time (R_T) and y dBm transmit power (T_P). The reactive jammer used only the fastest response time and largest transmit power in order to obtain the best performance, while the persistent jammer had various response times and transmit powers for comparison with the reactive jammer.

Figure 6(b) presents the effective throughput over the condition index from Table 1, as a function of the jamming speed and transmission power for reactive and persistent jammers. The results indicate that reactive jamming is significantly less effective than persistent jamming, which can significantly reduce the throughput of the target node in dense network conditions. The reactive jammer could not improve the jamming efficacy in the communication link even though it had the fastest response time and highest transmit power, while the persistent jammer could improve as the speed and power increased. As we presented in Section 2.1, due to the inefficiency and complexity, Wi-Fi devices use the reactive channel hopping schemes or passive-type channel switching scheme instead of the proactive channel hopping schemes. Therefore, in the current WLAN technologies, the target nodes change their channel frequencies slowly when link quality is degraded statistically. If we assume that target Wi-Fi devices can switch the channel very fast, channel scanning speed is important for persistent jamming attack. The jamming speed including channel scanning time and detection processing time is related to the jamming efficacy. The test results indicate that jamming efficacy could be improved as jamming speed is faster. Regarding the channel scanning time, there are three orthogonal channels in 2.4 GHz ISM and 19 channels in 5 GHz ISM band in 20 MHz channel unit. Therefore, it is possible to detect the target node when the attacker switches at most 5 times for full channel scanning because IEEE 802.11ac supports 80 MHz band operation.

Table 1. Experiment conditions

Condition index	Jamming type	Speed	Power	Speed+Power
1	Reactive	(0.125,0)	(2,20)	(0.125,20)
2	Persistent	(2,0)	(2,0)	(2,0)
3	Persistent	(1,0)	(2,5)	(1,5)
4	Persistent	(0.5,0)	(2,10)	(0.5,1.0)
5	Persistent	(0.25,0)	(2,15)	(0.25,15)
6	Persistent	(0.125,0)	(2,20)	(0.125,20)

4.2   Large-scale Emulation

Experimental Setup. In the developed prototype, it is difficult to evaluate the system in dense network conditions because it is necessary to have numerous hardware and software resources or expensive equipment. In order to overcome such problems, a software-based emulation environment can reduce the evaluation cost and experimental setup time. Therefore, the hardware behavior and performance can be emulated in the developed emulator. The hardware is manufactured using a hardware description language (HDL) in order to perform synthesis, place, and routing with various tools. Our FPGA prototype system was initially developed to be verified using a hardware-like C emulator. The emulator has been described with hardware architecture, and it has a cycle-true and bit-true description. That is, the emulator is programmed like a register

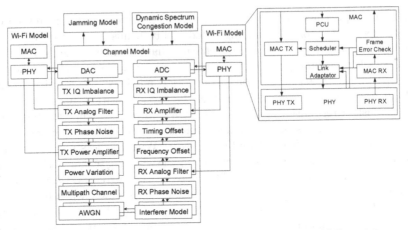

Fig. 7. Emulation environment, channel model, and MAC model

transistor level (RTL) description model, and it has timing and bit widths for all signals. This emulator was verified using a bit-matching process between the RTL and C model. The emulation performance curves are the same as the performance measurement results on the RTL targeted FPGA prototype system. In this way, we developed an emulation model that evaluates attack methods in dense networks.

Figure 7 presents the emulation model used to analyze the jamming effect in dense network conditions. The emulation model consisted of two Wi-Fi models for the sender and receiver, a channel model, a jammer model, and a dynamic spectrum congestion model. The Wi-Fi model had the same function and performance as the developed commercial hardware design. The channel model was developed with the IEEE 802.11 recommended channel model including RF/analog impairments. The dynamic spectrum congestion model randomly generated traffic from multiple nodes in the network. The jamming model could support one jamming strategy among the random, reactive, and persistent strategies. The target Wi-Fi model could mitigate the jamming effect and channel variation using channel hopping and link adaptation. This emulation model enabled the investigation of the jamming impact in dense network conditions.

There were three models in the simulation model: two Wi-Fi models for one AP and one station, and an interferer model for adjacent channel interference (ACI) or co-channel interference (CCI), which is generated using a jamming model and dynamic spectrum congestion model. The impairments that are analyzed include the multipath channel, mismatch between the in-phase and quadrature phase, carrier phase noise, carrier frequency offset, sampling phase noise, sampling frequency offset, signal amplitude variation, and adjacent channel interference variation. The channel models were modeled to have realistic RF/analog and wireless channel impairments. We applied a 50 ns root mean square (RMS) delay spread channel model. The channel model included a RAPP power amplifier with a 10 dB backoff. The phase noise was 104 dBc/Hz at 100 kHz, which was generated using the pole-zero model. The impairment model had a residual frequency error that is caused by oscillators with 8 ppm stability at the legitimate transmitter and receiver. Because the RF PLL and ADC clock use the same oscillator, the timing offset introduced by the ADC was 8 ppm. For simplicity of jamming efficacy comparison, we assumed that the packet size was 1,000 bytes and the packet interval was 16 μs. The SNR and signal-to-interference ratio varied randomly for every packet.

Figure 7 also presents the MAC model, which consists of a TX, RX, error counter, scheduler, power control unit (PCU), and link controller. In order to simulate the proposed scheme in a dynamically varying channel, a link adaptation scheme should be considered. The link adaptation algorithms are grouped into two classes: auto rate fallback (ARF) and SNR-based rate control [22, 31]. The ARF is a statistic-based scheme that has a slow response but simple implementation, whereas the SNR-based rate control is fast and uses the SNR as a good link quality indicator. However, the optimal rate and SNR are not correlated in certain link conditions. In this emulation, the combined scheme of ARF and SNR-based link adaptation was used as the jamming schemes. The link adaptation scheme is operated as an SNR-guided rate adaptation scheme [31] in order to manage the high fluctuations of the SNR, and it adjusts the transmission rate adaptively to the varying channel conditions according to the adaptive ARF. This type of combined rate control is effective in improving the link quality under dynamically interfered varying channel conditions.

Evaluation Results. We developed an emulation environment in order to evaluate the efficiency of the proposed attack strategy and conventional attack strategies in a dense network. The jammer can transmit packets using random jamming, reactive jamming, and persistent jamming strategies. In the emulation model, there are multiple BSSs with 8 access points. Each AP uses 8 different channels in the 5 GHz ISM band. There is one target node, one malicious node, and other legitimate nodes in multiple BSSs. There are up to eight legitimate nodes in the net-

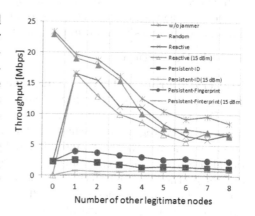

Fig. 8. Jamming efficacy: throughput vs. number of BSSs

work. The access point transmits 2,000 packets with a 1,000 byte length to the target node. The target node experiences varying channels in terms of SNR and interference levels.

Figure 8 presents the degraded throughput for the jamming schemes versus the number of BSSs. Increasing the number of BSSs causes more co-channel and adjacent channel interference in the target device when the jammer is transmitted at a small transmission power (0 dBm). As a result, if there is no malicious jammer, the target node is only affected by interference from other legitimate nodes in multiple BSSs. The random jammer has the worst performance. It is interesting that the reactive jammer is only effective if there are no other nodes, except the target node. However, the persistent jammer significantly degrades the throughput performance of a target node in dense network conditions. If the jammer transmits 15 dB higher jamming power, which is equivalent to 15 dBm transmission power at the output port of the RF amplifier, the measured throughput was close to zero for persistent jamming. This indicates that the effective throughput can be made zero through corrupting every packet being transmitted. In contrast, other jamming schemes were not significantly improved compared with the "w/o jammer" case. The evaluation results demonstrate that persistent jamming can improve the attack efficiency by approximately 80% in dense networks compared with reactive jamming schemes, and it can disconnect the link of the target node with a 20 dBm jamming power and 125 ms response time.

5   Defenses

In this section, we recommend four security defenses against the proposed persistent jamming attacks. In order to protect the ID information in the PHY header, we propose including a non-cryptographic device authentication and dynamic ID allocation mechanism during the standardization process for the next generation of WLANs. In addition, as potential countermeasures against the device fingerprint tracking, we recommend digital predistortion and friendly jamming techniques from an implementation perspective.

5.1   ID Protection

Non-cryptographic Device Authentication. In the current WLAN standards, the signal information in the physical layer header is not protected; thus, the ID in the signal field can be tracked by attackers. A complete solution would be to use a cryptographic mechanism that uses a shared key in the MAC layer in order to achieve authenticity, integrity, and confidentiality. However, the conventional cryptographic mechanisms require key management to distribute, refresh, and revoke the keys. Due to the inefficiency in terms of complexity and overhead, a non-cryptographic scheme in the PHY layer is required for device identification. For example, in a typical indoor wireless channel, the channel response decorrelates rapidly in space [27]. In addition, the channel reciprocity property between a transmitter and receiver can allow legitimate users to use the channel response as a shared key because an attacker, who is located in a different location to the legitimate users, has different channel frequency responses. The legitimate receivers can reliably extract the ID information based on the channel frequency responses of the received frame if the legitimate transmitter sends the ID information encoded using channel frequency responses.

However, the primary drawback of non-cryptographic device authentication using channel reciprocity is that the channel and nodes should be stationary. Thus, it is only applicable to typical indoor environments. Furthermore, from an implementation perspective, in order to fulfill the reciprocity principle at the

RF and analog transceivers that have different circuitry components, both transmission and reception paths should be calibrated for similarity in the transfer functions of the forward and reverse links. In order to achieve link equivalence, calibration schemes using additional circuitries and protocol or signal processing algorithms are required in the system design.

Dynamic ID Allocation. In the cellular network, temporary mobile subscriber identity (TMSI) can be tracked by eavesdroppers on the radio interface. Therefore, the cellular network can change the TMSI regularly in order to avoid the mobile node from being tracked [7]. However, in the latest WLAN standard such as IEEE 802.11ac/af/ah, there have not been considered the security issue of the unprotected frame header during the design of frame structure. The PAID is allocated to a station using an AP when the station associates with the AP, and the PAID is maintained until the station is deassociated. This static ID allocation allows an attacker to reliably snoop and capture the ID information in the wireless channel. However, if the ID is changed periodically based on a synchronized timestamp between the station and AP, it is difficult for the attacker to track the target. From an implementation perspective, dynamic ID allocation is feasible using the time synchronization function (TSF). An 802.11 station maintains a TSF, which is a timer with a modulus 264 counting in microseconds, and it synchronizes their TSF through transmitting and receiving beacons. Each beacon contains the timestamp value of a TSF at the AP, and all stations adjust their TSF considering the propagation and processing delay. As the timestamp value changes over time, if the AP allocates an ID periodically based on the synchronized timer, the stations can update their ID when they receive beacon frames. Furthermore, if the node or group of nodes updates the ID when it switches channels, it is more difficult to track the targets from the previous channel.

The primary drawback of dynamic ID allocation is that an adversary can still intercept the ID information during the same ID period. If the adversary can locate the ID update pattern through tracking the device based on an alternative scheme such as device fingerprints, it can analyze the ID update pattern. In order to reduce the duration of the same ID, the beacon interval should be shortened. However, a reduced beacon interval degrades the network efficiency due to the increased frame overhead and increases the number of wake-ups of power saving stations. Alternatively, in order to reduce the ID update interval, stations must update the ID based on their local timer. In this case, the TSF should be very accurate during a beacon interval because the IDs are determined based on the local timer value at the stations. Even though the dynamic ID allocation scheme is not a complete solution for persistent jamming, it can mitigate the success rate of attacks.

5.2   Fingerprint Protection

Digital Predistortion. The WLAN standards define the tolerance levels for impairments at the receiver. In order to support high data rates and QoS, all digital receivers are required to include compensation circuits for RF/analog and channel impairments. Specifically, WLAN receivers include compensating circuitries such as IQ mismatch correction, DC cancellation, carrier frequency offset correction, symbol synchronization, and sampling time/frequency phase tracking. Thus, if a legitimate transmitter predistorted the transmission signals using a specified amount of offsets for every packet that can be compensated at the legitimate receiver, it is difficult for an attacker to track the device finger-prints because the periodically changed offsets due to the digital predistortion scheme are hidden from others. For example, if the legitimate node randomly changes SNR and timing offset in the range of the tolerance level for every frame, the attacker cannot track the fingerprints due to the randomness while the legimitate receiver can reliably decode the frame.

The primary drawback of digital predistortion against malicious fingerprint detection is that it may degrade a legitimate node that has a residual estimation error and compensation error due to the finite hardware resolution. Therefore, we recommend adaptively using the digital predistortion scheme in frame trans-mission when the node switches channels due to persistent jamming attacks.

Friendly Jamming. The authors of [25] proposed that friendly jamming could not provide strong confidentiality because data can be extracted from the cor-related signals in certain conditions. According to [25], it is only true for simple modulation systems in narrow bandwidths and low radio frequencies. However, because the efficiency of the jamming signal cancellation is inversely proportional to the bandwidth and radio frequencies, it is difficult for an attacker to extract the device fingerprints from friendly jammed signals in WLAN systems that use OFDM modulation in wide bandwidths and high radio frequencies, if the tar-get node transmits friendly jamming signals during the unprotected PHY header transmission. In an implementation viewpoint, WLAN systems which adopt mul-tiple antennas for multiple input multiple output (MIMO) or non-contiguous carrier aggregation techniques can easily support the friendly jamming utilizing the existing hardware resources for transmitting independent spatial streams.

The primary drawback of friendly jamming is that the wireless devices must have extra hardware circuitries in order to generate the jamming signals and, consequently, they consume more energy and cost. This scheme may be only applicable for APs and not for mobile devices because the energy consumption is an important criterion when evaluating portable devices and sensors due to the impact on battery life. In addition, friendly jamming on the frame header field leads to degradation in the signal detection performance at the receiver side of the legitimate node. In order to mitigate this problem, the transmitter may localize the jamming attack [10] and send a friendly jamming signal using a transmit power control or beamforming transmission technique [4].

6   Conclusions

In this paper, we examined the limitations of the existing jamming schemes against channel hopping Wi-Fi devices in dense networks. Even though it is nat-ural for malicious jammers to attempt to identify target nodes in dense networks, it has not been investigated in jamming attack scenarios thus far. Therefore, we proposed and developed a persistent jamming attack to track and jam the target devices based on the PAID and device fingerprints in the frame header. Furthermore, we evaluated the effectiveness of the jamming schemes through empirical experiments and demonstrated that persistent jamming can attack target nodes in dense networks even though they adapt the channel frequency to avoid jamming signals. The evaluation results confirm the superior efficiency of the persistent jamming strategy in a dense network environment in dense network conditions. Finally, we recommended four security remedies to protect the PAID and device fingerprints.

Almost all modern wireless communication systems have the same security limitation in the frame formats which have the unprotected frame header. For low latency and high efficiency, the frame headers are not encrypted in typical wireless systems. Thus, any device can decode the signal information and detect the device fingerprints. However, the frame headers of the modern wireless communication systems include more information for advanced wireless connectivity. If the frame header is not protected, a persistent jammer can track and jam, or an eavesdropper can track and overhear the communication. As future work, this study will be expanded in order to improve the detection success rate of device fingerprints in various channel conditions, and we will implement and evaluate the defense schemes against the persistent jamming attack.

Acknowledgments. This work was supported, in part, by a National Research Foundation (NRF) of Korea grant funded by the Korean government (MEST) under contract numbers 2012R1A2A2A01008244 and 2012-0000979.

References

1. IEEE Standard 802.11h (2003)
2. IEEE Standard 802.11n (2009)
3. Cisco wireless lan controller configuration guide (2010), http://www.cisco.com/c/en/us/td/docs/wireless/controller/7-0/configuration/guide/c70.html
4. IEEE P802.11ac, Draft 7.0 (2013)
5. IEEE P802.11af, Draft 4.0 (2013)
6. IEEE P802.11ah, Draft 1.0 (2013)
7. Arapinis, M., Mancini, L.I., Ritter, E., Ryan, M.: Privacy through pseudonymity in mobile telephony systems. In: Network and Distributed System Security Symposium, NDSS (2014)
8. Benslimane, A., Bouhorma, M., et al.: Analysis of jamming effects on IEEE 802.11 wireless networks. In: International Conference on Communications (ICC), pp. 1–5. IEEE (2011)
9. Carious, L.: High-efficiency WLAN. IEEE 802.11-13/033lr5 (2013)
10. Chen, Y., Xu, W., Zhang, Y., Trappe, W.: Securing Emerging Wireless Systems. Springer (2008)
11. Fang, S.H., Hsu, Y.T., Kuo, W.H.: Dynamic fingerprinting combination for improved mobile localization. IEEE Transactions on Wireless Communications 10(12), 4018–4022 (2011)
12. Fang, S.H., Lin, T.N., Lee, K.C.: A novel algorithm for multipath fingerprinting in indoor WLAN environments. IEEE Transactions on Wireless Communications 7(9), 3579–3588 (2008)

13. Gaikwad, R.V., Moorti, R.T.: Apparatus and method for sampling frequency offset estimation and correction in a wireless communication system (2007), US Patent 7,177,374

14. Golmie, N., Rebala, O., Chevrollier, N.: Bluetooth adaptive frequency hopping and scheduling. In: Military Communications Conference (MILCOM), vol. 2, pp. 1138–1142. IEEE (2003)

15. Goth, G.: Next-generation Wi-Fi: As fast as we'll need? IEEE Internet Computing 16(6), 7–9 (2012)

16. Gummadi, R., Wetherall, D., Greenstein, B., Seshan, S.: Understanding and mitigating the impact of RF interference on 802.11 networks. In: Special Interest Group on Data Communication (SIGCOMM), pp. 385–396. ACM (2007)

17. Harjula, I., Pinola, J., Prokkola, J.: Performance of IEEE 802.11 based WLAN devices under various jamming signals. In: Military Communications Conference (MILCOM), pp. 2129–2135. IEEE (2011)

18. Jensen, T.L., Larsen, T.: Robust computation of error vector magnitude for wireless standards. IEEE Transactions on Communications 61(2), 648–657 (2013)

19. Jeung, J., Jeong, S., Lim, J.: Adaptive rapid channel-hopping scheme mitigating smart jammer attacks in secure WLAN. In: Military Communications Conference (MILCOM), pp. 1231–1236. IEEE (2011)

20. Lee, I.G., Choi, E., Lee, S.K., Jeon, T.: High accuracy and low complexity timing offset estimation for MIMO-OFDM receivers. In: Wireless Communications and Networking Conference (WCNC), vol. 3, pp. 1439–1443. IEEE (2006)

21. Mahmoud, H.A., Arslan, H.: Error vector magnitude to SNR conversion for nondata-aided receivers. IEEE Transactions on Wireless Communications 8(5), 2694–2704 (2009)

22. Makhlouf, A., Hamdi, M.: Practical rate adaptation for very high throughput WLANs. IEEE Transactions on Wireless Communications 12(2), 908–916 (2013)

23. Navda, V., Bohra, A., Ganguly, S., Rubenstein, D.: Using channel hopping to increase 802.11 resilience to jamming attacks. In: International Conference on Computer Communications (INFOCOM), pp. 2526–2530. IEEE (2007)

24. Pelechrinis, K., Broustis, I., Krishnamurthy, S.V., Gkantsidis, C.: A measurement-driven anti-jamming system for 802.11 networks. IEEE/ACM Transactions on Networking 19(4), 1208–1222 (2011)

25. Tippenhauer, N.O., Malisa, L., Ranganathan, A., Capkun, S.: On limitations of friendly jamming for confidentiality. In: Symposium on Security and Privacy (SSP), pp. 160–173. IEEE (2013)

26. Wilhelm, M., Martinovic, I., Schmitt, J.B., Lenders, V.: Short paper: Reactive jamming in wireless networks: How realistic is the threat? In: Proceedings on Wireless Network Security (WiSec), pp. 47–52. ACM (2011)

27. Xiao, L., Greenstein, L.J., Mandayam, N.B., Trappe, W.: Using the physical layer for wireless authentication in time-variant channels. IEEE Transactions on Wireless Communications 7(7), 2571–2579 (2008)

28. Xu, W., Trappe, W., Zhang, Y.: Channel surfing: Defending wireless sensor networks from interference. In: Proceedings on Information Processing in Sensor Networks (IPSN), pp. 499–508. ACM (2007)

29. Xu, W., Trappe, W., Zhang, Y., Wood, T.: The feasibility of launching and detecting jamming attacks in wireless networks. In: Proceedings on Mobile Ad Hoc Networking and Computing (MobiHoc), pp. 46–57. ACM (2005)

30. Yang, F., Zhang, X., Zhang, Z.P.: Time-domain preamble-based SNR estimation for OFDM systems in doubly selective channels. In: Military Communications Conference (MILCOM), pp. 1–5. IEEE (2012)
31. Zhang, J., Tan, K., Zhao, J., Wu, H., Zhang, Y.: A practical SNR-guided rate adaptation. In: International Conference on Computer Communications (INFOCOM). IEEE (2008)
32. Zhou, M., Tian, Z., Yu, X., Tang, X., Hong, X.: A two-stage fingerprint filtering approach for Wi-Fi RSS-based location matching. Journal of Computers 8(9) (2013)

On Emulation-Based Network Intrusion Detection Systems

Ali Abbasi[1], Jos Wetzels[1,2], Wouter Bokslag[2],
Emmanuele Zambon[1,3], and Sandro Etalle[1,2]

[1] Services, Cyber security and Safety Group, University of Twente, The Netherlands
{a.abbasi,emmanuele.zambon,sandro.etalle}@utwente.nl,
a.l.g.m.wetzels@student.utwente.nl
[2] Eindhoven University of Technology, The Netherlands
s.etalle@tue.nl, w.bokslag@student.tue.nl
[3] SecurityMatters BV, The Netherlands
emmanuele.zambon@secmatters.com

Abstract. Emulation-based network intrusion detection systems have been devised to detect the presence of shellcode in network traffic by trying to execute (portions of) the network packet payloads in an instrumented environment and checking the execution traces for signs of shellcode activity. Emulation-based network intrusion detection systems are regarded as a significant step forward with regards to traditional signature-based systems, as they allow detecting polymorphic (i.e., encrypted) shellcode. In this paper we investigate and test the actual effectiveness of emulation-based detection and show that the detection can be circumvented by employing a wide range of evasion techniques, exploiting weakness that are present at all three levels in the detection process. We draw the conclusion that current emulation-based systems have limitations that allow attackers to craft generic shellcode encoders able to circumvent their detection mechanisms.

Keywords: Emulation, IDS, Shellcode, Evasion, Polymorphism.

1 Introduction

Emulation-based Network Intrusion Detection Systems (EBNIDS) where introduced by Polychronakis et al.[1] to identify the presence of (possibly polymorphic) shellcode in network communication. The original motivation for introducing a new kind of NIDS was to overcome the limits of signature-based NIDS, which by definition can only identify known shellcodes, and are easily circumventable, e.g., by using polymorphism.

The main idea behind EBNIDSes is to check whether a given payload is actually malicious by trying to execute it in an instrumented environment, and checking whether the execution is possible and shows signs of being malicious. EBNIDSes work by turning the payload of a suspected network flow into a sequence of instructions and by simulating these instructions to determine what

A. Stavrou et al. (Eds.): RAID 2014, LNCS 8688, pp. 384–404, 2014.
© Springer International Publishing Switzerland 2014

they actually do. The resulting behavior is then analyzed with the help of specific heuristics.

After their introduction, we have seen a growing interest in this field, with a number of new proposals being introduced in a relatively short time-span [2–4, 6, 5, 7].

The goal of this paper is to investigate the actual practical effectiveness of EBNIDSes. In particular, in this paper

- we illustrate how EBNIDSes work by introducing three abstraction layers that allow us to describe all the approaches proposed so far,
- we investigate and question the actual effectiveness of EBNIDS, by providing evidence that present EBNIDSes have intrinsic limitations that make them evadable using standard coding techniques.

To substantiate the second point, we introduce simple coding techniques exploiting the implementation and/or design limitations of EBNIDSes, and show that they allow attackers to completely evade state-of-the-art EBNIDSes. Finally, we prove that it is possible to write a shellcode that evades EBNIDSes even in presence of a (theoretical) more complete implementation of the pre-processor and the emulator. In particular, we show it is still possible to evade both the emulation phase and the heuristics engine of EBNIDSes. These evasion techniques do not leverage implementation bugs of EBNIDSes (e.g., instruction set support) but exploit limitations in the concept of emulation and in the design of heuristics detection patterns.

Here we want to stress that we do not include in the research those intrusion detection systems relying on a precise memory image of the target, like Argos [7], because they are intrinsically different from EBNIDSes; indeed they are considered *host-based* (rather than *network-based*) NIDSes.

2   Detecting Shellcode on Emulation Based NIDS

In general, EBNIDSes detect encrypted shellcodes based on the following three steps: (1) pre-processing, (2) emulation and (3) heuristic-based detection (see Figure 1). We will now detail each of these steps.

2.1   Pre-processing

The main motivation for a pre-processing step is related to performance: emulation is resource consuming and it would not be feasible to emulate in real-time all the possible sequences of bytes extracted from the network. Therefore, the pre-processing step consists of inspecting network traffic, extracting the subset of traffic to be further investigated and transform (disassemble) it into an emulate-able sequence of bytes. Disassembly refers to a technique which machine instructions being extracted from the network streams. Zhang et. al. [8] propose a technique to identify which subset(s) of a network flow may contain shellcode by using static analysis. The proposed technique works by scanning

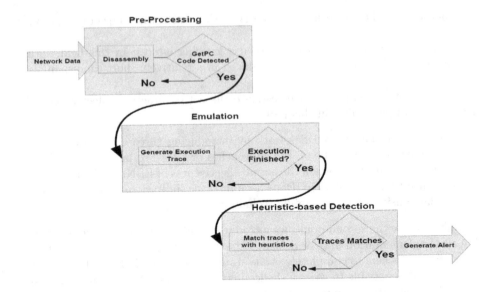

Fig. 1. Overview of Emulation Based Intrusion Detection System functionalities

network traffic for the presence of a decryption routine, which is part of any polymorphic shellcode. The authors assume that any shellcode, at some point, must use some form of GetPC instruction (such as CALL or FNSTENV) in order to discover its location in memory. There is only a limited amount of ways to obtain the value of the program counter, and by means of static analysis the seeding instructions for the GetPC code (e.g., CALL or FNSTENV instructions) are identified and flagged as the start of a possible shellcode. Although some of the early EBNIDSes (e.g., the approach proposed by Polychronakis et. al. [1]) do not implement the pre-processing step, follow-up extensions all include some form of pre-processing.

2.2 Emulation

The emulation step consists of running potential shellcode in an emulated and instrumented CPU or operating system environment. Instrumentation allows tracking the behavior of the emulated CPU during execution. In order to allow inspecting traffic in real-time, emulation is constrained by execution time, which imposes compromises on the implementation of emulators. Software-based emulators generally only support a subset of all hardware supported instructions for a restricted amount of hardware architectures. As an example, the approaches proposed by Polychronakis et. al. in [1, 9] support a subset of x86 instructions, which do not include floating point (FPU), MMX, and SSE instructions which are commonly available in modern CPUs or GPUs. In addition, the emulator does not know about the execution environment of the potential target of the shellcode (i.e., the machine on which the shellcode could run). For these reasons, it is not always possible to reliably emulate all shellcodes. To overcome this problem Polychronakis et. al. propose to employ a generic memory image [3]. By means of the generic memory image the emulator can read and jump to generic data structures and system calls, but still without guarantee that the values present at certain locations in memory will correspond to the values in the target memory.

2.3 Heuristic-Based Detection

The heuristic-based detection step consists of examining the execution trace produced by the emulator searching for known patterns of shellcode execution. If such patterns are found, the suspected network data is flagged as a shellcode and an alert can be raised by the EBNIDS. Three basic heuristics have been proposed over time to identify patterns of polymorphic shellcode in execution traces (see[1, 9]):

1. **GetPC code:** any shellcode must at some point obtain its own address in memory to read its own body and get environmental information, since such information can not be known prior to execution. This procedure is known as GetPC code. In its simplest form, the GetPC code consists of invoking CALL or FSTENV instructions. A heuristic to detect shellcode using GetPC code is built by searching for the GetPC seeding instructions and then ensuring that the execution trace of the code emulated starting from the GetPC instructions terminates.
2. **Payload read:** the decryption routine of polymorphic shellcode needs a large amount of memory accesses to read the encrypted payload. On the other hand, non-malicious code shows a limited frequency of unique memory reads. A heuristic to detect polymorphic shellcode is built by observing in an execution trace some form of GetPC code followed by a number of unique memory reads exceeding a so-called Payload Reads Threshold (PRT).
3. **WX instructions:** the decryption routine of polymorphic shellcode needs to write the decrypted instructions to memory. Executed instructions residing at memory addresses that were previously written are called WX instructions (write-execute instructions). A decrypted shellcode consists of such WX instructions, which may be allocated in a memory area different from the encrypted shellcode. A heuristic to detect polymorphic shellcode based on these observations consists of checking if, at the end of an execution trace, the emulator has performed W unique writes and has executed X WX instructions. In which case the payload is flagged as a non-self-contained polymorphic shellcode.

An extended set of heuristics is proposed in [3] to identify the presence of shellcode in arbitrary data streams. These runtime heuristics (which only cover Windows shellcodes) are based on "fundamental machine-level operations that are inescapably performed by different shellcode types" and are implemented in a prototype called Gene. Each runtime-heuristic in Gene is composed of several conditions which should all be satisfied in the specified order during the execution of the code for the heuristic to yield true.

1. **Kernel32.dll base address resolution:** most shellcodes require interacting with the OS through the system call interface or user-level API. In order to call an API function, the shellcode must first find its absolute address in the address space of the process. Kernel32.dll provides two functions (LoadLibrary and GetProcAddress) for this. Thus, a common fundamental operation in all above cases is that the shellcode has to first locate the base address of Kernel32.dll. Gene has heuristics recognizing two methods (using the Process Environment Block or Backwards Searching) of obtaining the Kernel32.dll base address. This particular heuristics focus on behavior specific to Windows shellcode.

2. **SEH-based GetPC code:** when an exception occurs, the system generates an exception record that contains the necessary information for handling it. In particular, the exception record contains the Program Counter (PC) value at the time the exception was triggered. This information is stored on the stack. A shellcode can register a custom exception handler, trigger an exception, and then extract the absolute memory address of the faulting instruction. Gene has a heuristic that detects any shellcode installing a custom exception handler, including polymorphic shellcode that uses SEH-based GetPC code.

3. **Process memory scanning:** some software vulnerabilities allow injecting only a limited amount of code, usually not enough for a fully functional shellcode. In most cases though, the attacker has the ability to deploy a second, much larger payload which will be stored at a random memory location (e.g., in a buffer allocated in the heap). The (first-stage) shellcode then needs to scan the address space of the process and search for the second-stage shellcode (also known as the *egg*), which can be identified by a long-enough characteristic byte sequence. This type of first-stage payload is known as *egg-hunt* shellcode. Blindly searching the memory of a process in a reliable way requires some method of determining whether a given memory address is valid and readable. Gene has a heuristic that recognizes shellcode attempting at retrieving information about paged memory through Structured Exception Handler (SEH) and syscall-based scanning methods.

3   Evading EBNIDSes

In this section we present a number of evasion techniques that can be applied to ensure that polymorphic shellcodes are not detected by state-of-the-art EBNIDSes. We present the evasion techniques based on the type of weakness in the EBNIDS that we exploit to avoid detection. We identify two types of weaknesses: (1) implementation limitations and (2) intrinsic limitations. While we acknowledge that the first type of weakness could be mitigated by investing more time and resources in the implementation of the EBNIDS (e.g. by a major security vendor), we think intrinsic limitations cannot be permanently fixed with the current design of EBNIDSes: There will always be an *emulation gap* that can be exploited to avoid detection. Given a target system T and an emulator E (integrated into the EBNIDS) seeking to emulate T, the emulation fidelity is determined by E's capacity to a) behave as T (e.g., by ensuring CPU instructions behave in the same way, or the same API calls are available) and b) have the same context as T at any given moment (e.g., the same memory image, CPU state, user-dependent information, etc.). We call *emulation gap* the behavior or information present in T but not in E. An attacker who is aware of this gap can use it to construct shellcode (e.g., an encoder) integrating this information in such a way that the shellcode will run correctly on T but not on E, thus avoiding detection.

We conduct a series of practical tests, consisting of implementing the different evasion techniques[1] and testing if state-of-the-art EBNIDSes are capable of detection. These tests will also give indications of the feasibility of implementing the different evasion techniques. We select *Libemu* and *Nemu* as our test EBNIDSes because they are broadly used as detection mechanisms as part of large honeynet projects [10, 11].

Libemu [12] is a library which offers basic x86 emulation and shellcode detection using GetPC heuristics. It is designed to be used within network intrusion prevention/ detections and honeypots. The detection algorithm of Libemu is implemented by iteratively executing the pre-processing, emulation and heuristic-based detection steps for each instruction, starting from an entry point identified by GetPC code seeding instructions. This process resembles the typical fetch-decode-execute cycle of real CPUs. Instruction decoding is handled by the *libdasm* disassembly library, while the emulation and heuristic-based detection steps are the core of the library implementation. We use Libemu in its default configuration, in which shellcodes are detected only by means of the GetPC code heuristic described in Section 2. We download Libemu (version 0.2.0) from the official project website, and use the *pylibemu* wrapper to feed our shellcodes to the EBNIDS.

Nemu is a stand-alone detector with the built-in capability of processing network traces both online and offline (e.g., from PCAP traces) as well as raw binary data to detect shellcode. Similarly to Libemu, the detection algorithm of Nemu is implemented iteratively by applying pre-processing, emulation and heuristic-based detection for each instruction. Also in this case, instruction decoding is handled by the *libdasm* disassembly library, while the emulation and heuristic-based detection steps are the core of the tool implementation. We receive Nemu from the author in 2014. When carrying out our tests we notice that the version of Nemu we received includes all the heuristics described in Section 2, except the one for detecting WX instructions, but including the additional heuristics related to resolving Kernel32.dll address and SEH-based GetPC code introduced in Gene [3]. The author confirms our finding. In more detail, a

---

[1] The authors plan to release all the implemented techniques as Metasploit plugins.

GetPC code heuristic is first used to determine the entry point of the shellcode. During emulation, eight individual heuristics detect Kernel32.dll base address resolution (seven targeting the Process Environment Block resolution method and one targeting the Backward Searching resolution method) and one heuristic detects self-modifying code using the Payload Read Threshold. Finally, a combination of the Process memory scanning and SEH-based GetPC heuristics is used after detection as a second-stage mechanism to reduce the amount of false positives.

To verify our evasion techniques, we first collect a set of samples that trigger the detection of both Libemu and Nemu. For Libemu, we create a simple shellcode consisting of GetPC instructions followed by a number of NOP instructions. For Nemu, we use eight shellcodes provided by the author as sanity tests, each triggering one of the Kernel32.dll heuristics. In addition, we write a simple self-modifying shellcode to trigger the Payload Read heuristic. To do this we encode a plain shellcode by XORing it with a random key and prepending a decoder which first performs a GetPC and then extracts the encoded payload on the stack and executes it. We then verify that both Libemu and Nemu can detect the shellcodes we created.

3.1   Evasions Exploiting Implementation Limitations

Limitations of the Pre-processor Implementation

In most EBNIDSes, static analysis is applied in the pre-processing step to determine which sequences of bytes should be emulated [2, 4, 8]. This makes these EBNIDSes susceptible to anti-disassembly techniques aimed at preventing the pre-processor to correctly decode the shellcode instructions.

For example, the EBNIDS presented in [8] proposes a hybrid approach which first uses static techniques to detect a form of GetPC code and then applies two-way traversal and backward data-flow analysis to pinpoint likely decryption routines which are then passed on to an emulator. Based on this approach, disassembly starts from the GetPC seeding instruction and, upon encountering an instruction that could indicate conditional branching or memory-writing behaviors, backward data-flow analysis is applied to obtain an instruction chain that fills-in all required variables. Conditional branching, self-modifying code and indirect addressing (using runtime-generated values) can be used to prevent this process to succeed.

Although the authors state that self-modifying code or indirect addressing is unlikely to appear before the GetPC code (since this would require a base-address for referencing) we argue that this is not the case. First, it is possible for an attacker to construct the shellcode on the stack in a dynamic fashion, including the GetPC code. Secondly, the attacker can avoid GetPC seeding instructions altogether and construct the entire shellcode on the stack. This would require a full emulation for detection, since it would be unfeasible to detect GetPC seeding instructions contained in a self-modifying code statically, especially if instructions are encoded using a randomized key. In the absence of the capacity to detect seeding instructions, subsequent analysis will fail as well.

Based on these observations, we create a shellcode encoder which consists of XORing the shellcode with a random key and prepending a decoder armored with anti-disassembly GetPC code. To build the anti-disassembly GetPC code we adapt four existing techniques proposed by Branco et. al. [13] and Sikorski et. al. [14] for preventing malware analysis:

1. *Use of garbage bytes and opaque predicates*: the insertion of garbage bytes after so-called opaque predicate instructions confuses some disassemblers into taking the bytes immediately after such an instruction as the starting point of a next instruction. Opaque predicates are logical tautologies or contradictions which are constructed in such a way that this can not be easily determined without evaluating them. For example, (GetUserID() xor 0x0A0A) is opaque for any instance evaluating it that does not know beforehand the result of GetUserID(), while an attacker can construct this when targeting user with id 0x0A0A specifically.

2. *Flow redirection to the middle of an instruction*: certain instructions are crafted to contain other instructions in the middle of their opcodes. During execution, the code flow is redirected to the middle of instructions to execute those "hidden" inside. This requires full emulation for proper disassembly.

3. *Push/pop-math stack-constructed shellcode*: instead of executing instructions directly, the opcodes are XORed with a static value, pushed onto the stack and control is transferred to the stack. This way, full emulation is required to obtain the instructions.

4. *Code transposition*: a piece of code is split into separate parts and re-arranged in a random order, tied together with several jumps. In addition, instead of returning to the original destination of a call operation (a characteristic of GetPC code), the destination pushed on the stack by the call operation is modified by the appropriate offset.

We evaluate these anti-disassembly techniques against Nemu and Libemu by encoding our test shellcodes with the anti-disassembly encoder described above. If the anti-disassembly encoder works, the pre-processor cannot correctly identify the GetPC code and the shellcode analysis will stop without raising alerts.

Table 1. Anti-disassembly techniques detection rate

	Garbage Byte	Flow Redirect	Push/Pop Math	Code Transposition
Nemu	9/9	9/9	8/9	8/9
Libemu	0/1	1/1	0/1	1/1

Table 1 shows the results of the tests. While we could bypass Libemu using Garbage bytes and Push/Pop math techniques, Nemu has better detection in most cases with the only successful evasion technique being Code Transposition and Push/pop math in one case. We believe this is due to the fact that Nemu did not properly disassemble all the instructions of our armored decoder. This impacts the emulation of such instructions, eventually preventing the correct execution of the decoding routine. As a result, the decoded shellcode cannot be completely emulated and this causes the failure of heuristics requiring the observation of a large number of instructions to trigger. However, we consider this is an exceptional case, while in general we conclude that the evasion techniques were ineffective against Nemu.

Limitations of the Emulator Implementation

Unsupported Instructions. Most EBNIDSes do not provide full emulation capabilities and only emulate a subset of the full instruction set. For example, the approaches presented by Polychronakis et. al. in [1, 9] use *libdasm* as disassembler and implement a subset of the IA-32 instruction set, including most general purpose instructions but no FPU, MMX or SSE instructions.

It is possible for an attacker to construct a shellcode which incorporates instructions not covered by the limited emulators, therefore causing emulation to stop when such instructions are encountered, and therefore preventing the heuristic-based detection. Additionally, it is possible to use the results of non-emulated instructions as an integral part of a self-modifying routine.

In addition to emulating only a subset of the IA-32 instruction set, all emulators provide only a subset of the complete system functionality, including syscall emulation, virtual memory and the presence of process images. These limitations in the implementation of system functionality emulation can be abused by an attacker in order to thwart successful emulation and thus detection.

Based on these observations, we create a shellcode encoder which consists of XORing the shellcode with a random key and prepending a decoder made with instructions which are not supported by some types of emulators. In more detail, we create five versions of the decoder, each using different types of instructions:

1. FPU instructions (using FNSTENV).
2. FPU instructions (using FNSAVE).
3. MMX instructions.
4. SSE instructions.
5. Instructions considered obsolete or undocumented by some disassemblers and emulators such as salc or xlatb instructions.

We evaluate these anti-disassembly techniques against Nemu and Libemu by encoding our test shellcodes with the anti-disassembly encoder described above. If the encoder works, the emulator cannot correctly execute the GetPC code and the shellcode analysis will stop without raising alerts.

Table 2 summarizes the test results. With the only exception of the FNSTENV FPU instruction, all other instruction sets prevented the emulator to successfully emulate the decoder and detect the shellcodes.

Emulator Detection. Emulator detection refers to a class of techniques which shellcodes can use to detect if they are run within an emulator. This approach relies on certain behavioral quirks present in all available emulators. A good example of these quirks is the method proposed in [9], in which the emulator initializes all its eight general purpose registers to hold the absolute address of the fist instruction of each execution chain. This introduces a detection vector, since this situation is highly unlikely to arise in a real-world scenario. While setting the stack pointer to point to the beginning of the shellcode most certainly does not affect its correct execution, shellcode could include emulation detection tricks which check the stack data preceding the shellcode (using the ESP as the base). The preceding data could be checked for valid stack frames or, better yet, data known to reside on the stack of the vulnerable program. This can be done through hardcoded addressing or through egg-hunting. The emulator would have to construct a legitimate program stack and mirror the vulnerable program in order to avoid being detected. A final limitation is that in various exploitation scenarios, including casual stack overflows, the EBP registers get overwritten with the 4 bytes preceding the new instruction pointer, yet the emulator initializes EBP to hold the shellcode base address. In this way an attacker could include 4 bytes crucial to successful execution of the shellcode before the new instruction pointer which the emulator would not properly handle. Research about emulator detection [15, 16] has shown that even mature, well-developed and maintained system emulators often provide only a subset of the functionality of the emulated platform or display behaviors that allow attackers to detect their presence. The examples we provided in our paper are specific to the tested EBNIDS emulators but the general principle remains: any difference of the emulated environment with regard to the target environment offers an attacker opportunities for evasion. Since we are dealing with network-based IDS especially the context part of the target environment will be infeasible and unscalable to completely mirror by the emulator for scalability reasons.

We propose three techniques to detect that the shellcode is being executed in Libemu or Nemu. In the case of Libemu all general purpose registers are initialized to the same value, something that virtually never occurs in a genuine exploited process. In the case of Nemu all general purpose registers are initialized to static values, even though the author mentions they are initialized to the address of the execution trace [3]. Also, for Nemu the CPUID instruction is decoded but not emulated. Usually, the CPUID instruction returns a CPU vendor string in certain registers when called. Nemu does not set these registers, hence providing a reliable way for detection. The third technique against all types of emulators is a timing attack. Since emulators perform slower than the actual CPU they seek to emulate, we can measure the timing difference for

Table 2. Unsupported instructions evasion detection rate

	FPU FN-STENV	FPU FN-SAVE	MMX	SSE	OBSOL
Nemu	9/9	0/9	0/9	0/9	0/9
Libemu	1/1	0/1	0/1	0/1	0/1

Table 3. Difference in actual running time (in milliseconds) between Nemu, Libemu and native CPU

	Opaque instructions	Intensive loop	Integrated loop	RDA
Nemu	6.80	9.08	37.81	52.90
Libemu	44.07	75.20	173.49	177.56
native	0.148	2.10	0.30	0.68

executing a series of instructions. We implement a timing attack using relative performance (instead of absolute performance which is very hardware dependent as well), executing two series of instructions (a NOP loop vs. a more intensive arithmetic loop) and take their ratio as a measure. On emulated environments the ratio will be far higher than on non-emulated environments. Table 3 shows an example of the running time difference between Nemu, Libemu and a native CPU when executing four different types of operations (see Section 3.2 for a description of the operations).

We create a shellcode encoder which consists of XORing the shellcode with a random key and prepending a decoder armored with emulator detection code. In more detail, the value of the decryption key is determined by the emulator detection code: in case the shellcode is being emulated, the key will be incorrect and the decoding will fail. Both Libemu and Nemu are unable to detect the modified shellcodes.

Limitations of Existing Heuristics

Evasion of Kernel32.dll Base Address Resolution Heuristics. We design two techniques to bypass the Kernel32.dll base address resolution heuristics of Nemu. An attacker only needs to use one of the following techniques to bypass Nemu.

The first technique consists of walking the Safe Exception Handler (SEH) chain until a pointer to ntdll.dll is found (see Figure 2). We scan the entire stack until we find a frame with value 0xFFFFFFFF, which precedes the pointer to the OS SEH record lying in ntdll.dll. To make sure a valid OS SEH pointer is found (and not some random 0xFFFFFFFF value) we compare the pointer value against the frame located 16 bytes away from it, which is always the return address of the top stack frame. Depending on the windows version, this address points either into ntdll.dll or kernel32.dll. Once we find an address in ntdll.dll, we do a backward scan from the discovered location until we encounter the PE header structure. We recognize this structure because its starting bytes are 0x4D, 0x5A (MZ in ASCII). The address of the PE header structure is the base address of any mapped library. Therefore, we now have a pointer to the base address of ntdll.dll. By using this information we can call the LdrLoadDLL function inside ntdll.dll. We use the LdrLoadDLL function to load Kernel32.dll and from there calling the LoadLibraryA function inside Kernel32.dll. It is worth mentioning that within different versions of the Windows OS, the distance between functions is static (even in existence of enabled ASLR, and that holds for all global return addresses).

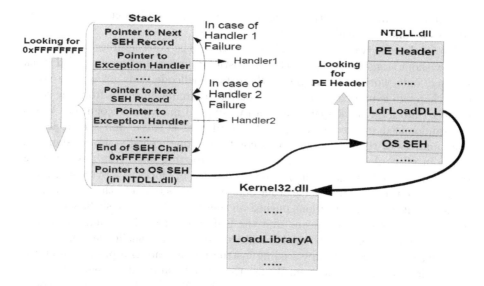

Fig. 2. SEH scanning technique for resolving the base address of Kernel32.dll

The second technique works in a more reliable way. In the x86 architecture the EBP register points to the current stack frame. Each stack frame starts with a pointer to the previous stack frame, all the way to the top stack frame. In Windows processes are created by the operating system using the NtCreateProcess API, which stores on the top stack frame as return address a pointer to ntdll.dll. Therefore, by walking the stack frames from the current stack frame to the top stack frame we have a pointer to ntdll.dll. We use this information in the same way described for the previous technique.

We use these two techniques to create two shellcodes that call the LoadLibrary function inside kernel32.dll and get the kernel32.dll base address. We then feed these shellcodes to Nemu, which does not trigger any alert. The reason why Nemu fails in the detection is that none of the eight different Kernel32.dll base address resolution heuristics in Nemu trigger on the operations we carry out. In more detail, we do not access any of the FS addresses (which are Nemu triggers), we do not perform memory reads on kernel32.dll (which is also a trigger for Nemu) and we do not access or modify any of the SEH handlers. Finally, we also notice that Nemu does not even seem to properly implement stack frames. In fact, EBP always points to unreadable memory.

Evasion of GetPC Code Heuristics. Both Libemu and Nemu use the GetPC code heuristic to identify a shellcode. Both Libemu and Nemu approach GetPC code detection in the same way, by checking whether the program counter is somehow stored in a memory location by means of a so-called seeding instruction subsequently read from that memory location. In practice, this means scanning for seeding instructions (for both systems only CALL and FSTENV/FSAVE are considered seeding instructions), emulating the trace and seeing if the stored address is somehow read and used.

We implement two different techniques to get the start address of the shell-code without triggering these GetPC heuristics. Our first technique, called stack scanner, only works with exploits where the shellcode ends up on the stack (and therefore is limited in scope). It works by scanning upwards from the stack pointer (into used stack space) until a randomized marker is recognized. When the randomized marker is recognized, its address is saved and serves as the start address of the shellcode. The second technique, called stack constructor, works in all exploit scenarios and involves converting any given payload to a stack-constructed payload. The payload is divided in blocks of 4 bytes which are pushed onto the stack in reverse order before a jump is taken to the ESP register (thus executing the instructions pushed on the stack). Since the shellcode is now located on the stack, this means that the ESP register (which points to the top of the stack) also is the current EIP, hence we know the shellcode starting address without resorting to any seeding instruction or reading a pushed/modified address from a memory location. We use these two techniques to create two shell-codes capable of performing a GetPC operation. We then feed these shellcodes to both Libemu and Nemu. As expected, none of them triggers any alert.

Evasion of Payload Read Heuristics. Nemu includes a heuristic for detecting self-modifying code called Payload Read Threshold (PRT). The heuristic consist of imposing a threshold on the number of unique read operations executed by the payload, combined with the presence of GetPC code. To circumvent this heuristic [17] proposes to use syscalls to execute read operations instead of reading directly in the payload shellcode. We implement a shellcode using this approach and notice that despite the fact that the technique has been public since 2009, the Nemu heuristic has not been updated to detect this technique. Note that Nemu has another heuristic, which imposes a threshold on the number of syscalls and could in principle trigger when this kind of evasion is used. However, the heuristic was designed to detect egg hunting, and as such the threshold imposed on the number of syscalls is way higher than the number of syscalls needed in the evasion payload. For this reason, even this second heuristic is ineffective against our implementation.

Evasion of WX Instructions Heuristics. A threshold of WX instructions is proposed as a heuristic in [9]. When a given piece of suspect input exceeds this threshold, a heuristic-flag is triggered. As stated by Skape in [18], Virtual Mapping can be used as a method to circumvent this heuristic. It involves mapping the same physical address to two different virtual addresses, using one for writing operations whilst using the other for execution thus disqualifying the code as being composed of WX instructions. In order to be able to do virtual mapping, the shellcode needs to invoke OS APIs, and this step could trigger the Kernel32.dll heuristic. However, an attacker can combine this technique with the technique to resolve the Kernel32.dll base address proposed above, which avoids triggering the corresponding heuristic.

Evasion of Process Memory Scanning Heuristics. An attacker could scan for a known fragment of instructions from the target code. Linn et. al. in [19] already introduced an attack which scans for a 17-byte sequence which forms the first basic block of the execve system call. Also, an attacker could generate a hash and then iterate through the suitable code-region and check the retrieved data against the hash. In this way, an emulator would have to brute-force the hash in order to determine what code fragment to prepare, something that cannot be done in a reasonable amount of time. Additionally, an attacker could construct (part of) the decryption key from code fragments obtained through hash-based searching.

3.2   Evasions Exploiting on Intrinsic Limitations

Limitations of the Emulator

Fragmentation. So-called Swarm or fragmentation attacks [20] are a class of attacks in which an attacker can create the shellcode decoder in the target process memory space using multiple instances of the attack, with each instance writing a small segment of the decoder at a designated location. After building the decoder in this fashion, the last attack instance hijacks the control of the attacked process to start the execution of the decoder while simultaneously including the shellcode cipher text. As such, swarm attacks could be considered a form of fragmented egg-hunting attacks. Swarm attacks can defeat all three components of EBNIDSes. It will be a severely complicated task to do static analysis for part of the decoder, in the pre-processor stage. Additionally, due to the fact that there is no fully valid shellcode present in any of the attack instances, the emulator is never capable of emulating the decoder and hence no heuristics are triggered. Attackers should take care, though, to keep the attack instances small and/or polymorphic enough to avoid triggering signature matching. Swarm attacks present a challenge to EBNIDSes but have the downside of being applicable only in specific exploitation scenarios (e.g., the application must keep all the different pieces of the shellcode in memory until the last piece of the shellcode is sent). Because of this we could not easily build a test to evaluate this evasion technique.

Limitations of faithful emulation

Non-self-contained Shellcode. It is possible for a shellcode to use code or data of the target system as execution instructions, and hence become dependent upon the state of the target machine. Such code is called non-self-contained and can involve the absence of classic heuristic triggers such as GetPC code or Payload Reads. Such code poses a problem for EBNIDSes which lack knowledge of the target machine state. Code depending on a particular machine state for successful execution not only requires full emulation of instructions, but also access to a potentially unknown amount of host-based information. While this might be relatively easy to implement on host-based IDSes, for EBNIDSes it is unscalable to keep up-to-date information about all possible target hosts in a network. The approaches in [1, 9, 8, 2–4] are all susceptible to armoring techniques involving some form of non-self-contained shellcode.

In addition, it is possible to generalize the principle of non-self-contained shellcode to the idea of Return-Oriented-Programming (ROP). ROP involves the re-using instructions or data in the memory of the target application in a way to compose an instruction sequence which performs the operations required by the attacker. Program data or code preceding a RET instruction is often chained to execute the desired behavior. As such, an attacker can seek out a sequence of instructions terminated by a RET instruction and note down their addresses. The actual shellcode would then consist of a series of PUSH operations pushing these addresses on the stack, followed by a final RET transferring control to the first ROP-chain segment. Thus, the actual shellcode transferred of the network would not contain any of the malicious instructions the attacker intends to execute.

The increasing proliferation of randomization techniques complicates matters and potentially renders non-self-contained shellcode fragile, something mentioned in [8]. An example of these techniques are Address-Space Layout Randomization (ASLR), which randomize the base address of loaded libraries and Position Independent Executables (PIE), which are compiled to be executable regardless of the base address they are loaded at and thus have a randomized image base. ASLR is enabled by default in modern operating systems. This however presents no problem when the ROP code is located in a program loaded at a static image base.

Even the latest efforts to address code reuse techniques in EBNIDSes [9] introduced in Nemu are unable to fully cope with non-self-contained shellcode. Nemu is outfitted with the program image of a real, albeit arbitrary, windows process in order to enable more faithful emulation. However, this only partially mitigates the problem, since attackers can craft shellcodes targeting only a specific OS version (and e.g., language pack) or a specific application.

In order to test the performance of Libemu and Nemu in detecting non-self-contained shellcode we modify our test shellcodes by dynamically building the entire GetPC code and the shellcode decoder out of ROP gadgets. Since these gadgets are only present at the target addresses on particular versions of a system (e.g. they vary from OS versions, service packs and language packs) any emulator that does not supply the correct image should not be able to execute this code. The fact that addresses vary between versions does not constitute a problem as addresses are static within each version. An attacker could build a database of addresses with the desired gadgets for each target platform much like Metasploit modules often do. Since ASLR is enabled in most operating systems for many libraries which are compiled with ASLR-compatible support, we ensure shellcode stability by leveraging the fact that ASLR varies the base addresses but not offsets of instructions from the base address. We therefore build a database of offsets, instead of addresses, and have the shellcode resolve the base address of the target library first. We gather the gadgets from ntdll.dll on x86 under Windows 7 and resolve the base address through the stackframe-walking technique explained in Section 3.1 to avoid triggering heuristics. We gather these gadgets using the RP++ tool [21]. It should be noted that our shellcode does not fully consist of ROP gadgets (only the GetPC and decoder stub) and as such the shellcode is still faced with traditional difficulties when dealing with an ASLR+DEP protected system. However, though most major applications and system libraries are compiled with ASLR support this is not always the case and often an attacker can still rely on static addresses from either the non-ASLR enabled target application image itself or from libraries compiled without ASLR support loaded by the target application. In order to bypass ASLR/DEP our shellcode would need to be modified by having the address-resolving stub consist of ROP-gadgets located in a non-ASLR-enabled image or library and subsequent ROP-gadgets derived from offsets to the resolved base address, or by resolving the library base address by using the SEH walk technique described in Section 3.1 . Neither Libemu nor Nemu we found capable of detecting our non-self-contained shellcode. In principle, recent approaches proposed for detecting ROP-based shellcode [23] could be more effective than Nemu and Libemu in detecting our bypasses. However we are still left with the open question of verifying the effectiveness of such new approach.

Execution Threshold. Real-time intrusion detection imposes the need to evaluate whether input is malicious or not within a reasonable amount of time. Shellcodes which take a large amount of time to be emulated pose a problem. Long loops have been used as an anti-debugging technique for a long time, and some of the detection techniques [1, 3, 4] use infinite loop detection and smashing or pruning to reduce the impact of execution threshold exceeding code. However, it is possible to employ techniques which force any emulator to spend a certain amount of time before being able to execute the actual shellcode.

One such technique is the use of Random Decryption Algorithms (RDAs) as described by Kharn [24]. RDAs essentially consist of employing encryption routines without supplying the decryption key and forcing the self-decrypting code to perform a brute-force attack on itself, thus creating a time-consuming decryption loop. An attacker could employ strong cryptographic algorithms and use a reduced key-space which can be brute forced in a timeframe which is acceptable for execution but not for detection. A more sophisticated approach, albeit more complex and implementationally limited, is the use of Time Lock Puzzles (TLPs) [25, 26]. TLPs, are cryptographic problems consisting of a cipher-text encrypted using a strong cipher and a puzzle, which requires a series of sequential, non parallelizable operations in order to retrieve the key. The authors of EBNIDS approaches almost invariably state that if attackers would start to employ evasion techniques aimed at exceeding execution thresholds, their method would still be useful as a first-stage anomaly detector since the appearance of loops exceeding the threshold in random code is rare. However, even if all streams exceeding execution thresholds would be passed on to a second-stage analysis engine, the problem of having to perform unacceptably time-consuming operations remains, forbidding analysis by second-stage engines as well, and leaving the malicious nature of the examined code undecided.

We modify our test shellcodes to evade EBNIDSes by exceeding their execution thresholds based on four techniques:

1. **Opaque loops:** we generate a loop that takes a long time to perform seemingly necessary operations (such as the calculation of certain values for code-branching operations used later on) while in reality the checks and calculation it performs are so-called opaque predicates (i.e. they always result in the same value and code-flow). Preceding the GetPC stub and decoder with such a loop lets 'linear' emulators timeout before they can get to the triggering code.

2. **Intensive loops:** similar to the opaque loops, intensive loops employ instructions (e.g.. FPU or MMX instructions) which are costly to emulate, taking a longer amount of time to execute in an emulated environment than on the target host. Again, this loop is prepended to the actual payload.

3. **Integrated loops:** as opposed to the opaque and intensive loops, the behavior of this stalling code is actually required for proper execution of the payload. The encoder key and the instructions of the GetPC code are split up in a loop-based calculation which takes a long amount of time. The shellcode will have to execute this code in order to obtain the key for proper decryption of the payload as well as the instructions of the GetPC code.

4. **Random Decryption Algorithm:** in this technique the payload is encrypted with a random key. The shellcode attempts to bruteforce the key and, after each attempt, checks the decrypted body against a hash value. The original RDA implementation [24] still needed plaintext GetPC code to know the address of the encrypted payload body. In our implementation we generate a second RDA key, XOR the GetPC instructions with the key and modify the decoder to first decrypt the GetPC as well.

Table 4 shows the results of our tests. Libemu cannot detect any of the modified shellcodes. On the other hand, the shellcodes modified with the first two techniques (opaque and intensive loops) could all be detected by Nemu. This is expected and is due to the fact that Nemu searches for potential shellcode entry points at every byte position within a payload and the execution of the stalling code is not required for execution of the shellcodes. However, by examining the source code, we observe that also Libemu should apply the same technique, and therefore should in principle be able to detect the same shellcodes. We believe the failure in the detection has to do with some implementation issue which is unrelated to the concept of execution threshold. None of the shellcodes modified with the integrated loops and RDAs techniques are detected, since the proper execution of the shellcode depends on the results of the execution of the stalling code.

Table 4. Detection of execution threshold evasion techniques against Libemu and Nemu

	Opaque loop	Intensive loop	Integrated loop	RDA
Nemu	9/9	9/9	0/9	0/9
Libemu	0/1	0/1	0/1	0/1

Context-keying. Information about the target host can be used as a cryptographic key to encrypt and decrypt the shellcode. This technique is known as Context-Keyed Payload Encoding (CKPE) armoring and has been proposed by Aycock et. al. to prevent the analysis of malware [27]. EBNIDS approaches [1, 9, 3, 8, 2, 4] are susceptible to evasion through CKPE armoring. The benefit of CKPE, compared to non-self-contained shellcode is greater stability, lower complexity and less effort on the side of the attacker.

Proper use of CKPE prohibits successful emulation of the shellcode by the EBNIDS and as such reduces the problem of evasion to ensure that the CKPE routine remains undetected. Strong CKPE armoring would involve producing a polymorphic key generator stub and decoder as well as avoiding the use of traditional hallmarks of self-decoding shellcode such as GetPC code or WX instructions. A context-based payload encoder is available in the Metasploit framework. Unfortunately, the Metasploit CKPE encoder can be detected by EBNIDSes since it includes GetPC code in the generated shellcode.

We improve the Metasploit CKPE encoder by adding a non-cryptographically secure hashing function that generates a hash based on the key and XORs 4 bytes of GetPC code with it before pushing it to the stack and transferring control to it. This way, the GetPC code is only executed if the key extracted by the system (which depends on context) hashes to the right value. We use CPUID information, values present at static memory addresses, system time and file information for context-dependent key generation in our tests as keys with which we encode our test shellcodes. Both Libemu and Nemu are not capable to detect any of the modified shellcodes.

Hash-armoring. A special case of CKPE is hash-armoring [28]. Hash-armoring uses a cryptographic hash function with a context-based key to hash an (arbitrary) salt. The technique consists of checking whether the resultant hash value for a given salt contains the instructions to be armored (called the *run*). Given a run, the armoring routine brute-forces all possible salts until a suitable hash is found, returning the positions between which the run is located in the hash together with the salt, forming a triple. This is repeated for the entire malicious body resulting in a collection of such triples. The unarmoring routine simply obtains the context-based key (in the correct environment) and concatenates the salt, generating the hash and extracting the run. The process is repeated this for all triples, thus (re)generating the original shellcode.

We implement this technique by creating a modified version of the Context_CPUID Metasploit key generator stub with modified GetPC code, similar to our CKPE implementation. The unarmoring routine consists of extracting the runs from the hashes obtained from combining the extracted context key with the information in the triples. Similarly to what we did for context-keying, we use CPUID information, values present at static memory addresses, system time and file information as context keys with which we armor our test shellcodes. Both Libemu and Nemu are not capable to detect any of the modified shellcodes.

4   Conclusions and Future Works

In this paper, we have shown how EBNIDSes work and we have pointed out that they suffer of important limitations. In particular, we have shown that all three steps of emulation-based detection (namely, pre-processing, emulation, and the heuristic-based detection) have limitations that make it relatively simple for an attacker to circumvent the detection. We tested two common EBNIDSes for a proof of concept and it showed us that it is possible to evade both systems in all the detection steps.

From the foundational viewpoint, we believe that the most interesting limitations are those regarding emulation and the heuristic-based detection. Indeed, we have demonstrated that *even assuming a bug-free pre-processor and emulator*, emulation can still be hindered and heuristic-based detection can be easily bypassed by a skilled attacker. We have shown that it is possible to write generic shellcode encoders which are able to completely bypass EBNIDSes by targeting their intrinsic limitations.

From the practical viewpoint, we think that the weaknesses resulting from the discrepancy between the emulated environment and the intended target of the shellcode is actually the easiest one to exploit for an attacker. Given that outfitting EBNIDSes with full host-based information would make the system completely unscalable, we believe it is unfeasible that EBNIDSes alone will ever be capable of bridging this particular gap either.

Finally, in addition to the structural problems faced by network-level emulators, the proposed pre-processing components often rely purely on static analysis techniques leaving them vulnerable to armoring methods.

Our results show that a sufficiently skilled attacker could armor his shellcode to bypass all investigated approaches or, even worse, develop an easy-to-use library to lower the barrier for armoring and provide other attackers with such an addition to their arsenal.

It is not in the scope of this paper to investigate how to mitigate these problems. We believe that promising avenues of research are those dealing with algebraic specification, hidden Markov-Models and neural networks. Regarding the limitations related to the incompleteness of the emulation environment but there has been research into the detection of ROP attacks such as [29–31] which would be crucial for any network intrusion detection system to implement.

Acknowledgement. The work of the second author has been partially supported by the dutch government national AVATAR project. The work of the fourth author has been partially supported by the European Commission through project FP7-SEC-285477-CRISALIS funded by the 7th Framework Program. The work of the fifth author has been partially supported by the European Commission through project FP7-SEC-607093-PREEMPTIVE funded by the 7th Framework Program.

References

1. Polychronakis, M., Anagnostakis, K.G., Markatos, E.P.: Network–Level polymorphic shellcode detection using emulation. In: Büschkes, R., Laskov, P. (eds.) DIMVA 2006. LNCS, vol. 4064, pp. 54–73. Springer, Heidelberg (2006)
2. Shimamura, M., Kono, K.: Yataglass: Network-level code emulation for analyzing memory-scanning attacks. In: Flegel, U., Bruschi, D. (eds.) DIMVA 2009. LNCS, vol. 5587, pp. 68–87. Springer, Heidelberg (2009)
3. Polychronakis, M., Anagnostakis, K., Markatos, E.: Comprehensive shellcode detection using runtime heuristics. In: Proc. of the 26th Annual Computer Security Applications Conference (ACSAC 2010), pp. 287–296. ACM (2010)
4. Snow, K., Krishnan, S., Monrose, F., Provos, N.: SHELLOS: Enabling Fast Detection and Forensic Analysis of Code Injection Attacks. In: USENIX Security Symposium (2011)
5. Egele, M., Wurzinger, P., Kruegel, C., Kirda, E.: Defending browsers against drive-by downloads: Mitigating heap-spraying code injection attacks. In: Flegel, U., Bruschi, D. (eds.) DIMVA 2009. LNCS, vol. 5587, pp. 88–106. Springer, Heidelberg (2009)
6. Gu, B., Bai, X., Yang, Z., Champion, A., Xuan, D.: Malicious shellcode detection with virtual memory snapshots. In: Proc. of IEEE INFOCOM 2010, pp. 1–9. IEEE (2010)
7. Portokalidis, G., Slowinska, A., Bos, H.: Argos: An emulator for fingerprinting zero-day attacks for advertised honeypots with automatic signature generation. In: Proc. of ACM SIGOPS Operating Systems Review, vol. 40(4), pp. 15–27. ACM (2006)
8. Zhang, Q., Reeves, D., Ning, P., Iyer, S.: Analyzing network traffic to detect self-decrypting exploit code. In: Proc. of the 2nd ACM Symposium on Information, Computer and Communications Security (CCS 2007), pp. 4–12. ACM (2007)
9. Polychronakis, M., Anagnostakis, K.G., Markatos, E.P.: Emulation-based detection of non-self-contained polymorphic shellcode. In: Kruegel, C., Lippmann, R., Clark, A. (eds.) RAID 2007. LNCS, vol. 4637, pp. 87–106. Springer, Heidelberg (2007)
10. Honeynet Project, Dionaea, a low-interaction honeypot (2008), http://www.honeynet.org/project/Dionaea
11. Markatos, E., Anagnostakis, K.: Noah: A european network of affined honeypots for cyber-attack tracking and alerting. The Parliament Magazine 262 (2008)
12. Baecher, P., Koetter, M.: libemu (2009), http://libemu.carnivore.it/
13. Branco, R., Barbosa, G., Neto, P.: Scientific but not academical overview of malware anti-debugging, anti-disassembly and anti-vm technologies. In: Black Hat Technical Security Conf., Las Vegas, Nevada (2012)
14. Sikorski, M., Honig, A.: Practical Malware Analysis: The Hands-On Guide to Dissecting Malicious Software. No Starch Press (2012)

15. Ferrie, P.: Attacks on more virtual machine emulators. Symantec Technology Exchange (2007)
16. Raffetseder, T., Kruegel, C., Kirda, E.: Detecting system emulators. In: Garay, J.A., Lenstra, A.K., Mambo, M., Peralta, R. (eds.) ISC 2007. LNCS, vol. 4779, pp. 1–18. Springer, Heidelberg (2007)
17. Bania, P.: Evading network-level emulation. arXiv preprint arXiv:0906.1963 (2009)
18. Skape, Using dual-mappings to evade automated unpackers (October 2008), http://www.uninformed.org/?v=10&a=1&t=sumry
19. Linn, C., Rajagopalan, M., Baker, S., Collberg, C., Debray, S., Hartman, J.: Protecting against unexpected system calls. In: Proc. of the 14th USENIX Security Symposium, pp. 239–254 (2005)
20. Chung, S.P., Mok, A.K.: Swarm attacks against network-level emulation/analysis. In: Lippmann, R., Kirda, E., Trachtenberg, A. (eds.) RAID 2008. LNCS, vol. 5230, pp. 175–190. Springer, Heidelberg (2008)
21. Overcl0k, RP++ ROP Sequences Finder (2013), https://github.com/Overcl0k/rp
22. kingcopes: Attacking the Windows 7/8 Address Space Randomization (2013), http://kingcope.wordpress.com/2013/01/24/attacking-the-windows-78-address-space-randomization/
23. Polychronakis, M., Keromytis, A.D.: Rop payload detection using speculative code execution. In: 2011 6th International Conference on Malicious and Unwanted Software (MALWARE), pp. 58–65. IEEE (2011)
24. Kharn: Exploring RDA (2006), http://www.awarenetwork.org/etc/alpha/?x=3
25. Rivest, R., Shamir, A., Wagner, D.: Time-lock puzzles and timed-release crypto. Massachusetts Institute of Technology, Tech. Rep. (1996)
26. Nomenumbra: Countering behavior based malware analysis (2009), https://har2009.org/program/track/Other/57.en.html
27. Glynos, D.: Context-keyed Payload Encoding: Fighting the Next Generation of IDS. In: Proc. of Athens IT Security Conference, ATH.C0N 2010 (2010)
28. Aycock, J., de Graaf, R., Jacobson Jr., M.: Anti-disassembly using cryptographic hash functions. Journal in Computer Virology 2(1), 79–85 (2006)
29. Davi, L., Sadeghi, A., Winandy, M.: ROPdefender: A detection tool to defend against return-oriented programming attacks. In: Proc. of the 6th ACM Symposium on Information, Computer and Communications Security (ASIACCS 2011), pp. 40–51. ACM (2011)
30. Chen, P., Xiao, H., Shen, X., Yin, X., Mao, B., Xie, L.: DROP: Detecting return-oriented programming malicious code. In: Prakash, A., Sen Gupta, I. (eds.) ICISS 2009. LNCS, vol. 5905, pp. 163–177. Springer, Heidelberg (2009)
31. Onarlioglu, K., Bilge, L., Lanzi, A., Balzarotti, D., Kirda, E.: G-Free: Defeating return-oriented programming through gadget-less binaries. In: Proc. of the 26th Annual Computer Security Applications Conference (ACSAC 2010), pp. 49–58. ACM (2010)

Quantitative Evaluation of Dynamic Platform Techniques as a Defensive Mechanism*

Hamed Okhravi, James Riordan, and Kevin Carter

MIT Lincoln Laboratory
{hamed.okhravi,james.riordan,kevin.carter}@ll.mit.edu

Abstract. Cyber defenses based on dynamic platform techniques have been proposed as a way to make systems more resilient to attacks. These defenses change the properties of the platforms in order to make attacks more complicated. Unfortunately, little work has been done on measuring the effectiveness of these defenses. In this work, we first measure the protection provided by a dynamic platform technique on a testbed. The counter-intuitive results obtained from the testbed guide us in identifying and quantifying the major effects contributing to the protection in such a system. Based on the abstract effects, we develop a generalized model of dynamic platform techniques which can be used to quantify their effectiveness. To verify and validate our results, we simulate the generalized model and show that the testbed measurements and the simulations match with small amount of error. Finally, we enumerate a number of lessons learned in our work which can be applied to quantitative evaluation of other defensive techniques.

Keywords: Dynamic platforms, platform diversity, quantitative evaluation, metrics, intrusion tolerance, moving target.

1   Introduction

Developing secure systems is difficult and costly. The high cost of effectively mitigating all vulnerabilities and the far lesser cost of exploiting a single one creates an environment which advantages cyber attackers. New active cyber defense paradigms have been proposed to re-balance the landscape and create uncertainty for the attackers [1]. One such paradigm is active defenses based on dynamic platform techniques.

Dynamic platform techniques (or simply, dynamic platforms) dynamically change the properties of a computing platform in order to complicate attacks. Platform properties refer to hardware and operating system (OS) attributes such as instruction set architecture (ISA), stack direction, calling convention, kernel version, OS distribution, and machine instance. Various dynamic platform techniques have been proposed in the literature. Emulation-based techniques change the calling sequence and instruction set presented to an application [2]; multivariant execution techniques change properties such as stack direction or machine description using compiler generated diversity and

---

* This work is sponsored by the Department of Defense under Air Force Contract #FA8721-05-C-0002. Opinions, interpretations, conclusions and recommendations are those of the author and are not necessarily endorsed by the United States Government.

A. Stavrou et al. (Eds.): RAID 2014, LNCS 8688, pp. 405–425, 2014.
© Springer International Publishing Switzerland 2014

virtualization [3–6]; migration-based techniques change the hardware and operating system of an application using containers and compiler-based checkpointing [7]; server diversification techniques rotate a server across multiple platforms and software stacks using network proxies [8]; self cleansing techniques change the machine instance by continuously rotating across many virtual machines and re-imaging the inactive ones [9–11].

Unfortunately, little work has been done on understanding and quantifying the impact of dynamic platforms on the security of a system. The impact of such techniques is often assumed to be intuitive and straight forward. Moreover, one cannot compare different features provided by different dynamic platforms in a quantitative way. For example, is it more effective to support multiple platforms that are running simultaneously and voting on the result (a.k.a. multi-instance), or to have one active platform, but support cleansing of the inactive ones (a.k.a. cleanup)?

In this work, we first identify the four major features proposed by different dynamic platforms in the literature. We then perform a set of experiments on a testbed with one such technique that is augmented to support these features in order to quantify its protection. The results from our testbed experiments are, in fact, counter-intuitive and complex. The complexity of the results suggest that various underlying effects contribute to such a system.

Based on our observations and the mathematical principles involved, we enumerate and analyze the various underlying effects in an abstract analysis of a dynamic platform system. To evaluate the completeness of our enumerated list of abstract effects, we develop a generalized model of dynamic platforms based on these effects and verify and validate the model by simulating the same experiments as the ones we performed on the testbed. The matching results and the small amounts of error validate our model and verify that we have at least correctly captured the main effects contributing to the protection provided by a dynamic platform. Finally, we enumerate a number of lessons learned that can be applied to the quantitative evaluation of other defensive techniques.

Our contributions are as follows:

- To the best of our knowledge, we perform the first quantitative evaluation of dynamic platforms as a defensive mechanism and illustrate the complexities and the counter-intuitive effects contributing to such a system. Moreover, we enumerate the major effects and their impacts.
- We develop a generalized model of dynamic platforms and simulate the results. We verify and validate the model by comparing the simulated results with the testbed experiments and show that they match closely.
- We demonstrate how testbed experiments, abstract analysis, and modeling and simulation can be used together to quantify the impact of defensive techniques. In our work, testbed experiments are used to uncover the complexities, abstract analysis is used to enumerate and describe such complexities, and modeling and simulation is used to check the completeness of the abstract analysis and to validate the results. We enumerate a number of lessons learned which can guide future evaluations of the defenses.

The rest of the paper is organized as follows. Section 2 provides a brief overview of dynamic platform techniques. Section 3 describes the threat model used throughout the paper. Section 4 discusses our testbed experiments and measurements performed on a real system. Section 5 discusses our abstract analysis approach and its results. Section 6 describes our generalized model of dynamic platforms. Section 7 presents the simulation results from the generalized model. Section 8 enumerates a number of lessons learned and discusses our findings. We discuss the related work in Section 9 before concluding the paper in Section 10.

2 Dynamic Platform Background

We briefly describe the defensive techniques based on dynamic platforms. We provide enough background for understanding the rest of the paper. More details about each technique can be found in its original publication.

Dynamic platform techniques change platform properties in order to make attacks more complicated [12]. They often rely on temporal changes (e.g. VM rotation), diversity (e.g. multivariant execution), or both (e.g. migration-based techniques) to protect a system. These techniques are often implemented using machine-level or operating system-level virtualization, compiler-based code diversification, emulation layers, checkpoint/restore techniques, or a combination thereof. Emulation-based techniques such as Genesis [2] often use an application-level virtual machines such as Strata [13] or Valgrind [14] to implement instruction set diversity. In some cases, multiple instances are executed and a monitor compares their results. Multivariant execution techniques such as Reverse stack [15] (also called N-variant systems [16]) use compiler-based techniques to create diverse application code by replacing sets of instructions with semantically equivalent ones. Migration-based techniques such as Talent [7] use operating system-level virtualization (containers) to move an application across diverse architectures and operating systems. A dynamic platform can also be achieved at a higher abstraction level by switching between different implementations of servers [8]. These techniques either do not preserve the state (e.g. a web server) or they preserve it using high level configuration files (e.g. DNS server). Finally, self-cleansing techniques such as SCIT [9] only change the current instance of the platform without diversifying it. The main goal, in this case, is bringing the platform to its pristine state and removing persistence of attacks.

We have identified four features that determine the protection provided by dynamic platform techniques. Later in our analysis, we show that these features can result in very different defensive benefits for each technique. The four features are:

Diversity. A dynamic platform technique provides diversity if it changes the properties of the platform used for running the application. For example, the Reversed Stack [15] technique provides diversity because it changes the direction of stack growth whereas SCIT [9] does not because it rotates the service among homogeneous virtual machines.

Multi-Instance. A technique is multi-instance if more that one platform instance is used to serve a transaction simultaneously. For example, multivariant execution [3] is a multi-instance technique because it runs a transaction on multiple different instances of the platform and compares the results, whereas Talent [7] is not, because it uses one instance at a time.

Table 1. Features of some of the dynamic platform techniques

Technique	Diversity	Multi-Instance	Limited Duration	Cleanup
SCIT [9]				✓
GA-Based Configuration [17]	✓		✓	
MAS [18]	✓			✓
Multivariant Execution [3]	✓	✓		
Reversed Stack [15]	✓	✓		
Talent [17]	✓		✓	
Machine desc. diversity [6]	✓		✓	
N-Variant System [16]	✓	✓		
Intrusion Tolerance for MCS [19]	✓	✓		
Intrusion Tolerant WS [8]	✓	✓		

Limited Duration. A technique has limited duration if the instance of the platform can change while processing a single transaction. Otherwise, we call it extended duration which means that the technique must finish processing a transaction before it can change the instance of the platform. For example, using genetic algorithms to change platform configurations [17] has limited duration because the the configuration can change while processing a transaction whereas moving attack surfaces [18] completes each transaction on the same instance on which it started (i.e. extended duration).

Cleanup. A technique supports cleanup if each instance is wiped and imaged into a pristine state before it is used again. For example, SCIT [9] supports cleanup whereas multivariant execution does not.

Table 1 shows a list of representative dynamic platform techniques and their features. We use one of the above techniques, Talent, to quantitatively analyze the effectiveness of dynamic platforms. Although Talent does not natively support multi-instance and cleanup, we augment it with these features to understand their impact. The main reason for using Talent was its code availability, but we show that our analysis can be generalized based on the features of the techniques.

In this work, our goal is not to provide arguments for merits or demerits of any of the proposed dynamic platform techniques. Rather, we strive to quantitatively evaluate dynamic platforms as a cyber defense mechanism and study various features that can significantly change their impact.

2.1 Talent

Talent [7] is a technique that allows live migration of applications across diverse platforms. It uses operating-system-level virtualization (OpenVZ [20]) to sandbox an application and migrate the environment. For internal process state migration, Talent uses a portable checkpoint compiler (CPPC [21]) to insert checkpointing instructions into a code. At the time of migration, it pauses a process, checkpoints its state, moves the state to the next platform, and resumes the execution. Some portions of the code are re-executed in order to construct the entire state.

Since it allows an application to run on different operating systems and architecture, Talent provides diversity. Also, it is a limited duration technique, because it can pause a process and resume it on a different platform. However, it does not natively support multi-instance since one platform is active at a time; it does not implement cleanup either.

Talent has been implemented on Intel Xeon 32-bit, Intel Core 2 Quad 64-bit, and AMD Opteron 64-bit processors. It has also been tested with Gentoo, Fedora (9, 10, 11, 12, and 17), CentOS (4, 5, and 6.3), Debian (4, 5, and 6), Ubuntu (8 and 9), SUSE (10 and 11), and FreeBSD 9 operating systems.

3 Threat Model

We discuss multiple threat models in this paper but analysis shows that they share common features. To make the analysis more precise, we explicitly describe the core threat model in this section. Variations upon the core threat model are described in the other sections as appropriate.

In our model, the defender has a number of different platforms to run a critical application. The attacker has a set of exploits (attacks) that are applicable against some of these platforms, but not the others. We call the platforms for which the attacker has an exploit "vulnerable" and the others "invulnerable." In a strict systems security terminology, vulnerable does not imply exploitable; without loss of generality, we only consider exploitable vulnerabilities. An alternative interpretation of this threat model is that the vulnerabilities are exploitable on some platforms, but not on the other ones.

The defender does not know which platforms are vulnerable and which are invulnerable, nor does she have detection capabilities for the deployed exploits. This scenario, for example, describes the use of zero-day exploits by attackers, for which no detection mechanism exists by definition.

Since there is little attempt to isolate the inactive platforms in dynamic platform systems, we assume that all platforms are accessible by the attacker, and the attacker attempts to exploit each one.

The attacker's goal is what creates the variations in our threat model. For example, one success criteria may be for the attacker to compromise the system for a given period of time to cause irreversible damage (e.g. crash a satellite), while a different success criteria gives the attacker gradual gain the longer the system is compromised (e.g. exfiltration of information). Different techniques with different features provide varying protections against these goals which we study in the subsequent sections.

4 Experiments

4.1 Experiment Setup

To understand the protection provided by dynamic platforms, we start by performing simple experiments with Talent and two real-world exploits. We observe that contrary to the naïve view, even these simple experiments result in very complex results which highlight a number of subtleties about dynamic platforms.

To perform the experiments, a notional application with C back-end and GUI front-end has been ported to Talent. The application's back-end performs attestation of machines within a local network and its front-end displays the result. However, the details of the application are unimportant for the evaluations done in this work, so for the sake of brevity we do not discuss them here.

On the testbed, we have a pool of five different platforms: Fedora on x86, Gentoo on x86, Debian on x86_64, FreeBSD on x86, and CentOS on x86. The application runs for a random amount of time on a platform before migrating to a different one (i.e. platform duration).

The attacker's goal in the experiments is to control the active platform for some time T. Since in a real scenario the vulnerability of the platform is unknown, we may consecutively migrate to multiple vulnerable platforms, in which case the attacker wins. To implement this scenario on the testbed, we launch two real exploits against Talent. The first is the TCP MAXSEG exploit which triggers a divide by zero vulnerability in `net/ ipv4/tcp.c` (CVE-2010-4165) to perform a DoS attack on the platform. Only the Gentoo platform is vulnerable to this attack. The second attack is the Socket Pairs exploit which triggers a garbage collection vulnerability in `net/unix/garbage.c` (CVE-2010-4249) to saturates the CPU usage and file descriptors. The Fedora and CentOS platforms are vulnerable to this attack. Our Debian and FreeBSD platforms are not vulnerable to these exploits.

In each configuration, we select $N \in (1, 5)$ platforms. For each trial, the application randomly migrates across those N platforms without immediate repeat. In the case of $N = 1$ (baseline), the application remains on the same platform during the entire trial. Without loss of generality, the duration on each platform (d) is chosen randomly and uniformly from $40 - 60$ seconds. Although we have no reason to believe that these are the appropriate values for a real-world application, we will show later that the actual values of the duration (d) and attacker's goal (T) are inconsequential to our experiments and can be parametrized.

One or both exploits become available to the attacker at random times during each trial. As a result, zero to three platforms can be compromised (zero when the exploit is not effective against the set of platforms and three when both exploits are available and Fedora, CentOS, and Gentoo are in the pool of platforms). When the exploit is launched, its payload reaches all of the platforms in the selected set at once (not one after another). This approach tries to model the behavior of network-based exploits that propagate to all machines within a network very rapidly. Each trial runs for 15 minutes. We collect 300 trials for each configuration. We also collect a central log which includes a timestamp, the status of each platform (up or down), and the active platform and a local log (for verification purposes) which also includes finer-grained CPU load for each platform.

Fig. 1 illustrates one trial with 3 platforms. The red arrows show when exploits are launched. In this case, platforms 2 and 5 are vulnerable to exploits 1 and 2 respectively. A shaded rectangle shows a compromised platform while a white rectangle shows an uncompromised one (vulnerable or invulnerable).

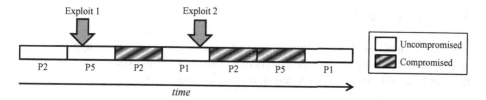

Fig. 1. A 3-platform trial

4.2 Experiment Results

We calculate the value of the metric, which is the percentage of time that the attacker is in control for longer than T and present these results in Fig. 2.

The results are completely perplexing. In fact, the results are so counter-intuitive that we initially thought that some mistakes have been made in collecting them. We can at least observe the following peculiarities in the results.

- The 1-platform result is very different than the others and seems to estimate a straight line for $T > 100$ sec.
- More platforms does not always result in lower chance of attacker success. Specifically for $60 < T < 120$, more platforms result in higher chance of success for the attacker.
- There are several downward steps in the curves for more than one platform at $T = 60, 120, 180, \ldots$.
- For $T > 120$, more platforms result in lower chance of attacker success and that remains the case for larger values of T.

The complexity of the results suggest that various effects should be in play which we explain one by one in the next section.

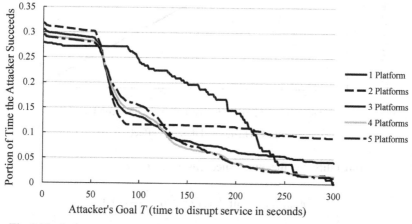

Fig. 2. Testbed measurements of the impact of dynamic platform on attacker success

5   Abstract Analysis

Much of the analysis of one system using dynamic platforms as a defense applies to any such system. First, we explain the effects that contribute to our experiment results and then we generalize our analysis to any dynamic platform technique.

5.1   Limited Duration Effect

The first effect contributing to the results is the limited duration effect. Let d be the duration of the transaction on a platform, T be the period that the attacker must be present, and s the start time of attack. If $T > d$, the attacker can never win. For $T < d$, the attacker can only win if she starts early enough during the $d - T$ interval. As a result, the probability of winning for the attacker is a decreasing linear function of T.

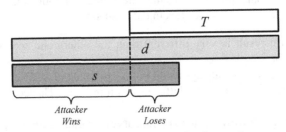

Fig. 3. Window of opportunity for the attacker

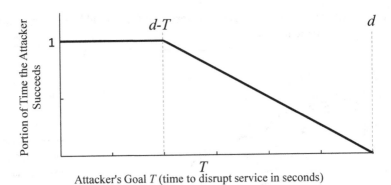

Fig. 4. The limited duration effect

Then the probability that the attack succeeds is given by

$$Pr_{success} = \min\left(1, \max\left(0, \frac{d - T}{s}\right)\right)$$

This explains the general decreasing trend for the probability of success as a function of attacker's goal in Fig. 2.

Counter-intuitively, this effect also explains the straight-line result for the 1-platform experiment in Fig. 2. Although in the 1-platform case, the platform never changes, the probability of success decreases linearly with time because the entire trial has a limited duration. The attacker cannot possibly win if she starts late even if that single platform is vulnerable. This explains the similarity of the 1-platform result in Fig. 2 and Fig. 4.

5.2 Diversity Effect

Informally speaking, the intuition behind the concept of diversity is that it is harder for an attacker to compromise different platforms than it is to compromise homogeneous ones. Since we assume that the platforms are all available and no separation exists between them, in the case of homogeneous platforms, they can all be compromised by an exploit that works against one of them. On the other hand, if the platforms are diverse (which is the case in our experiments), an exploit can work against some of them, but not the other ones.

In practice, diversity creates an effect which occurs when the required attacker goal T passes between various multiples of the duration of each platform d. For example, if the attacker goal passes from being a bit less than a single platform duration to a bit more, then instead of a single vulnerable platform, two need to be used consecutively. The same effect happens as we transition from two to three and so on. The result is downward steps in the curve when the required attacker goal passes multiples of the platform duration. Fig. 5 illustrates this impact when three out of five platforms are vulnerable. The first platform is trivially vulnerable with $\frac{3}{5}$ probability. Since we do not have immediate repeats, the subsequent platforms are chosen from the four remaining ones of which two are vulnerable, so the probability that the second platform is vulnerable if the first one is vulnerable is $\frac{2}{4}$. As a result, both the first and the second platforms are vulnerable with probability $\frac{3}{5} \times \frac{2}{4}$. If we extend the analysis, the first, second, and third platforms are vulnerable with probability $\frac{3}{5} \times (\frac{2}{4})^2$, and so on (see Fig. 5).

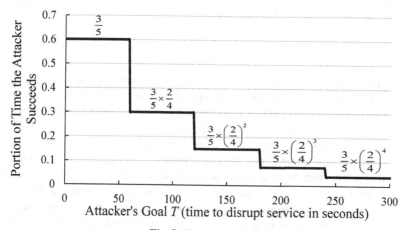

Fig. 5. The diversity effect

5.3 Multi-instance Effect

In the multi-instance case, the system is compromised if the majority of platforms are compromised. Although Talent does not natively support multi-instance, we augment it with a simple voting mechanism to analyze the impact of running multiple platforms simultaneously. With the same experiment setup as described in section 4 we analyze the probability of success when the application runs on multiple platforms and the majority of the platforms are compromised.

When the system is multi-instance, if there is no platform change, the case becomes trivial; that is, if the majority of the platforms are not vulnerable, the system as a whole is never compromised and the attacker never wins. On the other hand, if the majority of the platforms are vulnerable, the attacker wins as soon as the exploits are launched and remains in control indefinitely. As a result, we only show the effect when the platform change happens. Moreover, the 1-platform and 5-platform cases are also trivial, so we only show the results for a 3-platform setup. In this setup, the application runs on three platforms simultaneously. For each platform, the application migrates to a new platform uniformly randomly after spending 40-60 seconds. Thus, the migrations may be out-of-sync, but at each instance of time the application is running on three diverse platforms.

The multi-instance effect is shown in Fig. 6. The single instance result is the same as the 3-platform setup in Fig. 2.

Counter-intuitively, the multi-instance setup is less secure for small values of T. This arises from a combinatorial effect. Since three of the five platforms are vulnerable, there are three configurations in which the majority is not vulnerable (the two invulnerable platforms selected with one other vulnerable platform) which is expressed by $C(3,1)$ where $C(x,y) = \frac{x!}{y!(x-y)!}$ is the combinatorial choice function. The total number of choices is $C(5,3) = 10$. As a result, the defender wins with the probability of 30% and thus, the attacker wins with the probability of 70%. This is why the multi-instance case starts from 0.7. With the single instance case this probability is smaller because there is a higher probability of a combination with an invulnerable platform. In other words, when the majority of the platforms are vulnerable (3 out of 5 in this case), there is a higher probability that if we choose three platforms, two or more of them are vulnerable $(1 - C(3,1))$ than if we choose just one platform and that is vulnerable $(\frac{3}{5})$. We will explain this effect in more details in Section 6.1.

5.4 Cleanup Effect

A dynamic platform system supports cleanup if every inactive platform in restored into its pristine state. Talent does not natively support cleanup either, but we augment it with a cleanup capability to evaluate its impact. As discussed earlier, techniques such as SCIT [9] and MAS [18] implement cleanup.

The impact of cleanup is trivial if the exploit is only launched once and never repeated; the attacker may compromise the active platform for the remainder of the time on that platform, but when the platform changes, the system becomes pristine and the attacker never wins again. This is because the inactive platforms are being cleaned while the attacker attacks the active one. Consequently, in the case of a non-repeating exploit, the portion of time the attacker is in control amortizes with the duration of the trial.

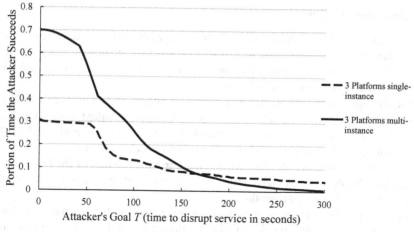

Fig. 6. The multi-instance effect

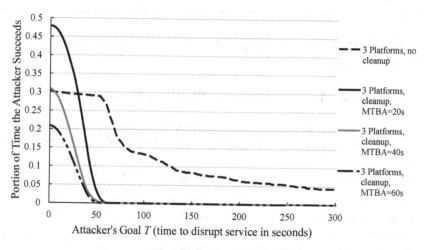

Fig. 7. The cleanup effect

Here, we evaluate the non-trivial case where the exploit is repeated frequently. We re-launch the exploit with mean time between attacks (MTBA) set at 20, 40, and 60 seconds. Fig. 7 illustrates the impact of cleanup. As can be observed, for any attacker goal of greater than 60 seconds, the chance of success for the attacker drops to zero. This makes sense because the inactive platforms are restored to their pristine state, so the application can never migrate to an already compromised platform. As a result, the attacker can only win if her goal is shorter than the maximum duration of time on a single platform, which is 60 seconds.

As the results suggest, cleanup can greatly improve the protection offered by dynamic platform techniques since it significantly reduce the window of opportunity for an attacker. It is advisable that all dynamic platform techniques should support cleanup.

5.5   Smoothing Effects

A few effects contribute to the smoothness of the edges of the curves depicted in Fig. 2. For example, the downward steps are not sharp transitions (similar to a step function). Rather, they are smoother curvatures. For the sake of completeness, we explain a few factors that contribute to this smoothness.

First, the time spent on a platform is not fixed; rather, it is a random variable uniformly selected between 40 and 60 seconds. This is an important smoothing factor because it makes the time on a platform non-deterministic and as a result, it makes the threshold for passing between multiples of the platforms also smooth.

Second, the exploits are also launched at random times instead of the beginning of the trial. This factor is not crucial in evaluating dynamic platforms and its only tangible impact is making the curves smoother.

Third, we assumed that as soon as the exploit is launched the vulnerable platforms are compromised. In reality, the time it takes for the exploit to successfully compromise a platform after reaching it is non-zero which also makes the results smoother. For example, the Socket Pairs exploit used in the experiments takes a few seconds to saturate the file descriptors.

Fourth, networking, OS scheduling, and various other delays also make the results smoother and in some cases noisier.

6   Generalized Model of Dynamic Platform Techniques

In this section, we use the knowledge of our experiments and the effects that we explained in the previous section to develop a generalized model of the dynamic platform techniques.

We can categorize the problem space according to a number of properties:

- The attackers control requirement can either be aggregate or continuous. In the aggregate case, any period of time during which the attacker controls a platform counts and *aggregates* towards the payoff. Data exfiltration attacks are an example of attacks that require aggregate control. In the continuous case, only the time since the most recent compromise during which the attacker has *continuous* control of the platform counts towards the payoff. For example, attacks that leak crypto keys through remote side channel attacks require continuous control since that key may only be valid for the most recent session.
- The attackers payoff can be either fractional or binary (all or nothing). In the fractional case, the attacker is rewarded more, the longer she controls the platform. Data exfiltration attacks are an example of fractional payoff. In the binary case, the attacker is not rewarded before a known period of control, and then she is fully rewarded at once. Attacks on critical infrastructure systems to cause a physical impact (e.g. to cause a blackout) are an example of binary payoff.
- The platform change model can include random with repeat, random without repeat, and periodic permutation.

We will define the abstract model of a dynamic platform system $\mathcal{P}$ as a system that migrates through a finite fixed collection of platforms $\{p_i\}$. Each platform either has or

Table 2. Notation describing dynamic platform system

α	Number of vulnerable platforms
β	Number of invulnerable platforms
p^k	Platform at migration step k
$v\left(p^k\right)$	Platform at migration step k is vulnerable
$\neg v\left(p^k\right)$	Platform at migration step k is not vulnerable
$Pr\left(v\left(p^k\right)\right)$	Probability that $v\left(p^k\right)$
Pr_{vv}	$P\left(v\left(p^{k+1}\right)\mid v\left(p^k\right)\right)$
Pr_{ii}	$P\left(\neg v\left(p^{k+1}\right)\mid \neg v\left(p^k\right)\right)$

does not have a property exploitable by the attacker which we call vulnerable. In the first approximation to the model we assume that the platforms are fully independent. We will use the notation presented in Table 2.

6.1 Attacker Aggregate Control

When the attacker requires only aggregate control, there are two main subcategories according to the attacker's payoff. The fractional case is trivially determined by the ratio of α and β. In the binary case, wherein the attacker wins by controlling a specified fraction of the vulnerable time, the defender may optimize via an initial subselection of platforms in a process reminiscent of gerrymandering. For example, if $\alpha = 3$ and $\beta = 2$ and the attacker wants to control greater than 50% of the time, then the defender should simply expect to lose should all platforms be utilized. By contrast if the defender randomly subselects two platforms then the defender can reduce the attacker's expectation of winning to

$$\frac{C\left(3,2\right)}{C\left(5,2\right)} = \frac{3}{10} = 30\%,$$

where $C\left(x,y\right) = \frac{x!}{y!(x-y)!}$ is the combinatorial choice function. Here the value of 2 as the number of platforms chosen.

Generally, if t is the percentage of time that the attacker requires for success and we subselect j platforms from the total $\alpha + \beta$, then the probability of attacker success is

$$Pr_{success} = \sum_{i=\lceil t \cdot j \rceil}^{\min(\alpha,j)} \frac{C\left(\alpha, i\right) \cdot C\left(\beta, j-i\right)}{C\left(\alpha + \beta, j\right)},$$

in the steady-state model.

6.2 Attacker Continuous Control

When the attacker requires continuous control, the defender can use the subselection strategy as above as well as leveraging conditional probabilities. These conditional probabilities are given in Table 3.

Table 3. Conditional Probabilities

Repeat	Vuln	¬Vuln	$Pr\left(v\left(p^{k+1}\right)\right)$	$Pr\left(v\left(p^{k+1}\right)\mid v\left(p^{k}\right)\right)$	$Pr\left(v\left(p^{k+j}\right)\mid v\left(p^{k+j-1}\right)\ \&\ldots\&v\left(p^{k}\right)\right)$
Without	α	β	$\dfrac{\alpha}{\alpha+\beta}$	$\dfrac{\alpha-1}{\alpha+\beta-1}$	$\dfrac{\alpha-j}{\alpha+\beta-j}$
With	α	β	$\dfrac{\alpha}{\alpha+\beta}$	$\dfrac{\alpha}{\alpha+\beta}$	$\dfrac{\alpha}{\alpha+\beta}$

Here, we observe that $\frac{\alpha}{\alpha+\beta} > \frac{\alpha-j}{\alpha+\beta-j}$ so long as β and j are both greater than zero. As such, migrating *without* immediate repeat, while not influencing the fraction of vulnerable platforms selected, tends to reduce successful sequences for the attacker. We note that the influence is greater when a smaller number of platforms is used. Our later experiment will use 3 vulnerable and 2 invulnerable platforms which is a sufficiently small number to have a strong influence upon the conditional probabilities.

This reduces to the Markov chain:

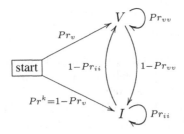

6.3   Attacker Fractional Payoff Model

The steady state of attacker control of the system can be modeled using Markov chains with states I and V referring to invulnerable and vulnerable respectively. While the simple Markov model describing the transitions $\{I, V\} \longrightarrow \{I, V\}$ describes the base behavior of the system, it does not naturally capture the notion of repeated vulnerable states. We can adapt this chain to one with a richer collection of states

$$\{I, IV, IV^2, \ldots, IV^{n-1}, V^n\} \longrightarrow \{I, IV, IV^2, \ldots, IV^{n-1}, V^n\}$$

which support runs of length n. The probability of invulnerable to invulnerable transition is given by

$$Pr_{ii} = Pr\left(\neg v\left(p^{k+1}\right)\mid \neg v\left(p^{k}\right)\right) = \frac{\beta-1}{\alpha+\beta-1}$$

and the probability of vulnerable to vulnerable transition is given by

$$Pr_{vv} = Pr\left(v\left(p^{k+1}\right)\mid v\left(p^{k}\right)\right) = \frac{\alpha-1}{\alpha+\beta-1}$$

The Markov model looks like

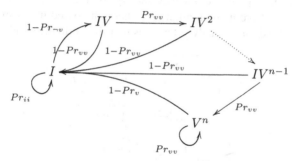

which has the $(n+1) \times (n+1)$ Markov transition matrix is given by

$$
\begin{bmatrix}
Pr_{ii} & 1 - Pr_{vv} & & & & & \\
1 - Pr_{vv} & & Pr_{vv} & & & & \\
1 - Pr_{vv} & & & Pr_{vv} & & & \\
1 - Pr_{vv} & & & & Pr_{vv} & & \\
1 - Pr_{vv} & & & & & \ddots & \\
1 - Pr_{vv} & & & & & & Pr_{vv} \\
1 - Pr_{vv} & & & & & & Pr_{vv}
\end{bmatrix}.
$$

This transition matrix has the steady state eigen-vector

$$
\begin{bmatrix} \frac{\beta}{\alpha+\beta} & a_v \cdot Pr_{vv} & a_v \cdot Pr_{vv}^2 & \cdots & a_v \cdot Pr_{vv}^{n-1} & a_v \cdot \sum_{i=n}^{\infty} Pr_{vv}^i \end{bmatrix}
$$

where

$$
a_v = \frac{\alpha}{\alpha + \beta} \cdot \left(\frac{1 - Pr_{vv}}{Pr_{vv}} \right).
$$

This can be used to compute the steady state behavior of the system. If the attacker success begins after n steps then the steady state is given by the right most term in the eigen vector $a_v \cdot \sum_{i=n}^{\infty} P_v^i = \frac{\alpha}{\alpha+\beta} - a_v \cdot \sum_{i=0}^{n-1} P_v^i$. If the attacker success includes the steps leading to a run of n steps then we must also include vulnerable states weighted by the probability that they will become a run of n vulnerable states and the contribution to the run: the probability that IV^{n-1} will become V^n is Pr_V, the probability that IV^{n-2} will become V^n is $2 \cdot Pr_V^2$ and so forth. Reducing that equation, we find that the expected period of attacker control $L(n)$ is

$$
L(n) = 1 - \frac{(1 - Pr_{\neg v})^{-1} + (1 - Pr_v) \sum_{i=0}^{n-1} i \cdot Pr_v^{i-1}}{(1 - Pr_{\neg v})^{-1} + (1 - Pr_v)^{-1}}
$$

which is one minus the percentage of time that the defender is in control.

6.4 Attacker Binary Payoff Model

In the binary payoff model with random selection (with or without immediate repeats), the attacker will eventually win so long as it is combinatorially possible in the same manner that a person flipping a coin will eventually observe a sequence of ten, or ninety-two, heads in a row. Here metrics might reasonably be based in the mean time until attacker victory. These can be analyzed in a fashion similar to the steady state model:

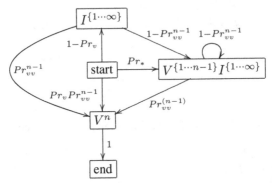

where $Pr_* = Pr_v \left(1 - Pr_{vv}^{n-1}\right)$. We can use this to evaluate the expected time $L'(n)$ to attack compromise as the probabilistically weighted sum of all path lengths

$$
\begin{aligned}
L'(n) = &n + \frac{1 - Pr_v}{1 - Pr_{ii}} + \\
&\left(Pr_{vv}^{1-n} - 1\right) \cdot \\
&\left(\frac{1 - n \cdot Pr_{vv}^{n-1} + (n-1) \cdot Pr_{vv}^{n}}{\left(1 - Pr_{vv}^{n-1}\right) \cdot \left(1 - Pr_{vv}\right)} + \frac{1}{1 - Pr_{ii}} \right)
\end{aligned}
\tag{1}
$$

Hence, in scenarios such as 'crash the satellite', Eq. (1) computes the expected time before the adversary is able to take down the service.

7 Simulation Results

In order to verify that we have captured the major effects in our analysis and that our generalized model of dynamic platforms is valid, we simulate the Markov chain that corresponds to our testbed experiments. Our testbed experiments assumed migration with no immediate repeat, continuous control, and fractional payoff which is modeled using the Markov chain in section 6.3. We run a Monte Carlo simulation on that model with the same parameters as our testbed experiments: $40 - 60$ second time of each platform, three vulnerable platforms out of five total, exploits launched at random times during each trial, and each trial runs for 15 minutes. The results are presented in Fig. 8. In the figure, the testbed measurements are also overlaid on the simulated results using dotted lines for comparison.

As can be observed, the simulation results match the testbed measurements very closely. This validates the fact that we have indeed captured at least the major effects that contribute to the effectiveness of dynamic platform techniques. Note that the smoothing effects (e.g. random duration on a platform and random exploit launch times) are captured in the simulation results since we have captured them in the model. However, various jitters and delays (e.g. networking, OS scheduling, etc.) are not in the

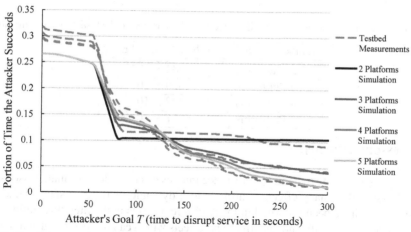

Fig. 8. Simulation results from the generalized model. The testbed measurements are also shown in dotted lines.

model which can explain the small amount of discrepancy between the simulated and measured results. Table 4 shows the mean squared error (MSE) of the simulation results compared to the testbed measurements.

7.1 Discussion

One important observation to be made for both the simulated and measured results is that for small attacker goals (T), fewer platforms actually perform better. This is due to the fact that in situations where the attacker wins quickly, more platforms present a larger attack surface. As a result, the attacker wins if she can compromise any of the platforms. In other words,

$\frac{T}{d} \rightarrow 0$: Attacker wins iff *any* platform is vulnerable

The value of dynamic platforms can only be observed for attacker goals that are large with respect to the duration of each platform ($T \gg d$). This is an important parameter when deploying dynamic platform systems; the duration of each platform must be selected short enough based on the service requirements of the system. For example, if the system has to survive and provide service within 5 minutes (i.e. the attacker goal is disrupting service longer than $T = 5$ minutes), the platform duration must be $d \ll 5$ min. In other words,

$\frac{T}{d} \rightarrow \infty$: Attacker wins iff *all* platforms are vulnerable

Note that there may be practical considerations when choosing small platform duration. If the platform changes too rapidly (i.e. very small d), it can disrupt the normal mission of the system.

Table 4. Mean squared error of the simulated model compared to the testbed measurements

Number of Platforms	Mean Squared Error
2 Platforms	634×10^{-6}
3 Platforms	329×10^{-6}
4 Platforms	322×10^{-6}
5 Platforms	257×10^{-6}

8 Lessons Learned

Our work in analyzing dynamic platform techniques has provided five main lessons.

The first is that many effects contribute to a dynamic platform system. Although these systems have been proposed in many different forms in the literature, little work has been done to identify and quantify these effects which can be very counter-intuitive. On the other hand, when these effects are studied and understood, even first-order models can closely estimate the system behavior.

The second is that experiments such as ours using real-world technologies on a testbed can shed light on some of the complex dynamics of active systems and can be used as a way to identify and quantify the major contributing effects of such systems.

The third is that threat models are crucial in understanding the protection provided by a defensive technique and they are also instrumental in quantitatively measuring such protections. As can be observed in our results, while a technique can provide significant protection against one type of threat (e.g. long-duration attacks that can have fractional gain for the attacker such as slow data exfiltration), it may actually degrade the security of the system for another one (e.g. short duration attacks causing an irreversible impact). In fact, threat models should be an integral part of metrics and measurements of effectiveness [22].

The fourth is that testbed experiments, abstract analysis, and modeling and simulation can be used together to perform quantitative evaluation of defensive techniques in general. These different approaches can identify subtle effects and dynamics. Moreover, they can provide the verification and validation necessary to ensure that the results are indeed correct.

The final lesson is that some features of the proposed techniques, such as cleanup, can significantly reduce the likelihood of success for attacks. When designing new techniques, quantitative evaluations such as what we have done in this paper can be used to decide the important features to support in order to provide the most protection with the least performance overhead.

9 Related Work

Various dynamic platform techniques have been proposed in the literature. As mentioned earlier, The Self-Cleansing Intrusion Tolerance (SCIT) project rotates virtual machines to reduce the exposure time. SCIT-web server [23] and SCIT-DNS [24] preserve the session information and DNS master file and keys, respectively, but not the internal state of the application. The Resilient Web Service (RWS) Project [25] uses a virtualization-based web server system that detects intrusions and periodically restores them to a pristine state. Certain forms of server rotation have been proposed by Blackmon and Nguyen [26] and by Rabbat *et al.* [27] in an attempt to achieve high availability servers.

High-level forms of temporal platform changes have been proposed by Petkac and Badger [28] and Min and Choic [19] to build intrusion tolerant systems although the diversification strategy is not as detailed in these efforts. Compiler-based multivariant [3–5, 15, 29] and N-variant systems [16] propose another way of achieving platform diversity. Holland *et al.* propose diversifying machine descriptions using a virtualization layer [6]. A similar approach with more specific diversification strategy based on instruction sets and calling sequences has been proposed by Williams *et al.* [2]. Wong and Lee [30] use randomization in the processor to combat side-channel attacks on caches.

On the evaluation side, Manadhata and Wind [31] propose a formal model for measuring a system's attack surface that can be used to compare different platforms. Evans *et al.* [32] develop models to measure the effectiveness of diversity-based moving target technique. They evaluate the probability of attack success given the time duration of attack probing, construction, and launch cycles and the entropy of randomness in the target system. They evaluate the impact of various attacks on moving target systems including circumvention, deputy, brute force, entropy reduction, probing, and incremental attacks.

There has been numerous modeling attempts in the literature for diversity systems or N-version programming such as those done by Popov and Mladenov [33], or Arlat *et al.* [34]. However, they focus on accidental faults, not malicious attacks.

10   Conclusion

In this paper, we have quantitatively studied cyber defenses based on dynamic platform techniques. We used testbed experiments to collect results from an actual technique. The unexpected and complex results motivated us to perform an abstract analysis to explain the various effects that contribute to the protection. We extended our analyses to the main features provided by the dynamic platforms proposed in the literature. Based on these effects, we then developed a generalized model of dynamic platforms. In order to ensure that we have captured the major effects, and to verify the model and validate our testbed results, we simulated the same sets of experiments using the generalized model. The closely matching results enhance the confidence in the results and validate the fact that we have at least captured the main effects.

Our results suggest that while dynamic platforms are useful for mitigating some attacks, it is of critical importance to understand the threat model one aims to defend against. While dynamic platforms can be effective against long-period attacks with gradual gains (e.g. data exfiltration), they can be detrimental for short-period attacks with instantaneous gains (e.g. a malware causing an irreversible impact in a control system).

The future work in this domain will focus on performing more experiments with such systems, extending the analysis to other dynamic platform techniques and other randomization and diversity approaches, and analyzing the second order behavior such as adaptive adversaries who change tactics based on the deployed defenses.

Acknowledgement. We would like to thank Charles Wright, Mark Rabe, Paula Dono-
van, and William Streilein for their insights and contributions to this work.

References

[1] Networking, F., Research, I.T., (NITRD), D.: Federal Cybersecurity Game-change R&D
Themes (2012),
`http://cybersecurity.nitrd.gov/page/federal-cybersecurity-1`

[2] Williams, D., Hu, W., Davidson, J.W., Hiser, J.D., Knight, J.C., Nguyen-Tuong, A.: Security
through diversity: Leveraging virtual machine technology. IEEE Security and Privacy 7(1),
26–33 (2009)

[3] Salamat, B., Jackson, T., Wagner, G., Wimmer, C., Franz, M.: Runtime defense against code
injection attacks using replicated execution. IEEE Transactions on Dependable and Secure
Computing 8(4), 588–601 (2011)

[4] Salamat, B., Gal, A., Jackson, T., Manivannan, K., Wagner, G., Franz, M.: Multi-variant
program execution: Using multi-core systems to defuse buffer-overflow vulnerabilities. In:
International Conference on Complex, Intelligent and Software Intensive Systems (2008)

[5] Jackson, T., Salamat, B., Wagner, G., Wimmer, C., Franz, M.: On the effectiveness of multivariant program execution for vulnerability detection and prevention. In: Proceedings of
the 6th International Workshop on Security Measurements and Metrics, vol. 7, pp. 7:1–7:8
(2010)

[6] Holland, D.A., Lim, A.T., Seltzer, M.I.: An architecture a day keeps the hacker away.
SIGARCH Comput. Archit. News 33(1), 34–41 (2005)

[7] Okhravi, H., Comella, A., Robinson, E., Haines, J.: Creating a cyber moving target for
critical infrastructure applications using platform diversity. International Journal of Critical
Infrastructure Protection 5(1), 30–39 (2012)

[8] Saidane, A., Nicomette, V., Deswarte, Y.: The design of a generic intrusion-tolerant architecture for web servers. IEEE Transactions on Dependable and Secure Computing 6(1), 45–58
(2009)

[9] Bangalore, A., Sood, A.: Securing web servers using self cleansing intrusion tolerance (scit).
In: Second International Conference on Dependability, pp. 60 –65 (2009)

[10] Huang, Y., Arsenault, D., Sood, A.: Incorruptible system self-cleansing for intrusion tolerance. In: 25th IEEE International on Performance, Computing, and Communications Conference, IPCCC 2006, vol. 4, p. 496 (April 2006)

[11] Arsenault, D., Sood, A., Huang, Y.: Secure, resilient computing clusters: Self-cleansing in-
trusion tolerance with hardware enforced security (scit/hes). In: Proceedings of the Second
International Conference on Availability, Reliability and Security, ARES 2007, pp. 343–350.
IEEE Computer Society, Washington, DC (2007)

[12] Okhravi, H., Hobson, T., Bigelow, D., Streilein, W.: Finding Focus in the Blur of Moving-
Target Techniques. IEEE Security & Privacy (March/April 2014)

[13] Scott, K., Davidson, J.: Strata: A Software Dynamic Translation Infrastructure. Technical
Report CS-2001-17 (2001)

[14] Nethercote, N., Seward, J.: Valgrind: A framework for heavyweight dynamic binary instrumentation. In: Proceedings of the 2007 ACM SIGPLAN Conference on Programming
Language Design and Implementation, PLDI 2007, pp. 89–100. ACM, New York (2007)

[15] Salamat, B., Gal, A., Franz, M.: Reverse stack execution in a multi-variant execution environment. In: Workshop on Compiler and Architectural Techniques for Application Reliability and Security (2008)

[16] Cox, B., Evans, D., Filipi, A., Rowanhill, J., Hu, W., Davidson, J., Knight, J., Nguyen-Tuong, A., Hiser, J.: N-variant systems: A secretless framework for security through diversity. In: Proceedings of the 15th Conference on USENIX Security Symposium (2006)

[17] Crouse, M., Fulp, E.: A moving target environment for computer configurations using genetic algorithms. In: 2011 4th Symposium on Configuration Analytics and Automation (SAFECONFIG), pp. 1–7 (October 2011)

[18] Huang, Y., Ghosh, A.K.: Introducing diversity and uncertainty to create moving attack surfaces for web services. In: Moving Target Defense, pp. 131–151 (2011)

[19] Min, B.J., Choi, J.S.: An approach to intrusion tolerance for mission-critical services using adaptability and diverse replication. Future Gener. Comput. Syst, 303–313 (2004)

[20] Kolyshkin, K.: Virtualization in linux. White paper, OpenVZ (September 2006)

[21] Rodríguez, G., Martín, M.J., González, P., Touriño, J., Doallo, R.: Cppc: A compiler-assisted tool for portable checkpointing of message-passing applications. Concurr. Comput.: Pract. Exper. 22(6), 749–766 (2010)

[22] Lippmann, R.P., Riordan, J.F., Yu, T.H., Watson, K.K.: Continuous Security Metrics for Prevalent Network Threats: Introduction and First Four Metrics. Technical report. MIT Lincoln Laboratory (May 2012)

[23] Bangalore, A.K., Sood, A.K.: Securing web servers using self cleansing intrusion tolerance (scit). In: Proceedings of the 2009 Second International Conference on Dependability, pp. 60–65 (2009)

[24] Huang, Y., Arsenault, D., Arun, S.: Incorruptible self-cleansing intrusion tolerance and its application to dns security. A Journal of Networks 1(5), 21–30 (2006)

[25] Huang, Y., Ghosh, A.: Automating intrusion response via virtualization for realizing uninterruptible web services. In: Eighth IEEE International Symposium on Network Computing and Applications, NCA 2009, pp. 114–117 (July 2009)

[26] Blackmon, S., Nguyen, J.: High-availability file server with heartbeat. System Admin. The Journal for UNIX and Linux Systems Administration 10(9) (2001)

[27] Rabbat, R., McNeal, T., Burke, T.: A high-availability clustering architecture with data integrity guarantees. In: IEEE International Conference on Cluster Computing (2001)

[28] Petkac, M., Badger, L.: Security agility in response to intrusion detection. In: 16th Annual Computer Security Applications Conference (ACSAC), vol. 11 (2000)

[29] Jackson, T., Salamat, B., Homescu, A., Manivannan, K., Wagner, G., Gal, A., Brunthaler, S., Wimmer, C., Franz, M.: Compiler-generated software diversity. In: Moving Target Defense, pp. 77–98 (2011)

[30] Wang, Z., Lee, R.B.: New cache designs for thwarting software cache-based side channel attacks. In: Proceedings of the 34th Annual International Symposium on Computer Architecture, ISCA 2007, pp. 494–505. ACM, New York (2007)

[31] Manadhata, P.K., Wing, J.M.: A formal model for a system's attack surface. In: Moving Target Defense, pp. 1–28 (2011)

[32] Evans, D., Nguyen-Tuong, A., Knight, J.C.: Effectiveness of moving target defenses. In: Moving Target Defense, pp. 29–48 (2011)

[33] Popov, G., Mladenov, V.: Modeling diversity in recovery computer systems. In: Mastorakis, N., Mladenov, V., Kontargyri, V.T. (eds.) Proceedings of the European Computing Conference. LNEE, vol. 27, pp. 223–233. Springer, US (2009)

[34] Arlat, J., Kanoun, K., Laprie, J.C.: Dependability modeling and evaluation of software fault-tolerant systems. IEEE Trans. Comput. 39(4), 504–513 (1990)

Some Vulnerabilities Are Different Than Others
Studying Vulnerabilities and Attack Surfaces in the Wild

Kartik Nayak[1], Daniel Marino[2], Petros Efstathopoulos[2], and Tudor Dumitraş[1]

[1] University of Maryland, College Park
[2] Symantec Research Labs

Abstract. The security of deployed and actively used systems is a moving target, influenced by factors not captured in the existing security metrics. For example, the count and severity of vulnerabilities in source code, as well as the corresponding attack surface, are commonly used as measures of a software product's security. But these measures do not provide a full picture. For instance, some vulnerabilities are never exploited in the wild, partly due to security technologies that make exploiting them difficult. As for attack surface, its effectiveness has not been validated empirically in the deployment environment. We introduce several *security metrics derived from field data* that help to complete the picture. They include the count of vulnerabilities exploited and the size of the attack surface actually exercised in real-world attacks. By evaluating these metrics on nearly 300 million reports of intrusion-protection telemetry, collected on more than six million hosts, we conduct an empirical study of security in the deployment environment. We find that none of the products in our study have more than 35% of their disclosed vulnerabilities exploited in the wild. Furthermore, the exploitation ratio and the exercised attack surface tend to decrease with newer product releases. We also find that hosts that quickly upgrade to newer product versions tend to have reduced exercised attack-surfaces. The metrics proposed enable a more complete assessment of the security posture of enterprise infrastructure. Additionally, they open up new research directions for improving security by focusing on the vulnerabilities and attacks that have the highest impact in practice.

1 Introduction

In order to improve the security of our software systems, we need to be able to measure how they are impacted by the various defensive techniques we introduce to protect them. Measuring security, however, is challenging. Many security metrics have been proposed, including the total count of vulnerabilities in source code, the severity of these vulnerabilities, the size of the attack surface and the time window between the vulnerability disclosure and the release of a patch. System administrators and security analysts often rely on these metrics to assess risk and to prioritize some patches over others, while developers use them as guidelines for improving software security. Practical experience, however, suggests that the existing security metrics exhibit a low level of correlation with

A. Stavrou et al. (Eds.): RAID 2014, LNCS 8688, pp. 426–446, 2014.
© Springer International Publishing Switzerland 2014

vulnerabilities and attacks, and they do not provide an adequate assessment of security [1, 2].

A vulnerability is a programming error that can be exploited by an attacker to subvert the functionality of the vulnerable software by feeding it malformed inputs (e.g., network packets or web form submissions that evade the program's error checks, allowing the attacker to execute arbitrary code on the host). For example, the vulnerability identified by CVE-2007-1748 [3] corresponds to a buffer overflow in the RPC interface for the DNS server included in several versions of Windows server. It allows remote attackers to execute arbitrary code by sending specially crafted network packets to the vulnerable host. The *total number of vulnerabilities* discovered in source code is commonly used as a measure of the system's security [1, 2]. However, this metric does not account for the fact that cyber attackers never make use of some of the discovered vulnerabilities, which may be hard to successfully exploit in the presence of security technologies such as data execution prevention (DEP) and address space layout randomization (ASLR). For example, CVE-2007-1748 was exploited in the wild, but there is no evidence of cyber attacks exploiting CVE-2007-1749.

Another popular metric is based on the observation that attacks can succeed only if the vulnerable software accepts input from potential attackers. For this reason, system administrators have long advocated turning off unnecessary system services to avoid exposure to exploits of unpatched or unknown vulnerabilities. For example, network-based attacks exploiting CVE-2007-1748 are unsuccessful—even if the vulnerability was not yet patched—if the DNS server is not running. This idea is formalized in the concept of *attack surface* [4, 5], which quantifies the number and severity of potential attack vectors that a system exposes by using a formula that takes into account the open sockets and RPC endpoints, the running services and their privilege level, the active Web handlers, the accounts enabled, etc. Reducing the attack surface, however, does not always improve security; for example, including security mechanisms in the OS may increase the attack surface, but renders the system more secure. Furthermore, the attack surface of software products changes after they are deployed in the field, as users install new applications and modify system configuration. To the best of our knowledge, the size and variability of attack surfaces has not been evaluated empirically in the field. It is, therefore, difficult to determine the effectiveness of this metric in capturing real-world conditions.

These examples illustrate that our ability to assess the security of systems that are deployed and actively utilized is currently limited by the metrics being used. In particular, the developers and the users may employ different security metrics. For example, one way of estimating the vulnerability density and the attack surface is to use existing tools that measure these properties by directly analyzing the code and the configuration of the system in question [6,7]. However, these measurements are conducted in lab conditions, and do not reflect the real-world security of systems that are deployed and actively used in the field.

For these reasons, users are ultimately interested in metrics that help them assess the effectiveness of these techniques in the field. Figure 1 illustrates this

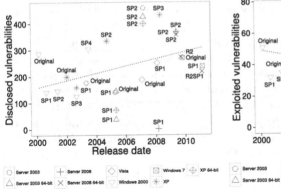
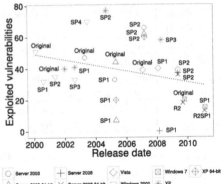

(a) All vulnerabilities disclosed publicly (from NVD [8]).

(b) Vulnerabilities exploited in the wild (cf. Section 4.2).

Fig. 1. Number of vulnerabilities disclosed and exploited for Microsoft Windows over 11 years of releases, with linear-regression trend lines

problem. The number of vulnerability exploits is not proportional to the total number of vulnerabilities discovered in Windows OSes, and the two metrics follow different trends (as suggested by the trend lines in Figure 1). Additionally, there is no apparent correlation between the number of vulnerabilities discovered, and the size of the OS code.[1] This suggests the existence of deployment-specific factors, yet to be characterized systematically, that influence the security of systems in active use.

Our *goal* in this paper is to propose new metrics that better reflect security in the real world and to employ these metrics for evaluating the security of popular software. Rather than measuring security in lab conditions, we derive metrics from field-gathered data and we study the trends for vulnerabilities and attack surfaces exercised in attacks observed in the real world. While the vulnerability count and the attack surface are metrics that capture the *opportunities* available to attackers, we instead focus on attempted, though not necessarily successful, attacks in the field. This new understanding, potentially combined with existing metrics, will enable a more accurate assessment of the risk of cyber attacks, by taking into account the vulnerabilities and attacks that are known to have an impact in the real world. For instance, although it is very important that *all* vulnerabilities be addressed, system administrators might find it useful to understand if some vulnerabilities are more critical than others, as a criterion for risk assessment and for prioritizing patch deployment.

A *meta-goal* of our study is to illustrate how this analysis can be conducted using data that is available to the research community for further studies, allowing other researchers to verify and to build on our results.

---

[1] Approximate lines of code, in millions: Windows 2000 $\simeq$ 30, Windows XP $\simeq$ 45, Windows Server 2003 $\simeq$ 50, Windows Vista, Windows 7 > 50 [9–11].

We make two contributions in this paper:

1. We propose field-measurable security metrics to identify *which* vulnerabilities are exploited (count of exploited vulnerabilities and exploitation ratio), quantify *how often* they are exploited (attack volume and exercised attack surface) and study *when* they are exploited.

2. We perform a systematic study of the exploited vulnerabilities and the exercised attack surfaces on 6,346,104 hosts. Our empirical findings include:

   - Few vulnerabilities are exploited in the real world: For Microsoft Windows, Adobe Reader, Microsoft Office and Microsoft Internet Explorer, fewer than 35% of the disclosed vulnerabilities are ever exploited. When the vulnerabilities for all these products are considered together, only 15% are exploited. Moreover, this exploitation ratio tends to decrease with newer product releases.
   - The exploitation ratio varies between products, implying that the number of vulnerabilities may not be a reliable indicator of real-world exploits and the security of a product.
   - The average exercised attack surface for Windows and IE has decreased with each new major release, and the latest versions of Reader have a far smaller exercised attack surface than earlier versions.
   - A significant portion of the average exercised attack surface of a host is due to products installed on the system and not the OS.
   - A few vulnerabilities (e.g. CVE-2008-4250 and CVE-2009-4324) account for a disproportionate number of attacks and influence our metrics.
   - Quicker upgrades to newer product versions are correlated with reduced exercised attack surfaces.
   - More than 93% of Windows and IE users are expected to remain unattacked at the end of four years. In contrast, only 50% Reader users are expected to remain unattacked for the same time period.

The rest of the paper is organized as follows. In Section 2 we review the related work on security metrics. In Section 3 we introduce our field-based metrics, and in Section 4 we describe how we measure them. Section 5 presents our empirical findings, and Section 6 discusses their implications.

2   Related Work

The total number of known vulnerabilities present in source code and their severity, as represented by the Common Vulnerability Scoring System (CVSS), are commonly used security metrics. For example, Rescorla [12] analyzes the number of vulnerabilities disclosed for 4 operating systems in order to determine whether the practice of vulnerability disclosures leads to reliability growth over time. Ozment et al. [13] study the rate of vulnerability finding in the foundational code of OpenBSD and fit the data to a vulnerability growth model in order to estimate the number of vulnerabilities left undiscovered. Clark et al. [14] examine the challenge of finding vulnerabilities in new code and show that the time to discover the first vulnerability is usually longer than the time to discover the second one (a phenomenon they call the "honeymoon effect").

Several studies employ vulnerability counts as an implicit measure of security. Shin et al. [1] evaluate code complexity, code churn and the developer activity to determine the vulnerable code locations in Linux. Bozorgi et al. [15] propose a machine learning approach for predicting which vulnerabilities will be exploited based on their CVSS scores. In consequence, the National Institute of Standards and Technology (NIST) recommends CVSS scores as the reference assessment method for software security [16]. Based on an empirical analysis, Ransbotham et al. suggest that vulnerabilities in open source software have an increased risk of exploitation, diffuse sooner and have a larger volume of exploitation attempts than closed source software [17].

Because programming errors are thought to be inevitable, reducing the attack surface was proposed a decade ago as an alternative approach to securing software systems [4]. In order to exploit a vulnerability, an attacker must have an opportunity to exercise the vulnerable code, for instance by sending a message to a service listening on a network port. Such an opportunity is known as an attack vector. Attack surface reduction works by decreasing the number and severity of potential attack vectors exposed by the OS and its applications. Like the vulnerability metrics, attack surface is typically measured by analyzing the source code or the configuration of the system. Howard [4] defines an attack surface metric as a weighted combination of targets, enablers, communication channels, protocols and access rights. The Microsoft Attack Surface Analyzer tool [6] estimates the attack surface from the system configuration and monitors changes over time. Manadhata et al. [5] define attack surface as a triple, where each element represents the sum of the damage potential-effort ratio for (i) entry and exit points, (ii) channels and (iii) untrusted data items. Kurmus et al. [18] define attack surface as a function of the call graph, a set of entry functions, and a set of barrier functions.

2.1   Problems with the Existing Security Metrics

Measurability. Some security metrics are difficult to assess. Code-based metrics have been shown to exhibit statistically significant, but small, correlations with security vulnerabilities [1,2]. Evaluating attack-surface metrics can require access to both the source code of the product and to the composition of its deployment environments [5]. In contrast, the metrics we propose can be computed from the typical telemetry collected by security products (e.g. anti-virus, intrusion-protection system) running on end-hosts around the world.

Representativeness. The existing metrics do not reflect security in the field. The CVSS "exploitability" subscore is not a good predictor for which vulnerabilities are exploited in the real world (though, most exploited vulnerabilities do have high exploitability) [19], and the CVSS-based risk evaluation does not fit the real attack data, as observed in the wild [20]. The attack surface metrics have not been validated empirically, in the deployment environment. In particular, the impact of user behavior (e.g. installing new software) on attack surfaces is unknown. In contrast, we focus on alternative metrics that better reflect the risk

Table 1. Summary of notations

Measurement subjects	
p	A software product.
h	A host.
v	A vulnerability.
m	A calendar month.

Sets of subjects	
$V_p(t)$	The set of vulnerabilities disclosed for a product p up to time t.
$V_p^{ex}(t)$	The set of vulnerabilities known to be exploited for a product p up to time t.
$V_p^{prog,ex}(t)$	The set of progressive vulnerabilities known to be exploited for a product p up to time t.
$H_{p,m}$	The set of hosts that have product p installed during month m.
$A_{h,m}^v$	The set of attacks against host h during month m attempting to exploit vulnerability v.

Vulnerability-based metrics	
$ER^p(t)$	Exploitation ratio for vulnerabilities of product p until time t.
$ER_{Prog}^p(t)$	Exploitation ratio for progressive vulnerabilities of product p until time t.

Attack-based metrics	
EP^p	Exploitation prevalence, the proportion of hosts with p installed that ever experience an attack exploiting p.
AV_p	Attack volume, the average number of attacks per machine-month for a product p.
$EAS_h(m)$	Exercised attack surface of a host h for month m.
$EAS_h^p(m)$	Exercised attack surface of a host h for month m w.r.t. p.
$AEAS_p$	Average exercised attack surface w.r.t p over all machine-months p was installed.
$AEAS(m)$	Average exercised attack surface over all hosts for all products during month m.
$AEAS_h^p$	Average exercised attack surface over all months p was installed on host h w.r.t p's vulnerabilities.

for end-users. These metrics include the *number of vulnerabilities exploited* and the *size of the attack surface exercised* in real-world cyber attacks. We also assess how the exercised attack surface varies from one host to another.

3 Proposed Metrics

In this section we introduce our proposed security metrics which, in contrast to existing metrics, are measured in the deployment environment. We consider this distinction important since security is a moving target once a system is deployed; attackers exploit new vulnerabilities (to subvert the system's functionality), vendors distribute software updates (to patch vulnerabilities and to improve security) and users reconfigure the system (to add functionality). Since our new metrics are derived from field-gathered data, they capture the state of system security as experienced by the end users. Table 1 summarizes the notations we employ.

The following metrics capture the notion of whether disclosed vulnerabilities get exploited.

1. *Count of vulnerabilities exploited in the wild.* For a product p, we consider the number of vulnerabilities known to have been exploited in the wild,

$|V_p^{ex}|$, to be an important metric. We combine information from NVD [8] and Symantec's databases of attack signatures [21, 22] to obtain the subset of a product's disclosed vulnerabilities that have been exploited. (These data sources are described in more detail in Section 4.1.) V_p^{ex} is the subset of the vulnerabilities listed in NVD that affect product p and which have at least one Symantec signature referencing the vulnerability's CVE identifier. Prior research has suggested that these signatures represent the best indicator for which vulnerabilities are exploited in real-world attacks [19].

2. *Exploitation ratio.* The exploitation ratio is the proportion of disclosed vulnerabilities for product p that have been exploited up until time t. It captures the likelihood that a vulnerability will be exploited.

$$ER^p(t) = \frac{|V_p^{ex}(t)|}{|V_p(t)|}$$

We also propose the following metrics that capture how often vulnerabilities are exploited on hosts in the wild.

1. *Attack Volume.* The attack volume is a measure that captures how frequently a product p is attacked. Intuitively, it is the average number of attacks experienced by a machine in a month due to product p being installed. It is defined as:

$$AV_p = \frac{\sum\limits_{m} \sum\limits_{h \in H_{p,m}} \sum\limits_{v \in V_p^{ex}} \left| A_{h,m}^v \right|}{\sum\limits_{m} |H_{p,m}|}$$

That is, the number of attacks that exploit a vulnerability of p against hosts with p installed, normalized by the total number of machine-months during which p was installed.

2. *Exercised Attack Surface.* We also define the *exercised attack surface*, $EAS_h(m)$, which captures the portion of the theoretical attack surface of a host that is targeted in a particular month. Intuitively, the exercised attack surface is the number of distinct vulnerabilities that are exploited on a host h in a given month m. We compute the exercised attack surface attributable to a particular product using the following formula:

$$EAS_h^p(m) = \left|\left\{ v \in V_p^{ex} \mid \left| A_{h,m}^v \right| > 0 \wedge h \in H_{p,m} \right\}\right|$$

That is, the cardinality of the set of p's vulnerabilities used in attacks against h in month m, or 0 if p is not installed on h during month m. We can now define the exercised attack surface for a host over all installed products as:

$$EAS_h(m) = \sum_{p} EAS_h^p(m)$$

We can then average these per host, per month metrics in various ways as listed in Table 1. In particular we can calculate an average exercised attack surface metric for a product p as follows:

$$AEAS_p = \frac{\sum\limits_{m} \sum\limits_{h \in H_{p,m}} EAS_h^p(m)}{\sum\limits_{m} |H_{p,m}|}$$

Intuitively, $AEAS_p$ represents the average number of vulnerabilities that are exploited for product p during one month on one machine. So, while AV_p captures the volumes of attacks against a product, $AEAS_p$ captures the diversity of those attacks.

4   Experimental Methods

4.1   Data Sets

Public vulnerability databases. The National Vulnerability Database (NVD) [3] is a database of software vulnerabilities which is widely accepted for vulnerability research. For each vulnerability, NVD assigns a unique identifier called CVE-ID. Additionally, we employ the Open-Sourced Vulnerability Database (OSVDB) [23] to determine the dates when proof-of-concept exploits are published for the NVD vulnerabilities.

Symantec signatures. Symantec security products include an extensive database of signatures. Attack signatures are described on a publicly-accessible web site [24], and they are employed by Symantec's intrusion-prevention systems (IPS) for identifying attacks in network streams—including attempts to exploit known OS or application vulnerabilities. Symantec also maintains descriptions of anti-virus (AV) signatures, used by anti-virus products to scan files for known threats [21]. For threats that involve exploits, these data sets indicate the CVE-ID of the vulnerability exploited. Prior research has suggested that these signatures represent the best indicator for which vulnerabilities are exploited in real-world attacks [19].

Worldwide Intelligence Network Environment (WINE). In order to analyze the attacks happening on different hosts running different products, we use WINE [25], which contains records of which signatures are triggered in the field and when. The binary reputation dataset within WINE provides information about all the binaries detected on end-user hosts by Symantec products such as Norton Antivirus. Each binary reputation record contains the filename, its version, a file hash, machine ID, and a timestamp for the detection event.

The intrusion-prevention telemetry dataset within WINE provides information about network based attacks detected by Symantec products. We define a network-based attack against a host as a series of network packets that: 1) carry malicious code, and 2) have not been prevented by other existing defenses (e.g. network or OS firewall). Each IPS entry contains the signature ID for the threat detected, a machine ID, a platform string and a timestamp for the event. Our study involves 298,851,312 IPS entries corresponding to 6,346,104 hosts over a period of 4 years. The average duration for which a host is present in our study is approximately 13 months.

4.2 Data Analysis Approach

The primary requirement for our analysis is to detect an attempt to attack a host running a vulnerable product. IPS telemetry does not indicate whether the vulnerabilities had been patched at the time of the attack. Moreover, these reports indicate attacks that were blocked by the IPS product, rather than successful infections. We exclude attacks against products that are not installed on a host, as they would not result in a successful infection.

Finding signatures used to exploit products. Using NVD, we first collect the disclosure dates and the vulnerable software list for all vulnerabilities—including vendor, product and version—and manually remedy any naming inconsistencies. We join this information with Symantec's attack signatures containing CVE numbers, so as to obtain entries of the form ⟨CVE, Prod, Sign⟩.

Selecting the hosts used in the study. We analyze Symantec's binary reputation reports in order to determine, for each host, what products are installed and the period of time during which they remained installed. We manually map the binaries to the corresponding product versions using externally available information. For instance, iexplore.exe corresponds to IE, and file version 8.0.6001.18702 corresponds to IE 8 [26]. Due to users enabling different features of their Symantec product at different times, the time period for which we have binary reputation data for a host may be different from the time period for which we have IPS telemetry reports (attack detections). Our metrics require both product presence and attack information, so we include hosts in our study only during the times when they are submitting both kinds of data.

Identifying an attack against a host. By joining the binary reputation and IPS dataset for all the hosts identified, we are able to discover all the products installed on a host and all the signatures triggered on the machine. We derive the operating system installed on a host from the platform string included in IPS telemetry submissions. If a vulnerable product is present when the corresponding signature is detected, we have an attack on the host. Of the 298,851,312 telemetry records, 40,954,812 correspond to one of the vulnerabilities that we study, and of these, 20,915,168 occur on a host with the vulnerable product installed.

4.3 Products Analyzed

At the time of this writing, NVD includes 61,387 vulnerabilities reported across all products. There are Symantec signatures corresponding to 1,406 of these vulnerabilities. We focus our study on Windows operating systems and on several applications that run on this platform because (i) they have been the primary target for cyber attacks over the past 10 years, and (ii) the platform has evolved in these 10 years and the versions we investigate incorporate considerable diversity, as many technical changes have been implemented between Windows

XP and Windows 7 SP1.[2] In particular, in this paper, we study the following software products:

- Microsoft Windows: XP (original, SP1, SP2, SP3), Vista (original, SP1, SP2), and 7 (original, SP1)
- Microsoft Office (referred to as Office) - Versions: 2000, 2003, 2007, 2010
- Internet Explorer (referred to as IE) - Versions: 5, 6, 7, 8
- Adobe Reader (referred to as Reader) - Versions: 5, 6, 7, 8, 9, 10, 11

There are 860 vulnerabilities in NVD for all the Windows operating systems we consider. Out of these, 132 vulnerabilities have seen exploits in the wild, according to Symantec's attack signatures. We exclude the 64-bit version of XP from our study as it belongs to the same product line as Windows Server 2003. There are 759 vulnerabilities reported for the versions of IE we consider. 108 of these vulnerabilities have seen exploits in the wild. For Office, 50 of the 163 vulnerabilities reported have been exploited. Finally, there are 337 vulnerabilities for the versions of Reader we analyze, out of which 44 vulnerabilities have seen exploits in the wild.

4.4   Threats to Validity

The biggest threat to the validity of our results is selection bias. The two databases we employ to characterize vulnerabilities and exploits, NVD and Symantec's attack signatures, respectively, may be incomplete. These databases include only the vulnerabilities and exploits that are known to the security community. Moreover, as WINE does not include telemetry from hosts without Symantec's anti-virus products, our field-data based measurements may not be representative of the general population of platforms in the world. In particular, users who install anti-virus software might be more careful with the security of their computers and, therefore, might be less exposed to attacks.

Although we cannot rule out the possibility of selection bias, we note that the NVD is generally accepted as the authoritative reference on vulnerabilities, and it is widely employed in vulnerability studies, and prior work found Symantec's signatures to be the best indicator for which vulnerabilities are exploited in real-world attacks [19]. Moreover, the large size of the population in our study (six million hosts) and the diversity of platforms suggest that our results have a broad applicability. However, we caution the reader not to assume that all systems will react in the same manner to malware attacks.

---

[2] While we do not know the amount of code these OSes have in common, it is widely accepted that a large amount of new code was introduced in Windows Vista, including security technologies such as software data execution prevention (DEP/SafeSEH), address space layout randomization (ASLR), driver signing improvements, user account control (UAC), or the Windows filtering platform.

5   Analysis of Exploited Vulnerabilities and Exercised Attack Surfaces

In this section, we evaluate the metrics introduced in Section 3 and discuss their implications. In particular, we focus on the following questions: *"How many of the disclosed vulnerabilities get exploited?"* (§5.1), *"How often do they get exploited?"* (§5.2), and *"When do they get exploited?"* (§5.3). The first question evaluates our vulnerability-based metrics under real-world conditions, while the second and third questions investigate our attack-based metrics and the deployment-specific factors that affect them.

5.1   How Many Vulnerabilities Get Exploited?

Exploitation Ratio. Table 2 shows the number of exploited vulnerabilities and the exploitation ratio for all OSes and products in our study. The exploitation ratios shown include vulnerabilities disclosed and exploited as of the end of the product's support period, or as of 2014 if the product is presently supported. We account for *progressive* and *regressive* vulnerabilities [14] separately. A progressive vulnerability is a vulnerability discovered in version N that does not affect version $N - 1$ or previous versions, while a regressive vulnerability is one found in version N that affects at least one of the previous versions. The progressive-regressive distinction is important for evaluating the software development process and for understanding the security of the new code added in each version—even though, from the users' point of view, it is important to study all the vulnerabilities that affect a product version. The table also includes the exploitation prevalence, EP^p, which helps to illuminate how likely a host is to experience an attack if a given product is installed. EP^p is defined as the proportion of the hosts with product p installed that experienced at least one attack targeting one of p's vulnerabilities. Note that this metric captures information not revealed by the exploitation ratio or the number of exploited vulnerabilities. For instance, Reader 9 has the same number of exploited vulnerabilities as IE 8, but its exploitation prevalence is far higher.

In aggregate, over all the software products we analyzed, about 15% of the known vulnerabilities have been exploited in real-world attacks. Note, however, that the exploitation ratio varies greatly across products and between versions of a product. This highlights the pitfall of employing the number and severity of vulnerabilities as a measure of security: a product with many high-impact vulnerabilities in NVD would be considered insecure, even if its exploitation ratio is lower than for other products. To further investigate whether the total count of vulnerabilities models the security of a software product, we compare the distributions of the disclosed and exploited vulnerabilities for each product using the Kolmogorov-Smirnov test [27]. The results suggest that we cannot reject the null hypothesis that the number of vulnerabilities and the number of exploits are drawn from the same distribution, at the $p = 0.05$ significance level, for any of the products studied. However, some differences stand out. For example, IE 5 has nearly three times as many reported vulnerabilities as Office 2000. Nevertheless,

Table 2. Exploitation ratio and exploitation prevalence of products. $ER(yr)$: exploitation ratio of the product for all vulnerabilities up to the year yr. EP_P: the ratio of machines experiencing an attack over the number of machines having the product installed. NA indicates that no machines in WINE had the product installed.

yr	Product	$ER^p(yr)$	$ER^p_{Prog}(yr)$	$\lvert V_p^{ex} \rvert$	$\lvert V_p^{prog,ex} \rvert$	EP^p
2006	IE 5	0.12	0.14	27	25	NA
2010	IE 6	0.17	0.16	73	33	0.035
2013	IE 7	0.13	0.07	36	4	0.002
2013	IE 8	0.13	0.15	29	10	0.0004
2009	Office 2000	0.32	0.32	27	27	NA
2013	Office 2003	0.35	0.36	43	21	0.0002
2013	Office 2007	0.27	0.18	18	2	0
2013	Office 2010	0.25	0	5	0	0
2009	Windows XP	0.21	0.15	39	8	NA
2006	Windows XP SP1	0.28	0.31	41	11	0.026
2010	Windows XP SP2	0.23	0.27	73	16	0.011
2014	Windows XP SP3	0.13	0.07	58	12	0.047
2012	Windows Vista	0.21	0.09	39	5	0.005
2011	Windows Vista SP1	0.16	0.06	40	6	0.004
2014	Windows Vista SP2	0.11	0.06	39	2	0.011
2014	Windows 7	0.07	0.25	20	2	0
2014	Windows 7 SP1	0.07	0	15	0	0.004
2008	Adobe Reader 5	0.18	0.2	4	1	NA
2008	Adobe Reader 6	0.22	0.17	5	1	NA
2009	Adobe Reader 7	0.17	0.09	11	4	0.177
2011	Adobe Reader 8	0.16	0.15	29	18	0.180
2013	Adobe Reader 9	0.11	0.10	29	10	0.242
2014	Adobe Reader 10	0.08	0.04	13	1	0.0002
2014	Adobe Reader 11	0.06	0	5	0	0

both have a similar number of exploited vulnerabilities. This is reflected in the much higher exploitation ratio for Office. This is one example of how field-gathered data which reflects the deployment environment can complement more traditional security metrics.

Another trend visible in Table 2 is that the latest versions of each product have a lower absolute number of exploited vulnerabilities than earlier versions (except in the case of IE). For instance, Windows 7 has fewer exploited vulnerabilities than Windows Vista, and Reader versions 10 and 11 have fewer than versions 8 and 9. One factor that has likely contributed to this decrease is the introduction of security technologies by Microsoft and Adobe that make exploits less likely to succeed, even in the presence of vulnerabilities (e.g., address space layout randomization and sandboxing). Another likely contributing factor is the commoditization of the underground malware industry, which has led to the marketing of exploit kits that bundle a small number of effective attacks for wide-spread reuse.

Time-to-exploit. The decrease in the number of exploited vulnerabilities over time could be caused by the fact that cyber attackers have had less time to find ways to exploit newer products. To investigate the influence of this confounding factor, we estimate the typical time that attackers need to exploit vulnerabilities in Windows after they are publicly disclosed. While the mention of these vulnerabilities in Symantec's AV and IPS signatures is an indication that an

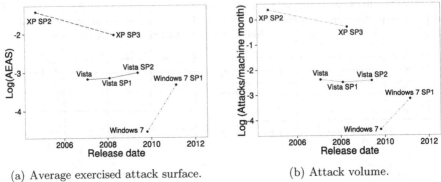

(a) Average exercised attack surface.   (b) Attack volume.

Fig. 2. Exercised attack surface and attack volume for Windows operating systems

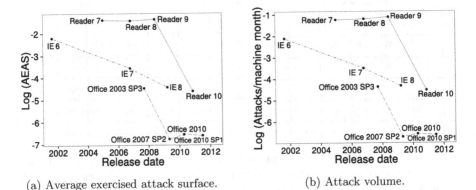

(a) Average exercised attack surface.   (b) Attack volume.

Fig. 3. Exercised attack surface and attack volume for Windows applications

exploit was, at some point, used in the real world, it is challenging to estimate the time that elapses between the vulnerability disclosure and the release of the exploit. We estimate the time-to-exploit using a combination of three methods: (i) the "exploit published" date from OSVDB; (ii) the "discovery date" from the anti-virus signature descriptions; (iii) the date when a signature is first recorded in the field data from WINE. We observe that 90% of exploits from anti-virus signatures and from attack signatures are created within 94 and 58 days after disclosure, respectively. Our observation is consistent with the prior work on this topic, which found that the exploits for 42% of vulnerabilities that are eventually exploited appear in the wild within 30 days after the disclosure date [28,29]. This shows that if a vulnerability is to be exploited, an attack will likely be observed soon after its disclosure.

5.2   How Often Do Vulnerabilities Get Exploited?

Average exercised attack surface. Figure 2 shows that the average exercised attack surface ($AEAS_p$) and the attack volume (AV_p) for OS vulnerabilities tend

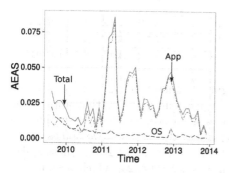

(a) Combined AEAS over time.

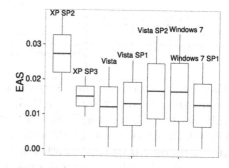

(b) Variation of combined AEAS for machines running different OSes.

Fig. 4. Average exercised attack surface (AEAS) due to OS and installed applications combined

to increase across minor releases of Windows (except XP), but they decrease considerably with each new major release. This could be explained by the fact that, over time, attackers become more familiar with the code and the mechanisms of an OS and they are more effective in finding and exploiting vulnerabilities [14]. However, major releases refactor the code and introduce new security technologies that make it more difficult to create exploits. For example, Windows Vista introduced address space layout randomization (ASLR) and data execution prevention (DEP), which render exploits less likely to succeed even if a vulnerability is present.

Figure 3 shows the average exercised attack surface ($AEAS_p$) and attack volume metrics (AV_p) for IE, Reader and Office. For IE, these values decrease with newer releases. Note the precipitous drop in exercised attack surface between Reader 9 and Reader 10 (three orders of magnitude). This can likely be attributed to *protected mode*, an enhancement that Adobe introduced in Reader 10 specifically to mitigate and prevent security vulnerabilities [30]. We also observe that the exercised attack surface values of Reader (except version 10) are about an order of magnitude higher than those of IE. This is somewhat surprising, since Table 2 shows that the various versions of IE have nearly as many or, in the case of IE 6, far more exploited vulnerabilities than any of the versions of Reader. Taken together, these observations suggest that vulnerabilities in Reader (prior to version 10) have proven easier for cyber criminals to successfully exploit.

We also note that some vulnerabilities affect the volume of attacks disproportionately. For OS vulnerabilities, the number of attacks due to CVE-2008-4250 (the vulnerability exploited by the Conficker worm) is three orders of magnitude higher than the number of attacks due to the next most targeted vulnerability. For product vulnerabilities, the number of attacks due to CVE-2009-4324 (a vulnerability in Adobe Reader) is almost 20× as high the number of attacks due to the next most targeted vulnerability.

Table 3. Average exercised attack surface in the presence of products

Reader	no	no	no	no	yes	yes	yes	yes
IE	no	no	yes	yes	no	no	yes	yes
Office	no	yes	no	yes	no	yes	no	yes
Average attack surface	0.00000	0.00002	0.00125	0.00068	0.02823	0.03130	0.03009	0.03195

Variation of exercised attack surface. Figure 4a shows the variation of the average exercised attack surface $(AEAS(m))$ over time. Notice that application vulnerabilities contribute to most of the attack surface, which suggests that the OS vulnerabilities are more difficult to exploit. Also, we see two spikes in the 2011-2012 time frame and another spike towards the end of 2012. These spikes are correlated with the attacks exploiting CVE-2009-4324, which account for the higher exercised attack surface measurement at those times. This illustrates the fact that, even against a background of diverse attacks, a single vulnerability that is attacked heavily can increase the average attack surface by reaching more hosts. Figure 4b shows the variation of exercised attack surface across hosts running the same operating system. We note that, in this case, both OS and application vulnerabilities contribute to the exercised attack surface. Thus, even if some hosts are running the same operating system, their exercised attack surface varies considerably based on the products installed on the system.

Impact of vulnerabilities on attack surface. Each host may have one or more products installed. Moreover this may change over time. Although it is hard to quantify the impact of specific vulnerabilities on a particular host, we can calculate the average exercised attacked surface for hosts with different combinations of the products in question. Table 3 shows the average exercised attack surface for hosts in the presence of IE, Reader, and Office. When none of the products in question is present, the average exercised attack surface is 0, since we have eliminated the effect of OS vulnerabilities, thus measuring only the impact of the products on the calculated attack surface. Furthermore, the calculation of each average attack surface value only considers hosts that have the exact product combination installed, and these hosts are not reconsidered for the calculation of any of the remaining values. We observe that the vulnerabilities present in each of the products have different impact on the average exercised attack surface. For instance, the telemetry data at our disposal suggest that the presence of Reader has a higher impact on the average attack surface of hosts than the presence of IE or Office.

How much can we reduce the attack surface? The overwhelming prevalence of attacks using CVE-2008-4250 and CVE-2009-4324, and the variability in the size of the exercised attack surface among the hosts in our study, prompt the question of whether attack surface reduction methods could be used to reduce the overall risk. In the case of application vulnerabilities, a user may reduce the attack surface by uninstalling the vulnerable product. For OS vulnerabilities, the user would have to disable the vulnerable component. We manually inspect the NVD entries for the top-10 OS vulnerabilities so as to determine if

Table 4. Most attacked OS vulnerabilities

CVE	# of Attacks	# of Hosts	Affected Operating Systems	Can be turned off?	NIST severity
2008-4250	17915163	66408	XP SP2/SP3/SP2 64 bit, Vista Original/SP/SP1, Server 2003 SP1/SP2	no	10
2006-3439	55998	2577	XP SP1/SP2/SP2 64 bit	yes	10
2011-3402	40598	21717	XP SP3, Vista SP2, Windows 7 SP1, Server 2003 SP2	no	9.3
2010-1885	36984	22337	XP SP3/SP2 64 bit	yes	9.3
2010-0806	25280	15539	XP SP3, Vista Original SP/SP1/SP2	no	9.3
2009-2532	20343	756	Vista Original/SP1/SP2, Server 2008 SP2	yes	10
2009-3103	20343	756	Vista Original/SP1/SP2, Server 2008 SP2	yes	10
2008-0015	6105	3897	XP SP2/SP3	yes	9.3
2010-2568	2182	360	XP SP3/SP2 64 bit, Vista SP1/SP2	no	9.3
2012-0003	93	71	XP SP2/SP3, Server 2003 SP2, Vista SP2, Server 2008 SP2	yes	9.3

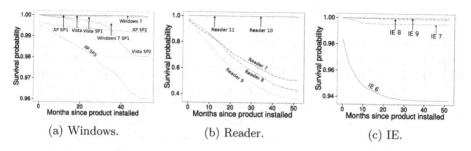

(a) Windows.   (b) Reader.   (c) IE.

Fig. 5. Time from installation to first attack

the vulnerable component can be disabled, while keeping the host operational. As seen in Table 4, 6 out of 10 of the intrusion vectors correspond to vulnerable services or components that could be disabled (assuming that the relevant service/functionality is not necessary), suggesting that there is potential for further reduction of the OS attack surface. Notice, however, that in certain cases the components that would need to be disabled or removed may severely affect the functionality of the system. To better understand the potential to improve security by disabling vulnerable components, we consider the volume of attacks for each vulnerability in Table 4. If we exclude the skew introduced by Conficker, we observe that the number of remaining attacks could be reduced by 67.3%, thus significantly reducing the size of the exercised attack surface.

5.3   When Do Vulnerabilities Get Exploited?

In this section we explore several time-related aspects of attacks. We presented the exploitation prevalence EP^p, which indicates how many of the hosts that install a product experience at least one attack due to that product, in Table 2. We now explore *when* that attack happens with respect to the installation of the product. Figure 5 plots the estimated survival probability versus the number of months since installation, where survival means not having experienced any

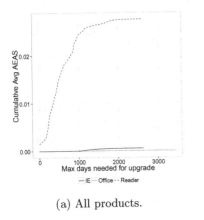

(a) All products.

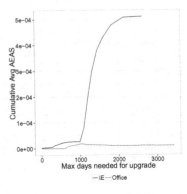

(b) Detail of IE and Office.

Fig. 6. Effect of product upgrade lag on a host's exercised attack surface $(AEAS_h^p)$

attack targeting one of the product's vulnerabilities. Our data set is right censored, meaning that some hosts leave our study (stop sending telemetry) without having experienced an attack; in this case, we know the period when these hosts were attack-free, but we don't know when they will experience their first attack. In statistical terms, these data points are right-censored. We estimate the survival probability using the Kaplan-Meier estimator [27], which accounts for censoring. The survival probability for most versions of Windows is nearly one even after four years of installation. Windows XP SP3 experiences more exploits, and so its survival probability drops with a fairly smooth slope down to about 0.96 after four years. The smooth slope seems to indicate that installation age is not strongly correlated with the likelihood of experiencing your first attack. Reader versions 7 through 9 also show a fairly smooth, though much steeper, drop in survival probability. Again, this indicates that a user has a similar probability of experiencing a first attack against Reader whether it's been installed for one month or ten months, though the slope does tend to decrease slightly as we move beyond twenty months. Hosts with IE 6 installed appear to have a higher probability of experiencing their first attack within the first ten months, after which the survival probability levels out with an estimated 94% of hosts experiencing no attack after four years. The plot for Office is not shown since all versions maintain over 99.9% survival for the entire period.

We now explore another time-related question: Does the length of time a user waits to upgrade after a new version comes out have an impact on exercised attack surface? To help answer this, we introduce the upgrade lag metric. In order to measure a user's upgrade lag with respect to a product version, we look at how long a user continues to use the version after a new version of the product is released. The user's upgrade lag for the product line is calculated as the maximum upgrade lag over all versions of the product. Note that even if only a single version of a product is ever installed on a machine, the upgrade lag is still defined. If a machine has only Reader 9 installed, and it is present for a period of time entirely before Reader 10 is released, the machine's upgrade lag for Reader is 0. If a machine has only Reader 9 installed, and it is present from one month after Reader 10 is released until six months after Reader 10 is released, then the upgrade lag would be six months.

In Figure 6a, we plot the upgrade lag in days versus the cumulative average exercised attack surface (that is, the average $AEAS_h^p$ for all hosts with a lag less than or equal to a given lag) for each of the product lines. So, for instance, if you consider all hosts that have a maximum upgrade lag for Reader that is less than or equal to 500 days, on average their AEAS with respect to Reader is about 0.015 vulnerabilities per machine per month. The steady increase in the curve for Reader from zero upgrade lag until 1000 days of upgrade lag is a strong indication that machines that wait longer to upgrade Reader tend to experience more attacks. In Figure 6b, we zoom in to show the detail for IE and Office. For both IE and Office, we see a modest increase in exercised attack surface as upgrade lag increases. The sharp increase in the slope of the IE curve after 1000 days can be explained by the fact that roughly 6% of hosts with IE installed have the most vulnerable version, IE 6, installed long after IE 7 was released. These hosts, which account for over 90% of attacks against IE, cause the rapid increase after 1000 days. These results suggest that the upgrade lag is one factor that affects the attack surface in the deployment environment.

6   Discussion

In this paper, we propose several metrics for assessing the security of software products in their deployment environments. For example, we observe that, for most products, the exploitation ratio and/or the number of exploited vulnerabilities decrease with newer versions. Interestingly, anecdotal evidence suggests that cyber criminals are starting to feel the effects of this scarcity of exploits. While zero-day exploits have traditionally been employed in targeted attacks [28], in 2013 the author of the Blackhole exploit kit advertised a $100,000 budget for purchasing zero-day exploits [31]. The zero-day exploit for CVE-2013-3906 was nicknamed the "dual-use exploit" after being employed both for targeted attacks and for delivering botnet-based malware [32].

Qualitative analysis. While the coexistence of several security mechanisms in a product prevents us from measuring the individual impact of each of these mechanisms, it is interesting to note that improvements in our metrics are often associated with the introduction of system security technologies. Improved security was a primary design goal for Windows Vista and we find a decrease in the number of progressive exploited vulnerabilities in Windows Vista and Windows 7. This seems to be associated with the introduction of security technologies like ASLR, DEP, User Account Control and the concept of integrity levels. Among products, there is a notable decrease in the exploitation ratio and number of exploited vulnerabilities in IE 7 and Reader 10. Both these products started running the application in a sandbox, which adds an additional layer of defense by containing malicious code and by preventing elevated privilege execution on the user's system [30]. IE 7 also removed support for older technologies like DirectAnimation, XBM, DHTML editing control in an attempt to reduce the surface area for attacks [33].

Operational utility of the proposed metrics. Our product-based metrics can be integrated in security automation frameworks, such as SCAP [16]. For example, knowing which vulnerabilities are exploited in the wild will allow system administrators to prioritize patching based on empirical data, rather than relying exclusively on the CVSS scores for this task. The exploitation ratios of different products can be incorporated in quantitative assessments of the risk of cyber attacks against enterprise infrastructures. The ability to determine whether a few exploits are responsible for most of the recorded attacks (as in the case of Conficker) will allow security vendors to focus on these vulnerabilities for reducing the volume of attacks against critical infrastructures in an efficient manner.

Our host-based metrics would be useful in infrastructures where not all hosts can be centrally managed, such as in enterprises that have *bring-your-own-device* (BYOD) policies. For example, the exercised attack surface metric captures the diversity of attacks against a host. This metric varies considerably from host to host, depending on the software installed and on the user behaviors; in particular, the exercised attack surface is correlated with a host's product upgrade lag. This information will allow administrators to subject the hosts more likely to be attacked to a higher level of scrutiny.

Agenda for future research. Our results illustrate the fact that, in the deployment environment, security is affected by factors that cannot be accounted for in the lab. Further research is needed to explore the opportunities for deriving security metrics from field data. For example, it is difficult to assess whether a single, potentially successful, attack exploiting vulnerability X is more or less devastating than a large number of attacks exploiting vulnerabilities other than X. As another example, the exercised attack surface metric cannot adequately capture the effects of a single powerful attack on a long-lived host H, since the effect of the attack on ES_H will be diluted by the amount of time H is under observation. To address this problem, we could define an *attack watermark* metric, which would represent the average number of unique vulnerabilities of a product P that are attacked on hosts running P during our observation period.

7   Conclusions

We believe that our ability to improve system security rests on our understanding of how to measure and assess security under real-world conditions. In this paper we analyze a large data set of security telemetry, available to the research community, to 1) expose trends in the exploitation of vulnerabilities, and 2) propose new field-measurable security metrics, capable of capturing the security of systems in their deployment environments, rather than in lab conditions. We focus on nine versions of the Windows operating system, and multiple versions of three popular applications. Our findings reveal that, combining all of the products we study, only 15% of disclosed vulnerabilities are ever exploited in the wild. None of the studied products have more than 35% of their vulnerabilities exploited in the wild, and most of these are exploited within 58 days after disclosure. We show that the number of vulnerabilities in a product is not a reliable indicator of the product's security, and that certain vulnerabilities may be significantly more impactful than others. Furthermore, we observe that, even though the security of newer versions of Windows appears to have improved, the overall exposure to threats can be significantly impacted by "post-deployment" factors that can only be observed in the field, such as the products installed on a system, the frequency of upgrades, and the behavior of attackers. The impact of such factors cannot be captured by existing security metrics, such as a product's vulnerability count, or its theoretical attack surface. To address this, we introduce new, field-measurable security metrics. The count of vulnerabilities exploited in the wild and the exploitation ratio aim to capture whether a vulnerability gets exploited. The attack volume and exercised attack surface metrics aim to measure the extent to which hosts are attacked. Finally, the calculated survival probabilities and our study of the impact of software upgrades to security aim to reveal real-world temporal properties of attacks. These metrics can be incorporated in quantitative assessments of the risk of cyber attacks against enterprise infrastructure, and they can inform the design of future security technologies.

Acknowledgments. We thank the anonymous RAID reviewers for their constructive feedback. Our results can be reproduced by utilizing the reference data set WINE-2014-001, archived in the WINE infrastructure. This work was supported in part by a grant from the UMD Science of Security lablet.

References

1. Shin, Y., Meneely, A., Williams, L., Osborne, J.A.: Evaluating complexity, code churn, and developer activity metrics as indicators of software vulnerabilities. IEEE Trans. Software Eng. 37(6), 772–787 (2011)
2. Zimmermann, T., Nagappan, N., Williams, L.A.: Searching for a needle in a haystack: Predicting security vulnerabilities for windows vista. In: ICST, pp. 421–428 (2010)
3. National Vulnerability Database, http://nvd.nist.gov/
4. Howard, M., Pincus, J., Wing, J.M.: Measuring relative attack surfaces. In: Workshop on Advanced Developments in Software and Systems Security, Taipei, Taiwan (December 2003)
5. Manadhata, P.K., Wing, J.M.: An attack surface metric. IEEE Trans. Software Eng. 37(3), 371–386 (2011)
6. Microsoft Corp.: Microsoft Attack Surface Analyzer - Beta, http://bit.ly/AO4NNO
7. Coverity: Coverity scan: 2011 open source integrity report (2011)
8. National Institute of Standards and Technology: National Vulnerability database, http://nvd.nist.gov
9. Microsoft Corp.: A history of Windows, http://bit.ly/RKDHIm

10. Wikipedia: Source lines of code, `http://bit.ly/5LkKx`
11. TechRepublic: Five super-secret features in Windows 7, `http://tek.io/g3rBrB`
12. Rescorla, E.: Is finding security holes a good idea? IEEE Security & Privacy 3(1), 14–19 (2005)
13. Ozment, A., Schechter, S.E.: Milk or wine: Does software security improve with age? In: Proceedings of the 15th Conference on USENIX Security Symposium, USENIX-SS 2006, vol. 15. USENIX Association, Berkeley (2006)
14. Clark, S., Frei, S., Blaze, M., Smith, J.: Familiarity breeds contempt: The honeymoon effect and the role of legacy code in zero-day vulnerabilities. In: Proceedings of the 26th Annual Computer Security Applications Conference, ACSAC 2010, pp. 251–260. ACM, New York (2010)
15. Bozorgi, M., Saul, L.K., Savage, S., Voelker, G.M.: Beyond heuristics: learning to classify vulnerabilities and predict exploits. In: KDD, Washington, DC (July 2010)
16. Quinn, S., Scarfone, K., Barrett, M., Johnson, C.: Guide to adopting and using the security content automation protocol (SCAP) version 1.0. NIST Special Publication 800-117 (July 2010)
17. Ransbotham, S.: An empirical analysis of exploitation attempts based on vulnerabilities in open source software (2010)
18. Kurmus, A., Tartler, R., Dorneanu, D., Heinloth, B., Rothberg, V., Ruprecht, A., Schröder-Preikschat, W., Lohmann, D., Kapitza, R.: Attack surface metrics and automated compile-time os kernel tailoring. In: Network and Distributed System Security (NDSS) Symposium, San Diego, CA (February 2013)
19. Allodi, L., Massacci, F.: A preliminary analysis of vulnerability scores for attacks in wild. In: CCS BADGERS Workshop, Raleigh, NC (October 2012)
20. Allodi, L.: Attacker economics for internet-scale vulnerability risk assessment. In: Proceedings of Usenix LEET Workshop (2013)
21. Symantec Corporation: A-Z listing of threats and risks, `http://bit.ly/11G7JE5`
22. Symantec Corporation: Attack signatures, `http://bit.ly/xQaOQr`
23. Open Sourced Vulnerability Database, `http://www.osvdb.org`
24. Symantec Attack Signatures, `http://bit.ly/1hCw1TL`
25. Dumitraş, T., Shou, D.: Toward a standard benchmark for computer security research: The worldwide intelligence network environment (wine). In: Proceedings of the First Workshop on Building Analysis Datasets and Gathering Experience Returns for Security, BADGERS 2011, pp. 89–96. ACM, New York (2011)
26. Information about Internet Explorer versions, `http://bit.ly/1oNMA97`
27. National Institute of Standards and Technology: Engineering statistics handbook, `http://www.itl.nist.gov/div898/handbook/index.htm`
28. Bilge, L., Dumitraş, T.: Before we knew it: An empirical study of zero-day attacks in the real world. In: ACM Conference on Computer and Communications Security, Raleigh, NC, pp. 833–844 (October 2012)
29. Microsoft security intelligence report, vol. 16, `http://download.microsoft.com/download/7/2/B/72B5DE91-04F4-42F4-A587-9D08C55E0734/Microsoft_Security_Intelligence_Report_Volume_16_English.pdf`
30. Adobe Reader Protected Mode, `http://helpx.adobe.com/acrobat/kb/protected-mode-troubleshooting-reader.html`
31. Krebs, B.: Crimeware author funds exploit buying spree (2013), `http://bit.ly/1mYwlUY`
32. FireEye: The Dual Use Exploit: CVE-2013-3906 Used in Both Targeted Attacks and Crimeware Campaigns (2013), `http://bit.ly/R3XQQ4`
33. A Note about the DHTML Editing Control in IE7+, `http://blogs.msdn.com/b/ie/archive/2006/06/27/648850.aspx`

Towards a Masquerade Detection System Based on User's Tasks

J. Benito Camiña, Jorge Rodríguez, and Raúl Monroy

Computer Science Department
Tecnológico de Monterrey, Campus Estado de México
Carretera al Lago de Guadalupe Km. 3-5, Atizapán, Estado de México, 52926, México
{a00965049,a00965439,raulm}@itesm.mx

Abstract. Nowadays, computers store critical information, prompting the development of mechanisms aimed to timely detect any kind of intrusion. Some of such mechanisms, called *masquerade detectors*, are often designed to signal an alarm whenever they detect an anomaly in system behavior. Usually, the profile of ordinary system behavior is built out of a history of command execution. However, in [1,2], we suggested that it is not a command, but the object upon which it is carried out what may distinguish a masquerade from user participation; also, we hypothesized that this approach provides a means for building masquerade detectors that work at a higher-level of abstraction. In this paper, we report on a successful step towards this hypothesis validation. The crux of our abstraction stems from that a directory often holds closely related objects, resembling a *user task*; thus, we do not have to account for the accesses to individual objects; instead, we simply take it to be an access to some ancestor directory of it, the user task. Indeed, we shall prove that by looking into the access to only a few such user tasks, we can build a masquerade detector, just as powerful as if we looked into the access to every single file system object. The advantages of this abstraction are paramount: it eases the construction and maintenance of a masquerade detection mechanism, as it yields much shorter models. Using the WUIL dataset [2], we have conducted two experiments for distinguishing the performance of two one-class classifiers, namely: Naïve Bayes and Markov chains, considering single objects and our abstraction to user tasks. We shall see that in both cases, the task-based masquerader detector outperforms the individual object-based one.

1 Introduction

Information is an extremely important asset. However, due to an increase in storage capacity, lots of critical information move around inside personal computer devices everyday. This makes information more vulnerable to be accessed by an unintended, third party. Several kinds of mechanisms have been proposed to get around from this threat, the one being of interest to this paper is known as a *Masquerade Detection System* (MDS). A MDS is especially designed to send an alarm whenever it detects an anomaly in the use of a computer device,

A. Stavrou et al. (Eds.): RAID 2014, LNCS 8688, pp. 447–465, 2014.
© Springer International Publishing Switzerland 2014

thus deducing that the device has come to somebody else's possession (presumably an intruder).

Due to the seminal work of Schonlau *et al.* [3], first MDS's profiled ordinary device usage considering the history of the commands executed by the owner user, thus the term user behavior. However, masquerade detection based on command usage has proven not to be powerful enough [4], driving research into looking for new opportunities of a source that can be used for user profiling. Example approaches for profiling user behavior in this vein are the use of I/O devices, such as the mouse or the keyboard [5,6], the use of specific applications, such as a document management system [7], and the characterization of certain kinds of user activities, such as search [8].

In [1,2], we introduced a new approach to masquerade detection. This approach claims that it is not the command or the activity carried out, but the object upon which it is performed what may separate a masquerade from genuine user participation. To support this claim, we have developed a masquerade dataset, called *WUIL*, which contains logs of the activity of a number of users, working on ordinary conditions; more importantly, WUIL also contains logs of simulated attacks, conducted on the actual user machines, and thus are more faithful than others reported on in the literature, *e.g.* [3,8].

In [2], we argued that our approach provides a richer means for building MDS's that could work at a higher-level of abstraction. In this paper, we further support such claim. We will introduce a MDS that is based on an abstraction of a *user task*, taken to be a directory holding a number of (allegedly) related file system objects. Thus, while using objects in a given user directory, we take the user to be working on the same task, and model the behavior of a user in terms of task activity, including task frequency and task transition.

Using the WUIL dataset [2], we have conducted two experiments for distinguishing the performance of two one-class classifiers, namely: Naïve Bayes and Markov chains. Each classifier was used as a MDS, considering both single objects and our abstraction to user tasks.

We have successfully validated that, even though it looks into the activity of only a few user tasks, our proposed MDS is just as powerful than the one that looks into each access to every single file system object underneath. The advantages of our task-based abstraction are paramount: it eases both the construction and the maintenance of the associated MDS, because it yields much simpler and shorter models. Further, notice that this kind of level of abstraction can hardly be achieved in other approaches, which either group command sequences into scripts, *e.g.* as in [9], or turn actual commands into generic ones, such as edit, compile, etc., *e.g.* as in [8]. Our results also show that our task-based abstraction can also be exploited in other masquerade detection approaches that also include file system usage, *e.g.* [8].

Overview of Paper. The remainder of this paper is organized as follows. First, in §2, we shall show the different approaches that have been studied for masquerade detection. Then, in §3 we will give an overview of the WUIL masquerade dataset, as well as our previous efforts on developing a masquerade detection mechanism based on user's File System (FS) navigation. There, we shall also introduce our abstraction of a user task, and how WUIL logs are transformed from FS object usage to task activities. Then, in §4, we shall show the experiment that we have designed to validate this paper's working hypothesis. Next, in §5, we shall present the results we have obtained through our experimentation. Finally, in §6, we report on the conclusions drawn from this experiment and provide guidelines for further work.

2   User Profile for Masquerade Detection

In terms of the approach used to profile user behavior, most existing MDS have made use of the history of commands that a user executes while working in an UNIX session [3]; some analyze the way a user drives an I/O device, like the mouse [5,10,11] or the keyboard [6,12]; and some study user search behavior [8,13]. In what follows, we provide an overview of these approaches to profile user behavior.

2.1   NIDES

(N)IDES [14], one of the earliest attempts at masquerade detection, is an expert-system that aims to detect a masquerade (and other types of intrusion) using a statistical behavior profile built from a diverse set of audit data from UNIX Systems. Audit data includes command usage, accesses to password protected directories, session information, CPU usage, the use of certain categories of applications like compilers or editors, and many others. Interestingly, NIDES considers grouping actions together into a sequence, and both the corresponding subject executing an action and the object upon which it is performed. NIDES has served as an inspiration by having profiles of normal usage and trying to discern between an intruder and a user by differences in behavior.

2.2   UNIX Commands

The most prominent approach to profile user behavior is that of Schonlau *et al.*, who suggested considering the commands that the user executes while working on an UNIX session. In order to validate this hypothesis, Schonlau *et al.* developed a masquerade dataset, known as SEA [15], which consists of a number of user logs, each of which is a sequence of commands, having got rid of any arguments.

SEA contains activity logs of 70 users. Each user log consists of a sequence of 15, 000 commands, and has been separated into 150 sessions with 100-command each. Masquerades are simulated by replacing a user's legitimate session with somebody else's. To this purpose, 50 users were designated to be honest, and the remaining 20 to be masqueraders. SEA identifies which user sessions are ordinary and which contaminated. Assessing the performance of a given MDS amounts to first building the MDS model using only ordinary user sessions (50), and then measuring how well the MDS did in distinguishing masquerader's sessions from user's ones (100).

Regarding the use of UNIX commands to masquerade detection, for the purpose of the work reported herein, two other pieces of research are worth mentioning. One, [16], redefines the experiment set by Schonlau *et al.*, and the other, [17], considers the used of enriched command lines. Unlike [3], [16] suggests evaluating the performance of a given MDS for a honest user by measuring how well it distinguishes as a masquerade every session of the remaining users. This yields a considerably larger number of test sessions upon which we may rest the validity of any statistical inference. For masquerade detection via enriched commands, [17] used Greenberg's dataset [18], which, for every user UNIX command, also includes the associated arguments. Greenberg's dataset contains activity logs of 168 users, divided in four categories: novice programmers, experienced programmers, computer scientists and non-programmers.

SEA was the first masquerade dataset that allowed a fair comparison among different MDS's, thus, yielding a significant amount of research (see [19,20] for a survey). However, SEA has a severe limitation, namely: it involves unrealistic masquerades, as they are made out of somebody else's ordinary behavior. Interestingly, even though this approach, we call *One Versus The Others* (OVTO), may not yield significant results to masquerade detection, it has prevailed in mostly datasets.

2.3   Mouse Usage

The use of I/O devices is another prolific approach to user profiling for masquerade detection. Given that the use of the mouse as an I/O device is widespread, it has attracted significant attention. For example, [5] has developed a dataset with information gathered from 18 users working on Internet Explorer. The dataset contains information about the coordinates of the mouse pointer after mouse movement, and other features like distance, angle, and time to travel between a pair of adjacent coordinates. [5]'s MDS is not *one-class*; *i.e.* model construction involves the use of both positive and negative examples, borrowed from somebody else's ordinary behavior.

In a similar vein [10], Garg *et al.* collected mouse usage information about a limited set of data of only three users. In particular, they measured the number of mouse clicks, the pointer distance between two consecutive clicks, mouse speed, and mouse angle, deriving from all this information 16 different features. Similarly, Weiss *et al.* [11] defined a 5x5 button matrix, and a set of button sequences that each participating user had to go through. They recorded activity logs for each user, gathering information of three mouse events: move, click, and drag, including key features such as time and coordinates.

Mouse usage to masquerade detection enables the possibility of contrasting users one against other in terms of the use of a standard device. However, so far, the masquerade scenarios that haven been considered are of little practical application, as they are constrained to an specific application. Moreover, further development on the masquerade dataset is required, as they involve only a few users. More importantly, [5,10,11] all follow an OVTO approach; thus, they do not consider faithful masquerade attempts.

2.4 Keyboard Usage

As for now, keyboards also are pretty common, and so may become a rather standard platform for user profile construction. Keyboard dynamics for masquerade detection is either static- or free-text. In the static-text approach, users are required to write the same piece of text. Killourhy & Maxion have rationally reconstructed a number of static-text MDS's reported on in the literature, and then carried out a fair comparison [6]. In their experiment, each MDS attempts to spot a masquerader looking into how a user types her password. For that purpose, they developed a dataset that contains the activity logs of 51 users. For each user, the dataset includes 8 sessions. Each session contains 50 records of the user typing the password, which is the same for every user; the information captured involves 31 different features of keystroke patterns.

By contrast, in the free-text approach, users type text at will. An example work in this vein is that of Messerman et al. [12], who have developed a dataset that contains logs of 55 users working in a web-mail application. The dataset involves mainly key downs and time stamps.

Though easy to implement, gathering information about keyboard usage might be intrusive. For example, in the static-text approach, a user must write the same text a number of times, and this might drive her not to abide to a change-password policy. While this remark is not applicable in the free-text approach, a user must be working with a designated application, thus, making the masquerade detection scenario unrealistic. Further, [6,12] both adopt an OVTO approach; thus, they do not consider faithful masquerades.

2.5 Search Patterns

In a different vein, Ben-Salem & Stolfo have developed a masquerade dataset [8], named *RUU*, which is used to profile a user in terms of search patterns. RUU contains activity logs of 18 users. Each log record involves 22 different features, some are user-level: browsing, communication, information gathering, etc., and some system-level: registry modification, process creation/destruction, file access, DLL usage, etc. In a follow-up paper, Song et al. [13] attempted to identify which RUU features best represent user search patterns.

In RUU, log recording is transparent; further, RUU involves a number of attacks. However, attacks were simulated in an external computer, *not* in the users'. This makes attacks rather unfaithful, since a user search pattern, indeed a collection of user actions, might drastically differ from one computer to other. This is attributable to issues, such as computer architecture, file system organization, and so on.

In conclusion, even though successful, existing approaches to masquerade detection all suffer from some limitations. A common problem is that MDS evaluation does not involve the use of faithfully simulated attacks (*e.g.* they adopt the OVTO approach). Other MDS's are limited to the output of a single application, overlooking the entire picture. We also stressed the relevance of making transparent activity recording.

3   WUIL and a Task Abstraction

As discussed above, user profile for masquerade detection is usually built out of a record of user actions (in the form of either I/O events, or running commands). Departing from this standard approach, in [1,2], we argued that not only is it the action, but it also is the object upon which the action is executed what distinguishes user participation. We introduced a novel MDS based on the way a user navigates the structure of her File System (FS). Also, we developed WUIL, a dataset that collects FS navigation from several users, but more importantly it collects a number of faithful masquerade attempts. This is also in contrast with existing datasets, such as SEA, which rely on a OVTO masquerade model.

In [2], we have also stated the hypothesis for which we provide further support in this paper, namely: our FS navigation approach to masquerade detection provides a richer means that could be made to work at a higher-level of abstraction. We shall introduce a MDS that is based on an abstraction to FS navigation, we call a *task*. Roughly, a task amounts to a FS directory holding a number of (allegedly) related file system objects. Thus, while using objects in that directory, we take the user to be working on the very same task, and model user behavior in terms of task usage, including task frequency and task transition. Apart from the notion of task, the FS navigation approach to masquerade detection enables further abstractions, including the principle of locality (which, roughly, states the likelihood that an object, or some object nearby, will be used next). We shall have more to say in §6. In what follows, we outline first WUIL, and then how we have abstracted out user FS navigation into task activity.

3.1   The WUIL Masquerade Dataset

FS navigation is universal in that it can be studied in virtually any PC, regardless of the underlying Operating System (OS). For the construction of WUIL, however, we recruited volunteers working with some version of MS Windows, since it is the most widely used OS. In WUIL, MS Windows versions range from XP to 7.

WUIL User Logs. Currently, WUIL contains log information about 20 different users. Each user log contains FS usage of the two most common directories: Desktop and My Documents. To gather these logs, we used the Windows tool audit, which inspects FS usage on the directories it is enabled. User logs have been preprocessed so that each entry consists of a tuple involving only a unique identifier, access date, access time, and the FS object itself: a FS path.

WUIL contains a heterogeneous mixture of users with different backgrounds, including students, senior managers, and departmental secretaries. We asked every user to fill in a survey with the aim of obtaining standard personal information like age, gender, and level of education. However, through this survey, we also collected subjective information, such as how skillful a user reckons herself about OS configuration, or how tidy she considers her personal file system to be and why. Overall, our aim is to research whether there exist certain kinds of users who are easier to protect from being harmed than others (we will have more to say on this later on in the text, *cf.* §6.)

WUIL Masquerade Logs. What makes WUIL most distinctive is that it contains close to real masquerade attempts. This is in contrast with existing masquerade datasets that use an OVTO approach, raising the concern as to what a given MDS actually achieves. This is because the 'intruder' has no intention to commit any intrusion, so any result is about the strength of the MDS as a classifier, but not as to how good it is at the masquerade detection problem.

By contrast, WUIL enables the study of a very specific intrusion scenario, namely: the access to a computer session that has been carelessly left unattended (which, in principle, is similar to a remote connection via privilege escalation). Accordingly, WUIL includes simulated masqueraders that are limited to be five minute long.

For each user, WUIL includes logs taken from the simulation of three different kinds of masqueraders: basic, intermediate, and advanced. In the basic attack, the masquerader has an occasional opportunity of using the victim computer; thus, he is not prepared for conducting the attack, lacking from any special tool or auxiliary equipment. In the intermediate attack, the masquerader aims at doing the attack, so he brings in an USB flash drive, but he has to manually gather whatever he reckons interesting, collecting everything into the USB flash memory. Finally, in the advanced attack, not only does the (more skillful) masquerader bring in a USB flash memory, but he also executes a script, which automatically extracts every file baptized with an interesting name (password, bank, personal, etc.), and attempts to take off any intrusion track. We remark that each of these simulated attacks have all been conducted in the user PC.

The WUIL masquerade attacks are both short and specific, yielding class unbalance (there are fewer attack sessions per user). Further, in the FS navigation approach, it is more difficult to synthesize an attack. As a machine file system changes, so should the masquerade detection model, yielding maintenance workload.

Currently, WUIL is under improvement, in order to include more users, with a focus on users running MS Windows 8 (in order to have a more up to date MS windows version repertoire). In the next section, §3.2, we shall explain the concept of task we are using and the way we processed WUIL to get the log's based on tasks accesses instead of objects accesses.

3.2   Task Abstraction

In an ideal setting, each user should define her own tasks, associating each of which to a specific directory in her file system. In WUIL, however, user logs do

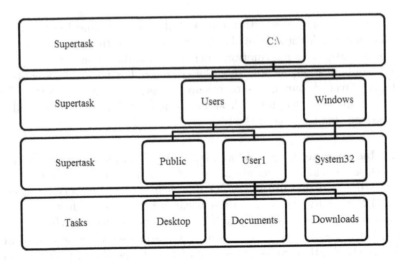

Fig. 1. A typical directory tree structure organized into tasks and supertasks, considering a depth cut point equal to four

not come with such information. Thus, we had to find a way to emulate this user definition. The rational behind our approach to such approximation is that we conjecture that user tasks are all at the same depth regarding the user FS tree directory. Thus, we only need to find out such depth, we call *depth cut point*.

Depth Cut Point. To approximate a depth cut point (DCP), we conducted sort of a backwards breadth-first search analysis about user task access rate. Our analysis makes three considerations. First, the resulting number of tasks should not exceed 100, as it would be odd for one to have 100 different roles. Second, the DCP should not be deeper than 10, because it would be odd for one to work that deep in the directory tree structure. And third, when searching upwards, we should not pass depth four, as that is the standard depth for both FS directories `Desktop` and `My Documents` (assumed to be the user working directories). Then, our procedure is as follows. Take a user. Set current depth to be the median of the user depth object access; if greater than 10, set current depth to 10. For each iteration, if current depth is greater than 4 and if the user task rate underneath current depth is less than 70%, decrement current depth and repeat. Otherwise, stop, yielding current depth. Set every directory above a user's DCP into a different task, we call a *super-task*, cf. Fig. 1.

Having identified a DCP, we mapped every WUIL log, both user and attack, from object access to its corresponding task access. This resulted in two separate sets, which were then used for both development and validation purposes. Tables 1 and 2 respectively show the DCP for each user, and contrast the number of different objects against that of different tasks, on a per user basis. From these tables, we observe both that the DCP often is five or six, and that the number of tasks per user is much fewer of that of objects. Looking more closely

Table 1. Users' depth cut point, as found experimentally

User	1	2	3	4	5	6	7	8	9	10	11	12	13	14	15	16	17	18	19	20
DCP	5	5	5	5	5	6	6	6	6	5	3	5	3	5	5	6	6	5	5	5

Table 2. A comparison of the number of different objects against that of different tasks, per user

User	Number of Objects	Number of Tasks
1	7886	12
2	1672	14
3	200	13
4	2555	61
5	40776	60
6	6642	69
7	9149	28
8	877	9
9	10321	49
10	655	8
11	3524	377
12	5616	31
13	151477	64
14	1809	15
15	4925	50
16	25718	39
17	7370	86
18	1385	9
19	620	9
20	1407	26
Average	14229	51

into these tables, we may notice that user 11 has a distinctively large number of tasks, 377, and that she has a DCP of three. This is because this user has a number of physical drive units, and, spreads her file system structure among them all. This actually makes it more difficult to protect her. We shall more to say on this and other limitations on our task-based abstraction below (see §5).

Below, §4, we shall describe the experiments that we have conducted to assess our working hypothesis, namely: that the performance of a task-based MDS is comparable to an object-based one.

4   Tasks vs Objects: An Experimental Comparison

With the aim of comparing the masquerade detection performance of a task-based model against an object-based one, we ran an experiment using two different classifiers: Markov chains and Naïve Bayes. The rationale behind the selection of these techniques is twofold. First, both techniques are suitable as a one-class classifier, as required in our problem setting. Second, they are complementary in that while Naïve Bayes commonly used for a *bag of words* model, where only the frequency of an event matters, Markov chain is used for an event sequence model, where each event depends on past events, accounting for temporal dependencies.

Table 3. Outputs used for assessing classifier performance

Window type	Classifier output	Assessment
User	User	True Negative (TN)
User	Masquerader	False Positive (FP)
Masquerader	User	False Negative (FN)
Masquerader	Masquerader	True Positive (TP)

Rounding off, our experiment forms a 2 × 2-matrix, involving an event class (task/object) and a classifier (Markov chain/Naïve Bayes). Each test was carried out on a per user basis.

4.1 Experiment Design

There are some parameters that need to be set before starting an experimentation. These parameters must be similar in all the experiments in order to make the results comparable. We explain each in turn below.

Construction and Validation Sets. For each user experiment we split the associated WUIL logs in two different sets: construction and validation. The construction set is composed with a certain percentage of the user log (ordinary behavior) and is used to create and train the classifier. The validation set consists of the remaining percentage of the user log, together with the full set of that user masquerade attacks, and is used to yield a classification performance.

For each experiment, we split the user log using different percentages for both sets, construction and validation, namely: 80-20, 70-30, 50-50, 30-70, and 20-80. The rationale behind this setting decision was studying how much information is needed to start having similar results, and how these proportions affect the performance of each classifier. We also conducted a five-fold cross-validation for the particular experiment that yielded the best classification result.

A Window-Based Analysis. We have divided every user validation set, whether task-based or object-based, using a *windowing approach*. We set both the window size and the window step to be 20. Windows are *not* mixed; they are filled in either with user events, or masquerader ones. Each time a window is analyzed, the classifier emits an evaluation, which might be correct, or not, yielding different assessments as shown in Table 3.

Threshold. To emit an evaluation, the classifier compares a *window score* against a *threshold*. A window is classified as *masquerade*, if the window score is greater than or equal to the threshold, and *normal*, otherwise. We vary the threshold to study the performance of a classifier, thereby drawing a so-called *Receiver Operating Characteristic (ROC)* curve. So, we start with a very low threshold, getting a lax classifier; then, we increase the threshold slowly until we get a very strict one. Doing so, we have got results from 100% False Positive (FP) with 0% False Negative (FN), to 0% FP with 100% FN, and with this information we identify the minimum misclassification point for each user (see section §5).

4.2 Markov Chains

For implementing a Markov chain-based MDS, we have followed the work of Maxion *et al.* [21]. In a Markov chain, each state comprehends a sequence of events (objects or tasks, in our case). Each event sequence is called an *n-gram*. N-grams are all the same size. A Markov chain is used to assess whether a sequence of state transitions conforms to a model (the user behavior, in our case). Notice how a Markov chain captures both event frequency (via a state transition) and event dependency (via the elements of an n-gram). For a correct operation, the Markov chain parameters must be tuned. We explain each of them, and how to fix them, below.

A User Log Is a Trace Sequence. For the construction and validation of a Markov chain model, we require a number of event sequences, each of which is called a *trace*. So, we split a user log into traces. We set a trace to include entries recording the activity of a calendar day. Whenever a user worked after midnight, we keep the next day events still as part of the current trace. To mark the end and the beginning of two adjacent traces, we have specified an idle time of at least two hours. Each masquerade attempt is an independent trace. Each trace is either construction, or validation, but not both. Every validation trace is divided into windows.

N-gram Size. To fix the size of the n-gram, we have used *divergence* [21], which measures how different an attack and a Markov chain model are. The more they diverge, the better the model is to detect an attack. We proceeded as follows. First, we randomly picked five pairs: user and attack. Then, working on one pair at a time, we initialized the n-gram size to one, and loop till 20, with increments of size one, in order to determine the n-gram size yielding maximum divergence. Finally, we set the n-gram size to be the average of all these values. It should be noticed, however, that for object-based masquerade detection, our computer (see below) was unable to handle models with n-grams greater than five, and, so for those we put a cap on size to that value.

Penalization. Penalization, Z, is the amount of bad points added to the score of a model, whenever that model does not involve a given state transition. In our case, following some experimentation, we fixed the penalization to be five.

Having set these parameters, we have built every Markov chain model as follows. Take a user trace. Create a new state; set it to be the current state and label it with an n-gram filled in with null events. Then, inspect the trace, from left to right, and, event by event, proceed as follows. Take the n-gram of the current state label, then remove the first event of that n-gram and append the current trace event. If there is not a state labeled with the resulting n-gram, create one, and then join the current state and the new state with a transition. Then, update the distribution probability of the state transition model, set the current state to be the new state with the resulting n-gram, and iterate this process as many times as the length of the current trace, creating and updating states and state transitions as required. This procedure is then repeated for every user trace, using the same Markov chain model.

Also following [21], we use each Markov chain model to classify every user validation trace using the procedure outlined below. Starting with the first state, filled in with null events, apply the above trace inspect procedure; however, instead of creating a state and its transitions, update X and Y, evaluation coefficients, as follows. First, using the trace, determine the next state. Then, there are two possible cases:

Model compliance: states current, e, and next, e', together with the associated transition, are in the model, and so:

$$X = X + 1$$
$$Y = Y + (1 - \Pr(e, e'))$$

where $\Pr(e, e')$ is the probability, according to the model, that e' follows e.

Model failure: e and e', together with the associated transition, are *not* in the model, and so:

$$X = X + 1$$
$$Y = Y + Z$$

Given a window, w, the classifier outputs a final evaluation, $\mu(w)$, given by $\mu(w) = Y/X$. For a given threshold, r, w is said to be *normal*, whenever $\mu(w) < r$, and *masquerade*, otherwise.

4.3   Naïve Bayes

Implementing a Naïve Bayes classifier for a particular user, u, (see, *e.g.* [16,17]), amounts to estimating the probability for an event (an object or a task access, in our case) c to have been originated from u, denoted $\Pr_u(c)$. Since Naïve Bayes is frequency-based, the associated probability distribution is computed out of the access information recorded in the training set. Thus, in symbols:

$$\Pr_u(c) = \frac{f_{uc} + \alpha}{n_u + \alpha \times K}$$

Where f_{uc} is the number of times user u has accessed task (respectively, object) c, n_u the length of u's training set, and where K is the total number of distinct tasks (respectively, objects). $0 < \alpha \ll 1$ to prevent $\Pr_u(c)$ from becoming zero; following [16,17], we set α to 0.01.

To evaluate a test window w, in which user u has allegedly participated, the cumulative probability of w, an access sequence of the form $c_1 c_2 \ldots c_n$, of length $n (= 20)$, is given by:

$$\Pr_u(w \equiv c_1 c_2 \ldots c_n) = \Pr_u(c_1) \times \cdots \times \Pr_u(c_n)$$

$\Pr_u(w)$ is then compared against a threshold: if it is above the threshold, the session is considered normal; otherwise, it is considered a masquerade.

Having explained our methodology, and how we have set each classifier parameter, we now turn our attention to show and analyze the results obtained throughout our experimentation.

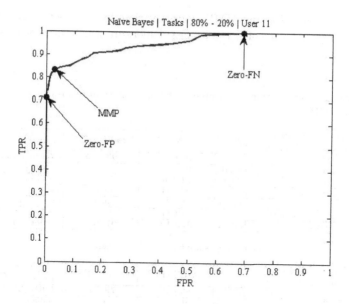

Fig. 2. An example ROC curve, annotated with the position of zero-FN, zero-FP, and MMP

5   Results

5.1   A Comparison of Classification Performance

We have used ROC curves, to understand the classification performance of all our MDS's. In order to compare these MDS's one another, we have used four different measurements: *Area-Under-the-Curve* (AUC), *Zero-False Negative* (Zero-FN), *Zero-False Positive* (Zero-FP), and the *Minimum Misclassification Point* (MMP). AUC denotes the area under a ROC curve. An AUC equal to one amounts to the perfect classifier, which correctly marks every window, as user or attack. Conversely, an AUC equal to zero corresponds to the worst classifier ever.

Zero-FN is the least False Positive rate (FP) at which we still work with a true positive rate of one, and, thus, masquerade windows are all classified correctly. We have borrowed zero-FN from [22]. By contrast, zero-FP is the least False Negative rate (FN) at which we still keep the false positive rate at zero, and, thus, user windows are all classified correctly. MMP corresponds to those values of FP and FN that minimize FP+FN. Fig. 2 depicts the zero-FN, zero-FP and MMP for a given ROC curve.

Tables 4 and 5 respectively show the overall performance evaluation of Naïve Bayes and Markov chains. Table 4(a) (respectively, Table 5(a)) shows the classification performance of Naïve Bayes (respectively, Markov chain) applied to object access. This applies similarly for Tables 4(b) and 5(b), but for task access.

Looking into Table 4, we may observe that the task-based Naïve Bayes classifier outperforms the object-based one. While the gain for AUC is marginal, that for zero-FN, zero-FP and MMP is greater than five percentage points. Recall that for the latter variables, the lower the measure, the better the classifier's performance.

Table 4. Average classification performance of Naïve Bayes in terms of AUC, zero-FN, zero-FP, and MMP

User's log division Construction% - Validation%	AUC	Zero-FN (FP%)	Zero-FP (FN%)	MMP	
				FP%	FN%
80 - 20	0.716	92.070	**93.425**	**22.149**	**26.229**
70 - 30	0.710	93.043	95.562	26.192	25.256
50 - 50	0.696	91.760	99.582	30.115	22.610
30 - 70	0.710	92.003	99.343	25.869	27.560
20 - 80	0.701	**91.260**	99.602	32.424	23.193
80 - 20 Cross Validation	**0.734**	91.934	99.498	23.366	26.198
Average	**0.711**	**92.012**	**97.835**	**26.686**	**25.174**

(a) Naïve Bayes applied to object access

User's log division Construction% - Validation%	AUC	Zero-FN (FP%)	Zero-FP (FN%)	MMP	
				FP%	FN%
80 - 20	0.758	**86.512**	79.093	**15.618**	**27.734**
70 - 30	0.758	86.728	80.354	14.356	30.738
50 - 50	0.741	86.553	88.633	16.791	29.762
30 - 70	0.736	89.819	91.221	17.267	29.723
20 - 80	0.719	88.713	91.253	19.884	29.174
80 - 20 Cross Validation	**0.763**	87.486	94.238	20.237	26.489
Average	**0.746**	**87.635**	**87.465**	**17.359**	**28.937**

(b) Naïve Bayes applied to task access

Similar remarks apply to the results reported in Table 5, except that the performance difference is not as drastic as for Naïve Bayes. For example, for the 80 - 20 (%) experiment, the task-based Markov chain classifier slightly outperforms the object-based one, except in the AUC measurement. However, as we shorten the amount of available training, the task-based classifier shows a more regular, stable performance behavior. Comparing the information reported in Tables 4 and 5, we may notice that, for our problem and regardless of whether task-based or object-based, Markov chains outperforms Naïve Bayes in all our measurements.

Summarizing, our experiments have yielded three key observations. First, a task-based approach to masquerade detection outperforms, though slightly, an object-based one. Second, Markov chain masquerade detection outperforms Naïve Bayes's for this scenario. This might be explained by that a Markov chain approach accounts for temporal relationships between accesses, giving more information to construct the user's profile. Third, and contrary to our expectations, shortening the amount of available training data does not severely affect the task-based approach to masquerade detection. This is in contrast with the object-based approach, where AUC, zero-FN, zero-FP, and MMP average values suffer notorious increments when we used a less percentage of a user log for training.

Table 5. Average classification performance of Markov chains, based on area-under-the-curve (AUC), zero-False Negative (zero-FN), zero-False Positive (zero-FP), and Minimum Misclassification Point (MMP)

User's log division Construction% - Validation%	AUC	Zero-FN (FP%)	Zero-FP (FN%)	MMP	
				FP%	FN%
80 - 20	0.838	**53.260**	**33.922**	13.159	13.017
70 - 30	0.829	58.304	42.888	16.536	12.383
50 - 50	0.837	65.911	42.910	15.032	14.437
30 -70	0.823	65.386	40.658	16.927	14.095
20 - 80	0.849	67.809	40.005	16.054	11.355
80 - 20 Cross Validation	**0.896**	55.484	41.165	**14.595**	**8.285**
Average	**0.845**	**61.026**	**40.258**	**15.384**	**12.262**

(a) Markov chain applied using object access

User's log division Construction% - Validation%	AUC	Zero-FN (FP%)	Zero-FP (FN%)	MMP	
				FP%	FN%
80 - 20	0.856	**43.844**	**33.655**	12.724	8.730
70 - 30	0.832	45.508	46.728	16.410	8.762
50 - 50	0.814	52.559	53.331	21.821	7.205
30 -70	0.803	53.690	52.520	17.268	13.215
20 - 80	0.831	51.318	57.233	17.387	10.173
80 - 20 Cross Validation	**0.874**	44.460	53.616	**11.814**	**8.492**
Average	**0.835**	**48.563**	**49.514**	**16.237**	**9.429**

(b) Markov chain applied using task access

Spotting the Difference. A careful analysis on our results reveals that for three users the Markov chains classifiers perform remarkably bad, in contrast with the good results exhibited for the other users. While this is an undesired result, it helps us understand the limitations and challenges of this approach. After closely examination of users 10, 12 and 13 logs, the problem seems to be that these users have a very odd file system structure. User 10 has very few file system objects; user 12 has all her files in a single directory, namely: Desktop; and user 13 has divided her file system into several physical or logical drive units. These issues make some users especially difficult to protect.

Due also to these users' odd file system structure, the automatic determination of what directories constitute a task, using the depth cut point procedure introduced in §3.2, selects directories that are not suitable as a task, or yields too few tasks to operate with. It is important to remark that the automatic task selection is an artificial construction because we do not have that information directly from the user on the WUIL dataset, suggesting the importance of a correct mapping between directories and tasks. More importantly, they suggest that an organization could fix and then enforce a set of policies (where to keep files, how many different directories to keep them in, etc.) so as to nudge users toward using reasonable file storage habits.

Benefits of a Task-Based Approach to Masquerade Detection. What makes the use of a task-based approach relevant is the size of the associated model, as it will always be much easier and faster to build and maintain a model that often is two orders of magnitude smaller. While one may easily anticipate

Table 6. Size of Markov chain models for every user at the 80 - 20% experiment

User	Objects	Tasks
1	88667	1674
2	14259	1406
3	3204	660
4	18440	906
5	177372	2822
6	50529	6371
7	62185	1725
8	26812	1575
9	58161	3604
10	27236	857
11	30466	10645
12	35220	3041
13	530691	4768
14	7653	1497
15	66079	3401
16	164725	8949
17	43798	4384
18	3340	592
19	8234	408
20	6650	961
Average	71186	3012

this benefit from Table 2, we list, in Table 6, the size of the Markov chain models that resulted from using the 80 - 20% experiment.

Also, the file system of a user is in constant change with files being created and deleted. Tasks are more resilient to change, because a user does not change her activities with a high frequency. So, most file system changes are transparent when using our task abstraction, making it less necessary for a constant update of the associated model. Thus, working with our abstraction demands fewer storage and computing resources, with a slightly better performance rate than working with pure objects.

5.2   Mean-Windows-to-First-Alarm

Another evaluation element is how many windows takes to a classifier to start detecting abnormal behavior. In order to analyze this, we used the concept of Mean-Windows-to-First-Alarm (MWFA) [21], that represents the average number of windows that must pass before a window is classified as abnormal. Table 7 shows the MWFA for each type of attack. MWFA can be used to anticipate how much information the masquerader can gain access to before the MDS detects him. From Table 7, we notice that, as the level of attack automation increases, Markov chains require more windows to detect an attack than Naïve Bayes. So, to quickly detect a masquerader, it seems that Naïve Bayes is better; however, one has to keep in mind that Markov chains detect attack windows more accurately than Naïve Bayes. Another important aspect to observe is that, in general, task-based classifiers detect more quickly a masquerade than the object-based ones.

Given that we work only with 20 users, we cannot guarantee that the underlying classification performance distribution is normal. So, for a statistical test, we used Wilcoxon signed rank to disprove the null hypothesis that the two

Table 7. Mean number of windows to first alarm per attack

Attack type	Markov chain		Naïve Bayes	
	Task-based	Object-based	Task-based	Object-based
Basic	2.4	2.1	4.02	6.03
Intermediate	18.2	58.45	2.59	5.19
Advanced	10.1	9.95	2.5	1.51

underlying distributions are related and not independent, meaning that the results between the two classifiers are statistically equivalent.

Applying the test for the AUC of task-based Markov chains against Naïve Bayes, we have found that the null hypothesis is rejected, with a $p - value$ of 0.0137. However, doing so for the AUC of task-based Markov chain against object-based Naïve Bayes, we have found that there is not enough evidence to reject the null hypothesis. With these results, we conclude that for our experiments the Markov chain classifier significantly outperforms Naïve Bayes, but that the performance difference from using task or object accesses is not significant. This result corroborates that the task-based approach for masquerade detection performs as well as the object-based one, but with a more stable, easier to maintain, and smaller representation of the user behavior.

Our experiments were all run on a HP EliteBook 6930p machine with 4GB of RAM (of which 3.84GB usable) running a 64 bits MS Windows 7 OS with an Intel® Core™ 2 Duo CPU P8400.

6   Conclusions and Further Work

We have conjectured that a file-system navigation approach to masquerade detection provides a means for reasoning at a higher-level of abstraction. Taking a step towards establishing this conjecture, we have introduced a task-based abstraction, where each task holds different but related objects. In order to evaluate the usefulness of our task abstraction, we have used the WUIL dataset and designed some experiments with two different classifiers: Markov chains and Naïve Bayes. First, we have found that a task-based MDS is as powerful as an object-based one. Second, we have found that Markov chains outperforms Naïve Bayes, because it accounts for event temporal relationships.

Even though a task-based MDS does not outperform an object-based one, if we take into account the size of a Markov chain model, the task-based approach provides a clear advantage. Also it is important to remark that the task-based approach provides secondary benefits: it encompasses a big part of the accesses, and it is more resilient to file system changes, meaning that the model has to be updated with less frequency than the object-based one. Considering all these advantages, we conclude that it is worth using our task abstraction.

In this paper, we have worked with a single abstraction, but in order to create a competitive MDS, other abstractions must be used. Fortunately, the file system navigation approach is a rich source of abstractions. Ongoing work, for example, explores using the *locality* memory-cache principle, which considers both time (temporal locality), and file location (spatial locality). Other abstractions that are worth exploring include file usage information (hot files against cold files), and the file system structure depth a user commonly works at.

At present, we are gathering data from new users for WUIL, especially MS Windows 8 users. We would like to test further how our task abstraction works with these new kinds of users. We would also like to explore any correlation between the performance of a classifier and some users' file system characteristics, like tidiness and organization. We would like to investigate whether it is possible to create some policies that a user has to follow, which could make it easier to protect her, and which at the same time would make it harder for a masquerader to steal critical information. Also, ongoing research is concerned with further analyzing our results, from a user perspective, giving, for example, the number of false alarms that may result per day, etc.

Acknowledgments. This paper has largely benefited from numerous discussions with Luis Ángel Trejo-Rodríguez. We thank both the anonymous referees, and the members of the NetSec group at Tecnológico de Monterrey, Estado de México, for providing invaluable, useful suggestions and advice on an earlier version of this paper. The first authors were respectively supported by CONACYT student scholarships 329962 and 376099, and by COMECYT with travel grants, while the third author was in part supported by CONACYT grant 105698.

References

1. Camiña, B., Monroy, R., Trejo, L.A., Sánchez, E.: Towards building a masquerade detection method based on user file system navigation. In: Batyrshin, I., Sidorov, G. (eds.) MICAI 2011, Part I. LNCS (LNAI), vol. 7094, pp. 174–186. Springer, Heidelberg (2011)
2. Camiña, J.B., Hernández-Gracidas, C., Monroy, R., Trejo, L.: The windows-users and -intruder simulations logs dataset (WUIL): An experimental framework for masquerade detection mechanisms. Expert Systems with Applications 41(3), 919–930 (2014)
3. Schonlau, M., DuMouchel, W., Ju, W., Karr, A., Theus, M., Vardi, Y.: Computer intrusion: Detecting masquerades. Statistical Science 16(1), 58–74 (2001)
4. Razo-Zapata, I., Mex-Perera, C., Monroy, R.: Masquerade attacks based on user's profile. Journal of Systems and Software 85(11), 2640–2651 (2012)
5. Pusara, M., Brodley, C.: User re-authentication via mouse movements. In: Proceedings of the 2004 ACM Workshop on Visualization and Data Mining for Computer Security, VizSEC/DMSEC 2004, pp. 1–8. ACM (October 2004)
6. Killourhy, K., Maxion, R.: Why did my detector do that?! - predicting keystroke-dynamics error rates. In: Jha, S., Sommer, R., Kreibich, C. (eds.) RAID 2010. LNCS, vol. 6307, pp. 256–276. Springer, Heidelberg (2010)
7. Sankaranarayanan, V., Pramanik, S., Upadhyaya, S.: Detecting masquerading users in a document management system. In: Proceedings of the IEEE International Conference on Communications, ICC 2006, vol. 5, pp. 2296–2301. IEEE Computer Society Press (June 2006)

8. Salem, M.B., Stolfo, S.J.: Modeling user search behavior for masquerade detection. In: Sommer, R., Balzarotti, D., Maier, G. (eds.) RAID 2011. LNCS, vol. 6961, pp. 181–200. Springer, Heidelberg (2011)

9. Posadas, R., Mex-Perera, J.C., Monroy, R., Nolazco-Flores, J.A.: Hybrid method for detecting masqueraders using session folding and hidden Markov models. In: Gelbukh, A., Reyes-Garcia, C.A. (eds.) MICAI 2006. LNCS (LNAI), vol. 4293, pp. 622–631. Springer, Heidelberg (2006)

10. Garg, A., Rahalkar, R., Upadhyaya, S., Kwiat, K.: Profiling users in GUI based systems masquerade detection. In: 2006 IEEE Information Assurance Workshop, pp. 48–54. IEEE Computer Society Press (June 2006)

11. Weiss, A., Ramapanicker, A., Shah, P., Noble, S., Immohr, L.: Mouse movements biometric identification: A feasibility study. In: Student/Faculty Research Day. CSIS, Pace University, pp. 1–8 (May 2007)

12. Messerman, A., Mustafic, T., Camtepe, S., Albayrak, S.: Continuous and non-intrusive identity verification in real-time environments based on free-text keystroke dynamics. In: Proceedings of the International Joint Conference on Biometrics, IJCB 2011, pp. 1–8. IEEE Computer Society Press (October 2011)

13. Song, Y., Ben-Salem, M., Hershkop, S., Stolfo, S.: System level user behavior biometrics using fisher features and gaussian mixture models. In: Security and Privacy Workshops, SPW 2013, pp. 52–59. IEEE Computer Society Press (May 2013)

14. Denning, D.E.: An intrusion-detection model. IEEE Transactions on Software Engineering 13(2), 222–232 (1987)

15. Schonlau, M.: Masquerading user data (Matthias Schonlau's home page) (1998), http://www.schonlau.net

16. Maxion, R., Townsend, T.: Masquerade detection using truncated command lines. In: Proceedings of the International Conference on Dependable Systems and Networks, DSN 2002, vol. 600, pp. 219–228. EEE Computer Society Press (June 2002)

17. Maxion, R.: Masquerade detection using enriched command lines. In: Proceedings of the International Conference on Dependable Systems and Networks, DSN 2003, vol. 22, pp. 5–14. IEEE Computer Society Press (June 2003)

18. gGreenberg, S.: Using Unix: Collected traces of 168 users. Technical Report 88/333/45, Department of Computer Science, University of Calgary (1988)

19. Salem, M.B., Hershkop, S., Stolfo, S.J.: A survey of insider attack detection research. In: Stolfo, S.J., Bellovin, S.M., Hershkop, S., Keromytis, A., Sinclair, S., Smith, S.W. (eds.) Insider Attack and Cyber Security: Beyond the Hacker. Advances in Information Security, pp. 69–90. Springer (2008)

20. Bertacchini, M., Fierens, P.: A survey on masquerader detection approaches. In: Proceedings of V Congreso Iberoamericano de Seguridad Informática, CIBSI 2009. Universidad de la República de Uruguay, pp. 46–60 (November 2009)

21. Jha, S., Tan, K.M., Maxion, R.A.: Markov chains, classifiers, and intrusion detection. In: Proceedings of the 14th IEEE Computer Security Foundations Workshop, CSFW 2001, pp. 206–219. IEEE Computer Society Press (June 2001)

22. Killourhy, K., Maxion, R.: Comparing anomaly-detection algorithms for keystroke dynamics. In: Proceedings of the International Conference on Dependable Systems Networks, DSN 2009, pp. 125–134. IEEE Computer Society Press (June 2009)

Poster Abstract: Forensically Extracting Encrypted Contents from Stego-Files Using NTFS Artefacts

Niall McGrath

Abstract. The research presents a method of investigating encrypted stego-files. The paper characterizes the encryption and steganography processes by establishing an event sequence signature based on the sequence of syscalls on the associated files. The syscall sequences are formally modelled and this provided the basis of implementing a successful search solution.

Introduction and Scope

Steganography with encryption is being used to commit fraud, terrorist activities and other illegal acts. It is has been demonstrated that there is a trend where it is used for the possession, storage and transmission of child pornography. Other illegal activity would include financial fraud, industrial espionage and communication within criminal or terrorist organizations. It is a fact that there is currently no tool or technique available to facilitate the investigation of stego-files with encryption. This is the research problem we are trying to solve here.

This research does not identify or detect the stego-files, this is already done by using contemporary stego-detection and analysis techniques implemented by the tools available. Embedded content is extracted by using contemporary stego-analysis techniques. The extraction of encrypted content in the stego-files is the focus here.

Materials and Methods

The stego-process was monitored to view the flow of IRPs between various applications and the NTFS driver. The file I/O events where classified into groups of event-types and from this we were able form event sequence signatures which were modeled formally. A performance-measure of the methodology's true-postive/false-positive rate was established which was achieved by following the Receiver Operator Characteristic statistical analysis method. The following tools were used in this research: Python 2.7.5, AccessData FTK Imager 2.5.1, WinHex 16.2 3, Process Monitor and MS FSUTIL.

Results and Conclusion

From the results of the ROC analysis it can be seen that the methodology yielded an excellent performance measure. The Null Hypothesis is completely rejected and this

A. Stavrou et al. (Eds.): RAID 2014, LNCS 8688, pp. 466–468, 2014.
© Springer International Publishing Switzerland 2014

proves that the methodology to be more powerful than a random rule. The outcome of this work is a formal methodology, which has been validated, and performance tested. The research problem has been solved. The modeling of the initial problem and back-tracking solution served as a basis for automating the methodology with Python. The methodology was proven to be compatible and interoperable with all tested types of encryption and steganography formats.

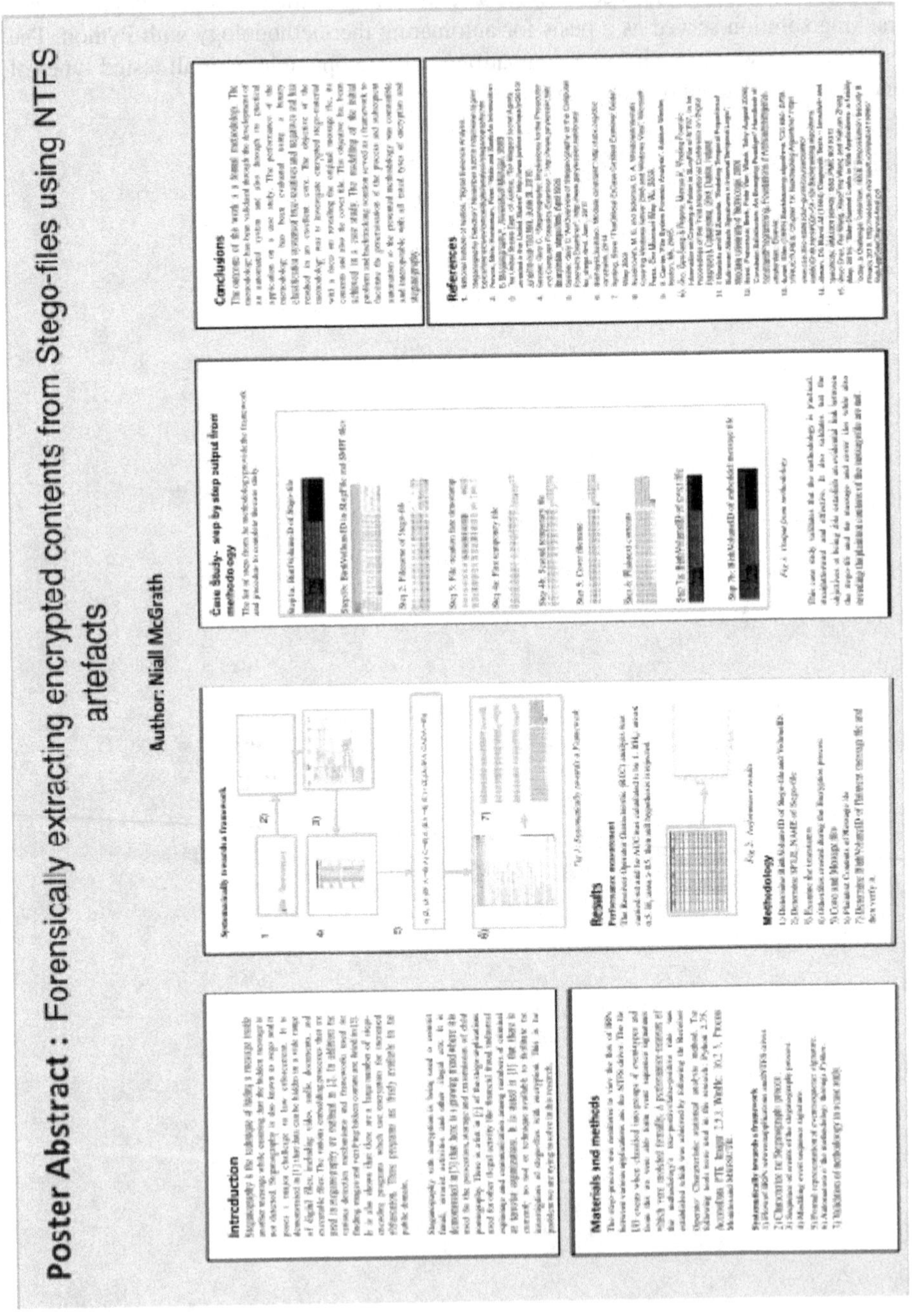

Poster Abstract : Forensically extracting encrypted contents from Stego-files using NTFS artefacts

Author: Niall McGrath

Introduction

Materials and methods

Systematically towards a Framework

Fig 1. Systematically towards a Framework

Results

Performance measurement

Fig 2. Performance results

Methodology

Case Study - step by step output from methodology

Fig 3. Output from methodology

Conclusions

References

Poster Abstract: Economic Denial of Sustainability (EDoS) Attack in the Cloud Using Web-Bugs

Armin Slopek[1,2] and Natalija Vlajic[1]

[1] Department of Electrical Engineering and Computer Science, York University, Toronto, Canada
[2] Department of Computer Science, Hochschule Bonn-Rhein-Sieg, St. Augustin, Germany
aslopek@yorku.ca, vlajic@cse.yorku.ca

Keywords: EDoS attack, Cloud, web-bugs, spam-email.

Introduction. Recently, a new form of security attack targeting Cloud-hosted web-sites/domains has been introduced ([1], [2]). In [1] this attack has been referred to as Economic Denial of Sustainability (EDoS) attack, while in [2] it is termed Fraudulent Resource Consumption (FRC) attack. From the technical, i.e., execution, point of view this attack appears as a version of low-volumetric application-layer DDoS attack. However, unlike its DDoS counterpart, EDoS attack does not aim to exhaust the victim's bandwidth or processing capability. Instead, the main goal of EDoS attack is to impose a significant financial burden on the victim through skillful and measured consumption of the victim's metered (pay-as-you-go) bandwidth. Small and medium size businesses, with limited web-hosting budgets, are the primary targets of EDoS attacks. As demonstrated in [3], even a simple non-intentional version of EDoS could result in monthly costs/losses in the order of tens of thousands of dollars.

Motivation. From the attacker's perspective, the most straightforward way to conduct an EDoS attack is by means of a custom-built or a rented botnet capable of executing application-layer DDoS [4]. (Examples of such botnets include: Dirt Jumper [5], BlackEnergy [6], WebHive [7], etc..) However, the main disadvantage of botnet-based EDoS/DDoS attacks – especially the ones that involve rented botnets – is the fact that they utilize the same family of compromised (bot-hosting) computers that might have been used in a number of previous attacks. For such computers, there is a high chance of their IP addresses already been identified as 'malicious' and publicly blacklisted. This would, in turn, result in a considerably reduced attack potential for the respective botnet ([8], [9]), and a considerably diminished overall payoff for the attacker.

A much more challenging (i.e., difficult to detect and thwart) variant of EDoS attack would assume the deployment of uncompromised computers - computers not infected by any form of malware and thus not publicly blacklisted. In other words, given that EDoS attack is conducted at the application-layer utilizing HTTP-based attack traffic, its most potent execution would be conducted by means of web-browsers of legitimate/trustworthy users.

A. Stavrou et al. (Eds.): RAID 2014, LNCS 8688, pp. 469–472, 2014.
© Springer International Publishing Switzerland 2014

Related Work. [10] is the first known study to discuss the possibility of deploying web-browsers of legitimate users for the purpose of application-layer DDoS. Namely, the authors of [10] propose that in order to conduct an application-layer DDoS attack, a set of HTML/JavaScript commands get embedded into a web-page of a high-traffic and otherwise legitimate web-site. The commands should not have any obvious visual manifestation - their sole purpose would be to instruct a browser to load objects from the target (victim) server. Put another way, every visitation/upload of such a site by a legitimate user/browser would result in one or multiple HTTP requests being sent towards the victim server.

Recently, in [11], a real-world implementation of the concepts from [10] and their consequent practical implications have been documented. The novelty of the work described in [11] is in the fact that the 'malicious' JavaScript commands were hidden in a skillfully crafted Web-Ad, which was then distributed to thousands of legitimate users through a known Ad Network.

Goal. The goal of our work is to investigate the technical feasibility of using spam-email with Web-bugs in order to engage the browsers of legitimated users in an EDoS attack. (Web bugs are small, usually invisible, HTML objects embedded in a web-page or an email, and are traditionally used for the purposes of user tracking and web analytics.) Note, though, that unlike the traditional Web-bugs, which cause HTTP-GET requests to be sent towards a legitimate user-tracking server, in our work these requests are directed towards the server targeted by the EDoS. To our knowledge, our work is the first one to look at the possibility of executing an EDoS attack using spam-email with Web-bugs, as well as to evaluate the overall pros and cons of such an execution for the attacker.

Method. A Web-bug embedded in a spam-email will successfully generate an HTTP-GET request only if the following three are satisfied: 1) the (HTML-enabeled) email tool does not quarantine the carrier spam-email; 2) the human recipient opens the carrier email; 3.a) the (HTML-enabeled) email tool automatically executes the embedded Web-bug code or 3.b) the human recipient is tricked into manually activating the embedded Web-bug code (e.g., through social engineering).

In our experimental study, we have looked at five different versions of Web-bug codes and five different HTML-enabled email tools (including Google, Hotmail and Yahoo), in order to determine the scenarios in which 1) and 3.a) successfully take place. Furthermore, we have employed 300 email addresses (i.e., email recipients) in order to determine the success rate of 2) and 3.b). The 'test' server targeted by our EDoS attack was set up on Amazon S3 Cloud.

Preliminary Results. The results of our study have shown that: a) EDoS using spam-mail with Web-bugs is a technically viable option; b) The overall attack potential of this approach (in terms of financial loss incurred by the victim) is in the low to modest range; c) Compared to the traditional execution scenarios involving botnets, EDoS using spam-mail with Web-bugs is financially far more affordable for the attacker while being increasingly more difficult to defend for the victim.

References

[1] Sqalli, M.H., Al-Haidari, F., Salah, K.: EDoS-Shield – A Two-Step Mitigation Technique against EDoS Attacks in Cloud Computing. In: 4th IEEE International Conference on Utility and Cloud Computing (UCC), Victoria, Austraila, pp. 49–56 (December 2011)

[2] Idziorek, J., Tannian, M., Jacobson, D.: The Insecurity of Cloud Utility Models. IEEE IT Professional Magazine 15(2), 22–27 (2013)

[3] (April 2012), http://www.behind-the-enemy-lines.com/2012/04/google-attack-how-i-self-attacked.html

[4] Manky, D.: Cybercrime as a service: A very modern business. Elsevier Computer Fraud & Security Journal 2013(6), 9–13 (2013)

[5] Andrade, M.M., Vlajic, N.: Dirt Jumper: A key player in today's botnet-for-DDoS market. In: IEEE World Congress on Internet Security (WorldCIS 2012), Guelph, Canada, pp. 239–244 (June 2012)

[6] (February 2011), https://blogs.mcafee.com/business/security-connected/evolving-ddos-botnets-1-blackenergy

[7] (April 2014), https://blogs.akamai.com/2014/04/cloudification-of-web-ddos-attacks.html

[8] Stone-Gross, B., Holz, T., Stringhini, G., Vigna, G.: The Underground Economy of Spam: A Botmaster's Perspective of Coordinating Large-Scale Spam Campaigns. In: 4th Usenix Workshop on Large-Scale Exploits and Emergent Threats, Boston (March 2011)

[9] Tringhini, G., Hohlfeld, O., Kreugel, C., Vigna, G.: The Harvester, the Botmaster, and the Spammer: On the Relations Between the Different Actors in the Spam Landscape. In: 9th ACM Symposium on Information, Computer and Communications Security (ASIACCS 2014), Kyoto, Japan, pp. 353–364 (June 2014)

[10] Antonatos, S., Akritidis, P., Lam, V.T., Anagnostakis, K.G.: Puppetnets: Misusing Web Browsers as a Distributed Attack Infrastructure. ACM Transactions on Information and Systems Security (TISSEC), 12(2) (December 2008)

[11] (August 2013), https://media.blackhat.com/us-13/us-13-Grossman-Million-Browser-Botnet.pdf

Economic Denial of Sustainability (EDoS) Attack in the Cloud Using Web-Bugs

1,2 Armin Slopek, 1 Natalija Vlajic

1 Department of Computer Science and Engineering, York University, Toronto, Canada
2 Department of Computer Science, Hochschule Bonn-Rhein-Sieg, St. Augustin, Germany

YORK UNIVERSITY

Introduction

How EDoS Attack Works

- victim is a web-server hosted in the Cloud
- attacking bots send legitimate looking HTTP requests
- like application-layer DDoS, but "slow and low" to avoid detection

EDoS Attack Objectives

- affecting QoS is not intended; instead ...
- goal is to impose long-term financial burden through skillful consumption of victim's pay-as-you-go bandwidth
- eventually, Cloud (Web) hosting becomes unprofitable

Problems of Botnet-Based EDoS Faced by the Attacker

- botnet must be either custom-built or rented
  a) custom-built botnet - less common
  - non-trivial and time-consuming to set-up
  - questionable success of bot-recruitment phase
  b) rented botnet - more common
  - $ cost may be very high, if botnet needed over longer period of time
  - same family of bot-hosting computers may have been used in previous attacks ⇒ high chance of blacklisting ⇒ diminished attack effectiveness

Alternatives to Botnet-Based EDoS (Related Work)

- employ web clients of legitimate users by injecting malicious code in a popular web-site
  - malicious code instructs browsers of visiting users to load objects from the 3rd party victim/target server
  - concept known as puppetnet
- 2013 real-world example: Million Browser Botnet
  - puppetnet formed through use of malicious Web-Ads

EDoS using Web-bugs

Goal of Our Work

- devise/examine a new type of EDoS attack that does not require use of botnets, and as such:
  - reduces cost of EDoS
  - is effective against blacklisting (i.e., harder to thwart)
- Web-bugs - small/invisible HTML objects embedded in a web-page of an email
  - traditionally used for user tracking and web analytics

- proposed EDoS attack: use email spam with Web-bugs to engage browsers of legitimate users in sending valid-looking HTTP requests towards the victim

- conditions required to activate an 'attack Web-bug':
  1) Webmail/email tool does not quarantine the spam email
  2) user opens the spam email
  3.a) email tool automatically executes Web-bug code, or
  3.b) user is tricked into manually activating Web-bug code through social engineering

Our Methodology & Results

Different Types of Examined Web-Bugs

- Image within an HTML image tag
- Image within an HTML iframe
- whole website incl. all elements within an HTML iframe
- pdf file within an HTML iframe
- JavaScript

Our Web-bugs in Different Webmail Tools

Type	img tag	img frame	page frame	pdf frame	JS frame	JavaScript	plain text
GMAIL	O	O	X	X	X	X	O
YAHOO	O	O	O	O	X	X	O
HOTMAIL	O	O	O	O	X	X	O
GMX	O	O	O	O	X	X	O
web.de	O	O	O	O	X	X	O

img tag - simplest and most successful Web-bug!

Gmail Image Proxy Technology

- introduced in December 2013
- images automatically uploaded by Gmail Image Proxy
  - aims to protect user privacy & enhance user experience
- perfect storm for our EDoS attack using Web-bugs

Experimental Setup: Victim Side

- main server on Amazon S3 Cloud
- back-up server in our department
- log-info saved on each server
  - HTTP-request ID
  - HTTP-request time-stamp
  - IP of requesting machine

Experimental Setup: Attacker Side

- 2 batches of spam/test email (300 emails total) sent
  - one on weekend - Feb 15, 2014
  - one during week - Feb 19, 2014
  - (20 emails to each of 5 free Webmail providers) x 2
  - (50 emails to CS Professors in Canada and US) x 2
- all email addresses were collected manually and semi-randomly off the Internet
  - to comply with Canadian/US Anti-Spam Laws

Experimental Results: % of Opened Emails and Successfully Activated Web-bugs

Results on weekend
incl. duplicates due
to email reopening

Results during week
incl. duplicates due
to email reopening

- 15 overall requests in total – 15%
- 2 overall requests from Yahoo – 10%
- 12 overall requests from Profs – 25%

- 27 overall requests in total – 18%
- 3 overall requests from Gmail – 15%
- 24 overall requests from Profs – 48%

Analytical Results: Attack Effectiveness

equations to compute $ cost of attack imposed on victim

# of activated Web-bugs: $A = N \cdot S$

N: # of spam mails sent
S: success rate - % of opened emails (HTTP-GET requests)

cost per e-mail: $\frac{\$}{mail} = \frac{GB}{mail} \cdot \frac{\$}{GB} + \frac{bugs}{email} \cdot \frac{\$}{request}$

cost per attack: $\$ = A \cdot \frac{\$}{mail}$

$ cost of attack for victim hosted on Amazon S3 Cloud

$Amazon \frac{\$}{GB} = \frac{\$0.085}{GB}$ $Amazon \frac{\$}{request} = \frac{\$0.004}{10,000 \; requests}$

Attack assumptions:
- each Web-bug requests a 2kB≈0.002GB image
- 1,000,000 spam mails sent over a prolonged interval of time

total $/DoS cost imposed on victim	S=15%	S=20%	S=25%	S=30%
10 Web-bugs per email	$295	$340	$425	$510
25 Web-bugs per email	$595	$890	$1082.5	$1275
100 Web-bugs per email	$2550	$3400	$4250	$5100

Poster Abstract: CITRIN: Extracting Adversaries Strategies Hidden in a Large-Scale Event Log

Satomi Honda, Yuki Unno, Koji Maruhashi,
Masahiko Takenaka, and Satoru Torii

FUJITSU LABORATORIES LTD.,
4-1-1, Kamikodanaka, Nakahara-ku, Kawasaki, Kanagawa, 211-8588, Japan

Keywords: Log Analysis, IDS log, Graph-mining.

1 Extended Abstract

In recent years, attacks on network systems become not only increase but also strategic. In many cases, attacks with high strategies are consist of different attack events as port scanning, brute force attacks, injecting malicious codes and so on. It is difficult to detect such strategical attacks with only conventional ways. Analyzing event logs like intrusion detection system(IDS) logs give great knowledge about adversaries' strategies to security analysts. Those logs include fragments of adversaries' strategies that consist of well-known attack events.

In extracting adversaries' strategies from a large-scale event log, the significant relations should be picked up from all existing combinations of factors. Most current analyses of relations are started from searching common IP addresses and applying anomaly detection techniques. In those classical analyses, the viewpoint is predefined and static. However, to counter the advanced attacks with high strategies, security analysts must start their analyses from searching all available factors worth analyzing their relations. In many cases, their work is with heuristic ways and cumbersome.

In this paper, we propose CITRIN, a graph-based analyzing method for extracting the relations in a large-scale event log. CITRIN enables the security analysts to grasp the multiple relations among individual attack events. By introducing the graph-based techniques with visualization, security analysts can accelerate the speed of searching available factors. In our approach, the records in the event log are clustered into subsets of records with similar attribute values based on information theory. The subsets of the records are represented as undirected graphs that consists of nodes and edges.

We also show the potentiality of extracting adversaries' strategies by our graph-based approach. We apply CITRIN to our actual IDS log from multiple sites. From the visualized graphs, we pick up a graph with unique shape. A graphical representation of connected records shows that host scanning is included in the subset of records that includes a kind of stealthy and distributed brute force attacks. As a result of our detailed analysis, we lead the basic adversaries' strategy, *scanning before attack*.

A. Stavrou et al. (Eds.): RAID 2014, LNCS 8688, pp. 473–474, 2014.
© Springer International Publishing Switzerland 2014

CITRIN: Extracting Adversaries Strategies Hidden in a Large-Scale Event Log

Satomi Honda, Yuki Unno, Koji Maruhashi, Masahiko Takenaka and Satoru Torii

FUJITSU LABORATORIES LTD.

Introduction

- Attacks on network systems become strategic
- Analyzing IDS logs gives great knowledge about adversaries' strategies
- Security analysts must search all available factors

> Analyzing logs is Cumbersome!

Our Approach

- A graph-based analyzing method for extracting the relations in a large-scale event log
- Security analysts can grasp the multiple relations among individual attack events
- Based on information theory, the event log are clustered into subsets of records

Extracting Adversaries' Strategies

- The subsets of records are visualized as undirected graphs
- From our actual IDS log, we lead the basic adversaries' strategy, *scanning before attack*

Source IP   Destination IP

Port   Information

Secure Shell Brute Force (Port 22)

Host Scanning (Port 22)

> A relationship between host scanning and brute force attacks!

The visualized subset of a kind of distributed brute force attacks

Our Analyzing Process

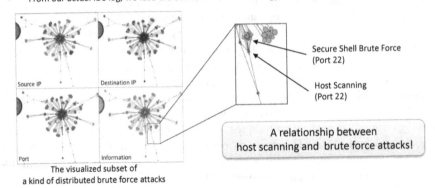

The visualized subsets

The IDS log

The subsets

xxxx, a.a.a.a, 22
y.y.y, b.b.b.b, 80

Clustering into subsets based on information theory

Visualizing the subsets as undirected graph*

The nodes represent unique records of a subset

The color variation depends on the values of attributes

*We visualize the subsets with graph analyzing software, *Gephi* (http://gephi.github.io/)

Poster Abstract: On Security Monitoring of Mobile Networks – Future Threats and Leveraging of Network Information

Michael Liljenstam, Prajwol Kumar Nakarmi, Oscar Ohlsson, and John Mattsson

Ericsson, Security Research, Stockholm, Sweden
{michael.liljenstam,prajwol.kumar.nakarmi,oscar.ohlsson,
john.mattsson}@ericsson.com

This work in progress explores security monitoring and protection technology specifically geared towards mobile network infrastructure. This includes both data correlation and presentation aspects of Security Information and Event Management (SIEM), as well as protection functions specifically for mobile networks – in this case, a proof-of-concept function to protect the control plane from a potential future threat of malicious signaling over the air interface. A second use case scenario concerns detection of smartphone malware for premium service charging fraud.

The emergence of open source baseband software [1] makes intentionally malicious air interface signaling a possibility [2]. Although nodes are already engineered for high availability and robustness, it nevertheless raises the question of whether some additional layer of protection could be justified. We have developed a proof-of-concept for the functional aspects of a flexible protection function for the GSM CS domain, conceptually similar to an IPS or ALG, to explore this question; and tested it against simulated examples of two types of DoS attacks. The first type is malformed or out-of-sequence signaling and the second type is flooding for resource exhaustion. The proof-of-concept operates on the RR and, parts of, RSL protocol layers to protect the BSC and is situated on the Abis interface, between the BTS and the BSC. The intention is to provide additional facilities for a quick response in case of an incident through the deployment of new protection rules.

The second type of scenario considered concerns malware. One way of monetizing malware for smartphones is through premium service fraud (see e.g., [3] p. 13). Existing solutions typically either monitor charges, e.g., Fraud Management Systems (FMS) or try to detect the malware (device- or network-based). As a first step in studying the possibility of leveraging more information from the network towards finding subscriber threats, we demonstrate correlation of indications from user plane traffic with simulated input from an FMS.

References

1. Welte, H., Markgraf, S.: Running your own GSM stack on a phone - Introducing Project Osmo-comBB (December 2010),
   http://events.ccc.de/congress/2010/Fahrplan/events/3952.en.html
2. Grugq, Base Jumping – Attacking the GSM baseband and base station (July 2010),
   https://media.blackhat.com/bh-ad-10/Grugq/BlackHat-AD-2010-Gurgq-Base-Jumping-slides.pdf

A. Stavrou et al. (Eds.): RAID 2014, LNCS 8688, pp. 475–476, 2014.
© Springer International Publishing Switzerland 2014

3. McAfee, McAfee Labs Threats Report Q4 2013 (March 2014),
   http://www.mcafee.com/sg/resources/reports/
   rp-quarterly-threat-q4-2013.pdf

ON SECURITY MONITORING OF MOBILE NETWORKS
FUTURE THREATS AND LEVERAGING OF NETWORK INFORMATION

Michael Liljenstam, Prajwol Kumar Nakarmi, Oscar Ohlsson, John Mattsson
Security Research, Ericsson

MOTIVATION

Mobile network infrastructure security is drawing increasing attention, while much of the work on tools and methods for network security focuses on enterprise environments, for instance when it comes to commercially available solutions for Security Information and Event Management (SIEM) and security functions deployed in the network. In this work we specifically address the production network of service providers, and in particular focus on mobile networks.

Research Questions

Addressing service provider environments, questions explored include:

- Technical gaps for monitoring mobile network infrastructure?
- New protection functions for mobile networks, or new ways to leverage network data for protection of subscribers?

Initially, these questions are explored for two scenarios:

i. Modified terminals are used to generate malicious signaling to disturb the network and the service
ii. Smartphone malware is used to perpetrate premium service charging fraud, e.g., by generating SMS messages to a premium number

PROTECTING THE CONTROL PLANE

Threat Landscape

Recent additions to the threat landscape from the air interface side relate to accessibility of Software Defined Radio (SDR) coupled with open source software to interact also with the control plane of the network.

The availability of these tools open up for the possibility of experimentation with malicious signaling behaviors against the network.

The figure to the right illustrates such possibilities. Currently the tools are limited to GSM, but it is reasonable to believe similar tools will emerge also for later generation systems.

Potential attacks
- Sending malformed signaling messages that upon interpretation by the target node causes system crash
- Flooding attacks (resource exhaustion attacks)

Infrastructure nodes are already built for high availability and robustness, but could it be justified to add an additional layer of protection?

Concept & Challenges

The idea explored here is the possible addition of a flexible protection function, using misuse-based detection and mitigation of threats – i.e., conceptually similar to an intrusion Prevention System or Application Layer Gateway, but for radio signaling protocols. The value provided is the possibility of a faster response through the application of a protection rule than the development and application of a product patch.

The challenges involved in creating such a protection function include:

- Protocol differences in mobile network control plane protocols compared to TCP/IP, for instance in terms of session tracking and how response actions can be taken.
- Finding the right balance between flexibility and performance

A Proof-of-Concept for GSM CS domain has been developed to demonstrate functional aspects.

- Misuse-based detection
  - describe rules to detect violations

Implementation & Evaluation

Functional tests for simulated attack instances of the two types of attacks previously mentioned: malformed/out-of-sequence messages and flooding

- Simulated attacks using OsmocomBB + own modifications
  - Use cases:
    - Protection against "unexpected message"
    - Rate limiting protection for some forms of the resource request flooding case

Example rule code for unexpected message case

```
signature classmark-enquiry-sig {
    rr-msg=type rr-cm-enqu
}

signature unexpected-funreq {
    requires-reverse-signature classmark-enquiry-sig
    rr-msg=type 0x44
    error "GSM Request following GSM Classmark Enquiry"
    firewall drop-channel
}
```

Conclusions and future work

Functional tests were performed to block the simulated malformed sequence attack, and to mitigate certain forms of the flooding attack.

Future work includes further study of the performance aspects of introducing this type of function, primarily meeting latency constraints, and how the function could be integrated into existing nodes where this is necessary due to encryption.

NETWORK INFORMATION FOR DETECTION OF SUBSCRIBER MALWARE

Explore additional sources of information beyond user plane DPI.

User Plane Inspection

Relatively simple approach, based on reputation feeds

- Primarily, network reputation: IP and domain reputation
- Secondary, file reputation of downloads

Additional Network Information

A first example explored here is

- Correlation with information about charging, for instance from a Fraud Management System / Fraud Detection System monitoring for abnormal charging patterns

SIEM correlates

- Sequences of events from user plane traffic inspection indicative of subscriber device malware infection: visit to suspect web site, download of untrusted app, outbound connections to suspected malware control site. WiFi/VPN access was used for demonstrator implementation. In a real deployment the function would reside on Gi/SGi interface or in Gateway node.

- Cross-correlation of user plane-based indications and events from fraud detection system based on charging data. (Lacking access to a charging system, fraud events were simulated in demonstrator implementation.)

Poster Abstract: Data Leakage Detection Algorithm Based on Sequences of Activities

César Guevara, Matilde Santos, and Victoria López

Complutense University of Madrid
Madrid, Spain
{cesargue,msantos}@ucm.es, vlopez@fdi.ucm.es

Abstract. In this paper we propose an algorithm for data leakage detection. This algorithm works with historical data of the activities of authorized users in a computer system. This information gathers data of the hour of the accesses, duration, day of the week, operation, table that has been accessed, etc. They have been provided by a governmental institution at Ecuador. The procedure has two phases. The first one is based on the calculation of the probability of each activity that is carried out by each user. These activities are for instance to modify a file, delete, copy, etc. The different activities at different times are codified by an integer or character. The Page Rank algorithm is used to calculate the probability of every activity. But the activities form sequences, that is, during a session (time between the user logs in and logs out), the user carries out different activities, one after another. These sequences of activities may have different length. The probability of each sequence of activities is then calculated by applying the Bayes' theorem. The minimum of these conditional probabilities is obtained and set as a threshold, r_{min}. If a new chain of activities, s_i, is introduced in the detection leakage system, first of all the page rank is applied and then the Bayes' law, so a probability of that particular sequence of activities for that user is obtained, let's say p_i. This probability, p_i, is compared to the threshold, r_{min}. If it does not surpass it, a leakage warning message is generated. Otherwise, the sequence of activities goes to the second phase of the procedure. The sequence of activities that is being tested is then compared to all the sequences of activities of that particular user that are stored in the historical database. Applying the Smith and Waterman algorithm, a similarity score is obtained for this sentence regarding the rest of the sequences previously carried out by the user. This algorithm determines similar regions between two strings comparing segments of all possible lengths and optimizes the similarity measure. If the score is higher than a second threshold, let' say that there are more than n characters (codified activities) that are the same than another sequence of the same user, the activity can be considered right; otherwise it may be a leakage. Although this algorithm is still being developing, its main contribution is the way it handles different lengths of the sequences and how it works with a behavioral pattern of each user.

Keywords: Data Leakage Detection, Page Rank algorithm, Bayes' Theorem, Smith and Waterman algorithm, behavioral pattern.

A. Stavrou et al. (Eds.): RAID 2014, LNCS 8688, pp. 477–478, 2014.
© Springer International Publishing Switzerland 2014

Poster Abstract: Data Leakage Detection Algorithm including Sequences of Activities

César Guevara (cesingu@ucm.es), Matilde Santos (msantos@ucm.es), Victoria López (vlopez@fdi.ucm.es)
Complutense University of Madrid. School of Computing, Department of Computer Architecture and Automatic Control
28040-Madrid,Spain

ABSTRACT

Information leakage is a current problem that worries institutions around the world. Data is one of the most important assets for an institution. Therefore it is important to design and implement computational tools in order to avoid leakage, loss or modification of crucial information. This problem is especially critical when data leakage is caused by authorized people.

In this paper we propose an algorithm for data leakage detection. The algorithm is based on the one hand on the probability of certain activities that authorized users usually do (such as modify a file, delete, copy, etc.). On the other hand, it also provides a ranking of similarity between the sequence of activities of particular users, that is, the frequency and order of these activities.

CURRENT SCENARIO (MATERIALS)

The public sector of the Republic of Ecuador, as any other government, has information systems of utmost importance. It is necessary to have an adequate control even of the authorized users' activities who have access to such information.

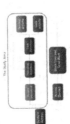

The information used in this study is the sequences of activities carried out by public servants who have authorized access to the governmental databases (modify a file, copy, insert, etc). This information gathers data of the hour of the accesses, duration, day of the week, operation, table that has been accessed, etc. It has been codified as a string of characters.

METHODS

- **Page Rank algorithm** allows us to obtain the probabilities of each of the activities undertaken by the users.
- **Bayes' Theorem** gives the conditional probability of a sequence of activities of a particular user.
- **Smith and Waterman algorithm** determines similar regions between two codified sequences of activities comparing segments of all possible lengths and giving a score.

USER BEHAVIOUR

The user behavior is dynamic and the number of activities during a session is variable

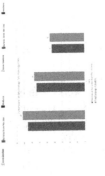

User Behaviour in a Computer System

Activities within a user session in a computer system has the following structure

ALGORITHM

Phase 1:

1) Page Rank: activity's probability $P_r(a_x)$

2) Bayes' Law: conditional probability of a sequence of activities of an user $P_r(s_x)$
   - Set a threshold as a minimum P_{min}

3) Evaluation of a new sequence of activities s_x
   - If $P_r(s_x) < r_{min}$ warning leakage otherwise go to Phase 2

Phase 2:

1) Smith & Waterman algorithm: score of similarity of that sequence $S(s_x)$
   - If $S(s_x) \geq O.T.$ warning leakage otherwise O.T.
   - If $S(s_x) < O.T.$ warning leakage otherwise

RESULTS

CONCLUSIONS

- The proposed algorithm handles different lengths of the sequences
- It works with a behavioral pattern of each user
- Preliminary results are encouraging

Poster Abstract: BPIDS - Using Business Model Specification in Intrusion Detection

João Lima[1], Nelson Escravana[1], and Carlos Ribeiro[2]

[1] INOV INESC Inovação - Instituto de Novas Tecnologias, Lisbon, Portugal
[2] INESC-ID, Instituto Superior Técnico, Universidade de Lisboa, Lisbon, Portugal

Problem Description and Goal. Despite the amount of research work developed in the area of intrusion detection, some effectiveness problems persist, either because the proposals are incapable of detecting new unidentified threats [1], or because they generate too many false alarms to be of any usefulness [1]. These problems have somehow hampered the application of intrusion detection systems to protect systems as those used by critical infrastructures, given their crucial need to be protected, also, from new threats, as well as due to the significant cost that false alarm handling might have [2].

The goal of this work is to, based on specification-based intrusion detection techniques, provide an IDS suitable to be used to increase the protection of critical infrastructures, featuring a negligible false-alarm rate and presenting simple and intuitive alert information.

Solution Description. The developed intrusion detection system is based on the description of the flow of activities carried by the monitored system's entities, i.e. the business processes, as well as the conditions that govern their execution, i.e. the business rules. The system features a centralized architecture, having multiple sensors monitoring either a given sub-network or some specific host, where each sensor is configured accordingly to the activities being executed by the hosts in its monitoring domain. The evidences captured from the distributed sensors are transformed into high-level, business process-related events. These high-level events are then analysed centrally against the specification of the acceptable behaviour and, if do not match, an alarm is raised.

Preliminary Results. The system was tested with data captured from a real-world mass transportation environment, as an instance of a critical infrastructure. The tests performed showed very promising results, by being able to detect new injected attacks, and exhibiting a negligible false alarm rate.

References

1. Axelsson, S.: The base-rate fallacy and the difficulty of intrusion detection. ACM Trans. Inf. Syst. Secur. 3, 186–205 (2000)
2. Mitchell, R., Chen, I.-R.: A survey of intrusion detection in wireless network applications. Comput. Commun. 42, 1–23 (2014)

A. Stavrou et al. (Eds.): RAID 2014, LNCS 8688, pp. 479–480, 2014.
© Springer International Publishing Switzerland 2014

BPIDS - Using business model specification in intrusion detection

João Lima[1], Nelson Escravana[1], Carlos Ribeiro[2]

[1]INOV Inesc Inovação, [2]INESC-ID, Instituto Superior Técnico, Universidade de Lisboa

MOTIVATION

Even though no major cyber attack has been reported to date, some attacks had already targeted Mass Transportation Infrastructures. Two examples of such attacks are an attack using a virus named Sobig that shut down the train signaling systems in Florida [1], and another attack in Poland where a boy, aged 14, de-railed four vehicles using a modified remote control [2]. Even though these attacks have not had severe consequences, they show how easy it is to cause major disturbances in MTIs. Moreover, the sensitive nature of these infrastructures and the evolving complexity and automation of the systems being deployed, while maintaining a lot of legacy systems, makes them increasingly susceptible to cyber attacks.

PROBLEM

Intrusion detection systems have been used for a while. It has faced effectiveness problems due to two main aspects:

- Incapability to detect new threats;
- Prohibitive amount of false alarms.

DETECTION PROCESS

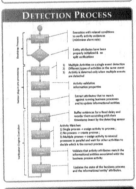

SOLUTION DESCRIPTION

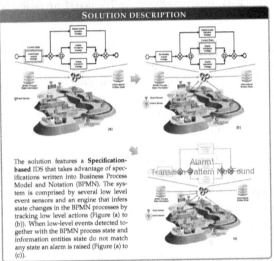

The solution features a **Specification-based** IDS that takes advantage of specifications written into Business Process Model and Notation (BPMN). The system is comprised by several low level event sensors and an engine that infers state changes in the BPMN processes by tracking low level event actions (Figure (a) to (b)). When low-level events detected together with the BPMN process state and information entities state do not match any state an alarm is raised (Figure (a) to (c)).

BPMN EXTENSION MODEL

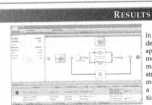

Business Processes are entities comprised by key attributes that uniquely identify each instance of a business process. **Informational Entities** are used to describe a real-world object that can be uniquely identified. **BPIDS Gateways** are extensions of the BPMN Gateways, with the code needed to verify the gateway condition. **BPIDS Activities** extend the BPMN Activity to extract information from it and to specify the conditions that must be met to infer the activity execution. **Business Rules** define the conditions that must be validated when some informational entity attribute is updated. **Hosts** entities represent the low level monitored entities. **Application Service** is defined as a set of operations implemented and executed by each Host that exposes it. **Activity Detection Sensor** element specifies the properties of the intrusion detection sensor being used.

REFERENCES

[1] Niland, M.:   Computer Virus Brings Down Train Signals.   http://www. informationweek.com/computer-virus-brings-down-train-signals/ d/d-id/1026461 (2003)

[2] Baker,   G.   Schoolboy hacks into city's tram system. http://www.telegraph.co.uk/news/worldnews/1575231/ Schoolboy-hacks-into-citys-tram-system.html (2008)

ACKNOWLEDGMENTS

This work was partially funded by the EU 7thFP project SECUR-ED.

www.secur-ed.eu

RESULTS

In order to assess the effectiveness of the developed intrusion detection system, we applied it to a demonstration environment, representative of part of a real-world mass transport infrastructure. The demonstration environment consisted of a multi-modal transportation terminal, combining a suburban railway station, a metro station, a ferryboat station and bus stops.

Poster Abstract: Highlighting Easily How Malicious Applications Corrupt Android Devices

Radoniaina Andriatsimandefitra and Valérie Viet Triem Tong

CIDRE research group,
SUPELEC
Avenue de la Boulaie, 35510 Cesson-Sévigné, France
{firstname.lastname}@supelec.fr

We propose an approach based on information flows to highlight how a malicious application corrupts an Android device. Basic attacks carried on by malicious applications often consist in leaking sensitive data to remote entities. Different works then focused on approaches to detect such attacks by analysing function calls or the access and the use of sensitive data (e.g [1,2]). However, there exist an other class of attack that threatens the integrity of the system itself or data it contains (e.g modification of the content of sensitive files or installation of new application). Such attacks tend to be overlooked and we propose here an approach to easily detect and highlight them.

To highlight these attacks, we first monitor how information from an application under analysis is disseminated in the whole system thanks to an information flow monitor named Blare [3]. Blare monitors information flow between system objects (process, file and socket) at system level and logs observed flow. From the log, we build a System Flow Graph [4] that describes the observed flows in a compact format. We then filter the edges of the SFG to only keep odd flows. As Android applications are all built in the same way, they have common behaviours, which means that some information flows they cause are the same (e.g information flow with the system_server process). By removing from the SFG the edges that describe information flows that are also present in SFG of benign applications, we therefore get the suspicious flows that can characterize an attack. We test our approach on 4 pieces of malware publicly known for corrupting Android devices and show that remaining edges of their SFGs describes the attack they are carrying.

References

1. Burguera, I., Zurutuza, U., Nadjm-Tehrani, S.: Crowdroid: Behavior-based malware detection system for android. In: SPSM 2011 (2011)
2. Enck, W., Gilbert, P., Chun, B.-G., Cox, L.P., Jung, J., McDaniel, P., Sheth, A.N.: Taintdroid: An information-flow tracking system for realtime privacy monitoring on smartphones. In: Proc. of the USENIX Symposium, OSDI (2010)
3. CIDRE: Blare, https://www.blare-ids.org
4. Andriatsimandetra, R., Viet Triem Tong, V., Mé, L. : Diagnosing intrusions in android operating system using system flow graph. In: Proceedings of WISG (2013)

A. Stavrou et al. (Eds.): RAID 2014, LNCS 8688, pp. 481–482, 2014.
© Springer International Publishing Switzerland 2014

Highlighting Easily How Malicious Applications Corrupt Android Devices

Radoniaina Andriatsimandefitra and Valérie Viêt Triêm Tông

CIDRE research group, SUPELEC/INRIA, Rennes, FRANCE

Goal

Discover quickly how a device was corrupted
- Monitor information flows involving data from applications under analysis
- Filter these flows to uncover the suspicious ones

Blare an information flow monitor

- Monitors information flow between system objects (process, file and socket) thanks to tainting
- Developed as a Linux Security Module
- Uses LSM hooks to intercept syscalls and observes information flows
- Logs any information flow involving tainted data (hard to analyse as its size grows quickly)

System Flow Graph

- Describes in a compact and more human readable way the information flows logged by Blare
- Directed graph $G = (V, E)$
- Each node represents a system object and has 3 attributes: type, name and identifier
- Each edge e from node $v1$ to node $v2$ represents a unique information flow between the system objects that $v1$ and $v2$ represent

Idea

Android applications share some common behaviours as they are built in the same way. Therefore, some of the information flows caused by Android applications are common between them. For instance, they all exchange data with the system_server process.

Approach

- Tag the .apk of the Android application to be analysed
- Monitor and logs how information from this application is disseminated thanks to Blare
- Build the corresping SFG
- Filter the edges of the SFG to keep only edges that we do not see in SFGs of benign applications

Experiments

- Malware : DroidKungFu1, DroidKungFu2, jSMSHider and BadNews
- Benign applications : 7 applications from Google Play

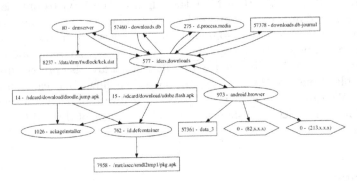

Figure : An excerpt from the filtered SFG of a Bad News sample

Contact: firstname.lastname@supelec.fr

Poster Abstract: Improving Intrusion Detection on SSL/TLS Channels by Classifying Certificates[*]

Zigang Cao[1,2], Gang Xiong[2], Zhen Li[2], and Li Guo[2]

[1] Beijing University of Posts and Telecommunications, Beijing, China
[2] Institute of Information Engineering, Chinese Academy of Sciences, Beijing, China
xionggang@iie.ac.cn

Abstract. There is no doubt that SSL/TLS is playing a very important role in today's Internet security. However, cyber criminals are making use of the encryption merit meanwhile to evade security inspections, posing a big challenge to intrusion detection systems. In view of this, we present a scheme to screen the evil SSL/TLS channels from massive network connections into a much smaller set by classifying server certificates. Combined with other information such as certificate attributes and visit counts, malicious connections can be further identified. Compared with the statistical methods based on packet length, burst bytes or packet intervals, ours is more suitable for large data sets, offering a new practical perspective for SSL/TLS intrusion detection.

1   Our Work

In our measurement, we found that among billions of SSL connections in the real world, only a very small number of server certificates account for most of the total visits. Thus, we propose to identify malicious SSL sessions by certificate classification, through which the majority of innocent connections can be excluded firstly, so the evil can be further dug out of the left much smaller set.

First, we categorize the certificates into popular certificates and normal ones, of which the former appear the most frequently and they are marked as good. Then, the normal ones are further divided into the valid and the invalid. A certificate is valid only if it can be verified successfully. Afterwards, the valid are further sorted by validation type into extended validation, organization validation, and domain validation (DV), of which the DV is not secure enough. And the invalid are classified into three sub classes, namely the forged, the self-signed and others, in which "forged" means that the signature is invalid, and "self-signed" means it is a self-made root certificate.

After classification, evil SSL conversations can be further identified out of the valid DV certificates and invalid ones largely, especially the forged and the self-signed. Experiment results on a campus network show that our scheme is able to identify forged popular certificates easily without verification or any feature signatures, just by certificate appearing counts and subject item comparison.

---

[*] Supported by the National Science and Technology Support Program (No. 2012BAH46B02, No. 2012BAH45B01); the National High Technology Research and Development Program (863 Program) of China (No. 2011AA010703).

A. Stavrou et al. (Eds.): RAID 2014, LNCS 8688, pp. 483–484, 2014.
© Springer International Publishing Switzerland 2014

Improving intrusion detection on SSL/TLS channels by classifying certificates

Zigang Cao[1,2], Gang Xiong[2], Zhen Li[2], and Li Guo[2]

[1](Beijing University of Posts and Telecommunications, China)

[2](Institute of Computing Technology, Chinese Academy of Sciences, China)

xionggang@iie.ac.cn

ABSTRACT

There is no doubt that SSL/TLS is playing a very important role in today's Internet security. However, cyber criminals are making use of the encryption merit meanwhile to evade security inspections, posing a big challenge to intrusion detection systems (IDS) since encryption makes it difficult to distinguish between malicious and innocent by feature-based techniques. In view of this, we present a scheme to screen the evil SSL/TLS channels from massive network connections into a much smaller set by classifying server certificates appearing in the handshake phase. Combined with other information such as certificate attributes and visit counts, malicious connections can be further identified. Compared with the statistical methods based on packet length, burst bytes or packet intervals, ours is more suitable for large data sets and dispenses with training. The identity based scheme offers a new practical perspective for SSL intrusion detection.

INTRODUCTION

SSL/TLS is widely used today in web browsing, web mail, E-commerce, and protecting personal privacy against abused network surveillance. However, it is used for malicious communications of attacks and malwares such as Trojan and botnet. As for SSL intrusion detection, traditional signature-based methods fails since the data encryption makes the original plaintext signatures invisible. Statistical methods make use of flow or packet attributes such as packet length and time intervals for encrypted web sites identification within very small data sets, which cannot be applied to big data sets. Therefore, it is essential to develop some new solution to the challenge.

CERTIFICATE CLASSIFICATION SCHEME

In our measurement [1], we found that among billions of SSL connections in the real world, only a small number of certificates account for most part of the total visits and a certain type of certificate called self-signed certificate is used frequently in many known advanced. Therefore, we propose to identify malicious SSL/TLS sessions by server certificate classification.

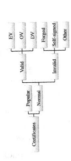

Fig.1 SSL server certificates categorization

The basic categorization of server certificates is shown in Fig.1. First, we categorize the certificates into popular certificates and normal ones, of which the popular ones are those that appear frequently in a lot of users' visits. Popular certificates are all marked as good. Then, the left are further divided into two classes: the valid and the invalid. A certificate is valid only if it can be verified successfully. Afterwards, the valid certificates are further sorted by validation type into extended validation (EV), organization validation (OV), and domain validation (DV), of which the relatively insecure DV certificates have been exploited by fraud sites. And the invalid ones are classified into three sub classes, namely the forged, the self-signed, and others. Here "forged" means that the certificate signature is invalid, and "self-signed" indicates that it is a self-made root certificate. By doing so, the majority of innocent connections can be excluded by certificates so that we can dig out the evil in the left much smaller set later.

Finally, evil SSL/TLS conversations can be further identified largely out of the valid DV certificates and invalid ones by other means, especially the forged and self-signed ones. Experiment results on a campus network show that we are able to identify forged popular certificates easily without verification or using any feature signatures, just by comparing the subject items of both popular certificates and normal ones.

REFERENCE

1. Cao, Z, Xiong, G., Zhao, Y.: X.509 certificate measurement based privacy analysis. Chinese Journal of Computers. 37(1), 151-164 (2014)

Poster Abstract: Using Financial Synthetic Data Sets for Fraud Detection Research

Edgar Alonso Lopez-Rojas and Stefan Axelsson

Blekinge Institute of Technology (BTH)
{edgar.lopez,stefan.axelsson}@bth.se

Abstract. Fraud detection research in the financial domain suffers from a serious problem which is the lack of public available data for the testing, evaluation and comparison of results using standard data sets. This problem is mainly due to onerous regulations, policies and the sensitivity of financial transactions that stop researchers to share and publish the result of their work.

Our aim is to address the problem of a lack of public data sets for fraud detection research in each of these domains, by providing a standard synthetic data sets as well as a method to first: replicate the normal transactional behaviour of the customers and second: to generate fraud scenarios such as money laundering, sales fraud (based on refunds and discounts), and credit card fraud that allows researchers to test, share and compare their methods. Public research concerning fraud detection in the financial domains is limited to general methods which in most cases can not be compared or their results independently replicated. As mentioned, one major reason for this is the secrecy and sensitivity of the customers data that is needed to perform the research.

We present a financial simulation framework that generates synthetic data sets of three real case studies of financial services based on real world data: Mobile Payments, Retail Stores, and Bank transaction systems. Our financial simulation framework consists of three social simulators for financial transactions that we named *PaySim, RetSim, and BankSim*. We used for our simulators the paradigm of multi agent-based modelling to represent the complexity of interactions between customers/clients and staff/merchants. Using statistics and social network analysis (SNA) on real data we can calibrate the relations between staff, merchants and customers, and generate verifiable realistic synthetic data sets.

These simulators enable us to generate synthetic transaction data of normal behaviour of customers, and also interesting known fraudulent behaviour, which can be used to further advance fraud detection research, without leaking sensitive information about the underlying data.

The generated data represents real world scenarios that are found in the original data with the added benefit that this data can be shared with other researchers for testing similar detection methods without concerns for privacy and other restrictions present when using the original data.

We used the *RetSim* simulator to investigate if threshold based detection could keep the risk of fraud at a predetermined set level, and while our results are preliminary, we argue that threshold based detection could keep the risk of fraud at a predetermined set level.

A. Stavrou et al. (Eds.): RAID 2014, LNCS 8688, pp. 485–486, 2014.
© Springer International Publishing Switzerland 2014

Using Financial Synthetic Data Sets for Fraud Detection Research

Edgar Lopez-Rojas & Stefan Axelsson
Blekinge Institute of Technology
Karlskrona, Sweden

Abstract

Fraud detection research in the financial domain suffers from a serious problem due to the lack of public available data sets for test, evaluate and compare results in standard datasets.

We present a financial simulation framework that generates synthetic data sets of three real case studies of financial services: Mobile Payments, Retail Stores, and Bank transactions systems. Our financial simulation framework consists of three social simulators for financial transactions that we named PaySim, RetSim, and BankSim.

These simulators enable us to generate synthetic transaction data of normal behaviour of customers, and also known fraudulent behaviour.

Introduction

- The defence against fraud in the financial services is an important topic that has seen some study.
- The characteristics of the methods used to defraud are constantly being modified by the fraudsters, which makes this problem interesting to study.
- One of the difficulties of doing research in this domain is the lack of available data sets to work on and compare results, this is why the generation of a synthetic data set is proposed as an alternative and effective way to deal with it.
- The main contribution, and focus, of this research is a method of generating anonymous synthetic data of diverse financial services from: mobile payments schema (PaySim), a retail store database (RetSim) and an aggregated transactional database of a bank payment system (BankSim). This synthetic data can then be used as part of the necessary input for the development and testing of fraud detection techniques.

Simulation of Financial Transactions

Multi-Agent Based Simulation is an approach that involves the use of autonomous and interactive agents and is it been used to model complex systems.

These agents are described by (sometimes simple) rules that describe their behaviour and interaction with other agents. Simulations has the benefits of:

- The data that represent realistic scenarios are easily available.
- The privacy of the customer is not impacted.
- The disclosure of results is not affected by policies or legal issues.
- The data set is available for other researchers to reproduce experiments.
- Different scenarios can be modelled with parameters controlled by the researcher.

Figure RetSim Use Cases

Figure BankSim Use Cases

PaySim: Mobile Money Payments Simulator

Figure PaySim State Diagram

- Mobile Money Payment Simulation (PaySim) is based on a real company that developed a service for phone users with the ability to transfer money between them using the phone as an electronic wallet.
- The service has not yet been implemented, therefore there was not transactional data available.
- PaySim was based only on the schema of the database and the described behaviour of the customers for the simulated system.
- Our research had the goal to provide a tool that detects suspicious transactions for money laundering and other fraud activities.
- Due to the lack of real data we turn to the generation of synthetic data as an alternative to develop, test, share and compare our methods.

Figure PaySim track of customers balance

RetSim: Retail Store Simulator

Figure RetSim screenshot

- RetSim is a general retail store simulator that started with the contribution of real data from one of the largest Nordic shoe retailers.
- RetSim is intended to be used for developing and investigating fraud scenarios at a shoe retail store, while keeping business sensitive and private personal information about customers consumption secret from competitors and others.
- Our first task was to build a simulator and calibrate the parameters given by the relation between customers and staff to fit the original data set.
- Parameters were extracted from original data using statistical analysis and social network analysis.
- We evaluated and verified that the generated synthetic data set was a realistic representation of the real data.

Figure Simulated data vs Real Data

Fraud Detection Research using RetSim

Figure RetSim

Figure BankSim

- We studied two fraud scenarios: Refunds fraud (fraudulent refund slips, keeping the cash refund for themselves) and Discounts fraud (registration of a discount on the sale without telling the customer).
- Current methods for detecting suspicious fraudulent staff are based on establishing fixed thresholds.
- We used the RetSim simulator to investigate if threshold based detection could keep the risk of fraud at a predetermined set level.

BankSim: Bank Transactions Simulator

Figure BankSim screenshot

Figure Generated categories

- BankSim was built on a sample of aggregated transactional data that one Spanish bank made available for a contest to encourage the development of applications in the big data.
- The aggregated data provided is rich enough to simulate with high granularity the consumption behaviour of customers in different merchants with segregation of gender, age and location including additional information of consumption patterns.

Conclusions

- When working with synthetic data there is always a risk of generating a data set that does not adequately represent the real world data set.
- A synthetic data set can simulate different scenarios that are not available for experimentation and analysis as they are restricted, private, unusual, catastrophic, etc.
- While our results are preliminary, we argue that threshold based detection could keep the risk of fraud at a predetermined set level.
- One of the biggest challenges for is to integrate all three simulators into one single Multi-Simulator that shares a common reference to the customers and can keep track of the transactions of a single agent across all simulators to investigate fraud that comprises multiple organizations.

Poster Abstract: Automatic Discovery for Common Application Protocol Mimicry[*]

Quan Bai, Gang Xiong, Yong Zhao, and Zhenzhen Li

Institute of Information Engineering,Chinese Academy of Sciences, Beijing, China
`xionggang@iie.ac.cn`

Abstract. With the development of Intrusion Detection Systems (IDS), some malicious applications begin to mimic common application protocol to get rid of detection. In the paper, we propose that we can automatic discover these protocol mimicry behaviours by measuring common applications and finding the general characteristics of their message structure. We formalize models and those who declare as common application protocol but do not match the general characteristics are recognized as mimicry.

1 Introduction

Mimicry of common application protocol is becoming more and more popular and brings great challenge to application recognition. Regular IDS can't deal with this case and we need a new method. In this paper, we propose a method based on measurement and statistical characteristics. Our approach is that, firstly we measure the traffic of a certain common application protocol; and secondly we summarize general characteristics of its message structure; finally those who declare as common application protocol but do not match the general characteristics are recognized as mimicry.

2 Our Work

In our work, we take web crawlers as an example. We measured the traffic of Google crawlers in real network [1]. We summarized the information of each field and the order of them. That is: HTTP message structure of Google crawler is in the order of:

GET →Host →Connection →Accept →From →User-Agent →Accept-Encoding

According to these characteristics, we found bogus behaviors of crawlers. And we think this method is useful to discover and verify other protocol mimicry behaviors.

---

[*] Supported by the National Science and Technology Support Program (No. 2012BAH46B02, No. 2012BAH45B01); the National High Technology Research and Development Program (863 Program) of China (No. 2011AA010703); the Strategic Priority Research Program of the Chinese Academy of Sciences (No. XDA06030200) . adfa, p. 1, 2014. © Springer-Verlag Berlin Heidelberg 2014

A. Stavrou et al. (Eds.): RAID 2014, LNCS 8688, pp. 487–488, 2014.
© Springer International Publishing Switzerland 2014

References

1. Bai Q, Xiong G, Zhao Y, et al. Analysis and Detection of Bogus Behavior in Web Crawler Measurement[J]. Procedia Computer Science, 2014, 31: 1084-1091.

Automatic Discovery for Common Application Protocol Mimicry

Quan Bai, Gang Xiong, Yong Zhao, Zhenzhen Li

Institute of Information Engineering, Chinese Academy of Sciences, Beijing, China

xionggang@iie.ac.cn

ABSTRACT

With the development of Intrusion Detection Systems (IDS), some malicious applications begin to mimic common application protocol to get rid of detection. In the paper, we propose that we can automatic discover these protocol mimicry behaviours by measuring common applications and finding the general characteristics of their message structure. We formalize models and those who declare as common application protocol but do not match the general characteristics are recognized as mimicry.

INTRODUCTION

Mimicry of common application protocol is becoming more and more popular and brings great challenge to application recognition. Regular IDS can't deal with this case and we need a new method. In this paper, we propose a method based on measurement and statistical characteristics. Our approach is that, firstly we measure the traffic of a certain common application protocol; and secondly we summarize general characteristics of its message structure; finally those who declare as common application protocol but do not match the general characteristics are recognized as mimicry.

OUR WORK

In our work, we take web crawlers as an example. We measure massive of web crawler traffic in the real high speed network during a long time. We summarize the most general characteristics of Google crawlers, including the information of fields and the order of them.

RESEARCH RESULT

The method based on measurement and statistical characteristics is shown below

The result of an certain example of discovery mimic common application protocol (Google crawler)

1. Measure the traffic of a certain application protocol

2. Summarize general characteristics

3. Match the general characteristics and recognize

Field	Most general characteristics
Request Method	GET
Host	(uncertain)
Connection	Keep-Alive
Accept	*.*
From	googlebot(at)googlebot.com
User-Agent	(User-Agent of Google)
Accept-Language	(NULL)
Accept-Encoding	gzip,deflate
Cookie	(NULL)
X-Forward-For	(NULL except for Googlebot-image/1.0)
Order of fields	Host->connection->accept->from->Use t-Agent->Accept-Encoding

CONCLUSION AND FUTURE

According to these characteristics, we found bogus behaviors of crawlers. And we think this method is useful to discover and verify other protocol mimicry behaviors.

REFERENCE

1. Bai Q, Xiong G, Zhao Y, et al. Analysis and Detection of Bogus Behavior in Web Crawler Measurement[J]. Procedia Computer Science, 2014, 31: 1084-1091.

Author Index